INTRODUCTION TO

Criminal Justice

A BRIEF EDITION

John Randolph Fuller
University of West Georgia

New York Oxford
Oxford University Press

Oxford University Press is a department of the University of Oxford. It furthers the University's objective of excellence in research, scholarship, and education by publishing worldwide. Oxford is a registered trade mark of Oxford University Press in the UK and certain other countries.

Published in the United States of America by Oxford University Press
198 Madison Avenue, New York, NY 10016, United States of America.

For titles covered by Section 112 of the US Higher Education Opportunity Act, please visit www.oup.com/us/he for the latest information about pricing and alternate formats.

Library of Congress Cataloging-in-Publication Data
Names: Fuller, John R., author.
Title: Introduction to criminal justice : a brief edition / John Randolph
  Fuller, University of West Georgia.
Description: First Edition. | New York : Oxford University Press, [2018]
Identifiers: LCCN 2017036142 (print) | LCCN 2017037979 (ebook) | ISBN
  9780190298197 (ebook) | ISBN 9780190298173 (paperbacl) | ISBN
  9780190858636 (looseleaf)
Subjects: LCSH: Criminal justice, Administration of. | Crime. | Criminal
law.
Classification: LCC HV7419 (ebook) | LCC HV7419 .F875 2018 (print) |
DDC
  364—dc23
LC record available at https://lccn.loc.gov/2017036142

9 8 7 6 5 4 3 2 1

Printed by LSC Communications, United States of America

For Amy
For Everything

Brief Contents

Contents

PART III   THE ROLE OF THE COURTS   197

CHAPTER 8 **THE COURTROOM WORK GROUP** **227**

CHAPTER 11   **PRISONS AND JAILS**   329

CHAPTER 12   **COMMUNITY CORRECTIONS**   367

PART V   CONTEMPORARY ISSUES   397

CHAPTER 13   JUVENILE JUSTICE   399

CHAPTER 14   CRIMINAL JUSTICE IN THE FUTURE: ISSUES AND CONCERNS   429

Preface

The field of criminal justice is undergoing constant change. As new laws are enacted, new technology developed, and offenders get more sophisticated in their lawbreaking methods, professionals in the criminal justice system must constantly adapt. These changes also require continual updates in what students who are interested in the criminal justice system need to understand.

Introduction to Criminal Justice: A Brief Edition has kept abreast of these many changes. There is a renewed emphasis on policing and technology, the militarization of the police, victimology, and white-collar crime, new concerns about how criminal justice policies are shaped by political considerations, and a host of new ways of responding to crime, particularly in the field of corrections where innovative methods for addressing the problems of offenders are always being introduced. Since the terrorist attacks of September 11, 2001, the field of criminal justice has become even more complex and challenging to study and to write about. The basic mission of some criminal justice agencies, such as the FBI, has been altered; the Department of Homeland Security was created; and state and local criminal justice agencies now have the additional duties of being first responders to terrorist attacks. Yet in spite of this ever-evolving threat, the fundamental job of the criminal justice system remains. Protecting individuals and property within the rule of law has always been a difficult mission. The delicate balance between thorough and effective public safety and protecting individual rights and liberties is being stretched anew by terrorist threats; the laws designed to address those threats, such as the USA PATRIOT Act and USA FREEDOM Act; and the emotions of citizens, which range from legitimate concern to paranoia.

It follows, then, that the criminal justice system is not as neat and orderly as is often portrayed; many factors, issues, and controversies must be put in context if we are to understand why some people break the law and how the criminal justice system responds when they do. This book is written with a critical perspective that recognizes the profound influence extralegal characteristics such as inequality, race, class, sex, and gender have on the criminal justice system and the quality of justice. Reflecting these contexts, this book is designed to help students grasp both the excitement of the field and the immense responsibility of serving the country and community. The mainstream narrative of this text provides instructors and students with foundational knowledge of the criminal justice discipline while helping students to separate fact from fiction and gain insight into the complexities of ethical decision making. It articulates the important issues of the field and supplies students with the basics necessary to work in this arena.

Introduction to Criminal Justice: A Brief Edition is designed to be, first and foremost, a standard text that covers the canon required in the first course that most criminal justice majors take. Additionally, the book serves as an introduction to the discipline for those students who have not yet chosen a major. The history and contemporary concerns of criminal justice are among the most interesting and necessary fields of study offered at universities. However, students often bring to these fields many myths about the criminal justice system that they have absorbed from television shows, as well as from media coverage of sensational cases. Students must not blindly accept the status quo when learning about the discipline; engaging in critical thinking is essential to fully understanding the field. This text is unique in that it encourages students' critical thinking skills beyond the memorization of facts and figures through a robust pedagogical framework. Students must appreciate the history of social control and the limits of the ability of science and government to respond to deviant behavior. Most important, students should be open to the many ways in which the criminal justice system might be effectively reformed as new challenges continue to emerge.

Criminal justice benefits from having students and instructors who have worked in the field, gained experience through internships, and interacted with the criminal justice system. These experiences enrich discussions in the classroom, and this text readily acknowledges the interplay between theory and practice in the criminal justice system. It is somewhat regrettable that the employment opportunities in criminal justice are so plentiful; it would be better for us all if crime were less prevalent. Nevertheless, good people who can solve problems, act ethically, and be trusted to use power responsibly are needed to fill the many positions in the criminal justice system. To the extent that this book facilitates the development of those types of individuals, it will be judged a success.

Organization of the Brief Edition

Introduction to Criminal Justice: A Brief Edition presents the latest available research, statistics, and developments in the field of criminal justice and is comprehensive yet concise enough for instructors who prefer a more economical option for their students without forgoing the primary advantages of a traditional longer text. This result has been achieved without sacrificing the kinds of features, images, tables, maps, and figures expected in this course. The brief edition is derived from the third edition of *Criminal Justice: Mainstreams and Crosscurrents*; each chapter has been streamlined, revised for more balanced coverage, and pedagogically strengthened to give students the tools they need to succeed. The following table illustrates how chapters from the third edition of *Criminal Justice: Mainstream and Crosscurrents* were streamlined to create the brief edition. Adopters will find the same content previously covered in 16 chapters now covered in 14 chapters and an appendix:

BRIEF EDITION CHAPTERS	THIRD EDITION CHAPTERS

Chapter 1: Crime and Criminal Justice	Chapter 1: Crime and the Problem of Social Control
	Chapter 2: The Nature and Measurement of Crime
	    Types of Crime
	    Offenses and Offenders

Chapter 2: How Crime Is Measured and Who It Affects	Chapter 2: The Nature and Measurement of Crime
	    The Nature and Measurement of Crime
	    Measurement of Crime
	Chapter 15: Victims of Crime and Victimless Crimes
	    Victims of Crime

Chapter 3: Criminal Law	Chapter 4: Criminal Law

Chapter 4: The History and Organization of Law Enforcement	Chapter 5: The History and Organization of Law Enforcement
	    A Brief History of the Police
	    Levels of Law Enforcement
	Chapter 7: Issues in Policing
	    Challenges to Traditional Policing

Chapter 5: Police Organization, Operation, and the Law	Chapter 5: The History and Organization of Law Enforcement Modern Police Organization Chapter 6: Policing and the Law

Chapter 6: Policing: Innovations and Controversies	Chapter 5: The History and Organization of Law Enforcement
	    Innovations in Policing
	Chapter 7: Issues in Policing
	    Sex and Race
	    Use of Force
	    Stress and Burnout

Chapter 7: The Courts	Chapter 8: The History and Organization of Courts
Chapter 8: The Courtroom Work Group	Chapter 9: Working in the Courtroom The Courtroom Work Group
Chapter 9: The Disposition: Plea Bargaining, Trial, and Sentencing	Chapter 9: Working in the Courtroom Pretrial Release Decisions Chapter 10: The Disposition: Plea Bargaining, Trial, and Sentencing
Chapter 10: The History of Control and Punishment	Chapter 11: The History of Control and Punishment
Chapter 11: Prisons and Jails	Chapter 12: Contemporary Prison Life Chapter 13: Corrections in the Community Jails

Chapter 12: Community Corrections	Chapter 13: Corrections in the Community
	    Community Corrections in Context
	    Diversion
	    Probation
	    Intermediate Sanctions
	    Parole

Chapter 13: Juvenile Justice	Chapter 14: Juvenile Justice
Chapter 14: Criminal Justice in the Future: Issues and Concerns	Chapter 16: Present and Emerging Trends: The Future of Criminal Justice
Appendix: Theories of Crime	Chapter 3: Theories of Crime

Features

Criminal justice is not black and white: it requires much situation-based decision making in shades of gray. Placing students in scenarios that reflect high-pressure, on-the-job circumstances is an ideal way to draw students into the field and prepare them to meet such challenges, whether in a courtroom or on the streets. To this end, *Introduction to Criminal Justice: A Brief Introduction* implements a robust pedagogical program to assist in teaching students the critical-thinking and ethical decision-making skills they need to understand and work in the criminal justice system.

> Each chapter begins with a **chapter-opening vignette**, which introduces a controversial case and/or event in the news that illuminates the chapter's major themes.

> **Learning objectives** describe the educational goals students are expected to come away with upon reading the chapter. Learning objectives

are keyed to each chapter-ending summary, as well as the major headings within the chapters.

› **Pause and Review** questions are knowledge-based review questions that now appear at the end of each major section to test students' memory and understanding of the chapter content.

› **A Closer Look** boxes encourage critical thinking in relation to various key topics discussed throughout the chapters, present relevant real-life examples, and expose common misconceptions about the criminal justice system.

› **Case in Point** boxes summarize landmark court cases relevant to the chapter discussion.

› **CJ Reference** boxes provide pertinent information, which students will refer to throughout their studies.

› **Focus on Ethics** boxes at the end of each chapter place students in on-the-job scenarios and ask them to respond to ethical dilemmas. The feature is accompanied by a set of "What Do You Do?" questions to help students understand the consequences of a potential decision (or these can be used to encourage in-class discussion). This feature also links to the book's companion website where students can watch videos that connect the scenarios to real-world situations.

› Each **Chapter Summary** is linked to the learning objectives and outlines the main concepts covered in each chapter.

› **Critical Reflection** questions appear at the end of each chapter. These questions are open-ended, and some may require further research.

› **Key terms** appear in the chapter margins where terms are first used, as well as in a chapter-ending list to help students recall the important concepts covered in the chapter.

› A rich **graphics program** of photographs and figures that illustrate the latest statistics helps students explore essential chapter themes.

Supplements

Oxford University Press offers a complete and authoritative supplements package for both instructors and students. When you adopt *Introduction to Criminal Justice: A Brief Edition*, you will have access to an exemplary set of learning resources to enhance teaching and support students' learning.

Ancillary Resource Center (ARC)

A convenient, instructor-focused destination for resources accompanies *Introduction to Criminal Justice: A Brief Edition*. Accessed online through individual user accounts (https://arc2.oup-arc.com/), the ARC provides instructors with access to up-to-date ancillaries at any time, while guaranteeing the security of grade-significant resources. In addition, it allows Oxford University Press to keep instructors informed when new content becomes available. The ARC for *Introduction to Criminal Justice: A Brief Edition* includes:

› **Instructor's Manual:** For each chapter of the textbook, the Instructor's Manual includes the following:

- Chapter Summaries: Full summaries of each chapter provide a thorough review of the important facts and concepts covered.

- Chapter Outlines: Detailed outlines give an overview of each chapter.
- Key Concepts
- Key Terms
- Media Connections: Suggestions are given for related books, movies, and television programs on which to focus discussion of the chapter topics, including questions to stimulate class discussion.
- Learning Objectives: These are based on the book.
- CNN Videos: These videos showcase news stories with summaries and questions.

> **Textbook Figures and Tables:** All of the textbook's illustrations and tables are provided for instructor use.

> **PowerPoint Resources:** Complete lecture outlines are presented, ready for use in class.

> **Computerized Test Bank:** A complete test bank provides instructors with a wide range of test items (approximately 50 questions per chapter), including multiple-choice, short-answer, true/false, and essay questions.

> **Sample Syllabi** for both semester and quarter terms.

> **Focus on Ethics Videos:** Designed to enhance the educational value of the Focus on Ethics features at the end of each chapter, these videos and accompanying exercises help students connect the scenarios presented in the chapters to real-world situations. Available on the text's companion website, the exercises guide students through a series of questions expanding the analysis of the ethical and practical implications of each Focus on Ethics scenario. They are ideal for use as lecture starters or as assignments.

> **Interactive Media Activities:** Designed to reinforce key concepts with real-world situations, each activity:

- Takes approximately 10 minutes to complete and produces unique results for each student.
- Enables students to see how criminal justice works, experiencing the decision making required on the job.
- Is optimized to work on any mobile device or computer.
- Ends with assessments to connect the activity to classroom discussions.

Interactive media activities will cover topics such as Discretion in the Criminal Justice System, Prosecutor Misconduct, Prison Contraband, Job Application Dilemmas, and Probation Internship.

> **Careers in Criminal Justice:** The book has extensive coverage of the careers available to criminal justice students. In addition to the chart on the inside front cover detailing 10 types of criminal justice occupations, the companion website presents an expanded version of the chart with greater descriptions of the occupations and the educational requirements necessary to pursue them. Additionally, the companion website presents an annotated list of 50 criminal justice agencies' websites that allows students to learn what each of these agencies requires for employment and what benefits they provide to their employees.

Student Companion Website

The free and open access companion website for *Introduction to Criminal Justice: A Brief Edition* (www.oup.com/us/fuller) helps students to review what they have learned from the textbook as well as explore other resources online. Resources include:

> **Chapter Summaries:** Full summaries of each chapter provide a thorough review of the important facts and concepts covered.

> **Chapter Outlines:** Detailed outlines give an overview of each chapter.

> **Practice Quizzes:** Each chapter includes a practice quiz (10 multiple-choice, 10 true/false, and 10 fill-in-the-blank questions, as well as approximately five essay/discussion questions), which students can use as a self-review exercise, to check their understanding.

> **Focus on Ethics Videos:** Designed to enhance the educational value of the Focus on Ethics features at the end of each chapter, these videos and accompanying exercises help students connect the scenarios presented in the chapters to real-world situations. Available on the text's companion website, the exercises guide students through a series of questions expanding the analysis of the ethical and practical implications of each Focus on Ethics scenario. They are ideal for use as lecture starters or as assignments.

> **Interactive Media Activities:** Designed to reinforce key concepts with real-world situations, each activity:

  - Takes approximately 10 minutes to complete and produces unique results for each student.

  - Enables students to see how criminal justice works, experiencing the decision making required on the job.

  - Is optimized to work on any mobile device or computer.

  - Ends with assessments to connect the activity to classroom discussions.

  Interactive Media Activities will cover topics such as Discretion in the Criminal Justice System, Prosecutor Misconduct, Prison Contraband, Job Application Dilemmas, and Probation Internship.

> **Careers in Criminal Justice:** The book has extensive coverage of the careers available to criminal justice students. In addition to the chart on the inside front cover detailing 10 types of criminal justice occupations, the companion website presents an expanded version of the chart with greater descriptions of the occupations and the educational requirements necessary to pursue them. Additionally, the companion website presents an annotated list of 50 criminal justice agencies' websites that allows students to learn what each of these agencies requires for employment and what benefits they provide to their employees.

> **What Agency Am I?** These activities test students' understanding of the duties of federal criminal justice agencies.

> **Crossword:** This feature consists of puzzles testing students' comprehension of key concepts.

> **In the News:** These activities help students connect concepts they learn in class to current events.

> **Flashcards:** Interactive flashcard activities are an effective way for students to learn and review all of the important terminology.

Dashboard

Dashboard (www.oup.com/us/dashboard) is Oxford University Press's nationally hosted learning management system. It features a streamlined interface that connects instructors and students with the functions they perform most often, simplifying the learning experience to save instructors time and put students' progress first. Dashboard's prebuilt assessments were created specifically to accompany *Introduction to Criminal Justice: A Brief Edition* and are automatically graded so that instructors can see student progress instantly. The Dashboard for *Introduction to Criminal Justice: A Brief Edition* includes:

> **Practice Questions:** There are 20 questions per chapter (10 multiple-choice, 10 true/false), distinct from what is offered on the ARC and Student Companion Website.

  • Each question is tied to a **learning objective** from the chapters.

> **PowerPoint Resources:** Complete lecture outlines are available, ready for use in class.

> **Interactive Media Activities:** Designed to reinforce key concepts with real-world situations, each activity:

  • Takes approximately 10 minutes to complete and produces unique results for each student.

  • Enables students to see how criminal justice works, experiencing the decision making required on the job.

  • Is optimized to work on any mobile device or computer.

  • Ends with assessments to connect the activity to classroom discussions.

  Interactive Media Activities will cover topics such as Discretion in the Criminal Justice System, Prosecutor Misconduct, Prison Contraband, Job Application Dilemmas, and Probation Internship.

> **Careers in Criminal Justice:** The book has extensive coverage of the careers available to criminal justice students. In addition to the chart on the inside front cover detailing 10 types of criminal justice occupations, the companion website presents an expanded version of the chart with greater descriptions of the occupations and the educational requirements necessary to pursue them. Additionally, the companion website presents an annotated list of 50 criminal justice agencies' websites that allows students to learn what each of these agencies requires for employment and what benefits they provide to their employees.

> **Flashcards:** Interactive flashcard activities are an effective way for students to learn and review all of the important terminology.

> **What Agency Am I?** These activities test students' understanding of the duties of federal criminal justice agencies.

> **Crossword:** Puzzles test students' comprehension of key concepts.

> **In the News:** These activities help students connect concepts they learn in class to current events.

> **Media Connections:** Suggestions are offered for related books, movies, and television programs on which to focus discussion of the chapter topics, including questions to stimulate class discussion.

> **Find it Online:** These activities are designed to expand students' awareness of Internet research and online government sources.

For more information about Dashboard, contact your Oxford University Press sales representative.

Course Cartridges

For instructors who wish to use their campus learning management system, a course cartridge containing all of the ARC and Dashboard resources is available for a variety of e-learning environments.

eBook

Introduction to Criminal Justice: A Brief Edition is available as an eBook via Redshelf, Vitalsource and Chegg.

Acknowledgments

The professionals at Oxford University Press have been delightful to work with. My editor, Steve Helba, has been instrumental in helping me refine the focus of the book to appeal to a broad range of students and professors. His wise counsel and sound judgment mean a lot to me, and I will be forever indebted for his commitment to this project. I am also indebted to John Challice, Vice President and Publisher, Higher Education; Frank Mortimer, Director of Marketing; Tony Mathias, Marketing Manager; Clare Castro, Marketing Manager and Head of Market Development; Larissa Albright, Assistant Editor; and Jordan Wright, Marketing Assistant, for their many helpful suggestions in developing and marketing this edition. I am especially indebted to Maegan Sherlock, my Development Editor, who made countless insightful contributions to this book. Finally, Amy Hembree, to whom this book is dedicated, deserves great credit for her hard work, wise counsel, sense of humor, and tolerance over these many years of working with me.

Manuscript Reviewers

I was lucky to have a set of reviewers who were not afraid to suggest ways that this edition could be improved. The following reviewers gave generously of their time and expertise, and I am grateful for their many wise suggestions:

Tina Adams, Worcester State University
Jonathan Appel, Tiffin University
Amin Asfari, Wake Tech Community College
Lauren M. Barrow, Chestnut Hill College
Allan Barnes, University of Alaska Anchorage
Curt R. Blakely, Truman State University
Bradley Carlton Bowen, Tri-County Technical College
Julie Campbell, University of Nebraska at Kearney
Serguei Cheloukhine, John Jay College of Criminal Justice, CUNY
Barbara Allison Crowson, Norwich University
Anthony Dangelantonio, Keene State College
Nicole Doctor, Ivy Tech Community College
Scott Duncan, Bloomsburg University of Pennsylvania
Laura Dykstra, Plymouth State University
Julie Globokar, Kent State University
Brian Gorman, Towson University
Jennifer D. Griffin, University of Delaware

Melchor C. de Guzman, Georgia Gwinnett College
Julia Hall, Drexel University
Diane Hartmus, Oakland University
Brittany Hayes, Sam Houston State University
Marilyn Horace-Moore, Eastern Michigan University
Shawn Keller, Florida Gulf Coast University
Erin M. Kerrison, University of Pennsylvania
Douglas Klutz, The University of Alabama
Barry Langford, Columbia College
John Mabry, University of Central Oklahoma
Waylyn McCulloh, Saint Ambrose University
Karen McCue, Central New Mexico Community College
Shana Mell, Virginia Commonwealth University
Eric Metchik, Salem State University
John Lincoln Passmore, University of Massachusetts, Boston
Patrick O. Patterson, Eastfield College
Lynn Pazzani, University of West Georgia
Cornel D. Plebani, Eastern Maine Community College
Marlene Ramsey, Albany State University
Joseph Schafer, Southern Illinois University Carbondale
Martin D. Schwartz, George Washington University
Pamela J. Segers, North Georgia Technical College
Quanda Watson Stevenson, Athens State University
Francis M. Williams, Plymouth State University
Wayne Thompson, Carthage College
J. Michael Vecchio, Loyola University of Chicago
Harold Wells, Tennessee State University
Bradley Wright, University of Connecticut
Jennifer R. Wynn, LaGuardia Community College

About the Author

John Randolph Fuller is Professor Emeritus at the University of West Georgia where he taught in the Department of Criminology for 33 years. He brings both an applied and a theoretical background to his scholarship and has been recognized by his students and peers as an outstanding teacher and scholar. In addition, he served as the university's Ombuds, where his knowledge in conflict resolution helped settle disputes among and between students, faculty, staff, and administrators.

Dr. Fuller served as a probation and parole officer for the Florida Probation and Parole Commission in Broward County, Florida, where he managed a caseload of more than 100 felons. In addition, he served as a criminal justice planner for the Palm Beach County metropolitan criminal justice planning unit. In this capacity, he worked with every criminal justice agency in a three-county area and wrote grants for the Law-Enforcement Assistance Administration that funneled more than $1 million into local criminal justice agencies. By working directly with offenders as a probation and parole officer and with criminal justice administrators as a criminal justice planner, Dr. Fuller gained significant insights that inform his writing about the criminal justice system.

Dr. Fuller has authored and edited numerous journal articles, chapters, and books on criminal justice, criminology, global crime, courts, and juvenile delinquency.

PART I

Crime: Problems, Measurement, and Law

Chapter 1

Crime and Criminal Justice

Pictured here are Kayla Laws, a victim of revenge porn, and her mother, Charlotte Laws. Revenge porn, or non-consensual pornography, remains a major technological, social, and legal issue. What are some obstacles to accomplishing legislative change regarding this issue?

In October 2011, 24-year-old Kayla Laws photographed herself at her home and e-mailed the pictures to herself. Laws says she never shared the pictures, some of which were of her nude from the waist up. In January 2012, she learned that one picture had been posted on a website called Is Anyone Up that was operated by Hunter Moore.[1] Since 2010, Moore had been posting nude photographs to the site. Many of the images, most of which were of women, were supposedly sent by people who wanted revenge against their former partners. Moore posted not only the photographs, but also personal identifying details of the people in them, including names, home addresses, phone numbers, and workplaces.[2]

Is Anyone Up was regularly receiving over 30 million page views and earning about $10,000 monthly in ad revenue.[3] In his defense, Moore cited the Communications Decency Act of 1996, which holds websites unaccountable for content submitted by users.[4] Although Moore claimed that all the site's photographs were sent to him, Kayla Laws was certain that no one else had seen her photographs. She told her mother, Charlotte Laws, what had happened.

Charlotte Laws wrote to Moore, asking him to remove her daughter's photo. When Moore ignored her, Laws wrote to his attorney, his web-hosting service, Facebook, and his Internet security company.[5] When none of this worked, Laws contacted the Los Angeles police, who said they could not help. Laws then called the Federal Bureau of Investigation (FBI). It was only when she explained that her daughter's computer had been broken into that the FBI acted. When the agency opened an investigation, Moore removed Laws's photo.[6] Eventually, the FBI found that many, if not most, of the site's photos were stolen from victims' computers by Charles Evens, whom Moore was paying. In some cases, the image of a victim's face had been pasted onto the body of a pornographic actor.[7]

Moore closed the site in April 2012.[8] The FBI arrested Moore and Evens in January 2014, and Moore, 28, pleaded guilty to unauthorized access to a computer, aiding and abetting unauthorized access of a computer, and identity theft. In December 2015, Moore was sentenced to 30 months in prison, and Evens received 25 months.[9] Twenty-seven states now have laws banning the posting of nude photographs of a person without his or her permission.[10]

THINK ABOUT IT > Why was it so difficult for Charlotte Laws to get assistance in this case? Why did Laws finally resort to the criminal justice system?

LEARNING OBJECTIVE 1

Define social control.

LEARNING OBJECTIVE 2

Outline how the U.S. criminal justice system protects individual rights.

LEARNING OBJECTIVE 3

Define crime and criminal justice.

What is Crime?

Social control consists of the rules, habits, and customs a society uses to enforce conformity to its norms. Imagine how chaotic society would be if there were no rules and everyone did whatever they wanted. Recall the opening case of Hunter Moore. One reason that Charlotte Laws was unable to get the images of her daughter removed from the website was that there was no state or federal law specifically prohibiting posting a person's image on the Internet without his or her consent. Only when Laws referenced federal laws concerning identity theft and unauthorized access to a computer was law enforcement able to act.

Communities and countries are composed of the citizens who live in them. In a democracy, not only do citizens decide which laws they want to govern them, but sometimes citizens must also ensure that the laws are enforced. This is an important aspect of social control in a democracy. The feature that sets the U.S. criminal justice system apart from those of many other countries is the way individual rights are protected as an integral part of the functioning of law enforcement. The criminal justice system must maintain a delicate balance between imposing order and preserving individual rights. This task, which is difficult in the best of times, becomes even more problematic in times of war and terrorism. Yet it would be a grave mistake to think of these issues as mutually exclusive. In other words, keeping people safe does not mean removing their constitutional rights. To successfully create and nurture meaningful communities, the government must control crime without turning the country into a police state. Achieving this balance is part of the Herculean task of the criminal justice system.

As we construct new responses to the threats of terrorism, this task will challenge all of us to appreciate the complexities and ambiguities of crime control in the 21st century. Although crime must be addressed within the rule of law, many practitioners recognize that more fundamental questions must be considered. These questions about the nature of justice in the United States include concerns of racial prejudice, the power of law enforcement to decide what to do with suspects, economic inequality, and the gaps in access to decision-making processes in all aspects of society.

Crime can be described as the violation of the laws of a society by a person or a group of people who are subject to the laws of that society. In this context, **justice** is the administration of a punishment or reward in accordance with morals that a given society considers correct. **Criminal justice** is a social institution that has the mission of controlling crime by detecting, detaining, adjudicating, and punishing and/or rehabilitating people who break the law. Most people envision crime as fairly straightforward, often sordid affairs, such as robbery, rape, and murder. For example:

> In 2012, an ATM security camera in Arizona recorded the image of a man driving a white Ford Focus making a withdrawal while wearing a horror mask. The ATM card belonged to an 18-year-old Alaska woman, Samantha Koenig, who had been reported missing. Later in Texas, police pulled over the car for speeding and arrested its driver, Israel Keyes, upon seeing his Alaska driver's license.[11] Charged with Koenig's murder and facing the death penalty and a pile of incriminating evidence, Keyes told police about his murderous career.[12] He had traveled around the country from his home in Anchorage, hiding cash, tools, and weapons to facilitate murders he would commit later. In the 2011 murder of Bill and Lorraine Currier, Keyes flew to Chicago, rented a car, and visited family in Indiana on his way to Burlington, Vermont. There, he spent three days looking for random victims. After kidnapping and killing the Curriers, Keyes flew home.[13] Similarly, after killing Samantha Koenig, he hid her body in a shed and went on a two-week cruise.[14] The murders of Koenig and the Curriers are the only ones Keyes gave details about. Keyes claimed responsibility for eight murders but hinted about at least three more. He committed suicide in his jail cell in December 2012.[15]

Many offenses involve the harm not of other people but of social order. Although order is a good thing to have in a society, sometimes the order itself is questionable.

> In 2015, Arnold Abbott, 90, was arrested in Ft. Lauderdale, Florida, for giving food to homeless people. Abbott, an activist and World War II veteran, had operated a charity that provides food to the city's homeless population since 1991. He said he would continue his work despite violating a recent ordinance that restricted giving food to homeless people. Police cited Abbott at least five times, with each citation bearing a fine of up to $500 and up to 60 days in jail. Weeks later, however, a judge temporarily halted the ordinance.[16]

social control—The rules, habits, and customs a society uses to enforce conformity to its norms.

crime—The violation of the laws of a society by a person or a group of people who are subject to the laws of that society.

justice—The administering of a punishment or reward in accordance with morals that a given society considers to be correct.

criminal justice—A social institution that has the mission of controlling crime by detecting, detaining, adjudicating, and punishing and/or rehabilitating people who break the law.

Samantha Koenig was one of the victims of serial murderer Israel Keyes who traveled the country looking for victims. Why is it so difficult to detect serial killers who kill in many different states?

Other offenses, such as espionage (spying), threaten not only society's laws but also its political stability. How these offenses are dealt with, however, is usually a result of the political mood of the times. In the last 10 years, those who have committed treasonous offenses have been sent to prison.

> In 2013, Edward Snowden, a then 29-year-old Central Intelligence Agency (CIA) contractor and computer analyst, left the United States and flew to Hong Kong to reveal a trove of classified National Security Agency documents to journalists. It is believed that Snowden may have downloaded as many as 1.7 million secret documents during his tenure as a CIA contractor. In June 2013, the *Guardian* newspaper reported that the U.S. National Security Agency (NSA) was collecting the telephone records of millions of Americans.[17] On June 14, 2013, the U.S. Department of Justice charged Snowden with violating the Espionage Act and theft of government property, offenses punishable by up to 30 years in prison.[18] The U.S. Department of State revoked Snowden's passport on June 22, 2013, one day before Snowden flew to Russia.[19] In 2014, the Russian government issued Snowden a residency permit that allows him to travel freely within Russia and to leave the country for up to three months. As of November 2017, Snowden continued to live in Russia.[20] He has stated that he has applied for asylum in 21 countries, including some in western Europe.[21]

Incidents such as these make rational discussion about crime difficult. The personal nature of crime further compounds this problem. In a society as diverse as the 21st-century United States, what is rational to one person might not be rational to another, and everyone has his or her own solution to crime based on what he or she considers rational.

Although Edward Snowden is accused of violating the law, many people believe he did the right thing by exposing U.S. surveillance practices. If Snowden ever returns to the United States, should he be prosecuted for his crimes or treated as a hero?

Taking these factors into account, a student of criminal justice can begin to understand how the apparently simple progression of crime → **arrest** → trial → punishment really represents many subtleties and complications. Still, as individuals we hold tightly to the perspectives that support our personal notions of fairness, justice, and goodness, even when we know those notions might be grounded in the privilege of middle-class values concerning race, class, sex, and gender. However, crime is a messy human problem that does not respond to simple, mechanical, or straightforward solutions.

The study of crime and the criminal justice system is not an exact science. In thinking about crime, we must use what sociologist C. Wright Mills called the **sociological imagination**, or the idea that we must look beyond the obvious to evaluate how our social location influences how we perceive society.[22] Mills encouraged us to step back from our personal experiences and examine issues apart from our social location. For example, could the father of a murdered daughter reasonably sit on a jury of the accused killer? Of course not. Likewise, according to Mills, each of us should attempt to look at crime and criminal justice policy from a neutral and objective position. The key word here is "attempt." It can be argued that no one can truly be neutral and objective when considering social issues. We must be honest and acknowledge that our social class, race, gender, sex, age, and other personal attributes affect our thinking. Only by explicitly stating our social location can we, and those we seek to convince, put our opinions in context and evaluate them.

arrest—When law enforcement detains and holds a criminal suspect or suspects.

sociological imagination—The idea that we must look beyond the obvious to evaluate how our social location influences how we perceive society.

PAUSE AND REVIEW

1. What is the feature that sets the U.S. criminal justice system apart from those of other countries?

2. What is crime? What is criminal justice?

3. What is the relationship between crime and justice?

LEARNING OBJECTIVE **4**

List the steps of the criminal justice process.

LEARNING OBJECTIVE **5**

Explain the major difference between the due process and crime control models.

LEARNING OBJECTIVE **6**

Describe the wedding-cake model of criminal justice.

The Criminal Justice System and Process

When the law is broken, the criminal justice system must respond in the name of society. The criminal justice system comprises various agencies from different levels of government, each with a mission to deal with some aspect of crime. Although some of these agencies appear to overlap in duties, and the system seems to be inefficient and cumbersome, it chugs along, processing a vast number of cases. However, the criminal justice system is often criticized by the public for being ineffective and failing to produce the justice that many people expect. Why do so many people perceive the criminal justice system in this way?

First, the system is not confined to one level of government. The criminal justice system spans the range from local governments to the federal government. The lines of authority and distinction between agencies are not always clear and in some cases must be negotiated according to the politics of the case. For example, tension exists between federal agencies such as the FBI and local law enforcement agencies. Depending on the case, investigators must decide whether federal or state laws have been violated and which agency has the primary responsibility for investigation. Although interagency cooperation is the stated norm, conflict does arise. (See A Closer Look 1.1 to learn more about interagency cooperation.) In addition, problems between different components of the criminal justice system may exist. The goals and missions of law enforcement are not always viewed as identical to those of the judicial system or the corrections system. Individual criminal justice practitioners might believe that other agencies are working against them. For example, the police sometimes believe that district attorneys and judges are working against them by helping offenders get plea bargains, light sentences, and **probation**. On the other hand, prison officials might think that lawmakers who legislate tougher, longer sentences are overcrowding the prisons.

Now let's examine how the criminal justice system is set up.

probation—The suspension of all or part of a sentence subject to certain conditions and supervision in the community.

The Criminal Justice Process

The criminal justice process is covered in great detail in the following chapters. However, this brief overview will provide some orientation as to how each component of the system is related to the process.

Cases move through the criminal justice system in a consistent manner. They begin with contact with a law enforcement agency and then proceed to the courts which determine guilt (if any) and prescribe a sentence for the guilty. The convicted then move to the correctional system where punishment and/or treatments are administered. At each step of the process criminal justice officials decide whether the case should continue to the next stage.

A CLOSER LOOK 1.1
A Comparison of Federal, State, and Local Law Enforcement

One of the most stubborn problems in U.S. law enforcement is getting agencies to work together. Although we call it a criminal justice "system," historic, structural, personal, and jurisdictional issues prevent or impede criminal justice agencies from freely exchanging information and resources. Local, state, and federal law enforcement agencies are all subject to individual agency cultures rather than one national law enforcement culture affecting individual law enforcement agencies. This philosophy had an especially tragic effect on September 11, 2001. Following the attacks, the National Commission on Terrorist Attacks Upon the United States, known as the 9/11 Commission, was created to investigate the circumstances surrounding the attacks. The Commission discovered that many major federal law enforcement and investigation agencies all held separate pieces of information regarding the terrorist plot but had not communicated them to one another.[23] The Commission concluded that had various agencies acted together, the attacks could have potentially been prevented.

A solution to this problem would be to create a large, federally mandated law enforcement agency, but this is unlikely to happen. Although other countries have this type of law enforcement structure, one of the intrinsic values of the United States is the idea that, when possible, government control should be vested at the level closest to the people. According to Sunil B. Desai, a U.S. Marine Corps major who served on the Council on Foreign Relations, four factors challenge the transition to greater interagency cooperation:

1. There is no formal, comprehensive concept of coordination for either routine or crisis situations.
2. There is no independent authority to develop and train personnel in interagency cooperation.
3. Individual agencies organize their policies and operations differently.
4. Personnel policies focus on developing personnel who are primarily dedicated to the individual agency rather than the community of agencies.[24]
5. Table 1.1 illustrates how the various federal, state, and local agencies are organized and funded, and what they do.

As shown in Table 1.1, law enforcement agencies at different levels of government have different resources, funding authorities, and mandates. Cooperation between these agencies is always a goal, but their differences are grounded in legal mandates. Also, agency cultures dictate that there will always be some degree of conflict, competition, and distrust between law enforcement agencies operating at different levels of government. Until the culture changes, our law enforcement system will be challenged to find ways to get federal, state, and local agencies to work together.

THINK ABOUT IT
1. What would you do to encourage law enforcement agencies to work together?
2. Should there be a national police force? Explain your answer.

TABLE 1.1 Comparison of Law Enforcement Levels of Jurisdiction

	FEDERAL	STATE	LOCAL
Agencies	• FBI • Immigration and Customs Enforcement • Secret Service	• State highway patrol • State investigative agencies	• Municipal police departments • County sheriff's offices
Mandate for Enforcing Laws	• Offenses on federal property and military reservations • Interstate crime	• Interstate highway systems • Offenses of local and state government officials	• State statutes within local jurisdictions
Funding	• Federal income tax	• State income tax • Sales tax • User taxes (driver's license, license plate fees, etc.)	• Sales tax • Property tax

LAW ENFORCEMENT

Police officers are typically the first responders to crime and thus make initial contact. Someone may report or alert them to the crime, or they may witnesses it themselves. Upon making contact, police officers seek to determine the causes and perpetrators of the crime through investigation. They gather evidence, preserve the crime scene, and interview victims and witnesses. Individuals suspected of breaking the law are arrested and taken into custody. They are advised of their constitutional rights, questioned, and subject to limited freedom until further processing. Once an individual is arrested, the booking process takes place. This includes several activities, including fingerprinting, the taking of photographs (mugshots), and in some cases the collection of DNA evidence from the suspect.

Role of law enforcement: initial contact → investigation → arrest → booking

COURTS

If the prosecutor's office decides that there is enough evidence to proceed with the case, it will charge the suspect with a specific crime. This is a major decision-making point at which the prosecutor may decide to dismiss the case. If the prosecutor decides to charge the suspect, a preliminary hearing is held. This process is designed to determine whether there is reason to think that a law has been broken. In some states and in the federal system, a grand jury makes this determination. At this stage, the defendant is brought before the court and the formal charges are read. The defendant is also informed of his or her constitutional right to be represented by legal counsel. A plea of guilty or not guilty is entered, and a trial date is set. Bail may also be considered at this point. Following arraignment, plea bargaining occurs. Here, the prosecutor and defense attorney discuss the case and attempt to agree on a resolution. Typically, the prosecutor seeks a guilty plea in exchange for a reduced sentence. Defense attorneys who believe that the case against their client is weak or that their client is innocent will reject a plea bargain and demand a jury trial.

If the case proceeds to trial, the prosecution and defense present their cases before a jury which decides whether the prosecution has presented enough evidence

The sentencing of a convicted person can be an emotional ordeal. Which key term best describes the movement of a case through the trial process?

to convict the defendant. A verdict of guilty or not guilty is returned. This is called **adjudication**. In cases in which a jury cannot decide on a verdict, the prosecutor must choose between releasing the defendant or requesting a new trial. If a guilty verdict is reached, the judge sentences the convicted party to a punishment, usually a fine, a treatment program, probation, incarceration, or some combination of these. In some serious cases, the sentence may be death.

Role of courts: charging → preliminary hearing → arraignment → plea bargaining → adjudication → sentencing

adjudication—To administer a legal process of judging and to pronounce a judgment.

CORRECTIONS

An offender may have to pay a sum of money as part of his or her punishment. In addition, an offender may be able to serve all or part of the sentence outside of prison or jail. The offender must agree to a set of conditions by which he or she will remain free and report to a probation officer. The offender may have to wear an electronic device that tracks his or her location.

Offenders serve sentences less than a year in a local jail and sentences longer than a year in prison. After release from incarceration, the corrections system attempts to ease the reintegration of the offender into the community. This is typically done through **parole** in which the rights and liberties of the former convict are restricted and requirements such as drug-testing, job counseling, and educational requirements may be imposed.

Role of corrections: fines and probation and/or incarceration → re-entry

parole—The conditional release of a prison inmate who has served part of a sentence and who remains under the court's control.

The Due Process and Crime Control Models

The criminal justice system has a complicated mission. People expect the system to operate efficiently and move cases through the system as expeditiously as possible, but also to protect the innocent, convict and punish the guilty, and deliver justice. Not only are these two expectations difficult to achieve consistently, but they are sometimes at odds. In the 1960s, legal scholar Herbert L. Packer created models to describe these two expectations: the **due process model** and the **crime control model**. The crime control model describes the expectation of an efficient criminal justice system. The due process model describes the expectation of a just and fair system. The tension between these two models can be described as a competition between two sets of values: one that seeks to control crime and one that seeks to protect the legal rights of individuals accused of violating the law. In truth, the criminal justice system exemplifies both of these value systems and seeks to create a balance in which crime is controlled while individual rights are protected.[25]

due process model— A model proposed by legal scholar Herbert L. Packer to describe the public's expectation of a just and fair criminal justice system.

The crime control model is based on the idea that the repression of crime is the most important function of the criminal process. This is because, according to this model, crime control is important to individual freedom. It is difficult to be truly free in a society that does not enforce laws, apprehend offenders, and convict the guilty. If individuals are always living in fear of being victimized, they cannot behave in a free manner, and thus the social order is threatened. So, under the crime control model, the justice process moves like an assembly line. Suspects are apprehended; the most likely suspects are charged and their guilt is ascertained, and the guilty receive an appropriate disposition. A free society is dependent on the criminal justice system doing this efficiently and well. In contrast, the due process model operates more like an "obstacle course," in comparison with the crime control model's assembly line. Each stage of the due process model is designed to obstruct the movement of suspects further along the justice process. This is because the due process model recognizes the role of human error. People make mistakes, or they can be corrupt. Thus, the due process model pursues informal,

crime control model—A model proposed by legal scholar Herbert L. Packer to describe the public's expectation of an efficient criminal justice system.

non-judgmental fact-finding that recognizes the right of a suspect or defendant to receive the most correct and just judicial process possible.[26] Some major distinctions between the two models are outlined in Table 1.2.

The application of these models is affected by the political climate at any given time. Two good examples are illustrated by the efforts of the Warren Court (the U.S. Supreme Court between 1953 and 1969 named for its Chief Justice Earl Warren) and the passage of the USA PATRIOT ACT in response to the terrorist attacks of September 11, 2001. Friendly to the due process model, the Warren Court left a lasting mark on U.S. criminal procedure with its decisions. Notable cases include *Gideon v. Wainwright*, which established that states must provide impoverished defendants with an attorney in felony cases (see Chapter 9) and *Miranda v. Arizona*, which established that police must inform arrestees that they do not have to answer questions and may have an attorney present during questioning (see Chapter 5). On the other hand, the USA PATRIOT ACT is an example of the crime control model. USA PATRIOT stands for Uniting and Strengthening America by Providing Appropriate Tools Required to Intercept and Obstruct Terrorism. This legislation greatly expanded the government's powers to investigate and process cases of terrorism while curtailing the legal protections of not only criminal suspects, but also, to a large extent, the general public.[27]

TABLE 1.2   The Crime Control Model versus the Due Process Model

CRIME CONTROL MODEL	DUE PROCESS MODEL
The repression of crime is the most important function of the criminal justice system and a necessary condition for meaningful communities and a free society.	The most important function of the criminal justice process is to deliver fundamental fairness of the law and due process.
The criminal justice system should be more concerned with the victim's rights than the defendant's rights.	Because the Bill of Rights expressly provides for protection of defendant's rights, the criminal justice system should concentrate on those rather than on the rights of victims.
Police should have expanded powers to investigate, arrest, and search suspects.	Police power should be limited to prevent oppression of individuals by the state.
Legal technicalities that obstruct the police should be eliminated.	Criminal justice authority should be held accountable to the rules, procedures, and guidelines embedded in the Constitution.
The criminal justice system should operate like an assembly line that moves cases efficiently toward disposition.	The government should not convict a person as guilty solely on the facts; a person should be found guilty only if the government has followed legal procedures in its processing of the case.
The main objective of the criminal justice process should be to discover the truth and establish the factual guilt of the accused.	The main objective of the criminal justice process should be to correctly follow legal procedure in establishing the factual guilt of the accused.

How Cases Move Through the System

With an appreciation of how complex the criminal justice system is, we now turn to how cases are processed. Only a small percentage of offenses result in someone going to prison. This is because the system is close to being overloaded. An even slightly larger percentage of cases would be nearly impossible for the system to process in a fair and legal manner given the resources currently available. Therefore, police officers, prosecutors, judges, and corrections officials use their judgment to decide which cases are pushed further into the criminal justice system and which ones are kicked out. It is useful to envision the criminal justice system as a large funnel in which cases move downward toward their final disposition (see Figure 1.1). The problem with the funnel, however, is that it is too small to hold all the cases, so a considerable amount of leakage occurs.

The criminal justice system is much more complex than suggested by the funnel analogy, and this complexity will be revealed in subsequent chapters that cover the system's components in greater detail. The analogy's goal is to indicate how the numbers dwindle drastically when we move down the funnel from offense to sentencing. This funnel analogy illustrates the relatively low number of offenders who are actually incarcerated. Many offenses that enter the system are excluded for several reasons. Briefly, these reasons include, but are not limited to, the following:

1. Cost. As a society, we simply cannot afford to spend the money and resources necessary to have a totally crime-free society. Although crime is a serious social problem, many other worthy items compete for our tax dollars. Increased spending on crime means that health care, national defense, education, highways, and a host of other legitimate and desirable services do not get enough of the resources they require to function effectively. For example, decisions must be made on which military aircraft are built because we cannot afford all of them. Similarly, most students must take out loans to pay for a college education because the government can fund only so many scholarships. The criminal justice system, by some estimates, could bankrupt the nation if funded for all its legitimate needs. This is especially true at the local level: local governments spend far more on criminal justice than state governments or the federal government. Therefore, only a relatively small percentage of offenses ever receive what the public believes to be "full justice."

2. Discretion. Criminal justice practitioners exercise a considerable amount of **discretion**—that is, the power to make decisions—in deciding what happens to individual cases. Although this discretion is constrained by resources, a good amount of personal philosophy and judgment also goes into deciding what happens to cases. This discretion is sometimes deemed problematic, and the influence of individual decision makers is curbed. For example, there can be wide disparity in sentencing across jurisdictions or even between judges in the same city. In an effort to ensure that similar cases are treated more equally, legislatures have passed laws mandating fixed sentences. Mandatory-minimum statutes and three-strikes laws greatly limit the discretion judges have in sentencing offenders. Similarly, some police departments are required to make arrests in domestic assault cases in which there is clear evidence of physical abuse. Some discretion is inherent in the criminal justice system, but its use is contested.

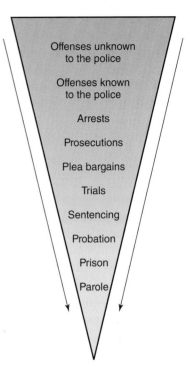

FIGURE 1.1 The Funnel Effect This figure represents the pattern of how cases move through the criminal justice system. The actual number of cases varies by jurisdiction, severity, and annual occurrence. At each point along the way, cases drop out of the system. Charges may be dropped; cases may be dismissed; offenders may abscond; or defendants may plea bargain. Relative to the number of suspects arrested, only a small percentage of offenders actually go to prison. Does the funnel illustrate the total number of offenses that catch the full implications of the public's perception of justice?

discretion—The power of a criminal justice official to make decisions on issues within legal guidelines.

3. Errors. Sometimes cases simply fall through the cracks. Criminal justice practitioners are human and can make mistakes. They are often over-worked and underpaid, and they experience a considerable amount of stress in doing a difficult job. Most jurisdictions do not have sophisticated computer systems that link all the components of the criminal justice system that would help ensure that cases are handled efficiently. Also, criminal justice practitioners might make errors in judgment. The police officer who gives a suspect a second chance or the judge who places a sex offender on probation can find himself or herself betrayed by offenders who do not or cannot appreciate the break they have been given.

The Perception of Crime and the Wedding-Cake Model of Criminal Justice

Not all crime is the same. Many offenses go undetected, and their harm to society is not generally perceived. Some offenses are just a step across the line of good, effective business practices and are considered the price we pay for a market economy. An example of this offense is insider trading (using confidential information about an investment instrument to buy and sell on the stock exchange). Other offenses, such as some murders, are sensationalized by the media and given such vast resources in their detection and prosecution that they distort the perception of the amount and seriousness of crime. Finally, there is the problem of **street crime**: small-scale, violent, and property offenses. These types of crime illustrate how complex and differentiated the issue really is. Making broad general statements about crime is difficult because so many behaviors are considered criminal offenses.

street crime—Small-scale, personal offenses such as single-victim homicide, rape, robbery, assault, burglary, and vandalism.

Crime in the United States has dropped steadily for the last several years. In 2016, property crime (burglary, larceny-theft, motor vehicle theft, and arson) continued to decline, and violent crime (murder, rape, robbery, and aggravated assault), though slightly up from 2015, continued its general decline (see Figure 1.2).[28] This drop in crime reveals an interesting disconnect between the occurrence of crime and the perception of crime. Street crime is often what most people fear and what they consider as needing the strictest social control. As such, prisons continue to be built, zero-tolerance policies enforced, and the **war on drugs** fought.

war on drugs—Governmental policy aimed at reducing the sale and use of illegal drugs.

The wedding-cake model of criminal justice differentiates types of cases based on the seriousness of the offense, the defendant/offender's criminal record, and the relationship between the victim and the defendant/offender.[29] This model also highlights the differences between types of cases based on how the media treats them and how the public considers them. The four layers are as follows (see Figure 1.3).

1. The top layer. As on a wedding cake, the top layer is the smallest but receives the most attention. Referred to as "celebrated cases," the cases in this layer are the ones that fascinate the public the most: unusual or gruesome murders; serial murders and mass murders; mysterious missing-persons cases; and cases that involve famous people. These cases may also interest the public for additional reasons: they may involve children or terrorism, or they may have significant racial or gender dimensions. Examples of such cases include the 2012 shooting of Trayvon Martin by George Zimmerman, the 2015 shooting of nine people at a historic black church in Charleston, South Carolina, or the 2016 Orlando nightclub shooting. The participants in these cases may also have defining qualities that are favorable to media coverage. For instance, in the O. J. Simpson murder case, Simpson, who was accused of murdering his wife and her friend, was a college and professional football star who had gone on to a successful career as a sportscaster and media personality. Top-layer cases differ from others in that they usually involve

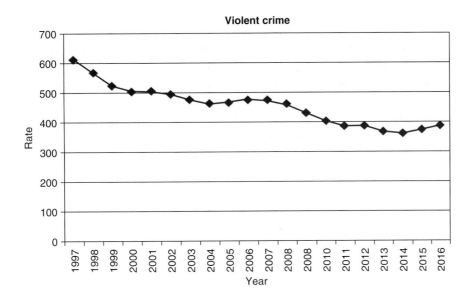

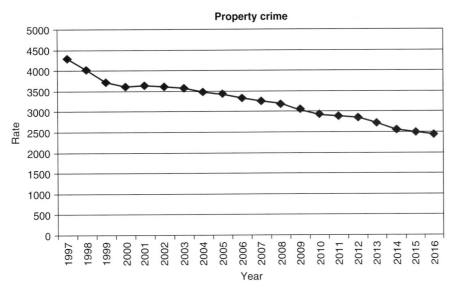

FIGURE 1.2   Violent and Property Crime Rates The rate of violent offending increased slightly in 2016, but the rate of property offending was down for the fifteenth year in a row. Give some possible reasons for the decrease in property offending and the increase in the rate of violent offending.

Source: Federal Bureau of Investigation, Uniform Crime Reports: Crime in the United States 2016, *Table 1, https://ucr .fbi.gov/crime-in-the-u.s/2016/ crime-in-the-u.s.-2016/ topic-pages/offenses-known- to-law-enforcement/tables/ table-1.*

a criminal trial and extensive publicity. It is through these cases that many people develop their opinions of the criminal justice system and their perceptions of how it operates. Although these cases receive a great amount of attention, they are relatively rare.

2. The second layer. The second layer comprises serious felonies, such as rape, murder, manslaughter, and robberies that result in fatalities. As with the first layer, the cases in the second layer often involve a gruesome offense and a criminal trial. Second-layer cases may receive local media coverage and attention but do not reach first-layer status because they involve more ordinary offenses and participants. For example, the robbery of a small-town jewelry store by some local youths who shoot and kill its owner would qualify as such a case.

3. The third layer. Less- serious felonies that typically do not involve fatalities, such as burglary and larceny, compose the third layer. These cases are sometimes dismissed, or defendants may be allowed to plea bargain. Convicted defendants may be placed on probation (the suspension of all or part of a sentence subject to certain conditions). The outcomes for defendants in this layer are less predictable

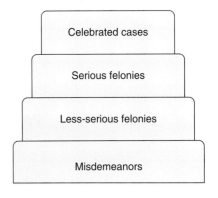

FIGURE 1.3   The Wedding-Cake Model How are celebrated cases different from the lower three layers?

The terrorist bombing at the 2013 Boston Marathon is an example of a celebrated case. Why do celebrated cases get the most media coverage even though they are relatively rare?

because the charges are not as serious. Trials become increasingly rare in this layer. Here, criminal justice proceedings are more routine and less dramatic, and usually the only people interested in them are those who are directly involved.

4. **The bottom layer.** The bottom layer consists of misdemeanors, or minor offenses, which include traffic violations, minor drug violations, shoplifting, and minor assault. Lower criminal courts usually deal with bottom-layer offenses, which are punishable by a fine or jail time up to a year, although there are so many of these offenses that they overwhelm some small courts. Defendants in these cases are not considered threats to public safety, and the typical outcome is a fine, probation, or jail.[30] Trials are rare: some defendants consider the proceedings an annoyance and prefer to just pay the fine for, say, a speeding ticket, rather than go to court. A more troubling outcome in these cases is that, although the offenses are minor, they constitute a major problem for the offenders. Many offenders are too impoverished to not only challenge the case, but also to pay the fine and/or any court fees. Instead, many go to jail and lose their jobs, sending themselves and their families deeper into poverty. In an economically disadvantaged community, enough of these cases can endanger the entire community.

The celebrated cases of the top layer represent the majority of media interest, even though they are relatively rare. At the bottom layer, the number of cases expands greatly. Few cases are unusual enough to command media attention, and the vast number of routine cases remains unseen, unknown, and unappreciated by the public.

PAUSE AND REVIEW

1. **What is the nature of the relationship between local, state, and federal levels of criminal justice?**
2. **What are the basic steps of the criminal justice process?**
3. **Discuss the difference between the due process and crime control models.**
4. **Describe the four layers of the wedding-cake model.**

Types of Crime

LEARNING OBJECTIVE **7**

Discuss why street crime receives more attention than corporate and white-collar crime.

Crime can be divided into different types. Sometimes crime is categorized according to a specific characteristic of the offense. For instance, as you study crime, you will see references to gang crime, victimless crime, environmental crime, sex crime, urban crime, rural crime, drug crime, hate crime, cybercrime, and so on. In these cases, the differentiation is itself worth studying. For example, the phenomenon of young people banding together to sell drugs, commit murders, wear specific colors, and defend neighborhood turf is an important characteristic of gang crime that is worthy of study and differentiates it from, say, hate crime.

This section divides crime into two broad types: street crime and corporate/white-collar crime. As discussed in the previous section, street crime is what most people worry about when they think of crime, probably because it sometimes involves violence. However, **corporate crime** and **white-collar crime** are just as damaging, perhaps even more so, but these types of crime get less attention because no violence is involved. This is essential to the measurement of crime because measures of crime are what help to generate criminal justice funding, media attention, and public concern. If there is little or no official measurement of a type of crime—as with corporate and white-collar crime—then that type of crime will likely receive less social attention. It is significant , then, that the differences between street crime and corporate and white-collar crime are discussed.

Street Crime

Street crime includes a wide variety of acts in both public and private spaces, including interpersonal violence and property crime. These offenses, which include homicide, rape, assault, **larceny**, **arson**, breaking-and-entering, **burglary**, **robbery**, and motor- vehicle theft, are the ones most often included in official measurements of crime. (We discuss official measurements of crime further in Chapter 2.)

A healthy fear of street crime is wise. The effect of rape, assault, and especially homicide may alter how a person and his or her loved ones relate to others and may require many years of recovery. However, street crime is still relatively rare. Most of us go about our daily lives without encountering danger, and we do not need to carry a weapon or distrust people most of the time. Some studies have found that those with the least likelihood of being victimized fear crime the most. Elderly citizens demonstrate the greatest fear of street crime, yet they are the least likely to encounter it. Conversely, young males are the most victimized, but they do not have a great fear of crime. In some ways, this disjuncture is understandable, but it also illustrates how distorted our concept of crime is.[31]

The crime rate does not always correlate with the public perception of the level of crime. During the 1990s, even as the national crime rate was declining, people felt that crime was one of the most important social problems.[32] Because the public is so concerned about street crime, many criminal justice resources are devoted to its prevention and prosecution. This emphasis on street crime is both understandable and problematic. We need to believe that the criminal justice system is doing all that can be done to protect innocent people from predatory criminals. The public clearly demands that the police "do something" to prevent crime and apprehend lawbreakers.[33] According to some criminologists, for example, aggressive control of the homeless is necessary for meaningful, safe communities. People who feel safe on the streets are engaged in public interaction to a greater degree, and this, in turn, means that the streets are populated by more lawful citizens.[34]

The emphasis on street crime is problematic because it drains resources from the prevention of other types of crime. Scholar Jeffrey Reiman contends that corporate crime is much more harmful to society than street crime, stating that the

corporate crime— Offenses committed by a corporation's officers who pursue illegal activity in the corporation's name.

white-collar crime— A nonviolent criminal offense committed during the course of business for financial gain.

larceny—A form of theft in which an offender takes possessions that do not belong to him or her with the intent of keeping them.

arson—Any willful or malicious burning or attempt to burn a dwelling, public building, motor vehicle, aircraft, or personal property of another.

burglary—Breaking into and entering a structure or vehicle with intent to commit a felony or a theft.

robbery—The taking or attempting to take anything of value from the care, custody, or control of a person or persons by force or threat of force or violence and/or by putting the victim in fear.

Larceny is one of the most common types of street crime reported to police. Why is street crime more likely to be reported to the police than other types of crime?

preoccupation of the criminal justice system with street crime is fueled by a racist and class-conscious society. Although street crime is significant to individuals, corporate crime is much more damaging to society as a whole. Reiman argues that individuals with the most money and power define crime and use the criminal justice system to protect their own interests.[35]

Corporate Crime and White-Collar Crime

Sometimes criminal offenders are conventional in all other aspects of their lives, and it is difficult to envision them as lawbreakers. Because harmful behaviors are not always defined as crime, envisioning how otherwise honorable citizens can be considered criminals is sometimes difficult. So-called pillars of society known for their charity, public service, and conventional behavior are sometimes the biggest crooks.

Corporate crime involves breaking laws in the otherwise lawful pursuit of profit. For example, an industrial company that does not follow safety standards in disposing of its industrial waste can do irreparable harm to the environment and to the health of many people. Although the intent of the company's officers may be simply to maximize profits and not to hurt anyone, the result can be devastating. The company's officers did not physically rob or assault the citizens, but the damage done to the community water supply may be much more harmful. Corporations can hurt individuals in a variety of ways. Yet when we look at the law and the response of the criminal justice system, we see that street crime is often met with greater penalties.[36]

Sometimes the terms *corporate crime* and *white-collar crime* are used interchangeably, but there are important distinctions between them.[37] Corporate crime involves the purposeful commission or omission of acts by individuals acting as representatives of a business. Their goal is to make money for the business, and the offenses they commit are related to making the company profitable. Corporate crime, then, may also include environmental crime if a corporation's criminal negligence results in an environmental disaster, such as an oil spill. White-collar crime, by contrast, usually involves employees harming the corporation. For example, the treasurer who embezzles money and the office manager who makes excessive long-distance phone calls are harming the company. Sometimes corporate and white-collar crime may be present in the same offense. It may be argued that the financial offenses of investor Bernard Madoff, who defrauded his investors of

Martin Shkreli, former CEO of Turing Pharmaceuticals, being escorted by federal law enforcement agents after being arrested for securities fraud in December 2015. What is the difference between corporate crime and white-collar crime?

at least $20 billion, were perpetrated by someone who was acting not only in his personal interest but also as the head of a company.[38]

There is no official program that measures corporate and white-collar crime. Without a thorough official measurement, it is difficult to estimate how much corporate and white-collar crime is being perpetrated and who the victims are. Unlike street crime, corporate and white-collar crime are difficult to investigate and difficult for laypeople to understand. Not only may it take years for an offense to be perpetrated, the investigation of a complicated scheme may take years to complete. Bernard Madoff perpetrated fraud for nearly his entire working life and was not caught until he was 71 years old. In contrast, a liquor store robbery may take only a few minutes to plan and execute, and the police may be onto the perpetrators within hours.

PAUSE AND REVIEW

1. **What are some examples of street crime?**
2. **How is corporate crime different from white-collar crime?**
3. **Why does street crime receive more attention than corporate and white-collar crime?**

Offenses and Offenders

The behaviors that offend our sensibilities can be categorized in many ways. We have rules, regulations, norms, folkways, and laws that dictate what is acceptable and what is punished. Laws attempt to define crime in a comprehensible manner, the most basic distinction being between misdemeanors and felonies. This distinction is a rather crude way to distinguish the seriousness of these actions, and it is not made until a law enforcement officer decides which law was violated by the action. The distinction between a **misdemeanor** (a minor criminal offense punishable by a fine and/or jail time for up to one year) and a **felony** (an offense punishable by a sentence of more than a year in state or federal prison and sometimes by death) might be blurred when the prosecutor decides what the formal charge will be. The process becomes even more complicated when, as a result of plea negotiations, the judge passes sentence.[39]

LEARNING OBJECTIVE **8**

Give examples of violent crime, property crime, and public-order crime.

misdemeanor—A minor criminal offense punishable by a fine and/or jail time for up to one year.

felony—An offense punishable by a sentence of more than a year in state or federal prison and sometimes by death.

Therefore, a man who gets into a fistfight may believe he is acting in self-defense, but he might also find that because he severely hurt his opponent, a police officer has charged him with misdemeanor assault. The prosecutor may decide to kick the charge up to a felony because of the use of a baseball bat, but after a plea negotiation the charge might once again become a misdemeanor. The relationship between a behavior and the legal designation ultimately attached to it is sometimes difficult to justify. Therefore, the legal categorizations of offenses are not the best indicators of the nature of crime.[40]

Another way to understand crime is to consider the victimization. Focusing on the victim or object of harm instead of the charge can provide a better measure of the level of crime. The following three-group typology elucidates the similarities and differences among the general classes of crime:

sexual assault—Sexual contact that is committed without the other party's consent or with a party who is not capable of giving consent.

1. Violent crime. These offenses include the violent personal offenses of homicide, rape, **sexual assault**, robbery, and assault.
2. Property crime. These offenses include burglary, arson, embezzlement, larceny-theft, and auto theft.
3. Public-order crime. These offenses include drug use, disturbing the peace, drunkenness, prostitution, and some forms of gambling.

Considering crime in this manner gives us a better idea of the harm caused by unlawful actions than does the simple misdemeanor/felony dichotomy. Although each of these categories spans the range of seriousness from minor irritation to extreme disruption, they group offenses in terms of who or what is harmed. Exploring this typology in greater detail reflects the type of harm done to victims. Each of these categories includes a continuum of offenses that differ in degree and may be either stringently punished or relatively neglected by the criminal justice system.

Violent Crime

rape—Sexual activity, usually sexual intercourse, that is forced on another person without his or her consent, usually under threat of harm. Also, sexual activity conducted with a person who is incapable of valid consent.

The most severe penalties, including capital punishment, are reserved for those who commit violent crime. Personal violent offenses such as murder and **rape** are the most devastating and the most feared of all offenses and receive the most media coverage.[41] These serious offenses occur much less frequently than do property offenses, but they are of the most concern to law enforcement and victims. When considering homicide and assault cases, we can discern certain motivations that apparently compel offenders to engage in this serious antisocial behavior.

› Interpersonal disputes. Sources of dispute can include disagreements over money, charges of infidelity, challenges to masculinity, or insults to moral character. Often, the difference between offender and victim is who is fastest on the draw; that is, there is sometimes no clear relationship between who is responsible for starting the dispute and who emerges the winner.[42] In some segments of society, a subculture of violence emerges in which assault or murder is expected as a way of resolving conflict.[43]

› Instrumental violence. Violence is sometimes used as a means to another criminal end. Drug dealers may kill competitors; robbers sometimes shoot convenience-store clerks, and carjackers sometimes attack drivers to steal automobiles.[44] Some forms of instrumental violence are premeditated. Intimidating witnesses or "teaching a lesson" to an informant employs violence as an extreme form of communication when "a message" needs to be sent.[45] Often, the motivation or message of instrumental violence is difficult to discern, such as when a bank robber successfully takes the money, then shoots the clerk on the way out of the bank.

› Group violence. Another source of motivation to commit violence can be found in the dynamics of certain groups. Assaults or homicides often occur in situations in which groups of young people conflict. Violence is often used in instrumental ways when youth gangs clash over territory or symbolic concerns such as colors of clothing or other displays of gang affiliation. Youths often feel a greater sense of bravado when surrounded by friends and may feel a greater need to demonstrate their courage and rebellion. Group dynamics might encourage and facilitate, and, in some cases, even demand, members' use of violence to address some real or imagined insult. When alcohol or drugs enter the equation, violence is even more likely.[46]

› Serial murder and mass murder. Sometimes violence is instrumental as a part of a larger pattern of crime, as with **serial murder** (the murder of several individual victims in separate incidents), and sometimes it seems random and indiscriminate, as with **mass murder** (the murder of three or more victims in a single incident). Often, this type of offender is the hardest to understand because there is no apparent motivation. Although serial murderers are rare, they usually have some underlying personal logic regarding their targets. Some, such as Ted Bundy, might kill young women with a certain hair color. Others, such as John Gacy or Jeffrey Dahmer, might exclusively kill young men.[47] Even though the motivation might be the result of a psychological problem, the serial murderer is often capable of committing many offenses and eluding detection and arrest. The typical mass murderer is not a chronic violent offender: his or her offense may be the only time the offender has ever broken the law. This is what makes mass murder so difficult for law enforcement to deal with—it is explosive, singular, devastating, and often makes little sense.

› Political violence. Some offenses are meant to send a message. This is the case with political violence, of which the most well-known type is **terrorism**. Terrorism can be domestic, as in the case of the 1995 bombing of the Murrah Federal Building in Oklahoma City, or it can be of the international variety, as in the suicide plane hijackings of September 11, 2001. Terrorism is often committed by intelligent, sincere people who believe violence is necessary for their voices to be heard.[48]

› Rape and sexual assault. Because the motivations for committing rape and sexual assault are often different from the motivations for committing other types of personal violent offenses, and because the effect on the victims can be so devastating, these offenses will be considered as unique forms of violence. Rape is just one of a number of sex offenses that has garnered more attention from criminologists in recent years.[49] Although rape has been a consistent occurrence throughout recorded history, the past 40 years have seen an increased awareness of the definition of what types of behavior constitute rape and sexual assault, as well as greater legal protections for victims. Women and children, once considered as not having individual rights when the perpetrator was a husband or father, are now protected by the criminal justice system.[50] In 2011, the Department of Justice changed the definition

serial murder—The murder of a series of victims during three or more separate events over an extended period of time.

mass murder—The murder of three or more people in a single incident.

terrorism—The use or threat of violence against a state or other political entity in order to coerce.

Serial killer Chester Turner, on death row for killing 10 women in the Los Angeles area, was convicted in June 2014, of four more murders. Why is Turner considered a serial murderer instead of a mass murderer?

The 1995 bombing of the Alfred P. Murrah Federal Building in Oklahoma City, Oklahoma, was a domestic terrorist attack that caused the deaths of 168 people. How do local, state, and federal law enforcement agencies work together to fight terrorism?

of rape from "the carnal knowledge of a female, forcibly and against her will" to "the penetration, no matter how slight, of the vagina or anus with any body part or object, or oral penetration by a sex organ of another person, without the consent of the victim."[51] This new definition expanded how the government collects rape statistics. Additionally, child molestation, date rape, acquaintance rape, the rape of males, and sexual harassment are now recognized as serious types of antisocial behavior and are dealt with in a more humane and serious manner by law enforcement and the courts.[52]

> Robbery. The FBI defines robbery as the taking or attempting to take anything of value from the care, custody, or control of a person or persons by force or threat of force or violence and/or by putting the victim in fear. Robbery varies by location, whether on the street (such as a mugging) or within an institution (such as a bank or a convenience store). Finally, even though carjackings involve the theft of a motor vehicle, they are considered robberies because of the force involved.

Property Crime

The accumulation of wealth and possessions is an important cornerstone of individual and group well-being in the United States, and laws protect the rights of those who own and control property. These laws range from prohibitions against theft to the copyrights that protect intellectual and creative endeavors. The types of property crime that are best measured by the criminal justice system are those in which the offender is a stranger to the victim. Although many laws address differences in opinion while transacting business, these conflicts are usually covered by civil law. Burglary, larceny-theft, motor vehicle theft, and arson are dealt with by the criminal law and measured by the FBI. The following are several points to understand when considering the measurement of property crime.

> Burglary is different from larceny-theft. When classifying the taking of another person's property, several distinctions determine whether the offense is larceny-theft or burglary. Burglary involves the unlawful entry of a structure to commit a felony. Larceny-theft involves the unlawful taking of another person's

Arson involves setting fire to a structure. What are some of the motivations that drive individuals to set fires?

property. Larceny-theft includes theft from a person by stealth such as pocket-picking, purse-snatching (when only minimal force is used), shoplifting, thefts of articles from motor vehicles, and thefts from coin-operated machines.

> Motor vehicle theft involves the theft of most self-propelled vehicles that run on land surfaces and not on rails. The theft of water craft, construction equipment, airplanes, and farming equipment is classified as larceny rather than motor vehicle theft.

> Arson involves purposely set fires. It does not matter whether the fire was started with the intent to defraud, only that it was willfully or maliciously set. Fires of suspicious or unknown origin are not treated as arson.[53]

Public-Order Crime

Some criminal offenses involve no discernible victim. **Victimless crime** involves consensual interactions or behaviors that offend the powerful groups of society who have succeeded in having their concerns and sensibilities elevated to the level of the criminal law. Although broad consensus exists on some of these behaviors, there is also a good deal of controversy about offenses that are a matter of values.[54]

Behaviors that fit into the category of offenses against the public order include drug use and sales, loitering, gambling, prostitution, vagrancy, disorderly conduct, and liquor law violations. These are often considered to be nuisance offenses, reflecting quality-of-life concerns for many people. The laws concerning these offenses are vigorously enforced in some places and almost completely ignored in others.[55] For instance, when vagrants, street people, and the homeless are considered to be interfering with the tourism trade, shopkeepers, hotel owners, and restaurant managers might ask the police to clear the streets.[56] It is worth noting that the police have broad decision-making powers in deciding how to enforce public-order laws. They might overlook the possession of small amounts of marijuana in one instance and decide to make an arrest in another if the offender does not show respect.[57]

victimless crime—
Behaviors that are deemed undesirable because they offend community standards rather than directly harm people or property.

PAUSE AND REVIEW

1. **What are some examples of violent crime, property crime, and public-order crime?**

Two women march for sex workers' rights in the Capital Pride Parade in Ottawa, Ontario, Canada. Who are the victims of public-order crimes such as prostitution?

FOCUS ON ETHICS   A Balance of Interests

In your job as a probation officer, you are assigned the case of a rich and successful accountant who is on probation for driving under the influence of alcohol. As part of her community service, the accountant has spent each Saturday morning at a local nursing home where she has been helping the residents fill out their tax forms. This accountant has secured thousands of dollars in tax refunds for these elderly citizens. In fact, one of the residents, who happens to be your grandmother, reports that not only is this accountant helping the residents save money, but she also has been coming to the nursing home during the middle of the week, on her own time, to talk to lonely and depressed residents.

You feel a little guilty that this accountant has developed a close relationship with your grandmother and that you have not been to the nursing home in months. Being suspicious, you investigate to see whether the accountant knows that you have a relative in the home. You discover that not only does she not know, but she has volunteered to serve as a member of the board of directors of the home and help the residents deal with confusing social service agencies such as Medicare and Social Security.

Late one night you get a call from the accountant. She is obviously drunk and informs you that she has just crashed her car into a tree and that she needs a ride home before the police come and arrest her. You know that if she gets another DUI, she not only will lose her license but will also have to spend 90 days in jail and might lose her job. Although you have little sympathy for people who cannot control their drinking, this young woman has been turning her life around and doing good works, especially for the elderly. You see potential in this client.

WHAT DO YOU DO?
1. Pick her up. You owe her for helping your grandmother, and this is one of the few things you can do to repay her help and kindness.
2. Call the police and report her. You are a court officer, and you cannot ethically do anything else. Also, you might get in trouble if you do not call.
3. Help her but make a deal stipulating that she will check herself into a clinic and get help for her drinking problem. Use this last incident as leverage to force her to confront her drinking.
4. Call your supervisor and ask to be relieved of the case because you can no longer be objective.

For more insight as to how someone might respond to such an ethical dilemma, visit the companion website at www.oup.com/us/fuller to watch a video that connects this scenario to a real-world situation.

Summary

LEARNING OBJECTIVE 1 Define social control.	Social control refers to the rules, habits, and customs a society uses to enforce conformity to its norms.
LEARNING OBJECTIVE 2 Outline how the U.S. criminal justice system protects individual rights.	The protection of individual rights is an integral part of the functioning of law enforcement. The government serves citizens' interests by finding methods to control crime without allowing law enforcement agencies to turn the country into a police state.
LEARNING OBJECTIVE 3 Define crime and criminal justice.	Crime is as an action taken by a person or a group of people that violates the rules of society to the point that harm is done to an individual or to society's interests. Criminal justice is a social institution whose mission is to control crime by detecting, detaining, adjudicating, and punishing and/or rehabilitating people who break the law.
LEARNING OBJECTIVE 4 List the steps of the criminal justice process.	Law enforcement: Initial contact, investigation, arrest, booking Courts: Charging, preliminary hearing, arraignment, plea bargaining, adjudication, sentencing Corrections: Fines and probation, incarceration, reentry
LEARNING OBJECTIVE 5 Explain the major difference between the due process and crime control models.	The crime control model describes the expectation of an efficient criminal justice system. The due process model describes the expectation of a just and fair system.
LEARNING OBJECTIVE 6 Describe the wedding-cake model of criminal justice.	The wedding-cake model of criminal justice differentiates types of cases based on the seriousness of the offense, the defendant/offender's criminal record, and the relationship between the victim and the defendant/offender. This model also highlights the differences between types of cases based on how the media treats them and how the public considers them. The top layer consists of cases that receive the most attention; the middle layers comprise grave felonies; and the fourth layer comprises less serious offenses.
LEARNING OBJECTIVE 7 Discuss why street crime receives more attention than corporate and white-collar crime.	People are more afraid of street crime because it is sometimes violent. It also gets more media attention and is easier for the public to understand. Corporate and white-collar offenses may take years to perpetrate and investigate, whereas most street crime happens relatively quickly.
LEARNING OBJECTIVE 8 Give examples of violent crime, property crime, and public-order crime.	Violent crime offenses include homicide, rape, sexual assault, robbery, and assault. Property crime offenses include burglary, arson, embezzlement, larceny-theft, and auto theft. Public-order offenses include drug use, disturbing the peace, drunkenness, prostitution, and some forms of gambling.

Critical Reflections

1. What is the proper role of the criminal justice system in maintaining social control? How does the criminal justice system share this responsibility with other institutions such as the school, family, and religious institutions?

2. Explain how different individuals can have wildly different opinions on what the goals of the criminal justice system should be. How may a person's social location (age, sex, race, gender, economic situation) influence how a person feels about the role of the criminal justice system?

Key Terms

adjudication **p. 11**
arrest **p. 7**
arson **p. 17**
burglary **p. 17**
corporate crime **p. 17**
crime **p. 5**
crime control model **p. 11**
criminal justice **p. 5**
discretion **p. 13**
due process model **p. 11**

felony **p. 19**
justice **p. 5**
larceny **p. 17**
mass murder **p. 21**
misdemeanor **p. 19**
parole **p. 11**
probation **p. 8**
rape **p. 20**
robbery **p. 17**
serial murder **p. 21**

sexual assault **p. 20**
social control **p. 4**
sociological imagination **p. 7**
street crime **p. 14**
terrorism **p. 21**
victimless crime **p. 23**
war on drugs **p. 14**
white-collar crime **p. 17**

Endnotes

1 Emily Greenhouse, "The Downfall of the Most Hated Man on the Internet," *The New Yorker*, January 28, 2014, http://www.newyorker.com/tech/elements/the-downfall-of-the-most-hated-man-on-the-internet.

2 Charlotte Laws, "I've Been Called the 'Erin Brockovich' of Revenge Porn, and for the First Time Ever, Here Is My Entire Uncensored Story of Death Threats, Anonymous and the FBI," XOJane, November 21, 2013, http://www.xojane.com/it-happened-to-me/charlotte-laws-hunter-moore-erin-brockovich-revenge-porn.

3 Megan Geuss, "Revenge Porn Site Operator Hunter Moore Pleads Guilty to Hacking, ID Theft," Ars Technica, February 18, 2015, http://arstechnica.com/tech-policy/2015/02/revenge-porn-site-operator-hunter-moore-pleads-guilty-to-hacking-id-theft.

4 Alex Morris, "Hunter Moore: The Most Hated Man on the Internet," *Rolling Stone*, November 13, 2012, http://www.rollingstone.com/culture/news/the-most-hated-man-on-the-internet-20121113.

5 Carole Cadwalladr, "Charlotte Laws' Fight with Hunter Moore, the Internet's Revenge Porn King," *theguardian*, March 30, 2014, http://www.theguardian.com/culture/2014/mar/30/charlotte-laws-fight-with-internet-revenge-porn-king.

6 Ibid.

7 Ibid.

8 Greenhouse, "The Downfall of the Most Hated Man on the Internet."

9 Motherboard, Revenge Porn King Gets Two Years in Prison, December 2, 2015, http://motherboard.vice.com/read/revenge-porn-king-gets-two-years-in-prison.

10 Cyber Civil Rights Initiative, http://www.cybercivilrights.org/revenge-porn-laws. Accessed April 2016.

11 Justin Peters, "Was Israel Keyes the Most Meticulous Serial Killer of Modern Times?," Slate, December 10, 2012, http://www.slate.com/blogs/crime/2012/12/10/israel_keyes_suicide_is_he_the_most_meticulous_serial_killer_of_modern_times.html.

12 Rick Anderson, "Israel Keyes: In Plane Sight," *Seattle Weekly News*, January 22, 2013, http://www.seattleweekly.com/2013-01-23/news/israel-keyes-in-plane-sight.

13 Peters, "Was Israel Keyes the Most Meticulous Serial Killer of Modern Times?"; Anderson, "Israel Keyes: In Plane Sight."

14 Peters, "Was Israel Keyes the Most Meticulous Serial Killer of Modern Times?"

15 Anderson, "Israel Keyes: In Plane Sight."

16 Peter Holley, "After 90-Year-Old Is Arrested, Florida Judge Halts Law That Restricts Feeding the Homeless," *Washington Post*, December 3, 2014, https://www.washingtonpost.com/news/post-nation/wp/2014/12/03/after-90-year-old-is-arrested-florida-judge-halts-law-that-restricts-feeding-the-homeless.

17 BBC, "British Spies 'Moved after Snowden Files Read,'" http://www.bbc.com/news/uk-33125068.

18 Peter Finn and Sari Horwitz, "U.S. Charges Snowden with Espionage," *Washington Post*, June 21, 2013, http://www.washingtonpost.com/world/national-security/us-charges-snowden-with-espionage/2013/06/21/507497d8-dab1-11e2-a016-92547bf094cc_story.html. David M. Herszenhorn, "Leaker Files for Asylum to Remain in Russia," *New York Times*, July 16, 2013, http://www.nytimes.com/2013/07/17/world/europe/snowden-submits-application-for-asylum-in-russia.html.

19 Kathy Lally, Anthony Faiola, and Jia Lynn Yang, "Edward Snowden Flees Hong Kong for Moscow, Asks Ecuador to Grant Him Asylum," *Washington Post*, June 24, 2013, http://www.washingtonpost.com/world/snowden-departs-hong-kong-for-a-third-country-government-says/2013/06/23/08e9eff2-dbde-11e2-a9f2-42ee3912ae0e_story.html.

20 Michael Birnbaum, "Russia Grants Edward Snowden Residency for Three More Years," *Washington*

Post, August 7, 2014, http://www .washingtonpost.com/world/europe/ russia-grants-edward-snowden- residency-for-3-more-years/201 4/08/07/8b257293-1c30-45fd- 8464-8ed278d5341f_story.html.

21 Gordon Hunt, "Edward Snowden: I've Applied for Asylum in 21 Countries," Silicon Republic, June 5, 2015, https://www.siliconrepublic. com/enterprise/edward-snowden-ive- applied-for-asylum-in-21-countries.

22 C. Wright Mills, *The Sociological Imagi- nation* (New York: Oxford University Press, 1959).

23 Sunil B. Desai, "Solving the Inter-agency Puzzle," *Policy Review* (February 1, 2005): 57–71.

24 Ibid.

25 Herbert L. Packer, *The Limits of the Criminal Sanction* (Stanford, Calif.: Stanford University Press, 1968).

26 Herbert L. Packer, "Two Models of the Criminal Process," *University of Penn- sylvania Law Review* 113, no. 1 (1964). [AU: Please provide pages. THERE ARE NO PAGES.]

27 Walter M. Brasch, *America's Unpatri- otic Acts: The Federals Government's Violation of Constitutional and Civil Rights* (New York: Peter Lang, 2005).

28 Federal Bureau of Investigation, *Crime in the United States 2015*, Table 1: Crime in the United States, https:// ucr.fbi.gov/crime-in-the-u.s/2015/ crime-in-the-u.s.-2015/tables/table-1.

29 Lawrence M. Friedman and Robert V. Percival, *The Roots of Justice: Crime and Punishment in Alameda County, California, 1870–1910* (Chapel Hill: University of North Carolina Press, 1981). Samuel Walker, *Sense and Nonsense about Crime, Drugs, and Communities*, 8th ed. (Stamford, Conn.: Cengage Learning, 2015), 43–54. Don M. Gottfredson, *Decision- making in the Criminal Justice System: Reviews and Essays* (Rockville, Md.: National Institute of Mental Health, Center for Studies of Crime and Delinquency, 1975).

30 Walker, *Sense and Nonsense about Crime, Drugs, and Communities.*

31 William G. Doerner and Stephen P. Lab, *Victimology*, 5th ed. (Cincinnati, Ohio: Lexis-Nexis, 2008), 289–299.

32 Alfred Blumstein and Joel Wallman, *The Crime Drop in America* (New York: Cambridge University Press, 2005).

33 Ronald D. Hunter and Mark L. Dantz- ker, *Crime and Criminality: Causes and Consequences* (Upper Saddle River, N.J.: Prentice Hall, 2002).

34 James Q. Wilson and George L. Kel- ling, "Broken Windows," in *Critical Issues in Policing: Contemporary Issues*, 2d ed., eds. Roger G. Durham and Geoffrey P. Alpert (Prospect Heights, Ill.: Waveland Press, 1993).

35 Jeffrey Reiman, *The Rich Get Richer and the Poor Get Prison*, 8th ed. (Boston: Allyn & Bacon, 2006).

36 Ibid.

37 Lewis R. Mizell, Jr., *Masters of Decep- tion: The Worldwide White-Collar Crime Crisis and Ways to Protect Yourself* (New York: Wiley, 1997).

38 "The Madoff Recovery Initiative," http://www.madofftrustee.com/. Accessed January 2016.

39 Ellen Hochstedler Steury and Nancy Frank, *Criminal Court Process* (Minneapolis/St. Paul, Minn.: West, 1996).

40 Maximo Langer, "Rethinking Plea Bar- gaining: Prosecutorial Adjudication in American Criminal Procedure," *American Journal of Criminal Law* 33, no. 3 (2006): 223–299.

41 Chris McCormick, ed., *Constructing Danger: The Mis/Representation of Crime in the News* (Halifax, Nova Scotia: Fernwood, 1995).

42 Lance Hannon, "Race, Victim Precipi- tated Homicide, and the Subculture of Violence Thesis," *Journal of Social Sciences* 41, no. 1 (2004): 115–121.

43 Albert K. Cohen, *Delinquent Boys: The Culture of the Gang* (New York: The Free Press, 1955).

44 Mitch Stacy, "Details Sketchy in Kill- ing of Charlotte County Prison Guard," *Florida Times Union*, June 12, 2003.

45 Frederic G. Reamer, *Criminal Lessons: Case Studies and Commentary on Crime and Justice* (New York: Columbia University Press, 2003). See especially Chapter 5, "Crimes of Revenge and Retribution," 97–119.

46 Malcolm Klein, *The American Street Gang: Its Nature, Prevalence, and*

Control (New York: Oxford University Press, 1997).

47 Eric W. Hickey, *Serial Murderers and Their Victims*, 4th ed. (Belmont, Calif.: Wadsworth, 2006).

48 Alex Schmid and Janny de Graaf, *Violence as Communication: Insurgent Terrorism and the Western News Media* (Newbury Park, Calif.: Sage, 1982).

49 Eric W. Hickey, ed., *Sex Crimes and Paraphilia* (Upper Saddle River, N.J.: Prentice Hall, 2006).

50 David Finkelhor and Kersti Yllo, *License to Rape: Sexual Abuse of Wives* (New York: Holt, Rinehart, and Winston, 1985).

51 Federal Bureau of Investigation, Attorney General Eric Holder An- nounces Revisions to the Uniform Crime Report's Definition of Rape, January 6, 2012, https://www.fbi. gov/news/pressrel/press-releases/ attorney-general-eric-holder- announces-revisions-to-the-uniform- crime-reports-definition-of-rape.

52 Dean G. Kilpatrick, David Beatty, and Susan Smith Hawley, "The Rights of Crime Victims: Does Legal Protection Make a Difference?" in *Victims and Victimization: Essential Readings*, eds. David Shichor and Stephen G. Tibbetts (Prospect Heights, Ill.: Waveland Press, 2000), 287–304.

53 Terence D. Miethe and Richard C. McCorkle, *Crime Profiles: The Anatomy of Dangerous Persons, Places, and Situa- tions* (Los Angeles: Roxbury, 2001).

54 Robert F. Meier and Gilbert Geis, *Victimless Crime? Prostitution, Drugs, Homosexuality, Abortion* (Los Angeles: Roxbury, 1997).

55 William H. Daly, "Law Enforcement in Times Square, 1970s-1990s," in *Sex, Scams, and Street Life: The Sociol- ogy of New York City's Times Square*, ed. Robert P. McNamara (Westport, Conn.: Praeger, 1995), 97–106.

56 John A. Backstand, Don Gibbons, and Joseph F. Jones, "Who's in Jail? An Exam- ination of the Rabble Hypothesis," *Crime and Delinquency* 38 (1992): 219–229.

57 Joseph Goldstein, "Police Discretion Not to Invoke the Criminal Process," in *The Invisible Justice System: Discre- tion and the Law*, eds. Burton Atkins and Mark Pogrebin (Cincinnati, Ohio: Anderson, 1978), 65–81.

Chapter 2

How Crime Is Measured and Who It Affects

Chicago Police Superintendent John Escalante (left) speaks during a news conference discussing crime in Chicago on December 30, 2015. Why are police chiefs sensitive to political pressure from mayors regarding crime statistics?

n July 2013, Chicago police found the naked, decomposed body of 20-year-old Tiara Groves on the floor of a vacant warehouse. Wire was draped over her hand and wound around the arms of a nearby chair. She had been gagged. Toxicology tests revealed non-lethal amounts of heroin and alcohol in her system. Police told Groves's mother, who had filed the missing-person report, that her daughter was murdered. The pathologist ruled Groves's death a homicide by "unspecified means," meaning that it was uncertain exactly what had killed the young woman. However, by December, police reclassified the case as a noncriminal death investigation, and the death of Tiara Groves escaped Chicago's murder statistics for 2013.[1]

Chicago has a crime problem. It also has a crime-reporting problem. In a two-part series about the city's crime, *Chicago* magazine found that the unbelievable drop in crime in Chicago was, well, unbelievable. The steep drops in serious crime were too good to be true. The reason for this reported decline was that some crimes were not being counted. This non-counting was achieved in several ways, such as assigning new codes to certain offenses so that they were recorded as less serious offenses; pushing the recording of offenses forward or backward in time so that the statistics were not reported in the current year; charging suspects with less serious offenses; and, finally, as in the Tiara Groves case, recategorizing cases entirely. It is possible, according to *Chicago* magazine, that serious crime in Chicago has not been accurately reported for many years.[2]

In April 2016, Groves's neighbor, Leondra Martin—who can be seen on a surveillance video arguing with Groves—and a man named Desmond Collins were convicted of concealing Groves's death.[3] The pair say they saw Groves die of a heroin overdose and hid her body. Groves's sister, Kenyatta, believes "they got away with murder."[4]

THINK ABOUT IT > How can the measurement of crime rates be made less political and more scientifically accurate?

LEARNING OBJECTIVE 1

Describe three logistical obstacles to measuring crime effectively and efficiently.

The Problems of Measuring Crime

Measuring crime is tricky. Criminal justice scholars, government officials, and the public all have different motivations, interests, and ideologies that dictate why and how crime should be measured. Whereas scholars and the public want a realistic picture of crime so that they can make informed decisions, some police administrators may have an occupational perspective. For example, if a police chief wants to make the case that his or her department needs more financial resources, a crime wave could be used as a justification. Conversely, if the police chief is in political trouble, that chief might determine that a drop in the crime rate would be evidence that he or she is doing a good job. In the case of Chicago's crime-reporting controversies, the city is under social pressure to do something about the rate of serious crime in order to make Chicago safer for its citizens. The logistical obstacles to measuring crime effectively and efficiently are daunting. These logistical problems, which we will cover in detail later in the chapter, include:

> Problems of definition: Although laws are written in a specific manner to minimize ambiguity, the interpretation of behaviors that seem to be criminal offenses can be problematic. For the legislator who writes the law in

the safety of his or her office, the circumstances might seem clear-cut and easily defined. For the police officer, the information needed to determine whether a criminal offense is committed might be conflicting, absent, or even false.

> Problems of resources: Thousands of criminal justice jurisdictions report official criminal justice statistics. Some large metropolitan or state agencies have teams of well-trained personnel dedicated to tracking crime, whereas other, smaller agencies do not. Consequently, the priority of maintaining these records varies significantly across jurisdictions based on the available resources, in terms of both finances and personnel.

> Problems of politics: Public officials do not want their communities perceived as high-crime areas. The economic and social effects of the perception of crime can cause city officials to pressure law enforcement agencies to minimize the reporting of crime. For this reason, aggravated assaults might be reported as simple battery, and motor vehicle theft might be deemed to be joyriding, depending on the political circumstances.

To understand crime's effect on individuals and society, we must understand how crime is conceptualized and measured. There is a big difference between a homicide and some children throwing rocks through the windows of an abandoned house. Similarly, there is a big difference between massive corporate fraud and the motorist whose license is suspended after three drunken-driving convictions.[5] The total number of criminal offenses, or even the crime rate, fails to capture the variability and deleterious effects of crime. Although crime measures are useful in any comparison of the relative safety of cities, states, or regions, the way crime is measured can provide misleading and inaccurate pictures of how it is distributed and how it affects people, especially victims.[6]

The victim performs an important role in the criminal justice system. The victim of a criminal offense is one of a triad of important actors. The perpetrator commits the offense; the victim is on the receiving end of the behavior; and the criminal justice system responds to the offense in the name of the state. This is an important point. Once a criminal offense has been committed, the criminal justice system sets the victim aside, and the prosecutor acts in the name of society rather than the victim. Because of this structure, many claim that the victim is forgotten in the criminal justice process.[7] For example, the police may decide not to arrest a criminal suspect; the prosecutor may decide to accept a lenient plea bargain or not to press charges at all; or a judge may dismiss the charges against a defendant or impose a lenient punishment on a convicted offender. Or, as may have happened in the case of Tiara Groves, the death may not be counted as a homicide for political reasons. These actions often occur without any input from the victim or victim's family, which is not only frustrating for those parties, but also makes the public cynical about the quality of justice meted out by the criminal justice system.[8]

This chapter will explore the role and perspective of the victim in several ways. First, we consider some typologies of victims. Next, we will look at categories of victims and how the criminal justice system responds to them, with a particular focus on programs aimed at alleviating harm.

PAUSE AND REVIEW

1. **What are three logistical obstacles to the effective and efficient measurement of crime?**

How Crime Is Measured

dark figure of crime—A term describing crime that is unreported and never quantified.

burglary (from Chapter 1)—Breaking into and entering a structure or vehicle with intent to commit a felony or a theft.

In this section, we will examine the various tools used for measuring crime and identify some of the issues and concerns raised by trying to measure the amount of crime in communities. Whenever there are variations in crime rates, care must be taken to ensure that these variations are the result of actual changes in crime and not measurement error. Besides definitional problems as to how to classify certain behaviors, there may also be perceptual problems about exactly when a behavior becomes a criminal offense. Kids who are fist fighting may think they are "just horsing around," but to the parent of the child with the bloody nose, it might look like bullying or an assault. To be included in the measurement of crime, the incident must be reported to law enforcement, which reports data to the Uniform Crime Reports and National Incident-Based Reporting System, or researchers who collect data for the National Crime Victimization Survey and self-report studies.

One of the problems in attempting to measure crime is that not all offenses are reported. If an offense is not reported, it will not be counted in the indices that comprise the official measures of crime rates. The offenses that actually occur but do not get reported are called the "**dark figure of crime**" (see Figure 2.1). A victim might not want to report an offense to the police for several reasons.

› An offense might be so subtle that it is never known to have happened. Suppose that a person uses a passkey to break into an apartment with the intent to steal a television belonging to the resident, then changes his mind and leaves, disturbing nothing. This action constitutes **burglary**—which is the breaking into and entering of a structure or vehicle with intent to commit a felony or a theft—but no one but the offender would ever know it happened.

› An offense might not be perceived as such. Suppose that in the course of a hockey game, a defenseman for the Philadelphia Flyers were to slash a star center of the Montreal Canadiens with his hockey stick, opening a large cut

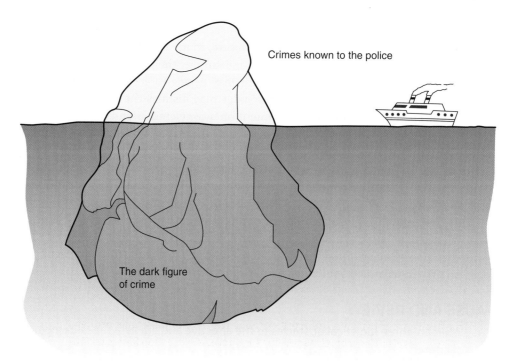

FIGURE 2.1 The Dark Figure of Crime Would efforts to shed light on the dark figure of crime infringe too much on individual civil rights?

New York Rangers' Colton Orr skates away after knocking out Philadelphia Flyers' Todd Fedoruk after a fight during a hockey game at Madison Square Garden in New York. Why is violence in professional sports seldom prosecuted in the criminal court?

over his eye. Such incidents occur in the heat of competition and are defined as major penalties within the context of the game. The incident described, of course, also constitutes a criminal offense that might be classified as an aggravated assault under the Uniform Crime Reports or as a wounding in the Canadian Crime Statistics. However, the event is unlikely to be perceived as a crime by either player, by either team, by the referees, or by the fans, and it is unlikely to be reported to the police. In the sport of boxing, a fighter who abides by the sport's rules might cause the death of the other fighter and face no sanctions from the criminal justice system, the referee, or the sport's ruling body.

› An offense might not be reported because the offender is a family member, a friend, or an acquaintance.

› An offense might not be reported because the victim believes that it was trivial or that the potential penalty is too grave for the harm done.

› An offense might not be reported because the victim fears reprisal.

› An offense might not be reported because the victim feels antipathy toward the police.

› An offense might not be reported because the victim may have broken the law as well or is embarrassed by the circumstances under which the offense occurred.[9]

Given these reasons for not reporting crime, does it make any sense to try to measure crime and then base criminal justice system policy on these flawed numbers? The answer is yes, but with caution. Although the dark figure of crime will always be unknown, an idea of the extent of crime can be surmised with the development of precise definitions and uniform reporting standards. Because crime rates are calculated every year and show a pattern of stability, criminal justice experts can assume that unreported crime varies at about the same rates.[10] However, a change in reporting can be mistakenly interpreted as a change in the level of crime.

For example, suppose a community establishes a new rape crisis center. As part of their duties, the center's staff begins an educational prevention and awareness project in which they visit schools and community groups and encourage victims to report rape and sexual assaults. The staff members also support victims in the ordeal of reporting their experiences to the police. Although the number of rapes in the community might remain constant, the rape crisis center has stimulated an increase in victim reporting that results in more arrests, prosecutions, and incarcerations. Rape may appear to be on the rise in the community, when in reality, more of the dark figure of crime is becoming known and crime measurement is becoming more accurate.[11]

Imperfect as they are, crime measurements are used by criminal justice officials to make several types of decisions. For instance, law enforcement officials can use the frequency and seriousness of crime statistics in their jurisdictions as justifications for staffing patterns and tactical decisions. When they find areas that have an unusual number of assaults, larcenies, or murders, they can use the statistics to commit more law enforcement resources to these areas. Additionally, criminal justice officials can approach legislatures or city council members for additional funding based on measures of crime.

Researchers within both government agencies, such as the Bureau of Justice Statistics, and academia use official measures of crime to construct the crime picture. These pictures, in turn, are used by officials to make funding decisions and, to a large extent, develop the public's perception of the frequency and seriousness of crime in their jurisdictions. However, research has shown that these official measures of crime may be severely flawed (see A Closer Look 2.1).

Sexual Assault Awareness Month demonstration and visual display on the lawn of the Lillis Business School on the University of Oregon campus. How might raising awareness about rape increase the level of reporting of this crime?

A CLOSER LOOK 2.1
Cracks in the Statistics

The data collected by the FBI's Uniform Crime Reports (UCR) system are not accurate because there will always be a dark figure of crime that cannot be measured. Researchers, statisticians, criminal justice professionals, and legislators use UCR data because it is the best available, but the picture of crime the UCR provides is like a photograph of shadows in a snowstorm. You can see faint outlines of figures that look like people, trees, and animals and guess at what may be there, but you cannot see the people's faces, count the number of trees, or identify the animals.

The UCR has always had its critics. In 1931, legal scholar Sam Bass Warner reviewed burglary and robbery data from the 1930 UCR and concluded that the publication of false and misleading criminal statistics is not merely a waste of government funds, but a perversion of the public consciousness regarding one of the most important functions of our government.[12]

Since then, criticism of the UCR has continued. The consistent complaints are:

- Many offenses are not included because citizens do not report them to the police, and citizen reporting varies.
- The police are biased and selective in reporting offenses.
- The UCR reflects the organizational interests of law enforcement agencies that may use the data to further their own interests.
- Some agencies do not report or report incompletely.
- Reporting procedures and definitions of crime are inconsistent across agencies.[13]

THINK ABOUT IT

1. Should the UCR program be continued if it provides such poor statistics? Why or why not?
2. Do you agree or disagree with Warner's critique?

Uniform Crime Reports

The FBI's **Uniform Crime Reports (UCR)** is the most extensive and useful measure of crime we have. This annual publication compiles the volume and rate of eight criminal offenses—four violent crimes and four property crimes (see Table 2.1)—for the states and many jurisdictions (for an example of regional crime rates, see Figure 2.2). The UCR program is a cooperative statistical effort of law enforcement agencies that voluntarily report data on the offenses they know about. The program's main objective is to provide reliable information for use in law enforcement administration, operation, and management. Scholars, legislators, urban planners, and the media also use the UCR for research and decision-making purposes. Additionally, the UCR keeps citizens informed about the level and seriousness of crime in their communities.

Uniform Crime Reports (UCR)—An annual publication by the Federal Bureau of Investigation that uses data from all participating law enforcement agencies in the United States to summarize the incidence and rate of reported crime.

TABLE 2.1 Federal Bureau of Investigation Crime Classification

VIOLENT CRIMES	PROPERTY CRIMES
Murder and non-negligent manslaughter	Burglary
Rape	Larceny-theft
Robbery	Motor vehicle theft
Aggravated assault	Arson

Regional Crime Rates, 2016
Violent and Property Crimes per 100,000 Inhabitants

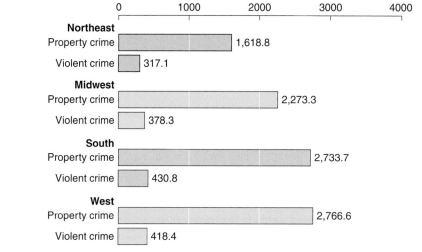

FIGURE 2.2   **Regional Crime Rates** Examine the differences in regional crime rates. Why might the rates of some regions be so much higher than others?

Source: Federal Bureau of Investigation, Crime in the United States, 2016, *Crime Map, https:// ucr.fbi.gov/crime-in-the.u.s/2016/ crime-in-the-u.s.-2016/figures/ region-map.*

Despite the numerous issues and concerns with how these records are compiled and used, they remain the best available picture of crime, even though that picture sometimes tends to be out of focus.[14] In 2016, more than 18,000 law enforcement agencies throughout the country voluntarily participated in the UCR program, representing about 98 percent of the U.S. population.[15]

Although the UCR provides a useful picture of crime in the United States, it is subject to unintentional and intentional error.[16]

> Unintentional sources of error. The UCR represents a massive collection effort. Thousands of law enforcement officers and clerks enter data into the system, leaving plenty of opportunity for simple errors.[17] For instance, homicide would seem to be the most unambiguous category of crime. Someone is dead, which means the offense will be reported and coded as such. Yet, in some cases, the victim dies in the hospital weeks after the case has been entered into the system. Some jurisdictions are better than others are when it comes to follow-up reporting of the subsequent death and the new homicide charge. Additionally, police officers might view certain offenses differently depending on their personal philosophies about gender roles. For example, variations exist within and across

jurisdictions in the categorization of rape if the parties involved are spouses or intimate partners. Also, researchers have found that few rapes are committed along with other offenses, such as a robbery and a rape. However, rapes that do co-occur with other offenses are more likely to be reported to police than rapes that occur as single offenses. This means that the source of error within rape statistics is probably higher than in statistics for other violent offenses.[18]

> Intentional sources of error. The UCR is an important social indicator that reflects the quality of life in a jurisdiction. Police chiefs, sheriffs, mayors, and other public officials are judged by the efficacy of their policies, and the UCR presents objective criteria on which to base pay raises, promotions, and firings. Because careers are based on these numbers, and the opportunity exists to influence these numbers, it is not surprising that sometimes "the books get cooked."[19] This can happen in two ways. For example, perhaps a sheriff wants to modernize a fleet of squad cars and so instructs the deputies to change their crime-reporting behavior by counting every trivial infraction, inflating the level of crime and thus bringing in more money. By contrast, a police chief who is worried about reappointment instructs officers to overlook crime so that the reported crime rate seems to indicate that the chief's policies have been effective in reducing crime.

These examples should not be interpreted to suggest that law enforcement officials are corrupt or that their staffs are incompetent. Rather, these examples demonstrate that many possible sources of error exist in the reporting of crime and that the extent of this error is unknowable.

The FBI calculates the crime rates for individual offenses as well as the rates for violent offenses and property offenses. Why not just compare the total numbers of offenses within jurisdictions? The UCR shows the actual number of criminal offenses in each jurisdiction, but jurisdictions with more people will always have more crime. Consequently, to compare the rates for a specific offense across jurisdictions, the **crime rate** is calculated (see Figure 2.3). Comparing the rate of crime per 100,000 people is a much more accurate way to illustrate the true picture of crime.

When considering the categories the UCR uses to conceptualize types of crime, we must remember that these categories do not reflect the actual criminal statutes in each jurisdiction. For instance, a misdemeanor drug possession in Bremen, Georgia, might qualify as a felony possession in the UCR. The reporting system collects data from thousands of jurisdictions, and the categories of crime are designed to quantify the criminal behavior in each jurisdiction, not to reflect which criminal laws have been violated. Because the UCR represents a limited agenda of counting offenses and comparing crime rates, it distorts the crime picture in the way it defines wrongdoing. This problem is most apparent when several offenses are committed in one incident.

Suppose someone breaks into your home, beats you up, steals your television set, kicks your dog, and smokes a marijuana cigarette while spray-painting obscene graffiti on your living room walls. You report the incident to the police, and

crime rate—The number of crime index offenses divided by the population of an area, usually given as a rate of crimes per 100,000 people.

$$\frac{\text{number of offenses}}{\text{population}} \times \text{per number of people}$$

For example, in the United States in 2016 . . .

$$\frac{9,167,220 \text{ estimated offenses}}{323,127,513 \text{ total U.S. population}} \times 100,000 = \begin{array}{c} 2,837 \text{ offenses} \\ \text{per } 100,000 \\ \text{people} \end{array}$$

FIGURE 2.3 The estimated U.S. population in 2010 was 308,745,538 and there were 10,329,135 total estimated offenses. What was the crime rate for the year 2010? By your calculations, did the crime rate in 2016 rise or fall?

Source: Federal Bureau of Investigation, Crime in the United States: 2016, *Table 1, https://ucr. fbi.gov/crime-in-the-u.s/2016/ crime-in-the-u.s.-2016/tables/table-1.*

hierarchy rule—When more than one criminal offense is committed in a given incident, but only the offense that is highest on the hierarchy list is reported to the FBI's Uniform Crime Reports.

after making the arrest, they charge the suspect with multiple offenses. What gets reported to the UCR system, however, is another matter. Because the UCR uses the **hierarchy rule** when dealing with multiple offenses, only the highest offense in the hierarchy is reported and the rest are ignored.[20] In this case, the robbery of your television set would be entered into the system, and the assault, vandalism, drug use, and abuse of your dog would not be counted. The offender may be prosecuted for each of the offenses (well, maybe not for kicking the dog), but only the robbery will be included in the official crime statistics. See CJ Reference 2.1 to understand how the hierarchy rule is applied.

Given the strengths and weaknesses of the UCR system, it should be evident that although the UCR provides a reasonably good picture of crime, it does not tell the whole crime story.[21] Fortunately, other measures supplement the UCR.

National Incident-Based Reporting System

National Incident-Based Reporting System (NIBRS)—A crime-reporting system in which each separate offense in a crime is described, including data describing the offender(s), victim(s), and property.

The UCR system is over six decades old, and although it has improved greatly, it still has some problems that make it deficient in providing the types of information necessary for a clear picture of crime in the United States. Therefore, the federal government has embarked on a more comprehensive crime-reporting system designed to rectify some of the UCR's shortcomings. The **National Incident-Based Reporting System (NIBRS)** gathers data on each criminal offense even if several offenses are committed at one time. This system is an improvement over the UCR because it compensates for the hierarchy rule.[22]

Developed in 1985, the NIBRS collects data on each single incident and arrest for 22 offense categories composed of 46 specific offenses in its Group A offenses. Additionally, arrest data are reported in 11 Group B offense categories (see Table 2.2).

CJ REFERENCE 2.1

The Hierarchy Rule

The UCR program refers to the occurrence of several offenses committed at the same time and place as a "multiple-offense situation." In this instance, the law enforcement agency must determine which offense occurs highest in the hierarchy and record that offense. The exceptions to the hierarchy rule are the offenses of justifiable homicide, motor vehicle theft, and arson. In cases in which arson occurs along with another violent or property offense, both offenses, the arson and the additional offense, are reported. Otherwise, the offenses in order of hierarchy are as follows:

1. Criminal Homicide
   a. Murder and Non-negligent Manslaughter
   b. Manslaughter by Negligence
2. Forcible Rape
   a. Rape by Force
   b. Attempts to Commit Forcible Rape
3. Robbery
   a. Firearm
   b. Knife or Cutting Instrument

    c. Other Dangerous Weapon
    d. Strong-arm—Hands, Fists, Feet, etc.
4. Aggravated Assault
   a. Firearm
   b. Knife or Cutting Instrument
   c. Other Dangerous Weapon
   d. Hands, Fists, Feet, etc.—Aggravated Injury
5. Burglary
   a. Forcible Entry
   b. Unlawful Entry—No Force
   c. Attempted Forcible Entry
6. Larceny-Theft (Except Motor Vehicle Theft)
7. Motor Vehicle Theft
   a. Autos
   b. Trucks and Buses
   c. Other Vehicles
8. Arson
   a.–g. Structural
   h.–i. Mobile
   j. Other[23]

TABLE 2.2   The National Incident-Based Reporting System Offense Categories

GROUP A OFFENSES

Extensive crime data for these offenses are collected in the National Incident-Based Reporting System.

Arson	Homicide offenses (murder and non-negligent manslaughter, negligent manslaughter, justifiable homicide)
Assault offenses (aggravated assault, simple assault, intimidation)	Human trafficking (commercial sex acts, involuntary servitude)
Bribery	Kidnapping/abduction
Burglary/breaking and entering	Larceny/theft offenses (pocket-picking, purse-snatching, shoplifting, theft from building, theft from coin-operated machine or device, theft from motor vehicle, theft of motor vehicle parts or accessories, all other larceny)
Counterfeiting/forgery	Motor vehicle theft
Destruction/damage/vandalism of property	Pornography/obscene material
Drug/narcotic offenses (drug/narcotic violations, drug equipment violations)	Prostitution offenses (prostitution, assisting or promoting prostitution, purchasing prostitution)
Embezzlement	Robbery
Extortion/blackmail	Sex offenses, forcible (rape, sodomy, sexual assault with an object, fondling)
Fraud offenses (false pretenses/swindle/confidence game, credit card/automatic teller machine fraud, impersonation, welfare fraud, wire fraud)	Sex offenses, nonforcible (incest, statutory rape)
Gambling offenses (betting/wagering, operating/promoting/assisting gambling, gambling equipment violations, sports tampering)	Stolen property offenses (receiving, etc.)
	Weapon law violations

GROUP B OFFENSES

Only arrest data are reported.

Bad checks	Liquor law violations
Curfew/loitering/vagrancy violations	Peeping tom
Disorderly conduct	Trespass of real property
Driving under the influence	Animal cruelty (data collection began in 2016)
Drunkenness	All other offenses
Family offenses, nonviolent	

The advantage of the NIBRS over the UCR is that it allows law enforcement to identify precisely when and where an offense takes place, its form, and the characteristics of victims and perpetrators.

Participation in the NIBRS requires that a state restructure how it collects and reports crime data.[24] This system of recording crime may produce some unintended consequences. One issue is the complexity of the reporting and coding procedures. Law enforcement agencies must invest increased resources and personnel in crime data-collection efforts. In the past, police administrators did the job of collecting and analyzing data, but the NIBRS may require skilled civilians to make the program work.

Another issue connected with getting states to adopt the system is that it is optional.[25] States and jurisdictions have been slow to adopt the NIBRS because setting up the process is complicated and expensive. Another issue is the effect that the NIBRS may have on the duties of street-level police officers. NIBRS requires a much greater level of detail in the reporting of offenses than the UCR, and some critics are concerned that street-level officers will consider this as interfering with "real" police work. Street-level officers might believe the NIBRS program to be more useful to researchers than to themselves. Finally, law enforcement officials might be concerned with what appears to be an increase in crime because the NIBRS reports each offense separately rather than reporting only one offense as does the UCR. The media and the public might not understand how changing the way in which crime is reported could result in the appearance of more crime. This could be a public-relations problem for police executives who are evaluated on how well they control crime in their jurisdictions.[26]

White-collar and corporate crimes constitute special cases as far as the measurement of crime is concerned. These types of crime damage society in the long term possibly as much as **street crime**, but more of it is represented by the dark figure of crime than street crime. This is important because it is impossible for the criminal justice system to address crime that goes unreported and remains unknown. On a large scale, the financial offenses that usually occur within the framework of white-collar and corporate crime can damage the country's economy, and on an individual scale they can hurt thousands of people, particularly those who are impoverished and struggling to get by.[27] Therefore, it is important that white-collar and corporate crime be measured with the same rigor as street crime. The NIBRS is better equipped than the UCR to do this, but measuring white-collar and corporate crime remains a difficult task for several reasons:

street crime (from Chapter 1)—Small-scale, person offenses such as single-victim homicide, rape, robbery, assault, burglary, and vandalism.

> Like the UCR, the NIBRS primarily reflects street crime. This is because local and state agencies, not federal agencies, were originally surveyed during the development of the NIBRS. Because of their concern with immediate public safety, local and state agencies are more concerned with street crime and want street-crime statistics so that they can improve policing.

> White-collar and corporate crime typically fall within the federal jurisdiction, so offenses that are not fraud, embezzlement, counterfeiting, or bribery—which are already represented in the NIBRS—are not as thoroughly represented in the NIBRS as street offenses.

> Much of the investigation and regulation of corporate and white-collar crime is done by regulatory agencies and professional associations, not by law enforcement agencies and legislation. This means that corporate and white-collar offenses are reported to the UCR and NIBRS only if criminal charges are filed, which is not always the case in corporate crime.

Many white-collar crimes are handled administratively instead of by the criminal courts. What other government agencies deal with crime that may not be reflected in the UCR crime reports?

> Common corporate offenses are typically classified as "All Other Offenses" in the NIBRS Group B offenses. Currently, there is no way to distinguish corporate offenses from the rest of the offenses in this category.

> Corporations might not report white-collar offenses perpetrated against them because doing so might harm the company's reputation. Also, major corporate offenses are often too complicated and widespread for most people to understand that they have been victims of a corporate offense.

> The UCR was developed at about the same time—during the 1920s and 1930s—as the concept of white-collar crime. Therefore, many of the laws that criminalize white-collar and corporate offenses did not yet exist.

The FBI is working to improve the NIBRS. Because the NIBRS is being directed to include more information on white-collar and corporate offenses, a type of crime that was once thought to be relatively rare might be discovered to be quite common and widespread. The measurement of white-collar and corporate crime is a good example of the collection of statistics shining a light on the dark figure of crime.

National Crime Victimization Survey

The **National Crime Victimization Survey (NCVS)** is the primary source of information on criminal victimization in the United States. The survey is administered annually by the U.S. Census Bureau and gathers data on the frequency, characteristics, and consequences of criminal victimization from a sample of about 90,000 U.S. households comprising nearly 160,000 people.[28]

Previous discussions of the UCR and the NIBRS have highlighted flaws and issues that each system has in developing an accurate picture of the nature and extent of crime in the United States. Because both systems require people to report criminal offenses to law enforcement, they miss unreported crime. The NCVS differs from the previously mentioned means of reporting crime in important ways.[29] As the name implies, the survey asks crime victims about their experiences. As such, the survey does not attempt to create a comprehensive account of

National Crime Victimization Survey (NCVS)—A survey that is the primary source of information on criminal victimization in the United States and attempts to measure the extent of crime by interviewing crime victims.

criminal offenses, but rather focuses on samples of the general public and specific types of crime.

Like the UCR and NIBRS, the NCVS has its flaws. Some types of offenses are not measured because the parties act in a consensual manner, and there is no reporting victim. For instance, the NCVS does not account for successfully completed drug transactions because buyers consider themselves satisfied customers, not crime victims, and thus do not report these offenses in victimization surveys. The same could be said of gambling and prostitution.[30] In addition, the NCVS does not study murder victims (because they cannot report their experiences) or victims under 12 years of age.[31]

White-collar and corporate offenses are also difficult to measure using victimization surveys because people are often unaware that they have been victims of subtle corruption or fraud. Because of the differences in the types of offenses that are measured, comparing the crime picture of the UCR with victimization surveys is problematic.[32] Rather than attempting to decide which method most accurately reports crime, it is more useful to think of them as measuring different aspects of crime. Used in conjunction, rather than in competition, these measures foster the development of a deeper appreciation of the types of crime that are committed and how crime affects communities.

Self-Report Studies

self-report study—
Research in which individuals are asked about criminal offenses they have committed, even those they have never been arrested for or charged with.

Another major technique for collecting data on unlawful behavior is **self-report studies**. In self-report studies, researchers, who are typically from universities, ask respondents to identify offenses they have committed. To do this, the studies use questionnaires, which are relatively inexpensive, standardized, and do not require personal contact. Studies may be conducted in person, by telephone, delivered by mail, or accessed online, although if the study is not conducted in person, the researcher can do little to ensure that the intended respondents are the ones actually answering the questions.[33] Often, the studies are conducted with high school and university students. However, some studies, particularly those concerned with juvenile delinquency, are conducted with correctional inmates or participants in rehabilitation programs.

Although some significant concerns about truthfulness arise when individuals are asked to admit to criminal behavior, there are also reasons to believe that these data provide a different and important picture of crime that is not supplied in government studies.[34] Self-report studies are important because they are not filtered through criminal justice system agencies. The UCR provides better measures of what the police do than of the amount of crime being committed. Victimization surveys provide the perspective of those who have suffered some loss, but they fail to record offenses without a direct victim. Self-report studies, however, provide a relatively accurate picture of crime without having to view the behavior through the lens of law enforcement agencies or victims, both of which may introduce bias.

So that respondents will feel comfortable answering questions, researchers make several assurances. The first is confidentiality. No one other than the researchers knows who answers the questions. The other type of assurance is anonymity. The names of respondents are not recorded, so specific answers cannot be linked to specific respondents. Projects that promise anonymity presumably will elicit answers that are more truthful because respondents can safely report their offenses without fear that anyone will be able to connect specific offenses to them.

Researchers have attempted to determine whether respondents tell the truth in self-report studies.[35] For example, in one study of drug use, subjects underwent urinalysis to determine whether their answers to questions about drug use were accurate. Over two-thirds of those who used marijuana lied about it to the researchers, and over 85 percent of those who used cocaine lied.[36] However, over repeated surveys, the same approximate level of dishonesty can be expected, and researchers can assume that the measures are comparable and valid. If responses are consistent over repeated surveys, researchers then assume that any differences in self-reported crime measure actual offenses rather than signify errors that have been introduced by lying respondents.[37]

Another concern about using self-report studies to examine the amount and degree of crime has to do with the issue of representativeness. Many early self-report studies were done with samples of convenience: researchers simply asked students in their classrooms to answer questionnaires. Generalizing to larger populations is difficult when the sample is constructed according to who shows up to class on a particular day. To correct for such a biased sample, researchers use probability theory to draw a sample that reflects the relevant characteristics of the population from which it is drawn. In this way, the researchers can be reasonably confident that the findings derived from their study of a small number of respondents are applicable to the larger population.[38]

Finally, there are some types of crime that self-report studies simply cannot reach. For example, although self-report studies have had some success in getting individuals to talk about their drug-taking behaviors, efforts to get them to talk about their drug-selling behaviors have been less successful. The larger the drug dealer's business, the less likely the dealer is to self-identify as such for fear that a response could lead to arrest.[39] An additional problem in gathering information from drug dealers is that it is difficult to know who they are. Researchers have limited or no access to the subculture of drug dealers who maintain unlisted phone numbers, live in dwellings registered to family members or friends, or are otherwise invisible to normal research techniques.[40]

Self-report studies and victimization surveys are powerful techniques for getting at the dark figure of crime, but these measures are not substitutes for the UCR or the NIBRS because they are not as comprehensive.[41] Taken together, however, these methods of collecting crime data give us the best picture we have ever had of crime. Although none presents the whole picture, each of these measures of crime concentrates on a different aspect of the problem.

The task of measuring crime with limited data collection methods is daunting, but the findings are essential to the functioning of society. Legislators, criminal justice administrators, law enforcement, and the public all make decisions based on their perceptions of how much crime exists and how it affects victims. Although scholars and government officials provide a limited picture of crime, the quality of this picture is improving, and it is better than relying on the media or public opinion for the information on which public policy is made and criminal justice system budgets are based.

By employing systematically gathered UCR and NIBRS data with the snapshots provided by victimization surveys and self-report studies, we are able to get a reasonably accurate idea of the scope and severity of the crime problem. Because crime is a socially constructed concept—that is, society agrees that there is such a thing as behavior that harms others that must be controlled—some ambiguity will always exist about what behaviors constitute crime and whether particular incidents fit those definitions. Additionally, even when we agree on the definitions of crime, there will always be incentives and motivations for individuals not to report.

LEARNING OBJECTIVE 5

Define "victim."

LEARNING OBJECTIVE 6

Differentiate between the idea of victim precipitation and the idea of the innocent victim.

LEARNING OBJECTIVE 7

Debate the advantages and disadvantages of victim-impact statements.

victim—"[A] person that has suffered direct physical, emotional, or pecuniary harm as a result of the commission of a crime."[42]

Victims of Crime

According to the Victims' Rights and Restitution Act, a **victim** is "a person that has suffered direct physical, emotional, or pecuniary [financial] harm as a result of the commission of a crime."[43] Typically, we think of a crime victim as someone who is completely innocent in an encounter with a predatory stranger. Much of the rhetoric that surrounds the pleas to elevate the victim's role in the criminal justice process offers a stereotypical view of the victim as innocent. However, victims sometimes play a much more complicated role in crime.[44] Sometimes the victim is simply the person who lost a fight.[45] This means that our analysis of victims requires a more nuanced and comprehensive view of the crime victim's role. The "innocent victim" concept is at the heart of the stereotype of what attributes a victim should possess. Criminologist Nils Christie outlined six attributes that we typically associate with the idea of an innocent victim.[46]

1. The victim is weak in relation to the offender. The "ideal victim" is likely female, sick, weak, old, young, or some combination of these.

2. The victim is, if not acting virtuously, then at least going about his or her legitimate, everyday business.

3. The victim is blameless.

Barbara Lloyd, of Charleston, South Carolina, cries during the singing of "We Shall Overcome" at a memorial service for nine victims of the shooting by Dylann Roof at Emanuel AME Church, in Charleston. Roof was convicted in December 2016 of all 33 federal hate-crime charges against him and sentenced to death. According to the FBI, why are most hate-crime victims targeted?

4. The victim is unrelated to and does not know the stranger who has committed the offense. This also implies that the offender is a person rather than a corporation and that the offense is a single incident.

5. The offender is unambiguously big and bad.

6. The victim has the right combination of power, influence, or sympathy to successfully elicit victim status without threatening (and thus risking opposition from) strong countervailing vested interests.

Examining this stereotype in more detail tells us a lot about how our society considers victims and how much sympathy to give them. Christie's description of the innocent victim is instructive for what it does not include. For instance, the most victimized group in American society comprises young black males, individuals who are often portrayed as the perpetrators rather than the victims.[47] However, the media tend to concentrate its victimization focus on young white females. This stereotypical view of crime victims does society, and other crime victims, a disservice because it diminishes the effects of crime on other types of victims.[48]

Typologies of Crime Victims

The two typologies discussed here are concerned primarily with the situational and personal characteristics of victims and the relationships of victims and offenders. One of the first scholars to develop a typology of victims was criminologist Benjamin Mendelsohn. His typology, developed in the 1950s, is controversial because Mendelsohn believed that most victims had an unconscious attitude that led to their victimization.[49] His typology included six types of victims (see Table 2.3).

In 1948, criminologist Hans von Hentig looked at homicide victims and developed a typology that differs significantly from Mendelsohn's. Whereas Mendelsohn considered situational factors, von Hentig considered biological, sociological, and psychological factors (see Table 2.4). Von Hentig's 12-point

TABLE 2.3	Mendelsohn's Typology of Victims
Innocent victim	This is the stereotypical victim detailed by Christie. This victim is viewed as someone who did not contribute to the conflict and is in the wrong place at the wrong time.
Victim with minor guilt	This victim does not actively participate in his or her victimization but contributes to it in some minor degree, such as frequenting high-crime areas.
Guilty victim, guilty offender	In this category, for example, the victim and the offender may have engaged in criminal activity together, after which one robs the other. The adage "there is no honor among thieves" applies here.
Guilty offender, guiltier victim	The victim in this case may have been the attacker, and the offender was simply more successful in the conflict. A good example would be if the victim picked a fight with an offender who was a superior fighter.
Guilty victim	In this case, a victim who instigated a conflict is killed by an offender who acted in self-defense. The term *victim* is used carefully in this situation because the victim caused his or her own demise.
Imaginary victim	Some people pretend to be victims.

TABLE 2.4   Von Hentig's Typology

The young	Young people are more susceptible to victimization because of their immaturity and vulnerability. Because young people are under adult supervision, adults are more likely to take advantage of them. Young people often lack the physical strength to protect themselves from assault, as well as the mental and emotional maturity to recognize when they are being sexually exploited.
Females	Females may not have the physical strength to ward off aggressive male attackers.
The elderly	The elderly are more likely to be crime victims because of their lack of strength. They may have low mental alertness, which makes them vulnerable to scam artists.
Mentally ill/ intellectually disabled	Those suffering from mental or intellectual problems are especially vulnerable to victimization. These individuals can easily be taken advantage of by bullies, scam artists, and sexual predators.
Immigrants	Immigrants to the United States may have problems understanding the English language and therefore may be easily taken advantage of. For those who are in the country illegally, the threat of deportation can become a leverage point for exploitation.
Minorities	Minorities are often marginalized individuals in a society. Many find themselves living in substandard housing and experiencing high unemployment.
Dull normals	In Von Hentig's typology, "dull normals" are otherwise reasonably intelligent people who are naive or vulnerable in some way. This population has trouble recognizing deception by others and so is more prone to victimization.
The depressed	Depressed people are easily victimized because they are not on guard to the possibilities of being taken advantage of. They are often gullible, easily swayed, and not vigilant.
The acquisitive	These individuals tend to be greedy and can be targets for scammers who would take advantage of their desire for financial gain.
The lonesome and the heartbroken	These individuals are particularly prone to victimization by intimate partners. They desire to be with someone at any cost. They are susceptible to manipulation by those who promise them companionship and intimate relationships.
Tormentors	These people are the primary abusers in relationships and become victims when those whom they assault finally turn on them.
Blocked, exempted, and fighting victims	These victims enter situations in which they are taken advantage of because of their own culpability. For example, a person engaged in criminal activity may be a victim of blackmail and be unable to report it because of her or his own vulnerabilities.

victim precipitation— A situation in which a crime victim plays an active role in initiating a crime or escalating it.

typology is the basis for later theories of **victim precipitation**.[50] According to the concept of victim precipitation, many victims play a role in their victimization. Most definitions of victim precipitation assert two major points: first, that the victim acted first during the course of the offense, and second that the victim instigated the commission of the offense.[51] Thus, the victim's actions "precipitated" the offense.

Table 2.4's list of victim types illustrates why someone could be considered a victim. What is particularly interesting is the idea that some victims are responsible for precipitating their own victimization. One important point about this list is that it refers only to the victims' personal characteristics. It does not consider the structural conditions that are responsible for the development of patterns of victimization.[52] For instance, victims of white-collar crime and terrorism are not on von Hentig's list.[53]

The Incidence of Victimization

As mentioned earlier in the chapter, the National Crime Victimization Survey records measurements of crime victimization of people age 12 and older. In 2014, the most recent statistics available, U.S. residents age 12 or older experienced about 5.4 million violent victimizations and 15.3 million property victimizations. People age 24 or younger had higher rates of violent victimization than older people, and urban residents continued to suffer slightly higher rates of total and serious violence. About half of violent victimizations were reported to police. As for property victimizations between 2013 and 2014, the number and rate of victimizations decreased from about 131 victimizations per 1,000 households to 118.[54]

Roughly half of offenses are not reported to police. Victims have several reasons for not reporting criminal offenses. These include:

> fear of reprisal or getting the offender in trouble;

> the belief that the police cannot or will not help;

> the offense simply is not important enough to the victim to report;

> the victim dealt with the offense in another way, such as reporting it to another authority, such as a guard, manager, or school official.

Many victims are unaware that when offenses go unreported, it affects how the system can assist them. Victims may not be able to obtain services to help them deal with the victimization, and the offender remains free to commit more offenses. Also, law enforcement resources may be misallocated or not allocated at all because the authorities do not have an accurate record of the total amount of crime.[55]

Categories of Victims

Anyone can be a crime victim, and victimhood can spread beyond the direct victim to indirect victims, such as family members, friends, neighbors, and the community. Here we will briefly consider some specific types of crime victims and the unique effects of their particular victimizations.

VICTIMS OF VIOLENT CRIME

Violent crime is perhaps the type of crime most people fear and what most people consider when thinking about crime. There are many types of violent crime, but all involve the injury or death of victims. Also, the "footprint" of violent crime—that is, the number of indirect victims or co-victims—can be quite large. Victims of murder, assault, and rape have family, friends, and neighbors who are affected by the loss or injury of the victim. Victims who survive violent crime may have trouble functioning afterward: they may be unable to remain employed, suffer post-traumatic stress, become dependent on drugs or alcohol, or become depressed. They may also have physical injuries that prevent normal functioning, such as traumatic brain injuries. Violent crime victims who survive the offense often need extensive care for the rest of their lives. In this section, we will look at three categories of violent victimization: the survivors of murder victims, or co-victims; domestic violence victims; and rape/sexual assault victims.

The families of murder victims lose not only a loved one but in some cases, a trusted parent, care provider, or breadwinner. The co-victims of murder victims often have several experiences unique to their status:

> The intent to harm. Co-victims must deal with the anger, rage, and violence that have been inflicted upon someone they love.

› Stigma. Society sometimes blames murder victims for their own deaths, which may extend to the victim's family when it is thought that they should have helped control the incident that led to the victim's murder.

› Isolation. Co-victims may not want to discuss the offense or may feel that no one could understand their grief. Some co-victims may be unwillingly isolated when acquaintances stop calling because they do not want to trouble the co-victim.

› The media. Co-victims may become the subjects of media stories. The intrusion into co-victims' lives is different than media reportage of deaths from accidents or other causes.

› The justice system. The legal players, jargon, and process of the justice system may feel like yet another violation for co-victims. Co-victims may even be suspects and witnesses, and instead of grieving their loss, they must defend themselves or spend hours recounting what they witnessed. The justice system, which is designed to protect the rights of the accused and prosecute the crime in the name of the state, may appear unmoved by the plight of co-victims.[56]

The effect on co-victims can be widespread. For instance, in the December 2012 mass murder at Sandy Hook Elementary School in Newtown, Connecticut, where 26 people were killed, including 20 six-year-old children, the victimization includes not only those who were slain but also indirectly their family members, the community, and society at large.[57] This incident has given rise to new efforts to invoke more stringent gun-control policies.

Domestic violence, which includes intimate partner and family violence, encompasses physical, sexual, and financial abuse, neglect and maltreatment of children, and elder abuse. Domestic violence incidents are usually not sudden or isolated but may involve years of emotional and physical abuse that increases in severity and frequency. A domestic violence victim is not only a crime victim but is in a difficult situation in that his or her offender may be a spouse and parent to his or her children. The offender may be the breadwinner, on whom the victim is

This school shooting memorial was created following the December 2012 massacre at Sandy Hook Elementary School in Sandy Hook, Connecticut. How has the mass killing of these children affected society's attitude toward firearms?

completely dependent. Domestic violence incidents often go unreported because the victim cannot live without the offender and may be unable to escape. The victim may be afraid that the authorities will not take the offense seriously and that the result will be worse reprisals from the offender.

Rape is one of the most underreported offenses in the United States. The stigma of being a victim of rape or sexual assault is still so strong that many victims do not want to go through the trauma of dealing with the criminal justice system. In fact, the criminal justice process is often called the "second victimization" of rape and sexual assault victims.[58] This is because the offense is sometimes difficult to prove in court, and until the advent of rape shield laws, the victim's integrity and personal history were often used against the victim by the defense. For example, a woman who was a prostitute, or had many boyfriends, or even wore a certain type of clothing might risk being accused of "asking for it." By calling the rape victim's character and integrity into question, law enforcement and medical personnel may re-victimize the victim.[59]

For males, the humiliation of admitting to being raped or sexually assaulted ensures that such cases rarely make it into the public eye, much less into a court of law. The idea of male rape was at one point considered so unlikely that it was not until 2012 that the U.S. Department of Justice changed its definition of rape to include males. FBI rape statistics counted only females; male victimizations were included in the sexual assault statistics. Today, the terms *rape* and *sexual assault* are almost interchangeable. However, some authorities consider sexual assault to constitute such activities as unwanted sexual touching, whereas rape includes penetration of the body.

In 2016, rape accounted for about 10 percent of violent offenses reported to the police and about 4.6 percent of arrests for all violent crime.[60] Victims of rape and sexual assault suffer significant mental health, medical, and social consequences. They have many concerns, including fears of being blamed by others, being found out by family and other people, becoming pregnant, contracting sexually transmitted diseases, and contracting HIV/AIDS.[61] Two general characteristics of rape victims' reactions are misunderstood, misinterpreted, and used to discredit them:

> › Immediately after the attack, victims typically act in ways that people do not expect. Many victims experience shock, resulting in an appearance of calm or a flat affect. Victims often find it difficult to concentrate and may appear confused or inattentive.

> › Later, as victims struggle to cope with the effects of the offense, they may have dramatic mood changes, which are often misinterpreted as indicators of inconsistencies in the victim's account of the offense. There is often a period of denial during which the victim may try to forget the incident. This may be evident in behaviors such as reporting the incident late, attempting to resume "a normal life," and avoiding anything that reminds the victim of the assault, including interacting with law enforcement, medical professionals, or other therapists.[62]

VICTIMS OF HATE CRIME

The 1990 Hate Crime Statistics Act defines hate crimes as "crimes that manifest evidence of prejudice based on race, religion, sexual orientation, or ethnicity." The law was amended in 1994 to include offenses motivated by bias against people with disabilities and in 2009 to include offenses based on gender or gender identity.[63] For the National Crime Victimization Survey to classify an offense as a hate

This memorial was placed outside of the gay rights landmark, The Stonewall Inn, in New York City for the victims of the mass shooting that occurred at Pulse nightclub, in Orlando, Florida, in June 2016. What groups of people are most at risk of being a target of hate crimes in the United States?

crime, the victim must report one of three types of evidence: the offender used hate language, the offender left hate symbols, or the police confirmed that the incident was a hate crime.[64] Although hate-crime legislation is sometimes criticized as being unnecessary, it has been found that a strong criminal justice reaction against hate crimes can stem riots and civil unrest that sometimes occur when a community perceives its members as being targeted.[65]

The victim of a hate crime may be an individual, a business, an institution, or society as a whole. In 2015, the FBI recorded 7,173 victims of hate crime.[66] Of all victims:

> 59 percent were targeted because of race, ethnicity, or ancestry.
> 18 percent were targeted for their sexual orientation;
> 20 percent were targeted for their religious beliefs;
> 1.7 percent were targeted because of gender-identity bias;
> 1.2 percent were targeted for their disability.[67]

More than 4,000 were victims of crimes against persons, and about 2,600 were victims of crimes against property. Eighteen people were murdered, and thirteen were raped; about 72 percent were victims of property damage.[68] One study sorted hate-crime offenders into four categories:

> Thrill-seeking: 66 percent of offenders were looking for excitement.
> Defensive: 25 percent committed hate crimes in response to perceived outsiders in their neighborhoods.
> Retaliatory: 8 percent were retaliating for a real or perceived hate crime.
> Mission: Only 1 percent committed hate crimes out of a strong commitment to bigotry.[69]

Another study found that hate crimes are disproportionately directed "downward"; that is, the offenders typically belong to a majority or powerful social group, and the victims to a minority social group.[70]

Hate-crime victims suffer the same physical, emotional, and financial plights as victims of offenses that are not hate crimes, but they carry the additional burden of knowing that they were targeted for the color of their skin, religion, nationality, gender identification, or sexual orientation. People who fear hate-crime victimization may find themselves avoiding certain neighborhoods or situations in which they believe an attack is likely. Victimization may occur at any time and any place, however. Because hate crimes ultimately seek to put fear into whole groups of people by attacking individuals, they are as damaging to society as to the individual.[71]

VICTIMS OF FINANCIAL CRIME

Financial crime encompasses many different offenses: identity theft, fraud, embezzlement, street scams, Internet scams, mail fraud, money laundering, Ponzi schemes, and so on. They may be committed by individuals or groups who come from all walks of life. There is no profile for a financial offender: he or she may be a white-collar worker who goes to the office every day in a suit, a young person hanging out on the street, or someone on the Internet whose face the victim never sees. As such, there is no typical victim either: the young, the elderly, the naïve, and even the financially savvy are all at risk.

Not all individuals who have experienced crime are direct victims. In many instances, the victim may never meet the offender and may never even realize that he or she has been a victim of crime. This is especially true for white-collar offenses in which price-fixing, embezzlement, and fraud go undetected.[72] There is considerable dissatisfaction with the criminal justice system because it often treats white-collar offenders more leniently than those accused of traditional street crime.[73] Because many of the victims of white-collar crime are unaware that they have been victimized or are unable to get the criminal justice system to take their victimization seriously, these victims often do not attempt to influence law enforcement to pursue white-collar offenders.

Unfortunately, the government does not keep statistics on the occurrence of financial crime and victimization to the extent that it does on street crime with the Uniform Crime Reports and the National Crime Victimization Survey. Because of the stigma of appearing "stupid," many victims likely never report the offense and just accept the financial loss and move on since they believe it is unlikely that they will ever recover their funds. Also, many types of financial offenses, especially those that occur in a white-collar or corporate environment, are difficult to investigate and prosecute because they are so complicated. It is often difficult to ascertain what the offense is, who is responsible, how much money is involved, and who the victims are.[74]

Victims of financial crime suffer different problems than victims of street crime, but this does not mean that their victimization is any less important or personally destructive. Victims of financial crimes can find their lifestyles, expectations, futures, and mental and physical health deeply affected. A good example of these consequences is the 2008 scandal in which trusted investor Bernard Madoff stole billions of dollars of his clients' funds. Unfortunately, it is common to paint victims of financial crime as greedy and thus deserving of their victimization. Some scam victims are taken in because they are presented with a prospect that is "too good to be true"; however, this does not make the offender any less criminal or the crime any less of a crime. Madoff presented himself as a careful and meticulous broker who offered his clients relatively small, steady returns. To inexperienced investors, the slim growth in their funds looked realistic, much like the interest on a bank statement. As a result, hundreds of people and charities deposited money with Madoff.[75]

Bernard Madoff was sentenced to 150 years in prison for carrying out the biggest financial fraud in Wall Street history. The 79-year-old financier cheated nearly 5,000 investors out of billions of dollars in a decades-long Ponzi scam. Is financial crime any less serious if it victimizes those who have a great deal of money?

Similar financial crimes occur but on a far less dramatic scale. Some occur on the street, when victims are approached by scammers perpetrating various types of cons. Many financial crimes occur online, such as advance-fee scams, in which scammers send out vast numbers of emails offering recipients money in exchange for assisting with a financial transaction. People posting items for sale online may also be the target for advance-fee scams. In such cases, sellers receive a response to their ad from a buyer who offers to send a cashier's check for more than the asking price in return for sending the balance to the buyer. When the victim cashes the fake check and sends the balance to the buyer (who never shows to pick up the item), the bank holds the seller responsible for the entire amount.

Often, victims of such minor scams suffer little more than embarrassment and the loss of some money. Sometimes, however, as in the Madoff case, they suffer the loss of their life savings and become impoverished. If the financial offense is big enough, it can bring down entire institutions. Such major financial offenses may also cause unexpected collateral harm. In 2010, Bernard Madoff's son, Mark Madoff, who worked for his father as a broker, committed suicide.[76]

THE ELDERLY AND CHILDREN

The elderly and children are two particularly vulnerable classes of victims because they usually have little or no control over their caregivers and because they may not understand the nature of their victimization. These victims may be confused, naïve, mentally or physically ill, or simply unable to understand what is happening. Both types of victim are particularly vulnerable to unscrupulous caretakers—whether they are parents, children, spouses, or guardians—who take physical, emotional, and/or financial advantage of their charges.

Sometimes the victimization may not even be purposeful: the caregiver may simply be exhausted, frustrated, and unable to cope with the stress of dealing with the victim on a daily basis. The caregiver may not have the financial or physical ability to properly care for the victim. Another aspect of this type of victimization is that it often goes unreported because the victims cannot contact law enforcement. The victim may also be afraid to report the victimization because he or she is dependent on the offender. The victim may also be unaware that the abuse is a criminal offense. We will briefly examine these forms of victimization.

The definition of elder abuse is inconsistent because there is no agreement on exactly what age constitutes "elderly" and what constitutes abuse. The term *elder abuse* may seem to apply to an independent 65-year-old man who is robbed, but not if the man's age was not a factor in the offense (for example, if the man would have been robbed if he were 25). Therefore, the typical definition of elder abuse involves a victim who is over the age of 60, is vulnerable, is dependent on a caregiver, and the victimization involves violation of trust between the victim and someone known to the victim.

Like other victims, victims of elder abuse may feel shame, helplessness, and depression about their victimization. Unlike children or the mentally disabled, an elder-abuse victim may be fully aware that he or she is being victimized, yet be too frail, vulnerable, or fearful to do anything about it. Most elder abuse occurs in the victim's residence, which may be a private home (even his or her own home), nursing home, assisted-living facility, or retirement community.

Child abuse is a familiar topic. Countless state, jurisdiction, and community services, including the juvenile justice system, focus on the welfare of neglected and abused children. Although children are certainly harmed and bullied by other children, child abuse is considered to be perpetrated by adults. Children are extremely vulnerable to abuse because they have no control over their caregivers, living situations, homes, neighborhoods, where they go to school, peer groups, and so on. The younger the child, the more vulnerable he or she is. Children from birth to 3 years of age account for the highest percentage of child abuse and neglect victims.[77]

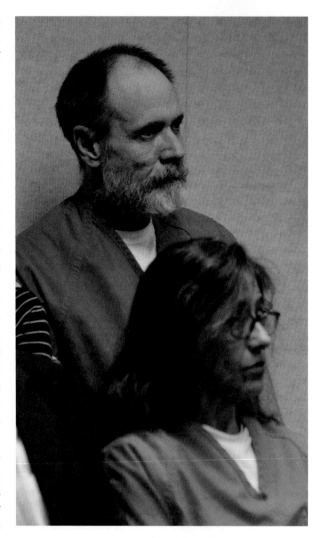

Phillip and Nancy Garrido, who pleaded guilty to the 1991 kidnapping of Jaycee Dugard, during their sentencing hearing. Phillip Garrido was sentenced to 431 years to life in state prison and Nancy Garrido to 36 years to life. What type of sentence do you believe these two individuals should receive for this crime?

Although children may be victimized in any way conceivable through either abuse or neglect, sexual abuse is considered a particular problem. A child may be abducted by a stranger and subjected to sexual abuse or abused by a caregiver. The child may be forced into prostitution or pornography or forced to become the sexual partner of an adult. For example, in 1991, 11-year-old Jaycee Dugard was abducted from a school bus stop by a husband-and-wife pair of kidnappers. Repeatedly raped, Dugard spent the next 18 years living in the backyard of her kidnapper and bore two of his children. Dugard and her two daughters were rescued in 2009.

The effects of child abuse are of particular concern to the criminal justice system because most abused children grow up to become adults, and the effects of their victimization can plague their adult lives and even make them more likely to become criminal offenders themselves. Research has shown that children who are physically abused are at a greater risk for mental illness, homelessness, crime, and unemployment, all of which affect the community and society.[78] Statistics estimate that as many as 10 million children are exposed to violence in their families and neighborhoods, which results in depression, anxiety, fear, anger, substance abuse, and poor school performance.[79]

The longer a child is physically abused, the more serious the effects. Chronic physical abuse can result in long-term physical disabilities, including brain damage, hearing loss, or eye damage. The age at which the abuse takes place is also important. Infants who are physically abused are more likely to experience long-term physical effects and neurological alterations such as irritability, lethargy, tremors, and vomiting. In cases in which the abuse was more violent or went on longer, the infant may experience seizures, permanent blindness or deafness, intellectual or developmental delays, coma, spinal cord injury, paralysis, and death.

Abused children also exhibit emotional, psychological, and social problems. They may have more difficulty with school work, self-control, self-image, and social relationships. They may be hyperactive, anxious, angry, hostile, afraid, or unable to express feelings. The social consequences of abuse may include an inability to make friends, poor social skills, poor cognitive and language skills, distrust of others, overcompliance with authority figures, and a tendency to solve social problems with aggression.

VICTIMS' RIGHTS AND ASSISTANCE

Services for victims of federal criminal offenses were introduced into victims' rights legislation during the 1980s and made law in 1990 with passage of the Victims' Rights and Restitution Act. Until recently, crime victims were a nearly forgotten part of the criminal justice process. Because the state prosecutes the criminal offense in the name of society, victims and their families were not consulted, asked how they felt about the process, or even notified of changes in the offender's status if he or she was released on parole or probation. This has changed with the introduction of victim-impact statements and regulations requiring that victims and/or their families be notified of the offender's activities.

A **victim-impact statement** is an account given by the victim, the victim's family, or others affected by the offense that expresses the effects of the offense,

victim-impact statement—An account given by the victim, the victim's family, or others affected by the offense that expresses the effects of the offense, including economic losses, the extent of physical or psychological injuries, and major life changes.

In 2016, serial killer Lonnie Franklin Jr. was convicted and sentenced to death for 10 murders commited in Los Angeles over several decades. Here, relatives of victim Mary Lowe (from left, Kenneitha Lowe, Cameron Wright, and Tracy Williams) give victims' statements before the sentencing. How might victim-impact statements affect an offender's sentencing?

including economic losses, the extent of physical or psychological injuries, and major life changes. The statement is provided to the judge before sentencing and may be read by the victim during the sentencing hearing. The defendant may see the victim-impact statement, which is often included with the pre-sentence report and may also provide information that helps the judge to determine restitution, if any. The victim-impact statement is intended to help give victims and co-victims a feeling of participation in the process and emotional release, as well as a sense of resolution and closure. If victims and co-victims can address the offender directly, it may assist with the grieving and healing process. The exact weight a judge gives to victim-impact statements when passing sentence is not known. However, judges must balance the victim's indignation with the offender's culpability and the resources available to the court. Many victims want the judge to impose the maximum sentence available under the law, but the judge is constrained in many ways. Notably the judge has to consider how other offenders in similar offenses have been sentenced, the availability of prison bed space, or the possibilities that the offender can be reintegrated into society with a rehabilitative sentence. The victim-impact statement is but one tool used by the court in sentencing offenders, and it must be recognized that the victim is not the best judge of what should happen. Victims have a strong personal interest in the sentencing and are often unable to look at the overall circumstances that the judge must consider.[80]

Victim-impact statements remain controversial in that they may affect an offender's sentencing. For example, in a child molestation case, the 16-year-old victim presented a statement that suggested that the offender should move from the neighborhood in which she and his other victims resided. The judge made the victim's suggestion part of the sentence.[81] A study that looked at victim-impact statements in capital cases found that jurors who heard a victim-impact statement were more likely to support a death sentence because the statements generated positive emotions toward the victim and the victim's family and negative emotions toward the offender. Other psychology and behavioral economics experiments have had similar results, showing that identified victims produce sympathy or empathy, leading to greater efforts to help the victim.[82]

Because most criminal offenders are eventually released into the community, many with little or no rehabilitation, reentry plan, or aftercare, many states have created a victims' "bill of rights." These rights typically include:

> The right to be informed. In many states, victims must be informed of the offender's earliest possible release date and of all parole hearings. This helps victims prepare for the defendant's release. Victims also have the right to be informed when an inmate is released. Depending on the state, victims may also be told where the inmate will be released, receive a recent photograph of the offender, be notified of any of the offender's name changes, and receive contact information for the agency that will supervise the offender upon release.

> The right to be heard. Victims generally have the right to provide input at some stages of the criminal justice process, including at sentencing and when an offender is considered for parole or other type of release.

> The right to restitution. Victims may seek restitution from an offender. In many states, payment is a condition of the offender's parole, and complying with restitution orders may be required for participation in a reentry program.

> The right to protection. Victims often have the right to be protected from the offender. States may prohibit offenders from contacting victims.[83]

Aside from establishing victims' rights, every state has some sort of victim-assistance program, and most have several. Some are public agencies, and some are community-based programs that receive federal and/or state funding. Victim-assistance programs ensure that victims are afforded their rights and provided with services. Assistance services include crisis intervention, emergency shelter and transportation, counseling, and criminal justice advocacy. For victims of federal crimes, the Federal Crime Victim Assistance Fund is available to assist victims with immediate services, such as transportation costs, emergency shelter, crisis intervention, and services to help victims participate in the criminal justice system.[84]

PAUSE AND REVIEW

1. **What is the definition of "victim"?**
2. **How does the idea of victim precipitation differ from the idea of the innocent victim?**

FOCUS ON ETHICS To Report or Not to Report

You are a married man, and you have made your share of mistakes, but now you are in a dilemma that threatens to ruin your reputation, your career, and your marriage. If you do nothing, all will be saved in your life, but it will be at the expense of public safety and might result in a life-or-death situation.

While your wife went to Des Moines to take care of her ailing grandmother, you strayed off the path of monogamy, fidelity, and loyalty. You met a young woman who was walking her dog in the park, and after some shameless flirting you accepted her invitation to meet her at a downtown bar that night. Because this bar was a place you would never have gone to on your own, you were unconcerned that your friends might see you out with another woman.

The time at the bar was a blur of drinking, flirting, and suggestive dancing. At 2:00 a.m., you drove her back to her apartment and agreed to go inside with her. Once inside, however, after much soul-searching, you decided that you could not violate your marriage vows. The woman then became angry and demanded the $200 that she said you agreed to pay her at the bar. You were shocked. You did not remember offering her any money. When you tried to leave, a man jumped out of the closet with a baseball bat and beat you senseless. After waking up in the hospital, you claimed that you were mugged in the park and did not get a good look at your assailant. Your wife flew home to take care of you, and as you began to heal, you renewed your determination to never again do anything that would hurt your wife.

Your unfortunate experience fades as the months pass, and you believe no one will ever discover your dalliance. Then one day as you are watching the local news, you see an exposé about how a number of men have been beaten with a baseball bat and dumped in the park. One man was beaten so badly he had permanent brain damage. The police chief tells the newscaster that it is only a matter of time before someone is killed by the man with the bat.

You remember the exact location of the apartment and the woman's name, and you can describe the man with the bat. You know you should tell the police what happened but realize that if you do so, your unfaithful behavior will be revealed. Because you are the vice president of your father-in-law's construction company, you may lose both your wife and your job. You are experiencing tremendous stress worrying that someone will be killed by this couple and that it is your moral responsibility to do something about it.

WHAT DO YOU DO?

1. Tell your wife the truth and hope she does not demand a divorce.
2. Go to the police and tell them what you know and beg them not to drag you into the case.
3. Write an anonymous letter to the police telling them what you know but protecting your identity.
4. Keep your mouth shut and let others worry about themselves.

For more insight as to how someone might respond to such an ethical dilemma, visit the companion website at www.oup.com/us/fuller to watch a video that connects this scenario to a real-world situation.

Summary

LEARNING OBJECTIVE 1 Describe three logistical obstacles to measuring crime effectively and efficiently.	Definitional Problems: Behaviors that seem to be criminal offenses are open to interpretation, thus skewing the definition of what constitutes a crime. Resource Problems: The priority of maintaining records of crime varies significantly across jurisdictions based on the available resources. Political Problems: The economic and social effects of the perception of crime can cause government officials to pressure law enforcement agencies to minimize the reporting of crime.
LEARNING OBJECTIVE 2 Explain what the Uniform Crime Reports program is, as well as its flaws.	The Federal Bureau of Investigation's Uniform Crime Reports (UCR) compiles the volume and rate of criminal offenses (four violent crimes and four property crimes) for the states and many jurisdictions. The UCR is a cooperative statistical effort of law enforcement agencies that voluntarily report data on the offenses they know about.
LEARNING OBJECTIVE 3 Understand why the National Incident-Based Reporting System is an improvement over the Uniform Crime Reports program.	The National Incident-Based Reporting System (NIBRS) gathers data on each criminal offense even if several offenses are committed at one time, thus compensating for the hierarchy rule. The NIBRS includes data describing the offender(s), victim(s), and property.
LEARNING OBJECTIVE 4 Compare and contrast the similarities and differences between the National Crime Victimization Survey and self-report studies.	The National Crime Victimization Survey (NCVS) is the primary source of information on criminal victimization in the United States and is administered annually by the U.S. Census Bureau. The NCVS attempts to measure the extent of crime by interviewing crime victims and gathers data on the frequency, characteristics, and consequences of criminal victimization from a large sample of people. Like the NCVS, self-report studies rely on respondents who are asked to identify offenses they have committed. Self-report studies provide a relatively accurate picture of crime without having to view the behavior through the lens of law enforcement agencies or victims, both of which might introduce bias.
LEARNING OBJECTIVE 5 Define "victim."	A victim is "a person that has suffered direct physical, emotional, or pecuniary [financial] harm as a result of the commission of a crime."

LEARNING OBJECTIVE **6** Differentiate between the idea of victim precipitation and the idea of the innocent victim.	The innocent victim is weak in relation to the offender; going about his or her own business; blameless; does not know the stranger who has committed the offense. The offender is unambiguously bad; and the victim has the right combination of power, influence, or sympathy to successfully elicit victim status without threatening strong countervailing vested interests. Victim precipitation occurs when a crime victim plays an active role in initiating a criminal offense or escalating it.
LEARNING OBJECTIVE **7** Debate the advantages and disadvantages of victim-impact statements.	Victim-impact statements may provide information that help judges to determine restitution, if any. The victim-impact statement is intended to help give victims and co-victims a feeling of participation in the process and emotional release, as well as a sense of resolution and closure. Victim-impact statements can affect an offender's sentencing. Victim-impact statements may influence jurors to be more sympathetic toward the victim and the victim's family and may generate negative emotions toward the offender.

Critical Reflections

1. Is it possible to accurately measure the incidence and severity of crime? Do you have suggestions for improving how crime is measured in the United States?

2. Can we assume that victims of crime are always innocent? Give an example of a situation in which victims might deserve what happens to them or in which they participated in their victimization.

Key Terms

burglary **p. 32**
crime rate **p. 37**
dark figure of crime **p. 32**
hierarchy rule **p. 38**
National Crime Victimization
   Survey (NCVS) **p. 41**

National Incident-Based
   Reporting System (NIBRS)
   p. 38
self-report studies **p. 42**
street crime **p. 40**

Uniform Crime Reports
   (UCR) **p. 35**
victim **p. 44**
victim-impact statement **p. 54**
victim precipitation **p. 46**

Endnotes

1 David Bernstein and Noah Isackson, "The Truth about Chicago's Crime Rates," *Chicago*, April 7, 2014. http://www.chicagomag.com/ Chicago-Magazine/May-2014/ Chicago-crime-rates/.

2 David Bernstein and Noah Isackson, "The Truth about Chicago's Crime Rates: Part 2," *Chicago*, May 19, 2014. http://www.chicagomag.com/ Chicago-Magazine/June-2014/ Chicago-crime-statistics/.

3 Jordan Owen, "Pair Sentenced in Death of Woman Featured in Chicago Magazine," *Chicago Sun-Times*, April 19, 2016. http://chicago.suntimes.com/news/

pair-sentenced-in-death-of-woman-featured-in-chicago-magazine/.

4 Rummana Hussain, "Pair Charged in Death of Woman Featured in *Chicago Magazine*," *Chicago Sun-Times*, March 13, 2015. http://homicides.suntimes. com/2015/03/13/pair-charged-in-death-of-woman-featured-in-chicago-magazine/.

5 Scott H. Decker, "Deviant Homicide: A New Look at the Role of Motives and Victim-Offender Relationships," in *Victims and Victimization: Essential Readings*, eds. David Shichor and Stephen G. Tibbetts (Prospect Heights, Ill.: Waveland Press, 2002), 170–190.

6 Harvey Wallace, *Victimology: Legal, Psychological, and Social Perspectives* (Boston: Allyn and Bacon, 1998).

7 S. Shepherd Tate, "The Forgotten Victim," *American Bar Association Journal* 65, no. 4 (April 1979): 513.

8 Ben Bradford, "Voice, Neutrality and Respect: Use of Victim Support Services, Procedural Fairness and Confidence in the Criminal Justice System," *Criminology and Criminal Justice: An International Journal* 11, no. 4 (August 2011): 345–366.

9 Paul Brantingham and Patricia Brantingham, *Patterns in Crime* (New York: Macmillan, 1984), 49.

10 William A. Bonger, *Criminality and Economic Conditions* (Boston: Little, Brown, 1916).

11 Peggy Reeves Sanday, *Fraternity Gang Rape: Sex, Brotherhood, and Privilege on Campus* (New York: New York University Press, 2007).

12 Sam Bass Warner, "Crimes Known to the Police: An Index of Crime?" *Harvard Law Review* 45, no. 2 (1931): 307–331.

13 Colin Loftin and David McDowall, "The Use of Official Records to Measure Crime and Delinquency," *Journal of Quantitative Criminology* 26, no. 4 (December 2010): 527–532.

14 J. Kitsuse and A. V. Cicourel, "A Note on the Uses of Official Statistics," *Social Problems* 11 (1963): 131–139.

15 Federal Bureau of Investigation, *Crime in the United States, 2016*, About UCR, https://ucr.fbi.gov/crime-in-the-u.s/2016/crime-in-the-u.s.-2016/resource-pages/about-ucr

16 Michael D. Maltz, "Crime Statistics: A Historical Perspective," *Crime and Delinquency* 23 (1977): 32-40.

17 James Nolan, Stephen Haas, and Jessica Napier, "Estimating the Impact of Classification Error on the 'Statistical Accuracy' of Uniform Crime Reports," *Journal of Quantitative Criminology* 27, no. 4 (December 2011): 497–519.

18 Lynn A. Addington and Callie Marie Rennison, "Rape Co-occurrence: Do Additional Crimes Affect Victim Reporting and Police Clearance of Rape?" *Journal of Quantitative Criminology* 24, no. 2 (June 1, 2008): 205–226.

19 Ron Martin, "Crime Stats: Questions Linger after Atlanta Audit," *Atlanta Journal-Constitution*, January 28, 1999.

20 Clayton J. Mosher, Terence D. Miethe, and Dretha M. Phillips, *The Mismeasure of Crime* (Thousand Oaks, Calif.: Sage, 2002).

21 David Seidman and Michael Couzens, "Getting the Crime Rate Down: Political Pressure and Crime Reporting," *Law and Society Review* 8 (1974): 457–493.

22 Michael Maxfield, "The National Incident-Based Reporting System: Research and Policy Applications," *Journal of Quantitative Criminology* 15 (1999): 119–149.

23 Federal Bureau of Investigation, *Uniform Crime Reporting Handbook* (Washington, D.C.: Government Printing Office, 2004), 10. Online at https://www2.fbi.gov/ucr/handbook/ucrhandbook04.pdf.

24 Cynthia Barnett-Ryan and Gregory Swanson, "The Role of State Programs in NIBRS Data Quality," *Journal of Contemporary Criminal Justice* 24, no. 1 (2008): 18–31.

25 David M. Bierie, "Enhancing the National Incident–Based Reporting System," *International Journal of Offender Therapy and Comparative Criminology* 59, no. 10 (September 2015): 1125–1143.

26 Mosher, Miethe, and Phillips, *Mismeasure*, 72.

27 Jeffery Reiman, *The Rich Get Richer and the Poor Get Prison*, 8th ed. (Boston: Allyn & Bacon, 2006).

28 Bureau of Justice Statistics, Data Collection: National Crime Victimization Survey (NCVS), http://www.bjs.gov/index.cfm?ty=dcdetail&iid=245. Accessed January 2016.

29 Douglas Eckberg, "Trends in Conflict: Uniform Crime Reports, the National Crime Victimization Surveys, and the Lethality of Violent Crime," *Homicide Studies* 19, no. 1 (February 2015): 58–87.

30 Meier and Geis, *Victimless Crime? Prostitution, Drugs, Homosexuality, Abortion.*

31 Bureau of Justice Statistics, Research and Development (National Crime Victimization Survey), March 2016,

32 Brantingham and Brantingham, *Patterns in Crime*, 76–79.

33 David P. Farrington and Maria M. Ttofi, "Criminal Careers in Self-reports Compared with Official Records," *Criminal Behaviour and Mental Health* 24(2014): 225–228. Marvin D. Krohn, Terence P. Thornberry, Chris L. Gibson, and Julie M. Baldwin, "The Development and Impact of Self-Report Measures of Crime and Delinquency," *Quantitative Criminology* 26 (2010): 509–525. Zack Cernovsky, Gamal Sadek, and Simon Chiu, "Self-Reports of Illegal Activity SCL-90–R Personality Scales, and Urine Tests in Methadone Patients," *Psychological Reports: Disability and Trauma* 117, no. 3 (2015): 643–648. Alex R. Piquero, Carol A. Schubert, and Robert Brame, "Comparing Official and Self-report Records of Offending across Gender and Race/Ethnicity in a Longitudinal Study of Serious Youthful Offenders," *Journal of Research in Crime and Delinquency* 51, no. 4 (July 2014):526–556. Francis L. Huang and Dewey G. Cornell, "The Impact of Definition and Question Order on the Prevalence of Bullying Victimization Using Student Self-Reports," *Psychological Assessment* 27, no. 4 (December 2015): 1484–1493. William S. Aquilino, "Interview Mode Effects in Surveys of Drug and Alcohol Use," *Public Opinion Quarterly* 58 (1994): 210–240.

34 Terence Thornberry and Marvin D. Krohn, "The Self-Report Method for Measuring Delinquency and Crime," in *Criminal Justice 2000: Measurement and Analysis of Crime and Justice* (Washington, D.C.: U.S. Department of Justice, 2000), 33–83.

35 Thomas Loughran, Ray Paternoster, and Kyle Thomas, "Incentivizing Responses to Self-report Questions in Perceptual Deterrence Studies: An Investigation of the Validity of Deterrence Theory Using Bayesian Truth Serum," *Journal of Quantitative Criminology* 30, no. 4 (December 2014): 677–707.

36 Thomas Gray and Eric Walsh, *Maryland Youth at Risk: A Study of Drug Use in Juvenile Detainees* (College Park, Md.: Center for Substance Abuse Research, 1993).

37 Gary Kleck, "On the Use of Self-Report Data to Determine the Class Distribution of Criminal and Delinquent Behavior," *American Sociological Review* (1982): 427–433.

38 Delbert Elliott, David Huizinga, and Barbara Morse, "Self-Reported Violent Offending: A Descriptive Analysis of Juvenile Violent Offenders and Their Offending Careers," *Journal of Interpersonal Violence* 1 (1986): 472–514.

39 Tom Mieczkowski, "Crack Dealing on the Street: Crew System and the Crack House," in *Drugs, Crime, and Justice: Contemporary Readings,* eds. Larry K. Gaines and Peter B. Kraska (Prospect Heights, Ill.: Waveland Press, 1997), 193–204.

40 Gary Potter and Larry Gaines, "Underworlds and Upperworlds: The Convergence of Organized and White Collar Crime," in *Readings in White-Collar Crime,* eds. David Shichor, Larry Gaines, and Richard Ball (Prospect Heights, Ill.: Waveland Press, 2002), 60–90.

41 David Huizinga and Delbert S. Elliot, "Reassessing the Reliability and Validity of Self-Report Delinquency Measures," *Journal of Quantitative Criminology* 2 (1986): 293–327.

42 42 U.S.C. § 10607(e)(2)(A). See www.law.cornell.edu/uscode/text/42/10607. Accessed December 2012.

43 42 U.S.C. § 10607(e)(2)(A). See https://www.law.cornell.edu/uscode/text/42/10607. Accessed April 2016.

44 Kay B. Warren, "Troubling the Victim/Trafficker Dichotomy in Efforts to Combat Human Trafficking: The Unintended Consequences of Moralizing Labor Migration," *Indiana Journal of*

Global Legal Studies 19, no. 1 (Winter 2012): 105–120.

45 Lance Hannon, "Race, Victim Precipitated Homicide, and the Subculture of Violence Thesis," *Social Science Journal* 41, no. 1 (January 2004): 115.

46 Nils Christie, "The Ideal Victim," in *From Crime Policy to Victim Policy*, Ezzat A. Fattah, ed. (Houndmills, Basingstoke, Hampshire, UK: Macmillan, 1986).

47 Dana L. Haynie and David P. Armstrong, "Race- and Gender-Disaggregated Homicide Offending Rates," *Homicide Studies* 10, no. 1 (February 2006): 3–32.

48 Sarah Stillman, "'The Missing White Girl Syndrome': Disappeared Women and Media Activism," *Gender and Development* 15, no. 3 (November 2007): 491–502.

49 Benjamin Mendelsohn, "The Origins of the Doctrine of Victimology," *Excerta Criminologicia* 3 (1963): 30.

50 Hans von Hentig, *The Criminal and His Victim: Studies in the Sociobiology of Crime* (New Haven, Conn.: Yale University Press, 1948).

51 Molly Smith and Leana A. Bouffard, "Victim Precipitation," *The Encyclopedia of Criminology and Criminal Justice*, Wiley Online Library, January 22, 2014, http://onlinelibrary.wiley.com/doi/10.1002/9781118517383.wbeccj309/abstract.

52 Toya Z. Like, "Urban Inequality and Racial Differences in Risk for Violent Victimization," *Crime and Delinquency* 57, no. 3 (May 2011): 432–457.

53 Elizabeth Moore, and Michael Mills, "The Neglected Victims and Unexamined Costs of White-collar Crime," *Crime and Delinquency* 36, no. 3 (1990): 408–418.

54 Jennifer L. Truman and Lynn Langton, *Criminal Victimization, 2014* (U.S. Department of Justice Office of Justice Programs Bureau of Justice Statistics, 2015). Online at http://www.bjs.gov/index.cfm?ty=pbdetail&iid=5366.

55 Lynn Langton, Marcus Berzofsky, Christopher Krebs, and Hope Smiley-McDonald, *Victimizations Not Reported to the Police, 2006–2010* (Washington, D.C.: U.S. Department of Justice Office of Justice Programs Bureau of Justice Statistics, 2012), 1–17. Available at http://www.bjs.gov/index.cfm?ty=pbdetail&iid=4393.

56 Office for Victims of Crime Training and Technical Assistance Center, Homicide, 2012, https://www.ovcttac.gov/views/TrainingMaterials/NVAA/dspNVAACurriculum.cfm.

57 Barry Paddock, Chelsia Rose Marcius, Michael J. Feeney, Larry Mcshane, Kerry Wills, and Matthew Lysiak, "Grisly Details Emerge in Sandy Hook Elementary School Shooting as Newtown, Conn. Mourns 26 Slain by Gunman Adam Lanza," *New York Daily News*, December 16, 2012, http://www.nydailynews.com/news/national/hunt-motive-sandy-hook-elementary-shooting-article-1.1220914#ixzz2LNRSfRzu.

58 Rebecca Campbell, Sharon M. Wasco, Courtney E. Ahrens, Tracy Sefl, and Holly E. Barnes, "Preventing the 'Second Rape': Rape Survivors' Experiences with Community Service Providers," *Journal of Interpersonal Violence* 16, no. 12 (December 2001): 1239.

59 Shana L. Maier, "Sexual Assault Nurse Examiners' Perceptions of the Revictimization of Rape Victims," *Journal of Interpersonal Violence* 27, no. 2 (January 15, 2012): 287–315.

60 Federal Bureau of Investigation, Crime in the United States, 2016, Table 1: Crime in the United States, https://ucr.fbi.gov/crime-in-the-u.s/2016/crime-in-the-u.s.-2016/topic-pages/tables/table-1. Table 18: Estimated Number of Arrests, https://ucr.fbi.gov/crime-in-the-u.s/2016/crime-in-the-u.s.-2016/topic-pages/persons-arrested/tables/table-18.

61 Dean G. Kilpatrick, Heidi S. Resnick, Kenneth J. Ruggiero, Lauren M. Conoscenti, and Jenna McCauley, *Drug Facilitated, Incapacitated and Forcible Rape: A National Study* (Charleston, South Carolina: National Crime Victims Research and Treatment Center, Medical University of South Carolina, 2007). Available at https://www.ncjrs.gov/app/publications/abstract.aspx?ID=240972.

62 Anne Seymour and Linda Ledray, Office for Victims of Crime Training and Technical Assistance Center, *Sexual Assault*, 2012, https://www.ovcttac.gov/views/TrainingMaterials/NVAA/dspNVAACurriculum.cfm.

63 Bureau of Justice Statistics, Hate Crime, http://www.bjs.gov/index.cfm?ty=tp&tid=37. Accessed April 2016.

64 Ibid., 4.

65 Michael Lieberman, "Hate Crime Laws: Punishment to Fit the Crime," *Dissent* 57, no. 3 (Summer 2010): 81–84.

66 Federal Bureau of Investigation, 2015 Hate Crime Statistics, https://ucr.fbi.gov/hate-crime/2015/topic-pages/victims_final.

67 Ibid.

68 Ibid.

69 J. McDevitt, J. Levin, and S. Bennett, "Hate Crime Offenders: An Expanded Typology," *Journal of Social Issues* 58, no. 2 (2002): 303–317.

70 Kathleen Deloughery, Ryan D. King, and Victor Asal, "Close Cousins or Distant Relatives? The Relationship Between Terrorism and Hate Crime," *Crime and Delinquency* 58, no. 5 (September 2012): 663–688.

71 Lieberman, "Hate Crime Laws: Punishment to Fit the Crime."

72 E. Moore and M. Millsap, "The Neglected Victims and Unexamined Costs of White-collar Crime," *Crime and Delinquency* 36, no. 3 (July 1990): 408.

73 Shanna Van Slyke and William D. Bales, "A Contemporary Study of the Decision to Incarcerate White-Collar and Street Property Offenders," *Punishment and Society* 14, no. 2 (April 2012): 217–246.

74 The Madoff Recovery Initiative, http://www.madofftrustee.com/. Accessed April 2016.

75 Ibid.

76 Bob Van Voris, "Mark Madoff's Widow Blames His Suicide on Father Bernard Madoff in Book," Bloomberg, October 21, 2010, http://www.bloomberg.com/news/articles/2011-10-20/mark-madoff-s-widow-blames-former-father-in-law-for-husband-s-2010-suicide.

77 Office of Juvenile Justice and Delinquency Prevention, Statistical Briefing Book, Juveniles as Victims: Child Maltreatment, 2010. Available at http://www.ojjdp.gov/ojstatbb/victims/qa02102.asp.

78 Mario Gaboury, Angela McCown, and Scott Modell, Office for Victims of Crime Training and Technical Assistance Center, *Child Abuse and Neglect*, 2012, https://www.ovcttac.gov/views/TrainingMaterials/NVAA/dspNVAACurriculum.cfm.

79 Kristen Kracke, *Children Exposed to Violence: The Safe Start Initiative* (Washington, D.C.: Office of Juvenile Justice and Delinquency Prevention, 2001). Available at https://www.ncjrs.gov/app/publications/abstract.aspx?id=187935. Alicia Summers, *Children's Exposure to Domestic Violence: A Guide to Research and Resources* (Reno, Nevada: National Council of Juvenile and Family Court Judges,

2002). Available at http://www .mincava.umn.edu/categories/883.

80 Ray Paternoster and Jerome Deise, "A Heavy Thumb on the Scale: The Effect of Victim Impact Evidence on Capital Decision Making," *Criminology* 49, no. 1 (February 2011): 129–161.

81 Rubén Rosario, "Victims' Statements Can Affect Sentencing," *St. Paul Pioneer Press* (Minnesota), August 7, 2006.

82 Paternoster and Deise, "A Heavy Thumb on the Scale: The Effect of Victim Impact Evidence on Capital Decision Making."

83 Susan Smith Howley, "Crime Victims and Offender Reentry," *Perspectives: The Journal of the American Parole and Probation Association*, Voice of the Victim issue, pp. 18–28. Available at https://www.appa-net.org/eweb/docs/ appa/pubs/Perspectives_2012_Spot-light.pdf.

84 Offices of the United States Attorneys, Services to Crime Victims, www.justice.gov/usao/briefing_room/ vw/services.html. Accessed April 2016.

Chapter 3

Criminal Law

FEATURES

Convicted sex offenders in Carson, California, have demanded the right to visit parks, libraries, and other public areas that they are prohibited from. Should registered sex offenders have limited constitutional rights?

W hen William Quarles comes home from work in the evening, he helps his wife make dinner, get the kids bathed and dressed for bed, and spends a little time with them reading or praying. At 9:30 p.m., he leaves his family and drives 12 miles to the end of a dirt road where he sleeps in his van until 6:00 a.m.[1]

Quarles does this because he is a convicted sex offender and, in the state of Florida where he and his family live, he cannot reside within 1,000 feet of a school, playground, park, or child-care facility. The problem with this requirement is that most residences are close to places where children may be. The only way Quarles and his wife are able to live within driving distance of their workplaces in a rental house that they can afford is for Quarles to sleep every night miles away in his car.

More than 15 years ago in Tennessee, Quarles molested two boys ages 6 and 8. After three years in prison, he participated in a sex-offender treatment program and today contends that his sexual deviancy is a thing of the past. Molested as a child himself, Quarles has tried to develop a normal lifestyle for himself and his family. Unfortunately, the criminal law designed to protect children is written in such a way that it places difficult obstacles in their quest for normalcy. Sex-offender laws have other unintended consequences. Each state has its own sex-offender legislation, and all have registries that require offenders to report to law enforcement for anywhere from five years to a lifetime.[2] Sex-offender laws are popular because they send a powerful message that sexual deviancy that involves children will not be tolerated. However, such laws have consequences not only for the offenders but also for their families.[3]

THINK ABOUT IT > Are there ways to protect society against sexual predators other than requiring them to stay away from potential victims?

LEARNING OBJECTIVE 1

Frame the development of the U.S. criminal law.

LEARNING OBJECTIVE 2

Evaluate the function of each of the four issues that guide precedent.

rule of law—In the context of criminal justice, the government cannot punish any individual without strict adherence to clear, fair, and defined rules, laws, and procedures.

The Development of the Criminal Law

The foundation for the criminal justice system is the criminal law. It protects society from predators and suspects from the whims of prosecutors and judges, and gives victims redress against those who have harmed them. The **rule of law** is an important differentiating feature between democratic societies and authoritarian ones. In a democratic society, this idea is captured by the Latin phrase *nullen crimen, nulla poena, sine lege*, which means, "there is no crime, there is no punishment, without law." However, this philosophy does not apply to authoritarian societies, where crime and punishment can exist without law.

In *The Gulag Archipelago*, Russian novelist and critic of totalitarianism Aleksandr Solzhenitsyn recounted life in the former Soviet Union, where the police basically operated without laws, arresting whomever they wished, often for no reason. For example, a man was with his wife at a train station when an unidentified man asked to speak to him in private. The two men stepped into an adjoining room, and the woman did not hear from her husband again for a decade. In another incident, a woman went to the police station to inquire about what she should do about her neighbor's daughter, a young girl who was left alone after the arrest of her parents. The police told her to wait, then arrested her a couple of hours later solely to meet their arrest quota. According to Solzhenitsyn, the Soviet

During the Soviet era, millions of people died of harsh labor and cruel treatment in the giant Gulag prison camp system. Here, Natalya Solzhenitsyn, the widow of Russian writer Alexander Solzhenitsyn, speaks at the opening of the Gulag history museum in Moscow, Russia. What laws ensure that U.S. citizens are not subjected to this type of treatment from the government?

police and courts were ruthless and operated with absolute authority and no oversight.[4] Without the system of checks and balances found in democracies, which allows each branch of government to prevent any one branch or government official from exercising too much power, a government could easily turn a country into a police state.

In a democratic society, laws must be enacted by the legislature, published in the criminal code, and enforced in a fair and even-handed manner by the authorities. Laws cannot be applied retroactively, and they are subject to review by appellate courts for their constitutionality. The criminal law specifies and clarifies the relationship between citizens and the government.

The criminal law performs many functions in society. It details what behaviors are punished and, as illustrated in the opening description of William Quarles, dictates how governments can go about issuing punishments. The criminal law supports citizens' strongly held values and, by omission, allows some people to engage in acts that others may find objectionable. An example would be burning the U.S. flag, which is not illegal but would offend some people. Therefore, we must remember that the criminal law is not a simple set of rules but a complex, ever-changing, and highly politicized tool of government.

This continuum ranges from mild controls, such as the table etiquette and manners taught to us by our parents, violations of which result in "that look from Mom" or a slap on the wrist, to the law that has the full force of the criminal justice system behind it, which can result in incarceration or even death. The continuum of proscribed behaviors is loosely matched by ever-increasing sanctions. One of the principles behind social control, therefore, is *proportionality*: The more serious the infraction of society's rules and sensibilities, the more severe the sanction.[5] However, as we will see throughout this chapter, one of the main challenges of the criminal justice system is the variation in how similar cases are treated according to wealth, skin color, culture, gender, and several other factors that demonstrate that justice is not always blind.[6]

The imperfections of the criminal justice system are less the result of the criminal law and more the result of its application. We can distinguish between the impartial law as it is written in the criminal code and the way it is enforced by human beings. Law enforcement officers, prosecutors, judges, and probation officers might be sincere in their application of the law but flawed in other ways. They might have personal biases; they might make mistakes, and some of them might be corrupt, all of which results in discrepancies between how the law is meant to be applied and how it is actually applied.

A democratic society has the opportunity to ensure that the criminal law reflects the values of all citizens. This is relatively easy to do when a consensus exists about which behaviors should be outlawed. Certainly, homicide, rape, embezzlement, and carjacking are behaviors we all wish to be protected from by the criminal law. We all agree that some dangerous individuals are best kept behind bars because of the harm they do. However, there are other behaviors for which there is no consensus, such as drug use, gambling, abortion, or pornography, and for which the criminal law is constantly in flux depending on which groups succeed in having their values addressed by the legislature and the courts.[7]

For example, several states prohibit people who have been convicted of felonies from voting. The individuals who would most like to see this type of law reversed are former felons. However, because ex-felons cannot vote in many states, they are unable to support candidates who may be sympathetic to their desires. Those who have been convicted of felony drug offenses are ineligible to vote for candidates who might legalize or decriminalize drugs. These are just a couple of examples of how those who have influence and power can best ensure that their values are encoded into the law.

Gambling laws are a good example of how economic and social values compete in the criminal law. In the not-too-distant past, Las Vegas and Atlantic City were the only places in the United States where gambling was legal. Now, many states permit various forms of gambling, and, in a turn of the criminal law that illustrates the differences between federal and state jurisdictions, many allow casinos only on federal lands controlled by American Indians. Citizens in many states have voted to allow lotteries that produce revenue to offset taxes. It is easy to see, then, that all laws are not equally grounded in the values of all citizens.

Here, the Secret Service blocks pro-marijuana protesters from carrying their 51-foot inflated marijuana joint in front of the White House. What do you predict the status of marijuana prohibition will be five years from now?

The process of developing the U.S. criminal law was and continues to be episodic, uneven, and political. Societies throughout history did not systematically build on the laws of previous cultures but instead chose elements consistent with their own values, religions, and economic structures and discarded elements that were not. Therefore, our own system is a hodgepodge of other societies' attempts to govern conduct through the criminal law.[8] A brief look at some of the previous systems of law provides insight into how our laws came to be structured as they are.

Early Legal Codes

In 1901, a stone tablet was discovered that bore the laws of ancient Babylonia as written by its king, Hammurabi. The tablet chiseled in the Akkadian language dates to about 1780 BCE and includes laws relating to a wide range of behaviors. The laws followed, literally, the "eye-for-an-eye" or *lex talionis* philosophy, an indication that severe penalties have always been part of legal codes. However, Hammurabi used this philosophy as a way of introducing some proportionality into the law. The **Code of Hammurabi** contained more than 250 laws that covered many economic, social, and criminal issues that reflect the values of the times. For instance, some of the laws make the penalties for the death or injury of slaves less severe than those for the death and injury of free people.

The Code of Hammurabi is not the earliest known legal code, but it is quite similar to the legal code of Lipit-Ishtar, king of Isin, a Mesopotamian city-state in what is now Iraq. Lipit-Ishtar's code is anywhere from 164 to 175 years older than Hammurabi's code and, like Hammurabi's code, encodes proportionality into the law. Unfortunately, archaeologists found only fragments of Lipit-Ishtar's code, so, unlike Hammurabi's code, it is largely incomplete.

Perhaps the most significant message to be learned from these codes has nothing to do with the actual laws—which, after all, apply to a society much different from ours—but rather, that legal codes existed more than 3,000 years ago. Archaeologists believe that the codes of Hammurabi and Lipit-Ishtar were likely only two of many that arose during that era and that there are other, possibly earlier, codes waiting to be found.[9] This tells us not only that the law has a long and fascinating history but that all complex human societies are likely to have some form of law.[10] Figure 3.1 provides a partial list of historical documents that have influenced the development of modern laws.

The Magna Carta

The English **Magna Carta**, a major document that contributed to U.S. law, limited the king's power and provided for the rights of citizens. King John signed the Magna Carta at Runnymede, England, on June 15, 1215, conceding a number of legal rights to the barons and the people. To finance his foreign wars, King John had taxed abusively. His barons threatened rebellion and coerced the king into committing to rudimentary judicial guarantees, such as freedom of the church, fair taxation, controls over imprisonment (**habeas corpus**), and the rights of all merchants to come and go freely, except in times of war. The Magna Carta has 61 clauses, the most important of which for our purposes is number 39: "No freeman shall be captured or imprisoned . . . except by lawful judgement of his peers or by the law of the land." This was the first time a king admitted that even he could be compelled to observe a law, with the barons allowed to "distrain and distress him in every possible way," which was just short of a legal right to rebellion.[11]

As the law developed over the centuries, it specified not only what rulers may do, but also what they may not do. The law limited the capricious decision-making powers of kings and dictated that people had certain protections from the

The Code of Hammurabi as inscribed on a basalt stele. These laws stand as one of the first written codes of law in recorded history. What is your interpretation of the "eye-for-an-eye" philosophy of this code?

Code of Hammurabi—An ancient code instituted by Hammurabi, a ruler of Babylonia, dealing with criminal and civil matters.

Magna Carta—"Great Charter"; a guarantee of liberties signed by King John of England in 1215 that influenced many modern legal and constitutional principles.

habeas corpus—An order to have a prisoner/detainee brought before the court to determine if it is legal to hold the prisoner/detainee.

Ur-Nammu's Code
The earliest known written legal code, from the Mesopotamian city of Ur, protects the poor, as well as deals with witchcraft, escaped slaves, and bodily injuries.

2100 BCE

c. 1750 BCE

The Code of Hammurabi
Babylonian King Hammurabi codifies a relatively sophisticated set of 282 case laws, including provisions for the regulation of commerce, slavery, marriage, theft, and debts. Its guiding principle is *lex talionis*, or the principle of "an eye for an eye, a tooth for a tooth."

The Ten Commandments
According to religious traditions, Moses receives these laws from God. Many commandments continue in the form of modern laws. Some scholars date the commandments between the 16th and 13th centuries BCE.

date unknown

Draco's Laws
Athenian politician Draco compiles the first comprehensive set of laws in Greece. The penalty for many offenses is death, and the code becomes infamous for its severity.

621 BCE

Solon's Laws
Solon makes important changes to the Athenian constitution and replaces Draco's laws with more humane codes. Solon's laws become the basis of the Athenian state.

c. 570 BCE

451–450 BCE

Laws of the Twelve Tables
Magistrates create these laws to appease the plebes, who complained that the oral laws weren't fair. Often modified, the laws are used for almost a thousand years. The tablets are destroyed by the Gauls in 390 BCE.

Code of Justinian I
Solon makes important changes to the Athenian constitution and replaces Draco's laws with more humane codes. Solon's laws become the basis of the Athenian state.

529–565 CE

604

The Seventeen Article Constitution of Japan
Crown Prince Shotoku Taishi issues to the ruling class laws based on Confucian concepts, including that of a unified state governed by a single ruler and a virtuous government that practices justice, decorum, and diligence.

T'ang Dynasty Law
Chinese Emperor Kao-tsu codifies a set of laws and administrative procedures that is used for the next seven centuries. The Ming Dynasty models its code on it, and it's adopted later by the Japanese, Koreans, and Vietnamese. Considered the oldest complete Chinese legal code.

624

1085–1086

Domesday Book
On the order of William the Conqueror, a general census of England is taken in order to refine taxation. "Domesday" means "doomsday" or "day of judgment."

Revival of Roman Legal Studies
Italian legal scholar Irnerius and other teachers lecture on rediscovered portions of Emperor Justinian's Corpus Juris Civilis and found a law school at Bologna, which eventually becomes the foremost in Europe.

1088

1166

Assize of Clarendon
In order to improve criminal law procedures, Henry II issues a number of articles, one of which is the establishment of the grand jury.

Magna Carta (Great Charter)
King John concedes a number of legal rights and liberties to the people under threat of civil war. The charter is altered in 1216, 1217, and 1225.

1215

1689

The English Bill of Rights
This predecessor to the American Bill of Rights limits the crown's legal rights and assigns political supremacy to Parliament. It is supplemented in 1701 by the Act of Settlement.

The Salem Witch Trials
In a Massachusetts Bay Colony town, a group of young women accuses three other women of practicing witchcraft, sparking a legal hysteria. Nineteen people are hanged, and 150 are imprisoned.

1692

1765–1769

Blackstone's Commentaries on the Laws of England
English jurist Sir William Blackstone publishes his lectures in a work that clarifies English law.

The American Declaration of Independence
On July 4, the Continental Congress announces the separation of the American colonies from Great Britain.

1776

1787–1789

The Constitution of the United States of America
In the summer of 1787, 55 delegates meet in Philadelphia to write the law of the U.S. government. The resulting document defines the government's nature and the basic rights of the country's citizens.

The American Bill of Rights
The first 10 amendments to the Constitution guarantee individual rights and limit federal and state governments.

1791

1803

Marbury v. Madison
The Supreme Court establishes the power of judicial review, by which courts may declare statutes unconstitutional.

Napoleonic Code
Napoleon appoints a commission to write a code embodying French private law and ancient Roman law. The first modern legal code of France, it's still in force today.

1808

1865

Thirteenth Amendment
Slavery is abolished.

Fourteenth Amendment
Defines national citizenship and guarantees the basic rights of citizens.

1868

1896

Plessy v. Ferguson
The Supreme Court rules that the equal protection clause of the Fourteenth Amendment deals with political, not social equality, thus declaring racial segregation constitutional.

Harrison Narcotics Act
Opium and non-narcotic drugs such as cocaine are restricted. It is replaced in 1970 by the Controlled Substances Act.

1914

1919

Volstead Act
Also known as the National Prohibition Act, the Eighteenth Amendment enforces prohibition of alcohol. It was passed by Congress over the veto of President Woodrow Wilson.

Twenty-First Amendment
Prohibition is repealed.

1933

1937

Marijuana Tax Act
Possession of marijuana is restricted to those who pay an excise tax for specific medical and industrial uses.

Brown v. Board of Education of Topeka, Kansas
The Supreme Court unanimously overrules *Plessy v. Ferguson*, stating that segregation in the public schools violates the equal protection principles of the Fourteenth Amendment.

1954

1966

Miranda v. Arizona
The Supreme Court holds that individuals in police custody must be informed of their rights concerning statements they make while in custody.

The Racketeer Influenced and Corrupt Organizations Act (RICO)
Congress enacts this statute to combat organized crime. RICO defines racketeering activities and provides extended penalties for crimes committed by criminal organizations.

1970

1984

Comprehensive Crime Control Act
Federal criminal laws are substantially reformed, overhauling the federal sentencing system, permitting pretrial detention of suspects considered dangerous, restricting the legal definition of insanity, requiring mandatory minimum sentences for career criminals, increasing fines for drug offenses, broadening drug forfeiture laws, and establishing a victim compensation program.

FIGURE 3.1   A Partial List of Historical Documents That Have Influenced the Development of Modern Laws

government. The law set forth numerous behaviors that citizens were told not to engage in, while also granting them rights and protections. These dual functions of the law are important in the modern criminal justice system. A major factor in this system is the **common law**, which was first developed in England and brought to the North American colonies, where it was modified to fit the new culture.

Common Law

Common law is different from **statutory law**. Instead of being expressly specified by a constitution or a legislature, the common law is based on the judiciary's past decisions. The term *common law* comes from England during the reign of King Henry II (1154–1189). During this time, the king's judges abided by the common customs of the kingdom rather than the particular traditions of each village. The "common law" was so called because it was the law common to all of England.[12]

Sometimes called case law, judiciary law, judge-made law, customary law, or unwritten law, common law is based largely on the doctrine of **precedent**.[13] This means that judges look to previous cases with similar circumstances to see how justice was meted out. The idea behind common law is that similar cases should be treated in a similar manner. Over the decades, thousands of cases came to form the foundation of common law. As precedents were set, lawyers and judges had to consider those precedents in the administration of cases. Today, four issues guide precedent:

1. Predictability. Predictability provides the concept of precedent with a certain level of order. By being consistent with the reasoning of previous cases and providing an outcome that fits with that reasoning, the common law gains legitimacy among people because they can understand how judgments are determined.

2. Reliability. Participants in the legal system expect the court to follow precedent. Even if some facts of the case are disputed, the court is obliged to consider how previous cases were decided. Reliability means that the court is using precedent as a guide.

3. Efficiency. Participants expect cases to be resolved in a reasonable time. Common law has created an expectation of how long cases should take to resolve. Although there are occasionally some extreme exceptions to the time it takes to try a sensational case, precedent defines when the time is becoming excessive.

4. Equality. Similar cases are expected to be treated in similar fashion. This is the most important function of the concept of precedent. The concept of justice depends on the perception that the court treats individuals fairly. To have vast differences in outcomes of similar cases violates the concept of equality.[14]

Courts are generally bound by the decisions of previous courts by this doctrine of precedent. This legal principle is known as **stare decisis**, whereby the precedent of a previous case becomes the standard by which subsequent cases are considered.[15] Part of the art of the practice of law is the attorney's skill in finding similar cases and convincing the court that the circumstances are so close to the present case that a similar decision should be imposed. The opposing attorney will dispute the similarity of the circumstances and find other similar cases with different outcomes to support a given position. Consequently, the law is not as cut and dried as is sometimes believed. The law is open to interpretation, and an attorney's legal reasoning, persuasive arguments, and reputation may play an

common law—Laws that are based on customs and general principles and that may be used as precedent or for matters not addressed by statute.

statutory law—The type of law that is enacted by legislatures, as opposed to common law.

precedent—A prior legal decision used as a basis for deciding a later, similar case.

stare decisis—The doctrine under which courts adhere to legal precedent.

important role in how a case is decided. Common law is important not only for the doctrine of precedent, but also because it has informed the development of other sources of law. As legislatures developed constitutions and statutes, they used the common law as a guide. In most areas, however, common law has been superseded by more formal and explicit sources of law. It is worth considering these in greater detail to gain a fuller understanding of how the criminal law operates.

PAUSE AND REVIEW

1. **In general, how did the U.S. criminal law develop?**
2. **What are the four issues that guide precedent?**

LEARNING OBJECTIVE 3

Identify and define the sources of the criminal law.

Sources of Law

The law is derived from no single source. Consequently, inconsistent principles, overlapping jurisdictions, and unclear nuances often appear in the criminal justice system. Ultimately, the U.S. Constitution defines the powers of the federal government. Conflicts between state and federal laws are dealt with by the Constitution's Supremacy Clause (Article VI, paragraph 2), which establishes the Constitution, federal statutes, and U.S. treaties as "the supreme law of the land." State constitutions and laws, then, are subject to federal law, and no laws may contradict the Constitution's principles.[16]

Considering the sources of the law can shed some light on this confusion. The primary sources of law are the U.S. Constitution and state constitutions; statutes enacted by legislative bodies (such as the U.S. Congress); court decisions (also known as case law); the rules of administrative agencies; and executive orders (see Figure 3.2).

Constitutions

In democracies, constitutions play a central and critical role in the development of criminal law. Constitutions express the will of the people. In a representative democracy, such as the United States, the Constitution binds elected legislators, the institutions of society, and the citizens to a system of government and laws. In the United States, the Constitution governs the nation. Each state also has a constitution that pertains to the citizens and businesses of that state. State constitutions

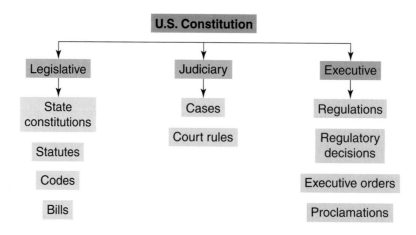

FIGURE 3.2   Sources of Law Which sources of law are you most familiar with? The least familiar with?

The Preamble to the Constitution. In what ways does the Bill of Rights serve as a foundation of the criminal law?

supplement but do not supersede the federal Constitution. This means that states cannot take away freedoms granted by the federal Constitution.

Although the U.S. Constitution does not proscribe many behaviors, it sets out some broad values that cannot be abridged by the criminal law. The Constitution specifies how the government is structured and the roles played by the various branches of government (see Figure 3.3). One of the first issues the framers of the Constitution dealt with was specifying how citizens were to be protected from the government. The first 10 amendments to the Constitution, also called the **Bill of Rights**, dictate the basic freedoms enjoyed by U.S. citizens (see CJ Reference 3.1). Later legislators did not stop there. The Constitution has been amended 27 times. Amending the Constitution is a cumbersome process, requiring the ratification of state legislatures, but the important point to remember is that the Constitution is a living and changing document, not an absolute one.

Bill of Rights—The first 10 amendments to the U.S. Constitution, which guarantee fundamental rights and privileges to citizens.

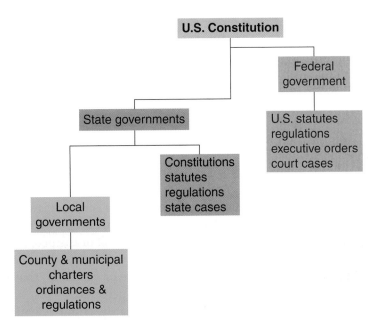

FIGURE 3.3 The Hierarchy of the U.S. Legal System Why might the hierarchy be structured this way? For example, why does the federal government rank higher than state governments?

CJ REFERENCE 3.1
The Bill of Rights

AMENDMENT I

Congress shall make no law respecting an establishment of religion, or prohibiting the free exercise thereof; or abridging the freedom of speech, or of the press; or the right of the people peaceably to assemble, and to petition the Government for a redress of grievances.

AMENDMENT II

A well regulated Militia, being necessary to the security of a free State, the right of the people to keep and bear Arms, shall not be infringed.

AMENDMENT III

No Soldier shall, in time of peace be quartered in any house, without the consent of the Owner, nor in time of war, but in a manner to be prescribed by law.

AMENDMENT IV

The right of the people to be secure in their persons, houses, papers, and effects, against unreasonable searches and seizures, shall not be violated, and no Warrants shall issue, but upon probable cause, supported by Oath or affirmation, and particularly describing the place to be searched, and the persons or things to be seized.

AMENDMENT V

No person shall be held to answer for a capital, or otherwise infamous crime, unless on a presentment or indictment of a Grand Jury, except in cases arising in the land or naval forces, or in the Militia, when in actual service in time of War or public danger; nor shall any person be subject for the same offence to be twice put in jeopardy of life or limb; nor shall be compelled in any criminal case to be a witness against himself, nor be deprived of life, liberty, or property, without due process of law; nor shall private property be taken for public use, without just compensation.

AMENDMENT VI

In all criminal prosecutions, the accused shall enjoy the right to a speedy and public trial, by an impartial jury of the State and district wherein the crime shall have been committed, which district shall have been previously ascertained by law, and to be informed of the nature and cause of the accusation; to be confronted with the witnesses against him; to have compulsory process for obtaining witnesses in his favor, and to have the Assistance of Counsel for his defence.

AMENDMENT VII

In Suits at common law, where the value in controversy shall exceed twenty dollars, the right of trial by jury shall be preserved, and no fact tried by a jury, shall be otherwise re-examined in any Court of the United States, than according to the rules of the common law.

AMENDMENT VIII

Excessive bail shall not be required, nor excessive fines imposed, nor cruel and unusual punishments inflicted.

AMENDMENT IX

The enumeration in the Constitution, of certain rights, shall not be construed to deny or disparage others retained by the people.

AMENDMENT X

The powers not delegated to the United States by the Constitution, nor prohibited by it to the States, are reserved to the States respectively, or to the people.

Statutes

statute—A law enacted by a legislature.

Federal and state legislative bodies have developed the common law into specific **statutes** that proscribe criminal behavior. These laws are debated and voted on by the legislative bodies and presumably represent the will of the people. For many behaviors, such as homicide, a consensus exists as to what the law should cover. However, there are other offenses, such as drug use or gambling, that many citizens contend should not be illegal. Regardless of personal beliefs, however, all citizens are expected to obey the law or risk entering the criminal justice system.

The advantage of statutes over the common law is that statutes are published in **penal codes** and therefore fit the principles of predictability, reliability, efficiency, and equality better than the doctrine of precedent. Statutes are easier to change than the Constitution, but new laws cannot violate rights given in the Constitution.[17] Consequently, new laws are often challenged on constitutional grounds. Laws may be challenged for constitutionality in two ways. The first is *unconstitutional per se*. In these cases, it is claimed that the law is unconstitutional under any and all circumstances. The other challenge is *unconstitutional as applied*, which is to claim that although the law may be valid, it is applied in a way that restricts or punishes the exercise of constitutional rights. This is an important distinction because a law that is found to be unconstitutional per se must be removed from the criminal code, whereas a law that is unconstitutional as applied requires only changes in the procedures of a criminal justice agency.

penal code—A code of laws that deals with crimes and the punishments for them.

Case Law

Cases decided by judges in state, local, and federal courts are all part of U.S. law. **Case law** operates under the principle of *stare decisis*; that is, similar cases are treated in a similar way. Case law enables the courts to prevent a vast disparity in judicial outcomes and ensure that a degree of uniformity exists across courts. Although case law depends on *stare decisis* to ensure that cases are in line with how past cases have been decided, it also evolves as new decisions are applied to new circumstances in each case. The legal reasoning of case law changes as appellate courts review the decisions of trial courts and note the reasons for their decisions that consequently guide future cases.

case law—The published decisions of courts that create new interpretations of the law and can be cited as precedent.

The issue of jurisdiction also heavily influences case law. Cases decided in one judicial circuit might not be as influential in other circuits. Although the decisions of the U.S. Supreme Court are important to every court, a decision of a court in Omaha might be less influential in a New York court than in a Nebraska court.[18]

Administrative Rules and Executive Orders

Federal, state, and local agencies have developed rules consistent with their responsibilities to oversee aspects of commerce and public protection. Health, environment, customs, and parole agencies all have the authority to enact rules that limit the freedoms of individuals operating within their spheres of influence. An example of an administrative rule in criminal justice would be rules specifying victim services. A rule set forth by the state of Utah, for instance, provides that emergency awards up to $1,000 can be granted to crime victims who need money for urgent expenses.[19] Another example in the state of Georgia from the Georgia Bureau of Investigation specifies the procedure for the disclosure and viewing of crime scene photographs and videos by members of the press.[20]

Sometimes administrative rules overlap with criminal statutes or constitutional rights and end up being contested in court. For instance, administrative rules about minority hiring practices or university admission policies have been found to be at odds with constitutional guarantees. In another example, parolees are subject to a host of conditions that require approval from one's parole officer, such as changing residences, traveling out of state, getting married, or drinking alcohol. These are all rules considered by the parole agency to be necessary to aid the parolee in the transition from incarceration to the free world. Violation of these conditions can result in the parolee returning to prison. Because these issues are administrative rules rather than legal statutes, the parolee is not accorded the full range of constitutional rights, as is the criminal defendant.

Executive orders are directives that the president issues to government officials and agencies. Executive orders have the force and effect of law but usually only affect the general public indirectly. The president, or a subsequent president, may repeal or modify executive orders, or they may have an expiration date. An executive order may also become obsolete when the purpose for which it was issued no longer exists. Executive orders are used in several ways, including:

> to issue binding pronouncements to units of the executive branch
> to make policy in fields such as security classification, governance of civil servants, foreign service and consular activities, and government contracting
> to initiate or direct legislation
> to delegate authority to other agencies or officers
> to reorganize agencies, eliminate existing agencies, or create new ones
> to manage federal personnel
> to control the military
> to manage foreign policy

State governors have authority similar to that of the U.S. president to issue executive orders concerning state administrative agencies and state military personnel.[21]

PAUSE AND REVIEW

1. **What are the sources of the criminal law?**

LEARNING OBJECTIVE **4**

Compare and contrast the similarities and differences between criminal law and civil law.

LEARNING OBJECTIVE **5**

Differentiate between substantive law and procedural law.

Types of Law

As a form of social control, the law performs many functions. In addition to defining socially unacceptable behaviors, it also regulates the rules of social conflict, dictates how authorities control behavior and maintain public order, and regulates how behavior is punished. Different types of laws accomplish these multiple functions. Here we will discuss the distinction between criminal law and civil law, followed by a discussion about substantive law and procedural law.

Criminal Law and Civil Law

The **criminal law** specifies the prosecution by the government of a person or people for an act that has been classified as a criminal offense. What criteria are used to determine that a behavior is so serious that it needs to be made a criminal offense and specified in the criminal law? Many objectionable behaviors are not covered by criminal law. Conversely, the criminal law covers some behaviors that many people believe it should not cover. Ideally, the criminal law is a mechanism of social control used only when other mechanisms (family, church, community) have failed and is used only for serious transgressions. Three criteria determine what behaviors are made criminal:

criminal law—The law specifying the prosecution by the government of a person or people for an act that has been classified as a criminal offense.

1. The enforceability of the law. Laws that cannot be enforced do little good. The prohibition of alcohol in the 1920s showed what happens when the law cannot be enforced. People continued to drink alcohol, but the government received no revenue from alcohol sales that could be used to combat the

negative effects of drinking. Many critics believe that the war on drugs is another example of laws that cannot be effectively enforced. Even as prison systems are overflowing with those convicted of drug-related offenses, illegal drugs continue to be bought and sold (see A Closer Look 3.1).

2. The effects of the law. Sometimes the cure is worse than the disease. During Prohibition, the consequences of attempting to enforce alcohol laws had a deleterious effect on society. Although alcohol was illegal, a great demand for it remained, bringing some unintended consequences in the form of organized crime and violence. Additionally, many otherwise law-abiding citizens were drawn into the criminal enterprise of alcohol production, transportation, and sales because of the lucrative alcohol trade. Perhaps even more harmful to society was the effect on the criminal justice system. Widespread corruption of judges and law enforcement officers seriously damaged the faith of citizens in the efficacy and fairness of government officials.

3. The existence of other means to protect society against undesirable behavior. Many people argue that even though drug and alcohol use have some unattractive features, the criminal justice system is not the most efficient and effective institution to control this behavior. Instead of attempting to discourage addictive behavior by punishment and deterrence, some experts contend that medical and psychological treatment would be more effective and not cause the harmful side effects of the war on drugs. Instead of using the criminal law as a weapon against drugs, the medical and mental health community could be better funded and expanded to address the problem. The repeal of Prohibition did not eliminate the problems of alcohol, but most would agree that by legalizing alcohol, the United States dealt more effectively with its health and social problems and spared the criminal justice system the temptations of corruption.[22]

The criteria for deciding which behaviors should be made criminal are not always heeded by legislators. The making of criminal law is as much a political enterprise as it is a legal one. Most citizens try to obey the law, but all of us are

In March 2016, then President Barack Obama met with people who had been incarcerated, mostly for drug-related offenses, and had their sentences commuted. Have existing drug laws been effective in reducing drug use?

guilty of choosing to disregard some laws. Think about the last time you exceeded the legal speed limit. Was it on your way to class today? Because of people like you, the government decided to repeal the once-universal 55-miles-per-hour speed limit on the interstate highway system. The trucking industry and those who traveled routinely broke the speeding laws, and ultimately, the federal and state governments were lobbied for a higher speed limit. From a safety perspective, the 55-miles-per-hour limit was useful, but it was ignored by too many citizens and eventually modified.

civil law—The law that governs private rights as opposed to the law that governs criminal issues.

There is an important difference between the criminal law and **civil law**. Both types of law try to control the behavior of people, and both can impose sanctions. Also, there is some considerable overlap in the types of behavior they address, such as personal assault or environmental pollution. The important difference between them, however, concerns the identity of the aggrieved party. In civil law, the case is between two individuals. In criminal law, the case concerns the defendant and the government. In criminal law, when someone is charged with assault, the dispute becomes the property of the government. The government greatly reduces the victim's role and prosecutes the case in the name of the state.[23] This aspect of the criminal law confuses and frustrates many victims who still consider the case a problem between themselves and the accused.[24]

A CLOSER LOOK 3.1
Drug Laws: More Expensive than Effective?

Lawmakers enact criminal laws with specific purposes in mind. For about the past 40 years, one of the government's goals has been to reduce the traffic in illegal drugs by establishing criminal consequences for using them. In the 1980s, lawmakers began to craft laws that increased the penalties for drug-related offenses, including the Sentencing Reform Act of 1984, which established that drug offenders were to spend 85 percent of their sentences behind bars, and compulsory sentence enhancements, such as doubling the penalties for repeat offenders.[25] The result has been a tremendous increase in the number of individuals incarcerated for drug-related offenses, and it has come at a steep price. The federal prison system now costs more than $6.7 billion a year, or about 1 in 4 dollars spent by the U.S. Justice Department. Today, researchers are asking whether the drug laws have been cost-effective in dealing with drug crime. According to a 2015 report by The Pew Charitable Trusts, the answer is no.[26]

Despite the tremendous amount of resources in terms of policing and prison spending that are thrown at the drug problem, there appears to be little evidence that drug laws have been effective in reducing drug use or lowering the rate of repeat offenders incarcerated for drug offenses. Between 1980 and 2013, spending on federal prisons increased 595 percent. Between 1980 and 2015, the number of federal inmates serving time for drug-related offenses increased from 5,000 to 95,000.

The increased incarceration of drug offenders has done little to stem the drug trade. Drugs are still readily available and less expensive than before this initiative to wage war on drugs. Although there has been a general decrease in crime, researchers attribute only 1 to 3 percent of the decline to increased incarceration. The deterrent effect of greater penalty for drug use has been negligible.[27]

Until the end of his presidency, President Barack Obama continued his administration's push for criminal justice system reform by encouraging some federal inmates—particularly those serving long sentences for non-violent, drug-related offenses—to petition for clemency. As of January 20, 2017, the Obama administration had commuted the sentences of 1,715 inmates.[28]

THINK ABOUT IT

1. Why have stricter punishments for drug crime not been an effective deterrent to drug trafficking?
2. What other ways might be more effective at reducing drug use in the United States other than incarcerating offenders?

At this point, the victim can invoke the civil law for redress and sue the offender for compensation for damages. Private attorneys, as opposed to the state prosecutor, represent the victim and offender. The court sentence is concerned with monetary damages, not with the prospect of incarceration. Civil law covers contracts, personal property, maritime law, and commercial law. **Tort law**, a form of civil law, covers personal wrongs and damage and includes libel, slander, assault, trespass, and negligence.[29]

An often-misunderstood principle of law called **double jeopardy** states that a person cannot be tried for the same offense twice.[30] This concept applies to the criminal law but also allows for legal actions from multiple jurisdictions. Therefore, double jeopardy does not preclude a crime victim from suing for private damages after the criminal trial has concluded, nor does it protect a criminal defendant from being prosecuted by both state and federal jurisdictions. For example, because of the distinction between the criminal law and civil law, the families of Nicole Brown Simpson and Ronald Goldman were awarded monetary damages from O. J. Simpson after he was acquitted of criminal charges. The standards of proof in a civil trial (**preponderance of the evidence**) are not as stringent as those in a criminal trial (**beyond a reasonable doubt**), which explains how two juries can consider the same case and produce different verdicts.[31] In another example, a defendant accused of breaking both state and federal laws may be prosecuted in both jurisdictions. Roberto Miramontes Roman was acquitted by a state court jury of the 2010 killing of sheriff's deputy Josie Greathouse Fox during a traffic stop. In 2016, the federal government tried Roman on the charge of killing a law enforcement officer, as well as several federal drug and weapons violations. A federal jury convicted Roman.[32]

Substantive Law and Procedural Law

Substantive law tells us which behaviors have been defined as criminal offenses. The "thou shall nots" of the criminal law, substantive laws are found in the criminal codes of the state and federal governments and are the result of generations of political and social development. Homicide, rape, assault, money laundering, and all the other behaviors that are against the law are proscribed by the substantive law. The substantive law also sets the parameters on the punishment for each type of offense. Once a suspect has been convicted, the judge does not have unlimited discretion in imposing a sentence. For example, few offenses are eligible for the death penalty. In the case of minor offenses, the judge can choose a short period of incarceration or decide that society is better served by placing the offender on probation.

Whereas the substantive law specifies what individuals are not allowed to do, the **procedural law** specifies how the criminal justice system is allowed to deal with those who break the law. The procedural law sets the rules by which the police, courts, and corrections systems process cases. Based to a large degree on the rights granted to accused individuals by the Constitution, procedural law protects citizens from arbitrary decision making of criminal justice professionals by dictating how cases are to be handled.[33] Procedural law specifies rules of arrest, search and seizure, rights to attorneys, and attorney–client privilege, as well as other "rules of the game."

Procedural laws change with the creation of new case precedents, new laws, or new court opinions. For instance, in the wake of the terrorist attacks on New York City and Washington, D.C., on September 11, 2001, the federal government decided that attorney–client privilege is not absolute and that the police may monitor communications to prevent future terrorist acts.[34] Whether this evidence

Tort law—An area of the law that deals with civil acts that cause harm and injury, including libel, slander, assault, trespass, and negligence.

double jeopardy—Prosecution of a defendant in the same jurisdiction for an offense for which the defendant has already been prosecuted and convicted or acquitted.

preponderance of the evidence—The burden of proof in a civil trial, which requires that more than 50 percent of the evidence be in the plaintiff's favor.

beyond a reasonable doubt—The highest level of proof required to win a case; necessary in criminal cases to procure a guilty verdict.

substantive law—Law that describes which behaviors have been defined as criminal offenses.

procedural law—Law that specifies how the criminal justice system is allowed to deal with those who break the law or are accused of breaking the law.

Police arrest a protester after an unlawful assembly formed on a street in El Cajon, California, near the site where police had shot an unarmed black man, Alfred Olango, 38. When do the police have the authority to arrest someone at a peaceful protest?

could be used against an accused terrorist in court is not clear at this time. This question will have to be decided by the courts.

PAUSE AND REVIEW

1. **What three criteria determine what behaviors constitute as criminal?**
2. **How are the criminal law and civil law alike? How are they different?**
3. **How does the substantive law differ from procedural law?**

LEARNING OBJECTIVE 6

Distinguish between felonies and misdemeanors and illustrate why the application of these labels is not always consistent.

LEARNING OBJECTIVE 7

Justify the need for inchoate offenses.

felony (from Chapter 1)—An offense punishable by a sentence of more than a year in state or federal prison and sometimes by death.

Types of Crime

The criminal law has categorized crime according to several different features. For instance, the difference in the seriousness of criminal offenses is captured by the felony versus misdemeanor distinction. Criminal offenses are also differentiated by who commits the behavior, as in the distinction of juvenile status offenses (underage drinking, for instance). Some statutes recognize criminal history in classifications for first-time offenders, career offenders, or sex offenders. In the sections that follow, we will discuss four types of crime: felonies, misdemeanors, inchoate offenses, and infractions.

Felonies

The **felony** is considered the most serious type of criminal offense. Felonies include murder, rape, assault, larceny, arson, and a host of other offenses at the state and federal level. The felony distinction is important because many agencies and corporations deny employment to those convicted of this type of offense. Felons are not allowed to run for public office, own a firearm, or enter certain professions, such as law enforcement or medicine. Also, the penalties are often more severe for felonies than for other types of offenses. Incarceration for felonies is usually more than one year, and life imprisonment or capital punishment is specified for some felonies.

Misdemeanors

Misdemeanors are less serious offenses than felonies and are subject to lighter penalties. Usually, the maximum incarceration for a **misdemeanor** is up to one year in jail. Misdemeanants spend their time in county jails or stockades as opposed to state prisons. More often than not, misdemeanants are placed on probation, fined, or required to do some type of community service rather than be incarcerated.

The distinction between felonies and misdemeanors can be confusing. An offense could be categorized as either, depending on the circumstances. Additionally, the prosecutor has wide discretion in deciding which type of offense to charge the offender with and may, as a result of plea bargaining, reduce the indictment from felony to misdemeanor. In some ways, this distinction gives the prosecutor immense power to coerce plea bargains from a defendant who is afraid of the vast consequences of being convicted as a felon as opposed to a misdemeanant.

When considering the differences between felonies and misdemeanors, it is important to note that a specific behavior may be a felony in one jurisdiction and a misdemeanor in another (or maybe not even a criminal offense at all). Gambling is a good example. Nevada has many types of legal gambling, whereas other states outlaw many types of gambling. For example, Georgia had no legalized gambling at all until the state decided that the revenue was so attractive that it instituted its own lottery system while continuing to prohibit other types of gambling.

Additionally, the differences between felonies and misdemeanors can be observed in drug laws in which the amount of drug in possession necessary to be a felony varies widely from state to state. Therefore, although the distinction between a felony and misdemeanor is important, the actual practice in the application of the label by the criminal justice system is sometimes inconsistent and problematic.

Inchoate Offenses

A crime does not always have to be completed for the offender to be arrested, charged, and punished. To limit the harm caused by crime and to deter individuals from planning and attempting wrongdoing, a category of crimes called **inchoate offenses** was created. There are three inchoate offenses: attempt, conspiracy, and solicitation. In attempt, an individual tries to break the law. In conspiracy cases, two or more people agree to break the law. In solicitation, one person encourages another to break the law.[35]

Although it is often difficult to prove, conspiracy to commit a criminal offense is a behavior that legislators have deemed to be so serious that it needs to be discouraged and punished. For example, if Timothy McVeigh, Terry Nichols, and Michael Fortier had been apprehended while collecting the materials and making the plans to bomb the Murrah Federal Building in Oklahoma City in 1995, they could have been charged with inchoate offenses. With the government's focus on preventing acts of terrorism, we can appreciate the need to have conspiracy laws available to incapacitate and deter individuals and groups intent on causing the type of mass destruction witnessed in the Oklahoma City bombing and the terrorist attacks on September 11, 2001.

The idea behind inchoate offenses is that the offender should not have to be successful in completing the crime before the criminal justice system can respond. For instance, if law enforcement is aware of a plan to kill the president of the

misdemeanor (from Chapter 1)—A minor criminal offense punishable by a fine and/or jail time for up to one year.

inchoate offense—An offense composed of acts necessary to commit another offense.

United States, they do not have to wait until it is completed before they arrest the conspirators.

Infractions

An **infraction** is usually an offense that is not serious enough to warrant curtailing an offender's freedom. For this reason, infractions do not merit jury trials or legal representation provided by the state. Judges decide the case in a bench trial, and the standard of proof is usually the lowest form required for civil procedures, preponderance of evidence. The most common punishment for an infraction is a fine and/or community service. In most jurisdictions, infractions are violations of a local ordinance, a municipal code, or a traffic law. Many states consider infractions to be a matter of civil law, although a few jurisdictions consider some infractions as criminal.

Exactly what behavior constitutes an infraction varies widely among jurisdictions, and these definitions are specified by state and local legislators. Nationwide, traffic offenses, such as speeding, are likely the most common form of infraction. Some states, such as California, have even reduced the possession of small amounts of marijuana to the status of an infraction. The exception to the civil nature of infractions is when an offender continues to commit them, and they pile up. For example, a large collection of unpaid parking tickets or speeding tickets may result in the offender being charged with a misdemeanor and serving a short time in jail.

PAUSE AND REVIEW

1. **In what ways is a felony different from a misdemeanor?**
2. **What are the three inchoate offenses?**

Features of Crime

Not all harmful acts are considered criminal offenses. Certainly, many automobile accidents have serious consequences for the victims, but unless the elements necessary for the legal definition of a crime are present, then the accident, no matter how serious, will not be considered by the criminal court. At least some of the following elements must be present in order for any act to be labeled a criminal offense:

1. The criminal act (***actus reus***) (must be present in all offenses)
2. The criminal intent (***mens rea***) (must be present in some offenses)
3. The relationship between *actus reus* and *mens rea* (also called **concurrence**)
4. Attendant circumstances (must be present in some offenses)
5. Result (criminal harm; must be present in some offenses)

Together, these elements constitute ***corpus delicti*** or the "body of the crime." This does not mean an actual dead human body, as is found at the scene of a homicide, but rather the aforementioned elements of the crime relevant to the case at hand. Most minor offenses do not require *mens rea*. Offenses composed only of *actus reus* typically require the element of **attendant circumstances**, which are additional conditions that define an offense. Consider, for example, a case in which a motorist is ticketed for driving 150 miles per hour down a highway.

In this instance, the excessive rate of speed is the attendant circumstance, and *mens rea* is not required for the driver to be sanctioned. Serious offenses, however, such as theft, burglary, assault, and murder, require *mens rea*. Offenses that require both *actus reus* and *mens rea* also need concurrence: the criminal act and the criminal intent must be present together. For example, the offense of burglary is defined as the breaking and entering of a structure with the intent to commit a felony. Finally, in some offenses, the results, such as a dead or injured person, are so serious that they are taken into account. These "results crimes," the best example of which is murder, require all five elements of a criminal offense. Now let's look a bit closer at the elements of *actus reus* and *mens rea*, as well as at the subject of strict liability.

Actus reus

Actus reus or "guilty deed" occurs when an individual (whether as principal, accessory, or accomplice) engages in a behavior prohibited by the criminal law. This behavior can involve either doing something wrong (commission) or failing to do something that is legally obligated (omission). The law requires that this commission or omission be an actual behavior as opposed to a thought. The criminal law does not punish thoughts. Those thoughts must be translated into some type of action or intentional inaction. For example, a bank teller is not criminally liable for considering embezzling money. However, when false accounts are created into which money is diverted, or when customers' deposited money is not recorded, then the requirements of the criminal act are met. Likewise, merely thinking about murder is not against the law. Attempting to commit murder by, say, poisoning a person is a physical act that meets the definition of *actus reus*.

Actus reus does not refer to someone's status. A person who is addicted to drugs or alcohol is not considered to have met the standard of *actus reus*. However, if a person carries illegal drugs around, sells drugs, or conspires with others to sell drugs, then it is reasoned that actual criminal acts have occurred, and the person could be arrested. Additionally, drunken drivers are punished not for their consumption of alcohol but because they committed the act of driving while impaired. To meet the test of *actus reus*, the behavior must also be voluntary. A person under the suggestion of hypnosis or some form of brainwashing is not aware of committing a criminal offense. Similarly, liability does not extend to one who is unconscious or is having a convulsion or other reflexive reaction that causes harm.

Actus reus is sometimes more difficult to prove when it involves the act of criminal omission. Failing to act when one is legally required to report child abuse is one example. People are also expected to take steps to save the life of a victim of some trauma. Allowing someone to die—even if for logical reasons and with the consent of the person, as in cases involving the terminally ill—can sometimes be considered the basis for *actus reus*.

Mens rea

In addition to considering the criminal act, the offender's state of mind is taken into account when deciding whether a behavior is a criminal offense. *Mens rea* or a "guilty mind" is considered present when a person acts purposefully, knowingly, recklessly, or negligently. The law distinguishes between general intent and specific intent when considering *mens rea*. General intent is present when the prosecution can prove that the defendant intended to do what the law forbids. Specific intent involves the intention of the defendant to accomplish a specific goal.

In the case of murder where the weapon is a gun, the prosecution often says that the defendant shot the victim with the *intent* to kill. It is possible that the defendant shot to wound the victim or sent warning shots into the air and struck the victim by mistake, but these conditions would need to be buttressed by other evidence to circumvent specific intent. For instance, if witnesses hear someone say, "Stop or I'll shoot you in the kneecap," and then that person shoots his target in the kneecap and the bullet ricochets into another person's head and kills that person, the intent might not have been "to kill" but simply to do "great bodily harm." Whereas shooting someone in the head allows the court to infer a specific intent to kill, shooting a person in the kneecap allows the court to infer intent to injure.[36]

Strict Liability

strict liability—
Responsibility for a criminal offense without intention to break the law.

Mens rea is not required for some statutory offenses; those that involve **strict liability**, or liability without fault, are an exception to the requirement of the presence of both *mens rea* and *actus reus*. Strict-liability offenses tend to be offenses in which the public's welfare is at issue, such as narcotics violations, health and safety violations, traffic violations, or sanitation violations. The offender need not have a guilty mind when breaking strict-liability laws. For example, many bars and restaurants have a sign that reads, "We Card Everyone, Every Time." If the bartender or waiter serves alcohol to an underage person, even if that person appears to be of legal drinking age, then the bartender is guilty of a criminal offense. Because a liquor license can be crucial to a restaurant, the owners cannot afford to depend on the discretion of a bartender. Requiring proof of age for every customer requesting an alcoholic beverage is the only way the establishment's owners can ensure that their employees do not put the business at risk of violating the strict-liability rules.

PAUSE AND REVIEW

1. What legal elements must be present in order for an act to be labeled a criminal offense?
2. What is strict liability?

Convenience stores, bars, and other establishments that sell alcohol and tobacco products typically display signs alerting customers to have identification ready when purchasing such products. Does displaying such warnings protect an establishment from strict liability offenses?

Criminal Responsibility and Criminal Defense

LEARNING OBJECTIVE 9

List the six arguments that can be employed in the defense against a criminal indictment.

The law recognizes that not all people are completely aware of the effect their behaviors have on others. Even though great physical harm or property damage might result from criminal behavior, the capacity of the offender to understand the ramifications of his or her behavior can produce mitigating reasoning that can excuse the individual from the full force of the criminal law. As such, the defense attorney will look for reasons to justify or excuse the criminal behavior. Essentially, six arguments can be employed in the defense against a criminal indictment:

1. My client did not do it.
2. My client did it, but my client is not responsible because he or she is insane.
3. My client did it but has a good excuse.
4. My client did it but has a good reason.
5. My client did it but should be acquitted because the police or the prosecutor cheated.
6. My client did it but was influenced by outside forces.

The last five of these defenses are affirmative defenses. An **affirmative defense** tries to persuade a jury to decide that the defendant is not guilty for a reason, even though he or she committed the offense. The defense is saying, "Yes my client did this, but here's why." The prosecution always bears the burden of proving that the defendant committed all of the elements of each offense charged. However, if the defendant admits that he or she committed the offense, but claims a good reason for doing so, then the defendant bears the burden of proving that reason.

affirmative defense—A defense in which the defendant must provide evidence that excuses the legal consequences of an act that the defendant has been proven to have committed.

My Client Did Not Do It

The best way to defend a client from a criminal charge is to show that the defendant did not do it. Unlike the rest of the defenses discussed in this section, this one claims that the defendant is completely innocent of the charges. An **alibi** can be an essential part of maintaining one's innocence, demonstrating that one was not at the scene of the crime. An alibi may be established in many ways, all of which hinge on credible evidence. Often, dated documents such as hotel receipts, credit card purchases, and cash withdrawals from an ATM can be used to help establish an alibi. In this age of surveillance, with so many cameras around to protect establishments against robbery or other offenses, a defendant might be able to show that she was in a store buying ice cream at the time the offense took place many miles away.

alibi—A defense that involves the defendant(s) claiming not to have been at the scene of a criminal offense when it was committed.

My Client Did It, but My Client Is Not Responsible Because of Insanity

In 2011, James Holmes opened fire at an Aurora, Colorado, movie theater killing 12 people and injuring 70 others. In 2015, a jury found him guilty. Holmes, who had a history of mental illness, pleaded not guilty by reason of insanity, which jurors rejected. If Holmes had been found to be insane, he would have been committed to a state psychiatric hospital. Instead, he avoided a death sentence when jurors could not agree and was instead sentenced to thousands of years in prison.[37]

In the district court of Cerro Gordo County, Iowa, Thomas Barlas Jr., was found not guilty by reason of insanity for the 2013 stabbing death of his father, marking what is believed to be the first time such a defense was successfully argued in that court. Why is the insanity plea termed an affirmative defense?

insanity defense—A defense that attempts to give physical or psychological reasons that a defendant cannot comprehend his or her criminal actions, their harm(s), or their punishment.

The **insanity defense** is based on the concept that although the defendant did commit the criminal act, he or she is not criminally responsible because of insanity (see Case in Point 3.1). The defendant did not appreciate that the behavior was wrong, that the behavior could hurt others, or that he or she was even committing the behavior. Today, the insanity defense is seldom used and seldom successful when it is used.[38]

Because insanity is a legal term and not a medical one, this criminal defense sometimes elicits confusion and bitterness.[39] However, mental illness alone does

---

CASE IN POINT 3.1

Durham v. United States (1954)

THE POINT

The Supreme Court created a new test for insanity.

THE CASE

In a trial without a jury, Monte Durham was convicted of breaking into a house. Durham's defense at the trial was that he was of unsound mind at the time of the offense. Before this conviction, Durham had spent years in prisons and mental institutions. In 1945 at age 17, Durham had been discharged from the Navy because he had "a profound personality disorder." In 1953, after the housebreaking incident, he was subjected to "subshock insulin therapy," released, and appraised by the hospital superintendent as "mentally competent to stand trial" on the housebreaking charge.

Given Durham's history, the D.C. Court of Appeals reversed the decision and remanded the case for a new trial. In setting forth a landmark new test for insanity, the court wrote that "an accused is not criminally responsible if his unlawful act was the product of mental disease or mental defect."

THINK ABOUT IT

1. Is the Durham rule an accurate test of criminal responsibility?

not relieve a person of responsibility for a criminal offense. For an insanity defense to be successful, the defendant must show evidence of mental illness as well as the connection between the mental illness and the offense.[40] Still, the public often believes that the defendant is faking insanity to escape the brunt of the criminal law or even the death penalty.

According to Richard J. Bonnie, a professor of law and psychiatry at the University of Virginia, the modern approach to the insanity defense is to avoid trial. In such cases, the prosecution and defense agree that the defendant is likely insane, so the issue never goes to trial. However, if the prosecution and defense disagree about a defendant's mental health and the case does go to trial, the insanity defense fails 75 percent of the time.[41] Most defendants will not even attempt the insanity defense because it is considered an admission to committing the offense. If the defense is unsuccessful, the defendant cannot negotiate for a lesser charge because he or she has already admitted to the offense.[42]

How is someone determined to be insane for the purposes of legal defense? The legal profession needs only to determine whether the defendant had the requisite mental capacity to have a guilty mind, so it uses its own standards to determine insanity. After the 1984 Insanity Defense Reform Act, most states and the federal government began placing the burden of proving insanity on the defendant; a few states still burden the prosecutor (the state) with proving the defendantis sane.[43] About half the states use some form of the M'Naghten rule; the rest use the Model Penal Code rule, except for New Hampshire, which uses the Durham rule. (For an overview of each of these legal standards and more, see Table 3.1.) Kansas, Montana, Idaho, and Utah have abolished the insanity defense completely.[44]

According to legal scholars, the insanity defense was successful fairly often until the attempted assassination of President Ronald Reagan in 1981 by John W. Hinckley, Jr. Hinckley was acquitted in 1982 and committed to a mental health facility until, according to a judge, he "recovered his sanity."[45] (Hinckley was released in July 2016 after doctors decided that he was no longer dangerous.[46]) Under the pre-1981 version of the insanity defense, a defendant was considered not guilty by reason of insanity if he or she lacked the capacity to appreciate the wrongfulness of his or her actions and was unable to "conform his conduct to the requirements of the law." By 1981, nearly all regional U.S. courts of appeals and many states were using this version of the defense.[47] After the Hinckley verdict, however, state and federal courts began to inch toward today's more stringent versions of the defense.

My Client Did It but Has a Good Excuse

A defense may use a number of other reasons or excuses to attempt to explain a defendant's culpability. These include duress, age, mistake, and intoxication. An excuse contends that the defendant should not be held legally responsible for the offense because of one of these personal disabilities.

> › Duress. Sometimes, according to the law, a person commits a criminal offense out of fear for his or her own life or fear of bodily injury. The 1975 Patty Hearst case is a good example of duress. Hearst was kidnapped by a group called the Symbionese Liberation Army, subjected to months of abuse and rape, and forced to participate in a bank robbery. Hearst's attorneys claimed she had been conditioned to fear her assailants. Although she could have run away from her captors during the robbery, she did not recognize this course of action as realistic.

TABLE 3.1	Some Legal Standards Used to Determine Insanity

M'NAGHTEN RULE

In 1843, Daniel M'Naghten was charged with murder after he shot and killed Edward Drummond, the assistant to the prime minister of Great Britain, Sir Robert Peel. M'Naghten believed he was being persecuted by Peel and, unfortunately for Drummond, mistook him for the prime minister. At the trial, evidence showed that M'Naghten was incapable of determining right from wrong at the time of the incident, and the jury found him not guilty. The House of Lords then produced a doctrine that the jury should acquit the defendant if it found that the accused "was laboring under such a defect of reason, from disease of the mind, as not to know the nature and quality of the act he was doing, or, if he did know it, that he did not know it was wrong." This test spread throughout the world where the British legal system had influence and became the foundation for the insanity defense.

IRRESISTIBLE IMPULSE RULE

In some states, an additional feature has been added to the M'Naghten rule standards. The irresistible-impulse rule states that although a defendant understands the nature and quality of the criminal act and understands that it is wrong, if a defendant experiences an irresistible impulse as a result of a mental disease that makes the person incapable of preventing himself or herself from doing the act, this is grounds for acquittal.

APPRECIATION TEST

The federal government has adopted a test that is similar to the M'Naghten rule in that it requires the defendant to be unaware of what he or she was doing or unaware that what he or she was doing was wrong. However, the defendant must also show that he or she had a lack of control.

DURHAM RULE

Based on a rule created in New Hampshire in 1871, the Durham rule was revived in 1954 in the case *Durham* v. *United States*. The rule asks the jury to decide whether the unlawful act was a product of the defendant's insanity. Unfortunately, little guidance is given to the jury in making this determination, and the Durham rule is used relatively infrequently. Also known as the "products test," the Durham rule is a legal construct, and without any clear criteria for making this determination, juries must depend on intuition rather than medical evidence or legal reasoning.

MODEL PENAL CODE TEST (OR ALI)

The Model Penal Code, created by the American Law Institute (ALI) in 1972, provides another criterion for determining whether the defendant is mentally ill. Sometimes called the "substantial capacity test," the code is not used by many states. It attempts to determine whether the defendant, as a result of mental disease or defect, lacks the substantial capacity either to appreciate the criminality of his or her conduct or to conform his or her conduct to the requirements of the law.

GUILTY BUT MENTALLY ILL

This verdict says that the defendant is factually guilty of the crime but was incompetent to control his or her behavior. This finding is not a justification or an excuse for the crime, but merely reflects society's frustrations with the line of legal versus medical reasoning that underlies the insanity defense. Under the guilty-but-mentally-ill concept, the judge can sentence the defendant to any sentence specified by the law. However, the judge is required to address three criteria in imposing the sentence: protecting society, holding offenders accountable for their offenses, and making treatment available to those with mental illness.

> Age. Common law has long established that children under age 7 are presumed incapable of having the necessary criminal intent for their unlawful acts to be considered crimes. For children between ages 7 and 14, however, this presumption can be challenged, and the prosecution can present evidence that the child had the capacity to form criminal intent.[48] This excuse of age, called **infancy,** is the foundation of the juvenile court system.

> Mistake. There is an old saying, "Ignorance of the law is no excuse." This position is reasonable because it would be impossible to prove that someone knew or should have known what the law is. For example, if you claim tax deductions that the law does not allow, even if you do not realize that the deductions are not allowed, the government can punish you. Part of participating in a democracy is knowing and obeying the law. Although ignorance of the law is seldom an effective excuse, ignorance of facts is. For example, suppose you buy a car, and you have good reason to believe that the seller owned the car. If, during a traffic stop, you discover that the car is stolen, then you might have a valid excuse. However, if the price you paid for the car was a fraction of what it was worth, then you are considered responsible for suspecting deviance. People can make honest mistakes, and the court will consider the possibility that the defendant acted honestly and in good faith.

> Intoxication. People who are drunk or under the influence of drugs might do things they would not normally do. However, this generally does not shield them from the law.

infancy—In legal terminology, the state of a child who has not yet reached a specific age; almost all states end infancy at age 18.

My Client Did It but Has a Good Reason

As a criminal defense, justifications contend that the harm caused by committing an offense was more desirable than the harm that would have been caused if one had done nothing. The justifications discussed here are self-defense, consent, and necessity.

> Self-defense. Self-defense has long been established to be a legitimate justification for violating the law. However, to be successful, the claim of self-defense is limited to certain conditions. First, the defendant must believe that physical force is necessary for self-protection or the protection of others. Second, this belief that physical force is necessary must be based on reasonable grounds. Third, the defendant must believe that the force used is necessary to avoid imminent danger. Finally, the force used cannot be in excess of that believed necessary to repel the unlawful attack. A key issue in the self-defense claim is the amount of force used. In a controversial 2012 case in Florida, George Zimmerman, 28, called 911 to report what he alleged was suspicious activity by Trayvon Martin, 17. Minutes later, Martin and Zimmerman became involved in an altercation in which Zimmerman said that Martin attacked him. At his trial on charges of second-degree murder, Zimmerman, who was armed with a gun, stated that he shot and killed Martin in self-defense because Martin was beating him.[49]

> Consent. The consent defense is often used in rape cases. For instance, the defendant claims the victim agreed to sex, whereas the victim claims there was either no consent or consent was given under duress or intoxication. For

Many people participated in marches throughout the country, calling for federal civil rights charges to be filed against George Zimmerman after his acquittal. Why do so many people believe that the amount of force used in this case was excessive?

statutory rape—
Sexual activity conducted with a person who is younger than a specified age or incapable of valid consent because of mental illness, mental handicap, intoxication, unconsciousness, or deception.

the consent to be legitimate, it must be given knowingly and freely. Children are not deemed capable of giving informed consent, and such actions will invoke a charge of **statutory rape**.

› Necessity. Defense based on the principle of necessity must show that the harm that would have resulted from compliance with the law would have exceeded that from its violation. For example, campers trapped in a mountain snowstorm might use the necessity defense to justify breaking into a cabin to keep warm as long as they later notify the owner and pay for the repairs.[50]

My Client Did It but Should Be Acquitted Because the Police or the Prosecutor Cheated

Some criminal defenses concentrate on the conduct of law enforcement authorities. Failing to follow procedural law, engaging in fraud or other misconduct, and treating defendants in a selective and discriminatory manner can all be reasons to challenge a criminal indictment. Examples of these behaviors include the following:

› Statute of limitations. A statute of limitations is a law applying to civil and criminal cases that holds that prosecution must take place within a specified period. Depending on the jurisdiction, many offenses have statutes of limitations. Murder, however, usually does not have a statute of limitations, and suspects can be charged decades after the crime.

entrapment—The use of extreme means by law enforcement to pressure someone to break the law.

› Entrapment. **Entrapment** occurs when the police use extreme means to pressure someone to break the law. Entrapment has been the defense of politicians caught accepting bribes or engaging in other illegal behavior. In the famous Abscam case, which lasted from 1978 to 1980, federal agents posing

An FBI agent carries out boxes of evidence following a search of a Chinatown fraternal organization in San Francisco. The FBI spent millions of dollars and used more than a dozen undercover operatives during the seven-year organized crime investigation. Many of the defendants, including a state senator and an aide caught up in the probe, claimed the FBI was guilty of entrapment. Is it possible for completely innocent people to be entrapped by the police?

as rich Middle Eastern sheiks offered public officials, including members of Congress, money for influencing legislation. The defendants were videotaped stuffing large amounts of cash into their pockets and were subsequently prosecuted. The defendants were unable to convince the court that they were victims of entrapment.[51]

› Double jeopardy. According to this defense, a defendant cannot be tried or punished twice for the same offense. Based on common law and the Fifth Amendment to the Constitution, the double jeopardy defense is designed to protect the defendant from repeated trials and excessive punishments. In a few circumstances, however, the same behavior may be considered for different purposes without violating the right against double jeopardy. In 1993, four Los Angeles police officers who were acquitted in the beating of motorist Rodney King were later tried in federal court on the charge of violating King's civil rights.[52] Two of the officers were found guilty.

› Police fraud or prosecutor misconduct. Law enforcement officials must play by the rules established by procedural law. Withholding evidence, making false statements, and putting forth evidence known to be false can be grounds for a defense claim of police fraud or prosecutor misconduct.

My Client Did It but Was Influenced by Outside Forces

Some defenses for criminal acts attempt to shift the blame from the defendant to something outside his or her control. A good example is the so-called Twinkie defense, which has become something of an urban legend. In November 1978, former San Francisco city supervisor Dan White entered City Hall through a basement window and shot and killed Mayor George Moscone and supervisor

Harvey Milk. White then turned himself over to police. At trial, White's attorneys claimed that White had severe depression before the shooting. A defense psychiatrist mentioned that the health-conscious White had eaten large amounts of junk food during his depression and that this radical change of behavior was a symptom of depression.[53] White's defense was that he was influenced by depression, not that a sugar high made him insane. A jury found White guilty of two counts of voluntary manslaughter, and White was sentenced to less than eight years in prison.[54]

PAUSE AND REVIEW

1. Which six arguments are commonly employed in the defense against a criminal indictment?

FOCUS ON ETHICS Changing the Substantive Law

Laws are made by elected legislators to reflect their constituents' wishes. In an ideal situation, communities enjoy a broad consensus as to what behaviors should be considered illegal and what the punishments should be for violating the law. However, citizens do not support some laws. These laws are broken regularly and sometimes enforced selectively.

Imagine that you are a state senator and that the majority party leader has told you that because of your hard work and your casting of several key votes, she can fix it with the rest of the party for you to have any law you want added to your state's criminal code. What behavior that is now legal in your state would you choose to make against the law? Does your new law address a significant social problem, or does it simply expose the rest of us to your personal aesthetic tastes, your religious sensitivities, or your individual pet peeves? For example, some people think that anyone smoking in public, even outdoors, should be arrested because of the danger of secondhand smoke.

On the other hand, what law that is currently on the books would you like to see removed? Why do you think this is a bad law, and what would be the social consequences of legalizing this behavior? For instance, if you are concerned with the right of people to choose to use marijuana and decide to repeal the marijuana laws, some unanticipated consequences might accompany this change. More people might use marijuana

in unsafe situations, such as while driving. Marijuana might become more easily available to children, and many people could develop health problems from long-term use.

Think through the possible ramifications of adding or deleting substantive laws. Even though no one would suggest that our system of laws is perfect, we do need to be cautious when we change the law. One of the foundations of a democracy is the confidence of the people in the wisdom and fairness of the law. The criminal justice system cannot maintain the order of society without widespread voluntary social control. Consider how the laws that you would add to the legal code and the laws that you would delete would affect the relationship between citizens and the government.

WHAT DO YOU DO?
1. What law(s) would you add?
2. What law(s) would you delete?
3. Should all new laws be subject to public vote? Why or why not?

For more insight as to how someone might respond to such an ethical dilemma, visit the companion website at www.oup.com/us/fuller to watch a video that connects this scenario to a real-world situation.

Summary

LEARNING OBJECTIVE 1 Frame the development of the U.S. criminal law.	The founders and subsequent generations of Americans chose to implement legal elements from previously established cultures that were consistent with their own values, religions, and economic structures and discarded elements that were not. As a result, U.S. criminal law is a hodgepodge of other societies' attempts to govern conduct through the criminal law and continues to evolve today.
LEARNING OBJECTIVE 2 Evaluate the function of each of the four issues that guide precedent.	(1) Predictability: predictability provides the concept of precedent with a certain level of order. (2) Reliability: participants in the legal system expect the courts to follow precedent. (3) Efficiency: participants expect cases to be resolved in a reasonable time. (4) Equality: similar cases are expected to be treated in a similar fashion.
LEARNING OBJECTIVE 3 Identify and define the sources of the criminal law.	Constitutions: In democracies, constitutions express the will of the people. In the United States, the federal Constitution governs the nation, and each state also has a constitution that pertains to the citizens and businesses of that state. Statutes: Developed from the common law, statutes proscribe criminal behavior. These laws are debated and voted on by legislative bodies and presumably represent the will of the people. Case law: Cases decided by judges in state, local, and federal courts are all part of U.S. law. Case law operates under the principle of *stare decisis* (similar cases are treated in a similar way). Administrative rules: Rules developed by federal, state, and local agencies to oversee aspects of commerce and public protection. Executive orders: Directives that the U.S. president or a state governor issues to government officials and agencies.
LEARNING OBJECTIVE 4 Compare and contrast the similarities and differences between criminal law and civil law.	The criminal law specifies the prosecution by the government of a person or people for an act that has been classified as a criminal offense. Civil law governs private rights as opposed to criminal issues. In civil law, the case is between two individuals. In criminal law, the case concerns the defendant and the government. Both civil law and criminal law try to control the behavior of people, and both can impose sanctions. Both overlap in the types of behavior they address, such as personal assault or environmental pollution.
LEARNING OBJECTIVE 5 Differentiate between substantive law and procedural law.	Substantive law tells us which behaviors have been defined as criminal offenses. Procedural law specifies how the criminal justice system is allowed to deal with those who break the law.
LEARNING OBJECTIVE 6 Distinguish between felonies and misdemeanors and illustrate why the application of these labels is not always consistent.	A felony is a criminal offense that calls for a minimum term of one year or more in state or federal prison. Felonies include murder, rape, assault, larceny, arson, and a host of other offenses at the state and federal level. A misdemeanor is a minor criminal offense (less serious than a felony) punishable by lighter penalties such as a fine and/or jail time for up to one year. An offense may be categorized as either a felony or misdemeanor depending on the circumstances of the offense, the prosecutor's use of discretion, and the laws of the respective jurisdiction.
LEARNING OBJECTIVE 7 Justify the need for inchoate offenses.	Inchoate offenses allow law enforcement to deter individuals and groups from causing harm and destruction. An offender should not have to be successful in completing a crime before the criminal justice system can respond.

LEARNING OBJECTIVE **8** Outline the elements of a criminal offense.	1. The criminal act (*actus reus*) (must be present in all offenses) 2. The criminal intent (*mens rea*) (must be present in some offenses) 3. The relationship between *actus reus* and *mens rea* (also called concurrence) 4. Attendant circumstances (must be present in some offenses) 5. Result (criminal harm; must be present in some offenses)
LEARNING OBJECTIVE **9** List the six arguments that can be employed in the defense against a criminal indictment.	(1) My client did not do it. (2) My client did it, but my client is not responsible because he or she is insane. (3) My client did it but has a good excuse. (4) My client did it but has a good reason. (5) My client did it but should be acquitted because the police or the prosecutor cheated. (6) My client did it but was influenced by outside forces.

Critical Reflections

1. **Which sources of law (the Constitution, case law, statutes) do you think should have precedence in the criminal justice system?**

2. **Explain how both the civil law and the criminal law are designed to control the behavior of individuals.**

3. **In your opinion, which of the six criminal defense explanations of criminal responsibility most mitigate an offender's unlawful behavior?**

Key Terms

actus reus **p. 80**
affirmative defense **p. 83**
alibi **p. 83**
attendant circumstances **p. 80**
beyond a reasonable doubt **p. 77**
Bill of Rights **p. 71**
case law **p. 73**
civil law **p. 76**
Code of Hammurabi **p. 67**
common law **p. 69**
concurrence **p. 80**
corpus delicti **p. 80**

criminal law **p. 74**
double jeopardy **p. 77**
entrapment **p. 88**
felony **p. 78**
habeas corpus **p. 67**
inchoate offense **p. 79**
infancy **p. 87**
infraction **p. 80**
insanity defense **p. 84**
Magna Carta **p. 67**
mens rea **p. 80**
misdemeanor **p. 79**

penal code **p. 73**
precedent **p. 69**
preponderance of the evidence **p. 77**
procedural law **p. 77**
rule of law **p. 64**
stare decisis **p. 69**
statute **p. 72**
statutory law **p. 69**
statutory rape **p. 88**
strict liability **p. 82**
substantive law **p. 77**
tort law **p. 77**

Endnotes

1 Stephen Yoder, "Collateral Damage: Harsh Sex Offender Laws They Put Whole Families at Risk," *Al Jazeera America*, August 27, 2015, http://america.aljazeera.com/articles/2015/8/27/harsh-sex-offender-laws-may-put-whole-families-at-risk.html.

2 Jane Shim, "Listed for Life," Slate, August 13, 2014, http://www.slate.com/

articles/news_and_politics/jurisprudence/2014/08/sex_offender_registry_laws_by_state_mapped.html.

3 Jill Levenson, Alissa R. Ackerman, Kelly M. Socia, and Andrew J. Harris, "Where for Art Thou? Transient Sex Offenders and Residence Restrictions," *Criminal Justice Policy Review* 26. no. 4 (June 2015): 319–344.

4 Aleksandr I. Solzhenitsyn, *The Gulag Archipelago 1918–1956* (New York: HarperCollins, 2002).

5 James Austin and John Irwin, *It's About Time: America's Imprisonment Binge*, 3d ed. (Belmont, Calif.: Wadsworth, 2001).

6 Jeffrey Reiman, *The Rich Get Richer and the Poor Get Prison: Ideology, Class, and*

Criminal Justice, 6th ed. (Boston: Allyn & Bacon, 2001).

7   Samuel Walker, *Sense and Nonsense about Crime and Drugs: A Policy Guide*, 4th ed. (Belmont, Calif.: West/Wadsworth, 1998).

8   Herbert A. Johnson and Nancy Travis Wolfe, *History of Criminal Justice*, 3d ed. (Cincinnati, Ohio: Anderson, 2003).

9   Ibid.

10 L. W. King, trans., "The Code of Hammurabi," The Avalon Project at Yale Law School, http://avalon.law.yale.edu/subject_menus/medmenu.asp.

11 Magna Carta, British Library, http://www.bl.uk/collections/treasures/magna.html.

12 David W. Neubauer and Henry F. Fradella, *America's Courts and the Criminal Justice System* (Belmont, Calif.: Wadsworth Cengage, 2011), 29.

13 Morris L. Cohen, "The Common Law in the American Legal System: The Challenge of Conceptual Research," *Yale Law School Legal Scholarship Repository*, 81, no. 13 (1989). Online at http://digitalcommons.law.yale.edu/fss_papers/2950/. The Robbins Collection, University of California at Berkeley School of Law, The Common Law and Civil Law Traditions, https://www.law.berkeley.edu/library/robbins/CommonLawCivilLawTraditions.html. Accessed April 2016. Joycelyn M. Pollock, *Criminal Law*, 9th ed. (New York: LexisNexis, 2009), 7. Kyle Scott, *Dismantling American Common Law* (Lanham, Md.: Lexington Books, 2007), 16. Oliver Wendell Holmes, Jr., *The Common Law* (New Brunswick, N.J.: Transaction Publishers, 2005), xiv.

14 Richard A. Wasserstrom, *The Judicial Decision: Toward a Theory of Legal Justification* (Stanford, Calif.: Stanford University Press, 1961).

15 Lief H. Carter, *Reason in Law*, 4th ed. (New York: HarperCollins, 1994).

16 Karla Castetter, "Chapter 1: Introduction," in *Locating the Law*, 5th ed. (Los Angeles: Southern California Association of Law Libraries, 2011), 1–12.

17 Kermit Hall, *The Magic Mirror: Law in American History* (New York: Oxford University Press, 1991).

18 Charles Rembar, *The Law of the Land: The Evolution of Our Legal System* (New York: Simon & Schuster, 1980).

19 Utah Department of Administrative Services, Division of Administrative Rules, Utah Administrative Code, Title R270. Crime Victim Reparations, Administration, Rule R270-1. Award and Reparation Standards, http://www.rules.utah.gov/publicat/code/r270/r270-001.htm.

20 Rules and Regulations of the State of Georgia, Georgia Bureau of Investigation, 92-5-.01, Rules for the limited disclosure and viewing of certain crime scene photographs and videos by bona fide members of the press, http://all.eregulations.us/eRegs_Georgia/Code/CHAPTER92/Chapter92-5//92501.pdf.

21 Alaine Ginocchio and Kevin L. Doran, *The Boundaries of Executive Authority: Using Executive Orders to Implement Federal Climate Change Policy* (Boulder, Colo.: Center for Energy and Environmental Security, 2008), 5–6. Available at http://www.climateactionproject.com/docs/CEES_PCAP_Report_Final_Feb_08.pdf.

22 John C. Klotter, *Criminal Law*, 6th ed. (Cincinnati, Ohio: Anderson, 2001), 6.

23 Nils Christie, "Conflicts as Property," *British Journal of Criminology* 17 (1977): 1–15.

24 Jennifer Eastman, "A Constitutional Amendment for Victims: The Unexplored Possibility," in *Victimology: A Study of Crime Victims and Their Roles*, eds. Judith M. Sgarzi and Jack McDevitt (Upper Saddle River, N.J.: Prentice Hall, 2003), 333–346.

25 Pew Charitable Trusts, Federal Drug Sentencing Laws Bring High Cost, Low Return, August 27, 2015, http://www.pewtrusts.org/en/research-and-analysis/issue-briefs/2015/08/federal-drug-sentencing-laws-bring-high-cost-low-return.

26 Ibid.

27 Ibid.

28 John Gramlich and Kristen Bialik, "Obama Used Clemency Power More Often Than Any President Since Truman," *Pew Research Center*, January 20, 2017, http://www.pewresearch.org/fact-tank/2017/01/20/obama-used-more-clemency-power.

29 Raymond J. Michalowski, *Order, Law, and Crime: An Introduction to Criminology* (New York: Random House, 1985), 139–141.

30 Frank A. Schubert, *Criminal Law: The Basics* (Los Angeles: Roxbury, 2004), 101–103.

31 Ibid., 10–13.

32 Pamela Manson, "After 7 Years and an Acquittal, Man Is Convicted of Killing Utah Deputy," *Salt Lake Tribune*, February 7, 2017, http://www.sltrib.com/home/4913508-155/jury-convicts-man-accused-of-killing.

33 James R. Acker and David C. Brody, *Criminal Procedure: A Contemporary Perspective* (Gaithersburg, Md.: Aspen, 1999).

34 Philip Shenon, "Lawyers Fear Monitoring in Cases on Terrorism," *New York Times*, April 28, 2008, http://www.nytimes.com/2008/04/28/us/28lawyers.html. Department of Justice, USA PATRIOT ACT, https://www.justice.gov/archive/ll/highlights.htm.

35 John Deigh and David Dolinko, ed., *The Oxford Handbook of Philosophy of Criminal Law* (New York: Oxford University Press, 2011), 126.

36 Schubert, *Criminal Law: The Basics*.

37 Ann O'Neill, Theater Shooter Holmes Gets 12 Life Sentences, Plus 3,318 years, CNN, August 27, 2015, http://www.cnn.com/2015/08/26/us/james-holmes-aurora-massacre-sentencing/. Amanda Paulson, "Why James Holmes Insanity Case Is So Unusual for Colorado," *Christian Science Monitor*, April 27, 2015, http://www.csmonitor.com/USA/Justice/2015/0427/Why-James-Holmes-insanity-case-is-so-unusual-for-Colorado-video.

38 Michael L. Perlin, "The Insanity Defense: Nine Myths That Will Not Go Away," in *The Insanity Defense: Multi-disciplinary Views on Its History, Trends, and Controversies*, ed. Mark D. White (Santa Barbara, Calif.: Praeger, 2017).

39 Eric Hickey, *Serial Murderers and Their Victims* (Belmont, Calif.: Wadsworth, 1991), 37–45.

40 Ira Mickenberg, "A Pleasant Surprise: The Guilty but Mentally Ill Verdict Has Both Succeeded in Its Own Right and Successfully Preserved the Traditional Role of the Insanity Defense," *University of Cincinnati Law Review* 55 (1987): 954–955 (citing In re Winship, 397 U.S. 358, 364 (1970)).

41 Joe Palazzolo, "John Hinckley Case Led to Vast Narrowing of Insanity Defense," *Wall Street Journal*—Online Edition, July 28, 2016.

42 John Q. La Fond & Mary L. Durham, "Cognitive Dissonance: Have Insanity Defense and Civil Commitment Reforms Made a Difference?" *Villanova Law Review* 39 (1994): 95.

43 Kathy McCabe, "N.H. Jurors Face Choice on Insanity Defense," Boston.com, February 28, 2011, http://www.boston.com/news/local/new_hampshire/articles/2011/02/28/nh_jurors_face_choice_on_insanity_defense/. Cornell University Law School, Legal Information Institute, 18 U.S. Code § 17 - Insanity defense, https://www.law.cornell.edu/uscode/text/18/17.

44 Warren Richey, "Supreme Court Rejects Idaho Case on Prohibiting

the Insanity Defense," *Christian Science Monitor*, November 26, 2012, http://www.csmonitor.com/USA/Justice/2012/1126/Supreme-Court-rejects-Idaho-case-on-prohibiting-the-insanity-defense.

45 Palazzolo, "John Hinckley Case Led to Vast Narrowing of Insanity Defense."

46 Shawn Boburg, "Would-be Reagan Assassin John Hinckley Jr. Is Freed after 35 Years," *Washington Post*, September 10, 2016,https://www.washingtonpost.com/local/public-safety/president-reagans-would-be-assassin-is-set-to-be-released-saturday/2016/09/09/

e1ad0e9e-75ca-11e6-be4f-3f42f2e5a49e_story.html.

47 Palazzolo, "John Hinckley Case Led to Vast Narrowing of Insanity Defense."

48 Klotter, *Criminal Law*, 514.

49 CNN, Trayvon Martin Shooting Fast Facts, February 11, 2015, http://www.cnn.com/2013/06/05/us/trayvon-martin-shooting-fast-facts/.

50 Klotter, *Criminal Law*, 540–542.

51 "Abscam bribery scandal," Source-watch, http://www.sourcewatch.org/index.php?title=Abscam_bribery_scandal.

52 Jim Newton, "Koon, Powell Get 2½ Years in Prison," *Los Angeles Times*, August 5, 1993.

53 Carol Pogash, "Myth of the 'Twinkie Defense,'" *San Francisco Chronicle*, November 23, 2003, www.sfgate.com/cgi-bin/article.cgi?f=/c/a/2003/11/23/INGRE343501.DTL; *People* v. *White*, 117 Cal. App. 3d 270, 172 Cal. Rptr. (1981).

54 White appealed and lost. He served a little more than five years, leaving prison in January 1985. He committed suicide that October.

PART II

Enforcing the Law

14395

Chapter 4

The History and Organization of Law Enforcement

This photograph of John Dillinger was taken at the Indiana Reformatory when he was 21 years old.
How was the lack of technology beneficial in Dillinger's success at avoiding law enforcement?

lthough many American criminals have become infamous, few have reached a level of notoriety that has transformed them into legends. Perhaps most infamous of these is John Dillinger.[1] Between September 1933 and July 1934, Dillinger and his gang robbed several banks in the Midwest, killed a sheriff, robbed police departments of weapons, and escaped from jail at least three times. Perpetrated during the Great Depression, this crime spree captivated the popular imagination and made Dillinger the first FBI "Public Enemy Number One."[2] One element that distinguished the "Dillinger gang" from most other criminal enterprises is the effect it had on the relationship between local and federal law enforcement agencies, as well as the eventual employment of technology to pursue criminal suspects. Most of all, Dillinger's exploits helped to make the FBI what its founding director, J. Edgar Hoover, wanted it to be: revered by the public, embraced by local law enforcement, feared by lawbreakers, technologically advanced, and a public-relations success. Dillinger made a well-funded national law enforcement agency seem like a good idea.[3]

On parole after serving eight years for robbery, Dillinger robbed an Ohio bank and was quickly arrested and jailed. He escaped when three friends of his who had escaped from the Indiana State Prison shot the local sheriff and freed Dillinger. Dillinger and his gang then went on a robbery spree. From three police arsenals in Indiana, they stole machine guns, rifles, revolvers, ammunition, and bulletproof vests, which they used to rob at least 12 banks.[4]

After being caught in Indiana and jailed again, Dillinger used a gun he whittled from wood to escape from a jail that was considered escape-proof. After forcing the guards into cells, he grabbed two machine guns and drove to Chicago in a stolen sheriff's car. Because Dillinger crossed state lines in a stolen vehicle, the FBI became involved in the case.[5]

The inability of law enforcement to capture Dillinger cast a harsh light on how inefficient and outgunned they were. The Dillinger gang was able to evade law enforcement largely because of a lack of communication technology, and they were as well armed as any police they did meet. Communication between agencies and individual officers was limited to the telephone and telegraph, and there was no radio communication between law enforcement vehicles. Often, by the time officers arrived at a location at which Dillinger had been seen, he was long gone.

In April 1934, FBI agents cornered Dillinger's gang at a Wisconsin resort. However, they opened fire on three innocent customers by mistake, killing one of them, while Dillinger's gang escaped out the back. By this time, the U.S. Justice Department was offering a reward of $15,000 (over $260,000 in today's dollars) for Dillinger's capture.[6] On July 21, 1934, FBI agents killed Dillinger as he walked out of a theater in Gary, Indiana.

THINK ABOUT IT > How did Dillinger's gang evade police for so long? Would they manage the same feat today? Why or why not?

What did the professionalization of the police and the expansion of the FBI contribute to law enforcement's ability to catch lawbreakers like Dillinger's gang?

A Brief History of the Police

As long as human beings have lived in large groups, we have needed social control. Much of this control was exerted through informal means, such as censure from families, friends, and other social institutions. However, as social groups became larger and less personally interconnected, formal means became required to deal with situations that did not respond to informal means, such as legal disputes and the control of violent people.

Even though we all realize the necessity of being policed, many of us still harbor some resentment at being controlled. If we have little or no respect for the person controlling our behavior, maybe due to her or his history of being unfair, this resentment may escalate into hostility and resistance. Ultimately, what determines the legitimacy of our own or others' policing behavior is the degree to which it is perceived as fair or just.

The institution of police is a relatively new phenomenon. Creating agencies devoted solely to maintaining order and apprehending lawbreakers entails a degree of occupational specialization that is available only in highly developed societies. However, like physicians, teachers, and farmers, police officers are needed for communities to function effectively. Although we commonly think of policing as a stable institution built on unchanging tradition, the police are, in fact, subject to rapid social change and constant challenges.[7] The way policing is done in the 21st century is the result of a long, uneven development that continues today.

Early Policing in England

The law enforcement function has existed in one form or another for thousands of years. Police in early history usually derived from a military connected with a government or ruler or from the community when citizens created informal groups to protect themselves. In the seventh century BCE, the Roman emperor Augustus created one of the earliest recorded organized police forces. In 17th-century Japan, each town had a military official, the samurai warrior, whose duties included acting as judge and chief of police. In Russia from 1881 to the revolution in 1917, the tsars' Okhranka was a police force that dealt with political terrorism and revolutionary matters.

The form of policing that most directly led to that of modern U.S. policing was the **frankpledge system** in England, which began in Anglo-Saxon England and continued until the 19th century. This system divided a community into tithings, or groups of 10 men who were responsible for the conduct of the group and ensured that a member charged with breaking the law would show up in court.

An important office in English policing was that of the shire reeve or sheriff. The sheriff led the shire's (or county's) military forces and judged criminal and civil cases. Later, the sheriff's duties became more restricted, and his job included trying minor criminal offenses, investigating offenses within the shire, and questioning suspects. (The office of sheriff in England continues to this day.)

In the 13th century, the Normans, invaders from France who eventually replaced the Anglo-Saxons as the ruling class of England, updated this system by adding the *comes stabuli*, or **constable**. Constables oversaw the **watch-and-ward system** that guarded the city's or town's gates at night. The actual job of enforcing the law was up to the citizens, who were expected to raise the alarm, or **hue and cry**, and catch people accused of breaking the law. Although the watch system lasted for hundreds of years, it had serious problems. Many citizens resented watchman duty and either refused to do it or did it poorly, and many were too elderly or infirm to do it.

LEARNING OBJECTIVE 1

Discuss the three enduring features of U.S. policing influenced by English policing.

LEARNING OBJECTIVE 2

Describe how the events of September 11, 2001, affected law enforcement.

frankpledge system—An early form of English government that divided communities into groups of 10 men who were responsible for the group's conduct and ensured that a member charged with breaking the law appeared in court.

constable—The head of law enforcement for large districts in early England. In the modern United States, a constable serves areas such as rural townships and is usually elected.

watch-and-ward system—An early English system overseen by the constable in which a watchman guarded a city's or town's gates at night.

hue and cry—In early England, the alarm that citizens were required to raise upon the witness or discovery of a criminal offense.

In the 17th century, Samurai warriors performed law enforcement duties in Japan. What other duties were the samurai responsible for?

Bow Street Runners— A police organization created circa 1748 by magistrates and brothers Henry Fielding and Sir John Fielding whose members went on patrol, rather than remaining at a designated post.

Thames River Police— A private police force created by the West India Trading Company in 1798 that represented the first professional, salaried police force in London.

Metropolitan Police Act— Created in 1829 by Sir Robert Peel, it was the first successful bill to create a permanent, public police force.

bobbies— A slang term for the police force created in 1829 by Sir Robert Peel's Metropolitan Police Act that was derived from the short form of Robert, Bob.

Around 1748, magistrates Henry Fielding and his brother Sir John Fielding created the **Bow Street Runners**, in which members were required to patrol specific areas rather than just sit in their watch boxes.[8] In 1798, the West India Trading Company created the first professional, salaried police force in London, the **Thames River Police**. This private police force, formed to prevent thefts from the port, was different from the frankpledge system in that officers patrolled to prevent crime, and officers were salaried and not allowed to accept any other payments. The police force worked so well that two years later the government added it to the public payroll.

Citizens accustomed to a system in which they were basically responsible for themselves were suspicious of a standing police force. However, London's social problems were mounting as a result of poverty and a burgeoning population. In 1829, British statesman Sir Robert Peel convinced the British government to pass the **Metropolitan Police Act**, the first successful bill to create a permanent, public police force. These "new police" carried out preventive patrols, were paid regular salaries, and wore uniforms. The police, who were nicknamed **bobbies** after their founder's nickname, "Bob," adhered to a strict military-type discipline. Although their jurisdiction was limited to London, the bobbies set a new standard of police professionalism.

The English tradition of law enforcement influenced three enduring features of American policing[9]:

1. Limited police authority. As opposed to other European countries, the Anglo-American tradition of policing emphasizes individual rights and liberties.

Sir Robert Peel created the first permanent police force in London in 1829. Why was this police force nicknamed the "Bobbies?"

2. Local control. Law enforcement agencies are, for the most part, local, city, or county institutions. The United States does not have a national police force. We do have many state and federal law enforcement agencies, but they are not like the national police forces found in many parts of the world where control is highly centralized within the government.

3. Fragmented system. There are more than 18,000 separate law enforcement agencies in the United States, ranging from federal (FBI, Secret Service) to state (highway patrol) to local (city police, county sheriff). These agencies are loosely coordinated, and the state and local agencies have little federal oversight.[10]

Early Policing in the United States

Many differences between the United States and England affected the development of their respective policing styles. One was the lack of a single, coherent philosophy. Whereas the English police were unified under the vision of Sir Robert Peel, local police organizations in the United States formed their own policies and procedures. A second factor was the large and ever-expanding political geography of the United States. As stakes were claimed and territories formed, government and law enforcement followed slowly. This led to the phenomenon of the "Wild West" in the 19th century. The farther the country developed from the cities and seats of government on the East Coast, the less controllable it became. A third factor was immigration. The constituency of the United States was (and continues to be) in constant flux, resulting in cities, states, and territories filled with people representing a vast array of cultures and languages. Conversely, the early

FIGHT BETWEEN THE METROPOLITAN AND MUNICIPAL POLICE.

This 19th-century drawing depicts a fight between the New York Municipal Police, which had been recently dissolved, and its replacement, the Metropolitan Police, which eventually became the New York City Police Department. Why did it take so long for big U.S. cities to create stable police forces?

English police were responsible for a static political and physical geography that had a shared culture and language.

In the United States, informal policing began in Boston in 1631 with the establishment of a night watch. In New York City in the 1650s, when the Dutch settlement was called New Amsterdam, the "schout fiscal" or "sheriff attorney" had such duties as settling disputes and warning the colonists of fire. A group of men called the "Rattle Watch" patrolled at night, carrying loud rattles to raise an alarm if anything was amiss. Policing continued this way for the next two centuries. It was not until 1833 that Philadelphia organized the first dedicated police force, followed by Boston in 1838.[11] The first New York City police agency, the Municipal Police Force, was created in 1845. Their copper star badges were so distinctive that the officers were nicknamed "coppers," which was later shortened to "cops." The modern New York City Police Department formed in 1898 when the state legislature ordered local cities, towns, and villages to consolidate into a single city called New York City and the Police Department of the Greater City of New York absorbed the smaller police agencies.[12]

Another important police force developed in Chicago around 1855. The city's police officers were not trained in the law, and the criminal justice system did not emphasize legal procedure. Chicago police were different from other police organizations in four respects:

1. The police and courts were highly decentralized and often reflected the values of local communities. Community standards rather than legal norms were expected to guide police behavior and check abuses.

2. The police, as part of a larger political system, were a significant resource at the command of local organizations. Police, courts, and prosecutors provided political leaders with jobs, were a source of favors for constituents, and were important agencies for collecting money that lubricated political campaigns.

3. Criminal justice institutions often operated organized illegal activities, providing the means by which police officers and other officials earned extra income.

4. Police officers and other criminal justice system personnel developed informal systems of operation that reflected what they wanted to do. These informal methods of operation bore, at best, only an indirect relationship to the formal legal system.[13]

The political nature of the Chicago police in the early 20th century resulted in a system in which the police regularly took bribes, solicited votes, harassed the homeless, beat suspects, and assisted gamblers. They also performed many duties now normally considered outside the responsibilities of crime control, such as taking injured people to the hospital, mediating family quarrels, rounding up stray dogs, returning lost children to their parents, and removing dead horses from city streets. One of the hallmarks of the professionalization of law enforcement over the past century is the degree to which the police mission has become less informal and more legally constrained.

The development of professional police departments in large metropolitan areas is important, but it is not the only contributing factor to the development of the police in the United States. In rural areas and small towns, particularly in the South and West, the vigilante tradition of taking justice into one's own hands was part of American life until the early to mid-20th century. In the newly developed areas of the frontier, the normal mechanisms of social control emerged slowly. Constraints on deviant behavior exercised by churches, schools, and cohesive community life were absent, and the formal system of law enforcement was inadequate. To protect property and social order from rogues and criminals, the elites established vigilante committees.[14] The justice meted out by the vigilantes was rough and included, but was not limited to, flogging, expulsion, and killing. These actions served not only as punishments, but also as warnings to others that a system of social order existed that everyone was expected to obey.[15]

The Introduction of Police Professionalism

At the start of the 20th century, law enforcement in the United States was caught in a web of inefficiency and corruption.[16] The police had become a tool of political interests, as politicians often recruited the officers. In return, the officers would encourage citizens to vote for some candidates, discourage them from voting for others, and help to rig elections. Police officers and administrators made up much of their pay from bribery and pay-offs, ignoring some crime in return for payments. Gambling establishments would send officers to collect debts, and the system became so entrenched that pay-offs became standardized according to police rank. For example, in New York City in 1900, a patrol officer could earn from $50 to $300 for protecting brothels and gambling establishments. Particularly lucrative positions, such as police captain, could be bought from local politicians.[17]

Politicians and heads of industry realized that maintaining popular support for the existing political and economic system required some changes. One such effort was the **Pendleton Civil Service Reform Act of 1883**. A response to public frustration with incompetence and corruption within the federal government, the act, according to its text, was passed to "regulate and improve the civil service of the United States." The act formed a civil service system that did away with patronage and administered employment and promotions based on merit rather than political connections. This legislation shook much of the corruption out of the U.S. civil service bureaucracy, including the country's budding police forces.

Pendleton Civil Service Reform Act of 1883—Law that established federal government positions would be awarded on the basis of merit rather than political affiliation.

Police arrest safe-crackers in a New York City bank in the 1870s. Why were police departments so slow in developing professional behavior?

Wickersham Commission report— The 14-volume report published in 1931 and 1932, which was the first comprehensive national study of U.S. crime and law enforcement.

The work of August Vollmer, a police chief of Berkeley, California, marks a highlight of the police reform movement. In 1908, Vollmer established formal training for his department's officers. He went on to author the federal **Wickersham Commission report** in 1931, which set the police reform agenda for the rest of the century, and he instituted many policies and practices that still influence law enforcement today. He was among the first police chiefs to recruit college graduates, and he organized the first police-science courses at the University of California. Many of his students went on to become police chiefs in other cities, where they extended his reform policies. Vollmer's police reform movement, which dominated the law enforcement agenda through the 1960s, focused on six issues:

1. Policing is defined as a profession in which the police serve the entire community on a nonpartisan basis.
2. Policing should be free of political influence.
3. Qualified executives should lead the police. This means that the chiefs of large cities should have some experience running large organizations.
4. The standards for being a police officer should be raised. Law enforcement personnel should be screened for intelligence, health, and moral character. (Although slow in developing, this increase in the quality of personnel resulted in specialized police academies where professional training is required.)

5. Modern principles of scientific management should be introduced that involve centralizing command structures so that the chief can better control officers.

6. Specialized units such as traffic, juvenile, and vice should be developed to increase the size and complexity of police agencies and allow officers to focus on particular types of crime. This reform opened up law enforcement to women, who were originally hired only for juvenile units.[18]

Other features of the progressive reform movement in policing included an emphasis on technology to help the police do their job. Of particular importance was the introduction of the patrol car, or, as Vollmer called it, "the swift angel of death."[19] The patrol car meant that officers could patrol larger areas of the jurisdiction more effectively and arrive quickly at locations to which they were called. Improved communications, advanced recordkeeping techniques, and the creation of crime-analysis laboratories were all new uses of technology that were introduced to law enforcement during this move toward professionalism.

Police professionalization also introduced preventive strategies that dealt with high-risk individuals such as juveniles before they had a chance to become career offenders. The police also engaged in public-relations activities to improve their image in the community. Such programs as "junior police" gave children positive interactions with law enforcement by teaching them military and marching drills, offering safety instruction, and having the "junior police" escort younger children back and forth to school and to playgrounds.

Finally, the move toward police professionalism involved removing functions not normally concerned with crime control. The police had been sort of a "catch-all" agency that, along with apprehending lawbreakers, chased stray dogs, licensed various enterprises, and enforced minor morals laws such as those prohibiting kissing in public.[20] Such activities became considered an inefficient use of police

J. Edgar Hoover is shown through the years in his post as director of the Federal Bureau of Investigation, which he was appointed to in 1924 and served until his death in 1972. Why was Hoover so successful at building the FBI into a premier law enforcement agency?

resources, so gradually the police were left with the sole job of maintaining public order and controlling crime.

Perhaps the most famous law enforcement administrator to champion professionalism was the Federal Bureau of Investigation's J. Edgar Hoover. Hoover built the FBI into one of the premier law enforcement agencies in the world with his skillful political maneuvering, masterful public-relations efforts, and surveillance of not only lawbreakers but also political rivals, politicians, and U.S. presidents. The agency he created is a cornerstone of law enforcement in the United States, but the abuses that he authorized of citizens' constitutional rights, which he used as leverage to keep himself in power, are as disturbing as they are legendary. Under Hoover's direction, FBI agents harassed civil rights and antiwar activists, ignored white-collar crime, and intimidated politicians.[21] Nevertheless, the FBI's crime labs, National Training Academy, Behavioral Analysis Unit, and administration of the Uniform Crime Reports all attest to its mission to bring coordination and professionalism to U.S. law enforcement.

Attempts to professionalize both police practices and police ethics have been a long-term concern for police reformers. History demonstrates that, as an institution, law enforcement has been plagued by political interference, corruption, and lack of resources. Nevertheless, police and elected officials continue to modernize, professionalize, and humanize law enforcement agencies.

The End of the 20th Century to Today: Crime Control, Communities, and Homeland Security

The 1980s and its popular theme of curtailing crime and drug usage at all costs boded well for police professionalization. As the front-line representatives in the get-tough-on-crime movement, the police began to use strategies that utilized community resources and residents—for example, by setting up neighborhood watches— to prevent crime and maintain order. Numerous police academics urged law enforcement executives to integrate research and scientific problem-solving strategies to analyze instances of crime in order to develop more effective response strategies and to democratize their services so that they would operate in partnership with the communities they policed. The federal government devoted an enormous amount of money to promote policing reforms (these will be discussed in detail in Chapter 6), and by the end of the 20th century, the police enjoyed unprecedented political, media, and public support.

The events of September 11, 2001, however, brought fundamental change to the criminal justice system. September 11 especially affected law enforcement, whose mission has been radically altered by demands to meet the threat of terrorism. Law enforcement, given these new demands, has changed in three ways:

> Role expansion. Federal, state, and local law enforcement agencies have been charged with responding to the terrorist threat. In addition to their normal duties, they must be on the lookout for suspected terrorists, design contingency plans for catastrophic terrorist events, and be prepared to deal with weapons of mass destruction. This new demand has greatly expanded the training necessary for officers at all levels and requires a new level of coordination between agencies.

> Racial and ethnic profiling. In responding to possible terrorist activities, there is the ever-present problem of racial and ethnic profiling. Because the September 11 terrorists were from Middle Eastern countries, there is a tendency to pay special attention to citizens and visitors who appear to be of Middle Eastern descent. Law enforcement agencies must ensure that, while

U.S. Customs and Border Protection is a federal law enforcement agency of the Department of Homeland Security. Here, Border Patrol agents search an undocumented immigrant who has crossed the border from Mexico into Texas. What are some of the challenges of enforcing immigration law?

protecting citizens against terrorism, they do not engage in activities that violate individuals' legal and civil rights.

> Immigration enforcement. Law enforcement agencies at all levels are responsible for enforcing U.S. immigration law. The federal government fundamentally changed its security structure by instituting the Department of Homeland Security, which is primarily responsible for immigration enforcement. Although many local law enforcement agencies do not wish to expend resources on enforcing federal immigration laws, they are periodically charged with investigating the immigration status of suspects and offenders.[22]

Such changes to federal, state, and local law enforcement have resulted in the need for greater financial investment in these agencies. This problem has been balanced somewhat by additional federal funding made available to all levels of law enforcement. It is still too soon to tell how the threat of terrorism will change the nature and mission of many law enforcement agencies, but it appears this will be an ongoing concern. One of the dangers of such a historic upheaval in law enforcement is that if the time comes when terrorism is no longer such a serious threat, law enforcement may continue to expend resources on terrorism, and ordinary citizens could become targets. When a bureaucracy builds infrastructure to deal with a specific threat, the infrastructure remains even after the threat is gone. With the relaxation of privacy afforded by federal antiterrorism efforts—such as the government's rebuffed demand in 2016 that Apple build a feature into its iPhones allowing law enforcement to bypass encryption—the danger exists that these laws could be used to undermine the constitutional protections provided to U.S. citizens long after the terrorist threat has waned.[23]

PAUSE AND REVIEW

1. What is the importance of August Vollmer and the Wickersham Commission report?

2. What three enduring features of U.S. policing did English policing influence?

LEARNING
OBJECTIVE **3**

Compare and contrast
the roles of the federal,
state, and local levels of
law enforcement and their
respective agencies.

Levels of Law Enforcement

We turn now to a brief examination of the many types of law enforcement agencies. Our goal is not to be exhaustive, but simply to demonstrate the range and complexity with which policing is organized at the federal, state, and local levels. There has been no centralized planning, and the pattern of federal, state, local, specialized, and private law enforcement agencies has developed according to historical accident, politics, special interests, and public welfare. However, what has been sacrificed in coordination and efficiency has been gained in responsiveness and accountability.

One of the founding principles of the United States is that control of government should be as close to the people as possible. For that reason, local governments have been allowed to enact laws that speak to their citizens' unique needs, and overall, an unorganized patchwork of ordinances reflects diversity instead of uniformity. This phenomenon is visible in the development of law enforcement agencies. There are nearly 18,000 state and local agencies nationwide.[24]

The three distinct levels of law enforcement in the United States are federal, state, and local. Federal law enforcement includes a multitude of agencies and jurisdictions. The Federal Bureau of Investigation is the country's foremost law enforcement agency and deals with most criminal offenses that occur on a nationwide basis (rather than within a single state). Additionally, many federal agencies that seem to have nothing to do with law enforcement have their own police forces that deal with offenses within those agencies' jurisdictions. State law enforcement agencies typically consist of state police, state highway patrols (except for Hawaii), and, sometimes, a state investigative agency. City and urban police departments, as well as county police forces (sheriff's offices), compose local law enforcement.

The duty of all law enforcement officers is to keep the peace, maintain order, ensure adherence to the law, and investigate when those laws appear to have been broken. This directive applies as much to the patrol officer who is trying to find out who is throwing rocks through shop windows as it does to the federal agent who is investigating a large, complicated financial offense. Now let us examine each level of law enforcement.

Federal Level

Federal law enforcement agencies are special-purpose agencies that have nationwide jurisdiction but concentrate on a specific, limited set of offenses. They are not general-service agencies that respond to 911 calls or engage in order-maintenance policing. For instance, an FBI agent will not arrest a person in connection with a traffic violation unless it somehow relates to a case he or she is working on. Similarly, a customs officer is not concerned with prostitution activities unless they involve international trade.

The best known federal domestic law enforcement agency is the **Federal Bureau of Investigation (FBI)**, followed closely by the U.S. Secret Service. However, the work of these agencies is often at odds with public perception. The romanticized popular conception of the FBI and the Secret Service leads many criminal justice students to desire a career in federal law enforcement. In truth, the work of these agencies is often not as exciting as that of local law enforcement agencies. Much of the work of federal law enforcement is concerned with criminal investigation and **white-collar crime**. Thus, the tasks of investigation are often more suited to the accountant than to the detective. For example, as a former part of the Department of the Treasury, the Secret Service spends more time and resources dealing with counterfeiting than protecting the president. For a list of the major federal law enforcement agencies, see CJ Reference 4.1.

Federal Bureau of Investigation (FBI)—The main federal law enforcement agency in the United States, which operates under the Department of Justice and deals with domestic crime that crosses state lines, as well as some types of significant crime within the states, such as terrorism.

white-collar crime (from Chapter 1)—A nonviolent criminal offense committed during the course of business for financial gain.

Department of Justice—The federal executive agency that handles all criminal prosecutions and civil suits in which the United States has an interest.

Although there are about 70 federal law enforcement agencies, the main ones are organized under just three departments: the Department of Justice, the Department of the Treasury, and the Department of Homeland Security.[25]

> Founded in 1870, the **Department of Justice** is responsible for enforcing federal laws. Its primary agencies are the Drug Enforcement Administration (DEA), the Federal Bureau of Investigation (FBI), and the U.S. Marshals.

> The **Department of the Treasury**, established in 1789, primarily enforces the collection of revenue. Its agencies include the Internal Revenue Service (IRS), the U.S. Mint, and the Inspector General.[26]

> The **Department of Homeland Security** was created after September 11, 2001 (see Figure 4.1). Under its auspices are several agencies that were transferred in whole or in part to Homeland Security because their duties are related to controlling terrorism. These agencies include U.S. Customs and Border Protection, U.S. Immigration and Customs Enforcement, and the U.S. Secret Service.

Federal officers are among the best paid law enforcement personnel, and competition for these jobs is stiff. Most federal officers train at the Federal Law Enforcement Training Center, which is headquartered in Glynco, Georgia. FBI and DEA agents also take some of their training at their respective academies in Quantico, Virginia. One aspect of this level of law enforcement is the likelihood that employees will be transferred around the country as they advance along their career path. Although there are many federal police agencies, the FBI and Secret Service are the ones that most people associate with federal law enforcement, so we will take a closer look at these agencies.

Department of the Treasury—The federal executive agency that is responsible for promoting economic prosperity and ensuring the financial security of the United States.

Department of Homeland Security (DHS)—A department of the U.S. government responsible for preventing terrorism and enhancing national security; securing and managing U.S. borders; enforcing and administering U.S. immigration laws; safeguarding and securing U.S. interests on the Internet; and assisting in the federal response to terrorist attacks and natural disasters within the United States.

Organization of the U.S. Department of Homeland Security

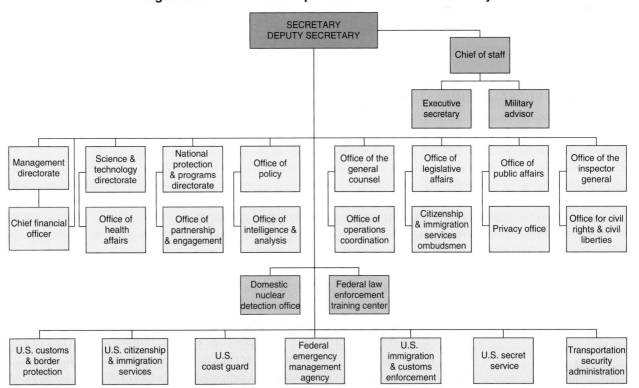

FIGURE 4.1 Organization of the U.S. Department of Homeland Security Which agencies within the U.S. Department of Homeland Security are most responsible for immigration enforcement? Which agencies were transferred to Homeland Security because their duties are related to controlling terrorism?

CJ REFERENCE 4.1
Federal Law Enforcement Agencies

BUREAU OF ALCOHOL, TOBACCO, FIREARMS, AND EXPLOSIVES (ATF)

The Bureau of Alcohol, Tobacco, Firearms, and Explosives is a principal law enforcement agency within the U.S. Department of Justice that enforces federal criminal laws, regulates the firearms and explosives industries, and investigates cases of arson and illegal trafficking of alcohol and tobacco products.

U.S. CUSTOMS AND BORDER PROTECTION (CBP)

U.S. Customs and Border Protection manages, controls, and protects the borders of the United States at and between official ports of entry. Located within the Department of Homeland Security, CBP combines the inspectional workforces and border authorities of U.S. Customs, U.S. Immigration, the Animal and Plant Health Inspection Service, and the U.S. Border Patrol.

DRUG ENFORCEMENT ADMINISTRATION (DEA)

The Drug Enforcement Administration, which is organized within the Department of Justice, enforces the controlled-substance laws and regulations of the United States. The agency also manages a national drug intelligence program, seizes assets used in drug trafficking, and enforces laws pertaining to legally produced controlled substances.

FEDERAL BUREAU OF INVESTIGATION (FBI)

The principal investigative arm of the Department of Justice, the FBI investigates major violent and financial crime and interstate crime and assists in terrorism investigations. Areas of investigation include computer-related crimes, cases of public corruption, hate crime, white-collar crime, and organized crime.

U.S. IMMIGRATION AND CUSTOMS ENFORCEMENT (ICE)

Immigration and Customs Enforcement is the largest investigative branch of the Department of Homeland Security. The agency was created in March 2003 by combining the law enforcement arms of the former Immigration and Naturalization Service and the former U.S. Customs Service.

U.S. MARSHALS SERVICE (FEDERAL MARSHALS)

Created in 1789, the U.S. Marshals Service is a federal police agency that protects federal judges and courts and ensures the effective operation of the judicial system. The agency also carries out fugitive investigations, custody and transportation of federal prisoners, security for government witnesses, asset seizures, and serving of court documents. Each of the 94 federal judicial districts has one U.S. Marshal.

U.S. SECRET SERVICE

The U.S. Secret Service protects the president of the United States, as well as other U.S. government officials and visiting officials. The agency also investigates financial fraud and counterfeiting.

THE FEDERAL BUREAU OF INVESTIGATION

The FBI has national jurisdiction to investigate federal offenses. The emphasis on which offenses get the most attention has shifted over the years as a result of political considerations and the leadership style of its directors. The FBI began in 1908 when President Theodore Roosevelt sent eight Secret Service agents to the Department of Justice to investigate violations of federal law. In the past century, it has grown into a large organization that also assists state and local agencies with expert help in training (FBI National Academy), criminalistics (FBI Crime Laboratory), crime measurement (Uniform Crime Reports), and consultation on difficult cases (Behavior Analysis Unit). Since September 11, 2001, the agency has shifted some of its focus to national security.

This scramble during the 1981 assassination attempt on President Ronald Reagan is what many people imagine what most Secret Service work is like. What do Secret Service agents actually do most of the time?

THE SECRET SERVICE

After September 11, 2001, the Secret Service was moved from the Treasury Department to the Department of Homeland Security. Its duties—protecting the president and other dignitaries and investigating counterfeiting and financial crimes—remain essentially the same but have been expanded somewhat to provide for defense against terrorism. The Secret Service's original task when it was created in 1865 was to control the proliferation of counterfeit money. Only in 1894 under President Grover Cleveland did the agency begin some protection services. A year after the assassination of President William McKinley in 1901, the Secret Service began full-time executive protection. In 1913, Congress authorized permanent protection of the president, and in 1917 the president's family began to receive protection. Security was gradually stepped up over the years, owing partly to the 1951 assassination attempt on President Harry S. Truman and the 1963 assassination of President John F. Kennedy. Gradually, the list of protectees came to include major presidential and vice presidential candidates, presidential widows, and visiting heads of state. Today, much of the agency's mission is protecting the country's payment and financial systems from financial and computer-based crimes. Most Secret Service agents spend most of their time on duties other than executive protection.

State Level

In many ways, state law enforcement agencies are overshadowed by local and federal agencies. State agencies have neither the numbers of officers that local agencies have nor the visibility of federal agencies. There are as many variations in how state law enforcement agencies are organized as there are states. Each state law enforcement system must be understood on its own terms because no two are exactly alike. This reflects the fact that the United States is a collection of united sovereign governments, with the elected government of each state deciding how that state is administered.

State police forces were developed to keep the peace in rural areas outside the jurisdictions of cities and towns. State highway patrol units became necessary as automobile usage increased and the state and interstate highway systems were developed.[27] Generally, there are two broad models of state law enforcement: the centralized model and the decentralized model. The centralized model combines investigative and highway patrol functions into one agency. The decentralized model separates these two functions. For example, the state of Georgia has a state highway patrol and an investigative agency, the Georgia Bureau of Investigation.[28] About half of the states have state highway patrols, and half have state police, with the exception of Hawaii, which has no state law enforcement agency.[29] Three western states, Texas, Colorado, and Arizona, have police agencies called "rangers" that are more than a century old and are among the first professional state/territorial law enforcement organizations in the United States. However, the Pennsylvania State Police, created in 1905, is recognized as the first uniformed, professional state police department.

State investigative bureaus have statewide jurisdiction for investigating criminal offenses, such as political corruption, in which local police might not be in a position to investigate their local bosses. State law enforcement agencies also provide a number of services to local law enforcement such as the coordination of multijurisdictional task forces, crime laboratory services, and, when requested, help in investigating offenses. Additionally, most state law enforcement agencies have police training academies that provide the basic instruction that is beyond the capabilities of all but the largest local police forces. Some states also have special agencies that deal with violations of alcoholic beverage or fish and wildlife laws.

Factors that may determine the simplicity or intricacy of a state police system include geography, population density, financial resources, and crime issues. Wealthy states with big cities may have state police agencies with special investigation units, community programs, and task forces. States with fewer resources might not have as many programs. A state's industry or culture can also dictate the type of programs it requires. For example, New Jersey's Department of Law and Public Safety has a gaming enforcement division to regulate the casino industry,

This Maryland State Trooper guards the Maryland State Senate chamber on the first day of the legislative session. How do state law enforcement agencies differ from federal ones?

and the Alaska Department of Public Safety has its Fish and Wildlife Protection division. Some states have placed all law enforcement divisions under one organizational umbrella, such as a department of public safety, whereas other states may separate these programs or lodge them within different bureaus of the state government. Given the wide variety of activities that the state can encompass, those interested in a law enforcement career should investigate opportunities within state agencies.

Local Level

Most of the country's crime is handled by local law enforcement agencies. Each state has a different configuration of political jurisdictions. Cities, counties (or parishes), and multijurisdictional agencies are vested with responsibility in varying ways, depending on the state law. What is most striking about how the criminal justice system is organized is the fact that most of the authority for law enforcement lies at the local level. Many people misunderstand the relationship among the three levels of police, believing that local police answer to state police, who, in turn, answer to federal police. This is not true. Generally, police departments answer to themselves, their communities, and the courts.[30] For a look at the employment distribution among local police departments, sheriff's agencies, and state police agencies, see Figure 4.2.

Much of local police work is especially concerned with order maintenance and problem-solving, such as resolving disputes, finding missing persons and runaways, and even dealing with small quality-of-life violations, such as telling the neighbors to turn the music down.[31] In many ways, local policing is where the action is. Each jurisdiction, whether big-city police department, county sheriff's office, or small-town police department, is the first responder to most criminal offenses. Additionally, these agencies have patrol and investigative duties in which they are often the only law enforcement agency involved in the case. Because local police handle most serious street-level crime, they are the ones we call when we "call the cops."

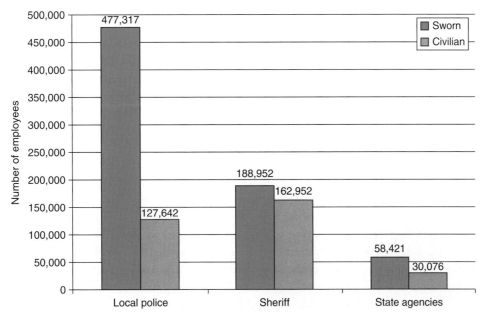

FIGURE 4.2 Number of Sworn and Civilian Employees in State and Local Law Enforcement Agencies Why do local police departments have so many more employees than either sheriffs' offices or state law enforcement agencies (such as state police or highway patrol agencies)?

Source: Andrea M. Burch, Sheriffs' Office Personnel, 1993–2013, Appendix Table 1 (U.S. Department of Justice Office of Justice Programs Bureau of Justice Statistics, 2016), 9. Available at https://www.bjs.gov/index.cfm?ty=pbdetail&iid=5622.

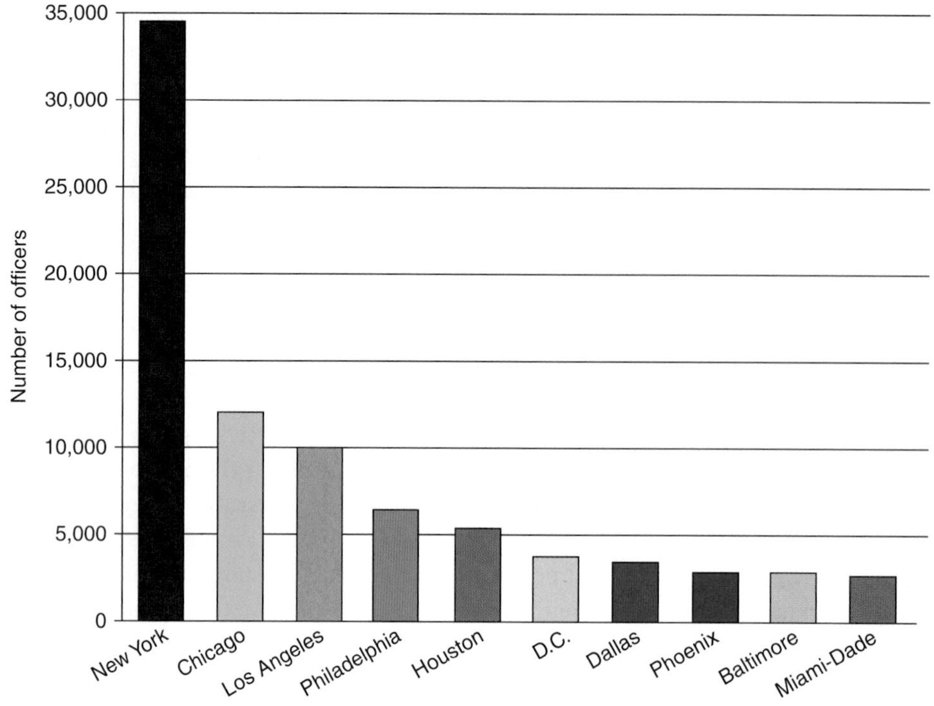

FIGURE 4.3   The 10 Largest Local Police Departments by Total Number of Full-Time Sworn Personnel, 2013 Why is the New York Police Department so much larger than any other police department in the United States?

Source: Brian A. Reaves, Local Police Departments 2013 *(Washington, D.C.: Bureau of Justice Statistics, 2015), 14. Available at http://bjs.ojp.usdoj.gov/index.cfm?ty=pbdetail&iid=5279.*

Most local police forces are operated by municipalities, with a few run by tribal and county governments. There are about 12,000 local police departments in the United States. The largest local police force in the country is the New York City Police Department. With more than 34,000 full-time officers, it is nearly three times the size of the next largest organization, the Chicago Police Department, which has just over 12,000 sworn officers.[32] (See Figure 4.3 for the 10 largest police departments in the United States.) At the other end of the spectrum, about half of local police departments employ fewer than 10 full-time officers. Not all local police officers are sworn (sworn means that they are certified, have powers of arrest, and have taken an oath to serve and protect the public).[33] Non-sworn department employees may work in technical support, administration, as records specialists, evidence specialists, or dispatchers, or in jail.

Local law enforcement agencies perform a wide range of duties. The most labor-intensive duty is routine patrol, in which officers travel around their assigned beats, respond to calls for service, and look for ways to keep the community safe. Some of the time that officers spend on patrol is used to interact with citizens who are not suspected of breaking any law. Officers talk to shopkeepers, watch for traffic infractions, cruise neighborhoods to show citizens they are being served, and investigate anything that looks suspicious or out of place. The business of apprehending suspects constitutes a small fraction of the officers' time. Local law enforcement agencies also devote resources and personnel to investigative duties, including homicide, burglary, auto theft, sex offenses, and juveniles. To a lesser degree, their duties may also include animal control, emergency medical service, and civil defense.

Larger departments operate special weapons and tactics (SWAT) and bomb disposal teams. Along with traditional car patrols, there has been a steady increase in bicycle and foot patrols. Large departments may assign officers to special units, such as horseback, bicycle, motorcycle, or boat patrols. Some police officers specialize in specific areas, such as forensic analysis, or in physical or firearms

Police officers spend a lot of time interacting with the community. Here, a young girl meets McGruff the Crime Dog, while Roanoke Police Academy recruits look on. How do such interactions help the public understand what their local police departments do?

training and instruction. Some departments may ameliorate officer shortages with supplemental and part-time personnel such as sworn reserve officers as well as nonsworn auxiliary officers, community service officers, police aides, and other types of volunteers. Each agency organizes its investigative duties and personnel according to its problems, resources, and needs, but each of them in some way must ensure that there is an investigative follow-up to reported crime.

Sometimes, law enforcement jurisdictions overlap. A person driving a car too fast within a city's limits may be pulled over and ticketed by a state patrol officer, a sheriff's deputy, or a city police officer. However, the state patrol or the county sheriff would unlikely be involved in investigating a homicide committed within a city's limits, which would likely be dealt with by the police agency responsible for that jurisdiction, with rare exceptions in special cases. An example of an exception would be the Atlanta child murders. From July 1979 to May 1981, 29 young black males were murdered in or near Atlanta, Georgia. Although the murders occurred mainly in the city of Atlanta and Fulton County, several agencies became involved in the investigation, including the local police, the sheriff's office, the Georgia Bureau of Investigation (GBI), and ultimately the FBI. (The federal agency, having no jurisdiction, became involved only by invitation from the local agencies.)

SHERIFF'S OFFICES

Sheriff's offices are the most common form of county law enforcement in the United States, with 3,063 offices.[34] Most sheriffs are elected officials and serve counties and municipalities without a police department. Their duties include performing routine patrols, investigating crime (some are responsible for crime lab services such as fingerprint and ballistics testing), executing arrest warrants, serving papers, and providing court security. Most offices operate at least one jail, and about half provide search and rescue services, as well as SWAT teams. Other services may include bomb disposal, animal control, emergency medical services, and civil defense. A few counties have two sheriff's offices (one for criminal matters and one for civil matters), whereas others have no sheriff's office. In cases in which a city occupies the entire county, as in the case of Miami-Dade, Florida, or several counties, as in the case of New York City, city and county law enforcement may be combined into one department.

REQUIREMENTS TO BECOME A POLICE OFFICER

Once upon a time, the requirements to become a police officer were simple and rather narrow: big, strong, young, healthy, brave, and male. Although some of these requirements still apply, they have been tempered in recent decades by the fact that the most important personal aspect an officer brings to the job is intelligence.[35] Officers, especially those on patrol, must meet specific levels of physical fitness and maintain those fitness levels, as well as maintaining proficiency with firearms. Speaking languages other than English is an asset, and, regardless of the level of service, officers must know how to write reports. Police officers who patrol beats and deal directly with offenses in progress must wear uniforms, whereas investigative officers and detectives do not.

Each department, be it statewide, urban, or rural, has its own set of requirements for applicants, but these tend to follow similar lines for physical conditioning and ability, age, education, and personal legal history.

> Education. Applicants usually must have at least a high school diploma, and some departments require at least two years of college. Some departments require a college degree.

> Training. Recruits usually attend police academy for about 21 weeks.[36] State and large urban agencies may have their own academies; recruits at small departments may attend a state or regional academy. Recruits learn constitutional and state law as well as local ordinances. They also train in accident investigation, patrol, traffic control, firearms, self-defense, first aid, and emergency response.

> Age, citizenship, physical, and residential qualifications. Applicants must be U.S. citizens and usually must be at least 20 years old. Departments typically have basic requirements for vision, hearing, strength, and agility. For example, a department may require that uncorrected eyesight cannot be weaker than 20/100 in each eye and must be corrected to 20/20 with glasses, contact lenses, or surgery. Some urban departments require officers to live in or near the city limits. For example, the Tallahassee (Florida) Police Department states: "Upon appointment you must reside within the state of Florida and within a 35-mile radius of the intersection of North Monroe and East Tennessee Streets."[37] This intersection is in downtown Tallahassee and represents the center of the city.

> Personal history. Departments may also extensively investigate their applicants' personal histories. Some agencies have candidates interviewed by a mental health professional, and candidates usually must take lie detector and/or drug tests.

> Disqualifications. An applicant may be automatically disqualified by any of the following: a felony conviction, misdemeanor convictions within the past few years, a specified number of moving violations within the past few years, a dishonorable discharge from the armed forces, convictions for certain offenses (such as domestic violence), or refusal to submit to polygraph, psychological, or drug testing.

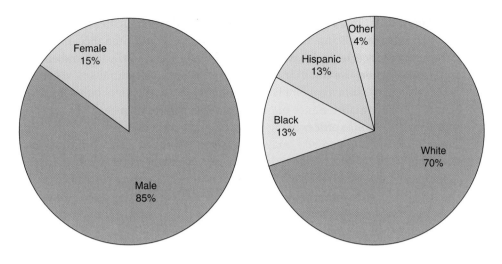

FIGURE 4.4 Law Enforcement Recruits Entering Basic Training Programs, by Sex and Race/Hispanic Origin Do the sex and race percentages of police recruits closely reflect their percentages in U.S. society?

Source: Brian A. Reaves, State and Local Law Enforcement Training Academies, 2013, *Appendix Table 17 (Washington, D.C.: U.S. Department of Justice Office of Justice Programs Bureau of Justice Statistics, 2016), 19. Online at http://www.bjs.gov/index. cfm?ty=pbdetail&iid=5684.*

Not mentioned in this list are several criteria that were once used to prevent individuals from entering law enforcement employment. Most prominent among these criteria were the requirements that applicants be male, white, and heterosexual. Like all agencies in federal, state, and local governments today, law enforcement agencies are prohibited from discriminating against applicants based on these criteria. See Figure 4.4 for a demographic look at police recruits entering training programs.

PAUSE AND REVIEW

1. **How are federal, state, and local levels of law enforcement alike? How are they different?**

Strategies in Policing

Not all police officers adopt the same style of interacting with the public, other members of the criminal justice system, and offenders. Each individual brings different personality traits, motivations, training, and objectives to the job. Additionally, not all law enforcement agencies are the same. The size of the community, the racial and ethnic diversity of the local population, the effects of local economic trends, and the history and political structure of the agency exert an influence on policing styles.[38] It is easy to see the differences between big-city departments and those of rural areas.[39] The nature of the crime problems is different, and citizens have varying expectations as to what constitutes optimal policing.

Wilson's Three Styles of Policing

First, we will discuss political scientist James Q. Wilson's classic typology of the three styles of policing: the watchman style, legalistic style, and service style. These styles illustrate important differences in how the police approach their tasks of maintaining order, controlling crime, and being of service to citizens.[40] These styles are important because they set the tone of civility between the police and the public. By looking at what the police consider their primary mandates, we can begin to appreciate the distinct differences among departments.

LEARNING OBJECTIVE **4**

Categorize the advantages and disadvantages of Wilson's three styles of policing.

LEARNING OBJECTIVE **5**

Define problem-oriented policing.

LEARNING OBJECTIVE **6**

Describe zero-tolerance policing and its relationship to the broken-windows perspective.

watchman style—A mode of policing that emphasizes the maintenance of order and informal intervention on the part of the police officer rather than strict enforcement of the law.

legalistic style—A mode of policing that emphasizes enforcement of the letter of the law.

service style—A mode of policing that is concerned primarily with serving the community and citizens.

› Watchman style. The **watchman style** of policing distinguishes between two mandates of policing: law enforcement and order maintenance. Law enforcement is concerned with discovering who has violated the law and either arresting or otherwise sanctioning that person (such as issuing a ticket for driving too fast). This mandate is the one that we usually associate with policing. The order maintenance mandate is also a primary concern of some departments.[41] A police officer using the watchman style may tolerate a certain amount of gambling and vice, may not arrest suspects in minor offenses, or may simply tell unruly people to leave an area even when law violations are suspected. The key is to preserve the social order in an effort to keep citizens happy.[42] Under the watchman style, certain extralegal factors such as age, race, appearance, or personal demeanor are used in deciding when to arrest and when to release suspects.

› Legalistic style. In many ways, the **legalistic style** is a positive style of policing because the focus is on treating all citizens alike, but it can be problematic. The legalistic style enforces the law by writing more tickets, making more arrests, and encouraging victims to sign complaints. Whereas the watchman style of officer may attempt to settle disputes informally, the legalistic officer will determine who is culpable, make an arrest, and allow the courts to resolve the incident.[43] Extralegal factors such as age, race, social status, and appearance are much less influential in this style of policing than in the watchman style.

› Service style. The **service style** of policing shares characteristics with the other two styles but is concerned primarily with service to the community and citizens. Like the legalistic style, it treats all law violations seriously, but the frequent result, as with the watchman style, is not to arrest. Instead, the department employs alternative strategies, such as official warnings or diversion programs.[44] The key to the service style of policing is that the individual officer may make decisions, but they are visible, subject to formal review and evaluation, and can be altered when circumstances require.

Other types of policing may be found in some departments, and a mixture of styles may occur within a department. For example, a department might provide officers with little discretion in dealing with domestic assault cases and grant wide latitude in handling drug cases. Although it is decades old, Wilson's typology is simply a guide. What has changed is the ability of police supervisors to consider how individual officers go about their work. Primarily because of advances in technology, the work of the officer on the street has become more visible.

In the past 30 years, new theoretical foundations concerning police organization have emerged. We will begin by examining community policing, problem-oriented policing, and zero-tolerance policing, three different approaches that challenge the notion of traditional policing. Each of these forms of policing suggests different levels of interaction between the police and the public, each of which is subject to criticism for what it fails to address as much as for what it successfully addresses.

Community Policing

One of the major new ways of thinking in terms of how to organize the police is the concept of community policing. More local police departments included a community policing section in their mission statements in 2013 than in 2003.[45] The Department of Justice's Community-Oriented Policing Services defines **community policing** as organizational strategies that support the systematic use of partnerships and problem-solving techniques to address the immediate conditions that give rise to crime, social disorder, and fear of crime.[46]

Community policing—which evolved from the 1979 Flint Foot Patrol Program—an experiment in which foot-patrol officers in Flint, Michigan, were assigned to areas that were usually patrolled by car—evokes the watchman style, in which the police officer is integrated into the community and has the advantage of being trusted by those being policed.[47] However, the concept of community policing is also different from the watchman style because both the police and communities have changed over the years. The watchman style of policing has its limitations, especially in affording equal justice to all citizens. In many cases, the watchman style simply reinforces the privileges of those in power while controlling youth and minorities.

Community policing also has elements in common with the legalistic style of policing in that it strives to treat all citizens equally according to their orientation with the law. However, the legalistic model emphasizes efficiency and exclusivity in the mandate for crime control. This exclusivity comes at a price in terms of distancing the police from the communities they serve. Community policing is viewed as a reform that breaks the monopoly of the police over crime-control activities and brings the citizen back into the equation as an active participant. Community policing is different from both the watchman and legalistic styles in content and scope, and it is worthwhile to consider its history and potential.[48]

The term *community policing* covers a range of police activities and programs. An exact definition is difficult to provide, but it is fair to say that community policing involves enlisting citizens to help solve law-and-order problems in their own communities.[49] Good policing requires citizen cooperation. If people do not report offenses, do not provide information to the police, and are unwilling to testify in court, then the police cannot effectively control crime. During the civil unrest of the 1960s, the police were forced to do a difficult job in controlling large groups of people. This violence revealed a deep fissure between old and young, workers and hippies, minorities and whites, and also between the police and the communities they served. Many people believed that the police were out of touch with those they served. For this and other reasons, the community policing approach was proposed.[50]

The goal of community policing is ambitious. It involves not only bridging the gap between the police and the citizens but also strengthening the bond among the citizens themselves. A good example of a community-policing style program is **Neighborhood Watch** in which citizens work together to watch over each other's safety and property. Instituted in 1972 by the National Sheriffs' Association, Neighborhood Watch (and, later, other such programs) "put more eyes on the street" to help prevent and report crime and cultivate strong community ties that can help address other neighborhood problems.[51] Another strategy of community policing is the use of foot or bicycle patrol, the goal of which is to foster a close relationship between the police and the public.[52] The patrol car is considered a barrier to communication between police and citizens. Taking the officers out of the cars and placing them in more direct contact with people makes the development of meaningful relationships more likely.

One problem with community policing is that not all communities are alike. Great variation persists among neighborhoods in terms of the socioeconomic,

community policing— A policing strategy that attempts to harness the resources and residents of a given community in stopping crime and maintaining order.

Neighborhood Watch— A community policing program that encourages residents to cooperate in providing security for the neighborhood.

Community policing programs like Neighborhood Watch allow residents to help keep their communities safe. What types of community policing efforts have you seen in your neighborhood?

racial, ethnic, and age compositions of the citizens. For example, a middle-class suburb inhabited by white-collar, middle-aged adults and their families and the elderly faces few crime problems compared to a low-income neighborhood populated with transients and drug dealers. It is much easier to institute a Neighborhood Watch program in affluent suburbs where the residents' comings and goings are less frequent and easier to monitor than in low-income neighborhoods where the pattern of social organization and movement is less obvious. Therefore, community policing can be said to work best in the communities that need it least. Nevertheless, studies have suggested that well-planned community policing efforts can achieve at least some of their goals.[53]

Lastly, getting the police to concern themselves with order maintenance and community-building can be problematic when many officers view themselves solely as crime-fighters. The inherent tension between the roles of "criminal catcher" and "social worker" may limit the potential for effective community policing.

Problem-Oriented Policing

problem-oriented policing—A style of policing that attempts to address the underlying social problems that contribute to crime by integrating research and scientific problem-solving strategies to analyze instances of crime with the goal of developing more effective response strategies.

A strategy related to community policing is **problem-oriented policing**. In many ways, problem-oriented policing can be thought of as simply an aspect of community policing, but it is important enough to be treated as its own topic. We give special attention to problem-oriented policing because it is designed to make more fundamental changes than community policing. Additionally, problem-oriented policing greatly expands the role of the police officer from one of reaction to one of proactive problem-solving. It allows police agencies to address crime on a more systemic level than traditional policing.[54]

For example, envision a downtown business district that is experiencing robberies and muggings. In addition to responding to these offenses, a problem-oriented police agency would analyze the causative factors. Included in this analysis might be a crime-mapping effort, which would reveal that the muggings are all in close proximity to a cluster of bars. On surveillance of these bars, the agency discovers that the bars are staying open well past the legal closing time and serving underage patrons. Going into these bars and enforcing the existing liquor laws could affect the robbery and mugging problem. Problem-oriented policing, then, is concerned with identifying and addressing the underlying issues that contribute to crime.[55] Within the scope of the law enforcement mission are many such opportunities that allow the police to do more than simply respond to crime.

Problem-oriented policing has different goals and techniques than community policing. In the long run, both types of policing may incur some of the same results, such as less crime and greater community support, but there are still important distinctions between these two styles. Problem-oriented policing is a more proactive process than community policing, and for this reason it is more likely to appeal to police officers. Instead of responding to calls for service, the problem-oriented officer analyzes the trouble areas of the community and designs tactics to address those problems.[56] Problem-oriented policing has a crime-prevention mission as well as a crime-responding mission. By intervening early and effectively when patterns begin to emerge, problem-oriented policing can address the causes of crime.[57]

Zero-Tolerance Policing and Broken-Windows Perspective

As promising as problem-oriented policing appears to be, some of its implementations, such as zero-tolerance policing, have been criticized. **Zero-tolerance policing** is the idea that if every little infraction of the law is met with an arrest, fine, or other punishment, offenders will refrain from more grievous activities. An important element of zero-tolerance policing is the controversial **broken-windows perspective** developed by law enforcement scholars James Q. Wilson and George L. Kelling who argued that crime follows community neglect.[58] They based this idea on the work of Stanford psychology professor Philip Zimbardo who conducted a fascinating experiment in 1969 in which he abandoned two cars, one in the Bronx, New York City, without license plates and its hood up, and a similar one in Palo Alto, California. Within 10 minutes, the car in the Bronx

zero-tolerance policing—A form of policing that punishes every infraction of the law, however minor, with an arrest, fine, or other penalty so that offenders will refrain from committing more serious offenses.

broken-windows perspective—The idea that untended property or deviant behavior will attract crime.

Broken-windows theory asserts that when a neighborhood appears to be run-down, vandalism and other criminal activity is likely to occur. Are there any problems with this theory?

was attacked, and within a few hours, it was totally destroyed. The car in Palo Alto sat for more than a week untouched until Zimbardo smashed it with a sledgehammer. Again, within a few hours the car was destroyed.[59]

According to the broken-windows perspective, vandalism and criminal activity occur when it appears that no one cares about a neighborhood. It is difficult to argue with Wilson and Kelling that untended property can draw vandals, especially when it is already damaged. However, Wilson and Kelling took this analogy a step further, suggesting that "untended" behavior also leads to the breakdown of community controls. When teenagers loiter in front of a convenience store or a drunk sleeps on the sidewalk, Wilson and Kelling assert that this signals that "no one cares," much as a broken window does. Citizens feel unsafe in their neighborhoods, and instead of being outside and involved in community activities, they hide in their homes. These actions leave the streets empty of many citizens engaged in the type of everyday pursuits that signify a healthy and involved community. According to Wilson and Kelling, this neglect of behavior is as damaging as leaving a broken window unfixed in terms of inviting crime into the community.[60]

The solution to this problem of the decline of the community is, according to the broken-windows perspective, to "fix" the "untended" behavior just as one would fix a broken window. This means arresting the public drunk, dispersing loiterers from the store or out of the mall, and otherwise "cleaning up" society. This approach becomes problematic when we consider that these individuals have not broken any laws and have not harmed anyone. Wilson and Kelling contend, however, that to maintain meaningful communities, police officers must address the issue of street people: "Arresting a single drunk or single vagrant who has harmed no identifiable person seems unjust, and in a sense it is. But failing to do anything about a score of drunks or a hundred vagrants may destroy an entire community."[61]

Many critics disagree with this prescription for social change. The following are three reasons to be cautious about adopting the broken-windows perspective:

1. Misreading of how communities were policed in the past. Criminologist Samuel Walker contends that there is no tradition of policing that encompasses the principles of the broken-windows perspective and that if Wilson and Kelling want to implement these ideas they have to start over.[62]

2. Concern for the rights of all citizens. Fixing a window or cleaning up a vacant lot can signal that people care about their neighborhood. Dealing with teenagers, drunks, the mentally ill, or the homeless presents a different set of problems. These issues cannot be solved by the police in a democratic country that values individual rights. For instance, if the deinstitutionalization of the mentally ill means that they are in the street, then housing programs, drug treatment facilities, and a host of other social services are needed.[63]

3. Problem of crime displacement. Removing undesirable people from a community does not mean that the associated problems will disappear.[64] These people may just reappear in an adjoining community. Additionally, by threatening to arrest street people and otherwise devaluing any positive contribution they might make to the community, we might actually accelerate their undesirable behaviors from nuisances to crime.[65]

The broken-windows perspective was behind the efforts of former New York City Mayor Rudy Giuliani's zero-tolerance policing policy during the early

1990s. By making misdemeanor arrests for panhandling, public drunkenness, prostitution, jumping subway turnstiles, and public urination, the New York Police Department aggressively sought to bring order and safety to the streets. In fact, serious crime did decrease, but critics point out that this was a national trend and could not be attributed solely to the police department's zero-tolerance policies.[66]

Although such zero-tolerance policies suggested by the broken-windows perspective are attractive to many politicians, law enforcement officials, and citizens, some important consequences must be considered.[67] The main targets of zero-tolerance policies tend to be low-income and impoverished people. Those who are

---

A CLOSER LOOK 4.1
Who Polices the Police?

Although it sometimes seems that police departments cannot be held responsible for abusive and violent practices, the federal government does have a remedy for those that continually abuse their communities. The 1994 Violent Crime Control and Law Enforcement Act allows the federal government to sue police departments if they show a "pattern and practice" of using excessive force and/or violating civil rights.[68] The law was passed after the 1991 beating of motorist Rodney King by four Los Angeles Police Department officers and the riots that occurred a year later in response to the officers' acquittal.[69]

To implement change, the government and the police department enter into a "consent decree," a plan that typically includes federal oversight of the department, as well as several reforms.[70] For example, in 2015, after protests over the acquittal of Cleveland, Ohio, police officer Michael Brelo of manslaughter, the city agreed to address what the government called the department's "systemic" use of excessive force.[71] (Brelo had been involved in a 2012 car chase in which he and other officers shot at two unarmed people over one hundred times, which resulted in their deaths.)[72] Included in the Cleveland reforms are:

- prohibition of pistol whipping, "neck holds," warning shots, and firing shots at moving cars;
- prohibition of uses of "retaliatory force" against suspects for fleeing or disrespecting officers;
- prohibition of racial profiling during stops-and-searches;
- training officers in community-policing principles;
- and training officers to deal with individuals with mental health issues.[73]

As of April 2017, 14 cities were under consent decree.[74] Police departments that are currently under or have been under a consent decree include Pittsburgh,

Los Angeles, Cincinnati, New Orleans, New York City, Detroit, Seattle, Albuquerque, Oakland, California, and Newark, New Jersey.[75]

Police departments do not always enter the arrangement willingly. After nine years of non-compliance by angry veteran officers, a federal judge ordered that the Oakland police department be placed under the management of a receiver, a person who is given complete control of a police department until it complies with reforms.[76] In Cincinnati in 2001, the strain between the receiver and the police became so extreme that officers kicked the receiver out of police headquarters. Cincinnati did not come into compliance until 2007.[77] New Orleans Mayor Mitch Landrieu and former New York City Mayor Michael Bloomberg were both unsuccessful in appealing their cities' consent decrees. Landrieu claimed that the New Orleans plan was too expensive. The New York City Police Department was placed under consent decree because its stop-question-and-frisk policy—in which police detain and question, and sometimes search, pedestrians—was deemed unconstitutional owing to the disproportionate number of racially disparate stops-and-frisks. Bloomberg asserted that this practice was necessary and constitutional, but a federal judge disagreed.[78]

Despite the protests, observers say consent decrees work. In 2014, Detroit's 11-year oversight ended after the police department complied with reforms.[79]

THINK ABOUT IT

1. What are some reasonable steps that cities can take to be released from a consent decree?
2. Have there been recent incidents of excessive force by police departments that would qualify a city for intervention by the federal government?

young, live on the street, or are drunk or mentally ill find that their minor legal transgressions are treated more severely than are the transgressions of others. Zero-tolerance policies aimed at reducing crime often result in the unequal treatment of those without power. Given the problems of increased legal judgments against police departments for the behavior of their officers, zero-tolerance policing might be more problematic than beneficial.[80]

For example, in the 2000s, the New York City Police Department (NYPD) and its zero-tolerance efforts were subjected to widespread criticism and intense public protests after some controversial actions. In 2011, the NYPD arrested 50,000 people for possessing small amounts of marijuana, as compared to 1,500 in 1980. New York's state legislature decriminalized possession of 25 grams or less of marijuana in 1977 but had deemed its public display a misdemeanor. The NYPD was accused of arresting people for possession after forcing them to "publicly display" the small amounts they carried.[81] For a look at a federal solution to police departments that appear to be abusing their public trust, see A Closer Look 4.1.

Perhaps the most fundamental problem with zero-tolerance policing is the adversarial relationship it seems to set up between the police and the public. By treating citizens with a heavy hand, the police alienate the very people who could help them solve more serious offenses. When people become angry and defiant, they are more likely to break major laws and less likely to be of assistance to the police.[82]

PAUSE AND REVIEW

1. **What are Wilson's three styles of policing?**
2. **How is community policing different from problem-oriented policing?**
3. **What are some of the issues associated with zero-tolerance policing?**

 **FOCUS ON ETHICS**   Righteous Vengeance?

As a police officer, you have been on the trail of a serial child molester who frequents the city's parks. You have a good idea of who it is, but this suspect has been smart enough to elude arrest for over 10 years. This morning you found your suspect dead, lying in a pool of blood with his skull crushed. After a search, you discover in a nearby trash can a baseball bat with the name of the son of a prominent politician printed on the bat handle. Blood and hair are matted on the bat. You know that this 17-year-old young man was a victim of molestation 10 years ago when this problem first surfaced in the community.

You strongly suspect that the teen killed the molester, but you also believe that the suspect deserved to be killed and that the teen did the community a service. If you hide the bat, there will be no way to trace the offense to this young man whom you think

had a good reason to commit this act. If you enter the bat into evidence, the boy could be convicted of murder and sent to prison for a long time. Because you have twin 8-year-old sons, you are happy this perpetrator will no longer prowl the city parks. Can you turn a blind eye to this crime? You know the correct procedure would be to arrest the teen, but a little voice inside your head is whispering something about a "greater justice," and you are tempted to dispose of the bat.

WHAT DO YOU DO?

1. Dispose of the bat and tell the boy's father so that he can protect you if you are found out and even help you get promoted.
2. Dispose of the bat, and tell no one.

3. Leave the bat where it is. Do your job and make your report, but say nothing about your suspicions. The crime scene techs will know what to do.
4. Tell your chief everything, and let her decide what to do.

For more insight as to how someone might respond to such an ethical dilemma, visit the companion website at www.oup.com/us/fuller to watch a video that connects this scenario to a real-world situation.

Summary

LEARNING OBJECTIVE 1 Discuss the three enduring features of U.S. policing influenced by English policing.	**Limited police authority:** The Anglo-American tradition of policing emphasizes individual rights and liberties. **Local control:** Law enforcement agencies are, for the most part, local, city, or county institutions. **Fragmented system:** The country's law enforcement agencies are loosely coordinated, and the state and local agencies have little federal oversight.
LEARNING OBJECTIVE 2 Describe how the events of September 11, 2001, affected law enforcement.	**Role expansion:** In addition to normal duties, police must be on the lookout for suspected terrorists, design contingency plans for catastrophic terrorist events, and be prepared to deal with weapons of mass destruction. **Racial and ethnic profiling:** Law enforcement agencies must ensure that while protecting citizens against terrorism, they do not engage in activities that violate individuals' legal and civil rights. **Immigration enforcement:** Many local law enforcement agencies must periodically investigate the immigration status of suspects and offenders.
LEARNING OBJECTIVE 3 Compare and contrast the roles of the federal, state, and local levels of law enforcement and their respective agencies.	The duty of all law enforcement officers is to keep the peace, maintain order, ensure adherence to the law, and investigate when those laws appear to have been broken. Federal law enforcement agencies are special-purpose agencies that have national jurisdiction but concentrate on a specific, limited set of offenses. The Federal Bureau of Investigation is the country's foremost law enforcement agency and deals with most criminal offenses that occur on a national basis. State law enforcement agencies typically consist of state police, state highway patrols, and, sometimes, a state investigative agency. State agencies do not have the numbers of officers that local agencies have, or the visibility of federal agencies. No two state law enforcement systems are exactly alike. City and urban police departments, and county police forces (sheriff's offices), make up local law enforcement. These agencies have patrol and investigative duties in which they are often the only law enforcement agency involved in the case because the specific jurisdiction is the first responder to most criminal offenses. Most of the country's crime is handled by local law enforcement. Much local police work is especially concerned with order maintenance and problem solving.

LEARNING OBJECTIVE 4 Categorize the advantages and disadvantages of Wilson's three styles of policing.	The watchman style of policing distinguishes between two mandates of policing: order maintenance and law enforcement. The law enforcement mandate is clear-cut: a person either did or did not break the law. Order maintenance may involve issuing warnings or other arrangements rather than outright arrest and extralegal factors such as age, race, appearance, or personal demeanor. The legalistic style concentrates on enforcing the law by writing more tickets, making more arrests, and encouraging victims to sign complaints. Its focus is on treating all citizens alike, but it is impersonal and disinterested. The service style of policing is concerned primarily with service to the community and citizens. Like the legalistic style, it treats all law violations seriously, but the frequent result is not to arrest.
LEARNING OBJECTIVE 5 Define problem-oriented policing.	Problem-oriented policing expands the police officer's role from one of reaction to one of proactive problem solving. It allows police agencies to address crime on a more systemic level than traditional policing. Instead of responding to calls for service, problem-oriented officers analyze trouble areas of the community and design tactics to address those problems. Problem-oriented policing also has a crime-prevention mission in that it intervenes when patterns begin to emerge.
LEARNING OBJECTIVE 6 Describe zero-tolerance policing and its relationship to the broken-windows perspective.	Zero-tolerance policing is the idea that if every infraction of the law is met with an arrest, fine, or other punishment, offenders will refrain from more grievous activities. An important element of zero-tolerance policing is the broken-windows perspective, which holds that crime follows community neglect. A criticism of zero-tolerance policies is that they often result in the unequal treatment of those without power.

Critical Reflections

1. Would law enforcement activities be more effective if there were simply one national police force? Why or why not? To what extent would an all-inclusive federal police agency be responsive to local customs, sentiments, and cultures?

2. Given the perceived increase of police–citizen conflict that we have seen in recent years, what are the most pressing issues that prevent the police from being effective in enforcing the law and in maintaining the trust of citizens? How would you design a research agenda to develop methods for making the police more effective? What programs would you suggest to rebuild trust between the police and the community?

Key Terms

bobbies **p. 100**
Bow Street Runners **p. 100**
broken-windows
   perspective **p. 121**
community policing **p. 119**
constable **p. 99**

Department of Homeland
   Security (DHS) **p. 109**
Department of Justice
   p. 109
Department of the
   Treasury **p. 109**

Federal Bureau of Investigation
   (FBI) **p. 108**
frankpledge system **p. 99**
hue and cry **p. 99**
legalistic style **p. 118**
Metropolitan Police Act **p. 100**

Endnotes

1 Evan West, "Our Gangster: John Dillinger," *Indianapolis Monthly*, March 27, 2013. http://www.indianapolismonthly.com/news-opinion/our-gangster-john-dillinger.

2 Ed Krayewski, "Eighty Years Ago Today, John Dillinger Helped Create the FBI," May 2, 2016. http://reason.com/blog/2014/07/22/eighty-years-ago-today-john-dillinger-he.

3 John A. Beineke, *Hooser Public Enemy: A Life of John Dillinger* (Indianapolis: Indiana Historical Society Press, 2014), 247–248.

4 Federal Bureau of Investigation: Famous Cases and Criminals: John Dillinger, https://www.fbi.gov/history/famous-cases/john-dillinger. Accessed October 2017. Krayewski, "Eighty Years Ago Today, John Dillinger Helped Create the FBI," *Reason*.

5 Ibid.

6 Charles Leroux, "John Dillinger's Death," *Chicago Tribune*, May 2, 2016. http://www.chicagotribune.com/news/nationworld/politics/chi-chicagodays-johndillinger-story-story.html.

7 Jonathan Rubinstein, *City Police* (New York: Farrar, Straus, & Giroux, 1973).

8 Rubinstein, *City Police*, 6.

9 Samuel Walker and Charles M. Katz, *The Police in America: An Introduction*, 4th ed. (Boston: McGraw-Hill, 2002), 25.

10 Ibid., 25. Walker and Katz provide a good discussion of why history is relevant to the understanding of the development of the police. They trace the political and social forces that were behind the major reforms of law enforcement.

11 David R. Johnson, *American Law Enforcement: A History* (St. Louis, Mo.: Forum Press, 1981).

12 Raymond W. Kelly, *The History of New York City Police Department*, 1993. https://www.ncjrs.gov/App/Publications/abstract.aspx?ID=145539.

13 Mark H. Haller, "Chicago Cops, 1890–1925," in *Thinking about Police: Contemporary Readings*, ed. Carl B. Klockars (New York: McGraw-Hill, 1983), 87–99.

14 Richard Maxwell Brown, "Vigilante Policing," in *Thinking about Police: Contemporary Readings*, ed. Carl B. Klockars (New York: McGraw-Hill, 1983), 58.

15 Ibid., 57–71.

16 Samuel Walker, *A Critical History of Police Reform* (Lexington, Mass.: Lexington Books, 1977).

17 Dean J. Champion, *Police Misconduct in America: A Reference Handbook* (Santa Barbara, Calif.: ABC-CLIO, 2001), 11–12.

18 Walker and Katz, *Police in America*, 34.

19 Center for Research on Criminal Justice, *Iron Fist*, 37.

20 Ibid., 39.

21 Thomas Barker, Ronald D. Hunter, and Jeffery P. Rush, *Police Systems and Practices: An Introduction* (Englewood Cliffs, N.J.: Prentice Hall, 1994), 77.

22 Walker and Katz, *Police in America*, 527–528.

23 Richard Trenholm, Tim Cook Hits Back at 'Chilling' Order for iPhone 'Backdoor,' CNET, February 17, 2016. http://www.cnet.com/news/tim-cook-apple-fbi-iphone-backdoor-terrorists-san-bernardino.

24 Brian A. Reaves, *Census of State and Local Law Enforcement Agencies, 2008* (Washington, D.C.: U.S. Department of Justice Office of Justice Programs Bureau of Justice Statistics, 2011), 2.

25 Brian A. Reaves, Federal Law Enforcement Officers, 2008 (Washington, D.C.: U.S. Department of Justice Office of Justice Programs Bureau of Justice Statistics, 2012), 1.

26 U.S. Department of the Treasury, June 2013. http://www.treasury.gov/about/organizational-structure/bureaus/Pages/default.aspx.

27 John S. Dempsey and Linda S. Forst, *An Introduction to Policing*, 4th ed. (Belmont, Calif.: Thomson/Wadsworth, 2008), 49.

28 Ibid.

29 Walker and Katz, *Police in America*, 71.

30 Randy L. LaGrange, *Policing American Society* (Chicago: Nelson-Hall, 1993), 54.

31 Samuel Walker and Charles M. Katz, *The Police in America: An Introduction*, 5th ed. (New York: McGraw-Hill, 2005), 231.

32 Brian A. Reaves, *Local Police Departments 2013* (Washington, D.C.: Bureau of Justice Statistics, 2015), 14. Available at http://bjs.ojp.usdoj.gov/index.cfm?ty=pbdetail&iid=5279.

33 Sworn officers are "police employees who have taken an oath and been given powers by the state to make arrests, use force, and transverse property, in accordance with their duties." Dean J. Champion, *The American Dictionary of Criminal Justice* (Los Angeles: Roxbury, 2001), 132.

34 Brian A. Reaves, *Census of State and Local Law Enforcement Agencies, 2008* (Washington, D.C.: U.S. Department of Justice Office of Justice Programs Bureau of Justice Statistics, 2011), 2. Available at bjs.ojp.usdoj.gov/content/pub/pdf/csllea08.pdf.

35 Dempsey and Forst, *An Introduction to Policing*, 49.

36 Brian A. Reaves, *State and Local Law Enforcement Training Academies, 2013* (Washington, D.C.: U.S. Department of Justice Office of Justice Programs Bureau of Justice Statistics, 2016), 4. Online at http://www.bjs.gov/index.cfm?ty=pbdetail&iid=5684.

37 City of Tallahassee Police Department Application for Police Officer, http://www.talgov.com/tpd/tpd-employee-po.aspx. Accessed May 2016.

38 Phillip B. Taft Jr., "Policing the New Immigrant Ghettos," in *Thinking about Police: Contemporary Readings*, 2d ed., eds. Carl B. Klockars and Stephen D. Mastrofski (New York: McGraw-Hill, 1991), 307–315.

39 William V. Pelfrey Jr., "Style of Policing Adopted by Rural Police and Deputies: An Analysis of Job Satisfaction and Community Policing," *Policing* 30 (October 1, 2007): 620–636.

40 James Q. Wilson, *Varieties of Police Behavior: The Management of Law and*

Order in Eight Communities (New York: Atheneum, 1968).

41   Ibid., 17–34.

42   Ibid., 140–171.

43   Ibid., 172–199.

44   Ibid., 200–226.

45   Brian A. Reaves, Local Police Departments, 2013: Personnel, Policies, and Practices (U.S. Department of Justice Office of Justice Programs Bureau of Justice Statistics, 2015), 8. Online at http://www.bjs.gov/index.cfm?ty=pbdetail&iid=5279.

46   U.S. Department of Justice, Community Policing Defined, 2014, https://ric-zai-inc.com/ric.php?page=detail&id=COPS-P157.

47   Robert C. Trojanowicz, Marilyn Steele, and Susan Trojanowicz, *Community Policing: A Taxpayer's Perspective*, (East Lansing, Mich.: National Center for Community Policing School of Criminal Justice Michigan State University, 1986). Available at http://msucj.bcpdev.com/assets/Outreach-NCCP-GB7.pdf.

48   David Alan Sklansky, "Police and Community in Chicago: A Tale of Three Cities," *Law and Society Review* 42 (March 1, 2008): 233–235.

49   Robert Trojanowicz, Victor E. Kappeler, Larry K. Gaines, and Bonnie Bucqueroux, *Community Policing: A Contemporary Perspective*, 2d ed. (Cincinnati, Ohio: Anderson, 1998).

50   Samuel Walker and Charles M. Katz, *The Police in America: An Introduction*, 4th ed. (Boston: McGraw-Hill, 2002), 202–203. Walker and Katz also stated three other reasons for this change: the police car patrol, the existing use of detectives, and the emphasis on response time. All were found wanting. Additionally, policing was recognized as a complex job that involved more than crime fighting, and citizens were co-producers of police services. Our discussion of these alternative forms of policing is heavily influenced by Chapter 7 of their book.

51   National Neighborhood Watch—a Division of the National Sheriffs' Association, http://www.nnw.org/about-national-neigborhood-watch. Accessed 2016. April Pattavina, James M. Byrne, and Luis Garcia, "An Examination of Citizen Involvement in Crime Prevention in High-Risk versus Low- to Moderate-Risk Neighborhoods," *Crime and Delinquency* 52 (April 1, 2006): 203–231.

52   Chris Menton, "Bicycle Patrols: An Underutilized Resource," *Policing* 31 (January 1, 2008): 93–108.

53   Wesley Skogan and Susan M. Hartnett, *Community Policing: Chicago Style* (New York: Oxford University Press, 1997).

54   Herman Goldstein, *Problem-Oriented Policing* (New York: McGraw-Hill, 1990).

55   Anthony A. Braga, Glenn L. Pierce, Jack McDevitt, Brenda J. Bond, and Shea Cronin, "The Strategic Prevention of Gun Violence among Gang-Involved Offenders," *Justice Quarterly* 25 (March 1, 2008): 132.

56   Michael D. White, James J. Fyfe, Suzanne P. Campbell, and John S. Goldkamp, "The Police Role in Preventing Homicide: Considering the Impact of Problem-Oriented Policing on the Prevalence of Murder," *Journal of Research in Crime and Delinquency* 40 (May 1, 2003): 194–225.

57   David Weisburd and John E. Eck, "What Can Police Do to Reduce Crime, Disorder, and Fear?" *Annals of the American Academy of Political and Social Science* 593 (May 1, 2004): 42–65.

58   James Q. Wilson and George L. Kelling, "Broken Windows: Police and Neighborhood Safety," *Atlantic Monthly*, March 1982, 29–38.

59   Ibid., 29–38.

60   Benjamin Chesluk, "'Visible Signs of a City out of Control: Community Policing in New York City," *Cultural Anthropology* 19 (May 1, 2004): 250–275.

61   Ibid.

62   Walker, "Broken Windows," 480–492.

63   D. W. Mills, "Poking Holes in the Theory of 'Broken Windows,'" *Chronicle of Higher Education* (February 9, 2001): A14.

64   Ronald V. Clarke, "Situational Crime Prevention: Its Theoretical Basis and Practical Scope," in *Crime Displacement: The Other Side of Prevention*, ed. Robert P. McNamara (East Rockaway, N.Y.: Cummings & Hathaway, 1994), 38–70.

65   NPR, "Drug Crime Displacement," *All Things Considered*, September 16, 1998.

66   Samuel Walker, "Broken Windows and Fractured History: The Use and Misuse of History in Recent Patrol Analysis," in *Critical Issues in Policing: Contemporary Readings*, eds. Roger G. Dunham and Geoffrey P. Alpert (Prospect Heights, Ill.: Waveland Press, 2001), 480–492.

67   Ralph B. Taylor, "Illusion of Order: The False Promise of Broken Windows Policing," *American Journal of Sociology* 111 (March 1, 2006): 1625–1628.

68   Joe Domanick, Police Reform's Best Tool: A Federal Consent Decree, The Crime Report, July 15, 2014, http://www.thecrimereport.org/news/articles/2014-07-police-reforms-best-tool-a-federal-consent-decree.

69   Ibid.

70   Ibid.

71   Ben Mathis-Lilley, Cleveland Police Agree to Extensive Reforms in Deal with Justice Department, Slate, May 26, 2015, http://www.slate.com/blogs/the_slatest/2015/05/26/cleveland_police_consent_decree_justice_department_and_city_agree_on_reforms.html.

72   Brandon Blackwell, "Cleveland Police Officer Michael Brelo Fired over Deadly 2012 Chase, Shooting," Cleveland.com, January 26, 2016, http://www.cleveland.com/metro/index.ssf/2016/01/cleveland_police_officer_micha.html. Holly Yan, "Brelo Verdict: Cleveland Officer Acquitted After Shooting Unarmed Couple - Now What?", CNN, May 26, 2015,http://www.cnn.com/2015/05/25/us/cleveland-police-verdict-up-to-speed/.

73   Mathis-Lilley, Cleveland Police Agree to Extensive Reforms in Deal with Justice Department.

74   John Seewer, "How City Police Departments with Consent Decrees Are Faring," The Associated Press, April 4, 2017, https://www.usnews.com/news/best-states/missouri/articles/2017-04-04/how-city-police-departments-with-consent-decrees-are-faring.

75   Ibid.

76   Ibid.

77   Saul A. Green and Richard B. Jerome, City of Cincinnati Independent Monitor's Final Report, December 2008, http://www.cincinnati-oh.gov/police/department-references/department-of-justice-agreement.

78   Domanick, Police Reform's Best Tool.

79   Elisha Anderson and Robert Allen, "Judge Lifts Federal Monitor's Oversight of Detroit Police," *Detroit Free Press*, August 25, 2014. http://archive.freep.com/article/20140825/NEWS01/308250153/Detroit-police-consent-agreement.

80 Amnesty International, *United States of America: Police Brutality and Excessive Use of Force in the New York City Police Department* (New York: Author, 1996).

81 Brent Staples, "The Human Cost of 'Zero Tolerance'," *New York Times*, April 28, 2012, http://www.nytimes .com/2012/04/29/opinion/sunday/ the-cost-of-zero-tolerance.html.

82 Lawrence Sherman, "Policing for Crime Prevention," *Preventing Crime: What Works, What Doesn't, What's Promising* (Washington, D.C.: National Institute of Justice, 1998), http://www.ncjrs.org/works/ chapter8.htm.

Police Organization, Operation, and the Law

A volunteer (facing) hugs a woman inside the police station in Gloucester, Massachusetts. The woman was one of the first people to benefit from the Gloucester Police Department's approach to the heroin epidemic. Should more intensive efforts be made to treat addicts rather than subject them to criminal penalties?

n the first three months of 2015, four people in Gloucester, Massachusetts, died of heroin overdoses. At a town meeting called to address the crisis, residents said they wanted drug users to be treated compassionately.[1] By June, the Gloucester Police Department announced a new plan. Under a new program called the Police Assisted Addiction and Recovery Initiative (PAARI), drug users who asked the police for help would be placed in a recovery program. There would be no arrests, no charges, no courts, and no jails.[2]

PAARI works simply. When a drug user arrives at the police department, an officer calls in a local volunteer to offer moral support to the drug user and to assist him or her during the placement process. The officer then takes the drug user's information and begins calling treatment facilities that can take the individual in and offer the appropriate treatment. Sometimes the facilities are local, but they may be as distant as California. According to the Gloucester Police Department, the process costs about $55 for each drug user, compared with $220 to arrest and jail a drug user for a single day.[3]

Not everyone thought the program was a good idea. The district attorney warned the police department in a letter that officers did not have the legal authority to decide whether to make an arrest if they knew a law had been broken.[4] The police department continued the program anyway, stating that PAARI is based on police discretion, and without an arrest there can be no charge.[5] By late 2016, PAARI had helped more than 500 drug users receive treatment at centers across the country, and 56 police departments in 17 states had started their own treatment programs.[6]

THINK ABOUT IT > What role does police discretion play in PAARI? Must police make an arrest every time they see a law has been broken?

LEARNING OBJECTIVE **1**

Recognize how the power of the police is constrained.

What We Expect of the Police

Law enforcement in a democratic society is accomplished with the greatest care and attention paid to how much authority is granted to the police. Although it may seem that the police simply enforce the legal statutes passed by the legislature, the reality of law enforcement in the United States is much more complicated, and for the student of criminal justice, far more interesting.

The individual police officer makes dozens of decisions each day that consider the rights of offenders, the opinions of citizens, the demands of supervisors, peer pressure from fellow officers, legal statutes, and the officer's own judgment as he or she decides how to act in what is a highly visible occupation. One important issue we will consider is police discretion. Discretion is mentioned in other chapters, but we will consider it here in more detail because it is at the core of the police officer's occupation.[7] The Gloucester Police Department's Police Assisted Addiction and Recovery Initiative uses police discretion to refrain from strict enforcement of the law in favor of assisting the community by helping drug addicts get treatment. Without recognition of the problems and issues surrounding the exercise of discretion, a precise understanding of policing is impossible.

In this chapter, we look at how the police are constrained in their efforts to keep order, provide services to citizens, and control crime. These constraints include legislative mandates that limit the power of the police, as well as court opinions that police officers must consider in their duties. By appreciating how the police are controlled by elements both inside and outside their agencies, we can begin to understand why policing is often as much an art as a science.

PAUSE AND REVIEW

1. **What constrains the power of the police?**

How the Police are Organized

LEARNING OBJECTIVE **2**

Specify how the job of supervising the police is different from that of supervising the military.

Police departments vary little in how they are organized. With the exception of some small departments, most departments are structured based on a quasi-military template complete with uniforms, ranks, hierarchical chains of command, and centralized decision making. For examples of the organization of modern police departments in small and large cities, see Figures 5.1 and 5.2.

A strict hierarchical chain of command accords status and responsibility according to rank, and uniforms display insignia that identify to both insiders and the public the exact social location of the officers. This quasi-military nature has some qualities that make it attractive to police organizations. Egon Bittner, a pioneer in the sociology of policing, identified three reasons why the military model is attractive to law enforcement administrators:[8]

1. Controlling force through discipline. Both the military and the police are in the business of using force, and the occasions for employing physical force are, as Bittner put it, "unpredictably distributed." Personnel must be kept in a disciplined state of alert and preparedness, with reliance on "spit and polish" and obedience to superiors.

2. Professionalization. The introduction of military-like discipline into police agencies in the 1950s and 1960s greatly professionalized departments that had been historically plagued by corruption and political favoritism and influence.

3. An effective model of organization. The police lacked other models of organization. Given that many officers had some sort of military background, it was easy to implement.

The military structure and culture of the police has resulted in some unintended and undesirable consequences. By having such a vast array of rules and regulations, police departments ignore the reality that individual officers must exert

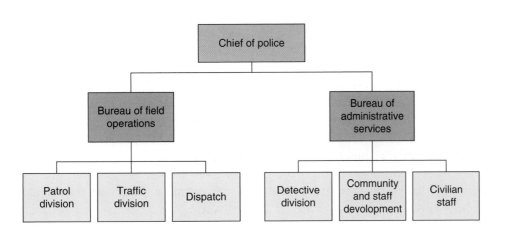

FIGURE 5.1 Organizational Chart of the Watertown, Massachusetts, Police Department, 2016 Watertown, Massachusetts, is a town in Middlesex County, six miles northwest of Boston. As of 2013, about 33,000 people lived in the city. Consider the organization of this particular department. Why might the detective division be under the Bureau of Administrative Services and not the Bureau of Field Operations?

Source: Watertown Police Department, http://watertownpd .org/about/administrative-services /organizational-structure.

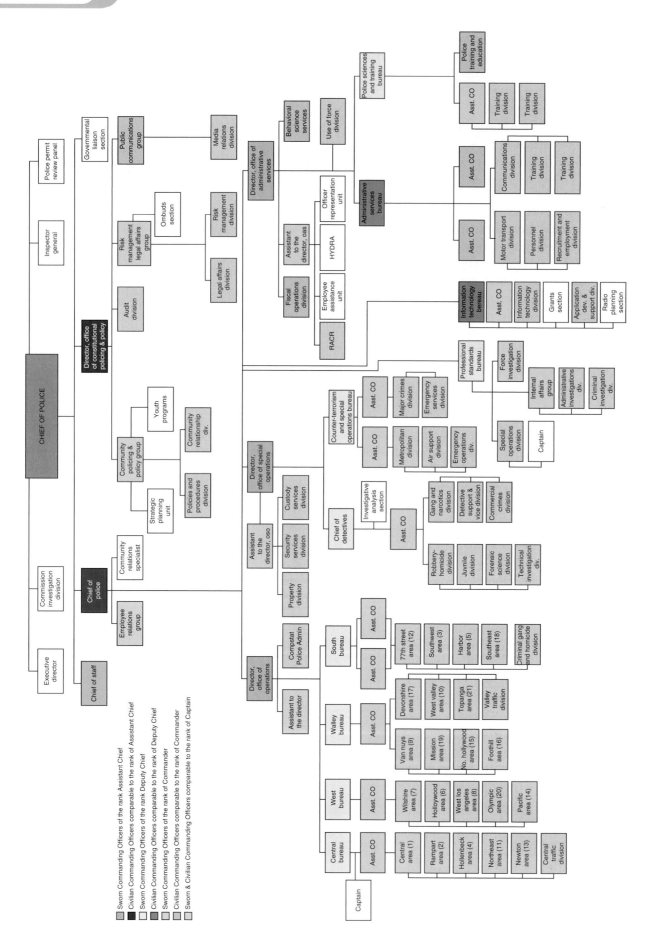

FIGURE 5.2   Organization of the Los Angeles, California, Police Department as of 2016   Los Angeles is the second most populous city in the United States with more than 3.8 million residents. What are some possible reasons for the chief of police answering to the Board of Police Commissioners?

Source: http://www.lapdonline.org/inside_the_lapd/content_basic_view/1063.

Sworn Commanding Officers of the rank Assistant Chief
Civilian Commanding Officers comparable to the rank of Assistant Chief
Sworn Commanding Officers of the rank Deputy Chief
Civilian Commanding Officers comparable to the rank of Deputy Chief
Sworn Commanding Officers of the rank of Commander
Civilian Commanding Officers comparable to the rank of Commander
Sworn & Civilian Commanding Officers comparable to the rank of Captain

New York City police officers are briefed in a subway station as they prepare to deal with a protest march. Although the military structure and culture of the police require many rules and regulations, individual officers must exert a substantial amount of discretion in the everyday performance of their duties. Can you think of an alternative structure for the police?

a substantial amount of discretion in the everyday performance of their duties. To meet the expectations of the department, a good deal of energy is spent conforming to regulations, and creative and effective decision-making is discouraged. According to Bittner, the police are beset with competing demands to stay out of trouble as far as internal regulations are concerned, while at the same time making arrests that "contain, or can be managed to contain, elements of physical danger."[9]

The analogy of the police as soldiers is inexact and faulty because there is a fundamental difference between how military organizations and police agencies deal with decision-making.[10] In military organizations, important decisions are made at the top of the chain of command and flow downward. In policing, essential discretion is vested in the judgment of the individual police officer, who determines when an offense has been committed and whether to make an arrest.

Even though the police agency has a hierarchical structure that, on the surface, resembles a military organization, the nature of discretion and the authority for decision making is actually reversed. Although police administrators can make broad policy and direct their officers' activities to some degree, police officers are dispersed widely, and each officer must decide individually when to invoke the criminal law. Modern communication has made the oversight of officers more efficient, but improved communications cannot mimic the type of organizational oversight that is available in the military. This is one reason that the selection and training of police officers is so important. They must be able to reason for themselves and interpret a given situation within a time frame that often precludes getting input from superiors. Some crucial differences between the police and the military make supervising the police a different, and in many ways more difficult, job than supervising the military. These differences can be categorized in terms of **discretion**, **visibility**, and **authority**.

1. Discretion. Perhaps the most fundamental difference between law enforcement and the military is the level at which discretion is exercised. In typical military units, the allowance for discretion is highest at the top,

discretion (from Chapter 1)—The power of a criminal justice official to make decisions on issues within legal guidelines.

visibility—A term that refers to the fact that police work is mostly easily observed by the public and that police are accountable to the public, police supervisors, and legislatures.

authority—The right and the power to commit an act or order others to commit an act.

and the individual soldier makes few decisions. A consistent and simple pattern of supervision exists in which the generals choose the battlefield strategy. The officers choose which units to commit to battle; the sergeants choose which soldiers will rush the machine-gun nest; and the soldiers do their duty, follow orders, and either succeed, retreat, or die. By contrast, in law enforcement organizations, most discretion is in the hands of the individual police officer. The chief can set some broad policies, and the supervisors can require the officers to keep them apprised of situations, but the individual police officer makes the important decisions. Determining whether a law has been broken, deciding to make an arrest, and giving advice to citizens are activities that are difficult for the command structure of police departments to control. In effect, each officer exercises a great deal of decision-making authority.

2. Visibility. The public observes police work on a daily basis. Officers must interact with citizens, have their decisions second-guessed by the media, and answer to the chief for any violations of procedure and laws. The military is not quite as exposed to the spotlight of public scrutiny. Battlefields are in other countries; the press is given extremely limited access (especially since the Vietnam War), and anonymity protects soldiers from having their actions judged by the public in all but the most egregious cases.

3. Authority. Military commanders have a great deal more authority over soldiers than police administrators have over police officers. If an officer fails to follow orders, he or she may be disciplined or dismissed. If a soldier fails to follow orders, he or she may be court-martialed. Additionally, many police departments are under collective-bargaining agreements that specify the terms of employment and disciplinary procedures. These collective-bargaining agreements are much more "worker-friendly" than the Uniform Code of Military Justice, which spells out the rights of military personnel.

PAUSE AND REVIEW

1. **Why is the military model an attractive model for organizing police departments?**

LEARNING OBJECTIVE 3

Summarize the three primary goals of police patrol.

LEARNING OBJECTIVE 4

Cite examples of extraordinary police duties.

What the Police Do

The job of police officer involves various activities. Many of these activities are well known and highly visible, such as patrol, whereas others are less obvious but equally vital, such as providing services to crime victims, helping individuals in distress, and answering calls for assistance about real and imagined problems. Police officers are among the first responders to natural disasters, accidents, emergencies, and criminal offenses.[11] To appreciate the complexity and range of activities performed by the police, it is useful to review the major functions of a typical police department.

Patrol

The most visible function of the police is patrol. The police patrol in squad cars or aircraft and on foot, bicycles, horseback, or motorcycle. Police patrol has three primary goals:

› To deter crime. When potential lawbreakers see police officers in the community, they are less likely to break the law. Because potential

Charleston, South Carolina, police officers set up a barrier during a hurricane to keep cars off a flooded street. What are some of the many roles police officers play during natural disasters?

lawbreakers do not know how close the police are and because they fear that a patrol car could show up at any moment, they can be deterred from spontaneously breaking the law. Although people often break laws without thoughts of getting apprehended by police officers, many other offenses are deterred because of the ever-present threat of an immediate police response.

› To enhance feelings of public safety. Police patrol gives ordinary citizens the confidence to go about their daily routines without fear of being attacked, robbed, or having their homes burglarized. Citizens who have confidence that the police are nearby are more likely to participate in recreational and civic activities and take advantage of public spaces such as parks and shopping malls. Feelings of security and public safety are essential for the development of meaningful communities where citizens interact with one another based on trust and courtesy rather than suspicion and fear.

› To make officers available for service. Think how inefficient and ineffective it would be if the police had to respond to calls for service in outlying areas of the community from a downtown police station. A good deal of time would be lost by traveling to crime scenes or other incidents, which would result in suspects leaving the scene, disagreements escalating into serious fights, and even people dying because the police took too long to arrive. By having officers patrolling assigned beats or sectors of the city, they can be dispatched more quickly to calls for service.[12] Some large cities even have district police stations and storefront precincts that decentralize law enforcement resources. Police patrol not only reduces response time, but also allows officers to become more familiar with a particular section of the city, where they get to know shopkeepers, street people, and local residents. This knowledge enhances the ability of the police to gather intelligence about troublemakers, gangs, and neighborhood bullies, and puts a human face on the police agency because citizens recognize individual police officers.[13]

Patrol officers enjoy facing new and different challenges each day. They are constantly bombarded with requests for services that can be either frivolous or serious. Because the police are first responders, they must assess situations and determine what type of resource should be committed to their resolution. Patrol officers are the public face of government and must deal with a host of situations that many would not consider to be serious police work, such as calls about overflowing sewers, loose dogs, strange smells, and requests to "do something about" the aggressive person on the street corner. When citizens do not know whom to call, or other businesses or services are not available, they call the police.[14]

The police employ several strategies for patrol that vary according to administrative policies, urban geography, and the availability of officers in patrol cars. These strategies are designed to best maximize their patrol functions within a given jurisdiction.

> › Single-officer patrol cars. Having single-officer patrol cars disperses more officers over a wider area. Many calls for service, such as responding to traffic accidents, involve mundane and routine activities for which only one officer is normally required.

> › Two-officer patrol cars. Many departments staff a patrol car with two officers because of safety concerns. When the police must respond to offenses in progress, gang activity, or domestic disputes, it is advisable to have two officers so that they can protect each other.

Police patrol is so popular primarily because the time it takes the police officer to get to the scene is assumed to be greatly reduced. However, research has not shown that a quick response time has any effect on the number of offenses solved by police. This is because response time is a more complicated matter than is generally thought. In fact, at least four aspects of response time must be considered:

1. Discovery time. Not all offenses are immediately detected. A great time gap can exist between when the offense is committed and when someone notices it. This is especially true in burglaries in which the home or business owner is away and returns only to discover that his or her house or business has been burglarized. In such cases, it makes little difference how quickly the police were notified because the perpetrator might be miles away by then.

2. Reporting time. People often delay calling the police after discovering an offense. This delay can occur for many reasons, including fear or embarrassment on the part of a victim, poor telephone service in rural areas, or the victim's thinking that he or she can solve the problem without police assistance. When such delays occur, the crime scene can go cold, perpetrators can escape, and witnesses can wander away.

3. Processing time. Once the police are notified, it might take some time for a car to be dispatched. The reasons for this time gap are an inadequate number of dispatchers, antiquated dispatch equipment, and lack of available officers in patrol cars.

4. Travel time. Depending on how patrol cars are dispersed throughout the community, it may take a while for them to get to the crime scene. Often patrol officers are already engaged in incidents in neighboring sections of the city, where they may be supporting other police officers in making arrests, quelling domestic disturbances, or simply taking a break for lunch. Travel time can vary greatly depending on the officers' distance from the crime scene or the difficulty in reaching the crime scene, such as heavy traffic or other delays.[15]

Additionally, patrol strategy may be useful for other reasons besides response time. In proactive policing, officers take the initiative to detect and respond to crime rather than reacting to calls for service (reactive policing). In these incidents, a patrol officer may **stop** suspicious individuals or cars and detect lawbreaking. Furthermore, proactive policing allows officers to keep an eye on areas that historically have a high crime rate and to intervene when they see someone breaking the law.[16] For all these reasons, police patrol is the most commonly used tactic for allocating law enforcement resources.

Alternative forms of patrol, such as foot and bicycle patrols, are encouraged in some situations and environments. Foot patrols have several advantages.[17] Officers can form a more intimate relationship with citizens and become sensitized to the ebb and flow of community life. They can enhance the quality of police–community relations while also acting as a deterrent on their beat. The obvious downside of foot patrol is the limited geographic area that one officer can physically patrol. Foot patrol is highly inefficient in cities that are spread out over many miles. However, in certain areas, such as shopping malls, parks that restrict motor vehicles, housing projects, and certain "hot spots," foot patrol can be more effective than patrol cars. Bicycle patrol has the advantages of expanding the range that police officers can cover and, like foot patrol, it allows police officers to patrol areas where motor vehicles are prohibited and keeps officers in close touch with the community.

A Honolulu, Hawaii, police officer patrols an area on his bike. How does an officer's mode of transportation affect his or her approachability?

Investigation

Another common function of the police is to investigate offenses. Detectives go to a crime scene after the patrol car has responded and take over the evidence gathering so that the patrol car can be released to resume patrol. Although detectives are often glamorized in the media and movies, their work is not as exciting as that of a patrol officer. A great deal of their time is spent questioning victims and witnesses and trying to re-create what happened.[18] Often many days, weeks, or months go by before the full picture can be put together and an arrest made. Unfortunately, all too often the detectives are unable to find out who committed the offense. At other times, the patrol officer has done everything necessary to make the case against the suspect, and the detective simply fills out the paperwork and ensures that the case is presentable to the prosecutor.

Several other individuals, including photographers, crime-scene technicians, and representatives of the coroner's office, help detectives investigate the case and put together the evidence. The coordination between patrol officers and detectives is handled by police administrators, with the overall goal of ensuring that criminal offenses are solved and that patrol officers are not unduly hampered in their primary duties.

stop—A temporary detention that legally is a seizure of an individual and must be based on reasonable suspicion.

Traffic Enforcement

Local police agencies and state highway patrols are responsible for ensuring safety on the roadways, including streets, roads, rural routes, interstate highways, and anywhere that automobiles are allowed. The activities of these agencies include responding to accidents, setting up roadblocks to detect drunk drivers or apprehend suspects, and enforcing traffic laws. Although not as glamorous as police patrol or investigation work, traffic duties most often bring police officers into face-to-face contact with citizens.

Enforcing traffic laws can be among the most dangerous aspects of police work. An officer never knows whom he or she is stopping, and citizens can resent being pulled over. In 2015, 15 percent of felonious police deaths ("felonious" meaning deaths as the result of criminal activity and not an accident or natural causes) occurred during traffic stops.[19] When making routine traffic stops, the officer might be tempted to let down his or her guard. However, the driver might be a person fleeing a crime scene, an escaped felon, impaired by drugs or alcohol, or all three. Additionally, many traffic stops are made at night when it is more difficult for an officer to accurately assess a dangerous situation.

Traffic enforcement policy can vary greatly by jurisdiction. For some agencies, traffic enforcement is a major source of revenue, whereas for others enforcing traffic laws is a low priority because they are busy with more serious offenses. At times police agencies make major initiatives to crack down on drunk driving.[20] On holiday weekends, when more people are expected on the highways, local agencies and state patrols step up efforts to enforce speeding and driving-under-the-influence laws to try to reduce the number of automotive fatalities.[21]

Peacemaking and Order Maintenance

Although enforcing traffic laws, patrolling the streets, and investigating offenses constitute the heart of police work, they do not encompass the varied and subtle duties that the police must perform. A major function of being a police officer is solving problems. Many issues routinely arise that may be better addressed by other agencies, but these often fall to the police because of the time of day, lack of resources, or the assumption that the police are the appropriate agency because of their authority. The following is a partial list of these extraordinary police duties:

> Domestic disputes. When spouses or partners, family members, roommates, or neighbors cannot reasonably solve an interpersonal dispute, sometimes the police are called to mediate. Nearly all local law enforcement agencies that serve 250,000 or more residents operate a full-time domestic violence unit (see Figure 5.3 for the actions the police most often take during their initial response to a domestic violence call).[22] Sometimes the mere presence of an officer is enough to quell the disturbance, and sometimes the arrival of police escalates the problem. Domestic disputes can be especially dangerous incidents for the police because emotions run high, and, all too often, drugs or alcohol are involved. However, police officers are trained to ease the tension and negotiate solutions. Often, a police officer can defuse the situation through a combination of reason, understanding, or threat of arrest.[23]

> Crowd control. Sociologists have long observed that people engage in collective behavior when they are part of a group, which may encourage them to do something that they would not do by themselves. This "mob mentality" can be witnessed at social protests, sporting events, and public celebrations. Police officers are dispatched to contain crowds and ensure that laws are not broken and people are not injured. This type of policing presents special

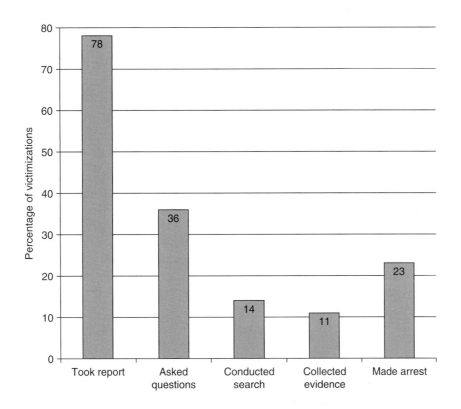

FIGURE 5.3 Police Actions during Initial Response to Domestic Violence Victimizations These are the actions that police officers took during the initial response to a call involving non-fatal domestic violence from 2006 to 2015. In 78 percent of the victimizations, the police took a report during their initial response. What are some reasons why relatively few arrests are made in non-fatal domestic violence calls?

Source: Brian A. Reaves, Police Response to Domestic Violence, 2006–2015 (U.S. Department of Justice Office of Justice Programs Bureau of Justice Statistics, 2017), 9. Available at https://www.bjs.gov/index.cfm?ty=pbdetail&iid=5907.

A police officer takes a photo of revelers playing in the confetti during a New Year's celebration in New York City's Times Square. It is part of the policing job to contain peaceful and celebratory crowds and ensure that laws are not broken and people are not injured. Why does this type of policing present special challenges for police agencies?

challenges for police agencies because it requires the coordination of a large number of officers. Normally, officers work alone or in pairs and are expected to use a great deal of discretion. In crowd-control situations, officers are required to act more as a military unit in which a commander makes a judgment, and individual officers work as a team to implement it. These situations require special training, coordination between numerous law enforcement agencies, and advanced communications technology.[24]

> Vice. Gambling, recreational drug use, and prostitution are just a few victimless crimes that police officers must deal with.[25] Vice laws vary by jurisdiction: for example, casino gambling is legal in Nevada but not in other states. Vice offenses, many of which are a response to supply-and-demand forces in the marketplace, are extremely difficult for police officers to deter, investigate, and prosecute. Nevertheless, police agencies do not get to select which behaviors are illegal. They are obligated to enforce every law. However, police agencies can decide that certain offenses are less of a priority than others and simply spend less time on them.

> Mental illness. One of the most perplexing problems that police officers must face is dealing with the mentally ill. The police are responsible for keeping the mentally ill from harming themselves and others while at the same time preserving their constitutional rights. Often, mentally ill people are unable to understand and accept reason and must be physically restrained. Although police officers may have sympathy for a mentally ill individual who is causing problems, the possibility of violence means that officers must always be prepared. Part of the problem is that many communities provide few alternatives for dealing with the mentally ill. Experts agree that, for the most part, the mentally ill are better treated in the community than in secure institutions, so the laws have specified that many people with mental health problems cannot be locked up. Therefore, it falls to the police to deal with the mentally ill, who are often poor, homeless, or hostile. Police require special training in the laws of dealing with the mentally ill, techniques for defusing individuals with a tenuous grasp of reality, and maintaining their own sanity when dealing with dangerous and unreasonable people.[26]

> Juveniles. In addition to enforcing the law, police officers must deal with juveniles who break the law and engage in behaviors that are prohibited because of their age, such as drinking alcohol, skipping school, and running away from home. Additionally, juveniles can commit serious offenses that the police must respond to without knowing the suspect's age. Dealing with juvenile suspects presents a host of legal, social, and moral dilemmas

Officers often must help children who are being neglected by their families or whose families have placed them in dangerous situations. A boy sits in a car behind his grandmother and her boyfriend, both of whom are unconscious from a drug overdose. A judge later turned over custody of the boy to other family members. What are some other situations in which police officers must deal with juveniles?

for police officers. Larger police agencies have officers specially dedicated to dealing with juveniles.[27] Officers may also have to help children who are being neglected by their families, and they may be the first responders to domestic situations in which children are removed from their primary caregivers.

› First response. In times of crisis, such as natural disasters, terrorist attacks, and other types of emergencies, the police not only are among the first officials to arrive on the scene but are also responsible for maintaining order, limiting damage and injury, and ensuring that the situation does not escalate further. This duty as a first responder is taken for granted by society until something goes drastically wrong.

› Use of force. Part of maintaining order is using force, sometimes deadly force. Police use of force is an issue on which reliable statistics are not collected. Thus, actions such as homicides committed by police officers in the line of duty are poorly understood (see A Closer Look 5.1 for more on this phenomenon). This subject will be discussed in greater detail in Chapter 6.

A CLOSER LOOK 5.1
The Police and Justifiable Homicide

It is estimated that in 2015, police killed 1,138 people in the United States.[28] Or 986.[29] These statistics, collected by news organizations from public reports of police justifiable homicides—the killing of a felon by a police officer in the line of duty—are unofficial.[30] Unfortunately, these are currently the most accurate counts of police homicides available because the federal government's current method for recording this information is based on voluntary reports from local agencies, which are collected by the FBI. About 3 percent of police departments nationwide participate. According to former FBI Director James B. Comey, the official measure of police homicides is "embarrassing."[31]

Thanks to social media, more police interactions with citizens, including violent encounters and homicides that would have remained local even a few years ago, have become infamous because of videos, photographs, and eyewitness accounts that are posted almost instantly on the Internet. This spotlight on police violence has spurred public officials to respond to calls for increased police accountability.[32] For example, New York State now requires a special prosecutor to investigate all police homicides. Texas has approved legislation requiring local police to report shootings by officers. California has made public a database containing information about deaths that have occurred in police custody during the last 10 years.[33] In October 2015, the

Department of Justice announced that it had begun for the first time to maintain a database of deaths in police custody.[34] According to the FBI, police committed 435 justifiable homicides in 2016.[35]

Of particular concern in this matter is the factor of race. Although more whites were killed by police in 2015, when adjusted for population, blacks were killed at about three times the rate of whites or other minorities.[36] In the *Washington Post*'s count, of the 986 people fatally shot by police in 2015, 26 percent were black.[37]

Concerned about the increasing attention to police homicides, some police chiefs have stated that their officers are becoming less proactive. Officers do not want to be featured on the Internet having a confrontation with a suspect, nor do they want to lose their jobs.[38] Additionally, their lives could be at stake if an assailant decides to take misguided revenge on random officers, as occurred in New York City in 2014 when a man shot two officers who were sitting in their squad car or in Dallas, Texas, in 2016, when an assailant shot and killed five officers.[39]

THINK ABOUT IT

1. How have social media increased our awareness of the number of police homicides?
2. In what ways might it be problematic for the police when citizens think there are too many police homicides?

1. **What are the three primary goals of police patrol?**

2. **What happens during investigation?**

3. **Why is traffic enforcement among the most dangerous aspects of police work?**

4. **Name a few examples of extraordinary police duties.**

LEARNING OBJECTIVE **5**

Evaluate the positive and negative aspects of police discretion.

LEARNING OBJECTIVE **6**

Illustrate the importance of the Fourth Amendment to regulating law enforcement.

procedural law (from Chapter 3)—Law that specifies how the criminal justice system is allowed to deal with those who break the law.

The Rules the Police Follow

In Chapter 3, we studied the distinction between substantive law and procedural law. As you will recall, the **procedural law** dictates how the government can go about discovering and prosecuting violations of the substantive law, or what constitutes criminal offenses. One way to consider procedural law is to think of it as the rules by which the government must play. Some people may think of procedural law as "tying the hands of the police" or "letting criminals go free because of technicalities," but the positive aspects of this control of government actions are extremely valuable in providing for a free and democratic state. Aspects of the procedural law were placed in the Constitution because its framers wanted to protect the people from government abuses such as those found in the European monarchies of the time.

Those who work in the criminal justice system sometimes get frustrated by the scope and complexities of the procedural law and often test the interpretation with aggressive crime fighting. The law is forever in flux, as new cases are brought before the courts for rulings concerning new technologies, changing community standards, evolving political pressures, and widening constitutional protections to more and more groups of people. Consequently, the law is a living, breathing, changing set of rules that is adjusted to the demands of society. However, the law is based on long-held principles that limit just how far it can be stretched, and it dictates that either the underlying values incorporated by the Constitution must be met or the Constitution must be amended.

Police Discretion

The police do not make an arrest every time they are legally authorized to do so. Police officers turn a blind eye to many violations and never engage in full enforcement of the law. If the police attempted to enforce all the laws, at least two bad things would happen. First, the criminal justice system would be swamped by the workload. The wheels of justice would grind to a halt under the weight of a system clogged by many times the number of cases it could reasonably process.[40]

Second, the most serious offenders would be obscured by the sheer mass of cases. The police would not have the time and resources to address the cases that represent the greatest dangers to society. Therefore, it is important to appreciate that the police, both as an organization and as individual officers, decide which laws to enforce, how much to enforce them, when to let some offenses slide, and when to devote attention to truly significant offenses.[41] These decisions on differential law enforcement are called discretion. Decisions to investigate, arrest, charge, and incarcerate are all made by the police in the legitimate performance of their duties. It is important to understand the dynamics that structure these decisions. For example, consider an interstate highway on which the posted speed limit is 55 miles per hour but where traffic generally moves at 70 miles per hour. The police do not enforce the posted limit because to do so would mean ticketing

The police do not make an arrest every time they are legally authorized to do so. This police officer is directing a jaywalking pedestrian to a crosswalk. Why do police officers often refrain from making arrests?

about 90 percent of the drivers. There is an unstated understanding between the police and the public that a pattern of non-enforcement is permissible.

In some incidents, the police use their discretion to engage in non-enforcement of the law. It might be fair to argue that the more trivial the offense is, the more likely the police will be not to practice full enforcement.[42] For instance, laws involving the possession of marijuana have long been subject to less enforcement than those involving heroin or cocaine. Additionally, the police are less likely to arrest two teenagers who fight at school than they are two adults who fight after a traffic accident. The context in which the violation occurs has a great deal to do with whether the police decide to invoke the criminal law.[43]

Although we might agree that the use of police discretion in deciding against full enforcement of the law is desirable, another side of police discretion is troubling. Police discretion also provides an opportunity for selective enforcement.[44] When the police use their judgment in deciding which infractions to pursue, bias, discrimination, and individual values may factor into how the law is enforced. When accusations of **racial profiling**, favoritism, corruption, or laziness accompany selective enforcement, the community begins to lose faith in the fairness of the criminal justice system.[45] Yet the police might feel the need to enforce the law selectively as a result of the inconsistencies and unpredictability of the criminal justice system.[46] According to legal scholar Kenneth Culp Davis, selective enforcement raises four questions:

racial profiling—
Suspicion of illegal activity based on a person's race, ethnicity, or national origin rather than on actual illegal activity or evidence of illegal activity.

1. Should the police make arrests when they know that the prosecutors will not prosecute the defendants or that the court will dismiss the case?

2. Do the police violate full-enforcement legislation when a law is broken in their presence but an arrest is (a) physically impossible, (b) less important than some other urgent duty, or (c) impossible because of limited resources?

3. Does insufficiency of police resources for full enforcement justify a system of enforcement priorities that takes into account all relevant reasons for enforcing or not enforcing? Or must the police indiscriminately try to enforce on any and all occasions, so that what remains unenforced will be so because of limited resources and not policy requirements?

4. Are the police always forbidden to make enforcement decisions on individual grounds?[47]

There are good reasons both for and against selective enforcement of the law. On the one hand, it violates the idea of fair play: that everyone who breaks the law should be treated equally. When the police use discretion to decide whom to arrest, it can appear discriminatory. On the other hand, there might be legitimate reasons to engage in selective enforcement, reasons that result in a community with less overall crime and less damage to citizens and property.[48]

Take the hypothetical case of the vice officer who arrests a drug user and finds out that the offender is responsible for several burglaries to get money to support drug purchases. Although we might reasonably expect that the vice officer would charge the drug user with the burglaries, the officer also has an interest in discovering the user's source of the drugs. The vice officer reasons that drying up the source of the drugs will prevent many more drug-related burglaries if there are fewer or no sellers to satisfy the demand for drugs. By encouraging the user to provide information on the seller in exchange for dropping the burglary charges, the vice officer can attempt to clean up the drug trade in that neighborhood. It becomes, then, a value judgment on whether this selective enforcement is justifiable. Certainly, the owner of a home that is burglarized would want the thief arrested and prosecuted. However, the homeowner might consider it a reasonable compromise to let the burglar go if that person could help eliminate drug sales in the homeowner's community.

Faced with these mixed messages sent by legislators, police administrators, and citizens, police officers must exercise a great deal of discretion in deciding which laws to enforce and how fully to enforce them.[49] Certainly, we do not want to give the police full rein to decide how to enforce the law because law enforcement without boundaries is a frightening prospect. While the law limits the actions of the police, it also allows them to exercise discretion on when to apply specific laws to certain situations. Even though we try to control discretion, it will always be a contested area of law enforcement.[50]

The Fourth Amendment

The procedural law that controls the activities of law enforcement is derived from the Fourth Amendment. Although many state laws, court cases, and departmental regulations specify how the police can go about investigation, interrogation, and arrest, all of these rules and regulations must be consistent with the Supreme Court's interpretation of the Fourth Amendment (see CJ Reference 5.1).

Although it constitutes only one sentence, the Fourth Amendment specifies a wide range of protections from police activity and essentially ensures that citizens

CJ REFERENCE 5.1
The Fourth Amendment

The right of the people to be secure in their persons, houses, papers, and effects, against unreasonable searches and seizures, shall not be violated, and no Warrants shall issue, but upon probable cause, supported by Oath or affirmation, and particularly describing the place to be searched, and the persons or things to be seized.

are not subject to the arbitrary actions of overzealous police officers. However, the Fourth Amendment does not completely tie the hands of the police. It is subject to interpretation by the courts, and its wording allows justices to include in their rulings their judgment about what the framers of the Constitution intended and what contemporary society demands. For instance, the interpretation of the word *unreasonable* is fraught with difficulty. What is reasonable to one individual may be unreasonable to another. Yet the police must have guidelines to ensure that the cases they present to the prosecutor are not considered unreasonable by the court. To appreciate the intricacies of the Fourth Amendment as a guide for procedural law, we must examine its language in greater detail.

SEARCH

Prosecuting criminal cases depends on information. Many times, the required information is readily available to police officers, but more often, they have to work hard at assembling the evidence necessary to secure a conviction. Suspects, especially the guilty ones, do not always cooperate fully with the officers who are investigating them. Suspects might hide, alter, or destroy evidence in their efforts to avoid detection and arrest. The police may **search** the suspect in a reasonable manner, but the court draws a line at the fuzzy concept of unreasonable searches, and the police must be trained in procedural law to judge which is which. A review of some of the concerns of the court is instructive.

search—An investigation of an area and/or person by a police officer to look for evidence of criminal activity.

1. Trespass doctrine. The trespass doctrine defines what constitutes a search. The court says that a search requires physical intrusion into a constitutionally protected area, specified by the Fourth Amendment as persons, houses, papers, and effects. The search of these areas must meet the requirements of the Fourth Amendment as being reasonable. Asking for a handwriting sample is not considered physically intrusive and is thus not a search protected by the Fourth Amendment. However, many people believe the government has no right to demand bodily fluids in its search for evidence because the Fourth Amendment protects our person.[51]

2. Privacy doctrine. In 1967, the privacy doctrine essentially replaced the trespass doctrine in *Katz* v. *United States*. This case held that people, not places, are protected from government intrusion whenever they have an expectation of privacy that society recognizes as reasonable. The police are given quite a bit of latitude in dealing with citizens on the street and in public places where privacy is usually not expected.[52]

3. Plain-view doctrine. The plain-view doctrine maintains that officers have a lawful right to use all their senses (sight, smell, hearing, and touch) to detect evidence of unlawful action. The plain-view doctrine also stipulates that such detection of evidence does not constitute a search because the police are not searching when they merely observe their surroundings. Thus, the plain-view doctrine holds that the Fourth Amendment does not protect such gathering of evidence because no search has actually occurred.[53] Three criteria must be met for the discovery of evidence to fall outside the Fourth Amendment's definition of a search: (a) the item must be in plain view of the officer; (b) the officer must lawfully be in the place where he or she discovered the evidence; and (c) the incriminating nature of the evidence must be immediately apparent.[54] Thus, when a police officer pulls a car over for speeding and sees a bag of marijuana on the passenger seat in plain view, the officer can arrest the driver for possession because no search was conducted.[55] Conversely, if the officer stopped the car because

the driver looked suspicious and, without asking the driver's permission, felt under the seat, and found a bag that contained marijuana, the officer's actions would be deemed an illegal search.[56] The court does not allow law enforcement to use sophisticated technology to enhance their natural senses in discovering evidence in plain view. Thus, the police may use flashlights, binoculars, and even airplanes to look for unlawful activity. In a recent case, the court drew the line at the use of thermal-imaging devices. The police used such a device to measure the heat emitted by special lights used to grow marijuana in a house as **probable cause** to secure a search warrant. The court ruled against the government, contending that such a device was beyond the plain-view doctrine.[57]

probable cause—A reason based on known facts to think that a law has been broken or that a property is connected to a criminal offense.

4. Open-fields doctrine. The right to privacy does not extend to open fields, even if the property is privately owned. For example, the police can arrest landowners for cultivating marijuana on private land even if the police were trespassing on that land.[58]

5. Public places. The Fourth Amendment does not protect individuals from being observed by the police using ordinary senses in public places. The street, parks, private businesses that are open to the public, and public areas of restrooms are all outside the protection of the plain-view doctrine of the Fourth Amendment.[59]

6. Abandoned property. The Fourth Amendment does not extend to abandoned property. Abandonment requires the individual to intend to permanently discard the property. For example, turning your car over to a valet parking attendant would not constitute abandonment because you expect to get your car back. Putting your household trash on the curb to be collected by the garbage service is another matter. Because we cannot expect that our trash will be free from the prying eyes of others, we are careful (or should be) to make sure credit card numbers and other sensitive information are destroyed before they go into the trash.[60]

The Constitution does not say the government cannot search, only that it cannot conduct unreasonable searches. Here, a SWAT team enters a private home in the search for a suspect in the Boston Marathon bombings. Was this search reasonable?

The legality of law enforcement searches is complex. The Constitution does not say the government cannot search, only that it cannot conduct unreasonable searches. For example, in *Illinois v. Gates* (1983), the U.S. Supreme Court set forth that the probable cause for a search does not demand proof beyond a reasonable doubt. In this case, an anonymous letter to police accused a married couple, Lance and Sue Gates, of buying and selling large amounts of illegal drugs. The police tracked the Gates's activities, obtained a warrant to search their home, and found large quantities of drugs. After their convictions, the Gates appealed to the Supreme Court, stating that because the police could not assess the reliability of the anonymous letter, no basis existed for the search warrant of their home. The Court stated that the "totality of circumstances"—meaning, in this case, how precisely the letter's specifics matched the Gates's activities—and not the letter itself justified the search warrant. The Gates's convictions were upheld.

Police officers must understand the parameters of lawful searching to ensure that their cases can withstand constitutional scrutiny.

We recognize the necessity for police officers to search for evidence, but we also understand that unreasonable searches are one of the most intrusive features of the criminal justice system. No one likes to have his or her person, home, or "stuff" searched, and the Court has tried to balance the privacy rights of citizens with the needs of law enforcement to collect evidence of crime. The police are restrained in their searches by the requirement that they have a warrant approved by a judge. A valid warrant requires probable cause, a specific description of the persons and places that are going to be searched, and a description of the items that are to be seized. Additionally, the officers must knock and announce their presence and give the occupants a brief time to answer before they enter the house to search.[61]

Two considerations exempt law enforcement from these Fourth Amendment provisions. The first is the problem of officer safety. If the police believe that an armed and dangerous subject is inside a home, should they be required to knock and announce their presence? To do so might invite a hail of gunfire. Second, by knocking and announcing their presence, the police may give suspects an opportunity to destroy evidence. Drugs can be flushed down the toilet, or documents can be burned before the police have time to secure the scene. The Court does not recognize any blanket exception such as a search of a dwelling where drugs might be used and sold, but it does recognize that, on a case-by-case basis, the knock-and-announce rule can be abbreviated.

As a practical concern, obtaining a judge's approval for a search warrant presents difficulties that can hinder a case. It can take a long time to get the warrant, time in which suspects can escape or destroy evidence. Consequently, far more searches are conducted without warrants than with legally secured warrants. The Court has recognized the following four major exceptions to the requirement that officers obtain warrants before conducting a search:

1. Searches incident to arrest. When the police arrest a suspect, it is reasonable, according to the Court, for them to search the suspect for weapons and incriminating evidence. However, in *Chimel v. California* (1969), the U.S. Supreme Court found that an arrest warrant allows only the search of a suspect's person and the immediate vicinity and that any further searches require a warrant.

2. Additionally, the police may search the immediate area under control of the suspect to further ensure their safety and prevent destruction of evidence. The legal issue of what constitutes "under immediate control" of the suspect does not allow the police to extend the search to the whole house. To do this, the police would need to secure a warrant. In the case of an arrest

grabbable area—The area under the control of an individual during an arrest in an automobile.

of an individual in an automobile, the area under the offender's control is deemed to be the **grabbable area**, which constitutes the inside of the passenger compartment but not under the hood or in the trunk.

3. Consent searches. Police officers may conduct a search without a warrant if they obtain the suspect's consent. Individuals may waive their right against a search as long as the police advise them that they have the right to refuse consent and that if the officers find incriminating evidence, it will be seized and used against them. This advisement regarding the waiver of consent is like the *Miranda* warning regarding self-incrimination. For a waiver of consent to be considered voluntary, it must be given by a suspect who feels free of coercion, promise, or deception.[62]

4. Exigent-circumstances searches or emergency searches. Sometimes events happen so quickly that it is unreasonable to expect the police to stop and get a search warrant to determine whether there is a danger to their safety, a chance of suspect escape, or the likelihood of the destruction of evidence (see Case in Point 5.1). For instance, if the police chase a suspect into a house, they are not required to get a warrant to search the immediate area, but the search would be limited to the room in which the suspect was caught. The police could not search the whole house.[63]

5. Vehicle searches. Historically, vehicles are exempt from the requirement of a search warrant. A person in a vehicle has a reduced expectation of privacy as compared to someone at home. This does not mean that the police are free to search a vehicle arbitrarily.[64] Probable cause would still be needed, but one's car is not considered as sacred as one's home. Additionally, objects in a car that could conceal items the police have probable cause to suspect, such as a purse, are also subject to a warrantless search.[65]

CASE IN POINT 5.1

Terry v. Ohio (1968)

THE POINT

Police have the right to search suspects to ensure their own safety and the safety of others if they think that the suspects are armed.

THE CASE

A Cleveland police officer who was in an area that he had patrolled for many years saw two men, John Terry and a man surnamed Chilton, walking back and forth repeatedly in front of a store and pausing to stare in the window. The officer reported that they did this about 24 times. After each pass, they met and talked on a nearby street corner. They were joined by a third man, who left the group, but met up with them again a few blocks away from the store. The officer suspected the three men of inspecting the store in order to rob it later. The officer went up to the men and identified himself as a policeman. Suspicious, he checked Terry

for weapons and felt a gun concealed in his coat pocket, and, in a further search, a gun in Chilton's pocket. Terry and Chilton were charged with and convicted of carrying concealed weapons. Terry appealed, the central argument in the case being whether police may search people who are acting suspiciously if they believe a criminal offense is being planned. The Supreme Court upheld Terry's conviction.

THINK ABOUT IT

1. Why were Terry and Chilton not also charged with burglary?

The procedural law attempts to strike a delicate balance between the rights of individuals to be protected from overzealous police officers and the needs of society to provide those officers with the flexibility and discretion to protect society. Although the Fourth Amendment requirement of a search warrant is highly desirable, it is not practical in all situations in which the safety of an officer or evidence preservation is at issue. Therefore, the court has allowed several exceptions. Other types of searches, called special-needs searches, pose legal issues that result in procedural law continuing to be contested.

SPECIAL-NEEDS SEARCHES

So far, our review of Fourth Amendment issues has dealt with how police officers must handle cases in which a law is believed to have been broken. In some circumstances, searches are allowed in an attempt to prevent crime rather than to catch suspects. This discussion of special-needs searches will demonstrate how the Fourth Amendment protects individuals other than criminal suspects from unreasonable searches. Although these searches can result in criminal prosecution and imprisonment and do not require warrants of probable cause, they must meet a standard of reasonableness that balances the needs of the government against the invasion of individual privacy.

In certain situations, however, individuals who are not suspected of breaking the law are subject to special-needs searches because of a special status such as student, prison inmate, or pilot. Examples of special-needs searches include the following:

1. Impound inspections. When the police impound property, they inspect it and give the owner a receipt. This process protects the police from accusations of theft and ensures that drugs, guns, or explosives are not unknowingly handled in a dangerous manner while in police custody. If in conducting these searches, illegal drugs, weapons, or incriminating evidence are found, the police are allowed to use this information to prosecute cases without having to meet Fourth Amendment requirements of probable cause or search warrants.

2. Border searches. The right to control what comes into or goes out of the country allows law enforcement to conduct searches at the border without probable cause or a warrant.[66] There are some limitations, however. **Reasonable suspicion** is necessary for strip searches, and probable cause is required for body-cavity searches.[67] In addition to the problems of drug smuggling, increased concerns about terrorist attacks make searches at borders more common and more rigorous.

3. Airport searches. Following a wave of airplane hijackings in the 1960s, the government instituted a process of inspecting all passengers with metal detectors before allowing them to fly. After the terrorist attacks of September 11, 2001, security at airports has become even more stringent. All carry-on and checked baggage is inspected. The searches apply to all passengers, so the Supreme Court does not consider these searches discriminatory. Also, notice is posted advising everyone that they will be searched, so individuals are free to not fly and not subject themselves and their luggage to intrusive inspections.[68]

4. Searches of inmates. Those who violate the law and are sentenced to jail or prison lose nearly all of their constitutional rights. The need to maintain a safe and orderly institution where weapons and contraband are constant threats allows prisons and jails to extend only a "diminished scope" of Fourth Amendment rights to prisoners (see Chapter 12 for more information).

5. Searches of probationers and parolees. Those on probation and parole do not enjoy the same Fourth Amendment rights as those who are not under

reasonable suspicion—A suspicion based on facts or circumstances that justifies stopping and sometimes searching an individual thought to be involved in illegal activity.

Passengers wait to have their bags screened at Denver International Airport. Why don't similar security screenings take place at train stations and bus depots?

the supervision of the court or corrections department because to secure their release from prison, they must sign a document waiving many of their freedoms. Therefore, any searches of probationers and parolees by a probation or parole officer are reasonable because they have consented to their restricted liberty.

6. Searches of students. School officials do not need probable cause or a search warrant to search students. Reasonable suspicion is enough.[69] Additionally, some students, such as athletes and those engaged in extracurricular activities, may be subjected to drug testing.[70]

7. Employee drug testing. Although not strictly a law enforcement matter, the illegal use of drugs is of concern to society for several reasons. With employee drug testing, the privacy of the individual from intrusion by the government must be balanced with the safety needs of society.[71] Those who are engaged in occupations that affect the safety of others, such as pilots, bus drivers, and train engineers, can be routinely and randomly tested for drug use to ensure that they are physically competent to operate their vehicles. Those charged with maintaining order, such as police and correctional officers, are also tested.[72]

SEIZURES

seizure—The collecting by police officers of potential evidence in a criminal case.

The Fourth Amendment does not allow evidence that the police have acquired in illegal **seizures** to be presented in court. The police have the right to stop individuals and ask questions, and those individuals have the right to decline to answer the questions and walk away. If citizens exercise this right, the police cannot use the refusal to talk to them as probable cause that something is amiss and search the citizen. The police must have some other objective evidence in order to seize an individual. Citizens may feel a moral obligation or a civic duty to talk to the police, and the Fourth Amendment does not cover this. However, if the police intimidate the suspect to the point that he or she does not feel free to leave, then an illegal seizure may be deemed under the Fourth Amendment (see Case in Point 5.2). Surrounding the suspect with several officers, display of a weapon by an officer, physical touching of the citizen, or the use of language or tone of voice indicating that compliance with the officers' request may be compulsory are the types of circumstances that could invoke a Fourth Amendment defense.[73]

STOP-AND-FRISK

From a procedural standpoint, the term **stop-and-frisk** encompasses two distinct behaviors on the part of police officers. The most basic way to think about them is to consider stops as seizures and frisks as searches. To conduct a lawful frisk, the stop must meet the conditions of a lawful seizure. It is useful to consider these actions individually to appreciate how they are related:

1. Two types of situations in which police officers stop suspects are of concern to the student of the Fourth Amendment. These two situations are **actual-seizure stops** and **show-of-authority stops**. Actual-seizure stops involve police officers physically grabbing a person and restricting his or her freedom. Show-of-authority stops involve the officers showing their authority (such as flashing a badge) and the suspects submitting to it. The Supreme Court uses a **reasonable stop standard** that considers whether a reasonable person would feel free to terminate the encounter in deciding whether the stop is constitutional. The legality of a stop is highly contextualized and has been codified into procedural law by decisions made in several cases.[74] The courts have ruled on the admissibility of stops in a wide range of circumstances. Some of the issues the courts have considered are as follows:

> The role of reasonable suspicion in an officer's decision to stop a suspect

> The use of an anonymous tip as a sufficient reason to make a stop

> Race as an indicator for reasonable suspicion

stop-and-frisk—A term that describes two distinct behaviors on the part of law enforcement officers in dealing with suspects. To conduct a lawful frisk, the stop itself must meet the legal conditions of a seizure. A frisk constitutes a search.

actual-seizure stop—An incident in which police officers physically restrain a person and restrict his or her freedom.

show-of-authority stop—An incident in which police show a sign of authority (such as flashing a badge), and the suspect submits.

reasonable stop standard—A Supreme Court measure that considers constitutionality on whether a reasonable person would feel free to terminate an encounter with law enforcement personnel.

CASE IN POINT 5.2

Florida v. Bostick (1991)

THE POINT

The test of what constitutes seizure is whether the suspect is free to decline an officer's request for a search and terminate the encounter.

THE CASE

In Broward County, Florida, sheriff's department officers boarded a bus at a scheduled stop and asked passengers for permission to search their luggage for drugs. Two officers asked Terrance Bostick if they could search his luggage and advised him of his right to refuse. Bostick gave his permission, and the officers found cocaine in his luggage. Bostick was arrested and charged with drug possession. However, the Florida Supreme Court held that the police officers' conduct was unconstitutional, reasoning that Bostick had been seized because the officers had cornered him at the back of the bus where he had been sleeping. Florida's attorney general appealed to the U.S.

Supreme Court, which reversed the lower court. The Court reasoned that the officers' actions did not constitute seizure under the Fourth Amendment because "taking into account all of the circumstances surrounding the encounter, a reasonable passenger would feel free to decline the officers' requests or otherwise terminate the encounter."

THINK ABOUT IT

1. According to the Florida Supreme Court, should Bostick have felt free to terminate the encounter with the officers? What was the reasoning of the U.S. Supreme Court?

A woman and children walk past a street mural listing an individual's rights during a stop-and-frisk. How does a stop differ from a frisk?

> ⟩ The use of pre-established profiles as valid reasons to make a stop
> ⟩ The stopping of individuals at international borders
> ⟩ The constitutionality of roadblocks

2. Although stop and frisk are closely linked, they are also quite different procedures that the law considers in great detail. Police officers may conduct a legal stop but engage in an illegal search. A frisk involves a light patting of a suspect's outer clothing with the intent to determine whether a weapon is present. However, if the officer detects contraband (such as drugs) during the frisk, then even though the frisk was initiated to detect weapons, an arrest can be made for drug possession or even intent to sell. At issue is the extent of the frisk. Frisks are considered the least invasive type of search; full body-cavity searches are the most invasive. The court will consider evidence obtained in a frisk only if it is confident that the evidence was discovered by officers conducting the frisk with the intention of detecting weapons to ensure their own safety.[75]

ARRESTS

An arrest is more invasive than a stop. It involves being taken into custody, photographed, fingerprinted, interrogated, and formally charged with a criminal offense. A suspect who is stopped and frisked may be released, but if the case proceeds to the arrest phase, then a temporary loss of liberty results. Because this loss of liberty can last anywhere from a few hours to a few days, a higher standard of suspicion of guilt is required. Although reasonable suspicion is sufficient for a stop-and-frisk, arrest requires the police officers to have probable cause that the suspect broke the law.[76]

The way in which police arrest suspects is also important. The amount of force used in the arrest should be consistent with maintaining the dignity of the suspect as much as circumstances allow. The Supreme Court has ruled that deadly force is constitutionally unreasonable if it is used simply because the felony suspect is fleeing. In order to use deadly force, the officer must believe the suspect to be a threat to others. The Court also has spoken to the need to have a warrant to arrest someone at home.[77] Although a multitude of circumstances and situations complicate the

Arrest requires police officers to have probable cause that the suspect broke the law. These officers are arresting a protester after he tried to climb barricades to enter private property. How does an arrest differ from a stop?

sanctity-of-the-home concept (such as when the police are chasing a suspect who runs into a residence), these exceptions must be considered in light of the language and intention of the Fourth Amendment's guarantee that people should be secure in their homes. To arrest someone at home, the court recommends four restrictions:

1. The offense should be a felony. This guards against arbitrary and abusive arrests and ensures that homes are invaded only for serious offenses.
2. The police must knock and announce. This allows the individuals to get dressed and open the door, thus assuring them of some degree of dignity.
3. The arrest should be made in daylight. The fear produced by someone pounding on the door in the middle of the night should be avoided.
4. The police must meet a stringent probable-cause requirement that the suspect is at home. This guards against the police entering the home and frightening others who live there or ransacking the home in their search for the suspect.[78]

Bear in mind that the criteria listed here refer to arrests in homes, not searches.

Interrogation and Confessions

One way in which the police gather information about criminal offenses is from the suspects themselves. By questioning suspects, the police can develop the required evidence to charge, prosecute, and convict lawbreakers. Although this interrogation of possible lawbreakers is exactly what we expect of the police, there are limits on exactly what methods can be used and on what types of help the suspects are entitled to. Even though the police might have good reason to suspect that an individual has broken the law, that person has constitutional rights that must be respected in the questioning process.[79] These rights stem from the Fifth, Sixth, and Fourteenth Amendments of the Constitution.

1. Fifth Amendment self-incrimination clause: "No person . . . shall be compelled in any criminal case to be a witness against himself."

2. Sixth Amendment right-to-counsel clause: "In all criminal prosecutions, the accused shall . . . have the assistance of counsel for his defense."

3. Fourteenth Amendment due process clause: "No state shall . . . deprive any person of life, liberty, or property without due process of law."

Defense attorneys and the court use these amendments to oversee how the police conduct interrogations, elicit confessions, and seize evidence. In some cases, the police might violate the law in conducting these activities, and the evidence gathered can be disallowed in court.[80]

PAUSE AND REVIEW

1. **What are some reasons to advocate for selective enforcement of the law? In what ways can police discretion have a negative impact on a community?**

2. **How does the Fourth Amendment limit the actions of law enforcement?**

FOCUS ON ETHICS   It's Only Marijuana

You are a police officer in a state that has not yet legalized marijuana. Although the laws seem to be changing across the country, your police department has not formulated any policy instructing its officers to overlook marijuana possession and use. As a police officer, you are constantly called on to use your discretion in deciding when to invoke the criminal law. To be honest, you do not make an arrest every time you have the opportunity because you do not want to spend all your time processing petty cases.

One evening you and your partner are called to a fraternity house on the local university campus after neighbors complained of loud partying at 2:00 a.m. You are admitted into the house by an obviously intoxicated fraternity president who says, "Come on in, ossifers. Look around all you want. Ain't nobody here but us chickens." As he giggles at his joke, you realize two things. First, he has given you permission to conduct a legal search of the house, and second, there is the unmistakable smell of marijuana emanating from both the fraternity house and its president.

As you and your partner conduct a cursory search, you easily find a water pipe, several half-full bags of marijuana, and about a dozen marijuana cigarettes that were tossed behind the couch, under chairs, and under the rug. You are about to gather all the marijuana to determine whether a felony case can be made when

your partner informs you that his wife's little sister, a high school junior, is present but passed out in one of the bedrooms. Your partner says his wife would kill him if her sister gets arrested, and he begs you to let everyone go with a warning. You are concerned about the number of youths who are engaged in underage drinking and drug use, but your partner is insistent and says, "Hey, it's only marijuana."

WHAT DO YOU DO?

1. Tell your partner that "the law's the law" and arrest everyone in the house on whom you think you can make a good case, including his wife's little sister.

2. Warn everyone to keep the noise down and that if the neighbors complain again and you have to come back, you will institute option 1.

3. Gather up all the marijuana and flush it down the toilet and send everyone home, thus ending the party.

For more insight as to how someone might respond to such an ethical dilemma, visit the companion website at www.oup.com/us/fuller to watch a video that connects this scenario to a real-world situation.

Summary

LEARNING OBJECTIVE 1 Recognize how the power of the police is constrained.	The police are constrained in their efforts to keep order, provide services to citizens, and control crime. These constraints include legislative mandates that limit the power of the police and court opinions that police officers must consider in their duties. The police are controlled by elements both inside and outside their agencies.
LEARNING OBJECTIVE 2 Specify how the job of supervising the police is different from supervising the military.	Discretion: In the military, the greatest allowance for discretion is located at the top of the command chain, but for the police it is with the individual officer. Visibility: The activities of the police are more visible to the public than those of the military. Authority: Military commanders have more authority over soldiers than police administrators have over police officers.
LEARNING OBJECTIVE 3 Summarize the three primary goals of police patrol.	(1) To deter crime. When potential lawbreakers see police officers in the community, they are less likely to break the law. (2) To enhance feelings of public safety. Feelings of security and public safety are essential for the development of meaningful communities. (3) To make officers available for service. By having officers patrolling assigned beats or sectors of a city, they can be dispatched more quickly to calls for service.
LEARNING OBJECTIVE 4 Cite examples of extraordinary police duties.	Domestic disputes; crowd control; vice; mental illness; dealing with juveniles; first response.
LEARNING OBJECTIVE 5 Evaluate the positive and negative aspects of police discretion.	Allowing the police to decide which laws to enforce, how much to enforce them, and when to let some offenses slide enables police to devote attention and resources to truly significant offenses, thus resulting in safer communities (in terms of less overall crime). If the police attempted to enforce all the laws, the criminal justice system would be swamped by the workload and the most serious offenders would be obscured by the mass of cases. However, police discretion also provides an opportunity for selective enforcement, in which bias, discrimination, and individual values may factor into how the law is enforced. This violation of fair treatment can cause a community to lose faith in the fairness of the criminal justice system.
LEARNING OBJECTIVE 6 Illustrate the importance of the Fourth Amendment to regulating law enforcement.	The procedural law that controls the activities of law enforcement is derived from the Fourth Amendment. It specifies a wide range of protections from police activity, including searches, seizures, stops, frisks, arrests, interrogations, and confessions, and essentially ensures that citizens are not subject to the arbitrary actions of overzealous police officers.

Critical Reflections

1. Suggest how law enforcement agencies might organize themselves and perform if they were not based on a quasi-military model.

2. How much discretion should law enforcement officers have in deciding what suspects and offenses to pursue? How might police discretion be monitored and evaluated?

Key Terms

Endnotes

1 Katharine Q. Seelye "Massachusetts Chief's Tack in Drug War: Steer Addicts to Rehab, Not Jail," *New York Times*, January 24, 2016, http://www.nytimes.com/2016/01/25/us/massachusetts-chiefs-tack-in-drug-war-steer-addicts-to-rehab-not-jail.html.

2 The Police Assisted Addiction and Recovery Initiative, http://paariusa.org/about-us.

3 Seelye, "Massachusetts Chief's Tack in Drug War."

4 Zachary Siegel, Cape Cod Police Opt Out of Police-Assisted Addiction Program, The Fix, March 11, 2016, https://www.thefix.com/cape-cod-police-opt-out-police-assisted-addiction-program.

5 Christian M. Wade, "DA: Don't Get Soft on Drug Crime," *Gloucester Times*, June 26, 2015, http://www.gloucestertimes.com/news/local_news/da-don-t-get-soft-on-drug-crime/article_7f8612bc-27af-5293-a7d0-6cc9ac2da0c9.html.

6 Ray Lamont, "Lawyer Looks to Ease Cops' 'Angel' Burden with Program Changes," *Salem News*, October 10, 2016, http://www.salemnews.com/news/lawyer-looks-to-ease-cops-angel-burden-with-program-changes/article_27add3a2-2443-5715-bbed-5e0ba213f95f.html.

7 Kenneth Culp Davis, *Police Discretion* (St. Paul, Minn.: West, 1975).

8 Egon Bittner, *The Functions of the Police in Modern Society* (Cambridge, Mass.: Oelgeschlager, Gunn & Hain Publishers, 1980), 53.

9 Samuel Walker and Charles M. Katz, *The Police in America: An Introduction*, 4th ed. (Boston: McGraw-Hill, 2002), 174–175.

10 Peter B. Kraska and Louise J. Cubellis, "Militarizing Mayberry and Beyond: Making Sense of American Paramilitary Policing," *Justice Quarterly* (December 1997): 607–629.

11 Willard M. Oliver, *Homeland Security for Policing* (Upper Saddle River, NJ: Pearson Prentice Hall, 2007), 114–116.

12 Larry K. Gaines and Victor E. Kappeler, *Policing in America* (Cincinnati, Ohio: LexisNexis, 2008), 183–185.

13 Walker and Katz, *The Police in America*, 195–196.

14 John S. Dempsey and Linda S. Forst, *An Introduction to Policing*, 4th ed. (Belmont, Calif.: Thomson Wadsworth, 2008), 230.

15 Ibid., 213.

16 Lawrence Sherman, Patrick Gartin, and Michael Buerger, "Hot Spots of Predatory Crime: Routine Activities and the Criminology of Place," *Criminology* 27 (1989): 27–55.

17 George Kelling, *Foot Patrol* (Washington, D.C.: National Institute of Justice, 1987).

18 William B. Sanders, *Detective Work: A Study of Criminal Investigations* (New York: Free Press, 1977).

19 Federal Bureau of Investigation, Law Enforcement Officers Killed and Assaulted 2015, Law Enforcement Officers Feloniously Killed Circumstance at Scene of Incident, 2006–2015, Table 23, https://ucr.fbi.gov/leoka/2015/tables/table_23_leos_fk_circumstance_at_scene_of_incident_2006-2015.xls.

20 H. Laurence Ross, *Confronting Drunk Driving: Social Policy for Saving Lives* (New Haven, Conn.: Yale University Press, 1992).

21 James B. Jacobs, *Drunk Driving: An American Dilemma* (Chicago: University of Chicago Press, 1989).

22 Brian A. Reaves, *Police Response to Domestic Violence, 2006–2015* (U.S. Department of Justice Office of Justice Programs Bureau of Justice Statistics, 2017), 9. Available at https://www.bjs.gov/index.cfm?ty=pbdetail&iid=5907.

23 Franklyn W. Dunford, David Huizinga, and Delbert S. Elliott, "The Role of Arrest in Domestic Assault: The Omaha Police Experiment," *Criminology* 28 (1990): 183–206.

24 Bittner, "Quasi-Military Organization," 171.

25 Robert F. Meier and Gilbert Geis, *Victimless Crime? Prostitution, Drugs, Homosexuality, Abortion* (Los Angeles: Roxbury, 1997).

26 Judy Hails and Randy Borum, "Police Training and Specialized Approaches to Respond to People with Mental Illness," *Crime and Delinquency* 49 (2003): 52–61.

27 John Fuller, *Juvenile Delinquency: Mainstream and Crosscurrents* (Upper Saddle River, N.J.: Prentice Hall, 2009), 395–429.

28 Guardian, The Counted, http://www.theguardian.com/us-news/ng-interactive/2015/jun/01/the-counted-police-killings-us-database#; *Washington Post*, Investigation: Police Shootings, http://www.washingtonpost.com/graphics/national/police-shootings/.

29 *Washington Post*, Investigation: Police Shootings, http://www.washingtonpost.com/graphics/national/police-shootings/.

30 Federal Bureau of Investigation, Expanded Homicide Data Table 5: Justifiable Homicide by Weapon, Law Enforcement, 2012–2016, Crime in the United States, 2016, https://ucr.fbi.gov/crime-in-the-u.s/2016/crime-in-the-u.s.-2016/tables/expanded-homicide-data-table-5.xls.

31 Aaron C. Davis and Wesley Lowery, "FBI Director Calls Lack of Data on Police Shootings 'Ridiculous,' 'Embarrassing,'" *Washington Post*, October 7, 2015, https://www.washingtonpost.com/national/fbi-director-calls-lack-of-data-on-police-shootings-ridiculous-embarrassing/2015/10/07/c0ebaf7a-6d16-11e5-b31c-d80d62b53e28_story.html.

32 Ibid.

33 Ibid.

34 Ibid.

35 Federal Bureau of Investigation, Expanded Homicide Data Table 5: Justifiable Homicide by Weapon, Law Enforcement, 2012–2016, Crime in the United States, 2016, https://ucr.fbi.gov/crime-in-the-u.s/2016/crime-in-the-u.s.-2016/tables/expanded-homicide-data-table-5.xls.

36 Kimberly Kindy, "Fatal Police Shootings in 2015 Approaching 400 Nationwide," *Washington Post*, May 30,

2015, https://www.washingtonpost.com/national/fatal-police-shootings-in-2015-approaching--400-nationwide/2015/05/30/d322256a-058e-11e5-a428-c984eb077d4e_story.html.

37 *Washington Post*, Investigation: Police Shootings.

38 Aaron C. Davis, "'YouTube Effect' Has Left Police Officers under Siege, Law Enforcement Leaders Say," *Washington Post*, October 8, 2015, https://www.washingtonpost.com/news/post-nation/wp/2015/10/08/youtube-effect-has-left-police-officers-under-siege-law-enforcement-leaders-say/.

39 Peter Holley, "Two New York City Police Officers Are Shot and Killed in a Brazen Ambush in Brooklyn," *Washington Post*, December 20, 2014, https://www.washingtonpost.com/national/two-new-york-city-police-officers-are-shot-and-killed-in-a-brazen-ambush-in-brooklyn/2014/12/20/2a73f7ae-8898-11e4-9534-f79a23c40e6c_story.html. Manny Fernandez, Richard Pérez-Peña and Jonah Engel Bromwich, "Five Dallas Officers Were Killed as Payback, Police Chief Says," *New York Times*, July 8, 2016, http://www.nytimes.com/2016/07/09/us/dallas-police-shooting.html.

40 Arthur Rosett, "Discretion, Severity and Legality in Criminal Justice," in *The Invisible Justice System: Discretion and the Law*, eds. Burton Atkins and Mark Pogrebin (Cincinnati, Ohio: Anderson, 1978), 24–33.

41 Ibid., 25.

42 Albert Reiss Jr., "Discretionary Justice in the United States," in *The Invisible Justice System: Discretion and the Law*, eds. Burton Atkins and Mark Pogrebin (Cincinnati, Ohio: Anderson, 1978), 41–58.

43 Melissa Schaefer Morabito, "Horizons of Context: Understanding the Police Decision to Arrest People with Mental Illness," *Psychiatric Services* 58 (December 1, 2007): 1582–1587.

44 Raymond Goldberg, *Drugs across the Spectrum* (Englewood, Colo.: Morton, 1997), 80.

45 Jerome H. Skolnick and Elliott Currie, *Crisis in American Institutions* (Boston: Little, Brown, 1973). See especially the sections on police and criminal law and corrections.

46 Aleksandar Tomic and Jahn K. Hakes, "Case Dismissed: Police Discretion and Racial Differences in Dismissals of Felony Charges," *American Law and Economics Review* 10 (April 1, 2008): 110–141.

47 Davis, *Police Discretion*, 83.

48 Clearly, the police develop strategies that target high-crime areas or events where crime is likely to appear. The difference between the police presence at a symphony orchestra performance and at a basketball tournament is likely to be significant even though the size of the crowd is the same.

49 Igor Areh, Bojan Dobovsek, and Peter Umek, "Citizens' Opinions of Police Procedures," *Policing* 30 (October 1, 2007): 637–650.

50 American Friends Service Committee, "Discretion," in *The Invisible Justice System: Discretion and the Law*, eds. Burton Atkins and Mark Pogrebin (Cincinnati, Ohio: Anderson, 1978), 35–40. This report argues that discretion should be removed from the criminal justice system so that constitutional protections of due process and equal application of the law will apply to everyone.

51 *Silverman v. United States*, 365 U.S. 505, 81 S.Ct. 679 (1961).

52 "Vehicle Search after Arrest Violated Driver's Rights, Rules Wyoming Supreme Court," *Lawyers USA*, June 2, 2008.

53 "A Bullet Box Observed in Plain View on a Person Gives Probable Cause for Arrest," *Narcotics Law Bulletin*, November 1, 2005, 4.

54 *Horton v. California*, 496 U.S. 128, 136–137 (1990).

55 "After Approaching Robbery Suspect, Police Spot Marijuana and Search Car," *Narcotics Law Bulletin*, May 1, 2003, 7–8.

56 Roadblocks used during DUI crackdowns are not illegal according to the Fourth Amendment because all cars are stopped. Probable cause is not an issue because no one is singled out for special treatment.

57 *California v. Ciraolo*, 476 U.S. 207, 106 S.Ct. 1809 (1986); *United States v. White*, 401 U.S. 745, 91 S. Ct. 1122 (1971).

58 *United States v. Dunn*, 480 U.S. 294, 107 S.Ct. 1134 (1987).

59 Samaha, *Criminal Procedure*, 112.

60 *Payton v. New York*, 445 U.S. 573, 100 S.Ct. 1371 (1980). White, Burger, and Rehnquist filed the dissenting opinion.

61 *Stanford v. Texas*, 379 U.S. 476, 85 S.Ct. 506 (1965); *Maryland v. Garrison*, 480 U.S. 79, 107 S.Ct. 1013 (1987); *Wilson v. Arkansas*, 514 U.S. 927, 115 S.Ct. 1914 (1995); *Richards v. Wisconsin*, 520 U.S. 385, 117 S.Ct. 1416 (1997).

62 *Schneckloth v. Bustamonte*, 412 U.S. 218, 93 S.Ct. 2041, (1973); *United States v. Rodney*, 956 F.2d 295, 297

(D.C. Cir. 1992); *Illinois v. Rodriguez*, 497 U.S. 177, 110 S.Ct. 2793 (1990).

63 *United States v. Santana*, 427 U.S. 38, 96 S.Ct. 2406 (1976); *Cupp v. Murphy*, 412 U.S. 291, 93 S.Ct. 2000 (1973); *Ker v. California*, 374 U.S. 23, 83 S.Ct. 1623 (1963).

64 Nicola Persico and Petra E. Todd, "The Hit Rates Test for Racial Bias in Motor-Vehicle Searches," *Justice Quarterly* 25 (March 1, 2008): 37.

65 *Carroll v. United States*, 267 U.S. 132, 45 S.Ct. 280 (1925); *Wyoming v. Houghton*, 526 U.S. 295, 119 S.Ct. 1297 (1999).

66 "Constitutional Law—Fourth Amendment—Ninth Circuit Holds That Destructive Search of Spare Tire at Border Is Constitutional.—*United States v. Cortez-Rocha*, 394 F.3d 1115 (9th Cir. 2005)," *Harvard Law Review* 118 (June 1, 2005): 2921–2928.

67 *United States v. Ramsey*, 431 U.S. 606, 97 S.Ct. 1972 (1977).

68 Michael G. Lenett, "Implied Consent in Airport Searches: A Response to Terrorism, *United States v. Pulido-Baquerizo*, 800 F.2D 899 (9th Cir. 1986)," *American Criminal Law Review* 25 (January 1, 1988): 549–575.

69 *State v. Hunter*, 831 P.2d, 1033 (Utah Ct. App. 1992); *New Jersey v. T.L.O.*, 469 U.S. 325, 105 S.Ct. 733 (1985).

70 "Search and Seizure—Suspicionless Drug Testing," *Harvard Law Review* 103 (December 1, 1989): 591.

71 Michael F. Rosenblum, "Security vs. Privacy: An Emerging Employment Dilemma," *Employee Relations Law Journal*, July 1, 1991, 81.

72 *Hester v. United States*, 265 U.S. 57, 44 S.Ct. 445 (1924); *Abel v. United States*, 362 U.S. 217, 80 S.Ct. 683 (1960); *California v. Greenwood*, 486 U.S. 35, 108 S.Ct. 1625 (1988).

73 Samaha, *Criminal Procedure*, 123; *California v. Hodari D.*, 499 U.S. 621, 111 S.Ct. 1547 (1991).

74 *Terry v. Ohio*, 392 U.S. 1, 99 S.Ct. 1868 (1968).

75 *State v. Morrison*, Ohio App. 8 Dist. (1999).

76 New York Civil Liberties Union, Stop-and-Frisk Data, http://www.nyclu.org/content/stop-and-frisk-data. Accessed October 2015.

77 David Cole, "The Usual Suspects," *Nation*, July 2/9, 2012, 4–6.

78 New York Civil Liberties Union, Stop-and-Frisk Data.

79 Craig M. Bradley, "Mixed Messages on the Exclusionary Rule," *Trial*, December 1, 2006, 56–59.

80 Samaha, *Criminal Procedure*, 355.

Policing: Innovations and Controversies

Bounkham Phonesavanh (left) is the father of Bounkham "Bou Bou" Phonesavanh who was severely burned by a flash grenade during a SWAT drug raid. Here, he and his family attend a vigil outside the Atlanta hospital where the toddler underwent treatment in 2014. What alternative tactic could the police have used in this situation to avoid injury?

On the night of May 27, 2014, the Habersham County (Georgia) Special Response Team (SRT) was preparing to execute a no-knock warrant. Earlier that day, a new informant for the sheriff's office had been sent to a residence to try to buy methamphetamine. The informant took along his wife and a roommate, neither of whom was working with the sheriff's department. According to the informant, two Mercedes SUVs were parked in the driveway of the house, with guards standing at the front and back doors. The informant's roommate bought the drugs while standing in the doorway, then left. No police surveillance was conducted to verify the purchase.

Deputy Sheriff Nikki Autry took an affidavit to a Habersham County magistrate judge swearing that the informant had made the purchase. The judge issued a no-knock search warrant for the residence and an arrest warrant for a man named Wanis Thonetheva, who had allegedly sold the drugs.[1] During the early hours of May 28, 2014, the SRT surrounded the home. The front door appeared to be blocked, so they rammed it open and, as instructed during their training, inserted a flash-bang grenade—a device that is intended to surprise, not cause injury or death—just inside the door.[2] The grenade detonated, and the team entered the home prepared to arrest Thonetheva.

Unfortunately, the item blocking the door was a playpen in which 19-month-old Bounkham "Bou Bou" Phonesavanh Jr. was sleeping. He and his parents, Alecia and Bounkham Phonesavanh, had brought their family from Wisconsin after their house burned down. Until they could find a new house in Wisconsin, they were staying with Bounkham's sister.[3] The Phonesavanh family was asleep in the front room of the house, when the grenade, which had landed in or near Bou Bou's playpen, detonated, blowing a hole in his chest and face. The boy, who was burned severely, survived the attack and was rushed to the hospital. The suspect Wanis Thonetheva, who did not live in the house, was not there during the raid and was arrested later. The sheriff's deputies were not charged with the use of excessive force, but the Habersham County drug task force was disbanded four months later.[4]

Although a grand jury declined to indict the SRT officers, Deputy Autry was charged with providing false information for search and arrest warrants but was acquitted in a federal trial.[5] Alecia and Bounkham Phonesavanh sued the county government and other agencies involved in the raid.[6] In April 2015, the county and the Phonesavanh family agreed upon a $1 million settlement.[7]

THINK ABOUT IT > What is the underlying rationale behind this type of policing practice, and how does this form of police behavior differ from traditional policing?

Use of Force

LEARNING OBJECTIVE | **1**

Identify some of the problems associated with the excessive use of force by police officers.

We expect a lot from our police, maybe too much. However, the police have claimed broad powers in staking out the mandate of their occupation.[8] The police have established a semi-monopoly on the core concerns of their profession, one of which is the **use of force**, which, according to the International Association of Chiefs of Police, is "the amount of effort required by police to compel compliance from an unwilling subject."[9] When situations get out of hand, we "call the cops" to exercise their professional skills and judgment to maintain order and ensure justice. The alternative would be anarchy in which everyone decided for themselves what constituted reasonable force and appropriate justice. In fact, most police contacts do not require the use of force, and the reality of law enforcement is much more routine. Although the police do engage in chases, gunfights, and careful sleuthing, these are rare events compared to a typical day's proceedings. Most police work resembles any other kind of work: it can be boring, tiresome, sometimes dirty, sometimes technically demanding, but not always dangerous.[10] Because of their use-of-force mandate, however, maintaining control of the police is a controversial issue.[11]

According to sociologist Egon Bittner, civilized society has been developing mechanisms to eliminate the legitimacy of all forms of force. From international diplomacy to the internal workings of the criminal justice system, the use of force has been relegated to last-resort status. Today, physical force is considered legitimate only under the following conditions:

use of force—"The amount of effort required by police to compel compliance from an unwilling subject," according to the International Association of Chiefs of Police.

1. Self-defense. Self-defense laws vary from state to state, but the generally accepted principle is that after exhausting all other means of avoiding harm, including retreat, force may be used to protect oneself or others.

2. Specifically deputized people against some specifically named people. In this case, Bittner was referring to agents such as mental hospital attendants and corrections officers. Here, the right to use force is given to those whose jobs may require them to deal with dangerous people in a special context. The right to use force does not extend beyond the confines of the job; their jurisdiction is limited to the hospital or the prison.

3. Police force. This last legitimate use of force is much broader than the previous two. According to Bittner, the formal restrictions of police use of force are as follows:

   a. Use of force is limited to certain types of situations. For example, in some jurisdictions, the police may shoot to kill dangerous fleeing felons but not those who have committed misdemeanors.

   b. The police may use force only in the performance of official duties, not to advance their personal interests or the private interests of others.

   c. The police may not use force maliciously or frivolously.[12]

Although these guidelines appear to limit the use of force by police, Bittner said they are essentially meaningless. No one really knows what is meant by the "lawful use of force" because each incident is different, and it is impossible to cover all the circumstances in which police may use force (see Figure 6.1 for a look at how and when a police officer might use force). Situations in which police use force are highly contextual, and it is difficult to determine what pressures police officers were under when they decided that force was necessary. We know that the police use force in making arrests and keeping order. For example, in the opening scenario, the police determined that dangerous drug deals were occurring inside a house, and thus they used force and surprise to enter the house. However, it is unclear how much the

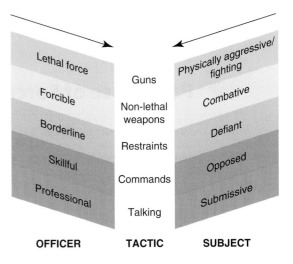

FIGURE 6.1 Use of Force Model This figure shows how a police officer may respond to a subject's behavior, and the tactics he or she may use. For example, an officer will take a professional tone and talk to a subject who is cooperative or submissive. A subject who is physically aggressive may require lethal force. What may an officer do if a subject is opposed to him or her? In the case of a subject who is combative?

police knew about who was actually inside the house at the time of entry. Based on their observations, they were clearly expecting hostile drug dealers. What they found was a sleeping family with small children. The problem is that we know little about exactly how police use force and how often the police decide to use force. For a summary of what we know about police use of force and where studies are still needed, see CJ Reference 6.1.

We call the police in situations that might require an outside party to mediate or use force on our behalf because they have been trained and are armed and authorized to do so. However, societal expectations put the police in a precarious position: on one hand, we expect them to use reasonable force when our interests are at stake; on the other hand, we decide what reasonable force is only after the fact. Because the legitimate use of police force is so dependent on the situation's context and because the police must make decisions in the heat of the moment and often under dangerous conditions, determining the lawfulness of the use of force is problematic.[13] This puts the police in a no-win situation. Failure to use appropriate force might risk injury or death to themselves or others. The use of too much force could result in disciplinary action. According to Bittner, we ask police to make a decision requiring the exercise of two conflicting parts of the nature of police work: the police must simultaneously balance their physical prowess with their professional acumen.[14]

The expectation of how much and what type of force an officer will use in a given situation varies according to a number of factors: the time of day, whether the officer is alone or working with a partner, the size and sex of the suspect, and the environment can influence whether, and how much, force is used. It is recommended that police officers use only the force required to bring order to a situation and no more (see Case in Point 6.1). This is a highly contingent judgment and one for which considerable variation can be expected. Additionally, if force is applied appropriately, we expect to see relatively low levels of force used more often than deadly force. In fact, most force used by the police is relatively minor. Given that the police are allowed and expected to use force, it should be of some comfort to realize that they use extreme force rarely. Cases of extreme use of force that are labeled police brutality create a negative perception of contemporary police work.

CJ REFERENCE 6.1
Police Use of Force

What we know with substantial confidence:

- Police use force infrequently.
- Use of force typically occurs at the lower end of the physical spectrum, involving grabbing, pushing, or shoving.
- Use of force typically occurs when a suspect resists arrest.

What we know with modest confidence:

- Use of force appears to be unrelated to an officer's personal characteristics, such as age, gender, and ethnicity.

- Use of force is more likely to occur when police are dealing with people who are under the influence of alcohol or drugs or are mentally ill.
- A small proportion of officers are disproportionately involved in use-of-force incidents.

What we do not know:

- The incidence of wrongful use of force.
- The effect of differences in police organizations, including administrative policies, hiring, training, discipline, and use of technology on excessive and illegal force.
- Influences of situational characteristics on police use of force and the transactional nature of these events.[15]

Here, activists march on behalf of the families of victims of alleged police brutality. What types of police use of force are likely to upset the community?

This problem of what constitutes appropriate police use of force has been exposed by the widespread availability of social media. Before nearly everyone was carrying a phone with a high-quality camera, the truth about police–citizen encounters was left to the police to disclose. Now, pictures and videos from these encounters routinely appear all over the media and become public knowledge almost

CASE IN POINT 6.1

Tennessee v. Garner (1985)

THE POINT

Deadly force may be used only if the suspect poses a threat to the lives of police officers or bystanders.

THE CASE

In 1974, Edward Garner, age 15, and a friend were in a house at night at which the owners were not present. A neighbor reported to police that someone had broken into the home. When the officers arrived, they saw someone running away, shouted warnings to stop, then shot at Garner, who was climbing a fence. The officer said that he was "reasonably sure" that Garner was unarmed but thought that once he got over the fence, he would elude capture. One of the bullets struck Garner in the back of the head, and he died later on the operating table. Because the officers suspected the boys of a felony—burglarizing the house—they believed they were justified in shooting at the boys to stop them.

Garner's father filed suit, claiming that his son's constitutional rights were violated. In 1985, the Supreme Court decided that the use of deadly force was not warranted. Justice Byron White wrote, "It is no doubt unfortunate when a suspect who is in sight escapes, but the fact that the police arrive a little late or are a little slower afoot does not always justify killing the suspect. A police officer may not seize an unarmed, non-dangerous suspect by shooting him dead."

THINK ABOUT IT

1. How did the police officers' actions violate Garner's constitutional rights?

instantly. Police officers have been recorded engaging in inappropriate, sometimes lethal, uses of force.[16] Sometimes these recordings are misleading because they do not show the full context of the encounter. Often, however, recordings show officers who are obviously greatly exceeding their use-of-force guidelines. Excessive use of force by the police is problematic in several ways. These include:

> Legal liability. Police departments risk legal liability when their officers use excessive force. Officers who severely injure or kill citizens expose the department and the locality to legal proceedings. If a judge or jury decides that the use of force was excessive, the financial compensation to the victim(s) may be substantial. Police departments cannot afford to let their officers have unfettered discretion in their use of force.

> Physical injury or death. The use of excessive force may injure or even kill people. From June 2015 through May 2016, about 1,900 arrest-related deaths occurred.[17] Although there are some instances in which the use of force is justified, there is a well-established principle that police officers should use just enough force to control situations and not as a form of dominance and intimidation. Police officers must decide in a short period of time exactly how much danger exists in a situation and apply reasonable force. This judgment, often made in a split second, can have severe consequences.

> Loss of citizen respect. Police officers must have the cooperation of citizens to do their job effectively and professionally. When they use excessive force, they forfeit that respect. This could have far-reaching implications for the enforcement of the law in the community. Citizens who would normally cooperate with law enforcement by pointing out dangerous situations and potential violators may remain silent because they object to the unreasonable force that police officers have used.[18] Without the respect and cooperation of citizens, the job of police officers becomes much more difficult. Additionally, lawbreakers or suspects who fear excessive use of force by police may engage in riskier behaviors, such as running away or even turning on police and initiating violence.[19] It is also worth noting that it is relatively rare for people who thought the police behaved improperly during a contact to file a complaint. For example, in 2011 (the most recent data available), 86 percent of people involved in traffic stops and 66 percent of people involved in pedestrian stops thought that the police behaved properly and treated them with respect during the stop. However, more people involved in pedestrian stops (25 percent) than those involved in traffic stops (10 percent) believed the police did not behave properly. Less than 5 percent of people who believed the police did not behave properly filed a complaint.[20]

> Community reaction. The actions of police officers, whether appropriate or inappropriate, can elicit negative reactions from dissatisfied and outraged citizens. Communities may engage in public protest, and, in some cases, the excessive use of force (especially if there is a record that clearly demonstrates police misconduct) has prompted rioting as a response.[21] For instance, on April 12, 2015, police in Baltimore, Maryland, arrested Freddie Gray, a 25-year-old black man, after he ran when he saw police officers. When Gray was caught, he said he had trouble breathing and asked for an inhaler, which police did not provide. Gray was placed in the back of a police van without a seat belt. After a stop during which police shackled Gray's hands and feet, the van continued. After a couple more stops, during which Gray requested medical help, the van arrived at the police station. There, a medic determined that Gray was no longer breathing, in cardiac arrest, and severely injured.

These demonstrators are protesting outside of the courthouse during the trial of Officer Caesar Goodson Jr., one of six Baltimore city police officers charged in connection with the death of Freddie Gray. What circumstances made this example of police use of force so objectionable to the community?

Gray, who had suffered a spine injury, fell into a coma and died on April 19, 2015.[22] Protests spread after Gray's funeral, some of which turned into riots. At least 20 police officers were injured, and 250 people were arrested. Hundreds of businesses were damaged, and vehicles and buildings were burned. Maryland Army National Guard troops were deployed, and a state of emergency was declared in Baltimore. On May 1, 2015, Gray's death was ruled a homicide, and charges were issued against the six officers involved in the incident, including a charge of second-degree murder against the officer driving the van. The state of emergency was lifted five days later.[23]

Police departments have traditionally struggled with controlling their officers' discretion and have instituted strategies to ensure that they enforce the law in a fair manner that enhances the safety of themselves and the community. These strategies to evaluate and control police officers' use of force include:

> Training. Police departments have constructed training programs that attempt to develop realistic scenarios in which police officers have an opportunity to consider when and how much force should be used in particular situations.[24]

> Identifying problem-prone officers. Not every police officer is equally equipped to engage in all forms of policing. Some officers are effective in dealing with the public, whereas other officers are better at dealing with drug dogs, directing traffic, or working a crime scene. Police records can reveal that some officers have repeated experiences in using force (sometimes excessive); those officers should receive special attention.

> Ethics education. The police officer's role is complicated. The officer must often make quick decisions that can have significant consequences not only for the maintenance of public order, but also for the probability of identifying perpetrators of crime and making lawful arrests. Many law enforcement administrators believe that ethics education reinforces officers' adherence to departmental policy and procedures and their ability to resolve moral dilemmas.[25]

LEARNING OBJECTIVE 2

Describe the issues inherent in the militarization of police departments.

posse comitatus— "The power or force of the county. The entire population of a county above the age of 15, which a sheriff may summon to his assistance in certain cases as to aid him in keeping the peace, in pursuing and arresting felons, etc." [26]

The Militarization of Police

Traditionally, major distinctions have been made between the roles of the police and those of the military. Police officers are tasked with serving citizens and protecting them from each other, whereas the military is responsible for protecting citizens from foreign threats. This distinction is somewhat codified by the 1878 Posse Comitatus Act (see CJ Reference 6.2).

Posse comitatus, according to *Black's Law Dictionary*, is "the power or force of the county. The entire population of a county above the age of 15, which a sheriff may summon to his assistance in certain cases as to aid him in keeping the peace, in pursuing and arresting felons, etc." [27] The original intent of the Posse Comitatus Act was to end the use of federal troops to monitor state elections in the former Confederate states. [28] In the 20th century, the act was extended to all domestic services with the enactment of Title 10 U.S. Code, Section 375. The act generally prohibits U.S. military personnel from direct participation in law enforcement. [29]

The act does not apply to the U.S. Coast Guard during peacetime; to the National Guard in Title 32 status (when a governor activates the Guard for law enforcement activities); or to the Guard in State Active Duty status (when a governor calls in the Guard in response to disasters or for Homeland Defense missions). [30] Congress has also enacted exceptions to the act that allow the military to assist civilian law enforcement agencies, such as in enforcing drug laws or suppressing insurrections. The act also allows the president to use federal troops to enforce federal laws when rebellion makes it difficult to enforce the law. Another exception allows for the enforcement of prohibitions regarding nuclear materials or biological or chemical weapons of mass destruction when it is determined that an emergency poses a serious threat and is beyond the capability of civilian law enforcement. [31]

CJ REFERENCE 6.2
What is the Posse Comitatus Act?

Section 1385 of Title 18, U.S. Code: The Posse Comitatus Act

Whoever, except in cases and under circumstances expressly authorized by the Constitution or Act of Congress, willfully uses any part of the Army or the Air Force as a posse comitatus or otherwise to execute the laws shall be fined under this title or imprisoned not more than two years, or both. [32]

Section 375 of Title 10 U.S. Code: Restriction on Direct Participation by Military Personnel

The Secretary of Defense shall prescribe such regulations as may be necessary to ensure that any activity (including the provision of any equipment or facility or the assignment or detail of any personnel) under this chapter does not include or permit direct participation by a member of the Army, Navy, Air Force, or Marine Corps in a search, seizure, arrest, or other similar activity unless participation in such activity by such member is otherwise authorized by law.

Despite these regulations, there seems to be nothing preventing the police from using military-style tactics and equipment to enforce the law, and the Posse Comitatus Act contains no language addressing this concern. As such, the general militarization of the police has been under way for a couple of decades.[33] This militarization can be observed in much of the equipment that the police use. Prior to the 1990s, police typically wore tactical gear, such as combat boots, helmets, and bullet-proof vests, only for particularly dangerous activities, such as controlling riots. Occasionally, a SWAT team (special weapons and tactics) was called in to deal with threats such as a hostage crisis or bank robbery. Now, it is quite common to see police dressed in tactical uniforms. During the 2014 riots and protests in Ferguson, Missouri, that arose over the shooting of Michael Brown, police were routinely photographed wearing camouflage uniforms, helmets, and gas masks, while patrolling the streets in heavily armored vehicles.[34] It is instructive to look at how this police militarization has evolved.

The Evolution of Police Militarization

The impetus for the increased militarization of policing was the terrorist attacks on the United States on September 11, 2001. The new "war on terror" and the resulting USA PATRIOT Act radically changed the environment in which police officers operated. Citizens were now willing to cede much more discretion to both national and local governments to prevent terrorism. Border security became a priority, and the police were enlisted to assist the federal government in fighting terrorism.[35] Police militarization has affected the nature of law enforcement in the United States in several ways:

› The relationship between the police and the community. Contemporary police departments have sought to bridge the gap between police officers and citizens. By adopting community policing strategies, police departments try to integrate the officers into the community, thus enabling them to recognize those who violate the law as well as enlist the support of law-abiding citizens in making the community safer. In many communities, however, police militarization has frustrated police officials in their attempts to integrate their officers into everyday community life. Instead of making police officers seem like approachable friends of the community, police militarization has made the police appear to be an invading force, aimed at suppressing everyone in the community, regardless of their orientation to the legal system. In many communities, the police do not live in the community, but rather come from outside of the community; as such, they are often viewed as occupying forces. For instance, in Ferguson, Missouri, protests in response to the 2014 killing of a young black man by a white police officer led to riots in which the majority white police force was challenged by a majority black community. Since then, several more deaths of black men at the hands of police have resulted in protests (sometimes peaceful, sometimes not), riots, and confrontations with the police.[36]

› Reorientation of the police identity. Rather than adopting community-oriented policing practices in which officers identify as part of the community, many officers have adopted the military model: an action-oriented culture in which all citizens are considered potential drug dealers, violent criminals, and terrorists. This military model is more proactive than reactive. Some officers consider community policing as being "soft" on crime and terrorism, especially in minority and immigrant neighborhoods. This attitude promotes an atmosphere of fear and intimidation rather than accommodation to community standards.[37]

> An increase in private policing. Another potential effect of police militarization may be the rise of private police forces in affluent communities. Much like the rise of private prisons to alleviate the problem of crowding in public facilities, there will likely be an increase in paramilitary security around businesses, neighborhoods, and schools.[38]

Police militarization often has the unintended consequences of alienating people from their own police. In our efforts to fight the wars on drugs and terrorism, we have engaged in a war upon ourselves.[39] However, although many citizens object to the presence of heavily armed police officers in public places, other citizens who are fearful of terrorist activities welcome the presence of officers who are equipped to handle situations in which extreme violence can occur.[40]

How should the police be equipped? In the past, the weapons that police departments possessed reflected limited local budgets. Now, armored vehicles, large-caliber rifles, and a variety of other types of military equipment have found their way into the arsenals of local police departments (see A Closer Look 6.1).

The militarization of the police and the war-on-crime analogy are most apparent in the SWAT divisions of police agencies. The SWAT team was first established in 1967 by Los Angeles Police Inspector Daryl Gates in response to the six-day-long 1965 riots that occurred in the Watts neighborhood.[41] Since then, SWAT and other paramilitary police teams have proliferated in response to the wars on drugs and terror, so that now 80 percent of towns with populations less than 50,000 have some form of paramilitary police team.[42] The types of situations in which a SWAT team may be used include, but are not limited to, the following:

1. Protecting police officers engaged in crowd control from sniper attack
2. Providing high-ground and perimeter security for visiting dignitaries

Many critics of police militarization say police officers should not have the same equipment as the military. Proponents of military gear for police say that they need such equipment because so many potential assailants are similarly armed. What is your opinion?

3. Rescuing hostages

4. Providing for the nonviolent apprehension of desperate barricaded suspects

5. Providing control-assault firepower in certain nonriot situations

6. Rescuing officers or citizens endangered by gunfire

7. Neutralizing guerrilla or terrorist operations against government personnel, property, or the general populace

Clearly, there are legitimate reasons to have SWAT teams. Police agencies are occasionally required to perform dangerous tasks. It makes sense to have specially trained officers to respond to unusual situations. However, some critics are concerned that merely having a SWAT team means that it will be employed in situations that can be handled in more routine ways.[47] SWAT deployments have increased more than 1,400 percent since the 1980s, with teams raiding organic

A CLOSER LOOK 6.1
Where Did All This Stuff Come From?

Police departments, especially SWAT teams, are increasingly looking more like military units. They are equipped with weapons and uniforms that make them appear to citizens like an invading army rather than public servants who are on the streets to "serve and protect." At a time when local budgets are stretched to the point of failing to provide for adequate schools, the maintenance of infrastructure, and other essential services, it seems odd that local police departments can afford sophisticated military-grade vehicles and weapons.

Where does all this stuff come from? The answer is the federal government.[43] Through a program called 1033, the government provides surplus military equipment at a steep discount to state and local law enforcement agencies purportedly to help them fight the wars on drugs and terrorism. With the winding down of the wars in Iraq and Afghanistan, millions of dollars' worth of expensive military equipment is no longer needed; therefore, much of this equipment has been made available to police departments. Apparently, the suitability of this equipment to policing civilian populations in the United States has received little consideration.

For example, Los Angeles County has received nine MRAPs (mine-resistant, ambush-protected vehicles) designed for combat operations. In addition to big-ticket items such as helicopters and cargo-transport planes, since 2006, the 1033 program has supplied local law enforcement agencies with 79,288 assault rifles, 205 grenade launchers, 11,959 bayonets, and over $124 million worth of night-vision equipment, including night-vision sniper scopes.[44] More than 8,000 participating agencies have received more than $5.1 billion worth of surplus military equipment since the inception of the 1033 program.[45]

This use of military equipment in the streets and neighborhoods of the United States has raised concerns from organizations across the political spectrum, ranging from the American Heritage foundation to the American Civil Liberties Union. American neighborhoods are not warzones, and police officers should not be treating citizens like enemy combatants. Yet, every year, billions of dollars' worth of military equipment flows from the federal government to state and local police departments. Because the federal government requires that agencies that receive 1033 equipment use it within one year of receipt, departments use the weapons in everyday policing.[46]

Police departments are tasked with the difficult problem of finding a balance between providing officers with sufficient firepower to deal with heavily armed drug dealers, gang members, and potential terrorists while providing day-to-day police services to ordinary citizens. This enabling of the militarization of local police forces competes with more benign law enforcement strategies such as community and problem-oriented policing. Although it is tempting for local officials to accept all this military equipment, many are now questioning the wisdom of the 1033 program.

THINK ABOUT IT

1. How might having military equipment change the way police departments view themselves?

2. How might a heavily armed police department be viewed by citizens of the community?

farms, nightclubs, barbershops, and poker games.[48] An American Civil Liberties Union (ACLU) study has revealed that it has become common for SWAT teams to execute search warrants in drug investigations. Of all the incidents the ACLU report looked at, 79 percent involved the use of a SWAT team to search a private home, and more than 60 percent of the cases involved searches for drugs. The study also found that SWAT teams forced entry into homes using a battering ram or similar device in 65 percent of drug searches. It is unclear how many of these situations were actually dangerous. The SWAT records provided for the study typically did not include information to explain why a situation was considered "high risk."[49] Most jurisdictions do not have policies governing the deployment of SWAT teams, nor do most police departments collect data on SWAT deployments in order to assess their efficacy.[50]

Because of the lack of data, rules, regulations, or laws concerning the use of SWAT teams, the accounts of raids-gone-wrong are often shocking. For instance, On January 5, 2011, a Framingham (Massachusetts) Police Department SWAT team arrived with a warrant to search an apartment rented by 68-year-old Eurie Stamps Sr., who lived there with his wife and her son, Joseph Bushfan, 20. The police wanted to arrest Bushfan whom they believed was a gang member who sold crack cocaine out of the apartment. Bushfan left the apartment minutes before the raid, and police arrested him. However, the officers were also looking for two associates of Bushfan, so they broke down the apartment door and entered. Stamps, who had been watching television in his pajamas, met the 12 officers in the hallway. He complied with their orders to get down on the floor and place his hands near his head. Eleven officers continued to search the apartment, while Officer Paul Duncan stood over Stamps, pointing an M4 rifle at him. Duncan said he was trying to secure Stamps's hands when he became tangled in the tactical apparatus he was wearing, and his rifle went off striking Stamps in the face and chest, killing him instantly.[51] Duncan was not charged in the incident.[52] The police chief disbanded the SWAT team in 2013.[53]

PAUSE AND REVIEW

1. **How has police militarization affected the relationship between police and the communities they serve?**

LEARNING OBJECTIVE 3

Identify the major problems associated with police stress and burnout.

LEARNING OBJECTIVE 4

Outline the four key elements of the policeman's working personality.

Stress and Burnout

In May 1792, Deputy Sheriff Isaac Smith was trying to arrest John Ryer at an inn in what is now the Bronx, New York City. Ryer, who was drunk, shot and killed Smith and fled. Arrested in Canada, Ryer was tried and hanged for the murder in New York in October 1793. Smith is believed to be the first law enforcement officer feloniously killed in the line of duty in the United States.[54]

Law enforcement can be a stressful career. Unlike many occupations, the threat of physical injury or death is a daily possibility. According to the FBI, 41 law enforcement officers were feloniously killed in the line of duty during 2015 (see Figure 6.2).[55] Because the police are the ones called when force must be used, they have the most to fear from violence. Police stress comes in many forms and can exert different types of strain on officers, their families, and the police agency.[56] It can be physical, emotional, social, marital, chemical, or occupational. At times, several types of stress can be experienced simultaneously. The job of police officer invites stress, and the way police agencies structure assignments, shifts, support, and discipline contributes to the anxiety and strain of the job.[57]

Pictured here are Columbus Police SWAT officers after loading the coffin of Officer Steve Smith during services in Westerville, Ohio. Smith was shot while trying to serve a warrant and died two days later. Is the prospect of dying on the job the most stressful circumstance that police face?

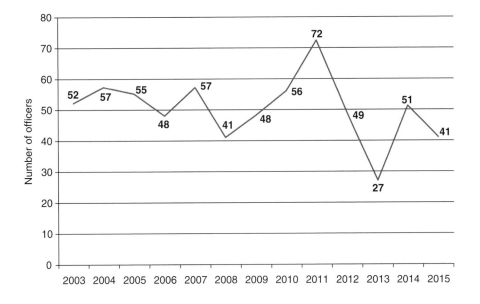

FIGURE 6.2 Number of Law Enforcement Officers Killed During the Commission of Felonies, 2003–2015 Between 2003 and 2015, what was the average number of law enforcement officers killed per year during the commission of a felony? Discuss how this relatively high statistic can contribute to stress.

Source: Federal Bureau of Investigation, Law Enforcement Officers Killed and Assaulted 2015, Law Enforcement Officers Feloniously Killed Circumstance at Scene of Incident, 2006–2015, Table 23, https://ucr.fbi.gov/leoka/2015/tables/table_23_leos_fk_circumstance_at_scene_of_incident_2006-2015.xls.

Police and Alcohol

Research has found that the stress of police work is highly related to alcohol abuse. Other coping mechanisms, such as emotional distancing (officers learn to objectify their emotions when faced with dead or injured people, victims, abused children, and so on) and cynicism, were found to be related to alcohol use either directly or indirectly. Studies found that alcohol was used as a method to relieve the inherent stress of police work 20 times as often as cynicism or emotional distancing. In fact, when those methods failed, alcohol use became more likely.[58]

The stress of police work might not be the only factor influencing police officers to turn to alcohol. The police subculture also tends to exert a powerful influence on drinking patterns, as it tests trustworthiness, loyalty, and masculinity.

Additionally, it might act as an obstacle to the reporting of a fellow officer with a drinking problem. Consider the following:

1. The police subculture might socialize new officers into accepting a pattern of after-shift alcohol consumption. New employees are anxious to fit into the group. In many occupations, the older workers want to know whether the new person can be trusted. In police work, in which the officer must depend on his or her partner, there is pressure to judge each other's reliability quickly. Learning what "makes the other person tick" through after-hours socializing is an important part of this judgment process. New officers are judged by their peers to "fit in" to the extent that they can hold their liquor; articulate the occupational worldview of the police subculture; and accept and participate in complaining about citizens, politicians, and superiors.

2. Socialization in the police subculture establishes that drinking alcohol is not deviant. Because "everyone drinks after work," alcohol consumption is soon viewed as normal behavior. Whereas in other circumstances, consistent and excessive alcohol consumption may be viewed as a problem, in police work it just means that an officer is "one of the guys." When embarrassing incidents happen or family problems emerge because of alcohol, these issues are turned into amusing stories that are told over and over in future drinking bouts as evidence that "civilians don't understand police work."

3. This normalization of alcohol consumption may preclude treatment because "all of my friends drink." One of the issues that can lead people to seek treatment for their drug or alcohol addiction is the embarrassment it can cause in the workplace. To the extent that alcohol use is the norm among one's contemporaries, its abuse is not a cause for concern, and its treatment may be viewed as a weakness or even a betrayal of the work group. When a fellow officer is forced to admit that alcohol is a problem, other officers might feel uncomfortable examining their own drinking patterns. A reformed drinker can sometimes help his or her friends, but often the friends continue to maintain their lifestyle, and an unspoken barrier is erected.

The effect of alcohol on the police has not been lost on police administrators.[59] As with many other agencies and corporations, personnel policies are geared toward ensuring that the police maintain good health and do not put the force at risk of lawsuits because of unfitness for duty. In the past several years, many public safety organizations have instituted drug and alcohol testing to ensure that police officers are capable of performing their assignments.[60] Assistance is offered to those who need help, and continued failures to meet departmental standards can be cause for dismissal. This extreme remedy is more likely to be used for those found to be taking illegal drugs than it is for those who abuse alcohol, but police agencies are more attuned to the effects of intoxication now than they have been in the past.

Family Problems and the Police

The individual police officer is not the only one affected by the stress of police work. Having a spouse or parent as a police officer can be a source of pride, but it can also be a source of worry and concern.[61] Often, family members experience several stressful concerns.[62] The first of these is the change in the personality of the police officer and his or her relationship with a spouse and/or children.

Police families experience stress when the police officer brings the job home and treats his or her spouse and children like potential suspects. The simple question, "Where are you going?" might be viewed as an interrogation rather than a normal concern. Children of police officers might be held to a higher standard of etiquette as the officer demands that they show proper respect and deference.[63]

Isolation is another issue that police officers and their families face, and it can take on two forms. The officer might not express the stress that comes from the job to the family, and he or she could appear withdrawn and uninterested in the family's concerns. Additionally, the family might be treated with hostility by neighbors who believe they are being watched by the police officer. On one hand, integrating into the community is desirable; on the other hand, it might become problematic when the members of the community see the police as a threat.

The dangers associated with police work can also be a source of stress for officers' family members.[64] Knowing that one's spouse or parent is potentially just one radio call away from a deranged person with a gun can keep one in an uneasy state of mind. If each phone call could be the police commissioner calling to say there has been a shooting, it is only natural that some family members would suggest the police officer find less dangerous work. Family members' pressure on the police officer about the job can create a dilemma. Feeling both loyalty to the job and responsibility to the family can result in the officer internalizing stress and, as a result, doing a bad job at both family life and policing.[65]

Police and Suicide

Suicide is an occupational hazard for police officers.[66] Several studies have shown that law enforcement has one of the highest suicide rates of any occupation. Small police departments have higher suicide rates than large departments owing to increased workloads and scarcity of mental health resources.[67] Given the preceding discussion about police stress and its contributions to alcohol abuse and family problems, it should not be too surprising to learn that suicide also concerns the police and their families. There is evidence that police officers are at a higher risk of committing homicide–suicide—killing a family member or members, then

In July 2016, five police officers were killed in Dallas, Texas, by a sniper. Pictured here are the widow and son of one of the slain officers. What other dangers do the family members of police officers worry about?

themselves—than civilians, with domestic violence and divorce or estrangement being prominent predictors.[68]

Five aspects of policing are associated with risk of suicidal ideation (thinking about suicide): organizational stress, trauma from critical incidents, shift work, relationship problems, and alcohol use and abuse. There is extensive evidence that people who have persistent, stressful traumatic experiences are at increased risk for suicidal ideation. Seeing human beings dead days or weeks after they are first reported missing can be stressful. Watching families fall apart because of poverty, drugs, or abuse can cause some officers to become depressed. Dealing with a mentally ill offender who is armed with a gun and having to shoot to protect other people can deeply affect police officers.

One study found that subjects who both experienced symptoms of traumatic stress and used alcohol were four times more likely to think about suicide. However, aspects of police work such as organizational stress and shift work may be more troublesome than is commonly believed. Erratic work shifts and insufficient sleep have long been identified as risk factors for suicidal ideation among physicians and other emergency personnel.[69] Additionally, the very nature of the criminal justice system can cause officers to become frustrated when they do their jobs well, only to find the offender set free to victimize others. The police must deal with the underside of society, and after a time, unless officers find ways to cope with the stress in a healthy manner, the job can become overwhelming.[70]

Why would police officers resort to suicide at rates higher than those in most other occupations? The answer lies in the types of stress we have already discussed and in the access the police have to handguns. Firearms are a constant feature in the lives of police officers. About 97 percent of officer suicides involve the officer's own service gun.[71] Police officers are trained in the use of guns, carry them on a daily basis, are prepared emotionally to use guns in the pursuit of lawbreakers, and so have been sufficiently desensitized to the effects of guns.

It is hard to think of any other occupation, including the military, in which guns are such a constant part of the job. In fact, the phrase "he ate his gun," is part of the police lexicon. It is unfair, however, to argue that the gun is solely responsible for police suicide rates. Although firearms are an efficient way to kill oneself, a determined person will find a way regardless of whether there is a convenient gun. It just happens that for police officers, there is always a convenient gun.

Dealing with the Stress of Policing

Although many occupations can stress their practitioners, policing seems to have some special features that, although recognized in the literature on policing, have been neglected by police agencies. Certainly, police departments' human resources divisions have implemented policies aimed at helping individual officers, and community programs that are available to all citizens are also available to the police, but police officers often shun these resources.[72] Within the police subculture, an attitude exists that to admit stress to the administration or to outsiders is a sign of weakness.

To successfully reduce police stress to manageable levels, police agencies, city or county administrations, and police officers themselves can use several strategies. Revisiting the effect of rotating officers' shifts is a first step in reforming policing. Officers have family responsibilities that suffer when the officer has no control over his or her working hours. The problems of sleep deprivation are known but sometimes appear to be ignored by police administrators. Making unattractive shifts more desirable for officers can be accomplished by paying more to those who are willing to assume the hardships.[73]

Another method of addressing the stress of police work is reducing the paramilitary focus that some departments have adopted. As was previously discussed, the military is a poor model on which to pattern a police department. Additionally, the police mission is considerably broader than the military mission, which concentrates on the use of force.

Finally, the move toward more community policing activities seems like a promising strategy to make police work less stressful. To the extent that the police become integrated into the community, it can be expected that their work will be not only more effective, but also more socially rewarding.

The Police Subculture

The style of policing adopted by an officer is influenced by that officer's personal characteristics in coping with the demands of the job and with family members and friends. Like many occupations, policing imposes a lifestyle that might set the police officer apart from civilians in terms of sociability, social integration, and social acceptance.[74] Sometimes police officers are not invited to parties because people fear their reaction to rowdy behavior. The police often do not want to interact socially with others because their occupation tags them with a status that causes others to treat them as a "cop."[75] Also, the police develop the policeman's working personality, which explains how police officers are drawn into a subculture that emphasizes a different set of values from those held by mainstream society.[76] Therefore, it is useful to consider the concept of the policeman's working personality in some detail by examining some of its key elements.

1. The symbolic assailant. Police officers must always be on guard. They are systematically trained and culturally reinforced to consider everyone a potential assailant until they can size up the situation and determine that an individual poses no threat. This is easy to do when confronted with a large, drunk, belligerent man wielding a knife. It is less easy when interacting with an elderly woman who seems lost and disoriented. Police officers will not relax until they are confident that the woman poses no harm to herself or others. They cannot assume that she is of no threat until they can independently establish that she is what she seems to be, which is accomplished based on behavioral and contextual clues. The situation of the knife-wielding man, on the other hand, alerts officers to keep their guard up.

2. Danger. Police work can be dangerous (see Figure 6.3). Although death in the line of duty and serious physical injury are relatively infrequent, the possibility of confrontation is always there. Actually, police are drawn to the more dangerous assignments, as a function of both job prestige and excitement.[77]

3. Social isolation. The public treats police officers differently. Whereas police officers may perceive an individual as a symbolic assailant, the public sees the police officer as a symbolic authority figure. Thus, even when an individual has done nothing wrong, he or she might be wary of an officer because of the perceived power the officer has to detain, question, search, and arrest. Social isolation causes many officers to limit their social interactions to situations in which other officers are around.

4. Solidarity. The combination of danger and social isolation creates a sense of solidarity in the police subculture. An "us against them" mentality exists to cope not only with law violators, but also with the public in general. The police may feel that the public takes them for granted and does not take enough responsibility for helping to fight the war against lawbreakers.[78]

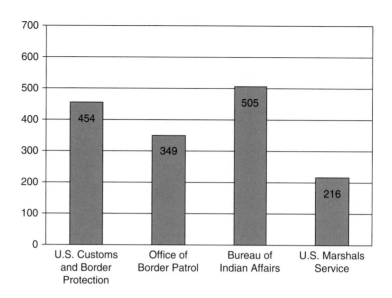

FIGURE 6.3   Federal Law Enforcement Officers Killed and Assaulted, 2015 The U.S. Customs and Border Protection Service, the Office of Border Patrol, the Bureau of Indian Affairs, and the U.S. Marshals Service are the four federal law enforcement agencies in which officers are most likely to be killed or assaulted. What are some possible reasons for this?

Source: Federal Bureau of Investigation, Law Enforcement Officers Killed and Assaulted, Table 123: Department and Agency by Number of Victim Officers and Known Offenders, 2014–2015, https://ucr.fbi.gov/leoka/2015/tables/table_123-fed_leos_k_and_a_department_and_agency_by_number_of_vos_and_known_offenders_2014-2015.xls.

The occupational culture of the police, like many other occupational cultures, fosters certain personality characteristics in its practitioners.[79] Danger, authority, potential symbolic assailants, and social isolation are features of the occupation that encourage the construction of the policeman's working personality. This process may have far-reaching implications for the recruitment, training, and control of police officers.[80] For example, how much money and resources should be spent on the selection and training of officers if the very nature of law enforcement occupations instills those individuals with an occupational perspective that dictates how they view the job and respond to suspects and the public?

Police Corruption

Although police corruption has been a significant problem for some agencies at particular times, it is likely not as pervasive as the issues of the policeman's working personality. However, the nature and extent of police corruption are worth our attention because of the constant temptations placed before police officers and because trust in the criminal justice system is one of the cornerstones of a democratic society.[81] The history of policing is replete with examples not only of corruption of individual officers, but also of the widespread, systemic corruption of entire departments and the municipal governments they serve.[82] Unfortunately, no official statistics are kept on the prevalence of police corruption, so it is difficult to estimate how much occurs.

In 1972, the Knapp Commission issued its report on police corruption in New York City. Based on the revelations made by undercover detective Frank Serpico, 19 officers were indicted for accepting payoffs. Subsequent investigations revealed even more violators. In examining this systematic corruption, the Knapp Commission distinguished between two types of corrupt police officers: "meat-eaters" and "grass-eaters." The grass-eaters took bribes but did not solicit them. The meat-eaters actively sought situations that they could exploit for financial gain.[83]

Not all police officers have equal opportunities to engage in corruption. The nature of the department, the community, and the particular assignment all influence how much temptation is placed in the officers' paths or how fertile the situation is for the meat-eater who aggressively seeks situations to exploit. Historically, illegal gambling, prostitution, substance prohibition, and other organized-crime activities have been major sources of police corruption. Presently, because of the war on drugs, tremendous amounts of money are changing hands, putting narcotics officers in positions to engage in corrupt acts. According to scholars Peter K. Manning and Lawrence John Redlinger, narcotics law enforcement can invite police corruption in at least seven ways.

1. Taking bribes. Officers can take bribes in several ways. They can provide advance warning of police raids, or they can take bribes not to arrest those caught using or selling drugs. Additionally, police officers are reported to have testified badly in a case in exchange for a bribe.

2. Using drugs. On occasion, police officers might use the very drugs they are mandated to suppress. Additionally, they might use other drugs to stay awake. The incidence of police officers using illegal drugs is probably not as serious a problem today as it might have been a generation ago. Many police agencies require random drug tests of employees, which deters illegal drug use.

3. Buying and selling narcotics. It may seem incredible that narcotics officers would deal in drugs, but in some circumstances, this type of corruption might seem reasonable to an officer. Police may give drugs to addicts to acquire their sworn testimony or to informers to pay them off. Given limited budgets for operating expenditures such as "buy money," enterprising narcotics agents might use drugs to finance operations the department cannot afford. However, these activities are still considered a form of corruption and are not sanctioned by police administrators. Finally, "meat-eating" officers have been known to sell narcotics and use the money for personal gain.[84]

4. Appropriating seized property. Property relevant to a criminal offense must be seized by the police department and held until the case is concluded, at which point the department determines whether to return it to its rightful owner, destroy it, or convert it to government use. The police must scrupulously account for all seized cash, drugs, guns, and automobiles. Although cash used by police to buy drugs is marked and the serial numbers are recorded, the cash seized from drug dealers is subject to theft by the arresting officers. Some of the cash and drugs seized at a crime scene might be diverted before they are officially logged as evidence.

5. Conducting illegal searches and seizures. Police can engage in corrupt misconduct in several ways when initiating searches and seizures on drug suspects. Lying about smelling marijuana or seeing drugs in "plain sight" is one method officers can use to claim probable cause to conduct a search. Officers may plant evidence on a suspect by "flaking," which consists of finding evidence the officer planted on the suspect, or "padding," the practice of adding drugs to a seizure to justify a raise in the charge from misdemeanor to felony. The police can use these practices to entice drug dealers and users to offer bribes of cash or sexual favors for lenient treatment.

6. Protecting informants. Sometimes the police are willing to tolerate a certain level of crime to battle more serious infractions. This becomes a judgment call that can lead to substantial harm to victims, the community, and the reputation of the law enforcement agencies. Both within and between criminal justice agencies there are rivalries, competition, and distrust. The narcotics division might overlook the burglaries of a confidential

informant if it is receiving good information that may facilitate the bust of a big drug dealer. A federal agency might hide the offenses of a snitch from a local police department if doing so furthers its agenda. Informants might coax all kinds of rewards, such as money, drugs, or reduced charges, from several agencies at the same time based on the promise of the same information.

7. Using violence. Narcotics officers might use unwarranted violence to cope with drug dealers. They might claim the suspect "went for his gun" and then kill the suspect. They might threaten to tell others in the drug trade that the suspect is an informant, ensuring that person's violent death at the hands of others. The police might use illegal force in a number of ways that enables them to prosecute or extort lawbreakers.[85]

These forms of police behavior all represent some type of corruption. They might sometimes be used to advance the cause of legitimate police work, but because they are illegal, they are of concern to police administrators and police scholars. A department that allows its officers to operate in devious ways inevitably exposes itself to the scandal of corruption and the problems of litigation.[86] Therefore, it seems prudent to consider these types of corruption as pressing issues within law enforcement.

PAUSE AND REVIEW

1. What factors, besides stress, influence police officers to turn to alcohol?
2. In what ways do the four key elements of the policeman's working personality contribute to the police subculture?

LEARNING OBJECTIVE 5

Argue for and against the use of less-than-lethal weapons.

LEARNING OBJECTIVE 6

Define information technology and describe how it may be incorporated into police work.

Policing and Technology

Many of the recent innovations in law enforcement are related to law enforcement transparency, citizen safety, and the ability to acquire and store information about law-abiding people, suspects, and offenders. For example, videos posted to the Internet and social media have revealed the controversial treatment of some suspects by police, including beatings and shootings, thus provoking a public call for greater police transparency in their activities. Efforts to control violent individuals and crowds in order to protect citizens have led to the development of less-than-lethal weapons. Finally, the need for increased national security and the desire for citizen safety have led to increased active acquisition of information about U.S. residents. Thus, body-worn cameras for police officers, less-than-lethal weapons, and information technology are new tools that have greatly affected policing in the United States.

Body-Worn Cameras

Body-worn cameras are devices that record interactions between police officers and the public. Officers usually wear the camera on the shoulder lapel or chest so that it can record the scene in front of the officer. Law enforcement can use these recordings to document statements, observations, and other evidence, and to deter inappropriate behaviors by both police officers and the public.[87]

In light of some recent controversial police shootings, and given the pace of technological advance in the last two decades, many observers assert that the obvious solution is for police officers to wear body cameras. One of the most highly regarded studies on body-worn cameras, conducted by the Rialto, California, Police

Department, found that equipping officers with cameras reduced use-of-force incidents by 50 percent and complaints against officers by 90 percent.[88] Another study revealed that some law enforcement administrators believe that body-worn cameras are useful for the following reasons:

> Cameras strengthen police accountability by documenting encounters between officers and the public, as well as provide video evidence for the public.

> Cameras prevent confrontations by improving officer professionalism and the behavior of the individuals who are being recorded.

> Camera recordings reveal internal agency problems by disclosing any officer misconduct.

> Camera recordings may be used for training and monitoring, as well as provide evidence for investigations and prosecutions.[89]

In May 2015, the Department of Justice awarded $23.2 million in grants to 73 local and tribal agencies in 32 states to expand the use of body-worn cameras and to research their effects.[90] Jurisdictions that received grants include Los Angeles, the District of Columbia, Miami-Dade County, Chicago, Detroit, and San Antonio, Texas.[91]

In jurisdictions in which officers are already wearing cameras, the handling of camera video has become increasingly contentious. States that restrict the public release of body-camera video say doing so could hinder investigations and trials by tainting witnesses and jurors. However, the ACLU asserts that not allowing the release of body-camera video defeats the purpose of recording it in the first place.[92] As of 2016, 30 states had passed legislation concerning police body-camera recordings.[93]

Meanwhile, videos of police confrontations, often recorded by bystanders on their mobile phones, continue to be posted on the Internet. Although the Internet contains many portrayals of the police assisting individuals, unfortunately it is the violent incidents that receive the most attention. As such, the public is demanding more scrutiny of the police and additional accountability in how they

Here, a Los Angeles police officer wears a body camera during a demonstration. Some jurisdictions allow police officers to control their cameras, turning them on or off when they wish. What are the possible reasons why police officers might have their cameras turned off?

do their jobs. Currently, the question seems to be not if police body-worn cameras will be implemented, but how quickly and what the policies will be. Each state will make its own laws governing the implementation of the cameras and the release of recordings. Many of these laws will likely see courtroom challenges over issues such as officer discretion in when they turn on their cameras, what the police department does with the video, and who—the police department or the state—gets to decide if and when to release the video. As such, the following is a partial list of policy recommendations from the U.S. Department of Justice based on research conducted by the Police Executive Research Forum and the Office of Community Oriented Policing.

> ❯ With some exceptions, officers should be required to activate their cameras during all law enforcement-related activities while the officer is on duty. Officers should be required to give their reasoning if they fail to record an activity that is required to be recorded.

> ❯ Officers should be allowed to review video of an incident in which they were involved prior to making a statement about the incident.

> ❯ Officers should be required to obtain crime victims' consent before recording interviews. Officers should have the discretion to deactivate their cameras while talking with witnesses and community members. However, because of the evidentiary importance of such statements, officers should attempt to record unless the person is unwilling to be recorded.

> ❯ Agencies should have clear and consistent rules for releasing video to the public and the media. Agency policy must comply with the state's public disclosure laws.[94]

Police Surveillance

The police use many methods to conduct surveillance on the public. Depending on the jurisdiction, the police may use automatic license plate readers; closed-circuit television; unmanned aerial systems (drones) carrying live-feed video and infrared cameras, heat sensors, and/or radar; microphones; cell-site simulators (sometimes called "stingrays") that track the locations of mobile phones; and software to monitor the Internet and social media.[95] Some jurisdictions may use only one of these methods, or a combination of some or all of them. For example, the Fresno, California, police department's Real Time Crime Center uses city, school, and traffic cameras; a vehicle license-plate database; a citywide microphone system to triangulate the location of gunshots; social media software that combs the Internet for threatening posts and communications; and software that assesses the threat level of individual suspects using information gleaned from arrest records, property records, and social media postings.[96]

It is not clear how much surveillance technology particular departments have or exactly how they are using it. However, every year an increasing number of local police departments are acquiring more and different types of technology from both the federal government and private companies. For example, cell-site simulators, which were designed for the government to track individuals suspected of terrorism, are now being used by local police departments to solve minor street crimes such as robberies, thefts, and fraud. The FBI, which provides police departments with cell-site simulators, requires that the departments keep them a secret. Rather than reveal that a police department is using a cell-site simulator, prosecutors often drop cases rather than answer questions about them in court. Although some jurisdictions require law enforcement to obtain a warrant before conducting such surveillance, police departments do not always do so and have even tried to hide their use of cell-site simulators.[97]

Because legislation typically lags behind technology, there are relatively few laws—and in some jurisdictions no laws—that specify exactly how police departments may obtain and use surveillance technology.[98] Often, police departments may acquire surveillance technology without the community's knowledge. In 2014, the Bellingham, Washington, city council had to hold a public hearing to discourage its police department from using a federal grant to purchase the same social media analysis software used in Fresno, California.[99] Meanwhile, jurisdictions across the country are introducing legislation to require community oversight of police acquisition and use of surveillance technology.[100] For instance, a Seattle, Washington, ordinance requires city council approval before any city department acquires surveillance equipment.[101] The issues concerning the use, incidence, and methods of police surveillance are still developing because the technology is evolving so quickly that it is allowing both federal and local law enforcement to utilize increasingly advanced methods to keep tabs on the activities of the American public.[102]

Less-Than-Lethal Weapons

For several decades, law enforcement has been looking for, developing, and testing weapons that immobilize and repel human beings but do not kill them. Although these types of weapons are known as nonlethal weapons, several of them have killed people. Therefore, the correct term for these weapons is less-than-lethal (LTL) because, although they might cause fatalities or serious injury, they are not intended to kill.[103] The ideal LTL weapon, one that never causes fatalities and is perfectly safe and easy to use in all situations, does not exist.[104] However, governments and private industry are still working with various tactics and substances to produce an effective LTL weapon. (See Table 6.1 for a brief history of the different types of LTL weapons.) The percentage of local police departments that authorized the use of conducted-energy weapons such as Tasers and stun guns rose from 7 percent in 2000 to 81 percent in 2013. Also in 2013, about 90 percent of departments authorized the use of pepper spray and batons.[105]

The arguments in support of LTL weapons point to the fact that they are not intended to cause fatalities while also protecting police. In many instances throughout the world, police have been outnumbered by rioting crowds and barely able to protect themselves, much less the property or the lives of others. Crowd control is a critical issue, especially in urban areas and at public events.

The primary critique of LTL weapons is that, although their use does result in fewer fatalities than the use of firearms, there is the potential for misuse and their adoption as substitutes for "intelligent and professional policing and soldiering."[106] Critics fear that instead of addressing the root of social problems, governments will simply rely on the use of reduced force through police departments and militaries—which are increasingly becoming involved in police-style actions—to control populaces.[107]

DNA Databases

Information technology is technology that helps to manage information by collecting it, storing it, retrieving it, and/or sending it. Several types of technology—not just computers or personal information devices—can be considered information

TABLE 6.1   Less-Than-Lethal Weaponry

	WEAPON	ERA	USAGE AND EFFECTS
Kinetic impact munitions	Guard rounds	World War II	Copper-clad bullets used by sentries that had fluted cartridges to lessen their impact. Shot with conventional guns, guard rounds were designed not to inflict injury in case a sentry accidentally shot a friendly soldier.[1]
	Rock salt	1930s	During the Great Depression, train guards loaded shotguns with rock salt to keep unauthorized riders off freight trains.[2]
	Teak-wood batons	1960s	In Hong Kong, British soldiers fired teak-wood batons from flare guns to disperse crowds. The batons were fired at the ground and skipped up to hit targets at the knees. However, a baton was known to have killed at least one person.[3]
	Rubber and plastic bullets, chemical filled "paintballs," beanbags, bird-shot	1970s–current	Fired from low-velocity shot guns and flare guns. Intended to cause pain and bruising with no permanent injury. Some projectiles might contain chemicals to cause stinging and burning on contact. At least one person has died from being struck with a beanbag in the chest. Some projectiles can penetrate the body.[4]
Chemical	CN gas (Mace)	1960s, with limited current use	Both are forms of tear gas. The newer CS is more potent and less toxic than CN. Both types of gas canisters are thrown by hand or fired from a special gun. CN and CS affect primarily the eyes and skin.
	CS gas	current	
	Pepper spray (oleoresin capsicum)	current	Causes a burning sensation in the mucus membranes, eyes, and skin. Usually safe, with few side effects. Originally made with a substance from chili peppers.[5]
	Superlubricants and superadhesives	current	"Goo" that is usually extremely sticky or extremely slippery.
Electroshock and microwave	Taser	Current	Uses a compressed-gas cartridge to launch two probes up to 35 feet. The probes have wires that attach to skin and clothing. The Taser can deliver 3,000 volts through about 2 inches of clothing.[6] The shock affects the voluntary nervous system and prevents coordinated activity.[7]
	Stun gun	1980s	The stun gun resembled an electric razor and has to touch the body to deliver a shock. In New York City, several officers and sergeants were charged with using stun guns on suspects during interrogations.[8]
	Active denial technology	developing	Generates and emits microwaves that cause a burning sensation in the skin in both crowds and targeted individuals.[9]
Audio and visual munitions	Flash-bang grenades, the Long Range Acoustic Device, laser blinding devices	current and developing	These "light–sound" devices divert or confuse targets. The Long Range Acoustic Device can make a sound that can inflict an instant headache on anyone within about 1,000 feet.[10] Laser blinding devices use light to temporarily blind or disorient targets.

	WEAPON	ERA	USAGE AND EFFECTS
Mechanical	Entanglements	current	Nets, usually launched by a low-velocity gun or other launch device.
	Water	current	High-pressure streams of water launched from cannons or hoses.

[1]Alan Dobrowolski and Sue Moore, "Less Lethal Weapons and Their Impact on Patient Care," *Topics in Emergency Medicine* 27, no. 1 (January–March 2005): 45.

[2-5]Ibid.

[6]Al Baker, "Tasers Getting More Prominent Role in Crime Fighting in City," *New York Times*, June 15, 2008, late edition, A25.

[7]Dobrowolski and Moore, "Less Lethal Weapons and Their Impact on Patient Care."

[8]Ibid.

[9]"The Future of Crowd Control," *Economist*, December 4, 2004, 11.

[10]Ibid.

technology. Over the past few decades, local police departments have gradually integrated information technology into their work. As the technology improves and becomes more economical to purchase and use, devices such as body cameras and in-vehicle computers are expected to become more common.

> As of 2013, about a third of local police departments used body cameras, and one-sixth used automated vehicle license-plate readers.

> In more than 90 percent of departments that served 25,000 or more residents, officers had in-vehicle computers to access vehicle records, driving records, and outstanding warrants.

> Among departments serving 10,000 or more residents, more than 90 percent maintained a website, and more than 80 percent used other forms of social media.[108]

One of the most important technological innovations has been the computerized database. Large police departments have their own computer networks. Small departments with lower budgets might hire a private, third-party company to maintain their databases. Some jurisdictions combine their databases or allow other jurisdictions access.[109]

A particularly useful and controversial type of database is the DNA database. DNA, or deoxyribonucleic acid, is the material in living organisms that determines heredity, and nearly every cell in a person's body has the same DNA. This makes DNA especially useful for identifying individuals. Currently, the military keeps DNA records of all in service, and, as of 2015, 28 states collect DNA from felony arrestees, with 22 states limiting samples to convicted offenders.[110]

The National DNA Index System (NDIS) grew out of the FBI's Combined DNA Index System (CODIS), a project begun in 1990. All 50 states and the federal government require some types of convicted offenders to provide a DNA sample for inclusion in CODIS and state databases.[111] Currently, more than 170 public law enforcement laboratories participate in NDIS, and more than 40 law enforcement laboratories in more than 25 countries use the CODIS software. CODIS has indices for convicted offenders, forensic evidence, arrestees, missing persons, and unidentified human remains. CODIS generates leads in cases in which biological evidence is recovered from a crime scene. For example, a profile that has matches in both the forensic evidence and convicted offender indices can provide a suspect's identity.[112]

Biologically related people share some DNA, so one person's DNA can provide information about his or her sibling, parent, or other biological relative. Some observers say that profiling DNA in this manner can target innocent people by placing them under police surveillance and violating their Fourth Amendment protection against unreasonable search and seizure.[113] However, DNA used in just this manner ended the 30-year killing spree of Dennis Rader (the BTK killer). The police, who suspected Rader, collected his daughter's DNA without her knowledge by acquiring a Pap smear specimen she had given five years earlier at a university medical clinic. The woman's DNA closely matched the DNA collected from Rader's crime scenes, suggesting that the woman was the killer's child and giving the police enough evidence to arrest Rader.[114]

PAUSE AND REVIEW

1. **In addition to the advantages provided by new technologies for detecting and dealing with crime, can you think of some possible problematic effects of these changes on society?**

LEARNING
OBJECTIVE **7**

Name arguments
historically used to exclude
women from policing
and criticisms of those
arguments.

LEARNING
OBJECTIVE **8**

Define the concept of
double marginality.

gender—The socially constructed roles, behaviors, actions, and characteristics that a society considers appropriate for males and females.

Sex and Race

Sex, **gender**, social class, and race are important issues in the study of law enforcement.[115] The quality of justice and the efficiency of police work are both dependent on, and a factor in, how well the police agency can win the confidence of the community. When the police are viewed as promoting and protecting only the interests of certain races, genders, or social groups, the criminal justice system is considered an instrument of the powerful and an oppressor of the weak.

It would be a mistake, however, to view the inclusion of women and minorities in police work as a simple matter of politics. Diversity in criminal justice personnel adds more than the appearance of sexual or racial equity. Including women and minorities in the criminal justice system provides a broader array of tools to control crime and develop meaningful communities. It is useful, then, to examine both sex and race as characteristics of both police officers and offenders.

Women as Police Officers

One of the main objectives of establishing social and economic equality for women has been to allow them access to previously all-male occupations. In the past 50 years, women have overcome barriers to employment in private professions, the military, and the criminal justice system. Female judges, prosecutors, and corrections administrators are so familiar in the 21st century that few ever remark on their suitability for their jobs. The same is becoming true of female police officers. Women are seen on virtually every large or medium-size police force, and they hold positions of leadership in many of them.

The road to equality for female police officers has been a rocky one, and for the most part, it is not yet complete.[116] Women make up only about 12 percent of the total number of officers in local law enforcement, and departments in larger jurisdictions employ higher percentages of women than do smaller jurisdictions.[117] The culture of the police force is still grounded in what many consider to be male

Many women around the country are moving into positions of leadership in law enforcement agencies. Are there still obstacles that females need to overcome to be accepted as law enforcement officers?

values, and the progress women are making in breaking down the barriers of sexism is incremental, sporadic, sometimes costly, and fraught with ambiguity. The resistance to female police officers from the public, male-dominated police administrations, fellow police officers, and even their own family members has caused many women to abandon their police careers.[118]

Before the integration of women into police forces, police officers saw their jobs as involving danger, violence, aggression, isolation, and authority.[119] These concerns were considered to be exclusive to men and legitimate reasons to keep women off the force. Women were stereotyped as being physically weak and emotionally fragile and thus ill suited for police work. The entries they did gain into police departments were as ancillary and support personnel, working as dispatchers or with youths and children.[120] The idea of women in uniform and on patrol was not seriously considered. Job qualifications for police officers stated that the applicant had to be male or referred to police officers as "him" and "he." The concept of female police officers was not seriously considered in almost all jurisdictions.

Of course, singling out policing for being reluctant to accord women full occupational equity is unfair because this form of sexism was the norm in society until relatively recently. It is interesting, however, to look at how police have responded to the demand for women's rights because police work had been considered one of the occupations that most justified that exclusion.[121] Arguments against women in policing included the following:

1. Women are not physically strong enough to be police officers. Police work can sometimes require the officer to fight a large, young, strapping, intoxicated, angry male offender. This is a dangerous task that often results in physical injury to the officer. Critics of this objection point out that only a few police officers can win a street fight with young, athletically gifted males. Police officers are required to use their powers of persuasion to make arrests without fighting, to use their weapons when their safety

or the safety of others is at risk, and to depend on other officers to help subdue the suspects, tasks of which women are capable. Female recruits must pass physical testing just as male recruits do, so properly handling a violent situation really depends on which police officers maintain their readiness.

2. Women bring different psychological attributes to police work. Critics of women in policing contend that "women, because they are more compassionate, less aggressive, and less competitive, see their job from a different perspective and hence adopt different policing styles than do men."[122] Advocates for women in policing agree, adding that the aggressive and competitive perspective brought to the street by male police officers is appropriate for only part of the police mission, and a small part at that. The emphasis on crime control must coexist with an emphasis on order maintenance and social support. The mindset brought by women who have been socialized into the roles of caregiving and nurturing significantly expands the nature of the police role.

In summary, the increased participation of women in policing has provided some important sociological lessons. There is more than one way to be a good police officer. According to some studies, the historically male-dominated police culture has been enriched by the inclusion of women, who bring different perspectives to the job. At one time, it was believed that the police subculture shaped recruits into a **policeman's working personality** that was determined by danger, violence, aggression, isolation, and authority. Now the culture appears to be changing as women introduce other values into the culture of policing.[123]

policeman's working personality—The mindset of police who must deal with danger, authority, isolation, and suspicion while appearing to be efficient.

Minorities as Police Officers

The United States has a checkered past in its treatment of minorities, and the criminal justice system has experienced its own stresses in accommodating the inevitable progress of opening occupations to people who have experienced prejudice and discrimination.[124] Historically, law enforcement has not led the way in providing equality to disenfranchised groups. However, some progress has been made, and the rate of improvement has increased with each passing decade.[125]

At times in the distant past, people of color worked as law enforcement officers, though only rarely and discontinuously. People of color were first employed as police officers in New Orleans in 1805. The officers were former African slaves who had won their freedom by serving with the French or Spanish militia, and they acted primarily to keep slaves under control and to catch runaways. These police gradually lost their jobs to whites and did not engage in law enforcement again until after the Civil War. During Reconstruction, former slaves enjoyed a brief period during which they performed the same type of law enforcement duties as whites. This period of occupational equality was also brief, and soon, as in other aspects of politics, law enforcement was completely dominated by whites. With the exception of tokenism brought on by political patronage in northern cities, police officers of color had few opportunities. Even when they were allowed into the occupation, their roles were greatly limited. People of color were responsible for policing their neighborhoods and were not allowed the full range of duties or to advance into administration.[126]

A new era of opportunity for people of color in all aspects of society began during the civil rights movement in the 1950s and continues today. Led by influential individuals such as Dr. Martin Luther King Jr., the civil rights movement called attention to the problems people of color experienced in the social, economic, legal, and educational arenas. Although far from complete, the civil rights movement has been successful in eliminating much of the institutional racism that had been part of the social fabric of American society.

Today, police officers of color can be found on virtually every large police force in the country. About 27 percent of local police officers are members of racial or ethnic minorities.[127] Some medium and small departments do not have minorities, but this may have more to do with location and population than with discrimination. Diversity has increased in all population categories since 1987.[128] The law no longer allows police agencies to exclude job candidates based on race. This march toward equality has not been easy. Many police officers of color were met with hostility when they sought to serve their communities. As police agencies began to integrate, police officers of color faced **double marginality**; that is, not only did their fellow police officers treat them differently, but other people of color also looked upon them with suspicion.[129] In larger cities, with more and more police officers of color, the double marginality issue has decreased. However, when we look at female police officers of color, we see a different type of marginality. These officers feel the dual prejudices against women and minorities as they attempt to develop a place for themselves in law enforcement.[130] The effects of racism are sometimes difficult to overcome because both whites and minorities must adjust to new ways of thinking about what police officers look like. In policing, the contributions of all Americans make the community not only more tolerant of others but also more supportive of our institutions.

double marginality—
The multiple outsider status of women and minority police officers as a result of being treated differently by their fellow officers.

PAUSE AND REVIEW

1. What are some arguments that have been used to exclude women from policing? What are some criticisms of those arguments?

2. Why do female police officers of color experience double marginality differently than their male counterparts?

In late 2016, the New York Police Department (NYPD) changed its uniform policy and began allowing Sikh officers to wear turbans and grow beards up to an inch long for religious reasons. Relaxing traditional grooming standards is one way that law enforcement can be more welcoming to minorities and create more diverse police departments. Which minorities may be underrepresented in U.S. police departments?

FOCUS ON ETHICS   To Trust a Partner

As a new female police officer, you have sailed through the police academy and in-service training with high marks, and you are excited to be teamed with one of the most popular and respected officers on the force. You find that the two of you work well together. He treats you with respect and increasingly gives you more authority in doing your job. You are developing mutual trust, and you could not be happier with your assignment. However, in the last few weeks you have begun to become concerned about your partner's emotional stability.

When the squad goes out for a drink after the shift, you notice that your partner has been getting quite drunk. One Saturday night after a particularly stressful shift that included a high-speed chase, shots fired, and the wrestling of a suspect to the ground, your partner confides in you that he is chronically depressed. After several beers, he admits that he and his wife are separating and that his children are the only passion he still has in life. Then the shocker comes. He looks around to make sure no other officers are listening and then tells you he has been having fantasies of "eating his gun." In the academy, they told you to take all talk of suicide seriously, but you are committed to maintaining the trust you have developed with your partner.

WHAT DO YOU DO?

1. Seek advice about your partner's depression from the police psychologist.
2. Try to counsel your partner, and tell no one about his depression.
3. Ask for a new partner.

For more insight as to how someone might respond to such an ethical dilemma, visit the companion website at www.oup.com/us/fuller to watch a video that connects this scenario to a real-world situation.

Summary

LEARNING OBJECTIVE 1 Identify some of the problems associated with the excessive use of force by police officers.	Legal liability. Officers who severely injure or kill citizens expose the department and the locality to legal proceedings. Physical injury or death. The use of excessive force may injure or even kill people. Loss of citizen respect. Police officers must have the cooperation of citizens to do their job in an effective and professional way. When they use excessive force, they forfeit that respect. Community reaction. The actions of police officers can generate dissatisfaction and outrage from citizens who engage in public protest, and, in some cases, riotous behavior as a response.
LEARNING OBJECTIVE 2 Describe the issues inherent in the militarization of police departments.	The relationship between the police and the community. In many communities, police militarization hinders policing strategies aimed at integrating officers into community life by making police appear unapproachable and alienating citizens. Reorientation of the police identity. Rather than adopting community-oriented policing practices in which officers identify as part of the community, many officers have adopted the military model, which views all citizens as potential violent criminals and promotes fear and intimidation. An increase in private policing. There will likely be more use of paramilitary security around businesses, neighborhoods, and schools.
LEARNING OBJECTIVE 3 Identify the major problems associated with police stress and burnout.	The stress of police work is highly related to alcohol abuse. The police officer may experience a change in his or her relationship with a spouse and/or children. Police families experience stress when the officer treats his or her spouse and children like potential suspects. Finally, law enforcement has one of the highest suicide rates of any occupation.

LEARNING OBJECTIVE **4** Outline the four key elements of the policeman's working personality.	The symbolic assailant. Officers are systematically trained and culturally reinforced to consider everyone a potential assailant until they can size up the situation and determine that an individual poses no threat. Danger. The possibility of confrontation is always present. Police are drawn to more dangerous assignments as a function of both prestige and excitement. Social isolation. The public treats police officers differently. Whereas police officers may perceive an individual as a symbolic assailant, the public sees the police officer as a symbolic authority figure. Solidarity. The combination of danger and social isolation creates a sense of solidarity in the police subculture. An "us against them" mentality exists to cope with not only law violators, but also the public in general.
LEARNING OBJECTIVE **5** Argue for and against the use of less-than-lethal weapons.	Less-than-lethal weapons are not intended to cause fatalities; they also protect police. However, despite the fact that their usage results in fewer fatalities than the use of firearms, there is the potential for misuse.
LEARNING OBJECTIVE **6** Define information technology and describe how it may be incorporated into police work.	Information technology is technology that helps to manage information by collecting it, storing it, retrieving it, and/or sending it. Several types of information technology have been incorporated into police work, such as body cameras, in-vehicle computers, automated vehicle license-plate readers, computerized databases, websites, and social media.
LEARNING OBJECTIVE **7** Name arguments historically used to exclude women from policing and criticisms of those arguments.	Women are not physically strong enough to be police officers. Critics point out that few police officers can win a fight against young, athletically gifted persons. Police officers must use persuasion to make arrests without fighting, use their weapons when their safety or the safety of others is at risk, and depend on other officers to help subdue suspects, tasks of which women are capable. Women bring different psychological attributes to police work. Advocates for women in policing assert that the aggressive and competitive perspective brought by male police officers is appropriate for only part of the police mission. The emphasis on crime control must coexist with an emphasis on order maintenance and social support. The caregiving and nurturing mindset brought by women significantly expands the nature of the police role.
LEARNING OBJECTIVE **8** Define the concept of double marginality.	Double marginality refers to the multiple outsider status experienced by both male and female minority police officers. As police agencies began to integrate, police officers of color were treated differently by their fellow officers and were viewed with suspicion by the people of color they policed.

Critical Reflections

1. **How has law enforcement performed relative to other occupations in providing women and minorities equal employment opportunities?**

Key Terms

double marginality **p. 189**
gender **p. 186**

policeman's working
    personality **p. 188**

posse comitatus **p. 168**
use of force **p. 162**

Endnotes

1 United States Attorney's Office, Northern District of Georgia, Former Habersham County Deputy Sheriff Charged for Her Role in Flash Bang Grenade Incident, July 22, 2015, http://www.justice.gov/usao-ndga/pr/former-habersham-county-deputy-sheriff-charged-her-role-flash-bang-grenade-incident.

2 Tina Chen, "Baby in Coma after Police 'Grenade' Dropped in Crib During Drug Raid," ABCNews, May 30, 2014, http://abcnews.go.com/blogs/headlines/2014/05/baby-in-coma-after-police-grenade-dropped-in-crib-during-drug-raid/.

3 Alecia Phonesavanh, A SWAT Team Blew a Hole in My 2-Year-Old Son, *Salon*, June 24, 2014, http://www.salon.com/2014/06/24/a_swat_team_blew_a_hole_in_my_2_year_old_son/.

4 Alison Lynn and Matt Gutman, Family of Toddler Injured by SWAT 'Grenade' Faces $1M in Medical Bills, ABC News, December 18, 2014, http://abcnews.go.com/US/family-toddler-injured-swat-grenade-faces-1m-medical/story?id=27671521.

5 Rebecca Lindstrom, Deputy Involved in Baby Bou Bou Raid Found Not Guilty, 11Alive, December 11, 2015, http://www.11alive.com/story/news/2015/12/11/nikki-autry-habersham-flash-bang-federal-court-jury/77151504/.

6 Paul Rea, "Habersham County Closer to Settlement in Phonesavanh Lawsuit," Now Habersham, August 20, 2015, http://www.nowhabersham.com/habersham-county-closer-to-settlement-in-phonesavanh-lawsuit2/.

7 Tyler Estep, "Official: Habersham- 'Baby Bou Bou' settlement 'fair as possible'," AJC.com April 22, 2015, http://www.ajc.com/news/news/report-family-of-baby-bou-bou-county-reach-964k-se/nkzmb/.

8 The police claim the right to use force to resolve societal problems as part of their mandate. The rest of us are mostly happy to let the police do this "dirty work" on our behalf. This relationship has been sanctioned by legislatures that pass laws giving the police their powers. As in most occupations, law enforcement officials guard their powers by forming unions, lobbying lawmakers, maintaining the image they present to the public, and ensuring that rival groups, such as the private security industry, are given only limited authority. For an excellent discussion of how occupations, especially the police, establish their mandates, see Peter K. Manning, "The Police: Mandate, Strategies, and Appearances," in *The Police and Society: Touchstone Readings*, 2d ed., ed. Victor E. Kappeler (Prospect Heights, Ill.: Waveland Press, 1999).

9 International Association of Chiefs of Police, Police Use of Force in America 2001, http://www.bjs.gov/index.cfm?ty=tp&tid=84, p. 1.

10 Manning, "The Police: Mandate, Strategies, and Appearances," 100–101.

11 Thomas Barker, Ronald D. Hunter, and Jeffery P. Rush, *Police Systems and Practices: An Introduction* (Englewood Cliffs, N.J.: Prentice Hall, 1994). These authors identified three primary roles for law enforcement: crime fighting, order maintenance, and service. They discussed the consequences of the crime-fighter image that they contended is promoted by the public, the media, and the police themselves. These authors said of the crime-fighter image: "in addition to creating unrealistic expectations about the police's ability to reduce crime, this narrow view prevents an informed analysis of the use of police resources" (p. 102).

12 Egon Bittner, *The Functions of the Police in Modern Society* (Cambridge, Mass.: Oelgeschlager, Gunn & Hain, 1980), 37–38.

13 James J. Fyfe, "The Split-Second Syndrome and Other Determinants of Police Violence," in *Critical Issues in Policing: Contemporary Readings*, 4th ed., eds. Roger G. Dunham and Geoffrey P. Alpert (Prospect Heights, Ill.: Waveland Press, 2001), 583–598.

14 Bittner, *The Functions of the Police in Modern Society*.

15 Kenneth Adams, "What We Know about Police Use of Force," in *Use of Force by Police: Overview of National and Local Data*, NCJ 176330 (Washington, D.C.: National Institute of Justice, October 1999).

16 Laurence Miller, "Why Cops Kill: The Psychology of Police Deadly Force Encounters," *Aggression and Violent Behavior* 22 (May 2015): 97–111.

17 Duren Banks, Paul Ruddle, Erin Kennedy, and Michael G. Planty, *Arrest-Related Deaths Program Redesign Study, 2015–16: Preliminary Findings* (U.S. Department of Justice Office of Justice Programs, Bureau of Justice Statistics, 2016), 2. Online at http://www.bjs.gov/index.cfm?ty=pbdetail&iid=5864.

18 Brad W. Smith and Malcolm D. Holmes. "Police Use of Excessive Force in Minority Communities: A Test of the Minority Threat, Place, and Community Accountability Hypotheses." *Social Problems* 61, no. 1 (February 2014): 83–104.

19 K. M. Lersch, "Police Misconduct and Malpractice: A Critical Analysis of Citizens' Complaints," *Policing: An International Journal of Police Strategies and Management* 21, no. 1 (1998): 80–96.

20 Lynn Langton and Matthew Durose, *Police Behavior during Traffic and Street Stops, 2011* (U.S. Department of Justice Office of Justice Programs Bureau of Justice Statistics, 2016), 1. Online at http://www.bjs.gov/index.cfm?ty=pbdetail&iid=4779.

21 Sheryl Gay Stolberg, Ron Nixon, Richard A. Oppel, Jr., and Stephen Babcock, "Clashes Rock Baltimore After Funeral," *New York Times*, April 28, 2015. A1-A15.

22 CBS News, Arrest to Death: What Happened to Freddie Gray, CBS News, May 1, 2015, http://www.cbsnews.com/news/arrest-to-death-what-happened-to-freddie-gray/.

23 Krishnadev Calamur, Maryland Governor Lifts State of Emergency in Baltimore, National Public Radio, May 6, 2015, http://www.npr.org/sections/thetwo-way/2015/05/06/404675117/maryland-governor-lifts-state-of-emergency-in-baltimore.

24 J. Niehaus, "Realistic Use-of-Force Training: The Technology Is in Place Today for an All-Inclusive Program," *Law and Order* 45, no. 6 (1997): 103–105.

25 Heather Wyatt-Nichol and George Franks, "Ethics Training in Law Enforcement Agencies," *Public Integrity* 12, no. 1 (2010): 39–50.

26 *Black's Law Dictionary*, http://thelawdictionary.org/posse-comitatus/. Accessed August 2015.

27 *Black's Law Dictionary*, http://thelawdictionary.org/posse-comitatus/. Accessed August 2015.

28 RAND Corporation, Preparing the U.S. Army for Homeland Security: Concepts, Issues, and Options, Appendix D: Overview of the Posse Comitatus Act, http://www.rand.org/pubs/monograph_reports/MR1251.html. Accessed August 2015.

29 U.S. Northern Command, Defending Our Homeland, The Posse Comitatus Act, May 16, 2013, http://www.northcom.mil/Newsroom/FactSheets/ArticleView/tabid/3999/Article/563993/the-posse-comitatus-act.aspx.

30 National Guard Association of the United States, NGAUS 101: Guard Duty Statuses, http://www.ngaus.org/advocating-national-guard/evolving-role-citizen-soldier. Accessed August 2015.

31 U.S. Northern Command, Defending Our Homeland, The Posse Comitatus Act, May 16, 2013, http://www.northcom.mil/Newsroom/FactSheets/ArticleView/tabid/3999/Article/563993/the-posse-comitatus-act.aspx.

32 Section 1385 of Title 18, United States Code.

33 Peter B. Kraska, "Questioning the Militarization of U.S. Police: Critical Versus Advocacy Scholarship," *Policing and Society* 9, no. 2 (April 1999): 141.

34 Jamelle Bouie, "The Militarization of the Police," *Slate*, August 13, 2014, http://www.slate.com/articles/news_and_politics/politics/2014/08/police_in_ferguson_military_weapons_threaten_protesters.html.

35 Abigail R. Hall and Christopher J. Coyne, "The Militarization of U.S. Domestic Policing," *Independent Review* 17, no. 4 (Spring 2013): 485–504.

36 Daryl Meeks, "Police Militarization in Urban Areas: The Obscure War Against the Underclass," *Black Scholar* 35, no. 4 (Winter 2006): 33–41.

37 John Murray, "Policing Terrorism: A Threat to Community Policing or Just a Shift in Priorities?" *Police Practice and Research* 6, no. 4 (September 2005): 347–361.

38 Martin Gill, "Senior Police Officers' Perspectives on Private Security: Sceptics, Pragmatists and Embracers," *Policing and Society* 25, no. 3 (2015): 276–293.

39 American Civil Liberties Union, *War Comes Home: The Excessive Militarization of American Policing* (New York: ACLU Foundation, 2014). Online at https://www.aclu.org/report/war-comes-home-excessive-militarization-american-police.

40 "Are Federal Programs That Provide Military Equipment to State and Local Police Departments Effective?" *Congressional Digest* 94, no. 2 (February 2015): 10–31.

41 Karena Rahall, "The Green to Blue Pipeline: Defense Contractors and the Police Industrial Complex," *Cardozo Law Review* 36, no. 5 (June 2015): 1785–1835.

42 Peter B. Kraska, "Militarization and Policing—Its Relevance to 21st Century Police," *Policing: A Journal of Policy and Practice* 1, no. 4 (2007): 501–513.

43 Defense Logistics Agency Disposition Services, Law Enforcement Support Office, http://www.dispositionservices.dla.mil/leso/pages/1033programfaqs.aspx. Accessed August 2015.

44 Arezou Rezvani, Jessica Pupovac, David Eads, and Tyler Fisher, MRAPs and Bayonets: What We Know about the Pentagon's 1033 Program, National Public Radio, September 2, 2014, http://www.npr.org/2014/09/02/342494225/mraps-and-bayonets-what-we-know-about-the-pentagons-1033-program.

45 Linda Feldmann, "Ferguson: How Pentagon's '1033 Program' Helped Militarize Small-town Police," *Christian Science Monitor*, August 16, 2014, http://www.csmonitor.com/USA/Politics/DC-Decoder/2014/0816/Ferguson-How-Pentagon-s-1033-program-helped-militarize-small-town-police-video.

46 American Civil Liberties Union, *War Comes Home*, 3, 16.

47 U.S. Federal News Service, "Cape Coral Police Department's VIN Unit, SWAT Team, Street Crimes Unit Execute Search Warrants on Suspected Marijuana Grow Houses," October 22, 2007.

48 Kraska, "Militarization and Policing—Its Relevance to 21st Century Police." Radley Balko, *Rise of the Warrior Cop: The Militarization of America's Police Forces* (New York: Public Affairs, 2013), 286, as cited in Krena Rahall, "The Green to Blue Pipeline: Defense Contractors and the Police Industrial Complex," *Cardozo Law Review* 36, no. 5 (June 2015): 1785–1835.

49 American Civil Liberties Union, *War Comes Home*, 3, 32.

50 Ibid., 4.

51 Richard K. Lodge, "Police Investigation Details the Night Eurie Stamps Sr. Died," *MetroWest Daily News*, May 1, 2011, http://www.metrowestdailynews.com/article/20110501/NEWS/305019966.

52 John M. Guilfoil, "Officer in Fatal Shooting Will Not Be Charged," Boston.com, March 10, 2011, http://www.boston.com/news/local/massachusetts/articles/2011/03/10/officer_in_fatal_shooting_will_not_be_charged/.

53 Norman Miller, "Framingham Police SWAT Team Disbanded," *MetroWest Daily News*, October 5, 2013, http://www.metrowestdailynews.com/article/20131005/NEWS/310059944.

54 Federal Bureau of Investigation, *Law Enforcement Officers Killed and Assaulted, 2003* (Washington, D.C.: U.S. Department of Justice, 2004), www2.fbi.gov/ucr/killed/leoka03.pdf.

55 Federal Bureau of Investigation, Law Enforcement Officers Killed and Assaulted 2015, Law Enforcement Officers Feloniously Killed Circumstance at Scene of Incident, 2006–2015, Table 23, https://ucr.fbi.gov/leoka/2015/tables/table_23_leos_fk_circumstance_at_scene_of_incident_2006-2015.xls.

56 "Justice Department Settles Employment Discrimination Lawsuit against the City of Virginia Beach, Virginia Police Department," U.S. Federal News Service, including U.S. State News, April 4, 2006.

57 Judith A. Waters and William Ussery, "Police Stress: History, Contributing Factors, Symptoms, and Interventions," *Policing* 30 (April 1, 2007): 169–188.

58 John M. Violanti, James R. Marshall, and Barbara Howe, "Stress, Coping, and Alcohol Use: The Police Connection," *Journal of Police Science and Administration* 13, no. 2 (1985): 106–110.

59 Charles Unkovic and William Brown, "The Drunken Cop," *Police Chief* (April 1978): 29–20.

60 Max T. Raterman, "Substance Abuse and Police Discipline," *Police Department Disciplinary Bulletin* (December 2000): 2–4.

61 Mary J.C. Hageman, "Occupational Stress and Marital Relationships," *Journal of Police Science and Administration* 6, no. 4 (1978): 402–412.

62 Laurence Miller, "Police Families: Stresses, Syndromes, and Solutions," *American Journal of Family Therapy* 35 (January 1, 2007): 21.

63 Clemens Bartollas and Larry D. Hahn, *Policing in America* (Boston: Allyn & Bacon, 1999). 199.

64 Peter E. Maynard and Nancy E. Maynard, "Stress in Police Families: Some Policy Implications," *Journal of Police Science and Administration* 10 (1982): 302–314.

65 Robert Henley Woody, "Family Interventions with Law Enforcement Officers," *American Journal of Family Therapy* 34 (March 1, 2006): 95–103.

66 Julia McKinnell, "Don't Let Their Only Friend Be a Gun," *Maclean's*, June 30, 2008, 59.

67 J. M. Violanti, T. A. Hartley, A. Mnatsakanova, and M. E. Andrew "Police Suicide in Small Departments: A Comparative Analysis," *International Journal of Emergency Mental Health* 14 no. 3 (2012): 157–162.

68 Vera A. Klinoff, Vincent B. Van Hasselt, and Ryan A. Black. "Homicide-Suicide in Police Families: An Analysis of Cases from 2007–2014." *Journal of Forensic Practice* 17, no. 2 (April 2015): 101–116.

69 Mark H. Chae and Douglas J. Boyle, "Police Suicide: Prevalence, Risk, and Protective Factors," *Policing* 36, no. 1 (February 2013): 91–118.

70 John M. Violanti, "Predictors of Police Suicide Ideation," *Suicide and Life-Threatening Behavior* 34 (October 1, 2004): 277–283.

71 Michelle Perin, "Police Suicide," *Law Enforcement Technology* 34, no. 9 (September 2007): 8.

72 Laurence Miller, *Practical Police Psychology: Stress Management and Crisis Intervention for Law Enforcement* (Springfield, Ill.: Thomas, 2006).

73 Göran Kecklund, Claire Anne Eriksen, and Torbjörn Åkerstedt, "Police Officers' Attitude to Different Shift Systems: Association with Age, Present Shift Schedule, Health and Sleep/Wake Complaints," *Applied Ergonomics* 39 (September 2008): 565.

74 John Von Maanen, "Kinsmen in Repose: Occupational Perspectives of Patrolmen," in *The Police and Society: Touchstone Readings*, 2d ed., ed. Victor E. Kappeler (Prospect Heights, Ill.: Waveland Press, 1999), 221; see also Victor E. Kappeler, Richard D. Sluder, and Geoffrey P. Alpert, "Breeding Deviant Conformity: Police Ideology and Culture," in *The Police and Society: Touchstone Readings*, 239.

75 "Master status" is a sociological term that refers to a status or a label that dominates all other positive or negative labels. For instance, if you introduced your boyfriend to your parents and mentioned that he had served time in prison for rape, nothing else you said could earn their trust of him. Conversely, a label such as "Medal of Honor winner" will supersede just about any other label.

76 Jerome H. Skolnick, *Justice without Trial: Law Enforcement in Democratic Society* (New York: Wiley, 1966).

77 Ibid., 47.

78 Ibid., 42–70.

79 Holly Bannish and Jim Ruiz, "The Antisocial Police Personality: A View from the Inside," *International Journal of Public Administration* 26 (June 1, 2003): 831–881.

80 Michael D. Lyman, *The Police: An Introduction* (Upper Saddle River, N.J.: Prentice Hall, 2002). Lyman provided an excellent discussion on the topic in his chapter "Personal Administration."

81 Sanja Kutnjak Ivkovic, "Police (Mis) behavior: A Cross-Cultural Study of Corruption Seriousness," *Policing* 28 (July 1, 2005): 546–566.

82 Lawrence W. Sherman, *Police Corruption: A Sociological Perspective* (Garden City, N.Y.: Anchor Books, 1974). See particularly Sherman's introductory chapter with its important typology of police corruption.

83 Knapp Commission, "An Example of Police Corruption: Knapp Commission Report in New York City," in *Police Deviance*, eds. Thomas Barker and David L. Carter (Cincinnati, Ohio: Pilgrimage, 1986), 28.

84 "Ringleader in Boston Police Corruption Case Sentenced to 26 Years in Prison," U.S. Federal News Service, including U.S. State News, May 16, 2008.

85 Peter K. Manning and Lawrence John Redlinger, "Invitational Edges," in *Thinking about Police: Contemporary Readings*, 2d ed., eds. Carl B. Klockars and Stephen D. Mastrofski (New York: McGraw-Hill, 1991), 398–413.

86 Lee Sullivan, "Drug Unit Corruption: Stopping the Scandal before It Starts," *Sheriff*, January 1, 2008, 27–29.

87 Body-Worn Camera Frequently Asked Questions, Bureau of Justice Assistance, 2015, https://www.bja.gov/bwc/topics-gettingstarted.html.

88 Barak Ariel, William A. Farrar, and Alex Sutherland, "The Effect of Police Body-Worn Cameras on Use of Force and Citizens' Complaints Against the Police: A Randomized Controlled Trial," *Journal of Quantitative Criminology* 31 (2015): 509–535.

89 Lindsay Miller and Jessica Toliver, "Implementing a Body-Worn Camera Program: Recommendations and Lessons Learned," *Community Policing Dispatch* 7, no. 10, October 2014, http://cops.usdoj.gov/html/dispatch/10-2014/body_worn_camera_program.asp.

90 United States Department of Justice, Justice Department Awards over $23 Million in Funding for Body Worn Camera Pilot Program to Support Law Enforcement Agencies in 32 States, September 21, 2015, https://www.justice.gov/opa/pr/justice-department-awards-over-23-million-funding-body-worn-camera-pilot-program-support-law.

91 U.S. Department of Justice, Bureau of Justice Assistance, Body-Worn Camera Program Fact Sheet, https://www.justice.gov/opa/pr/justice-department-awards-over-23-million-funding-body-worn-camera-pilot-program-support-law.

92 Zusha Elinson, Shibani Mahtani, and Valerie Bauerlein, "Charlotte, Tulsa Highlight Patchwork Approach to Releasing Body Camera Videos," *Wall Street Journal*, September 23, 2016, http://www.wsj.com/articles/police-shootings-expose-patchwork-approach-to-releasing-body-camera-videos-1474655168.

93 National Conference of State Legislatures, State Body-Worn Camera Laws, August 2016, http://www.ncsl.org/research/civil-and-criminal-justice/body-worn-cameras-interactive-graphic.aspx#/.

94 Lindsay Miller and Jessica Toliver, Implementing a Body-Worn Camera Program: Recommendations and Lessons Learned, Community Policing Dispatch 7, no. 10, October 2014, http://cops.usdoj.gov/html/dispatch/10-2014/body_worn_camera_program.asp.

95 Eric M. Johnson, "U.S. Cities Push for Local Laws to Oversee Police Surveillance," Reuters, September 21, 2016, http://www.reuters.com/article/us-usa-police-surveillance-idUSKCN11R304. Electronic Frontier Foundation, Surveillance Drones, https://www.eff.org/issues/surveillance-drones.

96 Justin Jouvenal, "The New Way Police Are Surveilling You: Calculating Your Threat 'Score'," *Washington Post*, January 10, 2016, https://www.washingtonpost.com/local/public-safety/the-new-way-police-are-surveilling-you-calculating-your-threat-score/2016/01/10/e42bccac-8e15-11e5-baf4-bdf37355da0c_story.html.

97 Brad Heath, "Police Secretly Track Cellphones to Solve Routine Crimes," *USA Today*, August 24, 2015, http://www.usatoday.com/story/news/2015/08/23/baltimore-police-stingray-cell-surveillance/31994181/.

98 Steven D. Seybold, "Somebody's Watching Me: Civilian Oversight of Data-Collection Technologies," *Texas*

Law Review 93, no. 4 (March 2015): 1029–1060.

99 Elizabeth E. Joh, "The New Surveillance Discretion: Automated Suspicion, Big Data, and Policing," *Harvard Law and Policy Review* 10, no. 1 (January 2016): 15–42.

100 Johnson, "U.S. Cities Push for Local Laws to Oversee Police Surveillance."

101 Cyrus Farivar, New California Bill Would Require Local Approval for Stingray Use, Ars Technica, April 16, 2015, http://arstechnica.com/tech-policy/2015/04/new-california-bill-would-require-local-approval-for-stingray-use/. Seattle, Wash., ordinance 124142 (March 27, 2013), http://clerk.ci.seattle.wa.us/~scripts/nph-brs.exe?s3=&s4=124142&s5=&s1=&s2=&S6=&Sect4=AND&l=0&Sect2=THESON&Sect3=PLURON&Sect5=CBORY&Sect6=HITOFF&d=ORDF&p=1&u=%2F%7Epublic%2Fcbor1.htm&r=1&f=G.

102 Stephen Rushin, "The Legislative Response to Mass Police Surveillance," *Brooklyn Law Review* 79, no. 1 (Fall 2013): 1–60.

103 Timothy C. Hardcastle, "What's New in Emergencies, Trauma and Shock? Pellets, Rubber Bullets, and Shotguns: Less Lethal or Not?" *Journal of Emergencies, Trauma and Shock* 6, no. 3 (2013): 153–154.

104 William P. Bozeman and James E. Winslow, "Medical Aspects of Less Lethal Weapons," *Internet Journal of Rescue and Disaster Medicine* 5, no. 1 (2005).

105 Brian A. Reaves, *Local Police Departments, 2013: Equipment and Technology* (Washington, D.C.: U.S. Department of Justice Office of Justice Programs Bureau of Justice Statistics, 2015), 1.

106 Brian Rappert, "A Framework for the Assessment of Non-Lethal Weapons," *Medicine, Conflict and Survival* 20 (2004): 51.

107 Ibid.

108 Reaves, *Local Police Departments, 2013*, 1.

109 Sharon Gaudin, "Pennsylvania Police Use Database as Crime-Fighting Tool," *InformationWeek*, January 19, 2007, http://www.informationweek.com/pennsylvania-police-use-database-as-crim/196902236.

110 Office of Justice Programs, National Institute of Justice, DNA Sample Collection from Arrestees, December 7, 2012, http://nij.gov/topics/forensics/evidence/dna/pages/collection-from-arrestees.aspx; Valerie Ross, Forget Fingerprints: Law Enforcement DNA Databases Poised To Expand, NOVA Next, January 2014, http://www.pbs.org/wgbh/nova/next/body/dna-databases/.

111 Office of Justice Programs, National Institute of Justice, DNA Sample Collection from Arrestees.

112 Federal Bureau of Investigation, CODIS brochure, https://www.fbi.gov/about-us/lab/biometric-analysis/codis/codis_brochure.

113 Richard Willing, "DNA 'Near Matches' Spur Privacy Fight," *USA Today*, August 3, 2007, 3A.

114 Ellen Nakashima, "From DNA of Family, a Tool to Make Arrests," *Washington Post*, Met 2d ed., April 21, 2008, A1, http://www.washingtonpost.com/wp-dyn/content/article/2008/04/20/AR2008042002388_pf.html.

115 Suman Kakar, "Race and Police Officers' Perceptions of Their Job Performance: An Analysis of the Relationship between Police Officers' Race, Education Level, and Job Performance," *Journal of Police and Criminal Psychology* 18 (April 1, 2003): 45.

116 National Center for Women and Policing, "Equality Denied: The Status of Women in Policing: 2000," National Center for Women and Policing, Feminist Majority Foundation, April 2001, http://www.womenandpolicing.org/statusreports.html.

117 Federal Bureau of Investigation, Crime in the United States, 2016, Table 25: Full-time Law Enforcement Employees by Population Group Percent Male and Female, 2016, https://ucr.fbi.gov/crime-in-the-u.s/2016/crime-in-the-u.s.-2016/topic-pages/tables/table-25. Brian A. Reaves, *Local Police Departments, 2013: Personnel, Policies, and Practices* (U.S. Department of Justice Office of Justice Programs Bureau of Justice Statistics, 2015), 4. Online

at http://www.bjs.gov/index.cfm?ty=pbdetail&iid=5279.

118 Jody Kasper, "Proven Steps for Recruiting Women," *Law and Order*, December 1, 2006, 63–67.

119 Jerome H. Skolnick, *Justice without Trial: Law Enforcement in Democratic Society*, 3d ed. (New York: Macmillan, 1994), 41–68.

120 Susan E. Martin, "Women Officers on the Move: An Update on Women in Policing," *Critical Issues in Policing: Contemporary Readings*, 4th ed., eds. Roger G. Dunham and Geoffrey P. Alpert (Prospect Heights, Ill.: Waveland Press, 2001), 401–422.

121 John R. Lott Jr., "Does a Helping Hand Put Others at Risk? Affirmative Action, Police Departments, and Crime," *Economic Inquiry* 38 (April 1, 2000): 239–277.

122 Alissa Pollitz Worden, "The Attitudes of Women and Men in Policing: Testing Conventional and Contemporary Wisdom," *Criminology* 31, no. 2 (1993): 203–240.

123 Larry A. Gould and Marie Volbrecht, "Personality Differences between Women Police Recruits, Their Male Counterparts, and the General Female Population," *Journal of Police and Criminal Psychology* 14 (April 1, 1999): 1–18.

124 J. J. Donohue III and Steven D. Levitt, "The Impact of Race on Policing and Arrests," *Journal of Law and Economics* 44 (October 1, 2001): 367–394.

125 Clemens Bartollas and Larry D. Hahn, *Policing in America* (Boston: Allyn & Bacon, 1999). See especially Chapter 12, "The Minority Police Officer," for a discussion of black, Hispanic, American Indian, and homosexual police officers.

126 Ibid.

127 Reaves, *Local Police Departments, 2013*, 1.

128 Ibid.

129 Nicholas Alex, *Black in Blue: A Study of the Negro Policeman* (New York: Appleton-Century-Crofts, 1969).

130 Susan E. Martin, "Outsider within the Station House: The Impact of Race and Gender on Black Women Police," *Social Problems* (August 1994): 389.

The Role
of the Courts

Chapter 7

The Courts

FEATURES

Jerry Hartfield spent over 30 years in prison. What sort of recourse should be available for offenders, like Hartfield, whose legal rights are violated?

n 1976, Jerry Hartfield was arrested in Wichita, Kansas, for a murder that was committed a few days before in Texas. Hartfield was convicted in 1977 and sentenced to death row, but the conviction was thrown out in 1980 because of a problem with jury selection. Without being retried, Texas's governor commuted Hartfield's death sentence to life imprisonment. Unfortunately, at the time, no one realized that Hartfield's death sentence could not be commuted because his conviction had been thrown out and no retrial had occurred. Hartfield's defense attorney stopped representing him after the commutation, and the prosecution believed that the life sentence was appropriate. Hartfield, who has an IQ of 51, never realized his incarceration was invalid. Therefore, despite the illegal sentence, Hartfield remained incarcerated.[1]

In 2013, it was discovered that Hartfield was in prison without a conviction, and a new trial was ordered. A state judge ruled that the speedy-trial provision of the Sixth Amendment had been violated because Hartfield had never requested a new trial. Prosecutors tried him again and secured a new conviction in 2015, although 35 years had passed since the crime was committed. Many of the 125 witnesses on the prosecution's list were dead or could not be found, and the murder weapon and the victim's car no longer existed. Some witness testimony from the 1977 trial was allowed into the new trial, but because this testimony was recited, the defense could not cross-examine. Because the Supreme Court abolished the death penalty for intellectually disabled people in 2002, Hartfield was sentenced to 5 to 99 years in prison. Hartfield and his attorneys appealed, arguing that his right to a speedy trial had been violated and he should be released. The Texas Court of Criminal Appeals agreed, ruling that only Hartfield's release could remedy that violation of his rights. In June 2017, Hartfield finally walked free.[2]

THINK ABOUT IT > What legal rights were compromised in this unusual case?

LEARNING OBJECTIVE | **1**

Identify the challenges facing the U.S. court system.

The Court System in the United States

Courts are a central feature in the U.S. criminal justice system. Typically, students of criminal justice are not as interested in courts as in law enforcement and corrections because working in the court requires legal knowledge. Many students go on to law school and successful careers as attorneys and judges, but to a college freshman that seems a long time in the future. However, students should consider careers in the legal system because the quality of justice in the United States is determined by the technical expertise, professional acumen, and ethical demeanor of those who work in the courts. Courts are responsible for determining whether a defendant is guilty or not guilty and for deciding on the disposition or sentence for defendants who are found guilty. Such processes occur according to a complex and ever-changing network of laws, personnel, and political pressures. Mistakes can affect the convicted and the victims, as well as reflect badly on the system itself. The case of Jerry Hartfield is a good example of how a case can slip through the cracks of the court system. The courts are besieged on all sides by those who observe an institution in crisis:

› Police officers, who complain that offenders are treated too leniently[3]
› Corrections officials, who lack room in their prisons for new inmates and are concerned about the severe sentences that keep inmates incarcerated for many years[4]

> The public, which sees the courts as an unfathomable machine that fails to provide justice when lawbreakers are released because of technicalities[5]

> Legislatures, which cannot provide the necessary financial resources to handle huge caseloads because tax dollars must be shared among many other government functions, including law enforcement and corrections[6]

> Offenders and defendants, whether guilty or innocent, as well as victims, who do not believe that the courts dispense justice in a fair manner[7]

The courts seem to be in a powerful position within the criminal justice system because it makes the important determinations of what happens to suspects, defendants, and offenders. However, the courts are actually at the mercy of outside forces. They do not control how they are financed, nor do they control how many cases they receive. They cannot ensure adequate resources to carry out sentences, and because courtrooms are open to the press, the courts cannot control their public image. In many ways, the courts are an institution that takes the blame for deficiencies not of their making.[8] For instance, when a police officer fails to read a suspect his or her Miranda rights or makes a mistake in the chain of custody of crucial evidence, the courts have no choice but to dismiss the case. This can cause the public to believe that the court released the offender on a technicality when, in fact, the court is obligated to interpret and implement the law. Citizen dissatisfaction with the court might be better directed at those whose job it is to educate the police. Additionally, citizens could petition their local representatives to change the law.

Another aspect of the U.S. court system that complicates its mission is the issue of professional orientation. Those who work in the court, including attorneys and judges, have a professional orientation, meaning that the practice of law and the dispensation of justice is a routine job. Each individual case is but one of many on the **docket** (the schedule of cases for a court), and they are typically handled in an assembly-line fashion, with all the court workers seeking to function smoothly together to process the cases. Each suspect, defendant, offender, and victim, however, likely considers his or her case to be of the utmost

docket—A schedule of cases in a court.

The courts seem to be powerful, but they are actually at the mercy of many outside forces. Here, police at Quincy (Massachusetts) District Court subdue and handcuff brawlers after a fight spilled out of a courtroom where four teens pleaded not guilty to murder charges stemming from the shooting death of 21-year-old Kyle McManus. What are some of the problems that the courts are subject to?

importance because his or her life is at stake. This is not the situation for the court workers. This professional orientation, which affects the image and functioning of the court, is a twofold problem:

adversarial process—A term describing the manner in which U.S. criminal trial courts operate; a system that requires two sides, a prosecution and a defense.

bench trial—A trial in which a defendant waives the right to a jury trial and instead agrees to a trial in which the judge hears and decides the case.

1. The U.S. criminal court system is an **adversarial process** in the sense that defense attorneys and prosecutors, as part of their professional orientation, represent the positions of two opposing parties. In the case of a trial, this process places the burden on the prosecutor, who must prove to a jury (or a judge, in the case of a **bench trial**, a trial heard by a judge and not a jury) that the defendant is guilty beyond a reasonable doubt. The defense attorney seeks to make the prosecutor prove the case and asserts the legal protections of the accused. The judge, a disinterested party, ensures that the two sides play by the rules. The adversarial process can sometimes seem to result in defense attorneys and prosecutors advocating for one side at the expense of the truth. The process requires attorneys to strike the most advantageous deal they can for their clients, even if they realize that other outcomes may better reflect the goals of justice.[9]

2. Because our legal system evolved over a long time and because it draws its inspiration and procedures from so many sources, the processes and language of the court may seem foreign to outside observers, especially defendants. Cynics might believe that the reason the courts are so unfathomable is to ensure that only those with a legal education can successfully negotiate the corridors of the courthouse.

The issues of professional orientation and lack of control over funding and image make the courts seem shrouded in mystery. This has resulted in a rather romantic view of the courts whereby the justice that is (or is not) dispensed is more a product of the courageous attorney and less a function of the criminal justice system process. This notion of how the courts work is inspired by television. Law-as-entertainment programs, in which celebrity judges preside over small-claims television courtrooms, further compromise this image. Such distorted images of a dashing defense attorney fighting valiantly against a corrupt and inefficient system or one of a short-tempered judge humiliating confused or naive people have little relevance to the actual practice of law. Such presentations of justice as entertainment portray a cynical and inaccurate vision of what courts actually do. Thus, much of the picture we have of the court system is imperfect. Our goal in these next three chapters is to show how courts fit into the larger context of the government and how they interact with the other components of the criminal justice system.

PAUSE AND REVIEW

1. **How does the professional orientation of those who practice law affect the image and functioning of the court?**

LEARNING OBJECTIVE **2**

Outline the importance of the Assize of Clarendon to the establishment of the jury.

LEARNING OBJECTIVE **3**

Describe trial by ordeal and its relationship to the jury trial.

LEARNING OBJECTIVE **4**

Describe the challenges faced by the courts in colonial North America.

The Historical Foundation of Modern U.S. Courts

A complete history of the evolution of the courts in the United States, from their English roots to now, is beyond the scope of this text and our limited concerns regarding the development of the criminal courts. However, some historical background is essential to understanding how the courts have evolved. Below we will discuss the early English foundations of the concept of the jury, as well as how the modern U.S. court system evolved from the inadequacies of the original 13 colonies.

Courts in England

The development of English courts between the 11th and 18th centuries provided the foundation for the courts of the United States. One of the first modern legal concepts was that of the **inquest**, considered to be the first type of jury. After a war, the reigning English monarch needed to determine which lands had been conquered and would therefore conduct an inquest in which men were summoned before the court to attest to the ownership of the land in the surrounding area. Gradually, the inquest was broadened to concerns other than land ownership, and the rudiments of a grand jury were developed whereby the crown would convene a court and suspect individuals would be charged with breaking the law.

In 1166, a law called the **Assize of Clarendon** was enacted to correct some of the problems and inefficiencies of the judicial process.[10] Accusers would often fail to follow through on their complaints because of the time, expense, and difficulty of achieving a guilty verdict. This was problematic because not only would the guilty go free and the community be left unprotected, but also the king could not collect a court fee. The Assize of Clarendon established the beginnings of the grand jury system. The jury, composed of 12 men from each jurisdiction, would inform the king's judges of the most serious offenses committed in each jurisdiction. This way, the decision to **charge** was taken from the individual accuser and given to civic-minded citizens who performed this duty as a community service. As such, offenses began to be regarded as public problems rather than as private wrongs. The Assize of Clarendon gradually developed from a process of simply identifying and charging wrongdoers to a body that determined whether evidence was sufficient to detain the accused before trial.[11]

The jury trial was created to fill a vacuum in the criminal justice process. In 1215, the Roman Catholic Church forbade priests to participate in **trials by ordeal**. Because the trial by ordeal was determined by divine intervention, and priests judged whether God did in fact provide a miracle to save the accused, the practice had to be stopped.[12] There were three main types of trial by ordeal: trial by cold water, trial by hot water, and trial by hot iron, or, as it was sometimes called, trial by fire.[13] Such trials often involved subjecting the accused to pain and/or danger. For example, in a trial by hot water, the accused had to reach into a cauldron of boiling water and pick a large stone off the bottom. Inability to lift the stone was evidence of guilt. If the accused lifted the stone, his or her wounded hand was bandaged. When examined three days later, the accused was declared innocent if the wounds were healing. However, if the wounds were festering, the accused was declared guilty, and a sentence was imposed.[14]

At first, people had a difficult time accepting the judgment of mere men, especially when the sentence could be death. They were more comfortable letting God decide such issues. However, with the church no longer sanctioning such spectacles, the judgment of 12 "good" men was gradually accepted. For the most part, the trial jury comprised the same men who sat on the grand jury that brought the

inquest—In archaic usage, considered the first type of jury that determined the ownership of land. Currently, a type of investigation.

Assize of Clarendon—A 12th-century English law that established judicial procedure and the grand jury system.

charge—Formal statement of the criminal offense the defendant is accused of.

trial by ordeal—An ancient custom in which the accused was required to perform a test that appealed to divine authority to prove guilt or innocence.

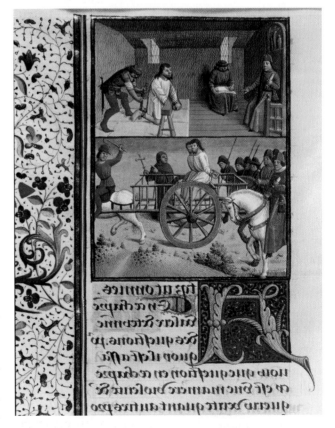

These illustrations depict victims being tortured in order to determine their innocence or guilt. What led to the end of trials by ordeal?

charge against the defendant. These jurors were expected to know the facts of the case, so little testimony was required. Guilt or innocence was determined by the accused's reputation and the intimate knowledge about the case that the jurors acquired when they first charged the accused. This process was gradually determined to be flawed, and eventually the two juries were separated. In many places, this required the use of jurors from outside the community, which resulted in the need for testimony to educate all the jurors about the case.[15]

It took 250 years for the jury to develop into the powerful institution it became at the end of the 15th century. In the 15th century, the common law that protected the rights of the accused came under attack. Political offenses and treason were especially problematic; therefore, a special judicial body, the **Court of the Star Chamber** (so called because the court met in a room with stars painted on the ceiling), was established to deal with offenses such as riots, unlawful assembly, perjury, criminal libel, and conspiracy.[16] The Court of the Star Chamber was notable for abuses such as:

> Secret interrogation of suspects

> The use of torture

> No right to a trial by jury

> Accusations brought without evidence

> The accused not informed of the identity of people making accusations[17]

Court of the Star Chamber—An old English court comprising the king's councilors that was separate from common-law courts.

During the Salem witch trials in colonial Massachusetts, many colonists were accused of practicing witchcraft; some were even executed. Why was each colony's court system different?

The Court of the Star Chamber is important because it demonstrated how a court without due process could violate citizens' human rights. It was abolished in 1641.

By the 18th century, many of the essential elements of modern criminal procedure were found in some form in English courts. Features such as a preliminary hearing, a grand jury, the opportunity for the defendant to challenge jurors who might be prejudiced against the case, and the idea that the jury's verdict is the final decision if the defendant is acquitted were added to the process. Eventually, the concept of an independent jury became firmly established in the English system, which today serves as a key check against the state's power to prosecute citizens.

Courts in Colonial North America

The development of courts in the North American colonies was an imperfect process. Because each of the 13 colonies was established under different motivations and conditions (for instance, Pennsylvania was founded by religious dissenters, whereas Virginia was founded by English gentry), the systems of government tended to vary widely. England made no effort to standardize practices among the colonies, so courts developed in response to the local economic, political, and social concerns of each colony.[18] Because many colonies were established by grants to individuals or corporations, early governors held court as they saw fit, and many of the legal protections that existed for defendants in England were absent in colonial North America. Complaints about the courts were frequent, and individuals often appealed to England to send trained judges to administer the law.[19]

One of the primary social forces that led to the American Revolution of 1776 was the colonists' belief that the English crown was treating them unfairly. The repressive measures England used violated the understandings many had about the rights of English subjects. These abuses of what many considered the common law included the practice of searching houses to find untaxed smuggled items and the use of admiralty courts in which trial by jury, right to counsel, and indictment by grand jury were absent. Given the second-class citizenship felt by many colonists, a move for independence seemed inevitable.[20]

An enduring consequence of independence from England is the U.S. Constitution, particularly the first 10 amendments, or the **Bill of Rights**, which were created to specify the relationship between the people and the state.[21] The framers of the Constitution recognized that conditions and situations change, and the process for amending the Constitution has allowed for expansion and a further delineation of rights. The courts were left to interpret how specific behaviors should be viewed, which has resulted in an important balance between the laws enacted by the legislature and the way those laws are applied.[22] In fact, although the Bill of Rights lists numerous rights and protections concerning criminal procedure, the only one that is also included in all state constitutions is the right to a jury trial.

> **Bill of Rights (from Chapter 3)**—The first 10 amendments to the U.S. Constitution, which guarantee fundamental rights and privileges to citizens.

PAUSE AND REVIEW

1. **Why was the Assize of Clarendon important to the establishment of the jury?**
2. **What is the Court of the Star Chamber?**
3. **Why were the colonial North American courts problematic?**

The Organization of Modern U.S. Criminal Courts

The U.S. criminal court system is the result of different developmental processes that have spawned a complex organizational structure that defies quick description. Unlike other countries, the United States has no centralized court system that uses equivalent terminology, jurisdictions, and personnel, which makes it difficult to understand how justice is meted out. This hodgepodge structure plays a large part in how the courts function and has the unintended consequence of subtly changing not only the style of justice, but also the quality of justice from one jurisdiction to another. This uneven system of justice presents a challenge for the observer of the courts to grasp the big picture. Therefore, we will examine the organization of the courts from several different angles with the intent of demonstrating its complexity.

> **LEARNING OBJECTIVE 5**
> Classify the three types of jurisdiction.

> **LEARNING OBJECTIVE 6**
> Outline the structure of the federal courts.

> **LEARNING OBJECTIVE 7**
> Outline the structure of state courts.

The Nature of Jurisdiction

Essential to our understanding of the courts is the concept of jurisdiction. **Jurisdiction** refers to the authority of the court to hear certain cases. The jurisdiction of any court depends on three factors: the seriousness of the case, the location of the offense, and whether the case is being heard for the first time or is on appeal. The three types of jurisdiction are subject-matter jurisdiction, geographic jurisdiction, and hierarchical jurisdiction.[23]

> **Subject-matter jurisdiction**. The nature of the case can determine which court will have jurisdiction. For example, many specialized courts handle only specific types of cases. Drug courts, traffic courts, and juvenile or family courts can be classified by subject-matter jurisdiction.[24] Sometimes

> **jurisdiction**—The authority of the court to hear certain cases.

> **subject-matter jurisdiction**—The authority of a court to hear a case based on the nature of the case.

limited-jurisdiction court—A court that has jurisdiction only over certain types of cases or subject matter.

general-jurisdiction court—A court that may hear all types of cases except for those prohibited by law.

geographic jurisdiction—The authority of a court to hear a case based on the location of the offense.

circuit court—A court that holds sessions at intervals within different areas of a judicial district.

hierarchical jurisdiction—The authority of a court to hear a case based on where the case is located in the system.

the distinction between felonies and misdemeanors will dictate the court to which a case is sent. **Limited-jurisdiction courts**—courts that have jurisdiction only over certain types of cases or subject matter—tend to handle misdemeanors, traffic cases, and low-value civil cases, whereas **general-jurisdiction courts**—courts that may hear all types of cases except for those prohibited by law—typically deal with more serious felonies. Depending on the state, some type of limited jurisdiction court may handle tasks such as issuing warrants, establishing bail, advising defendants of their rights, and setting a preliminary hearing date.

> **Geographic jurisdiction**. The location of an offense dictates which court will hear the case. Therefore, the political boundaries of cities, counties, and states can determine the geographic jurisdiction of a court. Depending on the state, jurisdictions may include courts in several counties that operate under a **circuit court**, which presides over different parts of a judicial district. Aimed at balancing the caseload according to population, a circuit might have one densely populated county or several less populated counties. Military bases and installations, American Indian reservations, and national parks are also subject to geographic jurisdiction. Offenses committed in these locations can be dealt with by courts established especially for the needs of these political structures. For instance, although a homicide committed on a military base may have happened within the jurisdiction of a state circuit court, it also occurred on federal land and thus would be handled by a federal court. Furthermore, if the defendant is military personnel, the case may be handled according to the Uniform Code of Military Justice rather than the federal court system.

> **Hierarchical jurisdiction**. A court's authority to hear a case is based on where the case is located in the system. For example, trial courts and appellate courts (which will be covered in more detail later) hear cases at different points in the system. Trial courts hear cases first, determine guilt, and impose a sentence. If a verdict is appealed, an appellate court reviews the work of the trial court and determines whether the case was handled within the constraints of the Constitution. If it is determined that the trial court judge allowed a mistake to occur, such as the presentation of illegally gathered evidence by the police, the appellate court can overrule the verdict and set aside the sentence. In terms of hierarchy, trial courts are responsible for implementing the substantive law, whereas appellate courts are responsible for ensuring that the trial courts follow procedural law.

These three ways of classifying jurisdiction alert us to the various organizational frameworks that compose our fragmented court system in the United States. As we delve deeper into the nature and structure of federal and state courts and confront the complex and overlapping terminology used to identify courts, it will be useful to remember that each court is somehow classified according to each of these three measures of jurisdiction. Each court is responsible for handling certain types of cases, according to the geographic location of the offense, and according to whether the case is being heard for the first time or is under appeal.

The Structure of the Federal Courts

The U.S. court system is divided into federal and state courts. We can think of this as a dual court system in which each part is further subdivided according to subject matter, geographic, and hierarchical jurisdiction. The federal courts get their power from Article III of the Constitution. Article III, Section 1 creates the U.S. Supreme Court and gives Congress the authority to create the lower federal courts. Thus, federal courts do not have general jurisdiction, as they may only hear cases that fall within the specifications of Article III. Federal courts comprise three main levels: U.S. district courts, U.S. courts of appeals, and the U.S. Supreme Court (for a look at how a case may move through the federal court system, see Figure 7.1). Federal courts hear the following types of cases:

1. Cases in which the U.S. government or one of its officers is a party

2. Cases involving violations of federal law or the Constitution

3. Cases between residents of different states if the dollar amount at issue exceeds $75,000

4. Cases involving bankruptcy, copyright, patent, and maritime law[25]

Additionally, state and federal courts may have *concurrent jurisdiction*. These cases typically involve circumstances in which a resident of one state sues a resident of another state. For the most part, however, the lines between federal and state court jurisdiction are clear except in cases in which the offense violates both federal and state laws. A high-profile example is the 2002 D.C. sniper case, in which the defendants, John Allen Muhammad and Lee Boyd Malvo, killed a federal agent and committed murders in the District of Columbia and other states. There is no law pertaining to such a situation, so the choice of where to prosecute Muhammad and Malvo fell to federal authorities, primarily because the two were in federal custody. After much political wrangling, the state of Virginia was chosen to prosecute the pair first. Both men were convicted. Muhammad was sentenced to death, and Malvo, who was a juvenile at the time of the murders, was sentenced to life in prison.[26] Generally, states may only initiate criminal prosecutions in state courts, and the federal government may only initiate criminal prosecutions in federal court.

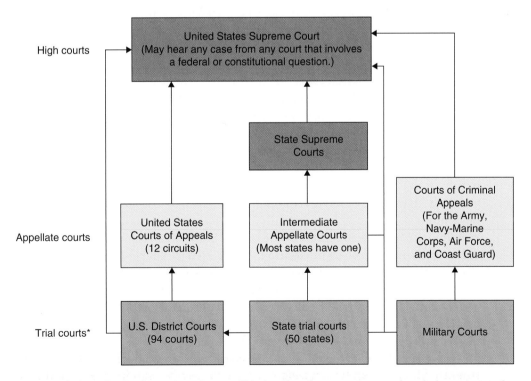

FIGURE 7.1   The Federal and State Court Systems   This chart shows how cases may move from the lower courts to the U.S. Supreme Court. The number of cases decreases at each level. For example, the U.S. Supreme Court hears relatively few cases. Why would the number of cases decrease at each level?

The U.S. Courts of Appeals also receive cases from the U.S. Tax Court, the U.S. Court of International Trade, the U.S. Court of Federal Claims, and the U.S. Court of Veterans Appeals.

John Allen Muhammad (in orange), was sentenced to death for the D.C. sniper attacks that resulted in the deaths of 10 people. In this case, why were the lines between federal and state court jurisdictions blurred?

racketeering—A federal crime that involves patterns of illegal activity carried out by organized groups that run illegal businesses or break the law in other organized ways.

Many types of criminal offenses trigger a federal charge. These include offenses involving drug trafficking, immigration, identity theft, child pornography, child molestation, explosives, offenses committed in federal facilities or on federal property, kidnapping, offenses that cross state lines, bank robbery, **racketeering** (offenses committed with the purpose of promoting an organization or business), organized crime, terrorism, fraud, bribery, extortion, and piracy. Each of the 94 federal judicial districts has a U.S. Marshal. Deputy U.S. Marshals oversee taking into custody suspects charged with a federal offense, including booking, processing and detention, court security, and prisoner transportation.

Once a suspect is charged, he or she goes through a process that is much like the state process (described in Chapter 9). The processing of a federal case begins with the 93 U.S. attorneys who are the chief federal law enforcement officers within their districts, and the grand jury. Federal law enforcement agencies are generally the source of most criminal investigations referred to the U.S. attorneys; however, state and local law enforcement agencies are also sources of referrals. The attorneys, who represent the United States in all criminal prosecutions, determine which cases to prosecute in their district courts (see Figure 7.2 for the number of suspects referred to the U.S. attorneys). The grand jury reviews the evidence from the U.S. attorney and decides whether it is enough to require a defendant to stand trial. A suspect must be brought before a judicial officer, usually a U.S. magistrate, upon arrest for an initial appearance. If a defendant pleads guilty immediately (90 percent do) and accepts a plea bargain, the court process stops there. If the defendant wishes to go to trial, the case can move from the district courts (trial courts), to the courts of appeals, and, finally, to the U.S. Supreme Court if the Court decides that the case involves a substantial question about the U.S. Constitution or federal law. A more detailed explanation of each type of court follows.[27]

U.S. DISTRICT COURTS

U.S. district courts are trial courts of general jurisdiction that try felony cases involving federal laws and civil cases in which the amount of money in controversy exceeds $75,000. Although civil cases constitute most of the district courts' workload, since 1980 drug and immigration prosecutions have risen significantly and now represent a large percentage of all federal criminal cases (see Figure 7.3).[28]

U.S. district courts are responsible for only a few types of cases that typically go to court. Most often, these are cases involving a federal question, an issue of diversity of jurisdiction, or a prisoner petition.

> Federal-question cases involve laws that are passed by the federal government, have constitutional implications, or involve treaties with other countries. Issues such as Social Security, antitrust laws, and civil rights violations also fall within the purview of the U.S. district courts.

> Diversity of jurisdiction involves cases between citizens of different states or with someone from another country. Although individuals have the option of suing in a state court, the opportunity to use the federal court system is attractive because of the presumed objectivity and the possibility of a greater reward. For this reason, the amount of money in dispute must exceed $75,000.[29]

> Prisoners in either federal or state prisons can file petitions in the U.S. district courts if they believe their rights under federal law are being violated. Typically, these cases allege violations of due process (such as lack of an effective attorney), cruel and unusual punishment (such as prison overcrowding or bad food), or inadequate medical care. Many of these cases are actually heard in a magistrate court (discussed later in this section), which then makes a recommendation to the U.S. district judge. Of the 94 U.S. district courts, 89 are located within the 50 states; the rest are in U.S. territories such as Puerto Rico and Guam, as well as in the District of Columbia. Each state has at least one district court, and some states, such as New York and Texas, have as many as four. No district court crosses state lines. The 94 districts have 667 district court judgeships that are distributed according to the population served and the political clout of members of Congress.[30] Judges are appointed to indefinite terms that depend on their good behavior; a judgeship can amount to a lifelong job unless a judge is caught breaking the law or brings scandal to the court. The reason judges are not given specific terms of four or six years is to allow them to be independent and objective. If they had to worry about reappointment or reelection, they might be concerned with the political effect of their rulings.

To assist the U.S. district courts with their caseload, Congress created the office of the U.S. magistrate in 1968. Magistrate court judges, who work within the district courts, are chosen by the district court judges and serve either as full-time judges (appointed to eight-year terms) or as part-time judges (appointed to four-year terms). The powers of federal magistrates are limited because their authority and independence are not explicitly delineated in the Constitution, as are the roles of other federal judges. For instance, they do not serve for life, nor are they selected by the president and confirmed by the Senate.[31]

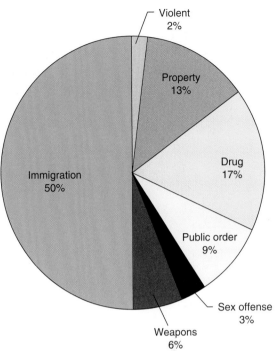

FIGURE 7.2 Number of Suspects Referred to U.S. Attorneys by Offense Type Most of the suspects referred to a U.S. attorney are involved in an immigration case. Typically, how many defendants plead guilty immediately and accept a plea bargain?

Source: Mark Motivans, Federal Justice Statistics, 2013–2014, *Table 6: Suspects in Matters Referred to U.S. Attorneys, by Offense Type and Federal District of Referral, 2010, 2013, and 2014 (U.S. Department of Justice Office of Justice Programs Bureau of Justice Statistics, 2017), 14. Available at https://www.bjs.gov/index.cfm?ty=pbdetail&iid=5885.*

U.S. district courts— Courts of general jurisdiction that try felony cases involving federal laws and civil cases involving amounts of money over $75,000.

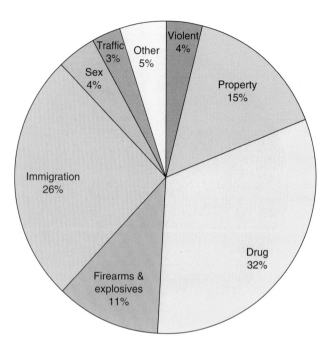

FIGURE 7.3   U.S. District Courts, Criminal Cases by Offense, 2016 Which offenses represent the largest portion of the district courts' workload?

Source: Federal Judicial Caseload Statistics, *Table D-2. U.S. District Courts—Criminal Defendants Commenced, by Offense, During the 12-Month Periods Ending March 31, 2012 through 2016. Accessed at http://www.uscourts.gov/report-names/federal-judicial-caseload-statistics.*

U.S. courts of appeals—Intermediate courts that dispose of many appeals before they reach the Supreme Court.

U.S. Supreme Court—The "court of last resort." The highest court in the United States, established by Article III of the Constitution, hears only appeals, with some exceptions.

writ of certiorari—An order from a superior court calling up for review the record of a case from a lower court.

Magistrate judges operate courts of limited jurisdiction that perform many of the court system's routine but essential tasks. For more serious felony cases that are typically handled by the district courts, magistrate judges assist with the preliminary work of sitting for initial appearances, conducting preliminary hearings, appointing counsel for those who cannot afford their own attorney, setting bail, and issuing search warrants. Additionally, the magistrate court handles misdemeanor cases by presiding over trials, accepting pleas, and passing sentences. In addition to its criminal case duties, the magistrate court performs a comparable set of duties for civil cases.

U.S. COURTS OF APPEALS

U.S. courts of appeals consist of 94 courts in 11 circuits, each of which encompasses several states, plus the District of Columbia Circuit and the Federal Circuit for a total of 13 circuits.[32] Judges are nominated by the president, confirmed by the Senate, and serve life terms, as long as their behavior is not called into question.[33] The U.S. courts of appeals serve as intermediate courts of appeals and can dispose of many appeals before they reach the Supreme Court. The Supreme Court hears relatively few cases each year, so for all practical purposes the U.S. courts of appeals are the "courts of last resort" for almost all federal cases.

In addition to criminal cases, the bulk of the U.S. courts of appeals caseload concerns civil rights violations, cases of sex discrimination, and cases of discrimination against the disabled. This requires each circuit to have a vast staff of lawyers and clerks and for each judge to have three law clerks. The process of screening and reviewing all the cases presented on appeal involves a substantial investment of resources and time to ensure that the U.S. district courts did not make procedural errors.

U.S. SUPREME COURT

The **U.S. Supreme Court** is at the top of the hierarchical jurisdiction for both the federal and state court systems (see CJ Reference 7.1 on how the Court got its power). Even when a case has gone through the entire state court process, including the state supreme court, appeal to the U.S. Supreme Court might still be a possibility, although a remote one. Although the Court may hear any case it wishes, as long as it involves federal or constitutional law, the typical case involves a "substantial federal question."[34] The Court grants plenary review (meaning that the Court independently examines the issue), with oral arguments by attorneys, in about 100 cases per term. Formal written opinions are delivered in 80 to 90 cases.[35] The Court does not attempt to serve as a court of last resort for all federal and state cases but instead seeks cases that have broad policy implications for important questions of the day.[36] The Court does have original jurisdiction in cases affecting foreign officials and those in which a state is a party. However, the Court has seldom heard cases involving foreign officials, and devotes its original jurisdiction to handling disputes between state governments.[37] In all other cases, the Court has appellate jurisdiction.

The procedure of the Supreme Court is to issue a **writ of certiorari** to a lower court that orders the case records to be sent to the justices so that they can decide whether the case presents the type of questions that should be decided by the

CJ REFERENCE 7.1
What Makes the Supreme Court Supreme?

Article III of the Constitution states that "[t]he judicial Power of the United States, shall be vested in one supreme Court, and in such inferior Courts as the Congress may from time to time ordain and establish." The U.S. Supreme Court was created in accordance with this provision in 1789 and organized on February 2, 1790.

However, the U.S. Supreme Court did not become the final arbiter of the nation's laws all at once. It achieved that status one case at a time. *Marbury* v. *Madison* (1803) established the judiciary as equal to the executive and legislative branches of government.[38] The issue in question was a minor decision concerning whether William Marbury should be given a commission as a justice of the peace as President John Adams had ordered. Because of an error, Marbury did not receive his commission, and the new president, Thomas Jefferson, ordered that the commission not be delivered.[39] Marbury did not get his commission, but the case is famous because Chief Justice John Marshall established the principle of judicial review, whereby the Supreme Court scrutinizes state and federal legislation and the acts of state and federal

executive officers and courts to determine whether they conflict with the Constitution.[40] Marshall also initiated the practice of presenting the justices' decisions as collective rather than separate opinions and providing written statements of the reasons why the court reached its decision.[41] Later, in *Martin v. Hunter's Lessee* (1816) and *Cohens v. Virginia* (1821), the Supreme Court reaffirmed the superiority of federal law over state law, upholding the Supremacy Clause in Article VI of the Constitution:

> This Constitution, and the laws of the United States which shall be made in pursuance thereof; and all treaties made, or which shall be made, under the authority of the United States, shall be the supreme law of the land; and the judges in every state shall be bound thereby, anything in the Constitution or laws of any State to the contrary notwithstanding.

The Court's decision thus established its power as the "final word" on all cases, and the Supreme Court became the court of last resort.[42]

Supreme Court. A **rule of four** exists whereby at least four of the nine Supreme Court justices must vote to hear a case before it is put on the docket.[43] All nine justices then hear the case, unlike the courts of appeals in which a panel of three justices hears a case. When a case is scheduled, attorneys file written arguments, as well as briefs on behalf of other parties called **amicus curiae** ("friend of the court") briefs, which allow an individual or a group that is not party to a case to give advice or testimony.[44] For instance, an organization such as the American Civil Liberties Union or Amnesty International may file an amicus curiae brief in a case involving the death penalty for someone who is mentally disabled.

SPECIALIZED FEDERAL COURTS

Most specialized federal courts hear civil cases.[45] However, a few types of courts hear criminal cases.

The U.S. Court of Appeals for the Armed Forces handles cases of military law in which questions of due process are raised in the implementation of the Uniform Code of Military Justice. Military justice imposes a broad set of rules and laws on military personnel to which civilians are not subject. Failure to follow orders or showing disrespect for an officer are violations of the Uniform Code of Military Justice and can result in punishments that include incarceration or discharge from the armed services. Armed forces personnel are not entitled to all the protections of the Constitution, and the due process afforded to suspected violators of military law is not as extensive as that afforded by civilian courts.[46]

Another specialized federal court that receives many criminal cases is the tribal court. American Indian tribes enjoy a certain level of self-determination

rule of four—A rule that states that at least four of the nine Supreme Court justices must vote to hear a case.

amicus curiae—A brief in which someone who is not a part of a case gives advice or testimony.

The Supreme Court of the United States. Seated from left are Associate Justice Ruth Bader Ginsburg, Associate Justice Anthony M. Kennedy, Chief Justice John G. Roberts, Associate Justice Clarence Thomas, and Associate Justice Stephen Breyer. Standing behind, from left, are Associate Justice Elena Kagan, Associate Justice Samuel Alito Jr., Associate Justice Sonia Sotomayor, and Associate Justice Neil Gorsuch. What is the process a case must go through in order to be heard by the Supreme Court?

and sovereignty on federal reservations. For example, in many states, American Indians have established casinos on reservations regardless of the approval of state governments. The tribal judicial system revolves around a core of five legal institutions: indigenous forums (also known as traditional courts), Court of Indian Offenses, intertribal courts, the courts of appeals, and tribal courts of general jurisdiction.[47] Tribal law is administered by American Indians and can be imposed in lieu of state law in some circumstances.[48] Especially for issues dealing with traditional American Indian concerns, such as hunting and fishing rights, tribal law can supersede state or federal law. Criminal jurisdiction on Indian lands varies by type of offense, whether the suspect/offender and/ or victim is a member of a tribe, and the state in which the alleged offense occurred. Offenses committed on Indian lands are often subject to concurrent jurisdiction among multiple criminal justice agencies. Six states—California, Minnesota (except the Red Lake Reservation), Nebraska, Oregon (except the Warm Springs Reservation), Wisconsin, and Alaska—have mandatory jurisdiction over offenses committed on Indian lands. The following states have optional jurisdiction either in whole or in part over Indian lands within their boundaries: Nevada, Idaho, Iowa, Washington, South Dakota, Montana, North Dakota, Arizona, and Utah. In other states, the federal government retains criminal jurisdiction for major offenses committed on Indian lands.[49]

Perhaps one of the most controversial types of federal court is the military commission: "a military court of law traditionally used to try law of war and other offenses. An alien unprivileged enemy belligerent who has engaged in hostilities, or who has purposefully and materially supported hostilities against the United States, its coalition partners or was a part of al Qaeda, is subject to trial by military commission under the Military Commissions Act of 2009."[50] Although military commissions have been around since the Revolutionary War, they came into regular use again after September 11, 2001, when President George W. Bush decided that terrorism suspects would be considered enemy combatants not subject to trial in criminal court.[51] Military commissions got off to a rocky start,

Pictured here is Chief Judge William Zuger, presiding over the Standing Rock Tribal Court. What are some of the functions of the tribal court?

however, when the U.S. Supreme Court set forth in *Hamdan* v. *Rumsfeld* (2006) that President Bush's 2001 Military Order was insufficient to conduct military commissions in a constitutional manner (see Case in Point 7.1).[52] Thus, the Military Commissions Act of 2006 was passed in response to *Hamdan*.

Military commissions are organized by a convening authority appointed by the U.S. Secretary of Defense. The military commission begins when the prosecution drafts charges against a person subject to the Military Commissions Act of 2009 (an updated version of the 2006 act). The convening authority decides whether to refer any or all of the charges to trial, which requires a finding of probable cause. If referred, a military commission is created. Individuals subject to trial by military commission are innocent until proven guilty beyond a reasonable doubt.[53]

The Structure of State Courts

The state court systems, which are established by the U.S. Constitution and each state's laws, address most of the legal disputes in the United States, both civil and criminal.[54] Like federal courts, **state courts** are generally divided according to a three-tier hierarchy.[55] At the lowest level are the courts of "first instance," state trial courts of limited and general jurisdiction. Some courts, especially those of limited jurisdiction and those with high caseloads, employ part-time judges or have staff hear cases as referees, commissioners, or hearing officers. These courts decide a case by examining the facts.[56] Further on, state intermediate courts of appeals review the trial court's application of the law to those facts.[57] Usually, an intermediate court of appeals reviews the cases of the lower courts before the court of last resort, the state supreme court, makes its final ruling. However, we use the phrase "final ruling" with caution because for a few cases, such as those with a "substantial federal question," there is always a chance that the U.S. Supreme Court could select them for review.

According to the Court Statistics Project, about 11,500 trial courts of general and limited jurisdiction reside within the authority of the United States. Each jurisdiction has different criteria for deciding what constitutes a court and thus has

state courts—General courts and special courts funded and run by each state.

CASE IN POINT 7.1

Hamdan v. Rumsfeld (2006)

THE POINT

The military commission as authorized after September 11, 2001, is insufficient to try terrorist suspects under the Uniform Code of Military Justice and the Geneva Conventions.

THE CASE

Salim Ahmed Hamdan, Osama bin Laden's former chauffeur, was captured by Afghani forces in 2001 and sent in 2002 to the U.S. military detention facility in Guantánamo Bay, Cuba. Hamdan challenged his detention by filing a petition for a writ of habeas corpus (a court order that directs the government to produce the prisoner and give a reason for his or her detention) in federal district court. Before the district court could rule on the petition, Hamdan received a hearing from a military tribunal, which designated him an enemy combatant.

The district court granted Hamdan's petition, ruling that he must first receive a hearing to determine whether he was a prisoner of war under the Geneva Convention before a military commission could try him. The D.C. Circuit Court of Appeals reversed this decision, finding that the Geneva Convention could not be enforced in federal court and that Congress had authorized the establishment of military tribunals.

The Supreme Court held that neither an act of Congress nor the inherent powers of the Executive in the Constitution expressly authorized the type of military commission at issue in *Hamdan*. Without such authorization, the commission had to comply with U.S. criminal law and the laws of war. The Supreme Court, then, could enforce the Geneva Convention, along with the statutory Uniform Code of Military Justice. Hamdan's exclusion from parts of his trial that the military commission considered classified violated both the Geneva Convention and the Uniform Code of Military Justice and was therefore illegal.

THINK ABOUT IT

1. Why did the military commission have to comply with U.S. criminal law, according to the U.S. Supreme Court?
2. Why was the president's order insufficient to conduct military commissions in a constitutional manner?

In this courtroom sketch, defendant Salim Ahmed Hamdan (left) watches as an FBI agent testifies about his interrogations of Hamdan during Hamdan's trial inside the war crimes courthouse at Guantánamo Bay U.S. Naval Base in Cuba. Why are military commissions controversial?

a different number of courts. For example, on the one hand, Texas considers each judgeship to be a court and so reports about 2,700 trial courts; on the other hand, California has 58 superior courts in its trial court system. Both states are among the largest in the union; however, they count courts differently.[58] For an example of the structure of a state court, see Figure 7.4.

JUVENILE COURTS

Although juvenile courts are part of the state court system, they differ in their goals and in the way they operate from courts that deal with adults. Whereas courts that try adults follow criminal law, juvenile courts follow civil law because the primary goal of juvenile courts is rehabilitation, not punishment. The relationship between state courts and their juvenile counterparts differs from state to state. However, only a few states operate completely separate juvenile courts. Most juvenile courts are attached to family courts or trial courts (although they are not trial courts). Juvenile courts will be discussed in greater detail in Chapter 13.

STATE TRIAL COURTS

State trial courts of limited jurisdiction are called **lower courts** or inferior courts. This refers simply to their place on the hierarchical ladder and not to the quality of justice they dispense. Technically, they are not part of the state court system because in most states the lower courts of limited jurisdiction are not funded by the state but instead receive their authority and resources from local county or municipal governments. There are more than 8,000 trial courts of limited jurisdiction in the United States. They handle most cases by either passing sentence or holding preliminary hearings and motions.[59]

Trial courts of limited jurisdiction have a variety of names depending on the state in which they operate. They are called city magistrates, justices of the peace, county courts, or city courts. They handle more than 67 million matters a year, mostly traffic cases, but also misdemeanors, small claims, and the preliminary stages of felony cases. These courts of limited jurisdiction are where most citizens come into contact with the court system. The geographic jurisdictions of limited-jurisdiction courts vary by state, having either county jurisdiction or jurisdiction limited to a city or town.[60]

Trial courts of general jurisdiction are referred to as "major trial courts" and are variously named circuit courts, district courts, superior courts, or courts of common pleas. These courts handle major cases in both the civil and criminal arenas. State trial courts of general jurisdiction hear most of the serious

lower courts— Sometimes called inferior courts, in reference to their hierarchy. These courts receive their authority and resources from local county or municipal governments.

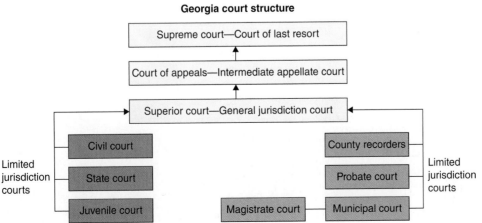

FIGURE 7.4 Court Structure of the State of Georgia Which are the courts of limited jurisdiction? Would these courts deal with serious felonies?

Source: Ron Malega and Thomas H. Cohen, State Court Organization, 2011 *(Washington, D.C.: U.S. Department of Justice Office of Justice Programs Bureau of Justice Statistics, 2013), 2.*

street-crime cases. Whereas federal courts deal with major white-collar offenders and large-scale drug dealers, state courts handle most cases involving rape, murder, theft, and small-scale drug dealing and drug possession.

Although the state trial court of general jurisdiction is popularly portrayed in the media when there is a jury trial, the bulk of the work of this type of court is conducted in hallways, judges' chambers, and over the telephone and via e-mail as prosecutors and defense attorneys negotiate plea bargains that eliminate the need for a trial.[61] These courts handle a variety of civil cases including those involving domestic relations, estates, and personal injury. General-jurisdiction trial courts are subdivided into circuits or districts. In some states, a single county serves as the judicial district, but most states have judicial districts composed of several counties.[62]

Finally, state attorneys general are the primary legal authorities of the states, commonwealths, and territories of the United States. Among other duties, they serve as legal counsel to government agencies and legislatures. The authorities of the attorneys general include the following:

› Prosecuting corporations that violate antitrust laws

› Representing state agencies and addressing issues of legislative or administrative constitutionality

› Enforcing air, water, and hazardous waste laws in most states

› Conducting criminal appeals and state criminal prosecutions

› Interceding in cases involving public utility rates

› Bringing civil suits[63]

STATE INTERMEDIATE COURTS OF APPEALS

Intermediate appellate courts are a relatively recent addition to the U.S. state court system. In 1957, only 13 states had permanent intermediate appellate courts. Currently, 41 states have such courts, which hear all appeals from the

Assistant State Attorney Laura Burkhart Laurie goes through a chronology during her closing arguments in the trial of Dalia Dippolito, who was convicted of attempting to murder her husband Michael Dippolito in Boynton Beach, Florida. What types of cases do state trial courts of general jurisdiction handle?

lower state courts. Only states with small populations do not have this level of courts. Intermediate appellate courts often have rotating panels of three or more judges to review cases.[64] Typically, these courts must accept all criminal cases but not necessarily all civil cases. Additionally, appellate courts often review the decisions made by administrative agencies.[65]

In most cases, the decision at the intermediate court of appeals level is the final decision because the state supreme courts, like the U.S. Supreme Court, select only a small percentage of cases to consider each year. The exception to this rule is death-penalty cases. In states with capital punishment, the filing of death-penalty appeals in the court of last resort is usually mandatory.[66] There are no jury trials at the appellate level because guilt is not the overriding issue. These courts are more concerned with the conduct of the lower court in providing due-process protections for the defendant and ensuring that the judge followed proper procedures.[67]

STATE SUPREME COURTS

Making general statements about state supreme courts is difficult because court systems vary across states. In states that have an intermediate level of courts of appeals, the state supreme court has a discretionary docket, which means it can select the cases it wishes to consider. For sparsely populated states with no intermediate court of appeals, the state supreme court hears appeals from the lower courts. Like the U.S. Supreme Court, the state supreme courts have all the justices hear each case instead of using rotating three-judge panels. All courts of last resort have an odd number of judges, with the most typical arrangement being a

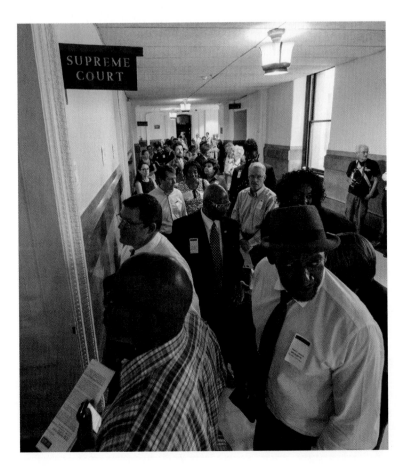

The state supreme court is the court of last resort for most cases. Here, people wait outside a courtroom of the Pennsylvania Supreme Court, which was hearing arguments in a case concerning school funding. An overflow courtroom that had been set up with video monitors was also filled, leaving many people waiting in the hallway. Which is more supreme: a state supreme court or the U.S. Supreme Court?

seven-judge court, as found in 28 states and Puerto Rico. Sixteen states have five-judge panels, and five have nine-judge panels.

The state supreme court is the court of last resort for all but a few cases that involve issues of constitutional or federal law that the U.S. Supreme Court decides are significant. The state supreme courts also have some authority to discipline lawyers and judges and often serve as a venue for judicial training.[68]

LOCAL AND COMMUNITY COURTS

There is a wide range of variation in the nature and organization of local courts across the United States. Although it is impossible to describe every type of community court here, we will highlight a few of these types of courts to show how they specialize in justice for specific problems. (For more on problem-solving courts, a type of community court, see A Closer Look 7.1.)

One of the primary features of U.S. government is that it should be close to the people. Therefore, each state has developed its own jurisdictional pattern to allow municipalities, counties, and neighborhoods to structure their local legal systems in a way that is most responsive to citizens' needs. The jurisdictional

---

A CLOSER LOOK 7.1
Problem-Solving Courts

Problem-solving courts are a recent innovation in the U.S. court system. A drug court in Florida's Miami-Dade County and a community court in Manhattan influenced the creation of similar courts throughout the country in the 1990s.[69] Today, the United States has more than 3,000 problem-solving courts. The most common types of problem-solving courts are drug courts (44 percent) and mental health courts (11 percent).[70]

Traditionally, the purpose of the U.S. courts is to process criminal and civil cases in the most objective manner possible. However, problem-solving courts approach some criminal matters from a different perspective in that they accommodate offenders with needs and problems that traditional courts cannot or will not adequately address, such as drug abuse, mental illness, veterans' issues, and domestic violence. These courts promote outcomes that will benefit not only society, but also the offender and the victim. Successful completion of a court program typically includes case dismissal or a suspended sentence.[71] Some common elements of problem-solving courts are:

- Focus on outcomes. Problem-solving courts are designed to reduce recidivism and create safer communities.
- Judicial involvement. Judges take an active approach to addressing problems and changing defendants' behavior.
- Collaboration. Problem-solving courts work with external parties, such as mental health providers and drug rehabilitation providers.

- Non-traditional roles. Problem-solving courts are less adversarial than traditional courts because personnel of problem-solving courts assume roles or processes not common in traditional courts.[72]

Often judges in problem-solving courts also work in, or have worked in, traditional courts, and thus may sometimes be uncomfortable with the problem-solving process. A more serious concern is that judges in problem-solving courts are often involved in ex parte meetings that exclude the defendant, a practice that is frowned upon or banned in some traditional courts.[73]

Another concern is the practice of "net-widening," which is when the criminal justice system pulls in people who would not normally be involved in the criminal justice process in an effort to help them. Drug courts, for example, have been criticized for processing drug users who would ordinarily have received only probation or no sanction at all. Although the drug court seeks to help the drug user, this might involve the person having to spend time in jail and make several appearances in court. Although the drug court is well intentioned, the process still stresses both the offender and the system.[74]

THINK ABOUT IT

1. Consider the issues of ex parte meetings and net-widening. In each scenario, how might there be some loss of a defendant's rights? Do the good intentions of problem-solving courts outweigh these concerns?

pattern of each state reflects different geographic features (urban versus rural), types of crime, and resources available to local governments.[75] Here are some types of community courts.

> Drug courts. Many local jurisdictions have adopted the philosophy that minor drug offenses, especially possession, clog the courts with trivial cases and drain resources from more serious offenses. Because drug users who are otherwise respectable citizens and do not pose a threat of violence to the community are usually handled by the imposition of a fine or sent to a treatment program, it is deemed unnecessary to employ the traditional criminal court. Drug courts are specialized or problem-solving courts that can siphon off many cases that are routinely treated more leniently than more serious cases. Drug courts allow the criminal justice system to accomplish several goals. First, the vast numbers of drug offenders can be treated more consistently. Having a court that specializes in low-level drug offenders ensures that cases with similar conditions are assigned similar sanctions. Second, drug-court personnel are more aware of treatment options available in the community.[76] This means that someone who would benefit from counseling or drug treatment is more likely to receive it.[77] Third, it is less expensive and more efficient to deal with low-level drug offenders in the specialized court, thus freeing up the criminal courts for handling more serious offenses.[78]

> Conflict-resolution programs. Many low-level offenses, such as burglaries or street fights, can be more efficiently dealt with by allowing offenders and victims to work out their disputes between themselves and not engaging the formal legal system.[79] Often, all that is required to satisfy victims is an apology, some restitution, and the feeling that offenders are being dealt with seriously. Because many offenders and victims have an ongoing relationship after the settlement of the case, conflict-resolution programs

Here, Faith Spriggs, a recent graduate of the Noble County (Indiana) Drug Court, shows her 2013 jail booking photo. What is the purpose of community courts, such as drug courts?

are useful because they can deal with some of the underlying issues that resulted in the offense.[80]

> Family courts. Many jurisdictions have family courts that deal with domestic assault, child abuse, and custody issues. Often, family courts are incorporated into the juvenile court, although in some jurisdictions they are freestanding. The advantage of family courts is that court personnel, including judges, can be more specialized in their knowledge of family dynamics and resources available to solve family problems. Given the focus of this type of court, family court judges are often better able to supervise personnel responsible for investigating child-abuse cases and monitor that the children in their cases are being adequately addressed.

> Magistrate courts. Magistrate courts handle minor offenses, preliminary court proceedings, and pre-trial intervention programs, and they establish bail. In many jurisdictions, the initial arraignment is now before the magistrate court. The magistrate court keeps minor cases out of the criminal justice system and often diverts them to alternative treatment programs designed to solve the underlying problems that resulted in the offense. By establishing bail, permitting release on recognizance, and by considering cases for dismissal, the magistrate court can relieve the local jail of the costly pretrial incarceration for those suspected of minor offenses.[81]

PAUSE AND REVIEW

1. **What are the three types of jurisdiction?**

2. **How are U.S. district courts different from U.S. courts of appeals?**

3. **What is the difference between state trial courts of limited jurisdiction and state trial courts of general jurisdiction?**

4. **How is the structure of the federal courts similar to the structure of state courts? In what ways do the two structures differ?**

blood feud—A disagreement whose settlement is based on personal vengeance and physical violence.

FOCUS ON ETHICS   Modern-Day Blood Feud

Your little brother has been dating a girl from another school for several months. Recently, during an argument, he got carried away and struck her. The next night he was shot in a drive-by shooting on the steps of your parents' home. You are certain your brother's killers are the girl's cousins, but the police have no solid evidence and are not close to making an arrest.

Although you know your brother was no saint and that striking another person deserves some punishment, his death has devastated your family, and you believe that, in part, it was racially motivated because your family is of Hispanic origin. The girl's cousins are part of a white-supremacy group that has continually hassled people of color in your county. However, the sheriff himself has

commented to reporters that your brother probably deserved what he got and that his office is too busy to expend more resources on this offense unless further evidence turns up.

You have lost faith in the local criminal justice system's ability and motivation to solve your brother's murder and bring his killers to justice. Your grandfather remarks that in his day, if someone was killed, it was the right, indeed the obligation, of the family to avenge the death themselves by killing the offender or a member of the offender's family. He looks at you in disgust and implies that you are a coward and a disgrace to the family. Engaging in a **blood feud** would likely lead to more violence and serve as encouragement for the killer's family to seek further revenge, and it could potentially set off a series of reciprocal acts of violence. As a criminal justice major at a local university, you know that modern courts evolved as a means of resolution from a long history of such feuds, skirmishes, and other types of conflicts that often caused more problems than they solved. You also have hopes of one day becoming an FBI agent, but the pull of family honor has you torn, and you think that you should make sure the killers do not get away with this.

WHAT DO YOU DO?

1. Do nothing. Even though you think the local criminal justice system has failed to properly investigate your brother's murder, there is little you can do that is within the law. Besides, you have your own life and career to think about. Even though your family expects you to seek justice, you are unwilling to continue the cycle of violence started by your hotheaded brother.

2. Uphold your family's honor and retaliate against the cousins of your brother's girlfriend. If the local criminal justice system does not care about your community, it is your duty to seek justice through revenge. If you do not, the Hispanic community will continue to be victimized by the powerful white majority.

3. Go to the FBI and make a complaint charging that this was a hate crime and that your brother's constitutional rights were violated. If the local criminal justice system refuses to act, make a federal case out of your brother's murder.

For more insight as to how someone might respond to such an ethical dilemma, visit the companion website at www.oup.com/us/fuller to watch a video that connects this scenario to a real-world situation.

Summary

LEARNING OBJECTIVE **1** — Identify the challenges facing the U.S. court system.	The court system does not control how it is financed; it does not control how many cases it receives; its financial resources are limited; and it cannot control its public image because proceedings are open to the press. The professional orientation of attorneys require them to strike the most advantageous deal for their clients, rather than outcomes that may better reflect justice. Outsiders have difficulty understanding court proceedings. Television presentation of justice as entertainment can portray the court system inaccurately.
LEARNING OBJECTIVE **2** — Outline the importance of the Assize of Clarendon to the establishment of the jury.	The Assize of Clarendon was a series of ordinances that established the beginnings of the grand jury system. Twelve men from each jurisdiction informed the king's judges of the most serious offenses committed in each jurisdiction. Gradually, the process evolved from simply identifying and charging wrongdoers to a body that determined whether the evidence was sufficient to detain the accused before trial.
LEARNING OBJECTIVE **3** — Describe trial by ordeal and its relationship to the jury trial.	There were three main types of trial by ordeal: trial by cold water, trial by hot water, and trial by hot iron (or fire). Trial by ordeal was determined by divine intervention, and priests judged whether God provided a miracle to save the accused. In 1215, the Roman Catholic Church outlawed the practice, which led to the development of the jury trial.
LEARNING OBJECTIVE **4** — Describe the challenges faced by the courts in colonial North America.	Each of the 13 colonies was established under different motivations and conditions, thus systems of government varied widely. England made no effort to develop or enforce standardized practices among the colonies, so courts developed in response to the local economic, political, and social concerns of each colony. Many of the legal protections that existed for defendants in England were absent in the colonies.

LEARNING OBJECTIVE 5 Classify the three types of jurisdiction.	Jurisdiction, the court's authority to hear certain cases, depends on three features: 1. The seriousness of the case (subject-matter jurisdiction) 2. The location of the offense (geographic jurisdiction) 3. Whether the case is being heard for the first time or is on appeal (hierarchical jurisdiction)
LEARNING OBJECTIVE 6 Outline the structure of the federal courts.	U.S. magistrate courts are the lowest level of the federal court system. U.S. district courts are courts of general jurisdiction that try felony cases involving federal laws and civil cases in which more than $75,000 is at stake. The U.S. courts of appeals consist of 11 district courts, each of which encompasses several states, as well the District of Columbia Circuit, and serve as intermediate courts of appeals. The Supreme Court is at the top of the hierarchical jurisdiction for both the federal and state court systems.
LEARNING OBJECTIVE 7 Outline the structure of state courts.	State trial courts of limited jurisdiction (also known as lower or inferior courts) are technically not part of the state court system because, in most states, these courts receive their authority and resources from local county or municipal governments. They handle most cases by either passing sentence or holding preliminary hearings and motions. State intermediate courts of appeals must accept all criminal cases but not necessarily all civil cases and often review the decisions made by administrative agencies. In states that have an intermediate level of courts of appeals, the state supreme court can select the cases it wishes to consider. For states with no intermediate court of appeals, the state supreme court hears appeals from the lower courts. Local and community courts vary in nature and organization across the United States according to their own jurisdictional pattern. This allows municipalities, counties, and neighborhoods to structure their legal systems to be most responsive to citizens' needs.

Critical Reflections

1. Discuss the possible ramifications if the federal government placed all state and local courts under federal jurisdiction.

2. In what ways has our concept of courts been influenced by religion, history, and the media?

3. In what ways can problem-solving courts actually solve the problems that result in crime?

Key Terms

adversarial process **p. 202**
amicus curiae **p. 211**
Assize of Clarendon **p. 203**
bench trial **p. 202**
Bill of Rights **p. 205**
blood feud **p. 220**
charge **p. 203**

circuit court **p. 206**
Court of the Star
    Chamber **p. 204**
docket **p. 201**
general-jurisdiction
    court **p. 206**
geographic jurisdiction **p. 206**

hierarchical jurisdiction **p. 206**
inquest **p. 203**
jurisdiction **p. 205**
limited-jurisdiction court **p. 206**
lower courts **p. 215**
racketeering **p. 208**
rule of four **p. 211**

Endnotes

1 Matt Ford, "The Retrial of a Texas Man Imprisoned Despite an Overturned Conviction," *Atlantic*, August 20, 2015, http://www.theatlantic.com/national/archive/2015/08/the-retrial-of-a-texas-man-imprisoned-despite-his-overturned-conviction/401876.

2 Andrew Cohen, "The Man Who Spent 35 Years in Prison Without a Trial," Marshall Project, June 12, 2017, https://www.themarshallproject.org/2017/06/12/the-man-who-spent-35-years-in-prison-without-a-trial.

3 Samuel Walker and Charles M. Katz, *The Police in America: An Introduction,* 4th ed. (Boston: McGraw-Hill, 2002), 41.

4 James Austin and John Irwin, *It's About Time: America's Imprisonment Binge,* 3d ed. (Belmont, Calif.: Wadsworth, 2001).

5 Frances Kahn Zemans, "In the Eye of the Beholder: The Relationship between the Public and the Courts," in *Courts and Justice: A Reader,* 2d ed., ed. G. Larry Mays and Peter Gregware (Prospect Heights, Ill.: Waveland Press, 2000), 7–24.

6 David Orrick, "Court Administration in the United States: The On-Going Problems," in *Courts and Justice: A Reader,* 2d ed., eds. G. Larry Mays and Peter Gregware (Prospect Heights, Ill.: Waveland Press, 2000), 207–227.

7 Stuart Nagel, "The Tipped Scales of American Justice," in *The Scales of Justice,* ed. Abraham Blumberg (New York: Transaction, 1970), 31–50.

8 Christopher Smith, *Courts, Politics, and the Judicial Process,* 2d ed. (Chicago: Nelson-Hall, 1997), 4–7.

9 Pamela A. MacLean, "Mixed Signals on Plea Bargains," *National Law Journal,* December 17, 2007, 7.

10 Lyon, *Constitutional and Legal History,* 295.

11 Barbara J. Shapiro, *"Beyond Reasonable Doubt" and "Probable Cause": Historical Perspectives on the Anglo-American Laws of Evidence* (Berkeley: University of California Press, 1991), 47.

12 Ibid., 73.

13 Robert Bartlett, *Trial by Fire and Water: The Medieval Judicial Ordeal* (Oxford, U.K.: Clarendon Press, 1986).

14 Steury and Frank, *Criminal Court Process,* 70–71.

15 Thomas Andrew Green, *Verdict According to Conscience: Perspectives on the English Criminal Jury Trial* (Chicago: University of Chicago Press, 1985).

16 Baker, *Introduction to English Legal History,* 591.

17 Steury and Frank, *Criminal Court Process,* 77.

18 Edwin C. Surrency, "The Courts in the American Colonies," *American Journal of Legal History* 11 (July 1967): 252–276.

19 Ibid., 256.

20 John Ferling, *A Leap in the Dark: The Struggle to Create the American Republic* (New York: Oxford University Press, 2003).

21 Robert Allen Rutland, *The Birth of the Bill of Rights* (Chapel Hill: University of North Carolina Press, 1955).

22 Bruce Ackerman, "The Living Constitution," *Harvard Law Review* 120 (May 1, 2007): 1737–1812.

23 Gary A. Rabe and Dean J. Champion, *Criminal Courts: Structure, Process, and Issues* (Upper Saddle River, N.J.: Prentice Hall, 2002).

24 Ron Malega and Thomas H. Cohen, *State Court Organization, 2011* (Washington, D.C.: U.S. Department of Justice Office of Justice Programs Bureau of Justice Statistics, 2013), 2. Online at https://www.bjs.gov/index.cfm?ty=pbdetail&iid=4802.

25 Federal Judicial Center, http://www.fjc.gov/federal/courts.nsf/autoframe?openagent&nav=menu1&page=/federal/courts.nsf/page/152. Accessed January 2017.

26 Sari Horwitz and Michael E. Ruane, "Jurisdictions Vied to Prosecute Pair," *Washington Post,* Oct. 9, 2003.

27 Administrative Office of the U.S. Courts, Understanding the Federal Courts, http://www.uscourts.gov/about-federal-courts/types-cases/criminal-cases. Accessed January 2017. Mark Motivans, *Federal Justice Statistics, 2011–2012* (Washington, D.C.: U.S. Department of Justice Office of Justice Programs Bureau of Justice Statistics, 2015), http://www.bjs.gov/index.cfm?ty=pbdetail&iid=5218.

28 David W. Neubauer, *America's Courts and the Criminal Justice System,* 7th ed. (Belmont, Calif.: Wadsworth, 2002), 68.

29 Larry Kramer, "Diversity Jurisdiction," *Brigham Young University Law Review,* 1990, pp. 3–66.

30 United States Courts, Authorized Judgeships, District Courts, http://www.uscourts.gov/judges-judgeships/authorized-judgeships.

31 Christoper E. Smith, "From U.S. Magistrates to U.S. Magistrate Judges: Developments Affecting the Federal District Courts' Lower Tier of Judicial Officers," in *Courts and Justice: A Reader,* 3rd ed., ed. G. Larry Mays and Peter R. Gregware (Long Grove, Ill.: Waveland Press, 2004), 53–66.

32 United States Courts, Court Role and Structure, http://www.uscourts.gov/about-federal-courts/court-role-and-structure. Accessed January 2017.

33 United States Courts, Chronological History of Authorized Judgeships—Courts of Appeals, http://www.uscourts.gov/judges-judgeships/authorized-judgeships/chronological-history-authorized-judgeships-courts-appeals. Accessed January 2017.

34 United States Courts, About the Supreme Court, http://www.uscourts.gov/about-federal-courts/educational-resources/about-educational-outreach/activity-resources/about.

35 Supreme Court of the United States, The Justices' Caseload, http://www.supremecourt.gov/about/justicecaseload.aspx. Accessed January 2017.

36 Robert A. Carp, Ronald Stidham, and Kenneth L. Manning, *Judicial Process in America* (Washington, D.C.: CQ Press, 2007). See pp. 28–30, "The Supreme Court as Policymaker."

37 Federal Judicial Center, History of the Federal Judiciary, Original Jurisdiction of the Supreme Court, http://www.fjc.gov/history/home.nsf/page/jurisdiction_original_supreme.html. Accessed January 2017.

38 *Marbury v. Madison,* 1 Cranch 137 (1803), 55, 56–57, 61.

39 Mary Ann Harrell and Burnett Anderson, *Equal Justice under the Law: The Supreme Court in American Life* (Washington, D.C.: Supreme Court Historical Society, 1982).

40 Mark Tushnet, "*Marbury v. Madison* and the Theory of Judicial Supremacy," in *Greatest Cases in Constitutional Law,* ed. Robert P. George (Princeton, N.J.: Princeton University Press, 2000), 17–54.

41 Laurence H. Tribe, *God Save This Honorable Court: How the Choice of Supreme Court Justices Shapes Our History* (New York: Random House, 1985).

42 Bernard Schwartz, *A History of the Supreme Court* (New York: Oxford University Press, 1993).

43 Eric M. Freedman, "Can Justice Be Served by Appeals of the Dead?" *National Law Journal,* October 19, 1992, 13.

44 Aaron S. Bayer, "Amicus Briefs," *National Law Journal,* February 25, 2008, 15.

45 Lawrence Baum, "Specializing the Federal Courts: Neutral Reforms or Efforts to Shape Judicial Policy?" *Judicature* 74 (1991): 217–224.

46 John R. Crook, "UCMJ Proceedings against U.S. Personnel Accused of Offenses against Civilians in Afghanistan and Iraq," *American Journal of International Law* 101 (July 1, 2007): 663–664.

47 Steven W. Perry, *Tribal Crime Data Collection Activities, 2012* (U.S. Department of Justice Office of Justice Programs Bureau of Justice Statistics, 2012), 11. Available at http://www.bjs.gov/index.cfm?ty=pbdetail&iid=4493.

48 Judith Resnik, "Multiple Sovereignties: Indian Tribes, States, and the Federal Government," *Judicature* 79 (1995): 118–125.

49 Steven W. Perry, Tribal Crime Data Collection Activities, 2016 (Washington, D.C.: U.S. Department of Justice Office of Justice

Programs Bureau of Justice Statistics, 2016), 1-2. Online at https://www.bjs.gov/index.cfm?ty=pbdetail&iid=5704.

50 Military Commissions, How Military Commissions Work, http://www.mc.mil/Aboutus.aspx. Accessed January 2017.

51 *The New York Times*, Military Commissions, October 2013, topics, http://topics.nytimes.com/top/reference/timestopics/subjects/d/detainees/military_commissions/index.html.

52 Office of Military Commissions, Military Commissions History, http://www.mc.mil/ABOUTUS/MilitaryCommissionsHistory.aspx. Accessed January 2017.

53 Ibid.

54 Administrative Office of the U.S. Courts, Understanding the Federal Courts, http://www.uscourts.gov/about-federal-courts/types-cases/criminal-cases. Accessed January 2017.

55 National Center for State Courts, http://www.ncsc.org/Information-and-Resources/Browse-by-State.aspx. Click on this map to find the structure of your state court. Accessed January 2017.

56 David B. Rottman and Shauna M. Strickland, *State Court Organization, 2004* (Washington, D.C.: U.S. Department of Justice, Bureau of Justice Statistics, 2006), 7, http://www.bjs.gov/index.cfm?ty=pbdetail&iid=1204.

57 Ibid.

58 S. Strickland, R. Schauffler, R. LaFountain, and K. Holt, ed., State Court Organization, National Center for State Courts, State Court Organization, Trial Courts, January 9, 2015, http://www.ncsc.org/microsites/sco/home.

59 Ibid.

60 Rottman and Strickland, *State Court Organization, 2004*, 7.

61 David Bjerk, "Guilt Shall Not Escape or Innocence Suffer? The Limits of Plea Bargaining When Defendant Guilt is Uncertain," *American Law and Economics Review* 9, no. 2 (October 1, 2007): 305–329.

62 Ibid.

63 The National Association of Attorneys General, http://www.naag.org/naag/about_naag/faq/what_does_an_attorney_general_do.php. Accessed January 2017.

64 Bjerk, "Guilt Shall Not Escape or Innocence Suffer?"

65 Rottman and Strickland, *State Court Organization, 2004*, 131.

66 Ibid.

67 Kevin M. Scott, "Understanding Judicial Hierarchy: Reversals and the Behavior of Intermediate Appellate Judges," *Law and Society Review* 40 (March 1, 2006): 163–191.

68 Hope Viner Samborn, "Disbarred—But Not Barred from Work," *ABA Journal* 93 (June 1, 2007): 57.

69 Bureau of Justice Assistance, Community-Based Problem-Solving Criminal Justice Initiative, www.bja.gov/ProgramDetails.aspx?Program_ID=53.

70 Suzanne M. Strong and Tracey Kyckelhahn, *Census of Problem-Solving Courts, 2012* (Washington, D.C.: U.S. Department of Justice Office of Justice Programs Bureau of Justice Statistics, 2016), 1. Online at http://www.bjs.gov/index.cfm?ty=pbdetail&iid=5744.)

71 Ibid.

72 Bureau of Justice Assistance, What Are Problem-Solving Courts?, www.bja.gov/evaluation/program-adjudication/problem-solving-courts.htm. Accessed January 2013.

73 Maria N. Greenstein, "Creative Judging: Ethics Issues in Problem-Solving Courts," *Judges' Journal* 51, no. 2 (Spring 2012): 40.

74 "Two Reports Criticize Drug Courts; NADCP Pushes Back," *Alcoholism & Drug Abuse Weekly* 23, no. 13 (March 28, 2011): 1–3.

75 Scott Henson, interview by Eileen Smith, "The Gritty Truth," *Texas Monthly* (February 2008).

76 Patricia Marinelli-Casey, Rachel Gonzales, Maureen Hillhouse, Alfonso Ang, Joan Zweben, and Judith Cohen, "Drug Court Treatment for Methamphetamine Dependence: Treatment Response and Posttreatment Outcomes," *Journal of Substance Abuse Treatment* 34 (March 1, 2008): 242.

77 "Utah Initiative for Offenders Links Treatment, Probation," *Alcoholism and Drug Abuse Weekly,* January 14, 2008, 1.

78 Sharon M. Boles, Nancy K. Young, Toni Moore, and Sharon DiPirro-Beard, "The Sacramento Dependency Drug Court: Development and Outcomes," *Child Maltreatment* 12 (May 1, 2007): 161–171.

79 Lorig Charkoudian and Carrie Wilson, "Factors Affecting Individuals' Decisions to Use Community Mediation," *Review of Policy Research,* July 1, 2006, 865–886.

80 Jon'a F. Meyer, "'It Is a Gift from the Creator to Keep Us in Harmony':

Original (vs. alternative) Dispute Resolution in the Navajo Nation," *International Journal of Public Administration* 25 (November 1, 2002): 1379–1401.

81 Stewart J. D'Alessio and Lisa Stolzenberg, "Unemployment and the

Incarceration of Pretrial Defendants," *American Sociological Review* 60 (June 1, 1995): 350.

The Courtroom Work Group

FEATURES

Here, Judge John Murphy sits with his attorneys, while a judicial panel hears his case. How are instances of judicial indiscretion handled?

On June 2, 2014, in Viera, Florida, at the Brevard County Courthouse, Judge John Murphy challenged assistant public defender Andrew Weinstock to a fight. Apparently upset at Weinstock's refusal to waive a speedy trial for his defendant, Murphy told Weinstock, "If I had a rock, I would throw it at you right now." Murphy then invited Weinstock to "go out back" and fight. A security video shows the two men exiting the courtroom into a hallway, where a scuffle ensued. Courtroom deputies separated the two combatants, and the public defender accused the judge of punching him.[1]

Judge Murphy contended that he was provoked by Weinstock, and the Florida Judicial Qualifications Commission found that "Mr. Weinstock was generally rude, disrespectful, incompetent and a highly unlikeable lawyer." Another judge testified that Weinstock "had been rude, disrespectful, moody and even appeared to be bipolar in her courtroom."[2]

The Florida Judicial Qualifications Commission suspended Judge Murphy for 120 days without pay and fined him $50,000, but recommended that he keep his post. After a month-long leave of absence, Murphy issued a public apology.[3] Weinstock resigned from the public defender's office following Murphy's return to the bench.[4] In December 2015, the Florida Supreme Court overruled the commission and fired Murphy.[5]

THINK ABOUT IT > In what ways is this case an example of the tensions that exist in the courtroom work group?

LEARNING OBJECTIVE **1**

Explain what a courtroom work group is.

The Courtroom Work Group

It is easy to think of the courts as an institution where justice is served in an assembly-line fashion. Individual defendants seem to be reduced to cases and are processed by court officials who appear to display little individual judgment but rather simply follow the procedures of the legal system. This chapter's aim is to humanize the court by illustrating that those who work in the courthouse pursue various personal and institutional agendas. Furthermore, in working together, they exhibit a form of individualized justice that is peculiar to each court. The people who work in the courtroom are a complex and fascinating set of actors who work together at various levels to fashion a product that is defined as "justice." Collectively, they form what we refer to as a **courtroom work group**.[6] Only by understanding how the courtroom work group is constrained by legal, social, and institutional factors can we fully appreciate how the court interacts with other components of the criminal justice system.

As illustrated by the incident between Judge John Murphy and public defender Andrew Weinstock, the criminal court can be a volatile place. On one hand, the processing of cases may look like a smoothly functioning system in which everyone "gets their day in court" and defendants are assured the full range of constitutional protections, as well as the guarantee that their voices will be heard and considered. On the other hand, below the surface of public scrutiny, the courtroom can be a chaotic place where attorneys and judges sometimes play fast and loose with the truth, individuals' rights, and justice itself. In an effort to move the docket—that is, to settle cases—justice is negotiated and bargained.[7]

Some people are alarmed by the dynamics of the courthouse, which differ vastly from the ideal of impartial justice being dispensed by wise judges. The notion of attorneys negotiating deals with the prosecutor to garner more lenient sentences for

courtroom work group— The judges, prosecutors, defense attorneys, clerks, and bailiffs who work together to move cases through the court system and whose interaction determines the outcome of criminal cases.

obviously guilty defendants violates our image of the courthouse as a place where truth prevails; the guilty get their just deserts; victims receive justice, and the innocent go free.[8] However, understanding courtroom politics is vital to comprehending the activities of those who compose the courtroom work group. In this chapter, we will identify the roles and responsibilities of those who handle the vast caseload that passes through the modern courthouse. We will start with the support personnel and then turn to the prosecutor's office and the various types of defense attorneys.

Not all courtrooms are the same. Different levels of jurisdiction (federal, state, and local) and different levels of responsibility (misdemeanors, felonies, and appeals) dictate different working arrangements among the participants in the courtroom work group. The following is a general discussion of the courtroom work group and the typical issues that arise in most courts.

The Prosecutor

The prosecutor, sometimes called a district attorney, has, in many ways, the most powerful position in the criminal justice system. The prosecutor functions as the major gatekeeper of the criminal justice process and not only decides which cases are formally defined as criminal offenses, but also argues those cases in court.[9] The prosecutor's position is powerful because the exercise of **discretion** rests with this office. In the case of the prosecutor, discretion is defined as the authority to decide which cases are inserted into the criminal justice system. With police officers pushing for charges against those whom they arrest, defense attorneys pleading for the best bargain they can get for their clients, and judges wanting to move the docket and bring cases to **disposition** quickly, the prosecutor's power allows him or her to inject personal philosophy and political interests into the justice system.[10] The prosecutor has the discretion to charge the case (or not), to decide what the charge will be, and to dismiss it if he or she so chooses. This pivotal actor has the most influence in plea bargaining.[11]

LEARNING OBJECTIVE 2

Recognize why the prosecutor is so powerful.

LEARNING OBJECTIVE 3

Outline the five categories of activities that divide the prosecutor's energies.

discretion (from Chapter 1)—The power of a criminal justice official to make decisions on issues within legal guidelines.

disposition—The final determination of a case or other matter by a court or other judicial entity.

Suffolk County Prosecutor David Deakin points to a map during the opening arguments of a murder trial in Suffolk Superior Court in Boston. Why is the prosecutor's position so powerful?

However, the prosecutor's discretion is not completely unfettered. Even though the prosecuting attorney has sole discretion in deciding which cases to prosecute, which offenses to charge a suspect with, and determining what sorts of deals the government will agree to, prosecutorial behavior is limited. During the trial stage, the prosecutor must act within established parameters of procedural law. For instance, if the prosecutor knows of evidence that might show the defendant to be innocent, he or she must share that evidence with the defense attorney.[12] However, defense attorneys are not expected to share evidence of their clients' guilt. The prosecutor must prove the case without the aid of the defense attorney and the defendant. This might seem unfair, but it is important to remember that the prosecutor has the resources of the state behind his or her efforts and that the Constitution protects the rights of the accused. Although the prosecutor represents the interests of the state (which includes the victim, police officers, and the ideal of justice), the idea of a free society under the law protects individuals from unrestricted state power.[13]

The Prosecutor at Work

Much of the prosecutor's work is invisible to the public, but this work occupies most of the prosecutor's time and, more important, forms the bulk of activities that determine exactly how justice is dispensed. Five categories of activities divide the prosecutor's energies:[14]

1. Fighting. Prosecutors work to prepare cases for court and possibly for trial. The police officer's efforts must be scrutinized to determine whether the case files are complete and, more important, whether the officer followed the procedural laws in arresting and interrogating the suspect. The prosecutor plans a legal strategy to present the strongest case possible and to deflect criticism by the defense. The prosecutor must have a good sense of how the judge and jury will react to the case and must consider the psychological and sociological dynamics of witnesses, defendants, and others affected by the cases. In short, the prosecutor must battle to ensure that the state's case is strong, complete, and coherent and satisfies the public's sense of justice.

2. Negotiating. Few cases ever go to trial. Most are **plea-bargained**, meaning that the defense attorney and the prosecutor strike a deal for a plea of guilty or no contest in return for a lighter sentence. Plea bargaining has been the subject of much controversy because it appears to the public as though defendants can escape the full responsibility for their actions. We will discuss plea bargaining in greater detail in Chapter 9, but it is prudent to say here that this practice is vital to the functioning of the criminal justice system. Because some defendants are guilty of the offenses the police charge them with, it is in their interests, as well as the state's, to settle the case as quickly and as economically as possible. The state cannot afford the time and resources required to take every case to a jury trial, and guilty defendants cannot afford to expose themselves to the maximum sentence available under the law. Therefore, a deal is struck in which each party considers the weight of the evidence, the likelihood of a conviction, and the expenses that would be incurred by a trial, and they negotiate a settlement. The prosecutor represents the state and/or the victim in these negotiations and must make several tactical decisions to ensure that the government is getting the best deal possible and that, in a greater sense, justice is being served. Negotiating a plea is an art, and experienced prosecutors must

plea bargain—A compromise reached by the defendant, the defendant's attorney, and the prosecutor in which the defendant agrees to plead guilty or no contest in return for a reduction of the charges' severity, dismissal of some charges, further information about the offense or about others involved in it, or the prosecutor's agreement to recommend a desired sentence.

act like poker players, sometimes revealing their evidence and sometimes attempting to bluff the defense attorney into believing that the state's or victim's case is stronger than it actually is.

3. Drafting. The drafting of legal documents is an important function of the prosecutor. Prosecutors must be careful to lay a paper trail of their activities to ensure that cases can be upheld on appeal. Prosecutors must also prepare several documents that enable other actors in the criminal justice system to perform their duties. For instance, the prosecutor drafts the search warrant, specifies which violations of the criminal codes defendants are charged with, and prepares documents that address motions made by the defense. Improperly prepared paperwork can have negative ramifications that include letting guilty suspects escape justice.

4. Counseling. Because the prosecutor occupies such a pivotal position, he or she must contend with the emotional and psychological needs of victims, witnesses, police officers, and other officials who compose the courtroom work group. If a police officer's case is weak, the prosecutor must explain why it cannot be taken to trial, and the police officer must be educated on the specific aspects of the law in which the case was inadequate. Victims may want the maximum penalty available imposed on their assailant, but the prosecutor might be restrained by other factors and must counsel the victim on why the plea bargain was the best outcome possible given the circumstances of the case.[15] Additionally, the prosecutor spends a considerable amount of time advising victims, witnesses, and law enforcement officers on how to testify at trial. A poorly prepared witness can be fatal to the state's case, and although the prosecutor will not advise anyone to tell a lie, he or she may advise the witness to answer the defense attorney's questions as succinctly as possible and not provide extra information that could be used as ammunition against the prosecution's case.[16]

5. Administering. The prosecutor's office is a modern bureaucracy and suffers from the same strains as any large organization. Personnel issues include hiring, supervising, and firing assistant attorneys, secretarial staff, and investigators. Prosecutors also play a large administrative role in keeping cases moving by ensuring that victims and witnesses are interviewed, briefed, and available should they be required to testify. Additionally, the prosecutor's office has to ensure that assistant district attorneys are available and present whenever a judge holds court.

The prosecutor's work is varied and complex. As the primary representative of the state in the courtroom, the prosecutor must fight for justice and ensure that the interests of the victim, the police, and the public are addressed. Sometimes these demands are complicated and may even conflict. For example, the prosecutor might decide that a case involving a young person charged with assault is relatively minor and that the offender would best benefit from probation and restitution, whereas the victim of the assault, who lost his or her front teeth, demands that the defendant be incarcerated.

As with any occupation, certain norms guide how cases are handled in the courtroom. However, the courtroom work group has some constraints that most organizations lack, constraints that make the prosecutor's work difficult to learn and do. Although each case must be decided individually, there are shared conceptions about how any particular case should be decided based on precedent. Legal variables such as the seriousness of the offense and the defendant's criminal record (if any) are also factored into the disposition.

What happens when the prosecutor insists on spending too much time and resources on a case? Because those who work in the courtroom work group want to maintain a regular routine in which they get to eat lunch and go home at a reasonable hour, they exert subtle influences on prosecutors who are unwilling or unable to keep the docket moving. The judge may complain about the backlog of cases that develops when the prosecutor is too stingy in the plea bargains offered to defendants. If too many cases require trials, then the court administrator must find courtroom time; the court clerk must empanel a jury; the court reporter must be put on standby; and attorneys, especially private attorneys, must juggle other commitments. Everyone understands that trials are sometimes required, but they also understand that there is a **going rate** by which other similar cases have been settled. When a prosecutor violates this well-understood norm, other members of the courtroom work group expect the case to be unique in some way. If it is not, they might complain. Promotions and reputations are gained according to conviction rates and how promptly and efficiently prosecutors dispose of cases. As such, the other members of the courtroom work group are always evaluating the prosecutor's role as a major gatekeeper of the criminal justice process.[17]

Additionally, organizational factors of the courtroom, such as the number of cases on the docket, the experience of the defense attorney, the presence or absence of the victim, and the remaining physical capacity of the local jail and the state prison system, are all elements that affect the shared expectations of the courtroom work group.

The prosecutor's office deals with various issues that include not only prosecuting cases but also representing the state's interests in other areas of the legal community.[18] In large jurisdictions with tremendous caseloads, the prosecutor's office is divided into bureaus, special units, and programs that address specific concerns and issues. For example, the Los Angeles County District Attorney's Office employs nearly a thousand deputy district attorneys (assistant prosecutors) and hundreds of support personnel in a bureaucracy that includes special units devoted to areas such as gangs, family violence, narcotics, sex crimes, juvenile delinquency, health care fraud, high-tech crime, white-collar crime, and public assistance fraud.[19] This division of labor allows attorneys to specialize in certain types of cases and allows the prosecutor's office to ensure that competent assistant prosecutors are assigned to difficult and complicated areas of the law.

Prosecution at the Federal Level

It is useful to distinguish between prosecutors at the state and federal levels because their differences are as important as their similarities. The U.S. Department of Justice, or Justice Department, is at the top of the federal hierarchy of prosecution. The U.S. attorney general is a cabinet-level officer who is appointed by the president and confirmed by the Senate through its advise-and-consent function. Lawyers working for the Justice Department are protected from political influence by their civil service status. Because so many of them spend their careers working for the government, they become experts in their particular branch of the law.[20] The U.S. Department of Justice is responsible for some programs, agencies, divisions, and bureaus not directly associated with the prosecution of criminal cases.[21] Here, the discussion will be limited to the three Justice Department offices that directly affect the prosecutorial aspect of the criminal justice process: the Office of the Solicitor General, the Criminal Division, and the U.S. Attorneys.

The **U.S. Solicitor General** is the person appointed to argue on behalf of the federal government in proceedings before the U.S. Supreme Court. The solicitor general also coordinates all appeals of cases that went against the federal

going rate—A term describing how similar cases have been settled by a given set of judges, prosecutors, and attorneys.

U.S. Solicitor General—The person who determines which cases the federal government will send to the U.S. Supreme Court for review and the positions the government will take before the Court.

government in the lower courts. The solicitor general's office decides whether a case is important enough to the federal government to merit the time and resources required to file an appeal. The case must have a high degree of policy significance and a reasonable legal argument that will stand a good chance of success before the solicitor general's office will accept the case. The solicitor general also imposes on cases in which the federal government is not a direct participant but has some policy interest.[22]

The **Criminal Division** coordinates the prosecution of all federal criminal statutes except those assigned to other divisions. It has a range of sections that deal with cases as varied as money laundering, child exploitation, and obscenity.

As we discussed in Chapter 7, the federal district courts have 93 **U.S. Attorneys** in 94 districts. Each state has one attorney for each of its districts (recall that some states have more than one district); the District of Columbia, Puerto Rico, and the U.S. Virgin Islands each have one attorney, and the districts of Northern Mariana Islands and Guam share an attorney (see Figure 8.1 for a map of the U.S. district courts). The U.S. Attorneys are responsible for most of the trial work in which the United States is a party. They prosecute criminal cases brought by the federal government; prosecute and defend civil cases in which the United States is a party; and collect debts owed to the federal government.[23] Although the U.S. Attorneys serve at the pleasure of the president and report to the attorney general, they often owe their jobs to senators or congressional representatives who recommended them for appointment.[24]

Prosecution in State Courts

State court systems are decentralized, with prosecution responsibility spread over state, county (or district), and local levels. This variety of organizational placements for prosecutors can result in an inefficient, overlapping, and often ineffective maze

Criminal Division— Part of the U.S. Department of Justice, the Criminal Division develops, enforces, and supervises the application of all federal criminal laws except those assigned to other divisions.

U.S. Attorneys—The principal litigators of the United States who conduct most of the trial work in which the United States is a party. They prosecute criminal cases brought by the federal government; prosecute and defend civil cases in which the United States is a party; and collect certain types of debts owed to the federal government.

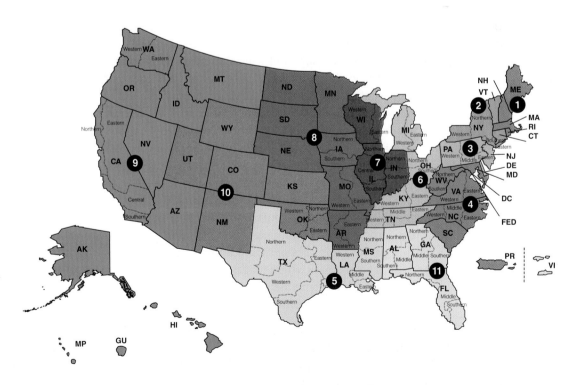

FIGURE 8.1 The U.S. District Courts The state of California is in the Ninth Circuit and has four districts. Which other states and/or jurisdictions have more than one district?

Source: U.S. Courts, Geographic Boundaries of the United States Courts of Appeals and United States District Courts, http://www.uscourts.gov/about-federal-courts/court-role-and-structure. Accessed March 2017.

of responsibility. Lawbreakers in large metropolitan areas might operate simultaneously in several jurisdictions, and prosecutors can be unaware of each other's efforts to bring them to justice. For instance, the Atlanta, Georgia, metropolitan area is overlapped by at least four counties.[25] This results in competition, rivalries, and obstructions among law enforcement agencies and courts. Savvy attorneys can manipulate gaps between jurisdictions to broker advantageous circumstances for their clients. Although considerable overlap in duties exists, the following three types of prosecutors are typically found in court systems across the United States: the state attorney general, the chief prosecutor, and local prosecutors.

The state attorney general is the chief legal officer for a state, and the state constitution usually delineates the duties of this office. The state attorney general represents the state in legal actions in which the state is a party. In most states, the power of the state attorney general is limited in criminal matters. Because local prosecutors are elected by the citizens of their districts, the state prosecutor can provide only minimal supervision over their work. For the most part, the state attorney general exercises most of the office's power in the civil area of the law. Prime examples of how state attorneys general prosecute civil cases on behalf of citizens are the lawsuits in the mid-1990s in which several states brought action against the major tobacco corporations.[26]

The chief prosecutor is the most powerful person in the criminal justice system. Depending on the state, this court officer is called the district attorney, the state attorney, or simply the prosecuting officer. This individual sits at the crossroads of the system between the police and the courts. There are more than 2,000 chief prosecutors across the country with a combined staff of more than 65,000 assistant prosecutors, investigators, secretaries, and other support staff, such as victim–witness advocates. Because chief prosecutors are elected officers in 95 percent of the districts, they are much attuned to the local political scene.[27] Working in the office of the chief prosecutor is a sought-after position by new attorneys. Securing a job as an assistant district attorney, deputy district attorney, or assistant prosecutor has several advantages. First, the prosecutor's office carries a certain amount of status. Second, the prosecutor's office affords new attorneys ample opportunity to practice courtroom law. Third, it provides a high degree of visibility in the legal community. Because of the large caseloads in many prosecutors' offices, a new attorney, often fresh out of law school, is thrown into a position of having to exercise considerable discretion, judgment, and power in the people's interest. This "on-the-job training" can be both stimulating and intimidating. Quick learners survive by depending on others in the courtroom work group to educate them on courtroom etiquette, protocol, and formal as well as informal procedures for a particular judge's court.[28] Assistant district attorneys are often recruited into large law firms after they have established a name for themselves as effective courtroom warriors. Additionally, after prosecuting a few high-profile cases, some assistant district attorneys opt to enter politics. The exposure gained from this position can be parlayed into a political career. This is especially true in states where judges are elected and the prosecutor can position himself or herself as someone who is tough on crime.[29]

Based at the city or county level, local prosecutors perform many duties that are concerned with either misdemeanor cases or the preliminary stages of felony cases. These are important actors in the criminal justice system because the vast numbers of cases they handle concern public drunkenness, petty theft, disorderly conduct, and minor assault. Depending on the size of the local jurisdiction, some of these local prosecutors work only part time.

The Defense Attorney

The defense attorney protects the interests of the accused and presents the case in the best possible light to ensure that the prosecution has adequately proved the charges. In an ideal world, the prosecutor would charge only the truly guilty, and the defense attorney would be successful in winning the cases of only the truly innocent. But the world of the criminal courts is not perfect, and the struggle between the defense and prosecution often ends not in justice but rather in negotiated settlements that leave everyone feeling dissatisfied.[30]

The image of the defense attorney has two parts. On the one hand, this officer of the court might be considered a valiant warrior against the injustice of the powerful and as such might be viewed as a stalwart of freedom in our country. On the other hand, the defense attorney might be viewed as a liar, a cheat, and a twister of the truth who will do anything to prevent a guilty client from facing justice.[31] The truth is, of course, somewhere in the middle of these two extremes.[32] Before we examine the profession of the defense attorney in detail, let's dispense with the most fundamental and significant issue that surrounds how legal defense is conducted in the United States: the effects of money.

LEARNING OBJECTIVE 4

Summarize the role of the defense attorney.

LEARNING OBJECTIVE 5

Describe the concept of "normal crimes."

Here, Bill Cosby and his defense attorney, Brian McMonagle (right), arrive at the Montgomery County Courthouse in Pennsylvania. In June 2017, Cosby's sexual assault case was declared a mistrial. What role can money play in securing a legal defense?

Not all defense attorneys are equally competent.[33] Many variables divide the successful from the unsuccessful, the ethical from the vile, the connected from the disenfranchised, and the one you want to argue for your life from the one you would not even let contest your parking tickets. These variables are the result of such factors as:

> The law school the attorney attended
> The law firm the attorney is associated with
> How long the attorney has worked in a particular jurisdiction
> How many cases the attorney has previously tried before a particular judge
> The attorney's relationship and history with the prosecutor
> Whether the attorney is a private attorney or a public defender
> Whether the attorney has other cases to settle with this prosecutor in the near future[34]

Given this list of variables that can influence an attorney's effectiveness, the single most important variable may well be how much money has been invested in getting the best representation possible. Although many reasonably priced private attorneys can provide an excellent defense, assembling the witnesses and legal and technical experts and constructing elaborate exhibits can become extremely expensive, and the client foots the bill for the cost of the defense.[35]

To illustrate the power of money, let's look at a high-profile example. In 2000, when Baltimore Ravens linebacker Ray Lewis was tried for murder in Atlanta, Georgia, he was able to provide his defense team with financial resources that most individuals could not muster. When the prosecution produced a witness who claimed he saw Lewis engage in the stabbings following a Super Bowl party in a nightclub, the defense undermined the credibility of the witness by producing evidence of past lies. The hostile witness had been convicted of identity theft and running up exorbitant charges on credit cards. In a dramatic and effective court-room maneuver, the defense attorney asked the witness if he had ever met the individual whose identity he had stolen and whose financial reputation he had besmirched, and then had that individual stand up in court to demonstrate to the jury that the witness had harmed a real person and not simply some abstraction.

The Ray Lewis defense team was able to fly this person across the country from California to Atlanta for the purpose of standing up in court for a mere 15 seconds to hammer home a point about the trustworthiness of a witness. The average defendant, who is not a multimillionaire football player, would have been unable to finance such a legal tactic. Prosecutors dropped the murder and aggravated assault charges against Lewis in exchange for his plea of guilty to misdemeanor obstruction of justice charges.

The Defense Attorney and the Courtroom Work Group

Although the defense attorney's first obligation is to provide the best defense possible for the defendant, this duty does not always result in a jury trial in which the truth is revealed and justice is done to the satisfaction of all. Despite the defense attorney's commitment to the interests of the accused, other pressures mediate how aggressively the prosecutor's case is challenged.[36]

The attorney who engages in criminal defense work on a regular basis becomes part of the courtroom work group. Although ideally the prosecutor's adversary, the defense attorney must develop a working relationship with the group to ensure that the group's goals are achieved. The wheels of justice never turn smoothly, but the obstinate defense attorney who causes them to grind to a halt by contesting

Here, Melissa Keeler demonstrates the beating she saw from her apartment window during the murder trial of Baltimore Ravens linebacker Ray Lewis and two other men. Why is it important that a wealthy defendant can provide financial resources for his or her defense that other defendants cannot?

and protesting every routine point of law and procedural ruling will quickly find that the judge, prosecutor, court reporter, and others in the courtroom work group will be less flexible and accommodating in their dealings with that attorney and that attorney's clients. An informal system of norms and relationships develops in the courtroom work group to efficiently move the docket and dispose of cases in accordance with expected outcomes.

The dealings of the courtroom work group are best explained by two classic studies of the court conducted by scholars David Sudnow and Abraham Blumberg. Sudnow introduced the concept of **normal crimes**, defined as cases that are considered in the context of how the court handled similar offenses.[37] Defense attorneys and prosecutors have a good idea about what the sentence will be for a particular offense by considering how that infraction compares to the court's pattern of sentencing. For the offender to receive a more severe or a more lenient sentence than the going rate, the offense's circumstances must be shown to be abnormal. Given this already established norm for sentencing, the defense attorney often encourages the defendant to plead guilty in return for a reduced sentence. When the defense attorney takes a normal crime to trial, he or she may be considered by the courtroom work group to be wasting the court's time and resources. Consequently, in the interests of conforming to the expectations of the defense of normal crimes, the defense attorney facilitates the criminal prosecution process rather than zealously advocates for the defendant.

This abdication of the responsibility to protect the defendant's interests might seem wrong, but we will see in the next chapter that plea bargaining is a complicated and complex issue. In many ways, the public defender is getting the best possible deal for a client when the case is handled as a normal crime.

normal crimes—
Routine cases that are considered in the context of how the court handled similar offenses.

Part of the client's difficulty in evaluating the contributions of the defense attorney lies in determining what can be attributed to the attorney's expertise and what can be attributed to the normal courthouse routine. The attorney may be working hard for the client, doing legal research, negotiating strenuously with the prosecutors, and developing treatment plans with probation officers, but the client has limited knowledge of this activity. In fact, according to Blumberg, the dynamics of the courtroom work group aid the defense attorney in erecting a facade of competence even when the attorney is simply "acting" in an effort to impress the client.

Although Blumberg alerts us to some interesting dynamics of how courtrooms actually operate, we should be cautious about becoming too cynical. All organizations have distinctions between what sociologist Erving Goffman called "front-stage" and "backstage" behavior, in which participants act one way when they are on public display and another when they are surrounded only by trusted co-workers.[38] Courts are no exception, and the defense attorney's dramatics performed for the defendant's benefit do not differ substantially from how judges, prosecutors, or even professors or physicians act when they are attempting to put the best face on their actions. The defense attorney is subject to organizational pressures from the courtroom work group. The defendant must understand that although the defense attorney negotiates with the defendant's best interests in mind, sometimes the best interests of the defense attorney differ from those of the defendant.[39]

The Best Defense: Private Attorney or Public Defender?

The quality of legal defense varies greatly for individuals accused of breaking the law. An attorney's competence might depend on the level of the court, the geographic location, the client's resources, and the way in which state and local governments fund indigent defense efforts. We commonly believe that private attorneys are automatically superior to those provided by the state, but in reality the issue is more complicated (see A Closer Look 8.1).[40]

Criminal defense work is not among the most lucrative specializations for private attorneys. In fact, few private attorneys can make a living practicing exclusively, or even primarily, criminal defense law. Many attorneys have more comprehensive practices in which they also practice tort law, family law, or business law.[41] Some of the most expensive and best attorneys confine themselves to specialties such as corporate law and seldom enter a courtroom. As such, a private attorney might not be the best one to represent a drug dealer or someone facing a capital charge of homicide.[42]

However, many successful private attorneys are excellent criminal defenders. Many former prosecutors or public defenders who go into private practice regularly do criminal defense work. In this way, they have an advantage in that they have been part of the criminal court's work group in the past and have already established relationships with the prosecutor's office and the judges. Depending on the reputation and experience of the private defense attorney, the cost of representation can be expensive. Because clients pay for private defense attorneys, the quality of the services rendered is expected to be superior to what is available from a public defender. However, if we can believe Blumberg, the private defense attorney may be likely to extend the case in order to charge a wealthy defendant as much money as possible.[43]

Public defenders have a precarious position in the criminal justice system. They are obligated to provide the best defense possible for the defendant, but their salaries may come from any number of sources. The indigent defense systems of 28 states and the District of Columbia are funded completely by the state or mostly by the state with some county funds. The rest of the states depend on county funds exclusively or on county funds, with some additional funds from the state. Several states supplement public defender funding with court fees assessed to indigent defendants

A CLOSER LOOK 8.1
(De)Funding Public Defenders

The Sixth Amendment ensures that criminal defendants not only have the right to a public trial without delay, but also the right to an attorney. In 1963, the U.S. Supreme Court ruled in *Gideon v. Wainwright* that not only the Constitution, "but also reason and reflection require us to recognize that in our adversary system of criminal justice, any person hauled into court, who is too poor to hire a lawyer, cannot be assured a fair trial unless counsel is provided for him."[44] However, the requirement that the state provide legal defense for indigent defendants is severely tested in many states because of budgetary constraints. For example:

- The city of New Orleans provides one-sixth of the budget for the public defender's office, and the state provides about one-quarter. The rest of the budget comes from fines and fees imposed upon defendants in a city where more than 27 percent of residents live in poverty. When impoverished defendants cannot pay these fines and fees, they are often jailed, thus creating even more defendants for the public defender's office.[45]
- The state of New York was sued by the New York Civil Liberties Union in 2007 for neglecting its duty to provide attorneys to impoverished defendants. In 2014, the state agreed to provide funding to ensure that attorneys have time to meet with their clients, visit them in jail, and thoroughly investigate their cases. The suit only provides services to five counties but is expected to provide a template for future reform statewide.[46]
- The American Civil Liberties Union has sued California for failing to provide adequate public defender services. For example, the Fresno County Public Defender's Office has an annual caseload of 42,000 and only 60 people on its staff.[47]
- In 2016, a county district judge in New Mexico found the state's chief public defender in contempt for the public defender's office's "failure and refusal to represent" defendants in some criminal cases. However, according to the office, the county's felony cases have more than doubled while the office has only four attorneys to work more than 1,000 cases.[48]

Many public defenders are skilled attorneys who are able to provide expert guidance to their clients. However, the massive volume of cases in many jurisdictions severely tests the public defender's ability to provide adequate counsel to his or her clients.

THINK ABOUT IT

1. Is it necessary for local and state governments to provide legal counsel for criminal defendants who cannot afford to hire their own attorney?
2. Does being defended by a public defender mean that the offender will not get adequate representation?

who plead guilty or are found guilty.[49] Additionally, because of the large caseloads experienced by many public defender offices, the time and resources available are seldom sufficient to provide the extended defense services that the public defender would like.[50] It is difficult to generalize the work of public defenders because of the variation in how they are structured and financed. (For more on the states' obligation to appoint attorneys for indigent defendants, see Case in Point 8.1.)

Each state has its own system for setting up the defense of indigent clients. These systems fall into three broad categories.[51]

> Assigned counsel. In small jurisdictions with limited resources, the judge may assign a practicing member of the bar to represent defendants who lack the financial means to hire a private attorney. There are drawbacks to this method of assigning attorneys. A limitation in many jurisdictions is that the judge draws from a pool that consists of attorneys who volunteer.[52] This volunteer pool usually comprises young attorneys developing their courtroom skills or less successful attorneys willing to take the reduced court fee just to make a living. Even in jurisdictions in which all the attorneys are in the selection pool, the defendant might end up with an excellent real estate lawyer who is not familiar with the demands of criminal defense work.

CASE IN POINT 8.1

Argersinger v. Hamlin (1972)

THE POINT

Defendants have the right to an attorney if an offense, regardless of its seriousness, is punishable by incarceration.

THE CASE

Jon Argersinger, an indigent, was charged in Florida with carrying a concealed weapon. With no attorney present, Argersinger was tried by a judge and sentenced to 90 days in jail. The court did not appoint an attorney for Argersinger, which the state supreme court upheld, holding that the right to court-appointed counsel extended only to offenses punishable by more than six months' imprisonment. The U.S. Supreme Court reversed this decision, holding that the right to counsel extended to defendants in any offense for which imprisonment can be imposed.

Scott v. Illinois (1979)

THE POINT

States may incarcerate offenders only if they have been represented by counsel; states are not obliged to appoint counsel for offenders who have not been sentenced to incarceration, even if incarceration is a possible punishment.

THE CASE

Aubrey Scott was convicted of theft by a judge and fined $50, although the maximum penalty was a $500 fine and/or one year in jail. Citing Argersinger, Scott appealed, contending that the Sixth and Fourteenth Amendments required the state to provide him with an attorney. The U.S. Supreme Court affirmed the original opinion and clarified Argersinger, holding that offenders could be incarcerated only if they had been represented by counsel. As Scott was not sentenced to incarceration, and could not be because he had not been represented by counsel, the state was not obliged to provide him with counsel.

THINK ABOUT IT

1. What is the main difference between these two cases in terms of incarceration and legal representation?

› Contract systems. In a contract system, law firms bid for the business of all indigent defense work. The advantage of this system is that the firm's attorneys quickly become proficient in dealing with the prosecutor and the courtroom work group. Opponents of this system contend that because of the competitive bidding process, the low bidder ends up with a caseload that does not provide enough revenue for the support system of secretaries, investigators, and attorneys that is necessary for a vigorous defense of all cases.

› Public defender. As a result of the decision in *Gideon v. Wainright* (see Case in Point 8.2), the public defender system has been implemented in 49 states and the District of Columbia.[53] Having a full-time public defender staff has several advantages. Attorneys who work in public defender offices quickly gain extensive experience working with the criminal law and become seasoned trial attorneys. Many attorneys like having a public defender office because it relieves their own firms of having to do *pro bono* work that drains their resources. Also, because of the permanence of public defender systems,

On weekday mornings, public defenders interview inmate clients at the Tulsa Jail in Tulsa, Oklahoma. This cooperative effort was established by the Sheriff's Office and the Tulsa County Public Defender's Office. How may such a program be beneficial to inmates?

relationships with other personnel in the criminal justice system have been developed so that the attorneys enter cases at an early stage, usually at the initial hearing.[54]

The image of the public defender is sometimes cast in a negative light when compared to that of private attorneys. This image is, paradoxically, both accurate and misleading. Certainly, someone with sufficient financial resources can hire an attorney who is experienced in criminal law and can provide the best legal defense money can buy.[55] However, many indigent defendants also receive excellent representation from competent, experienced, and dedicated public defenders.

CASE IN POINT 8.2

Gideon v. Wainwright (1963)

THE POINT

Indigent defendants have the right to court-appointed attorneys in felony cases.

THE CASE

In 1961, Clarence Gideon, an impoverished drifter, was charged with breaking and entering a poolroom, a felony under Florida law. Gideon went to court without money or a lawyer and asked the court to appoint counsel for him. The judge told him that counsel was appointed only if the punishment involved the death penalty. The case went to a jury trial in which Gideon defended himself. He was found guilty and sentenced to five years in prison. On appeal, the U.S. Supreme Court overturned his conviction and established that indigent defendants have the right to court-appointed attorneys in felony cases.

THINK ABOUT IT

1. What effect did the *Gideon* decision have on the public defender system?

This 1963 photo shows Clarence Earl Gideon after his release from a Panama City, Florida, jail. A unanimous Supreme Court issued its decision in *Gideon v. Wainwright,* declaring that states must provide defendants with "the guiding hand of counsel" to ensure a fair trial. How many states have a public defender system today?

PAUSE AND REVIEW

1. **What are some variables that can influence a defense attorney's effectiveness? Which variable is considered the single most important one and why?**

2. **Describe the concept of "normal crimes." How does this concept affect the courtroom work group?**

LEARNING OBJECTIVE | **6**

List several examples of the duties of judges.

LEARNING OBJECTIVE | **7**

Discuss the three methods of selecting judges.

The Judge

Judges occupy a unique space in the criminal justice system. On one hand, they are considered the most powerful actors in the system. On the other hand, judges are viewed as impotent referees who must act with neutrality, objectivity, and impartiality. They have neither the prosecutor's extensive power of discretion nor the prestige or salary of a successful defense attorney. The term *judge* encompasses many responsibilities from the local justice of the peace to a Supreme Court justice.

Judges perform several duties in the administration of justice. They act as a check and balance to the discretion of zealous prosecutors, as impartial arbiters in the contest between law enforcement and defendants, and as decision-makers in applying punishment or treatment to the guilty. Judges play a role at many points in the criminal justice system, including:

> Signing search warrants. Judges ensure that police officers do not violate suspects' rights against unreasonable searches by reviewing search warrants for evidence of probable cause.

> Informing defendants of charges. The judge informs the defendant of the charges the police officer has filed at the initial-appearance stage.

> Appointing counsel. For indigent defendants, the judge appoints a defense attorney. In many states, this is the public defender who is appointed to that judge's courtroom. In some jurisdictions, the judge appoints a private attorney whose turn it is to provide indigent defense.

> Setting bail. After hearing from the prosecutor who reviews the charges, the defendant's criminal history, and the likelihood that the defendant will appear at subsequent hearings, the judge gives the defense attorney an opportunity to rebut. Then, the judge either sets bail, releases the defendant on recognizance, or orders the defendant confined until trial.

> Taking a plea. At arraignment, the judge informs the defendant of the charges and allows the defendant to enter a plea of guilty, not guilty, or no contest.

> Ruling on motions. The judge rules on motions from the defense and the prosecution concerning the admissibility of evidence. These motions may concern illegal search and seizure issues, the interrogation of suspects, or the use of police lineups.

> Participating in or ruling on plea bargaining. Some judges take an active role in deciding a plea bargain between the defense and the prosecution. Other judges simply approve or disapprove the negotiated decision.

> Presiding at trial. The judge's role in a trial is to ensure that the defendant's due process rights are respected, to rule on the admissibility of evidence, to instruct the jury as to which laws are applicable in the case, and to ensure that all parties, including spectators, conduct themselves properly.

> Sentencing. Although many cases provide clear-cut choices between incarceration and liberty, the alternative options available to most judges are quite limited. Treatment options are scarce, and with prison crowding a serious issue in many states, judges are pressured to find dispositions other than incarceration.

Here, Judge Monte Watkins presides over the trial of Cory Batey, a Vanderbilt University student who was charged with raping an unconscious woman. What level of discretion do judges have in the administration of justice?

In the next section, we will discuss the methods of judicial selection. More important than the selection method, however, is the question of whether any method produces better judges than other methods.

Judicial Selection: Executive Appointments

At the federal level, judges are nominated by the president and confirmed by the Senate according to their advise-and-consent responsibility as stated in the Constitution. Although in the past this process has been a routine rubber stamp of the president's wishes, recently it has become quite politicized.[56] Controversial appointments are subjected to lengthy Senate hearings in which the nominee is grilled by senators about his or her character, legal history, and views on certain controversial issues that will likely come before the courts. A good deal of screening takes place to find candidates who reflect the president's worldview and yet are not controversial.

For U.S. district court judges, the senators of the state in which the appointment is to be made are commonly consulted as a courtesy. If a senator finds the nominee unacceptable, senators from other states (particularly those in the same party) might vote against the appointment. In this way, senators have both formal and informal influence on the selection of judges in their state. At the state level, the legislature has no comparable advise-and-consent function, so governors have more leeway in the selection of judges. At both levels, the influence of party politics is significant.[57] See CJ Reference 8.1 for the American Bar Association's guidelines for reviewing candidates for state judicial office.

Judicial Selection: Election of Judges

In an effort to democratize judicial selection, nearly half of the states elect judges (see Figure 8.2). It is assumed that judges who must run for re-election will conform to the wishes of the people rather than the dictates of the elite.[58] For the most part, the campaigns for judgeships have low visibility, and voters have little knowledge about the qualifications or temperament of the candidates. For this reason, incumbent judges have a distinct advantage over challengers, especially when the title "judge" is printed next to their names on the ballot. Some elections are hotly contested, especially seats on the state supreme court.[59]

CJ REFERENCE 8.1

American Bar Association Guidelines for Reviewing Qualifications of Candidates for State Judicial Office

These guidelines describe the minimum criteria for the evaluation of candidates for state and local judicial offices.

1. Integrity. A candidate should be of undisputed integrity.
2. Legal knowledge and ability. A candidate should possess a high degree of knowledge of established legal principles and procedures and have a high degree of ability to interpret and apply them to specific factual situations.
3. Professional experience. A candidate should be a licensed, experienced lawyer.
4. Judicial temperament. A candidate should possess a judicial temperament, which includes common sense, compassion, decisiveness, firmness, humility, open-mindedness, patience, tact, and understanding.
5. Diligence. A candidate should be diligent and punctual.
6. Health. A candidate should be in good physical and mental health.
7. Financial responsibility. A candidate should be financially responsible.
8. Public service. Consideration should be given to a candidate's previous public service activities.[60]

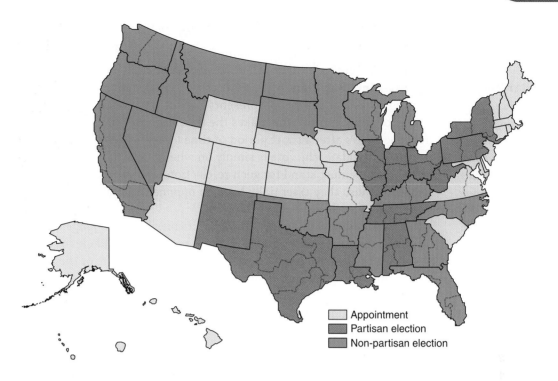

FIGURE 8.2 **The Methods for the Selection of General Jurisdiction Judges for an Initial Term** How many states appoint judges? How many hold partisan elections? Non-partisan elections? Which method does your state use?

Source: Ron Malega and Thomas H. Cohen, State Court Organization, 2011 (Washington, D.C.: U.S. Department of Justice Office of Justice Programs Bureau of Justice Statistics, 2013), 6. Available at https://www.bjs.gov/index.cfm?ty=tp&tid=26.

Candidate Eddie Treviño, Jr., won the seat of Cameron County Judge in Brownsville, Texas, in November 2016. What other ways are judges selected?

Judicial Selection: Merit Selection

Missouri Bar Plan—A form of judicial selection in which a nominating commission presents a list of candidates to the governor, who decides on a candidate. After a year in office, voters decide on whether to retain the judge. Judges must run for such re-election each term. Also called merit selection.

In an effort to remove politics from the judicial selection process, court reformers have adopted a system called merit selection or, as it is sometimes known, the **Missouri Bar Plan**. In this process, a judicial nominating commission comprising lawyers and laypeople presents a short list of qualified candidates (usually three) to the governor, who makes the final decision. Judges are then required to face the voters after a short period of time (one year). Instead of running against another candidate, the vote is simply on whether the judge should be retained in office. Judges must stand for such re-election each term, but they are seldom removed because they essentially have no opponents, and the voters seldom know of reasons why they should be removed.[61]

Each method of selecting judges has its merits. When judges are elected, they are considered more accountable to the voters and more likely to represent the interests of the average citizen rather than those of the elite of the legal profession. This admirable philosophy is pitted against the alternative of the appointment of judges, where, presumably free from catering to the voters, the judge can enjoy judicial independence and rule on the merits of the case.

Perhaps the most important and notable change in the judicial selection process is the increase in the number of women and minorities appointed to the bench. The profile of the judge as a white male is being radically changed without affecting other background characteristics such as judicial education. As more women go to law school and work their way up the ranks of prosecutors' offices and law firms, more of them are being elected or appointed as judges (see Figure 8.3). To a large extent, the same can be said for minorities, but because of the under-representation of black lawyers, there are fewer black judges. More minorities are on the bench in states in which judges are appointed than in states in which judges are elected.[62]

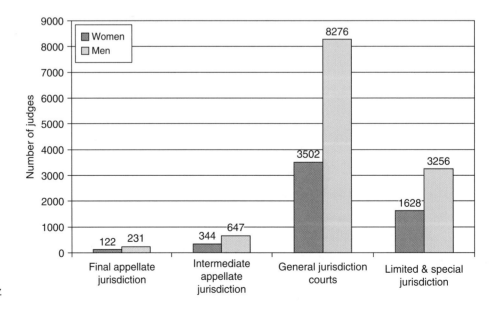

FIGURE 8.3   Gender of U.S. State Court Judges What are some reasons why general-jurisdiction courts have the lowest percentage of female judges?

Source: National Association of Women Judges, The American Bench 2016, Forster-Long, LLC, https://www.nawj.org/statistics/2016-us-state-court-women-judges. Accessed June 2017.

PAUSE AND REVIEW

1. **List five examples of the duties of judges.**

2. **What are the three methods of selecting judges?**

3. **How many states elect judges?**

The Participants

Although a certain adversarial atmosphere is present in the courtroom, those in the courtroom work group also exhibit a high level of cooperation.[63] The participants working in the courthouse, and, ultimately, in the courtroom, all come from disparate backgrounds, agencies, and ideologies. As in the criminal justice system in general, those who work in the courthouse have different sets of funding sources, constituents, responsibilities, and goals. These people, who sometimes seem to be working at cross purposes—for example, the prosecutor and the defense attorney have competing agendas regarding defendants— are in many other ways cooperating to move cases in a timely manner.[64] Consequently, there is a certain level of expectation of how each case will be settled based on the going rate.[65] In sociological terms, a routinization of work occurs whereby everyone (except the defendant) has a good idea about the ultimate outcome of the case. Nevertheless, each actor has a vested interest in seeing cases resolved according to his or her particular social and legal location within the courthouse. Let's review this variety of courthouse actors and the duties they perform in the courtroom.

Law Enforcement

Various types of law enforcement officers interact daily within the courtroom work group. First is the courthouse security officer, who is responsible for protecting everyone in the courthouse.[66] A second type of law enforcement officer working in the courthouse is the sheriff's deputy, who transports prisoners to and from jail. The courthouse usually has a holding pen where these deputies keep prisoners until they are required to be present in the courtroom. The **bailiff** is a court officer responsible for maintaining order in the courtroom.[67] In some jurisdictions, a bailiff works in a specific judge's courtroom. In other jurisdictions, bailiffs rotate from courtroom to courtroom as needed. Additionally, the constant parade of law enforcement officers who come to the courthouse to testify in trials are also integral participants. For the sake of efficiency, many courts have a senior law enforcement officer who coordinates with police agencies to ensure that officers do not spend all their time waiting in courthouse corridors for trials that might be canceled.

LEARNING OBJECTIVE **8**

Describe the two primary court functions that probation officers perform.

LEARNING OBJECTIVE **9**

Characterize the tasks of law enforcement, court support staff, corrections, and the public.

bailiff—Court officer responsible for executing writs and processes, making arrests, and keeping order in the court.

Two bailiffs escort a man from a courtroom. Besides attorneys and judges, who are some of the other essential courtroom actors?

Court Support Staff

Several courtroom support staffers work behind the scenes to ensure the smooth functioning of the court. The **clerk of the court** is an administrator with a large staff who keeps the court records and provides a sufficient pool of jurors for cases that go to trial. The **court reporter** makes a verbatim transcript of the proceedings. Given the ethnic diversity of many cities, the court employs translators to ensure that defendants, victims, and witnesses can have their testimony translated into English.[68] Many courts have partially replaced their court reporters with digital recorders, but court reporters are still an important part of the process in some courts. Besides recording the word-for-word account of a hearing or trial and transcribing cases, court reporters may also organize hearings, open or close the courtroom, and manage the exhibits. Finally, the **court administrator** handles the various administrative tasks necessary for the court to function, such as scheduling courtrooms, procuring furniture, improving case flow, creating calendars, and managing court personnel.[69]

Corrections

Probation officers perform two primary court functions. First, they interview offenders and write pre-sentence investigation reports in which the officers review the case and make sentencing recommendations to the judge.[70] Second, the probation officer supervises offenders who are placed on probation to ensure that they are following the judge's orders and are not breaking any further laws. Depending on the jurisdiction, the court may directly employ the probation officer via a statewide department of corrections or by a local government or private probation department. In some jurisdictions, pretrial services personnel—for instance, people who work for programs designed to divert defendants from the criminal justice system—work with judges to help identify individuals who could be safely released from custody pending further court proceedings.[71] Additionally, rehabilitation specialists, who typically work for the court, identify drug and alcohol treatment programs for qualified offenders.[72]

The Public

Several members of the public who have business with the court can be loosely identified as part of the informal courtroom work group. For-profit **bail agents** solicit offenders (or their families) who cannot afford the entire amount of their bail to use their services to get out of jail while awaiting trial.[73] News agencies have reporters covering the courthouse beat. Depending on their reputation for discretion, some reporters are allowed behind the scenes, where they might participate in the informal workings of the courtroom work group. Victim–witness program personnel, including staff members of rape crisis centers, are other informal participants in the courtroom work group.[74] These individuals advocate on behalf of crime victims and may introduce **victim-impact statements** to help the judge decide on an appropriate sentence.[75]

Juvenile courts often employ a **child advocate** to ensure that the best interests of the child, and not those of the state or the parents, are considered.[76] Many courts have members of the public who act as court watchers. These individuals may represent public-interest groups who advocate for better government, or they may simply be court aficionados who enjoy watching courtroom action. Perhaps the most important segment of the public that is constantly present in the courtroom are the jurors. Although no individual juror is a regular member of the courtroom work group, jurors are part of the proceedings and play an important role in court decisions.

As we can see, the informal courtroom work group comprises a variety of individuals who represent many, sometimes competing, interests.[77] All play important roles and are instrumental in the workings of the courts.

clerk of the court— The primary administrative officer of each court who manages non-judicial functions.

court reporter— A court officer who records and transcribes an official verbatim record of the legal proceedings of the court.

court administrator— An officer responsible for the mechanical necessities of the court, such as scheduling courtrooms, managing case flow, administering personnel, procuring furniture, and preparing budgets.

bail agent— An employee of a private, for-profit company that provides money for suspects to be released from jail. Also called a bondsman.

victim-impact statement (from Chapter 2)— An account given by the victim, the victim's family, or others affected by the offense that expresses the effects of the offense, including economic losses, the extent of physical or psychological injuries, and major life changes.

child advocate— An officer appointed by the court to protect the interests of the child and to act as a liaison among the child, the child's family, the court, and any other agency involved with the child.

Pictured here is volunteer Brenda Knaack (left) and Lindsey Jordan (right), director of the Grand Traverse Court Appointed Special Advocate program for the 13th Circuit Family Division in Traverse City, Michigan. What is the role of a child advocate?

PAUSE AND REVIEW

1. What two primary functions do probation officers perform for the court?
2. Name three examples of court support staff and describe their responsibilities.
3. In what ways does the going rate affect the various court participants?

Defendants, Victims, and Witnesses

Those working in the criminal courts learn the language, rituals, and protocols that dictate the pace and atmosphere of the court's daily routine.[78] These professionals must deal with civilians who are not knowledgeable about how the law is applied and how the courtroom works. Defendants, victims, and witnesses bring varying degrees of experience to the court and often leave with a sense of confusion, injustice, and bewilderment. It is useful to consider how each of these parties views the workings of the criminal court.

Defendants

Those who find themselves before a criminal court on felony charges are often the least able to understand the workings of the institution and feel powerless to affect the outcome of their case. Felony defendants are overwhelmingly male, young, poor, undereducated, and members of racial minorities.[79] Unless they are repeat offenders (and many are), they have little understanding as to what is happening to them as they are processed through the system. Many are illiterate and cannot comprehend even the simplest instructions or help their attorney prepare a defense.[80] Too many defendants come to court with problems that the criminal justice system is ill equipped to handle, such as drug addiction, mental illness, lack of education, or marital problems. Those who cannot secure bail before their appearance are attired in handcuffs, a jail jumpsuit, and slippers, which stigmatize them even further.[81]

LEARNING OBJECTIVE 10

Describe the experience of defendants, victims, and witnesses in the context of the courtroom work group.

LEARNING OBJECTIVE 11

Name some services that victim–witness programs provide.

The middle-class worldview of those in the courtroom work group is unsympathetic to the plight of those whose fates are being decided. The courtroom ritual serves to intimidate the defendant and impress on him or her the gravity of the situation. It is little wonder that many who experience "their day in court" often come away with a feeling of injustice and alienation.[82]

Victims

Perhaps the only people more disillusioned by the workings and results of the criminal court than the defendants are the victims.[83] Because a felony charge pits the defendant against the state, the role of the victim is sometimes diminished. Especially when cases are plea-bargained, the victim's interests might be slighted. Victims see their particular case as being serious and can become disillusioned when it is treated in the routine and bureaucratic manner that is the court's norm.[84] Victims are perplexed when, in lieu of a trial, in which they expect to explain how they were injured by the defendant's behavior, the prosecutor informs them that the case was settled with a disposition of probation rather than a long prison term. Many victims feel anger when they see defendants enjoying due process rights while their voices remain unheard.[85]

Witnesses

Those who witness crime or have other relevant testimony have less attachment to the case than the defendant or victim. Witnesses have an important role to play, however, and they often experience frustration in dealing with the court. Being required to travel to the court to provide testimony and finding the case postponed or having to wait long periods in uncomfortable hallways can cause a good deal of distress for witnesses. The loss of wages for time spent at court or having property kept for long periods of time as evidence can cause additional frustration. Perhaps the most stressful aspect of being a witness is the fear of retaliation from a defendant and the sense that criminal justice personnel are indifferent to the danger one feels.[86]

Witness Brooke Wilcox tearfully testifies during the murder trial for the late former New England Patriots football player Aaron Hernandez. What difficulties or stresses may some witnesses experience?

Victim–Witness Programs

The criminal justice system is not completely indifferent to the plight of victims and witnesses. Many jurisdictions have established victim–witness assistance programs to encourage cooperation in criminal cases and alleviate some of the inconvenience of appearing in court. Reducing the suffering caused by the offense and anticipating the confusion and frustration of dealing with the criminal justice system are the objectives of victim–witness programs.[87] Because each victim has different needs, programs are designed to provide many types of services, including:[88]

> Crisis intervention. Crime is a traumatic event for most victims. Especially in cases of violent crime, the victims and their families may need assistance in dealing with transportation to the hospital or court, notifying relatives, procuring money to buy meals, and understanding how and when the criminal justice system will handle the case.

> Follow-up counseling. The traumatic nature of offenses such as sexual assault may require ongoing counseling until the case is brought to court and, in some cases, long afterward. Counseling services might be provided by victim–witness staff or by referral to a psychologist. Some programs have established support groups to help victims deal with the effects of crime.

> Personal advocacy. Often, the victim is too traumatized to effectively plead his or her side of the case to the police, prosecutor, judge, or others. The victim–witness staff member asserts the victim's interests in the repeated telling of the effect of the offense on the victim. Victims can grow tired of pleading their woes and might feel that others perceive them as whining. A professional staff member, however, can advocate for the victim's best interests.

> Employer and landlord intervention. Victimization can have far-reaching and long-lasting effects. If the offense was committed in a workplace or rental residence, the employer or landlord might see getting rid of the victim as a solution to future violence. The victim–witness staff member can intervene to convince the employer or landlord that it would be morally unethical to fire or evict the victim.

> Property return. In cases of theft or armed robbery, the victim's stolen property may be used as evidence. Often the property is kept for long periods as the case winds through the court process. The victim–witness staff member can sometimes expedite the return of the property to the victim when the state has concluded the case.

> Intimidation protection. Victims and witnesses can be subject to intimidation from defendants or their families and friends. Sitting outside a courtroom waiting to testify can be frightening for the victim when the defendant, who is out on bail, or the defendant's family member is pestering him or her to drop the charge. Additionally, the defense attorney might give unsolicited advice to victims or witnesses that could border on intimidation.[89] The victim–witness staff member can act as a buffer for victims and witnesses and protect them from embarrassment or intimidation.

> Court orientation. For many victims and witnesses, their case represents the first time they have had to go to a courthouse. Seemingly insignificant issues such as parking, finding the correct courtroom, and what to wear are likely to be the subjects of questions for the uninitiated. Victim–witness staff members can answer questions and help prepare those who will be called to testify.

Victim–witness programs provide a range of services to those who must help the criminal justice system by testifying in criminal trials. Unfortunately, the level of services provided varies widely across the country, especially between large urban courts and smaller ones. There is no mandate for the state or federal government to provide these services. Although everyone may agree that victim–witness programs are beneficial, they are not required in the way that legal counsel for indigent offenders is. In lean budget years, victim–witness programs are one of the "frills" that courts can cut to save money.

PAUSE AND REVIEW

1. Describe some of the challenges faced by criminal defendants.
2. What are some of the stressful aspects of being a witness, and how can such stress negatively affect court proceedings?
3. What are some of the services that victim–witness programs provide, and how do such services positively affect court proceedings?

 **FOCUS ON ETHICS** Difficult Decisions for the Defense

As a defense attorney, you really dislike your client. He is a liar, a cheat, and a drug dealer and has been accused of killing a police officer. The prosecutor does not know about half the offenses your client has committed and has presented a case that, although convincing to many, has a major flaw that could set your client free. You are torn about what to do.

On one hand, you believe not only that your client deserves to go to prison for a long time but also that your community would be a lot safer if he were taken off the streets. After all, you have a family that you want protected from this type of pathological criminal. On the other hand, you realize that the prosecution's responsibility is to make the case against your client and that your obligation is to provide the best defense possible.

Unfortunately, the assistant district attorney has overlooked several pieces of critical evidence that can place your client at the scene of the crime and seal his fate. To complicate matters further, your firm's founding partners have all but assured you that if you win the case, you will jump over 10 senior associates and be made partner next year.

WHAT DO YOU DO?

1. Win the case. Your duty is to represent your client. It would be unethical to sabotage the case in any way or to give less than your best effort. Besides, this could be a major turning point in your career and could ensure your family's financial security.
2. Find an anonymous way to tip off the prosecutor to the critical evidence. This man is too dangerous to be put back on the street, and your family's financial security is meaningless if dangerous offenders like your client are roaming your community.
3. Resign from the case. Tell your senior partners that you cannot in good conscience represent such a despicable character. By making this choice, you realize not only that you risk the chance to make partner, but also that you could be fired.

For more insight as to how someone might respond to such an ethical dilemma, visit the companion website at www.oup.com/us/fuller to watch a video that connects this scenario to a real-world situation.

Summary

LEARNING OBJECTIVE 1 Explain what a courtroom work group is.	The judges, prosecutors, defense attorneys, clerks, and bailiffs who work together to move cases through the court system and whose interaction determines the outcome of criminal cases.
LEARNING OBJECTIVE 2 Recognize why the prosecutor is so powerful.	The prosecutor's position is powerful because the exercise of discretion rests with this office. The prosecutor decides which cases are formally defined as criminal offenses, whether or not to charge the case, what the charge will be, or chooses to dismiss it.
LEARNING OBJECTIVE 3 Outline the five categories of activities that divide the prosecutor's energies.	Fighting: Prosecutors must get a case in shape to take it to court and ultimately to trial. Negotiating: Most cases are plea-bargained, meaning that the defense attorney and the prosecutor strike a deal for a plea of guilty or no contest in return for a lighter sentence. Drafting: Prosecutors draft legal documents to record their activities to ensure that cases can be upheld on appeal and that enable other criminal justice system actors to perform their duties. Counseling: The prosecutor contends with the needs of victims, witnesses, law enforcement officers, and other officials who compose the courtroom work group. Administering: Prosecutors play an administrative role by making sure victims and witnesses are interviewed, briefed, and available should they be required to testify.
LEARNING OBJECTIVE 4 Summarize the role of the defense attorney.	The defense attorney provides the best defense possible for the defendant, protects the interests of the accused, and ensures that the prosecution adequately proves the charges.
LEARNING OBJECTIVE 5 Describe the concept of "normal crimes."	"Normal crimes" are cases that are considered in the context of how the court handled similar offenses. In these cases, attorneys have a good idea of what the sentence will be for a particular offense by considering how that crime compares to the court's sentencing pattern.
LEARNING OBJECTIVE 6 List several examples of the duties of judges.	Signing search warrants, informing defendants of charges, appointing counsel, setting bail, taking a plea, ruling on motions, participating in or ruling on plea bargaining, presiding at trial, sentencing.
LEARNING OBJECTIVE 7 Discuss the three methods of selecting judges.	Executive Appointments: Federal judges are nominated by the president and confirmed by the Senate. Election of Judges: Nearly half of the states elect judges. Merit Selection: A judicial nominating commission presents a list of qualified candidates to the governor, who makes the final decision. After about one year, the judges face the voters who decide whether the judge is retained.

LEARNING OBJECTIVE **8** Describe the two primary court functions that probation officers perform.	Probation officers interview offenders and write pre-sentence investigation reports in which they review the case and make sentencing recommendations to the judge. Probation officers also supervise offenders on probation to ensure that they follow the judge's orders and obey the law.
LEARNING OBJECTIVE **9** Characterize the tasks of law enforcement, court support staff, corrections, and the public.	Law enforcement: Courthouse security officers protect everyone in the courthouse. Sheriff's deputies transport prisoners and monitor them until they are required in the courtroom. Bailiffs maintain order in the courtroom. A senior law enforcement officer may coordinate with police agencies to schedule officers for trials. Court support staff: Court clerks keep court records and maintain the juror pool. Court reporters transcribe court proceedings. Translators translate testimonies. Court administrators handle administrative tasks. Corrections: Probation officers produce pre-sentence investigation reports and supervise offenders on probation. Rehabilitation specialists identify drug and alcohol treatment programs for qualified offenders. The Public: Bail agents solicit offenders who cannot afford their bail. Victim–witness program personnel advocate on behalf of victims and introduce victim-impact statements. In juvenile courts, child advocates support the best interests of the child.
LEARNING OBJECTIVE **10** Describe the experience of defendants, victims, and witnesses in the context of the courtroom work group.	Due to illiteracy, mental illness, poverty, age, or addiction, defendants often have trouble understanding the workings of the court and may feel powerless. Victims are sometimes diminished because a felony charge pits the defendant against the state and excludes the victim(s). Victims can become disillusioned when their cases are treated in the bureaucratic manner of the court. Witnesses may be inconvenienced by having to show up in court, lose wages at a job, and/or may fear retaliation from a defendant.
LEARNING OBJECTIVE **11** Name some services that victim–witness programs provide.	Crisis intervention, follow-up counseling, personal advocacy, employer and landlord intervention, property return, intimidation protection, referral to community resources, court orientation, court transportation and escort, public education, and legislative advocacy.

Critical Reflections

1. Is it fair that the prosecutor has so much power in the court?

2. What benefits do victim-witness programs provide?

Key Terms

bail agent **p. 248**
bailiff **p. 247**
child advocate **p. 248**
clerk of the court **p. 248**
court administrator **p. 248**
court reporter **p. 248**

courtroom work group **p. 228**
Criminal Division **p. 233**
discretion **p. 229**
disposition **p. 229**
going rate **p. 232**
Missouri Bar Plan **p. 246**

normal crimes **p. 237**
plea bargain **p. 230**
U.S. Attorneys **p. 233**
U.S. Solicitor General **p. 232**
victim-impact statement **p. 248**

Endnotes

1 John A. Torres, "Torres: Judge in Courtroom Scuffle 'Fights' for Seat," *FloridaToday*, September 15, 2015, http://www.floridatoday.com/story/news/local/john-a-torres/2015/03/29/torres-judge-courtroom-scuffle-fights-seat/70652794.

2 Florida Supreme Court, Inquiry Concerning Judge John C. Murphy, http://www.floridasupremecourt.org/pub_info/summaries/briefs/14/14-1582/Filed_05-19-2015_Findings_Conclusions_Recommendations.pdf. Accessed October 2015.

3 Dara Kam, "Brevard Judge in Viral Fight Video Suspended by Florida Supreme Court," *Orlando Sentinel*, October 21, 2015, http://www.orlandosentinel.com/news/breaking-news/os-brevard-judge-murphy-suspended-20151006-story.html.

4 Martha Neil, "Assistant PD Punched by Judge Resigns in Protest after Jurist Returns to Bench," *ABA Journal*, July 8, 2014, http://www.abajournal.com/news/article/public_defender_punched_by_judge_resigns_in_protest_of_jurists_return_to_be.

5 Sean Federico-O'Murchu, Florida Judge John C. Murphy Fired for 'Appalling Behavior', NBC News, December 18, 2015, http://www.nbcnews.com/news/us-news/florida-judge-john-c-murphy-fired-appalling-behavior-n482626.

6 James Eisenstein and Herbert Jacob, *Felony Justice: An Organizational Analysis of Criminal Courts* (Boston: Little, Brown, 1977).

7 Josh Bowers, "Punishing the Innocent," *University of Pennsylvania Law Review* 156 (May 1, 2008): 1117.

8 Máximo Langer, "Rethinking Plea Bargaining: The Practice and Reform of Prosecutorial Adjudication in American Criminal Procedure," *American Journal of Criminal Law* 33 (July 2006): 223–299.

9 William McDonald, "The Prosecutors' Domain," in *The Prosecutor*, ed. William McDonald (Newbury Park, Calif.: Sage, 1979).

10 Alissa Pollitz Worden, "Policy-making by Prosecutors: The Uses of Discretion in Regulating Plea Bargaining," *Judicature* 73 (1990): 335–340.

11 Talia Fisher, "The Boundaries of Plea Bargaining: Negotiating the Standard of Proof," *Journal of Criminal Law and Criminology* 97 (July 1, 2007): 943–1007.

12 *Brady v. Maryland*, 373 U.S. 83 (1963).

13 Bennett L. Gershman, "Why Prosecutors Misbehave," in *Courts and Justice: A Reader*, 2nd ed., ed. G. Larry Mays and Peter R. Gregware (Long Grove, Ill.: Waveland Press, 1999), 282–292.

14 David W. Neubauer, *America's Courts and the Criminal Justice System*, 7th ed. (Belmont, Calif.: Wadsworth, 2002).

15 Michael Booth, "Victim Need Not Be Told of Plea Bargain," *National Law Journal*, July 16, 2007, 15.

16 Resa Baldas, "Hot-Button Words Are Iced in Court," *National Law Journal*, June 16, 2008, 1.

17 Pamela Utz, "Two Models of Prosecutorial Professionalism," in *The Prosecutor*, ed. William McDonald (Newbury Park, Calif.: Sage, 1979).

18 Joan Jacoby, *The Prosecutors' Charging Decision: A Policy Perspective* (Washington, D.C.: U.S. Department of Justice, 1977).

19 Los Angeles County District Attorney's Office, Office Overview, http://da.co.la.ca.us/about/office-overview. Accessed January 2017.

20 Griffin Bell, "Appointing United States Attorneys," *Journal of Law and Politics* 9 (1993): 247–256.

21 The Department of Justice, Agencies, http://www.justice.gov/agencies. Accessed January 2017.

22 Rebecca Sudokar, *The Solicitor General: The Politics of Law* (Philadelphia: Temple University Press, 1992).

23 Offices of the United States Attorneys, Mission, http://www.justice.gov/usao/mission. Accessed January 2017.

24 Bell, "Appointing United States Attorneys."

25 KNOWAtlanta, Atlanta Metro Counties & Cities Map, http://www.knowatlanta.com/atlanta-metro-counties-cities.

26 "Key Events in State Suits against Tobacco Industry," CNN, November 16, 1998, http://www.cnn.com/US/9811/16/tobacco.timeline/.

27 Neubauer, *America's Courts and the Criminal Justice System*.

28 David Heilbroner, *Rough Justice: Days and Nights of a Young D.A.* (New York: Pantheon, 1990).

29 Neubauer, *America's Courts and the Criminal Justice System*.

30 David Lynch, "The Impropriety of Plea Agreements: A Tale of Two Counties," *Law and Social Inquiry* 19 (1994): 115–136.

31 William J. Price, "Make Sense of Your Client's Story," *Trial*, June 1, 2008, 66.

32 Rodney Uphoff, "The Criminal Defense Lawyer: Zealous Advocate, Double Agent or Beleaguered Dealer?" *Criminal Law Bulletin* 28 (1992): 419–456.

33 Stephen Bright, "Counsel for the Poor: The Death Sentence Not for the Worst Crime, but for the Worst Lawyer," *Yale Law Journal* 103 (1994): 1835–1884.

34 Michael J. McWilliams, "The Erosion of Indigent Rights: Excessive Caseloads Resulting in Ineffective Counsel for Poor," *American Bar Association Journal* 79 (1993): 8.

35 Larry J. Cohen, Patricia P. Sample, and Robert E. Crew Jr., "Assigned Counsel versus Public Defender Systems in Virginia," in *The Defense Counsel*, ed. William F. McDonald (Beverly Hills, Calif.: Sage, 1983).

36 Jerome Skolnick, "Social Control in the Adversary System," *Journal of Conflict Resolution* 11 (1967): 52–70.

37 David Sudnow, "Normal Crimes: Sociological Features of the Penal Code in a Public Defender Office," *Social Problems* 12 (1965): 209–215.

38 Erving Goffman, *The Presentation of Self in Everyday Life* (Garden City, N.Y.: Doubleday Anchor Books, 1959).

39 Brian Sullivan, "Canning Your Client," *ABA Journal* 94 (March 1, 2008): 46–52.

40 Roger Hanson, William Hewitt, and Brian Ostrom, "Are the Critical Indigent Defense Counsel Correct?" *State Court Journal* (Summer 1992): 20–29.

41 Carroll Seron, *The Business of Practicing Law: The Work Lives of Solo and Small-Firm Attorneys* (Philadelphia: Temple University Press, 1996).

42 Bright, "Counsel for the Poor."

43 Blumberg, "Practice of Law." "The real key to understanding the role of a defense counsel in a criminal case is to be found in the area of the fixing of the fee to be charged and its collection. The problem of fixing and collecting the fee tends to influence to a significant degree the criminal court process itself, and not just the relationship between the lawyer and his client" (p. 24).

44 *Gideon v. Wainwright*, 372 U.S. 335 (1963). Read the decision at https://www.law.cornell.edu/supremecourt/text/372/335.

45 Brentin Mock, The Many, Many Problems with New Orleans' Public Defender System, CityLab, September 23, 2015, http://www.citylab.com/crime/2015/09/the-many-problems-with-new-orleans-public-defender-system/406858.

46 Daniel Wiessner, New York State to Settle Landmark Suit Over Public Defenders, Reuters, October 21, 2014, http://www.reuters.com/article/2014/10/21/us-usa-lawsuit-newyork-idUSKCN0IA2L420141021.

47 Gabrielle Canon, "Can a Public Defender Really Handle 700 Cases a Year?," Mother Jones, July 27, 2015, http://www.motherjones.com/politics/2015/07/aclu-lawsuit-public-defense-fresno-california.

48 Dan Boyd and Katy Barnitz, "Lack of Funds Hits Public Defender Department Hard," Albuquerque Journal, December 19, 2016, https://www.abqjournal.com/911629/lack-of-funds-hits-public-defender-dept-hard.html.

49 Suzanne M. Strong, State-Administered Indigent Defense Systems, 2013 (U.S. Department of Justice Office of Justice Programs Bureau of Justice Statistics, 2016), 1. Online at https://www.bjs.gov/index.cfm?ty=pbdetail&iid=5826. Julia O'Donoghue, "Inadequate Representation: No More Money Expected for Public Defenders," NOLA.com, April 18, 2016, http://www.nola.com/politics/index.ssf/2016/04/public_defender_funding.html. Tim Lockette, "Lawyers on Layaway," Anniston Star, September 28, 2013, http://www.annistonstar.com/news/lawyers-on-layaway-alabama-bills-indigent-defendants-for-court-appointed/article_0a05b26b-7ecc-5e2d-ade7-5a7797ce2da7.html.

50 McWilliams, "Erosion of Indigent Rights."

51 Alissa Pollitz Worden, "Privatizing Due Process: Issues in the Comparison of Assigned Counsel, Public Defender, and Contracted Indigent Defense Systems," Justice Systems Journal 14 (1991): 390–418.

52 Gail S. Goodman, R.S. Edelstein, E.B. Mitchell, J.E. Myers, "A Comparison of Types of Attorney Representation for Children in California Juvenile Court Dependency Cases," Child Abuse and Neglect 32 (April 1, 2008): 497.

53 Lynn Langton and Donald J. Farole, Jr., Public Defender Offices, 2007-Statistical Tables (Washington, D.C.: U.S. Department of Justice Office of Justice Programs, 2010), 1.

Available at http://bjs.ojp.usdoj.gov/index.cfm?ty=pbdetail&iid=1758.

54 Neubauer, America's Courts and the Criminal Justice System, 179–182.

55 Arye Rattner, Hagit Turjeman, and Gideon Fishman, "Public versus Private Defense: Can Money Buy Justice?" Journal of Criminal Justice 36 (March 1, 2008): 43.

56 Sheldon Goldman and Elliot Slotnick, "Clinton's Second Term Judiciary: Picking Judges under Fire," Judicature 82 (1999): 264–285.

57 Terry B. Friedman, "The Politicization of the Judiciary," Judicature 82 (July 1, 1998): 6–7.

58 Paul Brace and Brent D. Boyea, "State Public Opinion, the Death Penalty, and the Practice of Electing Judges:[1]," American Journal of Political Science 52 (April 1, 2008): 360–372.

59 Philip Dubois, From Ballot to Bench: Judicial Elections and the Quest for Accountability (Austin: University of Texas Press, 1980).

60 Richard Watson and Ronald Downing, The Politics of the Bench and the Bar: Judicial Selection under the Missouri Nonpartisan Court Plan (New York: Wiley, 1969).

61 Ibid., 205.

62 Kathryn Fahnestock and Maurice Geiger, "We All Get Along Here: Case Flow in Rural Courts," Judicature 76 (1993): 258–263.

63 Abraham S. Blumberg, "The Practice of Law as a Confidence Game," Law and Society Review (June 1, 1967): 15–39.

64 Sudnow, "Normal Crimes."

65 Steven Goldspiel/American Bar Association, "Guidelines for Reviewing Qualifications of Candidates for State Judicial Office" (Chicago, Ill.: Judicial Administration Division Lawyers' Conference, 1987). Available at State of Nebraska Judicial Branch, court.cdc.nol.org/2410/american-bar-associations-guidelines-reviewing-qualifications-candidates-state-judicial-office. Accessed January 2017.

66 "Review Cites 8 Steps to Boost Court Security," Crime Control Digest, March 24, 2006, 4.

67 N. Gary Holten and Lawson L. Lamar, The Criminal Courts: Structures, Personnel, and Processes (New York: McGraw-Hill, 1991), 109–110.

68 Stacey Laskin, "Dramatic Drop in Court Reporters Causes Alarm," National Law Journal (July 23, 2007): 6.

69 Ibid., 111–112.

70 John Rosecrance, "Maintaining the Myth of Individualized Justice: Probation Pre-sentence Reports," Justice Quarterly 5 (1988): 235–256.

71 Gary A. Rabe and Dean J. Champion, Criminal Courts: Structure, Process, and Issues (Upper Saddle River, N.J.: Prentice Hall, 2002). Chapter 7 presents an excellent review of pretrial procedures.

72 Jennifer Eno Louden, Jennifer L. Skeem, Jacqueline Camp, and Elizabeth Christensen, "Supervising Probationers with Mental Disorder: How Do Agencies Respond to Violations?" Criminal Justice and Behavior 35 (July 1, 2008): 832.

73 Ronald Burns, Patrick Kinkade, and Matthew C. Leone, "Bounty Hunters: A Look behind the Hype," Policing 28 (January 1, 2005): 118–138.

74 Patricia Resick, "The Trauma of Rape and the Criminal Justice System," Justice System Journal 9 (1984): 52–61.

75 Robert Davis and Barbara Smith, "The Effects of Victim Impact Statements on Sentencing Decisions: A Test in an Urban Setting," Justice Quarterly 11 (1994): 453–469.

76 Ira Schwartz, Justice for Juveniles: Rethinking the Best Interests of the Child (New York: Lexington Books, 1989).

77 Erika Gebo, Nena F. Stracuzzi, and Valerie Hurst, "Juvenile Justice Reform and the Courtroom Workgroup: Issues of Perception and Workload," Journal of Criminal Justice 34 (July 1, 2006): 425–433.

78 Fahnestock and Geiger, "We All Get Along."

79 Marvin Free, African Americans and the Criminal Justice System (New York: Garland, 1997).

80 Arthur Rosett and Donald R. Cressey, Justice by Consent: Plea Bargains in the American Courthouse (New York: Lippincott, 1976).

81 John Irwin, The Jail: Managing the Underclass in American Society (Berkeley: University of California Press, 1985).

82 J. Dyer, The Perpetual Incarceration Machine: How America Profits from Crime (Boulder, Colo.: Westview, 1999).

83 Andrew Karnsen, Crime Victims: An Introduction to Victimology, 4th ed. (Belmont, Calif.: Wadsworth, 2001).

84 Emma Schwartz, "Giving Crime Victims More of Their Say: A Federal Law Has Created Tensions in the Legal System," U.S. News & World Report, December 24, 2007, 28.

85 Candace McCoy, *Politics and Plea Bargaining: Victims' Rights in California* (Philadelphia: University of Pennsylvania Press, 1993).

86 Kerry Healey, *Victim and Witness Intimidation: New Developments and*

Emerging Responses (Washington, D.C.: National Institute of Justice, 1995).

87 Peter Finn and Beverley Lee, *Establishing and Expanding Victim-Witness Assistance Programs* (Washington, D.C.: National Institute of Justice, 1988).

88 William G. Doerner and Steven P. Lab, *Victimology* (Cincinnati, Ohio: Anderson, 1995), 53–54.

89 Elizabeth Connick and Robert Davis, "Examining the Problems of Witness Intimidation," *Judicature* 66 (1983): 438–447.

Chapter 9

The Disposition: Plea Bargaining, Trial, and Sentencing

Oklahoma State Penitentiary inmate Richard Glossip is currently on death row. Given the nature of the case, do you agree with Glossip's conviction?

O n the night of January 6, 1997, in Oklahoma City, Oklahoma, Justin Sneed, a maintenance worker at the Best Budget Inn, used a master key to enter the motel room of his employer and motel owner, Barry Van Treese. Sneed then beat Van Treese to death with a baseball bat. Sneed admitted his role in the murder and, as part of a plea bargain, testified against motel manager, Richard Glossip. Sneed claimed that Glossip pressured him to kill Van Treese in exchange for thousands of dollars. Sneed told authorities that, with the motel owner dead, Glossip thought he could convince Van Treese's wife to let him manage both of the motels that Van Treese owned. With no physical evidence connecting Glossip to the murder, Glossip was convicted largely on the basis of Sneed's story and sentenced to death. For his testimony, Sneed received life in prison. On death row and fighting Oklahoma's attempts to execute him, Glossip maintains his innocence, saying that Sneed fabricated the story.[1]

THINK ABOUT IT > Why did Sneed, who admitted to committing the murder, get a lighter sentence than Glossip?

LEARNING OBJECTIVE | **1**

Summarize how sentencing disparities may negatively influence popular opinion about the criminal justice system.

The Criminal Court Process

The criminal court process has several important decision points that determine how justice is meted out. These decision points are plea bargaining, trial, and sentencing. In order to appreciate how defendants proceed through the courts to acquittal or conviction, we will consider how each of these decision points affects criminal cases.

The most dramatic and sensational decision point in the criminal justice system is the passing of the sentence. The passing of the sentence is considered to be the result of a deliberation process in which the evidence of the offense, the harm done to society (or other people), and the character of the defendant are weighed and a sentence prescribing a punishment is announced. The road to the disposition of a case is rocky and uncertain. Unlike the image presented by the media, the court's actions are ponderous, fickle, and they often seem unfair. For example, although the Glossip case seems unusual—a man accused of hiring another to commit a murder being sentenced to death while the actual murderer gets life in prison—this is the nature of plea bargaining. Defendants (even co-defendants) with identical charges, similar records, and equal culpability who appear before the same judge can receive drastically different sentences.[2]

Sentencing disparities among judges, courts, states, or regions of the country all elicit a sense that justice is not uniform.[3] The luck of the draw in determining which judge handles a case or which prosecutor is assigned may mean the difference between incarceration or probation, a long or a short prison sentence, even life or death. This is the inevitable result of funding limitations and political necessity. It is little wonder that many people are wary of the criminal justice process when they see such vast disparities in the outcomes of apparently similar cases.[4]

Despite the fact that court reforms are desired and needed, they are difficult to enact because of the complicated and interdependent nature of the criminal justice system. Reforming one part of the system will have ramifications and unanticipated consequences in other parts of the system. For instance, enacting the popular notion that every offender should serve every day of every sentence would have a profound and negative effect on the prison system. There is not enough prison space to accommodate all the offenders serving all their time.[5] Consequently, the criminal justice system, particularly the courts, must prioritize how to allocate the precious resource of prison beds. Therefore, the process of arriving at the sentence is fraught with difficulties and dissension. This chapter will examine some of the mechanisms that the criminal justice system employs as part of its quest for justice, including the plea bargain, the criminal trial, the concept of defendants' and victims' rights, and finally some of the broader issues concerned with sentencing patterns.

PAUSE AND REVIEW

1. **What are the decision points that determine how justice is meted out in the criminal court process?**

2. **Why are court reforms so difficult to enact?**

Pre-Trial Release Decisions

The criminal justice process takes time, often a long time. Suspects may be kept in jail if they are dangerous, or they may be released and told to return to court when the system is ready to consider their case.[6] The court must somehow decide which option is appropriate for each suspect. The pre-trial release decision is one of the most important crossroads of the criminal justice system. If innocent people are jailed for months before their cases are heard, then they are being punished unjustly, and if dangerous offenders are released, then they might continue to murder, rape, and rob.[7] Complicating this pre-trial release decision is the overcrowded condition of many jails. Courts have developed several types of systems for making this decision that attempt to ensure that the defendant will appear. These systems all involve some sort of bail/bond alternative:

> Cash bond. The judge sets a bail of a certain amount of money the defendant must give to the court in exchange for release pending trial. If the defendant shows up for the court proceedings, then the entire amount is refunded minus any fees charged by the court. This **cash bond** is meant to ensure that the defendant will come back to prevent losing the money. However, if the bail is too low or a severe punishment is likely, the defendant may flee anyway or "skip bail." The court then issues a warrant for the defendant's arrest, and the defendant forfeits the bail. Although the Eighth Amendment states, "excessive bail shall not be required," it is still difficult for many defendants to gather a large amount of cash in a short period.[8] Beginning in 1998, pre-trial releases that required bail became more common than nonfinancial releases, such as release-on-recognizance, because defendants on financial release were more likely to appear in court.[9]

> Property bond. By using a piece of property as collateral, defendants can avoid liquidating their assets to raise a cash bond. **Property bonds** favor the well-off who have equity in property. Defendants who fail to appear before the court forfeit their property.

> Release on recognizance. Defendants accused of minor offenses and who have ties to the community may be **released on recognizance (ROR)**, based on a promise to return to court. ROR programs evaluate how long defendants have lived in the community, how long they have been employed, whether they have family nearby, and other factors in an effort to determine whether

LEARNING OBJECTIVE 2

Identify alternatives to keeping a suspect in jail.

LEARNING OBJECTIVE 3

Contrast the competing values of presumption of innocence and preventive detention in the context of pre-trial release.

cash bond—A requirement that the entire amount of the bail cost be paid in cash.

property bond—The use of a piece of property instead of cash as collateral for bail.

release on recognizance (ROR)— When a defendant pays no money to be released from jail and promises to appear in court when required.

they are likely to flee.[10] For example, a South American drug lord who has no local address would probably not be granted ROR. The distinguishing feature of ROR is that the defendant does not need to pay money to be released.

> Surety bond. The most common method for securing bail is a **surety bond**, or the use of a bail agent who promises to pay the defendant's bail if he or she fails to appear for further court proceedings.[11] In exchange for the promise, the defendant pays the bail agent 10 percent of the bail as a fee and may put up some collateral. Thus, if the bail is $10,000, the bail agent makes $1,000. The bail agent does not give the court the bail at that time but must pay if the defendant fails to appear. The bail agent may then hire a bail enforcement agent (or "bounty hunter") to find the defendant and bring him or her back to court. If a bail agent thinks the defendant is likely to flee, the agent may revoke the bond and surrender the defendant to law enforcement.

surety bond—The use of a bail agent who promises to pay the defendant's bail if he or she fails to appear for further court proceedings.

Pre-trial release is a controversial issue. It must balance two strongly held values: presumption of innocence and preventive detention. On one hand, we believe that someone should not be incarcerated until he or she has been found guilty by a court of law. However, given the nature of the criminal justice system and the inevitable delays caused by crowded dockets and constitutional guarantees of due process, both the guilty and the innocent could spend months in jail before a trial.[12] If the defendant is found guilty and sentenced to incarceration, the period of time spent in jail awaiting trial is credited toward the sentence. Sometimes the sentence is simply "time served," in which case the defendant is released, having, in effect, served the sentence before the sentence was pronounced. In cases in which the defendant is acquitted or the charges are dropped, the period spent in jail waiting for the courts to process the case is time lost. The defendant, who has suffered the pains of being detained, may feel a sense of injustice.

The issue of presumption of innocence must be weighed against the responsibility of the state to protect society by keeping dangerous people behind bars while the court considers their cases. For example, in 2002 there was a case in

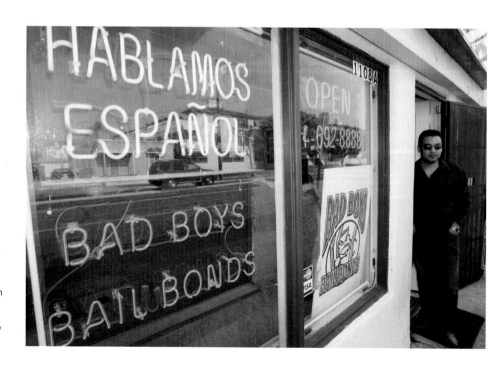

Suspects who cannot afford their bail can use a bail agent to get out of jail while awaiting trial. Suspects who sign a contract with a bail bondsman are considered to be in the bail bondsman's custody. What other types of bail/bond alternatives are there?

Washington, D.C., in which two males, an adult and a juvenile, were arrested on suspicion of shooting and killing several people with a high-powered rifle. In what became known as the "D.C. sniper case," the court refused to grant any type of pre-trial release because there was a reasonable fear that one of three bad things could happen.[13] First, because of the seriousness of the offenses, authorities feared that the defendants would attempt to flee the jurisdiction. Second, the defendants could harm more people. Third, given the terror caused by the shootings, it was feared that the defendants might be injured or killed by irate individuals. In fact, these concerns are so pronounced in such cases that those who are awaiting trial on murder charges that carry the death penalty are not allowed bail. Murder defendants, as well as those charged with rape, robbery, burglary, and motor vehicle theft, are typically the least likely to be released. Other factors affecting release are prior arrests, convictions, and whether the defendant is currently serving probation or on parole.[14]

There will always be a tension between the ideal of "innocent until proven guilty" and the need to protect society from potentially dangerous people. In some situations, it is clear that the defendant is dangerous. In other cases, it is not so clear, and the court must decide whether the suspect can be safely set free before trial. As the criminal justice system struggles with this balancing act, the possibility of class, racial, sex, and gender bias must always be kept in mind.[15] Are impoverished black males being held in preventive detention because they pose a threat or because of a stereotype held by those making the release decision?

PAUSE AND REVIEW

1. **What are some alternatives to keeping a suspect in jail?**
2. **Why is pre-trial release a controversial issue?**

The Plea Bargain

In 2009, Orville Lee Wollard fired a handgun inside his house to scare his daughter's 17-year-old boyfriend who, court documents state, had been abusing her and threatening the family. The bullet struck a wall, and Wollard's daughter and her boyfriend left the house. Wollard, who said he fired the gun in self-defense and in defense of his family, rejected two plea bargains. The first offered three years in prison and probation in exchange for a guilty plea. The second deal offered five years' probation. Not wanting a felony on his record, Wollard went to trial. The jury found Wollard guilty of shooting into a dwelling, child abuse, and aggravated assault with a firearm. Because of the mandatory minimum sentence specified in Florida's 10-20-Life law (during a criminal offense, the penalty for revealing a gun is 10 years in prison; firing a gun is 20 years in prison, and shooting a person is life in prison), Wollard was sentenced to 20 years in prison.[16]

The point in the criminal justice system at which there is the most attrition of cases is the plea-bargaining stage. A **plea bargain** is a compromise reached by the defendant, the defendant's attorney, and the prosecutor in which the defendant agrees to plead guilty or no contest in return for a reduction of the charges' severity, dismissal of some charges, further information about the offense or about others involved in it, or the prosecutor's agreement to recommend a desired sentence. There are many reasons for plea bargaining, and few are for the defendant's benefit.[17] The state has a lot to gain by disposing of cases quickly and efficiently. Prosecutors may decide that the case is weak and, rather than risking dismissal, opt for a negotiated plea that results in some type of punishment. Sometimes

LEARNING OBJECTIVE 4

Define plea bargain.

LEARNING OBJECTIVE 5

Compare and contrast the types of plea bargaining arrangements.

LEARNING OBJECTIVE 6

Argue for and against the abolition of plea bargaining.

plea bargain (from Chapter 8)—A compromise reached by the defendant, the defendant's attorney, and the prosecutor in which the defendant agrees to plead guilty or no contest in return for a reduction of the charges' severity, dismissal of some charges, further information about the offense or about others involved in it, or the prosecutor's agreement to recommend a desired sentence.

Pictured here is Orville Lee Wollard in the Apalachee Correctional Institute in Sneads, Florida. When, if ever, is it a good idea for an inmate to accept a plea bargain?

prosecutors accept a plea bargain from a lesser defendant who offers to help with the case to ensure conviction of a defendant accused of more serious offenses. Defense attorneys who see no realistic hope of having their clients acquitted are keenly interested in avoiding trial and limiting the sentence.

The Wollard case sheds some light on why a defendant would plead guilty to an offense he or she did not commit. A sentence received at a trial is usually much tougher than one received in a plea bargain, so from the defense's perspective, it may be a better option to plead guilty (even to an offense a defendant did not commit) rather than risk going to trial.

Defendants may also feel pressured to make a deal because they feel intimidated by the legal system and do not fully understand the consequences of a guilty plea.[18] It is important to understand that a guilty plea and a confession are not the same thing. A confession is only evidence; it does not automatically bring a judgment of guilt. The guilty plea is the source of the conviction because it is the defendant's formal agreement to a judgment of guilt. Therefore, a guilty plea is not a confession; it is a legal agreement.[19] When plea bargaining, defendants are simply making a legal agreement in order to gain their freedom sooner than if they risked a trial.

Plea bargains were uncommon until the end of the Civil War in 1865. Until then, a defendant would either plead guilty or go to trial. Upon conviction, the judge had broad discretion in sentencing, and that decision was subject to only cursory appellate review. After the war, social upheaval and increased immigration fueled crime rates, and plea bargains offered a way to move cases quickly without trials. By 1945, more than 80 percent of all criminal cases were resolved by plea bargaining. Population increases, namely, the Baby Boom, made plea bargaining an important tool for keeping the court system running relatively smoothly.[20] Later, the Supreme Court gave its official blessing to plea bargaining, determining in *Brady v. United States* (1970) that a guilty plea in exchange for a more lenient sentence is acceptable as long as the defendant has adequate counsel and has not been threatened or coerced. In *Santobello v. New York* (1971), the Court acknowledged that plea bargaining was essential to the criminal justice system because providing a trial for every criminal defendant would overwhelm the court system.[21] Today, plea bargaining is used much more than originally intended. It began as a way for some obviously guilty defendants to get a better deal from the state in return for resolving their cases quickly and without the expense of a trial.[22] As of 2012, 97 percent of federal cases and 94 percent of state cases were settled through guilty pleas.[23] To see the proportion of U.S. District Court cases that were disposed of by guilty plea in 2014, see Figure 9.1.

Issues That Affect Plea Bargaining

Given the size of the court system's caseload, plea bargaining is necessary and often desirable. If every defendant demanded a jury trial, the system would grind to a halt under the oppressive caseload. Defendants' right to a speedy trial would become impossible to accommodate, and vast amounts of money would be spent on cases that could otherwise be quickly disposed of. Additionally, without the reduced punishments inherent in the plea-bargaining process, the sentences meted out by judges would swamp the correctional system. If law enforcement is doing a good job, then most defendants are guilty, and the prosecutors have reliable evidence that is likely to stand up in court. There is no need for a trial, and by plea bargaining, the defense can strike a deal for a less-than-maximum sentence.

Plea bargaining affects the entire system. Diverse pressure (sometimes overt, sometimes subtle) is applied to the courts by law enforcement agencies, who want their collars to serve prison time, and correctional administrators, whose institutions are already filled to capacity. Added to these outside pressures are the dynamics of the courtroom work group, which has established patterns of plea bargaining. Additionally, the case's peculiarities will dictate just how wide a range

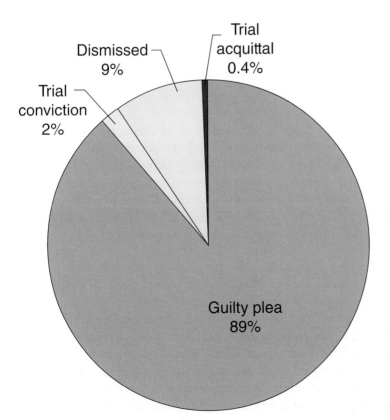

FIGURE 9.1 Dispositions in U.S. District Court The vast majority of cases in U.S. District Court are disposed by a guilty plea. Few cases go to trial, and even fewer defendants are acquitted at trial. Why do so many defendants plead guilty rather than go to trial?

Source: Mark Motivans, Federal Justice Statistics, 2013–2014, Table 15: Disposition and Sentence Received for Defendants in Cases Terminated in U.S. District Court, 2010, 2013, and 2014 (U.S. Department of Justice Office of Justice Programs Bureau of Justice Statistics, 2017), 27. Available at https://www.bjs.gov/index.cfm?ty=pbdetail&iid=5885.

of discretion can be applied. Political scientist David Neubauer has described three fundamental issues that guide the practice of plea bargaining.[24]

1. Presumption of factual guilt. By the time a case gets to trial, its merits have been reviewed many times, and it has been deemed a legitimate arrest with a good chance of a conviction. Most cases that get to this stage have a defendant who is, in fact, guilty of some charge. The police officer believed there was reason to arrest; the prosecutor believed the case to be strong enough for a formal charge, and the judge in the preliminary hearing deemed that sufficient reason existed to move the case forward. Therefore, prosecutors and defense attorneys negotiate which level of offense the defendant will be charged with while considering factors such as what evidence the state can produce, the nature of the victim, and the character of the defendant. There is little doubt, in most cases, that the defendant is guilty.

2. Costs and risks of trial. Failing to successfully negotiate a plea is risky and costly for all involved. Trials can last days for simple cases and months for more complicated ones. During this time, the courtroom work group, victim(s), and witnesses are all tied to the courtroom and cannot deal with the other demands of their jobs. Because trials are expensive and courtroom time scarce, few cases go to trial. Another reason plea bargains are considered preferable to trials is risk: the prosecutor risks an acquittal in which a guilty defendant might go free; the defendant risks a more severe sentence if convicted; and the defense attorney risks damage to his or her reputation if a guilty verdict is returned.[25]

3. What to do with the guilty. Plea bargaining increases the prosecutor's discretion in crafting a sentence appropriate to the offender. The willingness of an offender during the plea-bargaining process to enter a drug treatment program or do community service can give the prosecutor justification to consider a full range of alternatives to incarceration. If the case goes to trial, the defense attorney and the prosecutor lose their ability to influence the disposition, and if the defendant is convicted, the courtroom work group presumes that the judge will select a more punitive disposition than would have been negotiated between the prosecutor and the defense attorney.

Types of Plea Bargains

Not all plea bargains are the same. A prosecutor might decide that one type of bargain serves justice better than another, and the defendant might reluctantly accept one type while desiring an alternative. Often, there is no bargaining because the prosecutor may demand, "Accept my terms or forget it." Increasingly, the prosecutor wields the sledgehammer with habitual-offender laws carrying life terms for relatively minor offenses.[26] Although cases are negotiated in numerous ways, the following categorizations help to differentiate among the types of plea-bargaining arrangements.[27]

nolo contendere—A plea in which a defendant does not accept or deny responsibility for the charges but agrees to accept punishment. From Latin meaning, "I will not contest."

1. Vertical plea. This is perhaps the most advantageous plea for the defendant. By pleading guilty or ***nolo contendere*** (not accepting or denying responsibility for the charges but agreeing to accept punishment, which translates to "I will not contest") to a lesser charge, the defendant can reduce the potential for a harsh sentence. For instance, a homicide charge can be pleaded vertically downward to a manslaughter charge, thereby avoiding a potential death sentence and/or a longer prison term. The prosecutor might decide that the case does not have sufficient evidence to support a capital conviction and that a manslaughter plea would be better than an acquittal.

Additionally, many drug charges are pleaded down to misdemeanors, saving the offender from having a felony conviction on his or her record.

2. Horizontal plea. In this case, the defendant pleads guilty to a charge in exchange for other charges being dropped. It is not unusual for a burglar to be charged with multiple counts of breaking and entering and to plead to one count in order to have the others dropped. The defendant is then vulnerable only to the full penalty that the single charge carries. In many cases, this arrangement is advantageous to the state because the judge might have passed concurrent sentences for the multiple charges.

3. Reduced-sentence plea. The prosecutor and defense attorney, in consultation with the judge, might decide on a reduced sentence. For instance, if the charge carries a maximum five-year prison sentence, the agreement might be for a three-year sentence. This way, the defendant is assured of a specific less-than-maximum sentence, and the prosecutor gets a conviction without having to go to trial.

4. Avoidance-of-stigma plea. A defendant may plead guilty to a lesser charge in order to avoid a more serious charge that carries a stigma, such as "sex offender" or "habitual offender."[28] Several types of convictions do an extra measure of damage to a defendant's chances of receiving a light sentence. For instance, some states have "habitual offender" or "three-strikes" statutes that carry mandatory severe penalties.[29] Those convicted of relatively minor felonies sometimes find themselves facing life in prison because of offenses committed many years ago that also resulted in felony convictions. If the defendant's attorney is not successful in getting the charge reduced, the judge has no discretion in the case and must sentence the defendant according to the habitual-offender guidelines. This is a form of vertical plea, but because of the mandatory nature of these laws, the defendant has an extra incentive. Another type of avoidance-of-stigma plea concerns those facing sex-offense charges. Being adjudicated a sex offender can have long-term ramifications for the defendant even after the sentence has been served.[30] Conviction of a sex offense might lead to a defendant's identity being published in a public sex-offender database.

In 2015, actor Emile Hirsch was charged with assault in Park City, Utah. Hirsch agreed to a plea deal for misdemeanor assault and was ordered to serve 15 days in jail, pay a $4,750 fine, and perform 50 hours of community service in exchange for dismissal of the charge. What type of plea deal does Hirsch's case reflect?

Plea bargaining is not concerned with guilt or innocence. Rather, it allows the defendant and the prosecution to efficiently determine the amount of punishment without the expense of a jury trial.[31] In practice, plea bargaining obtains highly disparate results. Individuals in similar circumstances might receive widely varying punishments, as the proportionality of punishment to offense can become distorted by overcharging, draconian legislation, and political expediency. When a defendant is allowed to enter a plea of *nolo contendere*, in many ways, this is equivalent to entering a guilty plea in that the defendant waives the right to a jury trial and is sentenced as though there were a determination of guilt.[32] However, there are important differences between the *nolo contendere* plea and the guilty finding.

A *nolo contendere* plea cannot be used against a defendant in another case. In many jurisdictions, the court will allow the offender to enter a *nolo contendere* plea and will hold the actual sentence in abeyance while the offender completes some type of diversion program, pays restitution, performs community service, or engages in some other court-ordered activity. Once this activity is successfully completed, the court will drop the criminal charges, and the offender will escape the criminal justice system without a criminal record. This type of plea negotiation is used extensively with young offenders who commit relatively minor offenses. It allows the defendant to avoid the negative stigma of a criminal conviction and the frequent extralegal punishments of being denied access to schools or jobs.

Another benefit of pleading *nolo contendere* is that, unlike a guilty determination, this plea does not affect future civil court proceedings. If a defendant pleaded guilty and/or was convicted, there would be little leverage available for the defendant to contest a civil case. For example, if a defendant was involved in an accident while driving under the influence of alcohol and pleaded *nolo contendere* to the criminal charge, this plea could not be used as an admission of guilt by someone who might have been injured in that accident. The civil court case would need additional evidence such as witnesses or blood alcohol tests to determine culpability.

Should Plea Bargaining Be Abolished?

Although most criminal justice practitioners realize that plea bargaining is efficient and necessary, there is widespread opposition among the public, law enforcement officials, and crime victims.[33] These groups all consider plea bargaining as thwarting justice, with offenders being punished less than they deserve.[34] Still other people think that too many defendants are pleading guilty to offenses they did not commit just to get out of jail (for a look at an incident in which a defendant refused to plea and insisted on a trial, see A Closer Look 9.1). Some legal scholars argue that plea bargaining has made bail a critical stage in the criminal justice process because many indigent defendants cannot afford bail and therefore are faced with waiting in jail. If the prosecutor offers a plea bargain at or prior to the bail stage, an indigent defendant may accept the deal—for example, a guilty plea in exchange for time already served in jail—to avoid spending even more time in jail waiting for bail review or a trial.[35]

Occasionally, there are efforts to abolish plea bargaining and to require each case to be decided on its merits. Such efforts are usually short-lived; when plea bargaining is prohibited, several unintended consequences arise.[36]

The first and most drastic result of eliminating plea bargaining is the increase in the number of cases that defense attorneys are willing to take to trial. When no consideration is allowed for a guilty plea, there is no incentive for the defendant

A CLOSER LOOK 9.1

The Dark Side of Plea Bargaining

On May 15, 2010, 16-year-old Kalief Browder was accused of robbing a man of his backpack two weeks earlier in New York City. Browder, who was on probation for a juvenile offense, denied committing the robbery. He could not pay the $3,000 bail and was taken to Rikers Island, a jail notorious for its abominable conditions and violence.[37] Browder pleaded not guilty to charges of robbery, grand larceny, and assault, and was returned to jail without bail because the felony charges violated the terms of his probation. Browder insisted on a trial but instead spent two years in jail before prosecutors offered him a deal of three and a half years in prison in exchange for a guilty plea. Browder, who felt strongly about his innocence, rejected the plea, knowing that he could receive 15 years in prison if he were convicted at trial. In early 2013, a judge offered him another deal: get out of jail now in exchange for pleading guilty to two misdemeanors. Browder refused and asserted his right to a trial. Finally, months later, the same judge released Browder because his accuser had left the country and could not be located to testify. After three years in jail, about two years of which was spent in solitary confinement, Browder went home.[38] In 2015, after struggling with his mental health for two years, Browder committed suicide.[39]

About 2.2 million Americans are incarcerated in the United States. Many criminal justice system observers assert that the United States has the second highest incarceration rate in the world because for the last two decades prosecutors have used plea bargains to send more people to prison than ever.[40] Mandatory minimum sentencing (sentences determined by law that establish the minimum length of prison time that may be served for an offense) and sentencing guidelines (rules that direct the judge to consider certain facts about the case when

determining the sentence) have eroded judicial discretion. These trends have pushed more power to prosecutors who know that most defendants will plea bargain rather than risk a trial.[41]

The defendant and defense attorney are at a disadvantage during plea bargaining. The prosecutor decides if charges will be filed, which charges will be filed, and whether there will be a plea bargain at all. Prosecutors will often threaten to charge the most severe offenses possible to discourage the defendant from insisting on a trial.[42] The defense attorney must present the deal to the defendant, even if the offer is made only as a bargaining ploy. Not doing so would be to risk not providing effective counsel.[43] The plea deal is then made in private and is subject to little or no judicial review.[44]

Some criminal justice professionals assert that many defendants, especially those accused of minor felonies and misdemeanors, desire a plea bargain. It is not uncommon for a defendant to have an extensive record of minor offenses, so pleading guilty to stay out of jail is an attractive option. Still, critics of the plea-bargaining process maintain that many defendants, especially juveniles or the mentally disabled, do not fully understand the consequences of a guilty plea. Recall from the Kalief Browder case that he was on probation when he was accused of the robbery. Eight months prior, he had been charged with joyriding in a stolen delivery truck with friends. Browder said he had not taken the truck but thought that he had no defense, so he pled guilty.[45]

THINK ABOUT IT

1. Should the prosecutor's discretion and power be reduced? Is there any courtroom actor whose discretion and power should be enhanced?

to waive his or her right to a jury trial. He or she might as well take a chance on acquittal before a jury if the sentence is going to be the same anyway.[46]

Another consequence of abolishing plea bargaining is that the discretion inherent in the process is moved to another part of the criminal justice system where it might not be as visible and thus subject to increased abuse or corruption. For instance, abolishing plea bargaining in a higher court could result in discretion being shifted to the charging decision made by a prosecutor at the preliminary hearing in the lower court.[47] Victims, witnesses, and the public have less opportunity to comprehend how the system is arriving at its dispositions and, consequently, might become even more disillusioned with the process.

Kalief Browder's death sparked outcry and protests from prisoner's rights advocates. Here, protesters stand in front of New York City Hall demanding the closing of the institution on Rikers Island where Browder was held. In what ways is the defendant at a disadvantage during plea bargaining?

Finally, attempts to abolish plea bargaining might squeeze the prosecutor out of the process.[48] Defense attorneys can always attempt to negotiate directly with the judge to secure the best deal for the defendant. Judges faced with an increased caseload and under pressure to keep the docket moving are approachable by defense attorneys who can offer relief. One roles of prosecutors in the criminal justice process is to protect society's interests. When they are excluded from the plea-bargaining process, they have more difficulty ensuring that all cases are considered equally.

As students of the criminal justice system, we should realize that the law on the books and the law that is practiced in the courthouse are different. Although we tend to think that the criminal trial is the court system's main activity, in reality, plea bargaining is responsible for the disposition of most cases.[49] As courts are faced with caseloads that outstrip their resources, plea bargaining becomes a useful way to negotiate justice. However, calls for the reform of plea bargaining should not go unheard.[50] By opening the process to victims, police officers, and others who are affected by the sentence, plea bargaining can become a more acceptable tool.[51]

PAUSE AND REVIEW

1. **What are three issues that guide plea bargaining?**

2. **What are the four types of plea-bargaining arrangements?**

3. **What are some criticisms of arguments for the abolition of plea bargaining?**

LEARNING OBJECTIVE | **7**

Outline the steps of the pre-trial phase.

LEARNING OBJECTIVE | **8**

Analyze the role that the standard of reasonable doubt plays in the presentation of witnesses and evidence during the trial process.

The Trial

Few cases make it to the trial phase because most are settled during plea bargaining (see Figure 9.2 for a review of the criminal justice process). Of the cases that go to trial, few end up in guilty verdicts that allow further processing of the case. Some defendants are acquitted or found not guilty. Sometimes the case is dismissed because the prosecution is unable to present a viable case. Sometimes the case is dismissed because of prosecutorial misconduct that violates the defendant's rights. Regardless, the trial is what most people think about when they imagine justice in the United States. Unfortunately, the media image of U.S. courtrooms is rather distorted. Last-minute confessions on the witness stand by distraught, guilty individuals who are pressured or tricked by a crafty prosecutor do not accurately represent what actually happens in the courtroom. Most of the decisions are made behind the scenes, and excitement and drama in the courtroom are uncommon.

Criminal trials are relatively rare. Which cases make it to trial then? Certainly, we would expect innocent defendants to assert their right to a trial. Additionally, if the defendant does not like the prosecution's deal, the decision may be made to roll the dice. In any event, the trial is a pivotal point in the process because cases that fail to reach a plea bargain set the parameters for how justice is negotiated by the courtroom work group.

A few actions must happen before a trial can occur, two of which were covered in Chapter 1: arrest and booking. Briefly, police make an arrest once they become aware that a criminal offense has been committed and they have enough evidence. Arrests provide the rest of the system with cases. Police may continue to question a suspect after an arrest but must respect the suspect's constitutional rights. The booking process occurs at the police station, where a suspect's name, age, and address are recorded, as well as information on the time, place, and reason for arrest. Usually, a photograph and fingerprints are taken, the suspect's clothing and personal effects are stored, and the suspect is placed in a holding cell until he or she can be questioned further. The rest of the activities occur in the pre-trial and trial phases. Trials follow a specific format that is dictated by law, custom, and the administrative procedures established by the federal government and the states. In general, the trial process is conducted in the following steps:

1. Pre-trial phase
   a. Indictment
   b. Defendant's plea
2. Trial
   a. Prosecution opening statement
   b. Defense opening statement
   c. Witnesses and evidence presented
   d. Defense closing arguments
   e. Prosecution closing arguments
   f. Judge's instructions to jurors about procedures
   g. Judge's instructions to jurors about verdicts
   h. Final verdict
   i. Defendant released if acquitted or sentenced if convicted

The Pre-trial Phase

Several things must happen for a case to proceed through the criminal court process, and cases can be diverted at several points, including during the pre-trial phase, outlined as follows.[52]

> Filing of charges. Law enforcement first presents information about the case and the suspect to the prosecutor, who decides if formal charges will be filed. The suspect must be released if no charges are filed. A prosecutor can also decide to drop the charges later by entering a *nolle prosequi* (Latin for "we shall no longer prosecute"). A *nolle prosequi* must be made after charges are filed but before a plea is entered or a verdict returned. Usually, prosecutors

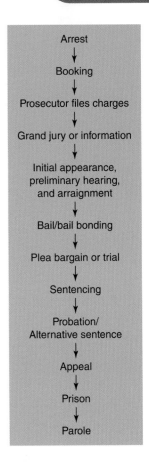

FIGURE 9.2   The Criminal Justice Process These are the basic steps of the criminal justice process. However, not everyone who enters prison is paroled or released. Some offenders are incarcerated for life, whereas others may be sentenced to death. What is the difference between a grand jury indictment and an information?

Arrest
↓
Booking
↓
Prosecutor files charges
↓
Grand jury or information
↓
Initial appearance, preliminary hearing, and arraignment
↓
Bail/bail bonding
↓
Plea bargain or trial
↓
Sentencing
↓
Probation/ Alternative sentence
↓
Appeal
↓
Prison
↓
Parole

must ask a judge's permission to enter a *nolle prosequi*. The prosecutor's decision to eliminate cases depends on several factors, the first of which is resources. The decision to prosecute depends on personnel, budget, space, and agency priorities. The prosecutor must prioritize cases according to importance and thus may decline to pursue certain ones. The prosecutor might decide that the police have not presented sufficient evidence to ensure successful prosecution of the case or that the police made procedural errors in the arrest that would result in a dismissal. Personal or agency priorities may also influence what types of cases are pursued. For example, political corruption cases might be encouraged or discouraged depending on the party affiliation of the state attorney versus the defendant.

› Initial appearance and preliminary hearing. After arrest, suspects must be brought before a judge within a reasonable time for an initial appearance. The suspect is formally charged with a crime and responds by pleading guilty, not guilty, or *nolo contendere* (no contest). Defendants are informed of their rights to bail and to an attorney. The judge or magistrate informs the accused of the charges and decides whether there is probable cause for further detention (i.e., whether the suspect is considered dangerous or likely to flee). A pretrial release decision can be made at this point; it also might occur at other hearings or be changed further along in the process. Those charged with a misdemeanor may enter a plea immediately. If the plea is guilty, the judge may impose the sentence. For serious offenses, the suspect is asked if he or she has retained counsel (an attorney); if the accused is indigent, counsel is assigned. Defendants charged with felonies usually do not enter pleas at this time. Also, they probably have not been able to consult an attorney before the hearing. At this point, the defendant is scheduled for a preliminary hearing, also known as the preliminary examination or probable cause hearing, where the prosecutor presents evidence to establish probable cause. The exception to this is when the defendant has been indicted by a grand jury, in which probable cause has already been established. In this case, the defendant's first court appearance is at an arraignment similar to the initial appearance.

› Grand jury. The grand jury hears the prosecutor's evidence and charges against the accused, presented as a **bill of indictment**, and decides if it is sufficient to bring the accused to trial. If the grand jury finds the evidence sufficient, it sends an **indictment**, a written statement of the facts of the offense charged against the accused, to the court. A grand jury returns a **true bill** if it decides that sufficient evidence exists to indict; if not, a **no-bill** is returned. A prosecutor may still file charges in the event of a no-bill. Prosecutors may also bring further evidence to the same jury or present the original evidence to a second jury. This system also works backward, in a sense. Instead of starting with a suspect and deciding whether to indict, a grand jury may investigate possible criminal activity. If probable cause is found, the grand jury issues an indictment, called a grand jury original, naming the suspects. Police then try to arrest the suspects. In some jurisdictions, prosecutors sometimes choose not to use a grand jury and instead file a criminal complaint. (For more on how grand juries work, see CJ Reference 9.1.)

› Indictments and informations. Some jurisdictions require grand jury indictments for felony cases. However, an accused may waive the indictment and accept an **information**, a formal, written accusation against a defendant submitted by a prosecutor, instead. Misdemeanor cases and cases when the offense is punishable by one year or less in prison might also proceed by the issuance of an information.[53]

bill of indictment—A declaration of the charges against an accused person that is presented to a grand jury to determine whether enough evidence exists for an indictment.

indictment—A written statement of the facts of the offense that is charged against the accused.

true bill—The decision of a grand jury that sufficient evidence exists to indict an accused person.

no-bill—The decision of a grand jury not to indict an accused person because of insufficient evidence. Also called "no true bill."

information—A formal, written accusation against a defendant submitted to the court by a prosecutor.

CJ REFERENCE 9.1

What Are Grand Juries and How Do They Work?

Grand jurors are usually selected from the same pool of people that provides trial jurors and are sworn in by a court. Typically, unlike trial juries, grand juries are not assembled for a specific case, but only for a period of time. The period may last for months, but the jurors only meet for a few days each month.

Grand jury proceedings are private and secret, and witnesses testify against the suspect without the suspect or the suspect's witnesses or suspect's attorney being present. This is to ensure that witnesses may speak freely without fear of retaliation and to protect the suspect's reputation if the jury does not indict. Grand juries do not require a unanimous decision to indict. Depending on the jurisdiction, a 2/3 or 3/4 majority is required. Grand jury investigations often target large, complex drug and conspiracy cases.[54] They are usually not used for minor felonies or misdemeanors.

The Fifth Amendment requires grand juries to be convened for indictments in federal felony cases. However, the Supreme Court held in *Hurtado v. California* (1884) that the Fifth Amendment grand jury clause does not apply to the states, nor does it violate the Fourteenth Amendment due process clause. Thus, the states are not required to use grand juries, although nearly all of them do. Forty-eight states and the District of Columbia use them to produce indictments. Only Connecticut and Pennsylvania do not use grand juries for criminal indictments. Connecticut replaced the grand jury with a hearing before a judge. Pennsylvania allows each county court to use informations instead of indictments to bring charges. However, both states use grand juries for investigations. Connecticut's grand jury is composed of between one and three judges, whereas Pennsylvania convenes grand juries from regular citizens.[55]

In some states, grand juries can only investigate offenses that are presented to them by a prosecutor or court. Grand juries in other states can investigate any suspected crime as long as the activity occurs within their jurisdiction. Finally, some state grand juries—sometimes called "special grand juries"—only investigate certain

These states (and district) require indictments for certain serious offenses.[56]	In these states, the use of indictments is optional. Most let prosecutors use either an indictment or an information to charge an offense.[57]
Alabama	Arizona
Alaska	Arkansas
Delaware	California
District of Columbia	Colorado
Florida	Georgia
Kentucky	Hawaii
Louisiana	Idaho
Maine	Illinois
Massachusetts	Indiana
Minnesota	Iowa
Mississippi	Kansas
Missouri	Maryland
New Hampshire	Michigan
New Jersey	Montana
New York	Nebraska
North Carolina	Nevada
North Dakota	New Mexico
Ohio	Oklahoma
Rhode Island	Oregon
South Carolina	South Dakota
Tennessee	Utah
Texas	Vermont
Virginia	Washington
West Virginia	Wisconsin
	Wyoming

types of crime, usually drug crime or organized crime.[58] State grand juries may investigate civil matters, the most common of which is the operation and condition of local jails and similar facilities.[59] At the federal level, grand juries investigate criminal activity, especially organized crime. They do not investigate civil matters.[60]

> Arraignment. After an indictment or information has been filed with the trial court, the accused is scheduled for **arraignment**. There, the accused is informed of the charges, advised of his or her rights, and asked to enter a plea. Sometimes the prosecutor and the defendant negotiate a plea bargain, in which the defendant pleads guilty.

arraignment—Court appearance in which the defendant is formally charged with a crime and asked to respond by pleading guilty, not guilty, or *nolo contendere*.

In November 2016, school bus driver Johnthony Walker was involved in a crash that resulted in the deaths of six children and injured 31 others. Walker's case was bound over to the grand jury after an hour and a half of testimony from two Chattanooga Police Department officers. What is the role of a grand jury?

> The plea. If the accused pleads guilty or *nolo contendere*, the judge either accepts or rejects the plea. No trial is held if the plea is accepted; the offender is sentenced either at this proceeding or at a later hearing. If the plea is rejected, the case proceeds to trial. For example, a guilty or nolo plea would go to trial if the judge believes that the accused is being coerced. If the accused enters a "not guilty" plea, a date is set for the trial, or the accused may request a bench trial (discussed later).

PRE-TRIAL MOTIONS

Prior to the opening statements of the prosecution and the defense, each side can file **pre-trial motions** that seek to gain the most favorable circumstances for their side and to limit the evidence the other side can present. Often the case is won or lost based on how the judge rules on the pre-trial motions. Some of the more frequent motions include the following:

pre-trial motion—A request made by the prosecutor or defense attorney that the court make a decision on a specific issue before the trial begins.

> Motion for dismissal of charges. The defense might ask that the case be dismissed because the prosecution has failed to present a sufficient case that has all the elements necessary to charge the defendant with the offense or because the case has some critical weaknesses. This can happen at the beginning of the trial or at any point along the way. Often, this motion is presented after the prosecution presents its case.

> Motion for continuance. This motion delays the trial. Often the defense or prosecution needs more time to prepare the case or to interview newly discovered witnesses. The defense is more likely to be granted such a continuance because the prosecution has an obligation to provide for a speedy trial.

> Motion for discovery. The defense has a right to obtain documents and a list of witnesses that the prosecution plans to call.

> Motion for severance of defendants. When more than one defendant is charged, each has his or her own defense attorney, who may wish to separate the cases so that each defendant has his or her own trial. This is often done when a conflict of interest exists in which one defendant is more culpable than the other is, or when the testimony of one defendant might incriminate others.

> Motion for severance of offenses. Defendants charged with several offenses might ask to be tried separately on all or some of the charges. The judge usually makes this decision.

> Motion for the suppression of evidence. The defense will attempt to prevent incriminating evidence from being presented during the trial. If the evidence was gathered illegally or a confession coerced by the police, the judge might rule it inadmissible (see CJ Reference 9.2). The defense might raise a number of due process issues that could result in motions to suppress evidence.

> Motion to determine competency. The defense can request that the judge rule that the defendant is not competent to stand trial. A defendant who cannot assist in the defense and does not understand the purpose and process of the proceedings might be mentally ill or intellectually disabled. Often, the court will order a psychiatrist to examine the defendant.

> Motion for change of venue. In offenses that draw a good deal of media coverage, the defense may claim that finding an impartial jury would be impossible. The court can move the case to another jurisdiction where those in the jury pool would not have heard about the case. Of course, offenses that receive national media coverage make it impossible to assemble a jury pool that has not been exposed to the case.

 CJ REFERENCE 9.2
The Exclusionary Rule

When a defendant goes free because of a legal technicality, the reason might be due to the exclusionary rule. Although the exclusionary rule dictates that the police must follow procedural law in the gathering of evidence, the issue is decided in the courts. The exclusionary rule covers three types of evidence:

- The identification of suspects
- Confessions in which the *Miranda* rules apply
- Searches in which the Fourth Amendment states, "The right of the people to be secure in their persons, houses, papers, and effects against unreasonable search and seizure, shall not be violated."

The law allows for the suppression of evidence that violates the exclusionary rule. As such, the prosecutor is prohibited from using illegally obtained evidence. The Supreme Court adopted the rule for three reasons.

1. If the courts used evidence that was illegally gathered, they would be participating in the violation of the defendant's rights. The courts must respect the rule of law if we are to have confidence in the quality of justice.
2. The exclusionary rule deters law enforcement officers from attempting to break the law. If they know evidence will be thrown out of court, they may be less likely to try to circumvent procedural laws.
3. The alternatives to the exclusionary rule are not feasible. Although a defendant might try to sue a law enforcement officer in civil court for damages stemming from police misconduct, this is a cumbersome and expensive process that is unlikely to have the desired effect of encouraging the police to play by the rules.

However, the court has allowed some narrow exceptions when the police make mistakes in "good faith."

This courtroom sketch depicts Boston Marathon bomber Dzhokhar Tsarnaev (right) standing before U.S. District Court Judge George O'Toole Jr., in federal court. Judge O'Toole denied Tsarnaev's request for a change of venue. Why might it be in a defendant's interest to be tried in a jurisdiction other than where he or she committed a crime?

The prosecution or the defense can present other types of motions, but this list illustrates how motions can be used to a defendant's advantage. These motions set the tone and limits of the trial and are extremely important even if they are not very visible in the process.

Opening Arguments

The prosecution is the first to make an opening argument, explaining why it believes that the defendant is guilty. Evidence is not presented at this time; the prosecution outlines the case and alerts the jury to the types of evidence to come. The goals of the opening statement are to present the defendant as the most likely perpetrator, convince the jury that the case against the defendant is strong, and stress that the prosecution can be trusted to ensure that justice is being pressed in the name of the people. The defense attorney then counters the outline of the case the prosecution has presented. Again, evidence is not presented, but the defense attorney attempts to put a more favorable spin on the prosecution's arguments and assure the jury that once it has seen all the evidence and heard all the facts, it will want to acquit the defendant on all charges.

The Prosecution's Presentation of Witnesses and Evidence

The prosecution begins presenting the case by introducing evidence and witnesses. The goal is to explain thoroughly the defendant's motive for breaking the law and his or her capability for carrying out the action. As the prosecution presents the case, the defense attorney may raise objections to the prosecutor's questions or a witness's answers.[61] The judge rules on these objections by either sustaining or overruling them. The objections can be on points of procedural law or on the competency of a witness to answer a question. For instance, if a police officer claims the defendant was drunk, the defense attorney may object, claiming that the officer could not know for sure that this was the case. The prosecutor may then ask the police officer if a breath test was administered to the defendant and what the result of that test was. Ideally, the process is designed to present the evidence and witness testimony in a factual and fair manner so that the jury can weigh them and reach its own conclusion.

Erath County District Attorney Alan Nash points out evidence during the murder trial of former Marine Cpl. Eddie Ray Routh, who was charged with the 2013 deaths of Chris Kyle and Chad Littlefield. How do the prosecution and the defense use evidence to build their cases?

After the prosecution questions a witness, the defense attorney has the opportunity to cross-examine. The right to cross-examine witnesses is derived from the Sixth Amendment and is one of the adversarial features of the trial. The defense attorney tries to **impeach**, or discredit, the witness by asking questions that undermine the prosecution's case. Sometimes the defense attorney can be successful in soliciting information from the prosecution's witness that is favorable to the defendant. Once the defense attorney has cross-examined the witness, the prosecutor may ask additional questions under the right to **redirect examination**. In turn, the defense attorney can ask for a re-cross-examination. Often, this tactic is used later in the trial after other witnesses reveal new evidence. The intent of cross-examining and redirecting is to give each side an equal opportunity to ask questions.

After the state presents its case against the defendant, the defense attorney can ask the judge for a **directed verdict of acquittal**, an order stating that the jury must acquit the accused because the prosecution has failed to present a compelling case documenting the defendant's guilt. Only in the most egregious cases would the judge be likely to make such a ruling. However, it costs the defense nothing to make such a motion. In some cases, the judge might believe the prosecution has failed so miserably to make a logical case that issuing a directed verdict of acquittal would not circumvent justice but save the court from having to sit through a trial with a foregone conclusion of acquittal.

Once the prosecution concludes the presentation of its evidence and witnesses, the defense may present its own evidence and witnesses. Because the burden of proof rests with the prosecution, the defendant enjoys a presumption of innocence. As such, the defense attorney need only present evidence that raises a reasonable doubt about the defendant's guilt. If the prosecution has a witness from the state crime lab who testified about blood samples or hair fibers, the defense will counter with other scientists to dispute the testimony. If the prosecution presents an eyewitness, the defense may attempt to impeach the testimony by showing that the witness's eyesight or memory is faulty.

After each side has presented its evidence and witnesses, the court allows both sides to present a summation in which they attempt to account for all the

impeach—The discrediting of a witness.

redirect examination—The questioning of a witness about issues uncovered during cross-examination.

directed verdict of acquittal—An order from a trial judge to the jury stating that the jury must acquit the accused because the prosecution has not proved its case.

beyond a reasonable doubt(from Chapter 3)—The highest level of proof required to win a case; necessary in criminal cases to procure a guilty verdict.

facts in a closing argument designed to put the best possible spin on their case. The prosecution gets the last word because of its burden to prove the defendant's guilt **beyond a reasonable doubt**, a legal yardstick that measures the sufficiency of the evidence. The prosecutor does not have to eliminate all doubt; lingering suspicions about the defendant's guilt might remain. New evidence may not be introduced at this stage because the opposing side does not have the opportunity to question it. Closing arguments can sometimes be flamboyant because the attorneys are not just presenting facts; they are trying to convince the jury that the defendant is a solid citizen or a criminal, sympathetic or disgusting, innocent or guilty. During the closing arguments portrayed on television dramas, culprits often blurt out a confession or the defense attorney brings the jury to tears with a dramatic and heartfelt speech. In reality, the closing arguments are not nearly so theatrical, but they can be extremely interesting and moving.

To convict a defendant, the prosecutor must build a case based on evidence. The reasonable doubt standard works in favor of the defendant, who needs only to raise questions about the quality of the prosecutor's case and does not have to prove anything.

In building the case, the prosecutor uses several different types of evidence. Some evidence is more convincing to the jury than other types, but the prosecutor must weave a convincing pattern that demonstrates that the defendant is guilty as charged. Evidence must conform to a set of rules that ensures that the defendant's rights are respected.[62] For instance, privileged communications between a doctor and patient or lawyer and client are not admissible in court, nor is illegally obtained evidence.[63] With these and other exceptions, however, the rules of evidence are geared toward obtaining the truth. Evidence is deemed trustworthy when every effort is made to ensure its veracity. For example, original documents are required because copies are too easy to alter. Additionally, young children or those suffering from mental illness might be judged by the court to lack competence, so their testimony would be inadmissible. This is true also for hearsay evidence, secondhand evidence in which someone reports that he or she heard someone say something, because it can be impossible to determine whether someone said what is reported. Other types of evidence, especially scientific evidence, can be discredited when new information is learned. Evidence can be classified in several ways.

> Real evidence. Real evidence consists of objects that can be readily observed. For instance, fingerprints, hair fibers, or blood can all be analyzed and certified by experts. Although opinions about the quality of the evidence or the chain of custody might be conflicting, experts can agree upon scientific standards. The courts are turning more and more to science to provide solid real evidence to determine guilt or innocence. Recent examples of death row inmates being released because of DNA evidence is a testament to how science can work both for and against the prosecution.

> Testimony. Testimony consists of statements that witnesses give under oath. Ideally, the prosecution will present witnesses who saw the defendant commit the offense. Lacking eyewitness testimony, the prosecutor might present someone who can place the defendant in the proximity of where the offense was committed at about the same time. Additionally, much real evidence requires expert interpretation. For example, hair fibers do not speak for themselves, so the prosecution must elicit testimony from an expert who is competent to evaluate them in relation to how the prosecutor contends they are connected to the offense.

A fingerprint can tie a defendant to the crime scene. In what ways has scientific evidence become an important factor in some cases?

> Direct evidence. Both real evidence and testimony can be considered direct evidence, which is ascertainable by the five senses: seeing, hearing, smelling, touching, and tasting. For instance, eyewitness testimony is defined as the witness seeing the defendant do something.

> Indirect evidence. Indirect evidence can also be termed "circumstantial evidence." When the prosecution fails to find the "smoking gun," then circumstantial evidence that demonstrates the defendant has bought a gun of the same caliber might be used to help establish the case. With enough circumstantial evidence, the prosecution can build a strong case. However, the defense has an easier time creating doubts with circumstantial evidence than with direct evidence.

The Case Goes to the Jury

Serving on a jury allows average citizens to participate in the criminal justice process in an important way that acts as a check-and-balance against government power. The jury can prevent an overzealous prosecutor from railroading a defendant. By having a jury comprising 12 citizens (this is the ideal number, but many states allow a jury of six for some types of cases) who consider the defendant's guilt, the dynamics of the courtroom work group are not as dominant as they would be if only criminal justice practitioners decided the cases.

The jury-selection process is a complicated and uncertain procedure that results in juries that might be partial to either the prosecution or the defense. Certainly, each side attempts to influence the jury selection to ensure that its arguments will find a sympathetic ear. The formation of a jury requires several steps.

> Master jury list. Each jurisdiction must develop a list of potential jurors. This list is compiled from voter registration records, driver's license lists, and utility customer lists. The goal is to develop a master jury list that is representative of the community in terms of race, sex, and social class.

Jurors discuss the February 2017 verdict of Pedro Hernandez, the man found guilty in the kidnapping and murder of six-year-old Etan Patz in the 1970s in New York City. How are jurors selected?

venire—The list or pool from which jurors are chosen.

voir dire—French for "to see, to speak"; a phrase that refers to the questioning of jurors by a judge and/ or attorneys to determine whether individual jurors are appropriate for a particular jury panel.

> *Venire.* A list of names is randomly selected from the master jury list to form the **venire** or the jury pool. The sheriff's office notifies these individuals by summons to appear at the courthouse for jury duty. Not all citizens who are summoned for jury duty will report. In some jurisdictions, the non-response rate is as high as 20 percent. Furthermore, many citizens request that they be excused from jury duty because of the inconvenience and hardship it imposes. Judges vary widely in their patterns of excusing citizens from jury duty. Juries are selected from this final, reduced jury pool.

> *Voir dire.* The prosecutor and the defense attorney have some input into which members of the jury pool wind up on the jury for an actual case. The **voir dire** ("to see, to speak") consists of the questioning of prospective jurors to determine whether they have the necessary qualifications to serve. The questions cover possible previous relationships potential jurors might have had with those involved in the case (for instance, the brother-in-law of the prosecutor would not be an appropriate candidate for the jury), knowledge about the case, attitudes about certain facts that could arise in the trial, and their willingness to be fair and impartial. The defense attorney or prosecutor can attempt to exclude someone from the jury by two means:

1. Challenge for cause. Potential jurors can be excused if it is suspected that they cannot be objective—for instance, if someone made a public statement about the case that clearly showed that he or she had already decided the defendant was guilty. Although challenges for cause are not often used and not often granted by the judge, this is an important safeguard against getting an obviously biased juror.

2. Peremptory challenge. Both the defense attorney and the prosecutor are allowed to have a certain number of potential jurors dismissed without providing reasons. For example, a defense attorney might decide that anyone who has experience working in the criminal justice system will not be sympathetic to the defendant, and therefore the defense attorney may

use **peremptory challenges** to exclude potential jurors who have been police officers, attorneys, criminology professors, or prison guards. However, using peremptory challenges to exclude individuals based on race or sex is prohibited (see Case in Point 9.1).

Depending on the case, serving on a jury can be satisfying, or it can be an arduous task. For instance, some juries are sequestered, and members must live in a hotel and avoid watching television or reading the local news. Some complicated and high-profile cases can cause jurors to lose months of work and exert a real hardship on their employers and families.

Jurors play a passive role during the trial. They must sit and listen to the prosecutor and the defense attorney present the case. They are not allowed to ask questions of the attorneys or the witnesses. Jurors who would like to have more control over their role and are not familiar with the legal procedures that underlie the trial process might find this role frustrating.[64] One feature that makes jury trials so interesting is that a conviction requires more than a majority vote. In fact, all jury members must vote; a jury that is deadlocked or unable to reach a unanimous verdict is a **hung jury**. When there is a hung jury, the prosecution has the option of trying the case again.

Not all cases get a jury trial. The exceptions are those in which the possible penalty is not serious (such as six months or less in jail), those in which the defendant is a juvenile, and those in which the defense requests a **bench trial**, a trial held before a judge who either decides for guilt or acquittal and passes sentence. A defense attorney might request a bench trial when the case involves technical or emotional issues, such as a child abuse case. Some believe that the chances for acquittal are better when a professional judge decides rather than a jury comprising ordinary citizens who might be more likely to become confused by the evidence or biased because of the nature of the case.[65]

peremptory challenges—The right of both the prosecution and the defense attorney to have a juror dismissed before trial without stating a reason.

hung jury—A jury in a criminal case that is deadlocked or that cannot produce a unanimous verdict.

bench trial (from Chapter 7)—A trial in which a defendant waives the right to a jury trial and instead agrees to a trial in which the judge hears and decides the case.

CASE IN POINT 9.1

Batson v. Kentucky (1986)

THE POINT

The Supreme Court established that the use of peremptory challenges to racially manipulate a jury violates the defendant's right to an impartial jury.

THE CASE

During James Batson's trial on burglary charges, the prosecutor used peremptory challenges to exclude four black jurors from the jury pool. The resulting all-white jury convicted Batson, who was black, of second-degree burglary. On appeal, the Supreme Court ruled that the use of peremptory challenges to racially manipulate the jury violated the equal protection rights of both Batson and the four excluded jurors. The case was remanded back to the trial court with the requirement that if "the prosecutor does not come forward with a neutral explanation for his action, our precedents require that petitioner's conviction be reversed."

THINK ABOUT IT

1. According to the Supreme Court, what was wrong with the use of peremptory challenges?
2. What effect did the use of peremptory challenges have on the jury in the Batson case?

The Defense Doesn't Rest

The defense considers many of the same issues as the prosecutor but has a competing mission of protecting the interests of the defendant. We will now look at these issues from the defense's point of view.

Once the prosecution has presented the evidence, the defense attorney must make an important decision. The defense can claim the prosecution has not proven beyond a reasonable doubt the defendant's guilt by asking for a directed verdict of acquittal and can decline to mount a defense. This is a risky gamble that defense attorneys do not often employ. The defense attorney might truly believe the prosecution's case is fatally flawed, but the jury will make its own decision, and the defense attorney will usually take the opportunity to rebut the evidence presented.[66] According to Neubauer, the defense may consider at least five strategies to counter the prosecution's case.[67]

› Reasonable doubt. The defense has the right to confront the witnesses and evidence through cross-examination and use this opportunity to attempt to poke holes in the case, thus raising a reasonable doubt about the defendant's guilt within the jury. By catching a witness in some contradicting testimony, or exposing how a witness might be motivated to lie, the defense attempts to weaken the prosecution's case. This is sometimes the defense's only strategy in the absence of any other plausible defense. According to Neubauer, this is the weakest type of strategy.

› Defendant testimony. The defendant is not required to testify. Although many jurors would like to see the defendant get on the witness stand and say, "I didn't do it," this strategy gives the prosecution the right to cross-examine. The Fifth Amendment protects defendants from self-incrimination, so the defense attorney must carefully weigh the risk of subjecting the defendant to questions from the prosecution against the problem of letting the jury wonder why the defendant does not take the stand to proclaim his or her innocence. One factor the defense attorney will consider is the believability of the witness and his or her ability to draw the jury's sympathy. In many cases, defendants can do themselves more harm than good by testifying. Although the direct examination by their own attorney can cast them in a positive light, this opens the door for the prosecutor to expose weaknesses in the character or in the alibi of the defendant.

› Alibis. The defense can present evidence that the defendant was somewhere else at the time of the offense. Having others testify that they saw the defendant miles from the offense at the time it was committed can raise doubt. According to Neubauer, some states require the defense to provide a list of witnesses who are going to present alibi testimony so that the prosecution can investigate their stories before the trial. The prosecutor's goal is to catch the witnesses in contradictory testimony or to impugn their honesty by showing that they are friends of the defendant and are likely to be untruthful.

› Affirmative defense. An affirmative defense essentially says that the defendant committed the offense but had a good reason that excuses his or her culpability. Examples include self-defense, duress, and entrapment. In each of these instances, the question of reasonable doubt is not challenged. Rather, the focus of the case shifts to the defendant's having a good reason for committing the offense. Perhaps the most recognizable affirmative defense is the insanity defense, in which the defendant admits to the offense but contends that he or she should not be held responsible because of mental illness.[68]

› Challenging scientific evidence. When the prosecution presents scientific evidence, it must also summon experts to explain it to the jury. Often, these experts are employees of the state or local crime laboratories that processed the evidence. The defense can present its own expert witnesses to cast doubt on the quality of the evidence or the interpretations of the prosecution's witnesses. The jury might be unfamiliar with the issues in dispute and incompetent to distinguish which set of experts is correct. This situation favors the defense, which must only raise a reasonable doubt in the minds of the jury to secure an acquittal.[69] The effect of science in the courts has been subject to debate as to whether popular television programs such as *CSI* have made jurors more demanding of the quality of physical evidence. This so-called CSI effect has not been shown to have any major influence on most jurors' expectations.[70]

There are no right answers when it comes to picking the best tactic to defend against criminal charges. Practicing law is as much an art as it is a science, and pleading a case before a jury can involve a bit of theater. Some might compare this process to a game because of its adversarial nature and because it is bound by a set of complicated rules. However, the stakes are too high to think of a trial as a game. Its effect on the lives of the defendants, the careers of those in the courtroom work group, and the public's sense of justice make this stage of the criminal justice system an extremely serious endeavor.[71]

Appeal

A written request to a higher court to modify or reverse the judgment of a trial court or intermediate-level appellate court is called an **appeal**. The process begins when a defendant who loses a trial files a notice of appeal, which usually must be filed within 30 days from the judgment date. The appellate court does not retry the

appeal—A written petition to a higher court to review a lower court's decision for the purpose of convincing the higher court that the lower court's decision was incorrect.

Convicted murderer Jermaine McKinney used bleach to get blood off his hands after killing two women to avoid leaving a blood trail. A criminalist from the Los Angeles County Sheriff's Department said the use of bleach, which destroys DNA, is no longer unusual in a murder thanks to television crime dramas like *CSI: Crime Scene Investigation*, which give offenders tips on how to cover up evidence. McKinney received two life sentences for the murders. In what other ways have crime dramas inspired real-life crime?

case. Rather, the defendant, now known as the "appellant," and the trial's winner, or "appellee," submit written arguments, or briefs, and sometimes make oral arguments addressing why the decision should be upheld or overturned. When appellate courts reverse lower-court judgments, it is usually because of prejudicial error, and the case is returned to a lower court for retrial. There is no constitutional right to appeal; however, some states have established the right to appeal by statute, whereas others have established it by custom.

PAUSE AND REVIEW

1. **What are the steps of the trial process?**
2. **What are the steps of the pre-trial phase?**
3. **How can motions be used to a defendant's advantage?**
4. **How does the reasonable doubt standard work in favor of the defendant?**
5. **What are some of the ways in which evidence can be classified?**
6. **In what ways can the prosecution and the defense influence the makeup of a jury?**

LEARNING OBJECTIVE 9

Distinguish between indeterminate and determinate sentencing and give an example of each.

LEARNING OBJECTIVE 10

Differentiate mandatory minimum sentencing from sentencing guidelines.

sentencing guidelines—A set of rules concerning the sentencing for a specified set of offenses that seek to create uniform sentencing policy by directing the judge to consider certain facts about the offense and the defendant when determining the sentence.

Sentencing

The criminal court process is twofold. The first part is concerned with determining the defendant's guilt. If the defendant is found guilty, or agrees to a plea bargain for a *nolo contendere* or guilty plea, the second part of the process begins. The judge must sentence the defendant (now the offender) to an appropriate disposition. When the judge has discretion, he or she considers the circumstances and seriousness of the offense, and the offender's attitude, as well as the prosecutor's recommendation and the probation office's pre-sentence report. Depending on the offense, a sentence can range from a fine and community service to several years in prison, life imprisonment, or death.

Depending on the nature of the case and the judge's philosophical concerns and motivations, the goal of the sentence might be treatment, punishment, incapacitation, restitution, revenge, or deterrence.[72] The judge's philosophical intention is not the only factor that guides the sentencing decision. The availability of prison beds or treatment programs, the defendant's demeanor or remorsefulness, and a host of factors that should have no bearing on the sentence, such as the offender's race, sex, gender, and social and economic status, can all influence the type and severity of the disposition.[73] The judge has, therefore, considerable discretion in deciding the appropriate sentence for each offender.[74]

It would be comforting if there were a uniform pattern in sentencing. If those who committed the most serious offenses and presented the greatest danger to society received the most severe sentences, the public's sense of justice would be satisfied. However, when sentences for offenders with similar cases and prior records differ significantly, the courts appear to be arbitrary and capricious.

Usually, the law limits the judge to a few options. **Sentencing guidelines** are rules for deciding sentences that classify offenses and offenders and prescribe punishments. According to the U.S. Sentencing Commission, the sentencing guidelines for federal offenses were created to ensure that "similar offenders of similar crimes would receive similar sentences."[75] An indeterminate sentence specifies a range of time that the offender must serve before parole can be granted (for example, a sentence of "10 years to life" for first-degree murder). This shifts the discretion for determining the offender's release from the judge to the parole board. In a capital case, in which the choice for the offender is either life in prison without parole or the death penalty, a jury chooses the sentence. A determinate sentence limits the judge's discretion in much the same way and is intended to limit sentencing disparity. Let's look at these types of sentencing in greater detail.

Indeterminate Sentencing

Is the judge the best person to decide how long an offender should spend in prison? When a case is plea bargained, is the courtroom work group the appropriate body to fashion a sentencing decision that affects not only the offender but also the agencies that must carry out the sentence? Perhaps the prison is better able to decide which inmates deserve to be there and which are good candidates for probation and parole. Perhaps the trial, where passions are high and the details of the crime vivid, is not the time to decide how long the offender should be incarcerated. Perhaps society would be better served if the actual length of an offender's sentence were predicated on how well that offender adjusts to prison life and on how safe society would be once the offender is released.[76]

The **indeterminate sentence** considers these issues and leaves it to the parole board's discretion to determine when the offender is ready to be released into the community. It views the judge as incapable of predicting when the offender is no longer a threat to society. At its most extreme, the indeterminate sentence sends the offender to prison for somewhere between one year and life. Based on the offender's behavior in prison and his or her rehabilitation, the parole board picks a release date.

The indeterminate sentence, which is based on the medical model of corrections, considers the uniqueness of each offender's offense and social background; the sentence is fashioned to address the diagnosed problems.[77] In a hospital, it would be inconceivable to handle a patient with a broken leg in the same way as one who has had a heart attack. The indeterminate sentence applies this medical analogy to the offender. By viewing unlawful behavior as a symptom of a social deficiency, the criminal justice system can prescribe a treatment, such as vocational training, drug or alcohol treatment, or counseling.

The indeterminate sentence is attractive if we assume that criminal behavior is comparable to physical illness. We can prescribe individualized justice in the same way we do individualized medicine and develop a "treatment" or a "cure" for the offender's criminal behavior. The time it takes to apply a cure to each offender is different, so the prison sentences are not fixed. That way, the offender is not released too soon or kept in prison too long. The parole board, in consultation with the prison staff, determines when the offender has been successfully rehabilitated and is safe to return to society.[78]

The indeterminate sentence enjoyed wide popularity during the 1950s and 1960s. A progressive attitude prevalent in correctional circles advocated rehabilitation over punishment. By shifting the discretion for deciding the length of incarceration from the judge to the prison staff and the parole board, the criminal justice system based treatment on the inmate's willingness to take advantage of rehabilitative services. The indeterminate sentence was predicated on three assumptions:

1. The offender is sick, and the prison staff can diagnose the problem.
2. The prison can provide the necessary treatment to correct the problem.
3. The prison staff and parole board can accurately determine whether the inmate has been successfully treated and is ready to return to society.[79]

indeterminate sentence—A prison term that is determined by a parole board and does not state a specific period of time to be served or date of release.

The indeterminate sentence was largely jettisoned in the 1970s and 1980s for four reasons.

1. There was little evidence that any of the three aforementioned assumptions were warranted. Considering antisocial behavior to be analogous to physical illness and subject to diagnosis and treatment did not prove to be accurate in many cases. As offenders deemed to be rehabilitated continued to break the law, citizens and politicians lost faith in the system.[80]

2. Indeterminate sentencing created wide disparities in incarceration times. Particularly when extralegal factors such as race and social class were correlated with length of incarceration, the inexact science of indeterminate sentencing began to look like a smokescreen for discrimination and the influence of political power.[81]

3. If the sentence was determined by how well inmates appeared to be rehabilitated, then it was in their interest to play the game. Inmates learned to act rehabilitated to convince prison officials they were ready to be released. They attended treatment programs and developed the positive vocabulary of rehabilitation to attain their goal of release.[82]

4. Some research was interpreted as revealing that participation in treatment programs did not significantly improve offenders' prospects for avoiding crime. Although the value of rehabilitation was, and continues to be, in dispute, the prevailing attitude at the time was that there was no evidence of effectiveness.[83] Consequently, the discretion for deciding how long the inmate would be incarcerated shifted from the prison staff and the parole board to the legislature and the prosecutor, with the introduction of the determinate sentence.

Determinate Sentencing

The effectiveness of rehabilitation will be discussed in Chapters 11, 12, and 13. For our purposes here, it is sufficient to say that there is widespread concern about its effectiveness and about the public's confidence in the criminal justice system. Although rehabilitation was considered a worthy goal, it was not deemed a sufficient foundation on which to base sentencing decisions. Legislators decided to pass laws that restricted the discretion that criminal justice decision-makers could exercise in an individual case. Sentencing guidelines were developed that stated that the length of time an inmate would serve would not be determined by the judge or the parole board but by the nature of the offense.[84] Sentencing guidelines forced judges to apply sentences within a narrow range of variability.[85] In 2004, the Supreme Court decided in *Booker* v. *United States* that the federal guidelines violated the Sixth Amendment right to trial by jury because they allowed judges to enhance sentences using facts not reviewed by juries. The Court set forth that the sentencing guidelines in federal courts would be advisory and not mandatory.

determinate sentence—A prison term that is determined by law and states a specific period of time to be served.

In its purest form, a **determinate sentence** gives a fixed sentence to each offender convicted of a particular offense. For example, an armed robbery conviction might call for a 30-year sentence. The judge has no discretion to alter the sentence, regardless of the circumstances of the offense or of the offender. One form of determinate sentencing, the **presumptive sentence**, allows judges limited discretion to consider aggravating circumstances (specifics about the offender or the case that worsen the offense) or mitigating circumstances (specifics about the offender or the case that lessen the severity of the offense) and depart from the guidelines. Some states employ voluntary guidelines, which allow judges the same departures. See Figure 9.3 for an example of a state sentencing guidelines table.

presumptive sentence—A sentence that may be adjusted by the judge depending on aggravating or mitigating factors.

Level	Illustrative offenses	Sentence range				
9	Murder	Life	Life	Life	Life	Life
8	Manslaughter (voluntary) Rape of a child with force Aggravated rape Armed burglary	96–144 Mos.	108–162 Mos.	120–180 Mos.	144–216 Mos.	204–306 Mos.
7	Armed robbery Rape Mayhem	60–90 Mos.	68–102 Mos.	84–126 Mos.	108–162 Mos.	160–240 Mos.
6	Manslaughter (involuntary) Armed robbery (no gun) A&B DW (significant injury)	40–60 Mos.	45–67 Mos.	50–75 Mos.	60–90 Mos.	80–120 Mos.
5	Unarmed robbery Stalking in violation of order Unarmed burglary Larceny ($50,000 and over)	12–36 Mos. IS-IV IS-III IS-II	24–36 Mos. IS-IV IS-III IS-II	36–54 Mos.	48–72 Mos.	60–90 Mos.
4	Larceny from a person A&B DW (moderate injury) B&E (dwelling) Larceny ($10,000 to $50,000)	0–24Mos. IS-IV IS-III IS-II	3–30 Mos. IS-IV IS-III IS-II	6–30 Mos. IS-IV IS-III IS-II	20–30 Mos.	24–36 Mos.
3	A&B DW (no or minor injury) B&E (not dwelling) Larceny ($250 to $10,000)	0–12Mos. IS-IV IS-III IS-II IS-I	0–15 Mos. IS-IV IS-III IS-II IS-I	0–18 Mos. IS-IV IS-III IS-II IS-I	0–24 Mos. IS-IV IS-III IS-II	6–24 Mos. IS-IV IS-III IS-II
2	Assault Larceny under $250	IS-III IS-II IS-I	0–6 Mos. IS-III IS-II IS-I	0–6 Mos. IS-III IS-II IS-I	0–9 Mos. IS-IV IS-III IS-II IS-I	0–12 Mos. IS-IV IS-III IS-II IS-I
1	Operating aft. suspended license Disorderly conduct Vandalism	IS-II IS-I	IS-III IS-II IS-I	IS-III IS-II IS-I	0–3 Mos. IS-IV IS-III IS-II IS-I	0–6 Mos. IS-IV IS-III IS-II IS-I
	Criminal History Scale	A No/Minor Record	B Moderate Record	C Serious Record	D Violent or Repetitive	E Serious Violent

Sentencing zones

- Incarceration zone
- Discretionary zone (incarceration/intermediate sanction)
- Intermediate sanction zone

Intermediate sanctions levels

IS-IV	24-hour restriction
IS-III	Daily accountability
IS-II	Standard supervision
IS-I	Financial accountability

FIGURE 9.3 Massachusetts Sentencing Grid Which offense/criminal history combinations are in the discretionary zone? Give some possible reasons that the sentencing for these offenses may be either incarceration or intermediate sanctions.

Source: Massachusetts Judicial Branch, Massachusetts Court System, http://www.mass.gov/courts/court-info/trial-court/sent-commission/ma-sentencing-grid-gen.html. Accessed February 2017.

The perceived advantage of the determinate sentence is uniformity. Similar cases are treated in the same manner, and, theoretically, such factors as social class, race, sex, and gender do not affect the sentencing equation.[86] These efforts to remove discretion from the criminal justice system have produced at least three unintended consequences that some consider detrimental to the welfare of offenders and society.

1. Determinate sentencing has removed the power to make decisions from those closest to the case. These participants are often in the best position to understand a case's complexities and weigh the conflicting interests of the welfare of society and the offender's punishment.

2. Legislators who espouse determinate sentencing policy are not always sensitive to the limitations of the criminal justice system to bear the demands of long prison sentences for a multitude of inmates. Even the most mundane criminal justice resources, such as prison beds, are limited. The civil and human rights of inmates are infringed upon when prisons are crowded, but criminal justice decision-makers, such as judges and parole board members, have little power to remedy the situation.[87]

3. By limiting the judge's sentencing discretion, determinate sentencing laws may affect the prosecutor's decision as to which charges will be filed, thus shifting power to the prosecution. Defense attorneys unwilling to expose their clients to long determinate sentences are pressured to accept plea bargains to lesser included offenses or in exchange for avoiding the stigma associated with drug or sex-offender convictions. The mandatory minimum sentences for these types of offenses provide the prosecutor with tremendous leverage in extracting plea bargains from defendants. Therefore, those in the best position to exercise discretion—the judge and the parole board—often find their hands tied by the determinate sentencing laws.

Mandatory Minimum Sentences

mandatory minimum sentence—A sentence determined by law that establishes the minimum length of prison time that may be served for an offense.

The **mandatory minimum sentence** is a form of determinate sentencing that addresses certain types of offenses that particularly rankle the public and receive little sympathy from the media or criminal justice practitioners.[88] Typically, mandatory minimum sentencing laws do not allow probation and stipulate incarceration for a specified number of years. Federal mandatory minimum sentences are not sentencing guidelines; thus, they are not subject to the *Booker* decision. Judges typically cannot impose a sentence shorter than the number of years set by Congress for offenses that carry a mandatory minimum.[89] The following are types of offenses that are likely to carry mandatory minimums:

› Weapons violations. Those who use a gun (or sometimes possess one) while committing a felony will find an additional prison term tacked on to the sentence. This guarantees that the case will not result in a probationary sentence.

› Repeated drunk driving. In some jurisdictions, those who persist in driving while intoxicated will be sentenced to mandatory prison or jail time.[90]

› Drug sales and drug kingpin laws. Many jurisdictions, including the federal government, have laws specifying mandatory prison time for the sale of illegal drugs. Some of these laws, aimed at drug kingpins, are especially punitive.

› Three-strikes laws. Aimed at the habitual offender, these laws result in mandatory incarceration for those who have two prior felonies. Judges are not allowed to consider the circumstances of the present offense and must sentence the offender to a prison term.

Pictured with his sons is music producer Weldon Angelos (center), who was sentenced to 55 years in prison as a result of mandatory minimum sentencing laws for possessing a firearm while selling marijuana. Angelos was released after 12 years on May 31, 2016. How should mandatory minimum sentencing laws be reformed?

> Truth in sentencing. These laws, which specify that the offender must serve a substantial portion of the sentence before being released, limit the flexibility of the parole board by ensuring that inmates spend most of the original sentence (often 85 percent) behind bars.[91]

The sentencing decision has become the primary way in which citizens evaluate the quality of justice meted out by the system because it is such a high-profile event. This is unfortunate because sentencing is just one of many decision-making points, and the reliance on this single event obscures the effects of the entire process. Efforts to limit judicial discretion have been frustrated due to the inevitable shift of decision-making power to other points in the system.[92]

PAUSE AND REVIEW

1. What is indeterminate sentencing?
2. What is determinate sentencing?

 **FOCUS ON ETHICS** Letting the Big Ones Get Away

As an assistant prosecutor, you are under orders from the chief prosecutor to rack up drug prosecutions to help make his reputation as a drug warrior in his campaign to run for Congress. You have been successful in putting several large-scale drug dealers behind bars, and you are in line for a promotion based on your success. In fact, when the total number of years for offenders' sentences is added up, your record is tied with your only competitor for the promotion. One of your current cases promises to vault you ahead if you can secure a reasonable plea bargain from the defense attorney.

Here's the problem: the drug dealer you have in your sights is a crafty and connected criminal. He has been charged before with several offenses and has always been able to avoid the clutches of the law. This time he has been caught with a kilo of cocaine at his girlfriend's house, and you have a perfect case if only she will testify against him. Because love makes fools of us all, she refuses to testify. She is pregnant with his child and does not want him to go to prison. His high-priced defense attorney comes to you with a deal. If you drop the charges against him, the drug dealer will testify that the cocaine belongs to his girlfriend. Because the girlfriend has had shoplifting and bad-check convictions from several years ago, the state's mandatory minimum sentence statutes will kick in, and you will be able to send her to prison for a 40-year term.

You really want to nail the drug dealer instead of the girlfriend, but she refuses to cooperate. She does not believe you when you tell her that her boyfriend has offered to roll over on her, and because the cocaine did not belong to her, she naively believes that she will not be prosecuted. Your chief prosecutor wants a big conviction, and this one would ensure your promotion.

WHAT DO YOU DO?
1. Teach her the most painful lesson of her life. Prosecute her for the cocaine and send her to prison for 40 years.
2. Dismiss the charges on both of them.
3. Explain your problem to the judge and ask him or her to try to talk some sense into the girlfriend.
4. Think of another creative way to try to bring justice to this case.

For more insight as to how someone might respond to such an ethical dilemma, visit the companion website at www.oup.com/us/fuller to watch a video that connects this scenario to a real-world situation.

Summary

LEARNING OBJECTIVE **1** — Summarize how sentencing disparities may negatively influence popular opinion about the criminal justice system.	Sentencing disparities elicit a sense that justice is not uniform but are the inevitable result of funding limitations and political necessity. Because of plea bargaining, defendants with similar charges, similar records, and equal culpability who appear before the same judge can be sentenced differently. Court reforms are difficult to enact because of the complicated nature of the criminal justice system.
LEARNING OBJECTIVE **2** — Identify alternatives to keeping a suspect in jail.	Cash bond: a certain amount of money set by a judge that the defendant must give to the court in exchange for release pending trial. Property bond: use of a piece of property as collateral in exchange for release pending trial. Release on recognizance: release of a defendant based on a promise to return to court. Surety bond: use of a bail agent, who pays a defendant's bail if he or she fails to appear in court.
LEARNING OBJECTIVE **3** — Contrast the competing values of presumption of innocence and preventive detention in the context of pre-trial release.	A pre-trial release decision must weigh the issue of presumption of innocence against the state's responsibility to protect society by detaining truly dangerous people in order to prevent possible further harm while the court considers their cases.

LEARNING OBJECTIVE 4 Define plea bargain.	A compromise reached by the defendant, the defendant's attorney, and the prosecutor in which the defendant agrees to plead guilty or no contest in return for a reduction of the charges' severity, dismissal of some charges, further information about the offense, or about others involved in it, or the prosecutor's agreement to recommend a desired sentence.
LEARNING OBJECTIVE 5 Compare and contrast the types of plea bargaining arrangements.	Vertical plea: By pleading guilty or *nolo contendere* to a lesser charge, the defendant can reduce the potential for a harsh sentence. Horizontal plea: The defendant pleads guilty to a charge in exchange for other charges being dropped. Reduced-sentence plea: The prosecutor and defense attorney, in consultation with the judge, decide on a reduced sentence. Avoidance-of-stigma plea: A defendant pleads guilty to a lesser charge in order to avoid a more serious charge that carries a stigma.

LEARNING OBJECTIVE 6
 	
Argue for and against the abolition of plea bargaining.
	For the abolition of plea bargaining:
	  – It allows offenders to thwart justice.
	  – It often ignores the voices of victims.
	  – The public has less opportunity to comprehend how dispositions are arrived at, causing disillusion.
	  – Some defendants, especially the indigent who cannot afford bail, may plead guilty to crimes they did not commit to get out of jail or avoid risking trial.
	Against the abolition of plea bargaining:
	  – It is inefficient; the number of cases that defense attorneys are willing to take to trial increases.
	  – The discretion inherent in the process could move to another part of the criminal justice system where it might not be as visible and thus subject to increased abuse or corruption.
	  – Doing so might squeeze the prosecutor out of the process because defense attorneys can attempt to negotiate directly with the judge to secure the best deal for the defendant.

LEARNING OBJECTIVE 7 Outline the steps of the pre-trial phase.	1. Filing of charges: Law enforcement agencies present information about the case and the suspect to the prosecutor, who decides if formal charges will be filed. 2. Initial appearance and preliminary hearing: After arrest, suspects are brought before a judge for an initial appearance. The suspect is formally charged and pleads guilty, not guilty, or *nolo contendere*. 3. Grand jury: This jury hears the prosecutor's evidence and decides if it is sufficient to bring the accused to trial. 4. Indictments and informations: Some jurisdictions require grand jury indictments for felony cases. An accused may waive an indictment and accept service of an information. Misdemeanor cases might also proceed by the issuance of an information. 5. Arraignment: The accused is informed of the charges, advised of his or her rights, and asked to enter a plea. 6. The plea: If the accused pleads guilty or *nolo contendere*, the judge either accepts or rejects the plea.
LEARNING OBJECTIVE 8 Analyze the role that the standard of reasonable doubt plays in the presentation of witnesses and evidence during the trial process.	The legal standard of "beyond a reasonable doubt" measures the sufficiency of the evidence. The prosecution has the burden of proof but does not have to eliminate all doubt. The defendant enjoys a presumption of innocence, so the defense attorney need only present evidence that raises reasonable doubt about the defendant's guilt. The defense confronts the witnesses and evidence through cross-examination, thus attempting to weaken the prosecution's case and raise a reasonable doubt within the jury about the defendant's guilt.

LEARNING OBJECTIVE 9 Distinguish between indeterminate and determinate sentencing and give an example of each.	An indeterminate sentence does not state a specific period of time to be served or date of release. An example is a sentence of "10 years to life" for first-degree murder. A determinate sentence is a prison term that is determined by law and states a specific period of time to be served. An example is an armed robbery conviction that calls for a 30-year sentence.
LEARNING OBJECTIVE 10 Differentiate mandatory minimum sentencing from sentencing guidelines.	A mandatory minimum sentence is a sentence determined by law that establishes the minimum length of prison time that may be served for an offense. Mandatory minimum sentences are not sentencing guidelines, which are a set of rules concerning the sentencing for a specified set of offenses. Judges typically cannot impose a sentence shorter than the number of years set by law for offenses that carry a mandatory minimum.

Critical Reflections

1. Why is the practice of plea bargaining considered to be a necessary evil?

2. What is the proper balance between the rights of a criminal defendant and the rights of the victim?

3. Should the discretion involved in criminal sentencing be vested in the hands of the prosecutor, the judge, or the legislature?

Key Terms

appeal **p. 283**
arraignment **p. 273**
bench trial **p. 281**
beyond a reasonable doubt **p. 278**
bill of indictment **p. 272**
cash bond **p. 261**
determinate sentence **p. 286**
directed verdict of acquittal **p. 277**
hung jury **p. 281**

impeach **p. 277**
indeterminate sentence **p. 285**
indictment **p. 272**
information **p. 272**
mandatory minimum sentence **p. 288**
no-bill **p. 272**
nolo contendere **p. 266**
peremptory challenges **p. 281**
plea bargain **p. 263**
presumptive sentence **p. 286**

pre-trial motion **p. 274**
property bond **p. 261**
redirect examination **p. 277**
release on recognizance (ROR) **p. 261**
sentencing guidelines **p. 284**
surety bond **p. 262**
true bill **p. 272**
venire **p. 280**
voir dire **p. 280**

Endnotes

1 Liliana Segura and Jordan Smith, "What Happened in Room 102," *Intercept*, July 9, 2015, https://theintercept.com/2015/07/09/oklahoma-prepares-resume-executions-richard-glossip-first-line-die.

2 John Hagan, "Extra-Legal Attributes and Criminal Sentencing: An Assessment of a Sociological Viewpoint," *Law and Society Review* 8 (1974): 357–381.

3 Thomas Austin, "The Influence of Court Location on Types of Criminal Sentences: The Rural-Urban Factor," *Journal of Criminal Justice* 9 (1981): 305–316.

4 Douglas Thomson and Anthony Ragona, "Popular Moderation Versus Governmental Authoritarianism: An Interactionist View of Public Sentiments Toward Criminal Sanctions," *Crime and Delinquency* 33 (1987): 337–357.

5 James Austin and John Irwin, *It's About Time: America's Imprisonment Binge*, 3d ed. (Belmont, Calif.: Wadsworth, 1997).

6 John Goldkamp, "Danger and Detention: A Second Generation of Bail Reform," *Journal of Criminal Law and Criminology* 76 (1985): 1–74.

7 Michael Corrado, "Punishment and the Wild Beast of Prey: The Problems of Preventive Detention," *Journal of Criminal Law and Criminology* 86 (1996): 778–814.

8 Michael J. Eason, "Eighth Amendment—Pretrial Detention: What Will Become of the Innocent?" *Journal of Criminal Law and Criminology* 78 (1988): 1048–1049.

9 Thomas H. Cohen and Brian A. Reaves, *Pretrial Release of Felony Defendants in State Courts* (Washington, D.C.: U.S. Department of Justice, Bureau of Justice Statistics,

2007), 1, https://www.bjs.gov/index.cfm?ty=pbdetail&iid=834.

10 Tim Bynum, "Release on Recognizance: Substantive or Superficial Reform?" *Criminology* 20 (1982): 67–82.

11 Mary Toborg, "Bail Bondsmen and Criminal Courts," *Justice System Journal* 8 (1983): 141–156.

12 Keith Hansen, "When Worlds Collide: The Constitutional Politics of *United States v. Salerno*," *American Journal of Criminal Law* 14 (1987): 155–225.

13 Robert Nagel, "The Myth of the General Right to Bail," *Public Interest* 98 (1990): 4–97.

14 Brian A. Reaves, *Felony Defendants in Large Urban Counties, 2009 - Statistical Tables* (Washington, D.C.: U.S. Department of Justice, Office of Justice Programs, Bureau of Justice Statistics, 2013), 15.

15 Stephen Demuth, "Racial and Ethnic Differences in Pretrial Release Decisions and Outcomes: A Comparison of Hispanic, Black, and White Felony Arrestees," *Criminology* 41 (August 1, 2003): 873–907.

16 Jason Geary, "A Single Shot, No One Hurt: Why 20 Years?" *Ledger*, June 19, 2009, http://www.theledger.com/news/20090619/a-single-shot-no-one-hurt-why-20-years. Steve Bousquet, "The Warning Shot That Condemned Orville Lee Wollard to Prison and Changed Florida," *Tampa Bay Tribune*, February 4, 2016, http://www.tampabay.com/news/politics/stateroundup/a-warning-shot-sent-a-man-to-prison-for-20-years-and-shockwaves-to-the/2264128.

17 Arthur Rosett and Donald R. Cressey, *Justice by Consent: Plea Bargains in the American Courthouse* (New York: Lippincott, 1976).

18 Stephanos Bibas, "Designing Plea Bargaining from the Ground Up: Accuracy and Fairness Without Trials As Backstops," *William and Mary Law Review* 57, no. 4 (2016): 1055–1081.

19 National Registry of Exonerations, Guilty Pleas and False Confessions, November 24, 2015, https://www.law.umich.edu/special/exoneration/Pages/False-Confessions.aspx.

20 Jed S. Rakoff, "Why Innocent People Plead Guilty," *New York Review of Books*, November 20, 2014, http://www.nybooks.com/articles/2014/11/20/why-innocent-people-plead-guilty/.

21 Lucian E. Dervan and Vanessa A. Edkins, "The Innocent Defendant's Dilemma: An Innovative Empirical Study of Plea Bargaining's Innocence Problem," *Journal of Criminal Law & Criminology* 103, no. 1 (2013): 1–48. Gregory M. Gilchrist, "Trial Bargaining," *Iowa Law Review* 101 (2016): 609–656.

22 Stephanos Bibas, *The Machinery of Criminal Justice* (New York: Oxford University Press, 2012), xix.

23 Mark Motivans, Federal Justice Statistics, 2013–2014, Table 15: Disposition and Sentence Received for Defendants in Cases Terminated in U.S. District Court, 2010, 2013, and 2014 (U.S. Department of Justice, Office of Justice Programs, Bureau of Justice Statistics, 2017), 27. Available at https://www.bjs.gov/index.cfm?ty=pbdetail&iid=5885. Missouri v. Frye, 132 S. Ct. 1399, 1407 (2012).

24 David W. Neubauer, *America's Courts and the Criminal Justice System*, 7th ed. (Belmont, Calif.: Wadsworth, 2002).

25 Talia Fisher, "The Boundaries of Plea Bargaining: Negotiating the Standard of Proof," Journal of Criminal Law & Criminology 97, no.4 (July 1, 2007): 943–1007.

26 B. Grant Stite and Robert H. Chaires, "Plea Bargaining: Ethical Issues and Emerging Perspectives," *Justice Professional* 7 (1993): 69–91.

27 N. Gary Holten and Lawson L. Lamar, *The Criminal Courts: Structures Personnel and Processes* (New York: McGraw-Hill, 1991).

28 Erving Goffman, *Stigma: Notes on the Management of Spoiled Identity* (New York: Simon and Schuster, 1986).

29 Jeffery T. Ulmer, Megan C. Kurlychek, and John H. Kramer, "Prosecutorial Discretion and the Imposition of Mandatory Minimum Sentences," *Journal of Research in Crime and Delinquency* 44, no. 4 (November 1, 2007): 427.

30 Linda A. Wood and Clare MacMartin, "Constructing Remorse: Judges' Sentencing Decisions in Child Sexual Assault Cases," *Journal of Language and Social Psychology* 26, no. 4 (December 1, 2007): 343.

31 Greg M. Kramer, Melinda Wolbransky, and Kirk Heilbrun,"Plea Bargaining Recommendations by Criminal Defense Attorneys: Evidence Strength, Potential Sentence, and Defendant Preference," *Behavioral Sciences and the Law* 25, no.4 (July1, 2007): 573.

32 Neubauer, *America's Courts and the Criminal Justice System*.

33 Jay S. Albanese, "Concern about Variation in Criminal Sentences: A Cyclical History of Reform," *Journal of Criminal Law and Criminology* 75 (1984): 260–271. William Rhodes, *Plea Bargaining: Who Gains? Who Loses?* (Washington, D.C.: Institute for Law and Social Research, 1978).

34 Jay S. Albanese, "Concern about Variation in Criminal Sentences: A Cyclical History of Reform," *Journal of Criminal Law and Criminology* 75 (1984): 260–271.

35 Charlie Gerstein, "Plea Bargaining and the Right to Counsel at Bail Hearings," *Michigan Law Review* 111 (June 2013): 1513–1534.

36 David Lynch, "The Impropriety of Plea Agreements: A Tale of Two Counties," *Law and Social Inquiry* 19 (1994): 115–136.

37 Michael Winerip and Michael Schwirtz, "Rikers: Where Mental Illness Meets Brutality in Jail," *New York Times*, July 14, 2014, https://www.nytimes.com/2014/07/14/nyregion/rikers-study-finds-prisoners-injured-by-employees.html.

38 Jennifer Gonnerman, "Before the Law," October 6, 2014, *New Yorker*, http://www.newyorker.com/magazine/2014/10/06/before-the-law.

39 Jennifer Gonnerman, "Kalief Browder, 1993-2015," *New Yorker*, June 7, 2015, http://www.newyorker.com/news/news-desk/kalief-browder-1993-2015.

40 Cynthia Alkon, "An Overlooked Key to Reversing Mass Incarceration: Reforming the Law to Reduce Prosecutorial Power in Plea Bargaining," *University of Maryland Law Journal of Race, Religion, Gender, and Class* 15, no. 2 (2015): 191–208. John F. Pfaff, "Escaping from the Standard Story: Why the Conventional Wisdom on Prison Growth Is Wrong, and Where We Can Go from Here," *Federal Sentencing Reporter* 26, no. 4 (April 2014): 265–270. Roy Walmsley, *World Prison Population List*, 11th ed. (London: Institute for Criminal Policy Research, 2016). Online at http://www.prisonstudies.org/research-publications. Michelle Ye Hee Lee, "Yes, U.S. Locks People Up at a Higher Rate Than Any Other Country," *Washington Post*, July 7, 2015, https://www.washingtonpost.com/news/fact-checker/wp/2015/07/07/yes-u-s-locks-people-up-at-a-higher-rate-than-any-other-country.

41 Jed S. Rakoff, "Why Innocent People Plead Guilty," *New York Review of Books*, November 20, 2014, http://www.nybooks.com/articles/2014/11/20/why-innocent-people-plead-guilty.

42 Alkon, "An Overlooked Key to Reversing Mass Incarceration." Rakoff, "Why Innocent People Plead Guilty."

43   Rakoff, "Why Innocent People Plead Guilty."

44   Ibid.

45   Gonnerman, "Before the Law."

46   Lynn Mather, *Plea Bargaining or Trial* (Lexington, Mass.: D. C. Heath, 1979).

47   Neubauer, *America's Courts and the Criminal Justice System.*

48   Thomas Church, "Plea Bargains, Concessions and the Courts: Analysis of a Quasi-Experiment," *Law and Society Review* 10 (1976): 377–389.

49   Jon'a F. Meyer and Diana R. Grant, *The Courts in Our Criminal Justice System* (Upper Saddle River, N.J.: Prentice-Hall, 2003).

50   Raymond Nimmer and Patricia Krauthaus, "Plea Bargaining Reform in Two Cities," *Justice System Journal* 3 (1977): 6–21.

51   Candance McCoy, *Politics and Plea Bargaining: Victims' Rights in California* (Philadelphia: University of Pennsylvania Press, 1993).

52   Bureau of Justice Statistics, "The Justice System: What Is the Sequence of Events in the Criminal Justice System?" https://www.bjs.gov/content/justsys.cfm. Accessed February 2017.

53   United States Attorneys' Manual, "When an Information May Be Used," http://www.justice.gov/usam/criminal-resource-manual-206-when-information-may-be-used. Accessed February 2017.

54   Ibid.

55   Ibid.

56   University of Dayton School of Law, Grand Jury Functions, http://campus.udayton.edu/~grandjur/stategj/funcsgj.htm. Accessed October 2015.

57   Ibid.

58   Ibid.

59   Ibid.

60   Ibid.

61   David A. Bright and Jane Goodman-Delahunty, "Gruesome Evidence and Emotion: Anger, Blame, and Jury Decision-Making," *Law and Human Behavior* 30, no. 2 (April 1, 2006):183-202.

62   Henry J. Abraham, *The Judicial Process*, 7th ed. (New York: Oxford University Press, 1998).

63   Steven Schlesinger, *Exclusionary Injustice: The Problem of Illegally Obtained Evidence* (New York: Marcel Dekker, 1977).

64   Steve Tuholski, "When Facts Don't Fit, Some Jurors Make Up New Facts," *National Law Journal* (February 4, 2008): S3.

65   J. Don Read, Deborah A. Connolly, and Andrew Welsh," An Archival Analysis of Actual Cases of Historic Child Sexual Abuse: A Comparison of Jury and Bench Trials," *Law and Human Behavior* 30, no. 3 (June 1, 2006): 259–285.

66   Barbara Reskin and Christine Visher, "The Impacts of Evidence and Extralegal Factors in Juror's Decisions," *Law and Society Review* 20 (1986): 423–439.

67   Neubauer, *America's Courts and the Criminal Justice System.*

68   Lincoln Caplan, *The Insanity Defense and the Trial of John W. Hinckley Jr.* (Boston: D. R. Godine, 1984).

69   Michael Freeman and Helen Reece, eds., *Science in Court* (Brookfield, Vt.: Ashgate, 1998).

70   Tom R. Tyler, "Viewing CSI and the Threshold of Guilt: Managing Truth and Justice in Reality and Fiction," *Yale Law Journal* 115, no. 5 (March 1, 2006): 1050–1085.

71   William Brennan, "The Criminal Prosecution: Sporting Events or Quest for Truth?" *Washington University Law Review* (1963): 279–294.

72   Peggy Tobolowsky, "Restitution in the Federal Criminal Justice System," *Judicature* 77 (1993): 90–95. See also Christy Visher, "Incapacitation and Crime Control: Does a 'Lock'em Up' Strategy Reduce Crime?" *Justice Quarterly* 4 (1987): 513–544.

73   Thomas Arvanites, "Increasing Imprisonment: A Function of Crime or Socio-economic Factors?" *American Journal of Criminal Justice* 17 (1992): 19–38.

74   Elizabeth Moulds, "Chivalry and Paternalism: Disparities of Treatment in the Criminal Justice System," *Western Political Science Quarterly* 31 (1978): 416–440.

75   U.S. Sentencing Commission, "Overview of the Federal Sentencing Guidelines," November 1998, www.ussc.gov. Tamasak Wicharaya, *Simple Theory, Hard Reality: The Impact of Sentencing Reforms on Courts, Prisons, and Crime* (Albany: State University of New York Press, 1995).

76   John Irwin, *Prisons in Turmoil* (Boston: Little, Brown, 1980). Irwin presents a scathing critique of the indeterminate sentence from a prisoner's point of view.

77   Ibid.

78   William Gaylin, *Partial Justice: A Study of Bias in Sentencing* (New York: Vintage Books, 1974).

79   Irwin, *Prisons in Turmoil.*

80   Steven P. Lab and John T. Whitehead, "From 'Nothing Works' to 'The Appropriate Works': The Latest Stop in the Search for the Secular Grail," *Criminology* 28 (1990): 405–418.

81   John Hagan, "Extra-Legal Attributes and Criminal Sentencing: An Assessment of a Sociological Viewpoint," *Law and Society Review* 8 (1974): 357–381.

82   James B. Jacobs, *Stateville: The Penitentiary in Mass Society* (Chicago: University of Chicago Press, 1977).

83   Francis T. Cullen and Karen B. Gilbert, *Reaffirming Rehabilitation* (Cincinnati: Anderson, 1982).

84   Pamala Grie, *Determinate Sentencing: The Promise and the Reality of Retributive Justice* (Ithaca: State University of New York Press, 1991).

85   Jeffery Ulner, *Social Worlds of Sentencing: Court Communities under Sentencing Guidelines* (Albany: State University of New York Press, 1997).

86   Darrell Steffensmeier, Jeffrey Ulmer, and John Kramer, "The Interaction of Race, Gender, and Age in Criminal Sentencing: The Punishment Cost of Being Young, Black and Male," *Criminology* 36: 763–798.

87   William McDonald, Henry Rossman, and James Cramer, "The Prosecutorial Function and Its Relation to Determinate Sentencing Structures," in *The Prosecutor*, ed. William McDonald (Beverly Hills, Calif.: Sage, 1979).

88   Ibid.

89   Families Against Mandatory Minimums, Understanding Booker and Fanfan: Federal Sentencing Guidelines Are Advisory, but Mandatory Minimum Sentences Still Stand, http://famm.org/Repository/Files/Booker_Fanfan_Fact_Sheet.pdf. Accessed February 2017. How Federal Sentencing Works: Mandatory Minimums, Statutory Maximums, and Sentencing Guidelines, http://famm.org/wp-content/uploads/2013/08/Chart-How-Fed-Sentencing-Works-9.5.pdf. Accessed February 2017.

90   Laurence H. Ross and James Foley, "Judicial Disobedience of the Mandate to Imprison Drunk Drivers," *Law and Society Review* 21 (1987): 315–323.

91   Paula Ditton and Doris Wilson, *Truth in Sentencing in State Prisons* (Washington, D.C.: Bureau of Justice Statistics, 1999). Available at https://www.bjs.gov/index.cfm?ty=pbdetail&iid=820.

92   Jeffery T. Ulmer, Megan C. Kurlychek, and John H. Kramer, "Prosecutorial Discretion and the Imposition of Mandatory Minimum Sentences," *Journal of Research in Crime and Delinquency* 44 no. 4 (2007):427.

PART IV

From Penology to Corrections and Back

The History of Control and Punishment

FEATURES

Protesters in Portland, Oregon, during a nationwide day of action against prison slavery on the 45th anniversary of the Attica Uprising. Why are some individuals opposed to the way the United States incarcerates offenders?

n September 2016, inmates in prisons throughout the United States went on a labor strike to protest low or non-existent wages, abusive corrections officers, overcrowding, and poor health care.[1] Although prison officials denied that the strike was widespread, activists say it involved thousands of inmates in at least 21 states.[2] Inmates used contraband cellphones to coordinate the strikes and post their demands on social media.[3]

Inmate labor is as old as American prisons. The Thirteenth Amendment bans "involuntary servitude" but makes an exception for work done "as a punishment for crime."[4] Most inmates are paid little or nothing, and wages vary by state. In at least three states—Texas, Arkansas, and Georgia—inmates are not paid at all. Federal inmates earn about 12 to 40 cents an hour. Most prisons require inmates to work, and most inmate labor is devoted to maintaining the prison, such as landscaping, cleaning, laundry, and kitchen work.[5] Inmates may also work for private corporations sewing clothing, making furniture, or working in call-centers.[6] California uses about 4,000 inmates to fight wildfires.[7] Inmates say they do not have a choice whether to work or not and those who refuse to work can lose all privileges and are often replaced with inmates who are willing to work.[8]

The inmates' concerns and demands varied by prison, but most included requests for real-world wages for private-industry jobs, better mental-health care, educational programs, and for their working days count toward time off their sentences.[9] One anonymous organizer wrote, "Prisoners are not looking for a lazy life in prison. They are not against work in prison—as long as they receive credit for their labor and good conduct that counts towards a real parole-validation."[10]

THINK ABOUT IT > What are the arguments for and against compensating inmates for their work?

LEARNING OBJECTIVE 1

Compare and contrast the two prison systems that emerged in the United States during the first half of the 19th century.

LEARNING OBJECTIVE 2

Describe the three most well-known examples of the Irish System of reform.

LEARNING OBJECTIVE 3

Summarize the three ways work was deemed beneficial during the early 20th century.

Prisons in the United States

Prison reform efforts in the United States have been aimed at making the institution more effective, humane, and palatable to the public. The results, however, have been serious, if unintended, consequences that have brought their own problems. Recall the opening case of the inmate strike. Work has long been considered rehabilitative for inmates and cost-effective for prisons. However, along with inmate labor comes issues concerning wages, working conditions, and the rights of inmate workers. To understand how U.S. prisons developed into today's bureaucratic institutions, we must trace their history from colonial times to the present, with an eye toward how well-intended reforms have not worked out as planned.[11]

Control in the Colonies and Early United States: 1770–1860

The North American colonies faced many of the same social control issues as England, but some major differences between the two led to the unique development of American incarceration. Early penal institutions were under local control and mixed various types of offenders; the accused were held with the convicted, civil violators with criminal offenders, and so on.

The idea of incarceration as the sole punishment for convicts took time to develop. Initially, corporal punishment, especially the stocks or whipping, was used in conjunction with jail to discourage crime. The Pennsylvania Quakers suggested that incarceration and hard labor were preferable to corporal punishment. Pennsylvania's 1786 penal code allowed inmates to work on public projects while chained to cannonballs and dressed in brightly colored clothing. However, because many objected to this public spectacle, hard labor was moved behind the walls of the institution.

Perhaps the most influential early carceral institution in the United States was Philadelphia's Walnut Street Jail. Built in 1773, it demonstrated all the shortcomings of early jails.

> Little attempt was made to reform the criminals. Segregation and classification were hardly known. Rations were poor and irregularly given. Escapes, riots and scenes of debauchery were common. The inmates were . . . offered little employment. Idleness, drunkenness, [shackles], prostitution and gambling were [the] companions of the corrupt keepers. . . . In general, it housed a conglomerate mixture of practices which are strongly denounced by penologists today.[12]

Used as a military prison during the Revolutionary War, the Walnut Street Jail was converted around 1790 into the country's first penitentiary, in which the most hardened convicts were kept in single cells. At this time, the institution's administration was revamped, and a board of inspectors, instead of the sheriff, was given authority over the jail's affairs. Part of the jail's new direction was to ensure that the inmates had meaningful work and steady employment.[13] The innovations at the Walnut Street Jail, now a prison, set the tone for the more formal prisons that were built in the next century.[14] The first institution to resemble a modern penitentiary was Castle Island in Massachusetts' Boston Harbor. Established by the Massachusetts legislature in 1785, it housed only convicted offenders from the state's various jails.[15] From 1785 to 1798, about 280 prisoners served time on Castle Island, with at least 45 escaping.[16]

LEARNING OBJECTIVE 4

Outline the circumstances that led to the advocacy of rehabilitation as a desirable goal for the field of corrections, as well as its subsequent demise.

This engraving depicts the Walnut Street Jail in Philadelphia, Pennsylvania, circa 1800. What types of offenders were incarcerated in this jail?

Two prison systems emerged in the United States during the first half of the 19th century, which attracted the attention of prison reformers. Both of these systems, the Pennsylvania System and the Auburn (New York) System (the names are based on their initial locations), emphasized regimens of silence and penitence.

THE PENNSYLVANIA SYSTEM

separate-and-silent system—A method of penal control pioneered by Philadelphia's Eastern State Penitentiary in which inmates were kept from seeing or talking to one another. This method is comparable to solitary confinement in modern prisons.

In 1829, the state of Pennsylvania opened a prison on the site of a cherry orchard outside Philadelphia. For years, the Eastern State Penitentiary, called Cherry Hill by locals, was characterized by the **separate-and-silent system**, by which it was reasoned that inmates would reflect on their offenses and reform if they were kept from seeing or talking to one another. By using such extreme procedures as having inmates wear hoods when outside their cells, the Eastern State Penitentiary administration believed it was facilitating the inmates' self-reflection and reform. By keeping the inmates from interacting with each other, the state hoped the inmates would not contaminate each other with antisocial thoughts and behavior. The Pennsylvania System viewed too much labor as interfering with rehabilitative meditation, so inmates did craftwork in their cells. Kept in solitary confinement, many inmates developed severe mental problems because of the oppressive boredom and lack of human contact. The inmates developed clever means of communicating, such as tapping codes on the water pipes in the cells, but for the most part they were kept as separate as possible by the prison's limited resources.[17] However, as the prison became more crowded, double-celling (having two inmates share a cell) became the norm and isolation was impossible. The separate-and-silent system was costly and soon met its demise, not only because of economics, but also because critics thought keeping anyone in isolation for so long was inhumane.

This lithograph depicts the Eastern State Penitentiary in Pennsylvania, circa 1855. What problems did the separate-and-silent system of this penitentiary present?

THE AUBURN SYSTEM

The Auburn Prison, opened in 1817 in New York, at first tried the separate-and-silent system. By 1823 though, it became apparent that this system caused more problems than it solved and that the inmates' mental and physical health issues were more punishing than the administration thought reasonable. Therefore, inmates were locked in separate cells each night but were allowed to eat and work together during the day. They were forbidden to talk to each other, however. This **congregate-and-silent system**, which prohibited face-to-face contact, required inmates to march in lockstep and keep their eyes downcast.[18]

Considerable debate surrounded these two prison systems. On one hand, the Pennsylvania System's supporters touted it as superior because it was easier to control inmates, was more conducive to meditation and repentance, and avoided the cross-contamination inherent when inmates are together. In contrast, proponents of the Auburn model argued that their methods and techniques of incarceration were superior because they were less expensive, could provide better vocational training, and were less harmful to the inmates' mental health. Additionally, the Auburn model used a factory-oriented labor system as opposed to the craft-oriented labor system of the Eastern State Penitentiary. Although neither of these systems was fully copied in other jurisdictions, they did serve as models for other prisons. Reformers adopted aspects of the Pennsylvania and Auburn models and introduced modifications that addressed changing political, economic, and social conditions.[19]

congregate-and-silent system—A style of penal control pioneered by the Auburn System, in which inmates were allowed to eat and work together during the day but were forbidden to speak to each other and were locked alone in their cells at night.

Age of Reform: 1860–1900

At the time that the penitentiary was developed in the United States, the penal practices of other countries influenced U.S. corrections. European countries experimented with techniques designed not only to punish, but also to give inmates a better chance at successfully returning to free society upon completing their sentence. This new emphasis on social reintegration was called the "Irish System," which was tried in the post–Civil War United States, despite having been used for decades abroad. Here, we will focus on the three most well-known examples of the Irish System of reform: those developed by Alexander Maconochie, Sir Walter Crofton, and Zebulon Brockway.

Prisoners at the State Prison at Auburn.

Prisoners marching at the State Penitentiary at Auburn, New York. Why did this prison abandon the separate-and-silent system?

ALEXANDER MACONOCHIE

In 1840, Alexander Maconochie, a retired British naval officer, was placed in command of the Norfolk Island penal colony off the eastern coast of Australia. Here, he developed a system to make inmates trustworthy, honest, and useful to society. This system was based on two fundamental beliefs:

1. Brutality and cruelty debase not only the subject but also the society that deliberately uses or tolerates them for purposes of social control.

2. The treatment of a wrongdoer during his sentence of imprisonment should be designed to make him fit to be released into society again, purged of the tendencies that led him to his offense, and strengthened in his ability to withstand temptation again.[20]

indeterminate sentence (from Chapter 9)—A prison term that is determined by a parole board and does not state a specific period of time to be served or date of release.

marks-of-commendation system—An incarceration philosophy developed by Alexander Maconochie in which inmates earned the right to be released, as well as privileges, goods, and services.

Central to Maconochie's philosophy of incarceration was the **indeterminate sentence** (see Chapter 9), in which the offender would be released when the prison officials believed he was reformed. A **marks-of-commendation system** was instituted in which inmates earned the right to be released. Additionally, privileges, goods, and services could be purchased with marks given for good behavior. The marks system enabled inmates to progress through various stages of social control, the goal of which was to give inmates some control over the pains of incarceration.

Maconochie's rational and systematic implementation earned high praise from prison experts. However, the Norfolk Island system was short-lived. Maconochie returned to England in 1844 and with him went the more humane treatment of inmates on Norfolk Island.

SIR WALTER CROFTON

A decade later, in 1854, Maconochie's progressive ways of treating inmates inspired Sir Walter Crofton, who was appointed director of the Irish prison system. In addition to Maconochie's marks system and the progressive stages of social control, Crofton implemented the concept of a completely open institution in which the inmates could gain experience in trust and avoiding temptation. Crofton is best remembered for instituting an early-release system called "ticket-of-leave," in which inmates were given a conditional release and supervised by local police. Inmates who violated the conditions of their release were returned to prison.[21] (This idea will be more fully discussed in Chapter 12.)

ZEBULON BROCKWAY

The ideas developed by Maconochie and Crofton were instituted by reformer Zebulon Brockway at the reformatory in Elmira, New York, from 1876 to 1900. Brockway used the 500-bed facility to house young men between the ages of 16 and 30 who were first-time offenders. A three-grade program was used in which inmates entered at the second grade. An inmate was promoted to the first grade after six months of good behavior or demoted to the third grade if he failed to conform. Only those who were in the first grade were eligible for release (they were sentenced to an indeterminate term with only the minimum amount of time being fixed). An inmate needed a year of good marks before being eligible for parole. The Elmira Reformatory used volunteers, forerunners of parole officers, to keep track of the released inmates. The important distinction between this accommodation and the Irish ticket-of-leave system is that police officers did not supervise the parolees. The modern separation of law enforcement and correctional activities is an enduring feature of this early program.[22]

Prison reform had its failures as well as successes. Penal reform did not progress in an uninterrupted manner from brutality to humane treatment because even reformers such as Zebulon Brockway had some unattractive ideas. For example, corporal punishment was such a stable feature of the Elmira Reformatory that Brockway was nicknamed "Paddler Brockway." In addition, the integrity of the classification system was difficult to maintain. Designed for young first offenders, the reformatories often housed seasoned offenders, and issues of violence, revolts, rape, smuggling, and arson often arose.[23]

For those who presented significant discipline problems, a form of solitary confinement was used. Brockway called this the "rest cure," but it included being shackled and fed nothing more than bread and water for months at a time. Although such treatment eventually led to the demise of the reform movement, the idea of reform has become a recurring theme in corrections. Many of the ideals of the age of reform are at the foundation of modern prison systems. The repeated imperfect implementation of these reforms speaks not to the inadequacy of the reforms but more to the economic, social, and political contexts that invariably frustrate the ideals of prison reformers.

A New Emphasis on Prison Labor: 1900–1930

The idea that work is healthy for both the inmate and society is as old as the prison. Even the Pennsylvania System, which viewed too much labor as interfering with rehabilitative meditation, had inmates do craftwork in their cells. Of particular interest is the degree to which work was viewed as a good thing in itself and when it was viewed as a means to other ends. Work was deemed beneficial in at least three ways:

1. It is a good way to keep inmates occupied. By doing work (sometimes backbreaking work), the inmates have neither the time nor the energy to cause trouble.

2. It has rehabilitative value. Because most prisoners eventually return to society, they benefit from work. They practice good work habits and sometimes learn useful skills.

3. It offsets the cost of incarceration. Inmate labor has been used to construct and maintain prisons, feed inmates, and at times make products that can be sold to other government agencies or even outside society.

The type of prison labor system that authorities choose is always subject to political and technological conditions. Decades ago, in southern states where counties rather than state governments controlled the prisons, the **convict lease system** was used extensively. Partly as a replacement for slave labor, this system allowed major landowners to employ inmates to do backbreaking work at wages that free people would not accept, such as harvesting cotton in Georgia and distilling turpentine in Florida.

convict lease system—A system in the late 19th and early 20th centuries in which companies and individuals could purchase the labor of prison inmates from state and county governments.

By the early 20th century, more than half of the states had adopted state-use laws regarding inmate labor. These laws prevented inmate-made wares from being sold on the open market and only allowed their use by the originating prison or by other state agencies. In 1934, President Franklin D. Roosevelt authorized the establishment of Federal Prison Industries, Inc. (FPI). The FPI system also prohibited the sale of inmate-made wares to the public, restricting sales to the federal government. By 1940, the Ashurst-Sumners Act and its amendment completely prohibited the interstate shipment of nearly all inmate-made wares. In 1977, FPI changed its name to UNICOR.[24] Today, UNICOR employs about 11,000

In 1910, this North Carolina convict chain gang lived in wagons, which were moved to different places so the convicts could work as needed. What types of labor did chain gangs provide for the government?

federal inmates.[25] The 1979 Private Sector Prison Industry Enhancement Certification Program eased some of the barriers to interstate shipment of inmate-made wares, allowing certified states to sell items on the open market under certain conditions. These conditions included paying inmates wages comparable with similar jobs outside the prison, collecting funds for a victim assistance program, and only using voluntary inmate labor.[26]

Today all state-level prison work for the private sector is regulated under the Prison Industries Enhancement Certification Program, which employs about 5,500 inmate workers.[27] Although hundreds of thousands of inmates work part- and full-time jobs, most do work to keep the prison running.[28] In fact, in many contemporary prisons, the only inmates doing any type of productive labor are those used to maintain the basic needs of the institution.[29] According to activist James Kilgore, who served six and a half years in prison, "[P]urposelessness and excruciating boredom, not overwork, are the dominant features of most prison yards."[30]

Age of Rehabilitation: 1930–1970

Rehabilitating inmates has always been a criminal justice system goal, but not until the 1930s did U.S. prisons acknowledge that rehabilitation was a primary goal. As far back as Maconochie, some advocated the prison's role in reforming individuals, but the state's responsibility for changing inmates' behavior was not widely recognized. Around 1930, several circumstances helped professionalize the field of corrections and allowed progressive reformers to advocate rehabilitation as a desirable and possible goal.[31]

A primary reason why rehabilitation became important at this time was the change in how science regarded illness. This change, in turn, affected how criminologists and correctional practitioners considered criminality. The germ theory of medicine that absolved the sick person of responsibility for contracting an illness spread to corrections. Crime was no longer viewed as simply a choice made by the offender. The idea that outside influences contribute to criminality led theorists and correctional administrators to speculate on how antisocial behavior is transmitted among individuals. A medical metaphor developed that viewed offenders as "sick," and rehabilitation efforts were dedicated to finding the causes of crime in the biological, psychological, and sociological deficiencies of the individual.[32] Once the cause was diagnosed, it was a simple matter to prescribe a "cure" of drug or alcohol treatment, family or individual counseling, more education, or anger-management classes. The medical model likened crime to disease and postulated that normal (law-abiding) behavior is within reach of all offenders and that the correctional practitioner can find the optimal treatment.

At the forefront of the effort to prioritize rehabilitation was the establishment of the **Federal Bureau of Prisons** in 1930. This agency eliminated political patronage in filling job vacancies, developed better trained and more professional staff, and greatly improved the conditions of confinement by way of new designs.[33] Prisons were constructed with the goals of facilitating the classification and treatment of offenders. Bureau of Prisons officials were committed to treating offenders as individuals and keeping them occupied in productive activities such as work and education.

Another factor that encouraged rehabilitation was the 1931 Wickersham Commission report, which prescribed a range of criminal justice reforms, including suggestions that rehabilitation be attempted in earnest. The commission documented the failures of prison labor systems and the idleness of inmates in most prisons in its quest to solve the penitentiary's systemic problems. The Wickersham Commission did not present new information, but the fact that it was a governmental fact-finding and policy-suggesting body gave its recommendations a legitimacy that previous reformers lacked.[34]

Although the theoretical foundations of treating offenders were further refined during the mid-20th century, several factors intervened to prevent rehabilitative practices from fully taking hold in prison systems. One of the leading causes was lack of resources. Keeping inmates confined and preventing them from hurting each other, as well as prison staff, soaked up most of the time, money, and creative energies of prison officials and staff. Treatment programs were considered luxuries in prison systems struggling to maintain minimal custody standards in states that would rather spend their limited tax dollars on education, infrastructure, and health care. In most prisons, the percentage of inmates who received any significant treatment was low. One observer called rehabilitation efforts during this time "token treatment," designed more for public relations purposes than for producing any real change in the attitudes and behaviors of inmates.[35]

Another reason why the rehabilitation era never fully developed effective methods for changing the lives of inmates and reducing crime was the lack of consensus regarding whether it was or could ever be effective. In a major study of treatment programs published in 1974, the unfortunate consensus was that "nothing works."[36] Even though this conclusion is more complex than initially reported, the correctional community jettisoned rehabilitation as an orienting perspective. Nevertheless, some claim that certain rehabilitative programs work for certain offenders and that although one course of treatment does not work for everyone, rehabilitation is still a worthy and attainable goal.[37]

The final reason why rehabilitation lost favor was the belief of some scholars that the medical model was a flawed metaphor for corrections. To view offenders as "sick" and in need of a "cure" was deemed problematic by many who favored a view that placed responsibility for antisocial behavior squarely on the shoulders of those who chose to violate the law. These scholars believed it was more accurate to think of felons as lazy, unmotivated, poorly socialized, or exploitive. Opponents

Federal Bureau of Prisons—Established within the Department of Justice in 1930, this federal agency manages and regulates all federal penal and correctional institutions.

of the medical model asserted that society did not need to "cure" inmates as much as inmates needed to learn that their unlawful behavior would have negative consequences. Therefore, they called for deterrence rather than rehabilitation.[38]

Retributive Era: 1970s to the Present

The movement away from the rehabilitation philosophy did not occur in a social vacuum. The events of the 1960s brought a number of changes in how our social institutions operated. A backlash to political protests, reported widespread drug use, relaxation of sexual mores, and general disrespect for authority and tradition manifested in ways that affected the prison.[39] One example of how events outside the prison found their way inside was the politicization of inmates. As minorities, youth, and women outside prison walls challenged how society treated them, inmates challenged the conditions of their confinement inside the prison.[40] For example, *Hope v. Pelzer* (2002) set guidelines for what constitutes cruel and unusual punishment in prison and the circumstances under which prison officials are liable for the mistreatment of prisoners. In 1995, Alabama inmate Larry Hope was handcuffed to a post for seven hours after fighting with a guard at a work site. Hope filed suit against three corrections officers, but the magistrate judge ruled that the guards were immune to the suit because they were unaware of any constitutional violations of their actions. The U.S. Supreme Court affirmed a lower court's judgment that Hope's treatment violated the Eighth Amendment and also held that the guards were liable for their actions and could be sued.

The courts traditionally had a "hands-off" policy concerning prison operations, but in the 1960s they started to specify exactly which constitutional rights, such as the expectation of privacy, inmates forfeited in prison.[41] This led to major changes in areas such as food and disciplinary procedures. For example, the prison must try to accommodate dietary requirements based on inmates' religious practices. As inmates organized to challenge the conditions of their confinement, a new, racial dimension appeared in the inmates' identity. The Black Panther Party and the Black Muslims agitated to have prisons recognize them as legitimate political organizations within the prison that spoke for minority inmates. The tensions caused by this politicization of inmates made rehabilitation efforts difficult to accomplish. When Black Muslim inmates defined themselves as political prisoners, they became unwilling to adopt the "sick" label of the medical model of rehabilitation and instead contended that society's institutions, particularly prisons, treated individuals unfairly. For example, in Stateville Prison in Illinois, troublesome Muslim inmates were not allowed to work in prison jobs, denied access to prison recreational and educational activities, and often placed in segregation.

With inmates rebelling against the conditions of their confinement, the courts questioning how prison officials did their jobs, and society losing faith in the promises of rehabilitation, a change in the basic philosophy of incarceration was inevitable. Retribution replaced rehabilitation as the primary goal of the prison. This had significant and widespread implications for how inmates were sentenced and treated in prison.[42] Some of the changes were as follows:

> › Determinate sentences. With rehabilitation no longer the prison's main goal, officials were no longer willing to certify when an inmate was safe to return to society. Therefore, indeterminate sentences were no longer desirable. **Determinate sentences**, or fixed terms of incarceration, were implemented in their place based not on inmates' needs but on the seriousness of their offenses and criminal record. In this way, inmates would be treated for what they did, rather than for some perceived deficiency in psychological makeup or social conditioning.[43]

determinate sentence (from Chapter 9)—A prison term that is determined by law and states a specific period of time to be served.

Pictured here is John Clark, leader of the Black Panthers, in 1970. Why did members of the Black Panther Party demand to be considered political prisoners?

> Voluntary treatment. With rehabilitation no longer a primary goal of incarceration, treatment services were offered on a voluntary basis because prison administrators believed that treatment was more effective for those who sought it without coercion or conditions. During the rehabilitation era, when inmates participated in treatment to impress a parole board, it was assumed they were "playing the parole game"; thus, their motivations were suspect.[44] Inmates who entered programs voluntarily were considered more likely to be sincere in their desires to learn new skills, acquire an education, or seek drug treatment. Additionally, there were presumably fewer "jailhouse conversions" when attendance at religious services (previously thought to be indicative of rehabilitative progress) was not considered at parole hearings.

> Abolition of parole. A by-product of a system that abandoned indeterminate sentencing and compulsory treatment has been the attempt to eliminate parole as an early-release mechanism. Although this has not been completely accomplished, many critics want inmates to spend their entire sentence behind bars and view parole as "soft on crime." Coupled with a surge in prison crowding, the elimination of parole is problematic, but several states and the federal government have eliminated discretionary parole.[45] Parole's primary function, like that of the prison, has shifted from treatment to supervision.[46]

The era of retribution may be about to change, however, if not end completely. Correctional budgets cannot afford to allow state and local governments to use mass incarceration as a correctional policy. It might be different if retributive corrections effectively deterred crime, rehabilitated offenders, and gave communities the confidence that justice is served in a fair and impartial manner. This is not the case, however. One study concluded that, at most, only 12 percent of the reduction in U.S. property crime rates since the 1990s could be attributed to higher incarceration rates.[47] There is no more crime in states with smaller prison populations than in states with larger prison populations.[48] Other studies have similarly concluded that the high incarceration rates of the past few decades did not cause the decrease in crime in the United States. Rather, lower crime rates have had more to do with demographic changes, such as an aging population, income changes, and decreased alcohol consumption.[49]

Many criminal justice system professionals, scholars, and observers agree that a new direction for U.S. corrections is needed. Several reforms have been advocated:

1. Sentences should be proportional to the severity of the crime. Although this idea goes back to the classical school of criminology, the United States has gotten away from proportionality with its use of mandatory sentences, especially "**three-strikes**" sentencing.

2. Incarceration should be used sparingly, utilizing a minimum level of punishment. This value addresses not only mandatory prison sentences, but also the practice of using incarceration for minor offenses that can be addressed in other ways.

3. Penal sanctions should not be so lasting as to permanently restrict a person's citizenship. Once an inmate has "paid his or her dues to society," he or she should be allowed to reintegrate into the community. Former inmates should be allowed to vote, not automatically be denied employment because of their status as former felons, or in other ways be stigmatized and ostracized.

4. The pains of imprisonment should not disproportionately burden any particular group of people, and prisons should equally distribute resources and opportunities to all groups. This would entail examining the processes that have resulted in the mass incarceration of peoples of color, as well as the economically disadvantaged.[50]

Cultivating retribution as the main value of the correctional system is counterproductive, but finding the appropriate balance between addressing crime and protecting the community is difficult. However, despite complications, some legislators are trying to do that. For example, in 2015, Kentucky's governor issued an executive order granting the right to vote to certain non-violent felons who had completed their sentences. Nearly six million former felons are prohibited by their states from voting.[51] Currently, 12 states restrict former convicted felons who have fully completed their sentences from voting; four states restrict prison inmates and parolees; 18 states restrict inmates, parolees, and probationers; and 14 states restrict voting only for prison inmates. Felons in Maine and Vermont have always had the right to vote at any point in the system and may do so as inmates from prison.[52] As the push for corrections reform continues, federal and state legislators will likely continue crafting laws that allow judges more leeway in sentencing, replace incarceration with alternative penalties and rehabilitation, and address penal conventions such as solitary confinement.[53]

This brief history of U.S. corrections highlights several themes. One is that many correctional practices that seem new and innovative are actually quite old. The ideas of work as useful in reforming individuals, rehabilitation geared to inmates' needs, and the value of keeping inmates busy have all been used in various eras of corrections. What has changed are not the ideas themselves but rather the resources and political will to support those ideas. This raises the question of whether rehabilitation has ever been given an honest chance. No jurisdiction has ever paid more than lip service to the idea of providing the counselors, modern

three strikes—In reference to criminal justice, a term that describes state laws that require an offender's third felony to be punishable by a severe sentence, including life imprisonment.

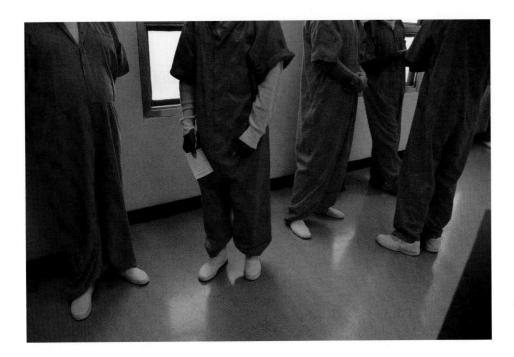

Inmates wait to cast their votes at the District of Columbia jail as part of early voting in the city's election in 2014. Washington, D.C., is one of only three jurisdictions in the United States that allows inmates to vote. Should incarcerated individuals be allowed to vote?

conditions, and aftercare necessary to effectively change the behavior of offenders who have learned to survive by way of a deviant lifestyle. In many ways, it is unrealistic to expect that participating in a few weeks' worth of rehabilitation activities will help an individual overcome a lifetime of poverty, discrimination, lack of education, and drug addiction. Yet, all too often, this is all society can afford in an attempt to change an inmate.

PAUSE AND REVIEW

1. What are the differences and similarities between the two prison systems that emerged in the United States during the first half of the 19th century?
2. What are the three most well-known examples of the Irish System?
3. In what ways was work deemed beneficial between 1900 and 1930?
4. What influences around 1930 helped professionalize the field of corrections?
5. What circumstances led to the rehabilitation era of corrections?
6. Why did the rehabilitative era of corrections evolve into the retributive era?

Capital Punishment

This overview of social control requires that we consider the use of **capital punishment**, the sentence of death for a criminal offense, as a method for compelling citizens to obey the law. This extreme form of control is controversial, with individuals and groups voicing impassioned opinions on both sides of the issue. Although whether the death penalty is cruel is subject to debate, from a historical point of view it is not unusual. Execution is older than incarceration. Although we cannot do justice to all the issues and ramifications of the death penalty, we will briefly consider some of the basic arguments. Easy answers to the issues surrounding the death penalty are elusive. Therefore, the goal of this section is to simply frame the issues.

LEARNING OBJECTIVE 5

Argue in support of capital punishment.

LEARNING OBJECTIVE 6

Argue against capital punishment.

capital punishment—The sentence of death for a criminal offense.

The execution chamber at the Utah State Prison. Utah allows for execution by firing squad if the drugs for lethal injection are not available. Bullet holes are visible in the wood panel behind the chair. Is the firing squad a humane method for executing offenders?

At the end of 2015, 33 states and the federal government held 2,881 inmates on death row, the 15th consecutive year that the number of condemned inmates has decreased. California, Florida, Texas, and Alabama held more than half of all inmates on death row, and 59 inmates were on federal death row. All executions in 2016 were by lethal injection, which is also the method used by the U.S. government.[54] See Figure 10.1 for the number of executions performed annually in the United States since 1930.

Capital Punishment in Historical Perspective

The concept of killing those who offend societal norms is probably as old as humanity. For example, the book of Leviticus in the Bible states, "And he that killeth

FIGURE 10.1   Executions in the United States, 1930–2016 In 1972, the U.S. Supreme Court invalidated capital punishment statutes in several states via *Furman v. Georgia* (1972), bringing about a moratorium on executions. Executions resumed in 1977 when the Court found in *Gregg v. Georgia* (1976), and other cases, that revisions to statutes in several states had addressed the issues of unconstitutionality. However, executions never resumed their peak numbers of the 1930s. What are some possible reasons why there are fewer executions now than in the 1930s?

Source: Tracy L. Snell, Capital Punishment, 2013—Statistical Tables (Washington, D.C.: U.S. Department of Justice Office of Justice Programs Bureau of Justice Statistics, 2014), 14. Available at http://www.bjs.gov/index.cfm?ty=pbdetail&iid=5156.

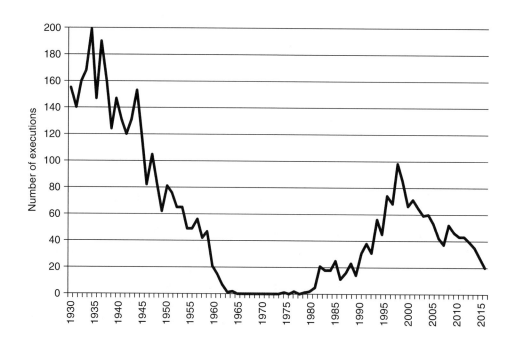

any man shall surely be put to death."[55] The reasons for such a stringent punishment include retribution, revenge, and general and specific deterrence. Killing a person can be easier than expending resources on rehabilitation and is a way for the state to show the extent of its power, organization, and control.

Before the 20th century, two major features of the death sentence were spectacle and pain. Spectacle proved to the aggrieved party that justice had been done and assuaged the desire for revenge. It proved that the offender was dead, achieved specific deterrence, and provided a visual aid for general deterrence. Spectacle displayed the blunt power of the state and its willingness to see justice done. It also entertained the masses. In many cases, the last thing the condemned would see would be a jeering crowd.[56] The other feature, pain, was inextricably linked to punishment. The offender was required to hurt while dying and hurt publicly. This satisfied the need for revenge and the desire that the offender be humiliated. Some means of inflicting pain were slow. Others, if the condemned was lucky, were quick.

Over the centuries, authorities have used various methods to kill the condemned. Often the executions were part of a public spectacle designed to demonstrate the consequences of violating the law. Burning, crucifixion, drowning, boiling, flaying, beheading, being impaled, being thrown to the lions, and an infinite variety of other creative and grotesque techniques were used to kill people.[57] The aspect of torture is difficult to appreciate today when society takes great pains to give the appearance that executions are physically painless.

Historically, the favored methods of execution in Europe were hanging, beheading, and, one of the most fearsome executions, burning. Many condemned were burned alive; more fortunate ones were burned after being hanged. Burning was considered a punishment that punished beyond death because it destroyed the body, which would not receive a proper burial. Only much later in European history did authorities seek to reduce the condemned's suffering. Before the 19th century, death by hanging depended on the "short drop." A rope was tied to the offender's neck, and he or she was either dropped or hoisted a short distance to die by slow strangulation. In the 19th century, British hangmen discovered that a "long drop," letting the offender fall a long distance from a platform, would break the neck and bring a quicker, more humane death.[58]

In 1792, France popularized the guillotine during the French Revolution. This mechanical device for lopping heads was considered humane, being quicker than hanging and less mistake-prone than an executioner wielding an ax or sword. However, concerns grew that a severed head might live and consciousness continue for several seconds or even minutes. Numerous experiments were done on severed heads, with reports of faces blushing when slapped or the victim's eyes responding to the sound of his or her name.[59] France continued to execute criminal offenders by guillotine until 1977, and finally abolished the death penalty in 1981.

The Search for Humane Execution

The organized call for humane execution in the United States began in the 19th century. Although "long-drop" hangings were supposed to be less painful, they were not always carried out properly, resulting in slow, painful deaths. In response, gallows were redesigned. One contraption called the "upright jerker" used weights and pulleys to draw the victim up, snapping the neck. The success of this method depended on the operator's skill and the condition of the machine and it still sometimes caused lingering asphyxiation rather than a quick death.[60]

The aspect of torture is difficult to appreciate today when society takes great pains to give the appearance that executions are physically painless. Methods of

The execution of Louis XVI in Paris, January 21, 1793. Is the guillotine a humane method of execution?

execution have changed to include more than the reduction of torture. The visibility of capital punishment has developed to the point that rather than having public ceremonies in which citizens can witness an execution, it is now done behind prison walls with only a few corrections staff, families of the condemned and victim(s), and a few members of the press present.[61] The relationship between capital punishment and the United States has also run hot and cold. In 1972, *Furman* v. *Georgia* set forth a moratorium on the death penalty, but *Gregg* v. *Georgia* (1976) reinstated it (see Case in Point 10.1 and 10.2). Below, we'll examine some of the varying methods of execution that are utilized in the United States today.

ELECTROCUTION

Thomas Edison insisted in 1887 that the best method of electrical execution was via alternating current, the preferred current of his rival, George Westinghouse. Despite Westinghouse's protests, the first electrical execution was performed with his equipment on William Kemmler at New York's Auburn Prison in 1890. Unfortunately, this execution was worse than hanging as electrocution science was poorly understood. Kemmler survived the first 17-second jolt, so the executioners let the second burst go for more than a minute. Blood seeped through the broken capillaries on Kemmler's face as his flesh burned, horrifying witnesses and officials.[62]

Officials continued to experiment until they hit on a satisfactory combination of electricity and time. Less than a year after Kemmler's execution, four inmates were executed in one day at Sing Sing Prison. By 1937, electrocution was the preferred method of execution by the federal government and many states.

GAS

In 1921, the Nevada legislature passed a bill allowing execution by gas. Advocates of gas specified that inmates should be asleep when the sentence was carried out, never knowing the exact date and time of their executions. This proved impractical

CASE IN POINT 10.1

Furman v. Georgia (1972)

THE POINT

The administration of the death penalty constituted cruel and unusual punishment, not the death penalty itself.

THE CASE

William Furman, a black man, shot and killed a homeowner through a closed door while trying to enter the house at night. Furman, 26, pleaded insanity and was committed to the Georgia Central State Hospital for a psychiatric examination. The staff who examined Furman concluded unanimously that Furman was mentally deficient with "psychotic episodes associated with Convulsive Disorder." They also said that although Furman was not currently psychotic, he also was not capable of helping his attorneys prepare his defense and needed further psychiatric treatment.

Later, the hospital superintendent concluded much the same, except he stated that Furman did indeed know right from wrong and was able to cooperate with his attorneys. Evidence that he was mentally unsound was presented at the trial, but Furman was convicted and sentenced to death. Furman appealed the conviction on the grounds that his Fourteenth Amendment rights were being violated. The Supreme Court concurred, saying that administration of the death penalty in Georgia was racially discriminatory and violated the Eighth and Fourteenth Amendments.

THINK ABOUT IT

1. How did Georgia's administration of the death penalty violate the Eighth and Fourteenth amendments?

CASE IN POINT 10.2

Gregg v. Georgia (1976)

THE POINT

The Supreme Court effectively reinstated the death penalty, finding that it did not constitute cruel and unusual punishment as long as its implementation was fair.

THE CASE

Troy Gregg was convicted of killing and robbing two men and sentenced to death. Four years earlier in *Furman v. Georgia*, the Supreme Court found the process by which the death penalty was imposed to be cruel and unusual. After *Furman v. Georgia*, the state implemented bifurcated trials, in which guilt or innocence is determined in the first stage, and the penalty is determined in the second. During the penalty phase, the jury is required to consider both mitigating and aggravating circumstances, and if aggravating circumstances are overriding, then the death penalty is to be imposed. The law also prescribed an automatic appeal. Upon appeal, the Supreme Court found all procedures to be correctly followed and that all were constitutional and violated neither the Eighth nor the Fourteenth Amendment. In this case, the Court affirmed that the death penalty itself was not cruel and unusual, as long as its implementation was judged to be fair. Therefore, Gregg's death sentence was upheld.

THINK ABOUT IT

1. Why was Gregg's death sentence upheld in this case?

for two major reasons: executions required witnesses, and the inmate would have to live in a special gas-ready cell for several days, thus spoiling the surprise. Officials eventually settled on something resembling the modern gas chamber: a chair in a room with a window for spectators. In 1924, Chinese immigrant Gee Jon became the first inmate to die by gas. Jon's execution went smoothly, and at least 11 states had gas chambers by 1955.

LETHAL INJECTION

As of 2008, lethal injection has been the preferred method of execution in almost all states that have a death penalty, plus the military and federal government. A few states (see Table 10.1) have alternatives to lethal injection, which either may be chosen by inmates or used if lethal injection is ever ruled unconstitutional or the injection drugs become unavailable. Although the first lethal injection execution was performed by the state of Texas in 1982, the first lethal injection law was passed in Oklahoma in 1977. At the time, the state's electric chair needed expensive repairs, and building a gas chamber was even more costly, so state Representative Bill Wiseman, with the help of state medical examiner, Dr. Jay Chapman, began to develop methods to administer lethal drugs intravenously. Wiseman and Chapman worked out a two-drug formula and process for lethal injection involving, according to Chapman, a "an ultra-short-acting barbiturate in combination with a chemical paralytic." Chapman said later that he did not research drug combinations, only that he knew what was needed from having been under anesthesia

TABLE 10.1   States with Alternative Methods of Execution

STATE(S)	METHOD(S) OF EXECUTION
Alabama, South Carolina, and Virginia	Inmates can request electrocution
Arizona	Inmates sentenced before November 15, 1992, may choose gas
Arkansas	Inmates who committed their offense before July 4, 1983, may choose electrocution
Florida	Choice of injection or electrocution
Kentucky	Choice of injection or electrocution for inmates convicted before March 31, 1998
Missouri	Injection or gas
New Hampshire	Hanging is used if injection is problematic
Oklahoma	Electrocution is used if injection becomes unconstitutional; firing squad is used if both injection and electrocution become unconstitutional
Tennessee	Choice of injection or electrocution for inmates who committed their offense before December 31, 1998; electrocution is used if injection is not possible
Washington	Choice of injection or hanging
Wyoming	Gas is used if injection is not possible
Utah	Firing squad is used if injection is not possible; condemned inmates who chose firing squad before May 3, 2004, may still be entitled to that method

Source: Tracy L. Snell, Capital Punishment, 2013—Statistical Tables, Table 2 (Washington, D.C.: U.S. Department of Justice Office of Justice Programs Bureau of Justice Statistics), 7. Available at https://www.bjs.gov/index.cfm?ty=pbdetail&iid=5156.

himself. Chapman said that he thought lethal injection should involve two drugs, both in individual doses potent enough to kill a human being, "to make sure if one didn't kill . . . the other would." Chapman later added potassium chloride to the cocktail to increase its lethality, warning that improper administration of lethal injections may cause extreme pain in recipients.[63]

Until 2009, the three drugs most used in lethal injection were sodium thiopental as a sedative, pancuronium bromide as a paralytic, and potassium chloride to stop the heart. Experts say that just one of these drugs can kill a human being, but that in any particular execution it is unknown which drug actually causes death. In recent years, the supply of some of these drugs has dwindled owing to a European Union ban on the export of pentobarbital and sodium thiopental, and the halt in the production of sodium thiopental by its only U.S. manufacturer, Hospira Pharmaceuticals.[64] States have been forced to either find new drugs, use two or only one of the drugs instead of all three, or adopt different methods of execution.[65] In 2015, when Arizona attempted to illegally import sodium thiopental, federal agents intercepted the shipment at the Phoenix airport. At least three other states, Nebraska, Ohio, and Texas, have also attempted to import sodium thiopental and other similar drugs. In 2015, Arkansas successfully procured lethal-injection drugs, but refused to reveal the source.[66] In April 2017, Arkansas executed four inmates in eight days because one of the execution drugs was about to expire. The state had planned at least four more executions, but these were blocked by court orders.[67]

Some states have tried to use the sedative midazolam instead of sodium thiopental, but the drug has been criticized for causing botched executions that violate the Eighth Amendment prohibition on cruel and unusual punishment. In June 2015, the U.S. Supreme Court ruled in *Glossip v. Gross* that midazolam did not result in botched executions. According to the Court, the Oklahoma death row inmates who brought the case failed to identify a "known and available alternative method of execution" that would carry a lesser risk of pain, a requirement under the Court's previous ruling upholding lethal injection.[68]

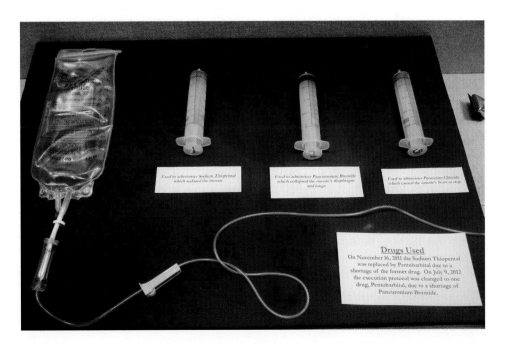

This exhibit at the Texas Prison Museum shows the three-chemical mixture used by Texas prison officials for lethal injections from 1982 until 2012, when it was replaced by a single drug. Is lethal injection a more humane method of execution than previous methods?

Arguments Supporting Capital Punishment

The deterrence argument is at the foundation of support for capital punishment. Two varieties of deterrence are used to justify the death penalty. Although considerable debate surrounds one of them, the other is obvious. **Specific deterrence** says that if a condemned individual is put to death, then he (most of those executed have been men) will never break the law again. There is no arguing with this logic. However, in practice, only a small percentage of those who commit murder are ever executed. As a policy, then, specific deterrence is of limited value. On the other hand, **general deterrence** says that if murderers are executed, the rest of us will see the ramifications of this behavior and will refrain from murder because we fear the consequences.

Although it seems logical to embrace the deterrence argument when considering most offenses and punishments, there is considerable debate as to whether it is useful when applied to murder and capital punishment.[69] Opponents of capital punishment say the general deterrence argument is questionable for several reasons.

> › For deterrence to be effective, we each must weigh the risks of getting caught and punished against the benefits of successfully committing the offense. Few circumstances exist in which most citizens would risk their lives, fortunes, and reputations for the possible benefits of an offense. In short, general deterrence works well on those who have something to lose but may not be as effective for those who have little invested in the status quo. The idea that drug dealers, professional assassins, gang members, and jealous spouses rationally calculate the prospects of the death penalty is not assured.

> › According to those who oppose the death penalty, the prospect of life in prison without parole is likely to deter as effectively as capital punishment.[70]

> › Many murders are crimes of passion in which deterrence likely does not enter into the offender's motivation. Those in a blind rage may not consider the death penalty or may even reason that they are so incensed that only by exposing themselves to the ultimate punishment can they adequately express their outrage.[71]

> › Deterrence is difficult to validate empirically because it is difficult to measure something that does not happen. Given the multiple variables that go into someone's decision to kill another person, it is extremely difficult to isolate the deterrent effect of death penalty laws.[72]

The deterrence argument is impossible to prove given our current laws. According to deterrence theory, we must do more than simply raise the severity of the punishment. Swiftness and certainty of punishment are also factors that offenders supposedly take into account when contemplating their offenses. In the case of the death penalty, neither swiftness nor certainty is guaranteed. Many executions occur 10 or more years after the offense (see Figure 10.2). Given the restrictive wording of statutes, plea bargaining, and the reluctance of some judges or juries to impose the death sentence, under present conditions, deterrence theory has not had a fair opportunity to demonstrate its potential. To fully assess the effect of deterrence, we would need to see some fundamental changes in the criminal justice system. By making capital punishment mandatory for some offenses, limiting the number of appeals and time allowed for appeals, and thereby executing a larger number of offenders in a swift and certain manner, capital punishment laws would be perceived as having some teeth and could possibly be a deterrent.

specific deterrence— A method of control in which an offender is prevented from committing more crimes by either imprisonment or death.

general deterrence— A method of control in which the punishment of a single offender sets an example for the rest of society.

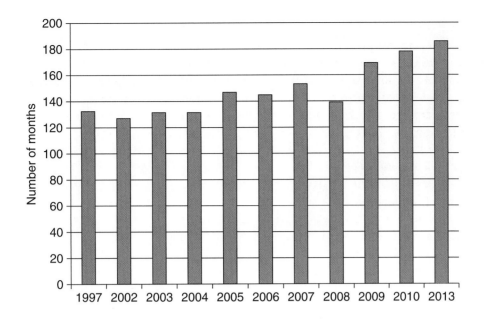

FIGURE 10.2 Average Elapsed Time from Sentence to Execution (in months) What are some possible reasons why the number of months between sentence and execution is increasing?

Source: Tracy L. Snell, Capital Punishment, 2013, Table 10 (Washington, D.C.: Bureau of Justice Statistics, 2014), 14. Capital Punishment, 2010—Statistical Tables. Available at bjs.ojp.usdoj. gov/content/pub/pdf/cp10st.pdf.

Supporters of the death penalty point to the **just deserts** argument as a justification for this form of punishment. This argument asserts that some people commit acts so heinous that only by killing them can a society fully express its values. In a sense, this argument maintains that some people deserve to be executed because of their antisocial behavior. This is a **retribution model** that embraces the "eye-for-an-eye" concept that many believe is the basis of justice handed down throughout history and that is deeply ingrained in some religious and philosophical teachings. According to this perspective, not executing killers in some way cheapens the victim's life. This outlook may speak to individuals who might take the law into their own hands if the government did not punish wrongdoers appropriately. The desire for revenge is a strong motivator for many, and the prospect of vigilante justice is always a concern. If the government fails to uphold the law and deal with offenders, some individuals will act as their own judge, jury, and executioner. For many, justice means that serious offenders "get what they deserve."

just deserts—A philosophy that states that an offender who commits a heinous crime deserves death.

retribution model—A style of control in which offenders are punished as severely as possible for a crime and in which rehabilitation is not attempted.

Arguments against Capital Punishment

Those who oppose the death penalty do so for many reasons.[73] Some people take to heart religious or philosophical proscriptions on murder, such as the Buddhist Eightfold Path, which encourages "right behavior," by which the follower should not engage in activities that harm others, including taking life.[74] In another example, the Sixth Commandment found in the Old Testament of the Bible states, "Thou shall not murder." Other capital punishment opponents point to the evidence on deterrence and conclude that capital punishment does not make society safer. Still others are concerned with the way in which some offenders are selected for capital punishment, while others escape it. They point to social class, race, sex, and gender as factors that determine whether the death penalty is applied in a given case.[75] These are but a few of the concerns of those who oppose capital punishment. It is useful to explore some of these issues in more detail because they are inherently complicated and significantly important to our understanding of the criminal justice system.

In April 2017, Arkansas had scheduled the execution of eight inmates in less than two weeks because lethal injection drugs were to expire at the end of the month. Four of the executions were blocked by court orders. Protesters gathered outside the state Capitol building in Little Rock to voice their opposition to the executions. What are the justifications for abolishing capital punishment?

An old axiom concerning capital punishment asks, "Why do we kill people to show people that killing people is wrong?" This statement is revealing on a number of levels, not the least of which is the perceived irony of the state modeling the very behavior it is attempting to discourage. Despite the fact that the death penalty has been modified over the centuries to inflict as little pain as possible, the process of execution is now so formalized, routinized, and bureaucratic that it has become a surreal procedure that some opponents consider a violation of the Eighth Amendment's proscription against cruel and unusual punishment. Other critics say the process dehumanizes both the offender and the executioner.[76] Death penalty supporters, however, contend that the death penalty should brutalize the offender just as the offender brutalized the victim. To be an effective deterrent, capital punishment should be unpleasant, according to its proponents. In fact, there are those who would return capital punishment to the days when it was a public spectacle in order to enhance what they believe to be its deterrent effects.

Many people who are opposed to capital punishment are not necessarily opposed to the idea of the death penalty, but rather to the state's seeming inability to impose it in a fair and impartial manner because of a perceived unfairness in the way certain categories of people are selected for that punishment (see Figure 10.3). When minorities and indigent people are executed at greater rates than whites and wealthy people, who escape with incarceration or less, the procedure's fairness is called into question. If everyone is equal under the law, then there should not be patterns of discrimination in how the death penalty is administered.[77]

Unfortunately, the historical evidence is unambiguous. Blacks and Hispanics are executed in greater proportions than whites: of the 2,979 condemned inmates at the end of 2013, 56 percent were white, 42 percent were black, and 13 percent were Hispanic. That means nearly half of inmates on death row were black, which is an astonishing number considering that black people compose only about

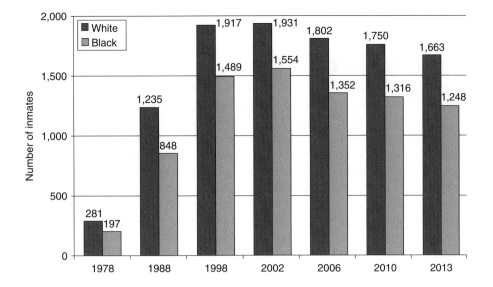

FIGURE 10.3 Inmates Under Sentence of Death by Race Which year saw the lowest percentage differential between black and white inmates on death row?

Sources: Tracy L. Snell, Capital Punishment, 2013—Statistical Tables, Table 4, (Washington, D.C.: U.S. Department of Justice Office of Justice Programs Bureau of Justice Statistics, 2014), 9. Tracy L. Snell, Capital Punishment, 2010—Statistical Tables, (Washington, D.C.: U.S. Department of Justice Office of Justice Programs Bureau of Justice Statistics, 2011), 8. Available at bjs.ojp.usdoj.gov/content/pub/pdf/cp10st.pdf. Thomas P. Bonczar and Tracy L. Snell, Capital Punishment, 2002 (Washington, D.C.: U.S. Department of Justice Office of Justice Programs Bureau of Justice Statistics, 2003). Available at bjs.ojp.usdoj.gov/content/pub/pdf/cp02.pdf. Tracy L. Snell, Capital Punishment, 2006—Statistical Tables, December 1, 2007, bjs.ojp.usdoj.gov/index.cfm?ty=pbdetail&iid=689.

12 percent of the total U.S. population and whites about 73 percent (see Table 10.2).[78] Another feature of racial bias is evident in how those who kill white victims are more likely to receive the ultimate sanction than those who kill minorities. Is a white life more valuable than a black life? That is what the evidence on the racial bias of the death penalty suggests.[79] Additionally, one study has shown that there is a "chivalric" bias in the administration of the death penalty: women found guilty of capital murder were less likely than men to be sentenced to death, and convicted murderers who killed women were far more likely to be sentenced to death than those who killed men.[80]

Social class is also an influential factor in terms of who receives the death penalty. Those with financial means who can afford to hire private lawyers and employ investigators have a decided advantage over the impoverished when charged with capital offenses. This is not to say that many public defenders cannot mount a credible defense in a capital case, but rather that the impoverished often lack the financial resources necessary to provide a first-class defense.[81]

Finally, a compelling reason to object to the death penalty is the problem of executing the innocent (see A Closer Look 10.1). Whereas defendants have

TABLE 10.2 Death Penalty and Race

	TOTAL U.S. POP. AS OF 2013 (ESTIMATED)	% OF TOTAL U.S. POP.	PRISON POP.	% OF U.S. TOTAL POP.	DEATH ROW POP.	% OF U.S. PRISON POP.
TOTAL	**316,128,839**	**100%**	**1,574,700**	**.50%**	**2,979**	**.19%**
Black	39,167,010	12.4%	549,100	.17%	1,248	.08%
White	230,592,579	73%	505,600	.16%	1,663	.11%
Hispanic	51,786,591	16.4%	332,200	.11%	389	.02%

Sources: United States Census, American FactFinder, https://factfinder.census.gov/faces/nav/jsf/pages/index.xhtml. Accessed February 2017. E. Ann Carson, Prisoners in 2013, Highlights, Table 7 (Washington, D.C.: U.S. Department of Justice Office of Justice Programs Bureau of Justice Statistics, 2015), 2, 8. Available at http://www.bjs.gov/index.cfm?ty=pbdetail&iid=5109. Tracy L. Snell, Capital Punishment, 2013—Statistical Tables, Table 9, Table 12 (Washington, D.C.: U.S. Department of Justice Office of Justice Programs Bureau of Justice Statistics, 2014), 9, 12. Available at http://www.bjs.gov/index.cfm?ty=pbdetail&iid=5156.

A CLOSER LOOK 10.1
The Innocence Project

Many convicted people insist that they did not commit the offenses for which they were convicted, and indeed, new evidence and technological advances have revealed that some of these people have been falsely accused and wrongly imprisoned. Given the large caseloads of most prosecutors' offices, little effort is exerted to look at past cases to determine whether mistakes were made.

In 1992, attorneys Barry Scheck and Peter Neufeld founded the Innocence Project, a program that initiates new looks at old cases to see whether justice has been served and to free the wrongly convicted. To date, more than 300 people have been exonerated, most by DNA evidence that established that the convicted individual was blameless.[82]

For example, in August 2015, a Pennsylvania judge reversed the conviction of Lewis Fogle, 64, who had served more than 34 years for the rape and murder of 15-year-old Deanna Long. In 1976, a neighbor discovered Long's body in the woods near his home. The day before the discovery, Long's younger sister was approached at her home by an unknown man who wanted to speak with Long. After the man left, Long's sister saw her walking home from a friend's house nearby. Long stopped to speak with the man and left with him in his car. Long's sister described the man to police, who produced a sketch. Days later, the man was identified as Earl Elderkin. Over the next five years, Elderkin, who was in a psychiatric

facility, was interrogated five times. Eventually, he implicated Fogle under hypnosis. At Fogle's trial in 1982, the prosecution depended on the testimony of three incarcerated informants who claimed that Fogle confessed while in jail. The prosecution presented no physical evidence linking Fogle to the murder. Fogle testified that he had spent the afternoon with his parents and brothers and that evening had gone to a friend's house and a bar. Although Fogle's parents verified his testimony, he was convicted and sentenced to life in prison. DNA testing of newly discovered evidence excluded Fogle, pointing to an unidentified male as the likely perpetrator.[83]

The Innocence Project is more than just an effort to free wrongly convicted people. By demonstrating that the person in prison is not guilty, the Innocence Project alerts the criminal justice system to the need to re-open investigations and attempt to find the actual perpetrators. For victims and their families, real closure cannot be obtained when the wrong person is punished.

THINK ABOUT IT

1. Who should pay for DNA testing offenders who want to challenge their convictions?
2. The Innocence Project is funded by individual donations, foundations, benefit activities, the Cardozo School of Law, and corporations. Should it receive federal funding?

---

numerous opportunities for appeal and review of their cases, condemned inmates do not. If a mistake is made in determining a defendant's guilt, a prison term, unlike death, can be rescinded. DNA evidence has exonerated several individuals who were convicted of capital offenses.[84] For example, in 1984, Kirk Noble Bloodsworth, a Maryland man with no criminal record, was accused of the rape and murder of a 9-year-old girl by his neighbor who thought he looked like a police sketch she saw on television. Because the murder was so heinous, police and prosecutors were under extreme pressure to solve the case. A jury found Bloodsworth guilty although five witnesses testified that he was home at the time of the murder. Bloodsworth spent nine years on Maryland's death row before managing to get a DNA test—still a new practice at the time—that proved someone else had committed the offense.[85] In 2004, Kimberly Shay Ruffner—who was already in prison for another conviction—pleaded guilty when authorities matched DNA from the crime scene to Ruffner's, which was in a database of convicted felons.[86]

Is the Death Penalty Dead?

Although capital punishment is politically popular in the United States, there are appeals to discontinue it.[87] Fifteen states and the District of Columbia do not even have the death penalty (see CJ Reference 10.1). Given the questions raised about

Alfred Swinton (middle) walks out of Hartford Superior Court with Innocence Project lawyers after a Superior Court judge approved a new trial in his conviction in the 1991 murder of Carla Terry. After serving 18 years, Swinton, 68, was released on a promise to appear in court. What factors may lead to innocent individuals being sentenced to death?

its effectiveness, fairness, and morality, many people contend that capital punishment is not an enlightened policy. Occasionally, it looks as though the courts will strike down this form of social control, but they seem to be unable to find the constitutional grounds to do so.

In *Ford* v. *Wainwright* and *Atkins* v. *Virginia*, the U.S. Supreme Court limited executions by determining that an offender's mental state must be considered when imposing a death sentence. In *Wainwright* (1986), the Court banned the execution of the insane. In 1974, Alvin Bernard Ford was convicted of murder in Florida and sentenced to death. Although Ford appeared mentally sound during his trial and sentencing, as well as at the time of the offense, his behavior changed while he was on death row. Ford's attorney had him examined by two psychiatrists, both of whom determined that Ford was not competent to undergo execution. The governor appointed three psychiatrists who interviewed Ford and determined that, although he had mental problems, he was fit for execution. Eventually, the U.S. Supreme Court concluded that the Eighth Amendment prohibits the execution of the insane.

CJ REFERENCE 10.1
States/Jurisdictions without a Death Penalty

Alaska	Maine	New York
Connecticut	Maryland	North Dakota
Delaware	Massachusetts	Rhode Island
District of Columbia	Michigan	Vermont
Hawaii	Minnesota	West Virginia
Illinois	New Jersey	Wisconsin[88]
Iowa	New Mexico	

In *Atkins* (2002), the U.S. Supreme Court established limits for the execution of the intellectually disabled. In 1996, Daryl Renard Atkins and William Jones abducted Eric Nesbitt at gunpoint, eventually killing him. Jones and Atkins both testified at Atkins's trial. Their descriptions of the incident agreed, except that each blamed the other for killing Nesbitt. Atkins's defense relied on one witness, a psychologist who said Atkins was "mildly mentally retarded," a conclusion based, in part, on a standard intelligence test that indicated Atkins had an IQ of 59. The jury found Jones's testimony more articulate and credited Atkins with the murder and sentenced him to death. The U.S. Supreme Court reversed, holding that executing intellectually disabled offenders violates the cruel and unusual punishments clause in the Eighth Amendment. According to the Court, a "significant number of states" have rejected capital punishment for intellectually disabled offenders, and that "the practice is uncommon" even in states that do. The Court cited evidence that an IQ of 70 or less indicates intellectual disability.

Two primary reasons for limiting executions because of the condemned's mental state are deterrence and the condemned's understanding of the execution and the reason for it. According to the Supreme Court, executing a mentally ill or intellectually disabled offender will not deter other offenders who have similar incapacities. Also, there are questions about the justice of killing those who do not understand what they are alleged to have done or even that they are being put to death.

However, the Supreme Court has upheld the constitutionality of lethal injection as a form of administering the death penalty.[89] In *Baze v. Rees* (2006), the court ruled that the possibility that a method of humane execution would be incorrectly administered and hurt the condemned does not violate the Eighth Amendment ban on cruel and unusual punishment. This ruling left the door open for states to continue their capital punishment practices.[90] However, the future promises even more challenges to capital punishment. The Supreme Court is in a pivotal position to decide policy on this issue. Those who are selected to fill vacancies on the Supreme Court are an important factor in whether capital punishment will continue.

PAUSE AND REVIEW

1. **How are specific and general deterrence used as arguments to justify capital punishment?**

2. **Which argument(s) against capital punishment are most compelling to you? Explain your answer.**

3. **Which two cases limited capital punishment based on the offender's mental state?**

 **FOCUS ON ETHICS**   Capital Punishment: Some Immodest Proposals

Almost everyone is dissatisfied with the death penalty for one reason or another. Liberals think that it is applied in a discriminatory manner and that it fails to act as a deterrent. Conservatives say that it is used too sparingly and that the time between crime and execution is too long. Families of victims feel left out of the decision-making process, and murderers eventually believe that they are the ultimate victim. If we were to redesign how we execute people, what might we do differently? Here are some proposals that would change the face of capital punishment in the United States. How many of them would you vote for?

- Take the guesswork out of who gets executed. Make capital punishment mandatory for all first-degree murders. This would address two concerns. First, claims of racial, sex, and social class bias would be eliminated because anyone convicted of a capital offense would receive the death penalty. An expensive lawyer, an emotional appeal, or a liberal judge could not intervene in such a process. Perhaps people would not kill if their conviction guaranteed the death penalty.
- Limit the number and time frame of appeals. The execution would take place one year after sentencing. This would discourage the defense from delaying the process. Perhaps people would not kill if death sentences were carried out promptly.
- Make executions public. This was once done to show people the consequences of crime. Now the execution has been moved behind prison walls, and only a few witnesses are allowed. If executions were televised, say at halftime of the Super Bowl when millions of people are watching, then everyone would have an opportunity to observe what happens to criminals. Major corporations might pay millions of dollars to sponsor such executions, and the money could be used for the victims' families.

- To have the maximum deterrent effect, capital punishment should not be painless. Instead of searching for humane ways to kill, the criminal justice system should bring back torture. Offenders would die in painful, protracted, and public ways.
- Allow family members of victims to participate in the execution. Victims' families should have a measure of retribution and revenge in the process. Allow a victim's family to pull the switch starting a lethal injection, for example.

WHAT DO YOU DO?

1. Are these suggestions extreme? Ask your classmates, family members, and friends what they think. Is there agreement on how offenders should be executed?
2. How far have we come from the times when these proposals were practiced? Are you willing to go back?

For more insight into how someone might respond to such an ethical dilemma, visit the companion website at www.oup.com/us/fuller to watch a video that connects this scenario to a real-world situation.

Summary

LEARNING OBJECTIVE 1 Compare and contrast the two prison systems that emerged in the United States during the first half of the 19th century.	The Pennsylvania System. The Eastern State Penitentiary was characterized by the separate-and-silent system, keeping inmates from seeing and talking to each other, the goal of which was to prevent the spread of antisocial thoughts and behavior. Solitary confinement caused many inmates to develop severe mental problems because of boredom and lack of human contact. The Auburn System. The Auburn Prison was characterized by the congregate-and-silent system, which locked inmates in separate cells each night, but allowed them to eat and work together during the day. This system prohibited face-to-face contact and required inmates to march in lockstep and keep their eyes downcast.
LEARNING OBJECTIVE 2 Describe the three most well-known examples of the Irish System of reform.	1. Maconochie's system was based on the ideas that brutality and cruelty debase not only the subject, but also society; and the treatment of a wrongdoer during his sentence of imprisonment should be designed to make him fit to be released into society again. 2. Crofton advocated the concept of a completely open institution in which inmates could gain experience in trust and avoid temptation. Crofton is best remembered for instituting the ticket-of-leave system. 3. Brockway used a three-grade program in which inmates entered at the second grade; an inmate was promoted to the first grade after six months of good behavior or demoted to the third grade if he failed to conform. Only those in the first grade were eligible for release. An inmate needed a year of good marks before being eligible for parole.

LEARNING OBJECTIVE **3** Summarize the three ways in which work was deemed beneficial during the early 20th century.	1. Work kept inmates occupied. 2. Work had rehabilitative value. 3. Work offset the cost of incarceration.
LEARNING OBJECTIVE **4** Outline the circumstances that led to the advocacy of rehabilitation as a desirable goal for the field of corrections, as well as its subsequent demise.	Changes in how science regarded illness led criminologists and correctional practitioners to adopt the medical model, which compared crime to disease and postulated that law-abiding behavior is within reach of all offenders and that rehabilitation was the optimal treatment. The creation of the Federal Bureau of Prisons in 1930 eliminated political patronage in filling jobs, developed better trained and more professional staff, and improved the conditions of confinement. The 1931 Wickersham Commission report further encouraged rehabilitation and condemned the failures of prison labor systems and the idleness of inmates. However, lack of resources, disagreement regarding its effectiveness, and the medical model's disregard for personal responsibility led to the rise of deterrent and retributive practices in lieu of rehabilitation.
LEARNING OBJECTIVE **5** Argue in support of capital punishment.	At the foundation of support for capital punishment is the deterrence argument. An offender is deterred, or prevented, from committing more crimes by being put to death (specific deterrence), which sets an example for society, thus encouraging others to refrain from antisocial behavior (general deterrence). The philosophy of just deserts also asserts that an offender who commits a heinous crime deserves death.
LEARNING OBJECTIVE **6** Argue against capital punishment.	Some people argue against capital punishment for religious and philosophical reasons involving proscriptions against murder. Other critics say deterrence does not work because not everyone considers the risks of punishment and deterrence is challenging to validate empirically because it is difficult to measure something that does not happen. Patterns of discrimination in how the death penalty is administered suggest that factors such as race, social class, sex, and gender determine whether the death penalty is applied. Lastly, due to the flaws of the criminal justice process, innocent people are sometimes condemned to death.

Critical Reflections

1. **Have the correctional policies in the United States become more enlightened and civilized over the past two centuries?**

2. **What do you see as the future for capital punishment in the United States?**

Key Terms

capital punishment **p. 309**
congregate-and-silent system **p. 301**
convict lease system **p. 303**
determinate sentence **p. 306**
Federal Bureau of Prisons **p. 305**

general deterrence **p. 316**
indeterminate sentence **p. 302**
just deserts **p. 317**
marks-of-commendation system **p. 302**
retribution model **p. 317**

separate-and-silent system **p. 300**
specific deterrence **p. 316**
three strikes **p. 308**

Endnotes

1 Jaweed Kaleem, "'This Is Slavery': U.S. Strike in What Activists Call One of the Biggest Prison Protests in Modern History," *Los Angeles Times*, October 28, 2016, http://www.latimes.com/nation/la-na-prison-strike-snap-story.html.

2 Kanyakrit Vongkiatkajorn, "Inmates Are Kicking Off a Nationwide Prison Strike Today," *Mother Jones*, September 9, 2016, http://www.motherjones.com/politics/2016/09/national-prison-strike-inmates. Kaleem, "'This Is Slavery'"

3 Kaleem, "'This Is Slavery.'"

4 Ibid.

5 Vongkiatkajorn, "Inmates Are Kicking Off a Nationwide Prison Strike Today."

6 Kaleem, "'This Is Slavery.'"

7 Lindsey Bever, "California Decides to Keep Violent Prisoners Off Inmate Firefighting Force," *Washington Post*, October 14, 2015, https://www.washingtonpost.com/news/post-nation/wp/2015/10/13/hot-debate-in-california-tinderbox-violent-criminals-may-join-inmate-firefighting-force.

8 Aimee Picchi, "Why Prisoners Nationwide Are Striking," CBS News, September 9, 2016, http://www.cbsnews.com/news/why-prisoners-nationwide-are-striking; Nicky Woolf, "Inside America's Biggest Prison Strike: 'The 13th Amendment Didn't End Slavery,'" *Guardian*, October 22, 2016, https://www.theguardian.com/us-news/2016/oct/22/inside-us-prison-strike-labor-protest.

9 E. Tammy Kim, "A National Strike Against 'Prison Slavery,'" *New Yorker*, October 3, 2016, http://www.newyorker.com/news/news-desk/a-national-strike-against-prison-slavery.

10 Carimah Townes, 'Enough Is Enough': Prisoners Across the Country Band Together to End Slavery for Good, ThinkProgress, June 15, 2016, https://thinkprogress.org/enough-is-enough-prisoners-across-the-country-band-together-to-end-slavery-for-good-32b03c4d133d.

11 David J. Rothman, *The Discovery of the Asylum: Social Order and Disorder in the New Republic* (Boston: Little, Brown, 1990).

12 Rex A. Skidmore, "Penological Pioneering in the Walnut Street Jail, 1789–1799," *Journal of Criminal Law and Criminology* 39, no. 2 (1948): 167–180.

13 Ibid.

14 Harry Elmer Barnes, *The Evolution of Penology in Pennsylvania: A Study in American Social History* (Montclair, N.J.: Patterson Smith, 1968).

15 Phillip L. Reichel, *Corrections: Philosophies, Practices, and Procedures,* 2d ed. (Boston: Allyn & Bacon, 2001), 72.

16 J. Hirsch, *The Rise of the Penitentiary: Prisons and Punishments in Early America* (New Haven, Conn.: Yale University Press, 1992).

17 Barnes, *The Evolution of Penology in Pennsylvania.*

18 Harry Elmer Barnes and Negley K. Teeters, *New Horizons in Criminology*, 3d ed. (Englewood Cliffs, N.J.: Prentice Hall, 1959).

19 Rothman, *The Discovery of the Asylum.*

20 J. V. Barry, *Alexander Maconochie of Norfolk Island* (Melbourne, Australia: Oxford University Press, 1958), 72.

21 Reichel, *Corrections,* 82.

22 Barnes and Teeters, *New Horizons in Criminology.*

23 Thomas G. Blomberg and Karol Lucken, *American Penology: A History of Control* (New York: Aldine de Gruyter, 2000), 76.

24 Unicor, *Factories with Fences,* https://www.unicor.gov/FPIHistory.aspx. Accessed February 2017.

25 Unicor, Federal Prison Industries, Inc., Fiscal Year 2016, Annual Management Report, November 15, 2016, https://www.unicor.gov/Reports.aspx.

26 William Stone, "Industry, Agriculture, and Education," in *Prisons: Today and Tomorrow*, ed. Joycelyn M. Pollock (Gaithersburg, Md.: Aspen Publishers, 1997), 116–157.

27 National Correctional Industries Association, Certification and Cost Accounting Center Listing, Third Quarter 2016 Certification Listing Report, http://www.nationalcia.org/piecp-2/quarterly-statistical-reports.

28 Beth Schwartzapfel, "Modern-Day Slavery in America's Prison Workforce," *American Prospect*, May 28, 2014, http://prospect.org/article/great-american-chain-gang.

29 John Irwin, *The Warehouse Prison: Disposal of the New Dangerous Class* (Los Angeles: Roxbury, 2005).

30 James Kilgore, "The Myth of Prison Slave Labor Camps in the U.S.," *Counterpunch*, August 9, 2013, http://www.counterpunch.org/2013/08/09/the-myth-of-prison-slave-labor-camps-in-the-u-s.

31 Blake McKelvey, *American Prisons: A History of Good Intentions* (Montclair, N.J.: Patterson Smith, 1977).

32 John Irwin, *Prisons in Turmoil* (Boston: Little, Brown, 1980). See especially 2, "The Correctional Institution."

33 John W. Roberts, "The Federal Bureau of Prisons: Its Mission, Its History, and Its Partnership with Probation and Pretrial Services," *Federal Probation* 61, no. 1 (1997): 53–58.

34 Larry E. Sullivan, *The Prison Reform Movement: Forlorn Hope* (Boston: Twayne, 1990).

35 James B. Jacobs, *Stateville: The Penitentiary in Mass Society* (Chicago: University of Chicago Press, 1977).

36 Robert Martinson, "What Works? Questions and Answers about Prison Reform," *Public Interest* 35 (1974): 22–54.

37 Ted Palmer, "The 'Effectiveness' Issue Today: An Overview," in *The Dilemmas of Corrections: Contemporary Readings,* 4th ed., ed. Kenneth C. Hass and Geoffrey P. Alpert (Prospect Heights, Ill.: Waveland Press, 1999).

38 David Fogel, *We Are Living Proof: The Justice Model for Corrections* (Cincinnati, Ohio: Anderson, 1975).

39 Todd Gitlin, *The Sixties: Years of Hope, Days of Rage* (New York: Bantam Books, 1993).

40 Leo Carroll, *Lawful Order* (New York: Garland, 1998).

41 Jacobs, *Stateville.* See especially Chapter 5, "Intrusion of the Legal System and Interest Groups," pp. 105–137.

42 Irwin, *Prisons in Turmoil.*

43 Pamala Griset, *Determinate Sentencing: The Promise and the Reality of Retributive Justice* (Albany: State University of New York Press, 1991). See also James Austin and John Irwin, *It's About Time: America's Imprisonment Binge,* 3d ed. (Belmont, Calif.: Wadsworth, 2001).

44 Irwin, *Prisons in Turmoil.*

45 Bureau of Justice Statistics, Reentry Trends in the U.S., http://www.bjs.gov/content/reentry/releases.cfm. Accessed February 2017.

46 Robert Martinson and Judith Wilks, "Save Parole Supervision," in *Correctional Contexts: Contemporary and Classical Readings,* 2d ed., eds. Edward J. Latessa (Los Angeles: Roxbury, 2001), 422–427.

47 Inimai M. Chettiar, Michael Waldman, Nicole Fortier, Abigail Finkelman,

"Solutions: American Leaders Speak Out on Criminal Justice" Brennan Center For Justice, April 27, 2015, https://www.brennancenter.org/publication/solutions-american-leaders-speak-out-criminal-justice.

48 *Economist*, "Jailhouse Nation," June 20, 2015, http://www.economist.com/news/leaders/21654619-how-make-americas-penal-system-less-punitive-and-more-effective-jailhouse-nation.

49 Council of Economic Advisors, Economic Perspectives on Incarceration and the Criminal Justice System, April 2016, https://obamawhitehouse.archives.gov/the-press-office/2016/04/23/cea-report-economic-perspectives-incarceration-and-criminal-justice. Oliver Roeder, Lauren-Brooke Eisen, and Julia Bowling, *What Caused the Crime Decline* (New York: New York University School of Law Brennan Center for Justice, 2015). Available at https://www.brennancenter.org/publication/what-caused-crime-decline.

50 *Economist*, "Jailhouse Nation."

51 Erik Eckholm, "Kentucky Governor Restores Voting Rights to Thousands of Felons," *New York Times*, November 24, 2015, http://www.nytimes.com/2015/11/25/us/kentucky-governor-restores-voting-rights-to-thousands-of-felons.html.

52 The Sentencing Project, 6 Million Lost Voters: State-Level Estimates of Felony Disenfranchisement, 2016, Table 1, http://www.sentencingproject.org/publications/6-million-lost-voters-state-level-estimates-felony-disenfranchisement-2016.

53 Leon Neyfakh, "In Sweeping Speech, Obama Calls for Enfranchising Felons and Limiting Solitary Confinement," *Slate*, July 14, 2015, http://www.slate.com/blogs/the_slatest/2015/07/14/obama_calls_for_fundamental_criminal_justice_reforms_in_major_naacp_speech.html.

54 Tracy L. Snell, *Capital Punishment, 2014–2015* (Washington, D.C.: U.S. Department of Justice Office of Justice Programs Bureau of Justice Statistics, 2017), 1. Available at https://www.bjs.gov/index.cfm?ty=pbdetail&iid=5908.

55 Leviticus 24:17 (King James Version).

56 George Olyffe, An Essay Humbly Offer'd, for an Act of Parliament to Prevent Capital Crimes (London: J. Downing, 1731), 6–7, in *The Death Penalty: An American History*, Stuart

Banner (Cambridge, Mass.: Harvard University Press, 2002), 70.

57 Edward Peters, *Torture* (New York: Blackwell, 1985).

58 Robert M. Bohm, *Deathquest: An Introduction to the Theory and Practice of Capital Punishment in the United States* (Cincinnati, Ohio: Anderson, 1999), 73.

59 Alister Kershaw, *A History of the Guillotine* (New York: Barnes & Noble Books, 1993), 81.

60 Stuart Banner, *The Death Penalty: An American History* (Cambridge, Mass.: Harvard University Press, 2002), 171–172.

61 Stuart Banner, *The Death Penalty: An American History* (Cambridge, Mass.: Harvard University Press, 2002).

62 Ibid., 186.

63 Virginia Leigh Hatch and Anthony Walsh, *Capital Punishment: Theory and Practice of the Ultimate Penalty* (New York: Oxford University Press, 2016), 144.

64 Spiegel Online International, Death Penalty Opposition: EU Set to Ban Export of Drug Used in US Executions, December 12, 2011, http://www.spiegel.de/international/europe/death-penalty-opposition-eu-set-to-ban-export-of-drug-used-in-us-executions-a-803238.html. Jon Stone, America is Running Out of Lethal Injection Drugs Because of a European Embargo to End the Death Penalty, Independent, March 13, 2015, http://www.independent.co.uk/news/world/americas/america-is-running-out-of-lethal-injection-drugs-because-of-a-european-embargo-to-end-the-death-10106933.html.

65 Robert Barnes, "Supreme Court Upholds Lethal Injection Procedure," *Washington Post*, June 29, 2015, https://www.washingtonpost.com/politics/courts_law/supreme-court-upholds-lethal-injection-procedure/2015/06/29/2b5cee6e-1b3c-11e5-93b7-5eddc056ad8a_story.html. Pam Belluck, "What's in a Lethal Injection 'Cocktail'?" *New York Times*, April 9, 2011, http://www.nytimes.com/2011/04/10/weekinreview/10injection.html.

66 Associated Press/Guardian, "Arizona Tried to Illegally Import Lethal Injection Drug Not Approved in the US," October 23, 2015, http://www.theguardian.com/us-news/2015/oct/23/arizona-illegally-import-lethal-injection-drug. Steve Barnes, Arkansas Buys Lethal Injection Drugs, Aims to End Execution Hiatus,

Reuters, August 12, 2015, http://www.reuters.com/article/2015/08/12/us-usa-execution-arkansas-idUSKCN0QH2QW20150812.

67 Mark Berman, "Fourth Arkansas Execution in Eight Days Prompts Questions about Inmate's Movements," *Washington Post*, April 21, 2017, https://www.washingtonpost.com/news/post-nation/wp/2017/04/27/arkansas-readies-to-carry-out-last-planned-execution-before-drugs-expire.

68 Robert Barnes, "Supreme Court Upholds Lethal Injection Procedure," *Washington Post*, June 29, 2015, https://www.washingtonpost.com/politics/courts_law/supreme-court-upholds-lethal-injection-procedure/2015/06/29/2b5cee6e-1b3c-11e5-93b7-5eddc056ad8a_story.html.

69 Scott H. Decker and Carol W. Kohfeld, "The Deterrent Effect of Capital Punishment in the Five Most Active Execution States: A Time-Series Analysis," *Criminal Justice Review* 15 (1990): 173–191.

70 Marla Sandys and Edmund F. McGarrell, "Attitudes toward Capital Punishment among Indiana Legislators: Diminished Support in Light of Alternative Sentencing Options," *Justice Quarterly* 11 (1994): 651–677.

71 Robert M. Bohm, "Retribution and Capital Punishment: Toward a Better Understanding of Death Penalty Opinion," *Journal of Criminal Justice* 20 (1992): 227–236.

72 Robert M. Bohm, *Deathquest: An Introduction to the Theory and Practice of Capital Punishment in the United States* (Cincinnati, Ohio: Anderson, 1999). See especially Chapter 5, "General Deterrence and the Death Penalty," 83–101.

73 Alison Tonks, "US States Experiment with Lethal Injections in an Ethical Vacuum," *British Medical Journal* 336 (June 21, 2008): 1401.

74 Oriental Philosophy, Oriental Philosophy: Buddhism: The Eightfold Path, http://philosophy.lander.edu/oriental/eightfold.html.

75 Samuel R. Gross and Robert Mauro, *Death and Discrimination: Racial Disparities in Capital Sentencing* (Boston: Northeastern University Press, 1989).

76 Robert Johnson, *Deathwork: A Study of the Modern Execution Process* (Monterey, Calif.: Brooks/Cole, 1990), 136.

77 Elizabeth Rapaport, "The Death Penalty and Gender Discrimination,"

in *A Capital Punishment Anthology*, ed. Victor L. Streib (Cincinnati, Ohio: Anderson, 1993), 145–152.

78 Snell, *Capital Punishment*, 2013.

79 James R. Acker, "Impose an Immediate Moratorium on Executions," *Criminology and Public Policy* 6 (November 1, 2007): 641.

80 Steven F. Shatz and Naomi R. Shatz, "Chivalry Is Not Dead: Murder, Gender, and the Death Penalty," *Berkeley Journal of Gender, Law and Justice* 27, no. 1 (Winter 2012): 64–112.

81 Jeffrey Reiman, *The Rich Get Richer and the Poor Get Prison: Ideology, Class, and Criminal Justice,* 6th ed. (Boston: Allyn & Bacon, 2001).

82 The Innocence Project, The Cases: DNA Exoneree Profiles, http://www.innocenceproject.org/cases/lewis-fogle/. Accessed February 2017.

83 Innocence Project, With Consent of District Attorney, A Pennsylvania Court Vacates Murder Conviction Based on DNA Evidence Pointing to Innocence, August 13, 2015, http://www.innocenceproject.org/with-consent-of-district-attorney-a-pennsylvania-court-vacates-murder-conviction-based-on-dna-evidence-pointing-to-innocence.

84 Michael L. Radelet, Hugo Adam Bedau, and Constance E. Putnam, *In Spite of Innocence: Erroneous Convictions in Capital Cases* (Boston: Northeastern University Press, 1992).

85 Scott Shane, "A Death Penalty Fight Comes Home," *New York Times*, February 5, 2013, http://www.nytimes.com/2013/02/06/us/exonerated-inmate-seeks-end-to-maryland-death-penalty.html.

86 Stephanie Hanes, "Guilty Plea Closes '84 Case of Rosedale Girl's Murder," *Baltimore Sun*, May 21, 2004, http://articles.baltimoresun.com/2004-05-21/news/0405210277_1_ruffner-dawn-hamilton-bloodsworth. Stephanie Hanes, "'84 Investigation Quick to Overlook the Culprit," *Baltimore Sun*, May 22, 2004, http://articles.baltimoresun.com/2004-05-22/news/0405220166_1_ruffner-dawn-hamilton-bloodsworth.

87 "Amnesty International Calls for End to Death Penalty in United States," *Preview Nation's Health* 38 (June/July 2008): 8.

88 Death Penalty Information Center, States with and without the Death Penalty, http://www.deathpenaltyinfo.org/states-and-without-death-penalty. Accessed February 2017.

89 Linda Greenhouse, "Justices Uphold Lethal Injection in Kentucky Case," *New York Times*, April 17, 2008, 1.

90 Carmen Gentile, "Florida: Inmate Is Executed," *New York Times*, July 2, 2008, 13.

Chapter 11

Prisons and Jails

FEATURES

Pictured here is Lawrence Phillips, in September 1997, as a running back for the St. Louis Rams.
How might a brain injury have contributed to Phillips's legal troubles?

// "I feel myself very close to snapping," wrote Lawrence Phillips in a March 2015 letter to his mother from prison. "I feel my anger is near bursting and that will result in my death or the death of someone else." In April, the body of Phillips's cellmate, Damion Soward, was found in the cell the two men shared.

Lawrence Phillips was a star player in the National Football League. He first played for the St. Louis Rams, and his coach called him potentially the best running back he had ever worked with. Phillips later played with the Miami Dolphins, NFL Europe, the San Francisco 49ers, the Arena football league, and the Canadian football league. At each stop, he alienated coaches, violated team rules, or got into trouble with the law. By 2015, Phillips was serving a 32-year prison term in California for driving his car into a group of teenagers in Los Angeles and assaulting his former girlfriend.[1]

Phillips wrote to one of his high school coaches that the prison was crowded and rife with drugs and weapons. He said that he had conflicted with gang members and had agreed to solitary confinement as an alternative to sharing a cell with a gang member. After being transferred to another cell for the 16th time since his incarceration, he wrote, "Sometimes I just want to hurt one of these people. They just will not let you rest."[2]

Phillips was charged with the first-degree murder of Soward in September 2015. On January 13, 2016, Phillips was found unresponsive in his cell and later pronounced dead at the hospital. His death was ruled a suicide.[3] Phillips's lawyer believes that a brain injury Phillips suffered during his football career may have contributed to his legal troubles.[4]

THINK ABOUT IT > What are some of the pains of imprisonment that Lawrence Phillips experienced?

LEARNING OBJECTIVE 1

Define the concept of a total institution as it relates to prisons.

LEARNING OBJECTIVE 2

Describe the five pains of imprisonment.

LEARNING OBJECTIVE 3

Frame how gangs affect the informal inmate social structure and prison security efforts.

LEARNING OBJECTIVE 4

Identify how prison violence and overcrowding are dealt with.

Prison Life

The field of corrections includes many types of facilities and programs ranging from local jails to federal prisons. Included in this array of correctional efforts are diversion programs, probation programs, parole, and a host of secure institutions. However, when we think of corrections, usually the first thing that comes to mind are prisons and jails, which remain the centerpiece of the U.S. criminal justice system's attempts to detain, punish, and rehabilitate criminal suspects and offenders. Unfortunately, U.S. prisons and jails are responsible for much more than this. They must deal with inmates who are mentally ill, intellectually disabled, and/or physically disabled. Consider the story of Lawrence Phillips. Given his history and his own statements, it is possible that his mental condition was deteriorating. Would attention to Phillips's mental health have saved his life and that of his cellmate?

This chapter will examine prisons and jails in light of several important issues that illustrate how these institutions affect inmates and correctional workers. We will examine inmates' social roles and legal rights, the occupation of the correctional officer, the problems and dangers associated with imprisonment, and finally the move to privatize this traditionally public service.

How U.S. Prisons Work

The United States has about 1,800 state and federal correctional institutions.[5] These institutions take a number of forms and have various titles. For example,

Texas has a system of facilities called state jails. Other states have correctional facilities or correctional institutions, and many states have rehabilitative facilities, transitional facilities, work camps, boot camps, and inmate medical facilities. Several states have one or two facilities especially for women, and all have one or more youth or juvenile institutions. The number of facilities a state has varies widely. For example, Michigan has 32 state correctional facilities, whereas Utah has 2; most states fall somewhere in between.[6] As of December 2015, state prisons housed more than 1.3 million inmates and federal institutions nearly 200,000 (see Figure 11.1).[7]

Generally, state prisons have at least three security levels: low, medium, and maximum. However, each state and the federal prison system has its own set of security-level classifications and specifications for each security level. For example, prisons in the state of Georgia have three security classifications: minimum, medium, and close (high security).[8] The state of California designates five security levels. These range from security-level 1 facilities with open dormitories and a low-security perimeter up to security-level 5 facilities that have secure perimeters with armed guards both inside and outside the facility.[9]

Federal prison inmates consist of defendants awaiting trial for federal offenses and offenders who have been convicted of a federal offense. Federal prisons also hold offenders who have been convicted of a felony in the District of Columbia. In special cases, state inmates may be held in a federal prison.[10] The federal government operates five security levels among its 122 prisons.

> Minimum-security institutions. Also called federal prison camps, these have dormitory housing, a relatively low staff-to-inmate ratio, and little or no perimeter fencing. Some institutions have a small, minimum-security prison camp next to a larger main facility to provide inmate labor to the main facility and to off-site work programs. As of 2017, about 17.5 percent of federal inmates lived in minimum-security institutions.

> Low-security institutions. These have fenced perimeters and dormitory or cubicle housing. The staff-to-inmate ratio in these institutions is higher than in minimum-security facilities. As of early 2017, about 37.4 percent of federal inmates lived in low-security institutions.

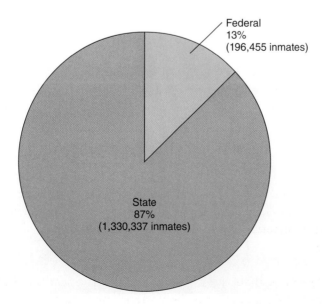

Federal
13%
(196,455 inmates)

State
87%
(1,330,337 inmates)

FIGURE 11.1 Number of Inmates in the United States as of December 31, 2015 Why are there so many more state than federal inmates?

Source: E. Ann Carson and Elizabeth Anderson, Prisoners in 2015, Table 1, (Washington, D.C.: U.S. Department of Justice, Office of Justice Programs, Bureau of Justice Statistics, 2016), 3. Available at https://www.bjs.gov/index. cfm?ty=pbdetail&iid=5869.

› Medium-security institutions. These have fenced perimeters, often with electronic detection systems, mostly cell-type housing, and a higher staff-to-inmate ratio and greater internal controls than lower security facilities. As of 2017, about 29.9 percent of federal inmates lived in medium-security institutions.

› High-security institutions. These United States Penitentiaries have highly secured perimeters with walls or reinforced fences, cell housing, a high staff-to-inmate ratio, and strict control of inmate movement. As of 2017, about 11.5 percent of federal inmates lived in high-security institutions.

› Administrative facilities. These specialized institutions hold pretrial detainees; treat inmates with serious or chronic medical problems; and/or hold extremely dangerous, violent, or escape-prone inmates. All administrative facilities, except for the ADMAX (administrative maximum) facility in Florence, Colorado, can hold inmates in all security categories.[11]

Federal correctional complexes are composed of several facilities with different missions and security levels located close to one another. Among other functions, these complexes increase efficiency by sharing services and give staff experience at different security levels. Additionally, the Bureau of Prisons operates four female facilities, all of which are correctional complexes with various security levels.[12]

Every state and the federal government has intake facilities or procedures that classify incoming prisoners by security level, as well as other factors, and sends them to the appropriate facilities. For federal prisoners, the court sends the judgment to the U.S. Marshals who request a prison designation from the Designation and Sentence Computation Center (DSCC) in Grand Prairie, Texas. The DSCC uses data about the judgment and the prisoner to determine the appropriate facility.[13] An interesting detail about the federal system is that many prisoners are not taken into custody upon conviction but are allowed to self-surrender. A few weeks after their conviction, these prisoners are notified by mail of the institution

Clinton Correctional Facility is a maximum-security state prison located in Dannemora, New York. What are the five federal prison security levels?

they must travel to and the date and time they must arrive there. Prisoners usually have about 90 days to turn themselves in.[14] State prisoners are typically taken into custody upon conviction and sent to an intake facility to determine the appropriate facility. Most state intake facilities perform the following functions:

> Identify the prisoner and establish the prisoner's record

> Interview the prisoner and determine custody level based in part on the severity of the current conviction, history of institutional violence, and escape history

> Assess the prisoner's medical and mental health

> Assess the prisoner's security requirements

> Identify sex offenders, sexual predators, vulnerable inmates, and gang members

> Assign housing and cells. In some states, the intake facility recommends housing and cell assignments. Other states leave this decision to the facility to which the prisoner is sent.[15]

The Pains of Imprisonment

The prison is what sociologist Erving Goffman called a total institution.[16] Much like the military, some religious monasteries, and secure mental health hospitals, the prison is a **total institution** in which everything is tightly controlled and highly structured. The inmates' ability to influence the conditions of their confinement is limited, and escape is almost impossible. This total control of inmates' lives, including who their cellmates are, what they eat, and when they can bathe, is designed to help the prison run efficiently, maintain order, and deprive the inmates of the discretion often taken for granted in free society. It is also designed to punish offenders by depriving them of goods and services and relationships with others. Unintentionally, inmates are often deprived of their physical security as well. In an effort to protect society from criminal offenders, the prison places these potentially dangerous people together in a place where they can prey on one another, often in brutal ways.[17]

Although confinement in a small cell may be uncomfortable to many, it is not the worst thing that can happen to a person.[18] Instead, deprivations are largely what define a prisoner's lifestyle. Sociologist and criminologist Gresham Sykes, in his seminal book *The Society of Captives*, argued that maximum-security prisons make incarceration a painful experience by depriving inmates of some basic freedoms, stating that "the modern pains of imprisonment are often defined by society as a humane alternative to the physical brutality and the neglect which constituted the major meaning of imprisonment in the past."[19] Sykes further noted that the pains of imprisonment can be destructive to the psyche and pose profound threats to the inmate's personality and self-worth. Because of deprivation, we have come to believe that incarceration is a sufficient punishment and that physical brutality in the form of corporal punishment is not required to achieve justice. However, this does not mean that inmates do not experience brutality at the hands of each other. Sykes described the five **pains of imprisonment** in this way:

1. Deprivation of liberty. The inmate is confined to an institution and then further confined within that institution. This loss of freedom is the most obvious feature of incarceration, but to adequately understand its effect on the inmate, we must appreciate that not only does it include being restricted to a small space such as a prison cell but also that this restriction is

total institution—A closed environment in which every aspect, including the movement and behavior of the people within, is controlled and structured.

pains of imprisonment—Deprivations that define the punitive nature of imprisonment.

involuntary. Because friends and family are prohibited from visiting except at limited times, the bonds to loved ones are frayed and sometimes break.[20]

2. Deprivation of goods and services. Inmates do not have access to the food, entertainment, and services that free people routinely enjoy.[21] To be sure, this deprivation is relative, and for some inmates "three hots and a cot" is an improvement over their disadvantaged lives on the outside. Having a dry place to sleep and a government-guaranteed calorie count are things that many in this world would consider an improvement in lifestyle. However, the inmates' perception is subjective, and, according to Sykes, some inmates view the impoverishment that incarceration brings as the prison acting as a tyrant to deprive them of the goods and services they should reasonably have. More often, inmates may see their poverty as a consequence of their behavior and a result of their own inadequacies.

3. Deprivation of heterosexual relationships. Living in a single-sex society such as a prison is stressful. The deprivation of heterosexual activities is one of the most visible and controversial because it sometimes leads to sexual deviation within the prison. Homosexual activities and rape are often associated with incarceration. This is particularly true in male prisons, where, as Sykes contended, the self-concept of men is bound up in their sexuality.[22] Without women to provide feedback for displays of masculinity, the inmates create an atmosphere that is sexually charged and difficult to negotiate. Men do not lose their sex drive when incarcerated; it becomes a type of hypermasculinity that demands that some men be subservient to others.[23] In 2003, Congress enacted the Prison Rape Elimination Act (PREA) to address the problem of sexual abuse of inmates. PREA sets standards for the detection, prevention, reduction, and punishment of prison rape. Federal facilities must comply with PREA standards, and the act awards grants to help state and local governments implement the act's provisions.[24]

4. Deprivation of autonomy. The inability to make decisions about some of the most basic tasks, such as walking from one room to another, is a particularly galling deprivation. Being subject to a bureaucratic staff's rules, whims, and preferences is a humbling experience. Having to ask for everything reduces the inmate to the status of a child. Some inmates argue or bargain with the staff, but their position is so weak that they have little leverage in a well-run prison free of guard corruption.

5. Deprivation of security. This is perhaps the most disturbing pain of imprisonment. Most of those confined to a maximum-security prison have already proven themselves violent, aggressive, and untrustworthy. Having to cope with such cellmates can be an anxious experience, even for those who are violent themselves. There are few places in the prison where one can feel secure. Inmates constantly test each other for physical or emotional weaknesses. Those without the courage or nerve to protect themselves are quickly victimized by others if they cannot find a protector.

These pains of imprisonment define the prison experience. Even in the best-managed prisons, with well-trained guards and adequate resources, these deprivations are present. However, with the exception of being deprived of security, these are not unintended consequences. Prisons are meant to be uncomfortable for inmates and lack the niceties of home. Many people do not feel sorry for inmates who suffer these deprivations.[25] However, these pains of imprisonment are real to inmates, and to understand prison dynamics we must appreciate not only

Here, David Whaley, an inmate at the Wabash Valley Correctional Facility in Carlisle, Indiana, visits with family. Inmates suffer deprivations of liberty, which pose a threat to familial bonds. What other types of deprivations do inmates suffer from?

how these deprivations affect inmates but also how they cope with this lifestyle. The 1971 Stanford Prison Experiment (see A Closer Look 11.1) sought to investigate how incarceration might affect inmates, staff, and administrators, but the study has since been deeply criticized for flawed methodology and conclusions. A 2007 study found that people who volunteered for a similar prison experiment ranked much higher on measures of aggressiveness, authoritarianism, narcissism, and social dominance—all characteristics related to abuse—than did a control group.[26] It is possible that the Stanford Prison Experiment ended like it did because of who responded to the newspaper ad asking for "guards" and "inmates."

Prison Gangs

To fully appreciate how the contemporary prison's informal inmate social structure shapes the lives of inmates and staff, we must consider the effect of prison gangs. Although not all correctional systems have severe gang problems, and not all gangs are as violent as the ones discussed here, gangs are a concern because without proper vigilance they can form and take partial control of a prison.

Here, we will discuss the California prison gang problem. Although not every inmate is affiliated with a gang, the prison gang problem is most serious in California. The signature feature of the California prison gang structure is that it is based on skin color and ethnicity. Currently, there are at least four major prison gangs:[27]

> Mexican Mafia. The oldest of the prison gangs, the Mexican Mafia, has been traced to the 1950s when a group of Mexican juveniles from Los Angeles was incarcerated together in the Deuel Vocational Institution in Tracy, California. The gang, also called "La Eme," appropriated the number 13 and the letter "M," the 13th letter in the alphabet. They began preying on white and black inmates by extorting and robbing them. They also attacked Mexican inmates from northern California whom they considered to be "farmers." In an effort to destabilize the gang, prison authorities dispersed members to prisons across the state where they recruited other Mexicans. The gang became a vertically integrated organization with considerable power both inside and outside the prison.

A CLOSER LOOK 11.1
The Stanford Prison Experiment

In 1971, Stanford psychology professor Philip Zimbardo created an experiment to test the effects of prison life on inmates and staff. He recruited 24 young men, 9 to act as inmates and 9 as guards in a makeshift prison (the other 6 remained on call if replacements were needed). The experiment was scheduled to last two weeks. It ended in six days.[28] In August 1971, in Palo Alto, California, police arrested nine students who had answered a newspaper ad offering to pay them $15 a day to participate in an experiment on prisons. The nine men assigned as inmates were booked and fingerprinted at a real jail, then blindfolded and driven to the Stanford campus to a "prison" located in the basement of a school building. The students assigned as guards received no training, only uniforms and instructions to control the prison as they saw fit without using violence. The prison had three cells with steel bars, but no windows. Videotaping equipment was installed, and a small closet was converted into a solitary confinement chamber. The cells were bugged via an intercom system.[29]

Upon their arrival at the prison, the "warden" established the seriousness of the inmates' offenses and their status as inmates. The inmates were strip-searched and de-loused in order to imitate real prison procedures and to humiliate them. Wearing only smocks (no underwear) printed with their ID numbers and rubber sandals, each inmate had a heavy chain bolted to each ankle, and his head was covered with a nylon stocking. Although the chain, smock, and stocking are not features in actual prisons, they were introduced to quickly stimulate a sense of humiliation and oppression. The inmates were called only by their ID numbers and could refer to themselves only by their numbers.[30]

The guards were divided among three eight-hour shifts to oversee the inmates. The guards counted the inmates several times a day, including waking the inmates for counts at 2:30 a.m. The guards also devised, with no input from the staff running the experiment, the punishment of push-ups, often placing their feet on the backs of inmates sentenced to do them.[31]

The inmates staged a revolt on the second day, removing their stocking caps and numbers and barricading themselves inside their cells. All nine guards responded by forcing the inmates away from their cell doors with blasts from a fire extinguisher and then stripped the inmates. The inmate leaders were forced into solitary confinement, while the remaining inmates were harassed. To break inmate solidarity, the guards set up a "privilege" cell in which the three inmates least involved in the rebellion were allowed to wash, dress, and eat a special meal in front of the other inmates, who were not allowed to eat. After a few hours, the guards put the innocent inmates back in the regular cells and the scheming inmates in the privilege cell, creating confusion and distrust among the inmates. A staff consultant who had been a former inmate in a real penitentiary confirmed that correctional officers actually used such tactics.[32]

According to Zimbardo, the guards continued to dehumanize the inmates. After 10:00 p.m. bathroom visits were not allowed, forcing the inmates to use buckets in their cells. Occasionally, the guards would not allow inmates to empty the buckets. Although it may seem that the guards were overplaying their roles for the researchers, some guards were videotaped continuing to abuse the inmates even when they thought the researchers were not watching.[33]

The inmates became so stressed that the staff released five of them early, but not easily. The staff themselves, according to Zimbardo, had begun thinking like prison officials. When one inmate began to show signs of mental distress, they thought he was trying to "con" the staff. Instead of offering him release, the guards asked him to inform on the other inmates in exchange for better treatment. He was released only when his signs of distress increased. The staff also manipulated the inmates' parents and friends who visited. After sprucing up the prison and the inmates, they forced the visitors to comply with an assortment of rules much like those in a real prison. Although some of the parents complained, they all complied, even though some remarked that they had never seen their sons looking so stressed or fatigued.

Zimbardo, who was the prison's superintendent, admitted becoming so consumed by his role as a prison official that he tried to quash a rumored mass escape plot by going to the Palo Alto police and asking to use their old jail to hold the student inmates. (The police turned down the request, much to Zimbardo's frustration.) Even a former prison chaplain invited in to evaluate the situation fell into his role and offered to get lawyers for the inmates. Some of the inmates' parents' called the staff to request attorneys to bail their sons out of "jail."[34]

After six days, according to Zimbardo, "The prisoners were disintegrated, both as a group and as individuals." The guards had total control of the prison and commanded the blind obedience of each inmate. The study ended prematurely because the organizers concluded they had created a situation in which inmates were withdrawing and behaving pathologically, and the sadistic behavior of the guards had become concerning.[35]

THINK ABOUT IT

1. Should experiments like this be allowed to be conducted?
2. Would you participate in such an experiment?

> La Nuestra Familia. This Mexican gang draws its members from northern California and is constantly at odds with La Eme. Some of the gang's younger members spun off and created the Northern Structure, which, in addition to feuding with La Eme, has also clashed with the old guard of La Nuestra Familia. Together, La Nuestra Familia and the Northern Structure represent the state's largest prison gang. The gang has a military structure and educates new members about how to identify the enemy and how to resist interrogations. Members who are released must set up "regiments" in their hometowns.

> Black Guerrilla Family. This gang of black inmates originates from the 1960s, when members of the Black Panther Party were incarcerated in California prisons. Back then, the inmates were extremely political and adopted a Marxist rhetoric that cast them as political prisoners of an unjust capitalist state. They espoused revolution, but as the years passed, many became gangsters in their own right, and instead of robbing drug dealers, they became drug dealers. Today the Black Guerrilla Family is composed of black lifers. Younger inmates who join gangs are more likely to be affiliated with inmates who belong to the Bloods or Crips street gangs.

> Aryan Brotherhood. These white gang members employ Ku Klux Klan symbols and Nazi swastikas as evidence of their racial identity. The Aryan Brotherhood is among the most violent and fights hard for its share of prison-yard drug dealing, extortion, and prostitution scams.[36] The Aryan Brotherhood occasionally aligns with La Eme in its ongoing conflict with La Nuestra Familia to the extent of conducting assassinations.

This list of gangs is incomplete because of the changing nature of gang identity and the efforts of prison officials to combat gangs. Gangs mutate over time, changing their names and leadership, but racial identification is a constant. One may think that the prisons could stop gang activity by isolating leaders, punishing those who display gang insignia, and transferring those who refuse to cooperate.

An inmate at California State Prison in Lancaster is tattooed with the "Black Hand" of the Mexican Mafia. What are some other prison gangs?

These techniques have been partially successful in the short run, but the diffusion of gang activity to other prisons has complicated efforts at gang control.[37]

It has been somewhat cynically suggested that it is not entirely in the prisons' interests to eliminate gang conflict. Prison officials reportedly keep gangs in a state of perpetual conflict by allowing rival gang members to use the exercise yard at the same time. At California's Corcoran institution, this practice was routinely a source of amusement for the guards. Not only were rival gang members placed in the same yard, but when the ensuing fight took place, the guards placed bets on which inmate would win.[38]

For the most part, prison officials are forced to make difficult decisions in attempts to stem gang violence. On the one hand, they attempt to segregate inmates who are members of rival gangs and different races to avoid violence. On the other hand, they hope to allow inmates to learn to get along with one another and promote the values of diversity espoused in society. Charges of discrimination can be leveled when inmates are racially separated, but when inmates are allowed access to each other and violence ensues, there can be charges of failing to protect the weak. One solution has been to build extremely expensive prisons, known as supermax prisons, where all the inmates are separated from one another in a modern version of the separate-and-silent system.[39]

Supermax Prisons

supermax prison—An extremely secure type of prison that strictly limits inmate contact with other inmates, correctional staff, and the outside world.

The modern **supermax prison** is based on the federal penitentiary at Marion, Illinois, which the Bureau of Prisons opened six years after Alcatraz closed in 1963. Like Alcatraz, Marion was a high-security institution, designed to hold the federal system's most dangerous inmates. As inmate violence at Marion intensified throughout the 1970s, prison administrators added a maximum-level unit to provide for the long-term separation of violent inmates. Marion became the first stand-alone supermax prison in the United States in 1983, when two correctional officers were killed in one day. The prison's administration locked down the facility permanently, confining all inmates in their cells for 23 hours a day. Today Marion is a medium-security institution, and the U.S. Penitentiary Administrative Maximum Facility in Florence, Colorado, serves as the federal supermax prison.

Throughout the 1980s and 1990s, other state institutions assumed the supermax model. Today, several states have at least one supermax prison or a prison with a supermax unit. An excellent example of such an institution is Pelican Bay State Prison, a maximum-security state prison located in Crescent City, California, which recalls the separate-and-silent system utilized in the first prisons in Pennsylvania and Auburn, New York (see Chapter 10).

Constructed in 1989, shortly after the conversion of the federal penitentiary in Marion, Illinois, the Pelican Bay prison architecture is designed to ensure almost total isolation of inmates as well as minimal contact with the staff. The prison itself is such a bleak, stark, and monotonous environment that inmates suffer severe disorientation, depression, and suicidal behavior.[40] High, gray concrete walls surround the exercise yards and totally block out the surrounding national forest. Inmates are confined to their cells with no work, recreation, or contact with anyone other than a cellmate who is equally deprived. When going to the shower (three times a week) or the exercise yard, the inmates are shackled and can move only with the escort of two baton-wielding correctional officers. The prison's security housing unit (SHU)—the term the California prison system uses to designate solitary confinement—is reserved for the state's supposedly most recalcitrant inmates. Until 2015, most of those inmates allegedly belonged to gangs, and the only way out of the unit was to identify other inmates as gang members.

However, after an inmate lawsuit, California agreed to end the indefinite isolation of inmates. At one point more than 500 inmates had been in the unit for more than 10 years.[41] Here is an excerpt from Pelican Bay inmate Gabriel Reyes's account of life in the SHU:

> For the past 16 years, I have spent at least 22½ hours of every day completely isolated within a tiny, windowless cell. . . . for alleged "gang affiliation." It is a living tomb. I eat alone and exercise alone in a small, dank, cement enclosure known as the "dog-pen." When another prisoner is the subject of a debrief, he is not informed of the content, so he is punished with no means to challenge the accusations.[42]

Pelican Bay prison is successful in several ways. It keeps the most dangerous offenders securely incapacitated, ensuring both their safety and the safety of the prison staff. This is a significant feat because it usually takes some degree of cooperation from the inmates to run a truly safe prison. Pelican Bay maintains order mechanically by using technology and prison design, giving inmates absolutely no opportunity to assemble outside their cells. However, this total control comes at a price. This type of prison is costly to operate, demanding a high degree of technology. Keeping an inmate in an SHU is expensive, nearly double the cost of an inmate in the general population. Most states can afford such treatment for only a small percentage of extremely dangerous offenders.[43] For the bulk of the prison population, less expensive prisons, with less control of the inmates, are the norm.

Violence and Overcrowding

The prison is a delicate social system that includes not only inmates but also guards and administrators and, to a lesser extent, the legislators and politicians responsible for funding and personnel decisions. Although inmates are presumed to be powerless in their captivity, they often employ many techniques to address the conditions of their confinement. Inmates may write letters to correctional officials, complain to their congressional representatives, petition the parole board, file briefs in the courts, or simply act out in ways that range from bothersome to seriously violent.

Some of these techniques are more effective than others. The bottom line, however, is that regardless of how frustrated inmates may feel in a correctional institution, they cannot leave. Those of us in society can drop out of school, move out of our parents' houses, quit our jobs, or dump our significant others when we have "had enough." Inmates do not have these options. Being incarcerated means that problems and frustrations can accumulate until a breaking point is reached. This breaking point can be a mental collapse, a fight with a fellow inmate, violence against a guard, or simply retreating from prison life by being so ornery that solitary confinement is required.[44] These are daily occurrences in the prison, and, for the most part, they are handled with established procedures that are understood by all involved.

Occasionally, the inmate's frustrations are shared by others, and the institution's authority is seriously challenged. Inmates acting together can overwhelm the guards and take over the institution in a full-scale prison riot in which people are injured or killed and property is destroyed. Sociologists use the term **collective behavior** to explain how the actions of the individual are transmitted into group actions that can go well beyond what any of the individuals in the group intended.[45] This "herd mentality" can cause even law-abiding citizens to engage in destructive actions. (A good example of this mindset is the riots that sometimes occur after sports championships.)[46]

collective behavior— A sociological term that describes how an individual's actions are transmitted into group actions that can exceed what any of the individuals in the group intended.

In the prison, collective behavior can not only have deadly consequences but also temporarily invert the social structure and shatter the bonds of social control.[47] With the administration no longer controlling the institution, the oppressed become king, the protected become vulnerable, and anyone caught in the middle can become a victim. The prison's most antisocial individuals are, for a limited time, free to wreak havoc.

In 2015, two California institutions experienced several riots. At Folsom prison in August, about 70 inmates began fighting with "shanks," or inmate-made weapons. The fight resulted in the death of Hugo Pinell, 71, who had been incarcerated for 50 years and was involved in a 1971 escape attempt at San Quentin State Prison that killed three correctional officers and three inmates.[48] In a 2016 riot, an inmate was stabbed by several other inmates and accidentally shot by a correctional officer who was trying to control the incident.[49] Such incidents are often caused by gang or personal rivalries. In a May 2015 incident at the medium-security California State Prison, Solano, inmate Nicholas Rodriguez disappeared during a riot. Officials thought he had escaped until his body was found sawed nearly in half with many of its organs removed, and stuffed in a garbage can near his cell.[50]

Studies on the causes and prevention of prison riots have made it clear that despite many commonalities, each institution has its own limitations, atmosphere, and vulnerabilities.[51] However, scholars point to several reasons for riots and other types of violence among inmates. One study revealed that aggressive inmates committed more assaults in institutions that were overcrowded and had a higher percentage of young inmates.[52] Overcrowding occurs when a facility is holding more people than it is designed for. Some prisons operate dormitories where the beds are so close that inmates can reach out and touch the beds next to them. Over the years, the federal and state governments have continued to build facilities that are crowded as soon as they open. The federal prison population has increased by about 800 percent since 1980, and federal prisons are operating at nearly 40 percent over capacity.[53] Overcrowding is unhealthy

Pictured here is the crowded reception area at the California State Prison in Lancaster. What are some consequences of prison overcrowding?

and stressful not only for inmates, but also for prison staff and correctional officers. Understaffed facilities with overworked staff endanger everyone within the facility.[54]

In an effort to keep facilities within capacity, state and local jurisdictions, as well as the federal government, are simply letting inmates go, often by changing the law. In 2014, the U.S. Sentencing Commission altered its sentencing policies for federal offenses, thus qualifying for early release about half of the 100,000 drug offenders in federal prison. In 2015, early release was granted to about 6,000 federal inmates. An additional 8,550 inmates were set for release in the following months.[55] In January 2015, California finally met a federal order to reduce its inmate population, assisted by a new law that reclassified some felonies as misdemeanors (see Case in Point 11.1).[56] By March 2015, California had released 2,700 inmates.[57]

Local jails are also employing relief strategies. Since 2000, 95 percent of the increase in jail inmate population has been due to an increase in the number of inmates who have not been convicted of any crime but are awaiting court processing.[58] To comply with state requirements to operate within capacity, one crowded facility in Michigan lowered some inmates' bond amounts and released other inmates a few days early.[59]

CASE IN POINT 11.1

Brown v. Plata (2011)

THE POINT

The court-mandated population limit in California prisons is necessary to remedy the violation of prisoners' constitutional rights and is authorized by the Prison Litigation Reform Act.

THE CASE

In April 2001, several inmates filed a class-action lawsuit alleging that overcrowding in California prisons violated the Eighth Amendment ban on cruel and unusual punishment. A panel of three federal judges determined that overcrowding in California prisons was the primary cause of violations of the Eighth Amendment. The court ordered the release of enough inmates—between 38,000 and 46,000 inmates—to reach 137.5 percent of the prisons' total design capacity. The U.S. Supreme Court affirmed this decision with a 5–4 majority.

THINK ABOUT IT

1. According to the inmates, what was the problem with overcrowding in the prisons?

PAUSE AND REVIEW

1. Why are prisons total institutions?
2. Name Sykes's five pains of imprisonment.
3. What are the pros and cons of operating supermax prisons?
4. What efforts are being made at the federal, state, and local levels to keep prisons within capacity?

LEARNING OBJECTIVE **5**

Outline how Elizabeth Fry improved prison conditions for women.

LEARNING OBJECTIVE **6**

Discuss some of the health issues associated with women's prisons.

Women in Prison

Women's prisons are much like men's prisons. They have the same high-, medium-, and low-security levels with the same security features, such as fences, razor wire, and electronic detection systems (depending on the security level), as men's prisons. The inmates have been convicted of breaking the same criminal laws as men, although far fewer women than men are in prison generally because they commit fewer violent offenses (see Figure 11.2). Some institutions house both men and women in separate facilities.

As of 2015, females made up about 7 percent of the state and federal prisoner population.[60] Regardless of race, female prisoners ages 30 to 34 had the highest rate of imprisonment. However, black females were up to four times more likely to be imprisoned than white females at any age.[61] Male and female state prison inmates differ in the types of offenses for which they are sentenced, although the percentage of females serving time for murder (11 percent of all sentenced females) was close to that of males (13.2 percent). More females than males were serving sentences for manslaughter, property offenses (except burglary), and drug offenses.[62]

A Short History of Women's Prisons

Women's prisons are a relatively new development. In early England and the North American colonies, male and female prisoners were housed together, and male staff supervised all prisoners.[63] This began to change in the 19th century with the involvement of the Quakers, a Christian religious denomination. In 1813, Quaker Elizabeth Fry visited England's Newgate Prison and was appalled at the conditions. Hundreds of women lived with their children in two filthy rooms, with some sleeping on the floor and others in hammocks. There was little clothing, and Fry was shocked at the sight of two women taking the clothes off a dead child to clothe another child. Fry made improving prison conditions her mission and not only provided clothes and bedding for the prisoners, but also began lecturing about the

FIGURE 11.2 Male versus Female Inmates, 2005–2015 There are far more male than female inmates in the United States. Generally, what is the rate of male-to-female imprisonment?

Source: E. Ann Carson and Elizabeth Anderson, Prisoners in 2015, Table 1 (Washington, D.C.: U.S. Department of Justice, Office of Justice Programs, Bureau of Justice Statistics, 2016), 3. Available at https://www.bjs.gov/index.cfm?ty=pbdetail&iid=5869.

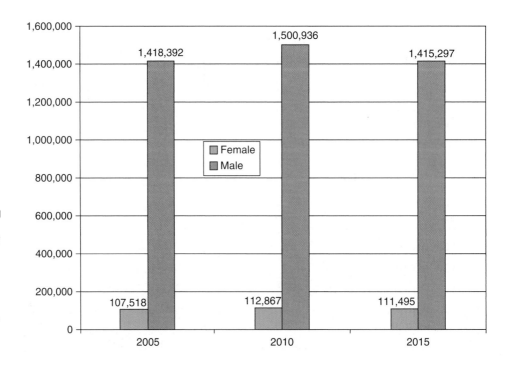

prison's conditions. She also advocated that women should not be guarded by men but by female staff only. Other English prisons adopted her reforms, including separate facilities for women, female staffing, prisoner education, and less hard labor.[64] Fry visited the United States, and in 1825, her efforts there inspired the creation of a separate wing for female juveniles at the New York House of Refuge.

The first completely separate institution for females in the United States was likely at Mount Pleasant, New York, near the Sing Sing male prison in 1835. In 1863, Zebulon Brockway opened a women's unit with female staff at the Detroit House of Correction. The first federal prison for women opened in 1926 in Alderson, West Virginia.[65]

Until the late 20th century, female inmate labor was restricted to what was traditionally considered "women's work": making clothing, cooking, and cleaning. As late as the 1990s, women's education in prison still revolved around training for domestic work and stereotypical women's vocations, such as cosmetology, sewing, food service, and clerical work.[66] In 2001, some women inmates at Utah State Prison sued for access to the same vocational courses offered to men, such as courses in auto repair, electrical work, and construction work. At the time, the only two courses available to women inmates were courses in visual art and design and cooking.[67]

Life in Women's Prisons

The culture in women's prisons is different from that in men's prisons. Male inmates tend to be isolated, and their interactions with other inmates focus on control and domination. Female inmates, on the other hand, are more concerned with forming relationships with each other and the staff. In the past, women inmates even went so far as to form **pseudofamilies**, in which there were "mothers," "fathers," and "children."[68] However, scholars say that these arrangements are disappearing due to the changing inmate population, the nature of offenses, sentence lengths, and increased inmate access to actual family members.[69]

A crucial element of female incarceration is the barrier it poses to proper health and reproductive care. Female inmates are reported to be particularly vulnerable to cervical cancer because the prison environment renders the screening process—the

pseudofamilies— Groups established by women in prison to imitate familial roles in society.

This illustration depicts prison reform advocate Elizabeth Fry reading to female prisoners at England's Newgate Prison. In what ways did Fry influence prison reform in the United States?

common and relatively inexpensive Papanicolaou (Pap) test—difficult. In one study, inmates reported that the administration of the test was rough, inhumane, painful, invasive, and performed with inappropriate equipment in slovenly conditions. Some inmates stated that they even avoided or refused Pap testing at their particular facility. Follow-up care and treatment was also uncoordinated among multiple providers, and, for some inmates, health care information was provided in a language that they could not understand. The provisions for testing were also uneven. Some women were automatically called in for an annual test, while others had to submit a written medical request form and a $5 fee.[70]

Another health issue is related to menstruation. Women inmates in some prisons have reported that staff restrict the availability of sanitary pads. One former inmate reported that at her last institution, sanitary pads were so limited that there were not enough to allow for regular changes, so a single pad had to be used continuously. Inmates who have enough money may purchase extras (if any are available at the commissary), but indigent women cannot do so and must make do with what the institution provides.[71]

Most incarcerated women are of reproductive age, and many women inmates often become pregnant after visits from husbands, consensual sex with staff or volunteers, or being raped by staff or volunteers.[72] A 2012 complaint filed with the Department of Justice alleges that sexual misconduct by male correctional staff at Alabama's Tutwiler Prison for Women is common and has resulted in numerous inmates becoming pregnant. Inmates reported being coerced into performing sexual favors in exchange for contraband and being raped by a male correctional officer while another male officer served as a lookout.[73] Incarcerated women are also likely to have chronic health problems, including mental illness and drug and/or alcohol addiction, and to have experienced physical or sexual violence at some point in their lives.[74]

About 4 to 5 percent of women are pregnant when they enter prison or jail.[75] Women's medical care, especially for pregnancy, is notoriously problematic because institutional medical regulations are not available to the public, and facilities often do not adhere to standards because the standards are not enforced.[76]

An inmate hugs her daughter in the visitation room at a Pennsylvania prison. What pains of imprisonment are unique to women?

Women inmates are commonly shackled during labor and childbirth.[77] Abortion care is also problematic because abortions are not provided within the facilities, so inmates must travel outside the prison for the procedure. At the same time, women have reported being pressured to have abortions, especially when the man who got them pregnant works for the prison. Unfortunately, Elizabeth Fry's recommendation that female staff supervise female inmates has gone by the wayside in the modern U.S. prison.[78]

Generally, women suffer many of the same pains of imprisonment as men. They struggle with addictions and illnesses, they miss their families, and they desire rehabilitation and education. Like men, they are overwhelmingly impoverished, of color, and from disadvantaged backgrounds. Many suffer from post-traumatic stress disorder as a result of abuse earlier in their lives, and the situation does not improve once they are imprisoned. When a federal review panel investigated the Fluvanna Correctional Center for Women, a maximum-security state prison in Troy, Virginia, one inmate testified that the warden, a woman, would tell correctional officers "that if she took anything and everything from us including our humanity maybe we would not return to prison."[79]

PAUSE AND REVIEW

1. How did Elizabeth Fry help improve the conditions of women's incarceration?
2. What are some health issues that women may experience in prison?

Courts and the Prison

Should inmates have legal rights while they are incarcerated? This might seem like a silly question. On one hand, inmates are viewed as having forfeited their rights as citizens, and many people believe that one of the consequences of incarceration is that inmates are stripped of the privileges and legal protections that other citizens enjoy. On the other hand, some believe that inmates should not lose all of their rights. In fact, inmates are still protected by the Constitution. Their legal rights, though necessarily attenuated, are not totally restricted. Inmates are only supposed to lose rights consistent with their confinement and the maintenance of institutional safety. Since 1996, the ability of inmates to bring civil rights actions against the government has been hampered by passage of the **Prison Litigation Reform Act** (see CJ Reference 11.1). The law has seen some recent challenges, however, owing to overcrowding and the deplorable conditions of some prisons.

Before the 1960s, the courts cultivated a **hands-off doctrine** toward inmates' rights.[80] It was thought that offenders had legal rights granted to them in the arrest and trial phases of the criminal justice process and that incarceration was primarily an administrative matter concerning the internal workings of the prison and not subject to a great degree of judicial oversight. There were a few significant reasons for this hands-off doctrine. First, the decisions made about the conditions of confinement were viewed as a technical matter that judges were not educationally equipped to consider. Second, because of the separation of powers, decisions about prisons were considered a matter for the executive branch of government, not the judicial branch. Third, the public did not really care about what went on in the prison and were content to allow prison administrators wide latitude in the treatment of inmates. Finally, the treatment

LEARNING OBJECTIVE 7

Recognize the contributions of the Eighth and Fourteenth Amendments to inmate rights.

Prison Litigation Reform Act—
Legislation that restricts litigation by prison inmates based on the conditions of their confinement.

hands-off doctrine—
The judicial attitude toward prisons before the 1960s in which courts did not become involved in prison affairs or inmate rights.

CJ REFERENCE 11.1
The Prison Litigation Reform Act

The 1996 Prison Litigation Reform Act (PLRA) provides a case-management plan for prison inmate civil rights lawsuits.[81] Critics of the act say it makes it more difficult for inmates to file lawsuits, thus curtailing their Eighth Amendment rights by limiting the means by which those rights could be asserted and the remedies that courts could provide.[82] The PLRA focuses on court practices for processing *in forma pauperis* (as an impoverished person) suits, as most of these inmate suits are filed *pro se* (for oneself). (Scholars have noted that inmates who file *pro se* cases have substantially lower success rates than inmates who have legal representation.[83]) Because most inmate civil rights complaints are decided without trial, the PLRA places most of the administrative burden on the district courts during the initial screening and pre-trial processes. Other provisions of the act are as follows:

- The PLRA tightened the requirements to file *in forma pauperis*, including stricter requirements to pay court filing fees.[84]
- Inmates are required to try to resolve their complaints via the prison's grievance procedure, and they must exhaust all avenues.[85]
- A strike is counted for each lawsuit or appeal that is dismissed because a judge decides that it is improper. After three strikes, an inmate cannot file again *in forma pauperis*. The only exception is if the inmate is at risk of imminent serious physical injury.[86]
- Federal courts must screen all inmate suits against government employees and all *in forma pauperis* cases at the beginning of the litigation. Frivolous or malicious cases, cases that fail to state a claim that may be relieved, and cases that seek damages from defendants immune from damages must be dismissed. [87]

of inmates was considered a product of privileges rather than legal rights. For these reasons, the courts were historically reluctant to involve themselves with the conditions of confinement.[88]

The social upheavals of the 1960s that advocated for the rights of marginalized groups, such as the civil rights and women's movements, influenced many aspects of society, including the prison. Inmates and those concerned with the welfare of inmates began to petition the courts to address several issues they deemed problematic. For instance, in Stateville Prison in Illinois, Christian inmates were allowed to read the Bible, but Muslim inmates were forbidden to possess the Qur'an.[89] Prison officials were successfully sued in *Cooper v. Pate* (1964), which began a new era in prison litigation by helping to end the judicial hands-off doctrine toward prisons and allowing inmates to sue for civil rights violations. This new interventionism resulted in the courts considering a range of prison issues and fundamentally changed the relationship between the courts and corrections. Inmates found the courts receptive to their complaints about the arbitrary ways in which prisons operated. Prison administrators were forced to treat inmates more uniformly, keep better records, and run their institutions according to well-defined and ascertainable criteria.[90]

From where did the courts draw their authority to enter the realm of inmate rights? Inmates' lawyers turned to the Eighth and Fourteenth Amendments to persuade the courts to reconsider prisoners' rights.

Eighth Amendment

As we discussed in Chapter 10, the Eighth Amendment prohibits "cruel and unusual punishments" (see CJ Reference 11.2). However, there is considerable debate as to what should be considered cruel or unusual. The courts have ruled on thousands of cases in which prison administrators were faulted for various policies concerning food, heating, and discipline. Although we cannot discuss all these issues, it has been suggested that the Supreme Court has not provided a clear statement about what constitutes "cruel" or "unusual." Rather, the Court has provided a general statement in which it likens a given situation to that which "amounts to torture, when it is grossly excessive in proportion to the offense for which it is imposed, or that is inherently unfair; or that is unnecessarily degrading, or is shocking or disgusting to people of reasonable sensitivity."[91]

Fourteenth Amendment: Due Process and Equal Protection

The court system has little time to consider cases involving the internal workings of the prison; however, inmates abused by prison officials need somewhere to turn to have their concerns heard. The Fourteenth Amendment states that the due process granted to citizens by the Constitution is also applicable to the states (see CJ Reference 11.2). The concept of incorporation prevents states from restricting rights granted by the federal government. The courts determined in *Wolff v. Mc-Donnell* (1974), which defined the processes required for prison disciplinary proceedings, that inmates are allowed some level of due process.

The equal protection clause of the Fourteenth Amendment addresses racial and sex-based discrimination in the prison. Individuals cannot be treated differently based on their race or because they are male or female.[92] Discrimination that is prohibited in society is similarly not permitted in the correctional institution. Cases that involve religious freedom are also applicable here in that the prison cannot allow certain religions to be practiced while excluding others.[93] Of course, given the multiplicity of religions, there are some limits as to just how far the prison can go in accommodating inmates' needs. For security, economic, and commonsense reasons, not all of the inmates' desired religious requests can be granted. For instance, the prison cannot keep kitchens open 24 hours a day to feed inmates who might have different eating concerns based on religion, nor can prisons cater to the exact dietary restrictions of all religions.[94] Nevertheless, prisons are obligated to make reasonable efforts to address the different legitimate religious needs of a substantial number of inmates.

CJ REFERENCE 11.2
The Eighth and Fourteenth Amendments

EIGHTH AMENDMENT

Excessive bail shall not be required, nor excessive fines imposed, nor cruel and unusual punishments inflicted.

FOURTEENTH AMENDMENT

Section 1.

All persons born or naturalized in the United States, and subject to the jurisdiction thereof, are citizens of the United States and of the state wherein they reside. No state shall make or enforce any law which shall abridge the privileges or immunities of citizens of the United States; nor shall any state deprive any person of life, liberty, or property, without due process of law; nor deny to any person within its jurisdiction the equal protection of the laws.

Inmate Renzee Standberry preaches to fellow Muslim inmates at the Indiana State Prison chapel in Michigan City, Indiana. What efforts are prisons required to make to meet the religious needs of inmates?

Prisons are a unique environment, and the expectations of privacy granted by the Constitution and its amendments are only partially available to inmates. For instance, the standards of privacy in the home do not extend to the prison cell.[95] Although the inmate lives in the cell, there is no constitutional guarantee that it cannot be searched for contraband. The prison has a security imperative to make the institution safe for other inmates and staff that overrides any demand for privacy. Cells may be searched without warning (prior notice would give the inmate time to dispose of drugs, weapons, or other contraband), as may inmates' personal effects, such as books, papers, clothing, and mail.

The inmate's body is also a point of contention, according to the courts. Under what circumstances, and to what degree, can the inmate's body be searched? The inmate's body has only slightly more protection than does the cell and personal effects. The courts have deemed routine strip and body-cavity searches necessary for the institution's safety.[96] However, body-cavity searches that are abusive, unhygienic, or unreasonably degrading are prohibited. The right to privacy of the body is also a concern when the situation involves male guards and female inmates or female guards and male inmates. It sounds reasonable to prohibit cross-sex supervision of inmates, but the courts consider the matter more complex. For instance, although modesty and privacy are important concerns, the cost of same-sex guards for the prison might be prohibitive. Additionally, male inmates might object to a homosexual guard watching them shower, or female inmates might feel uncomfortable in the presence of a lesbian guard. The courts have determined that there are simply too many possibilities for potential embarrassment to get involved.

Courts have an additional reason to be reluctant to intervene in sex and gender issues. To prohibit women from supervising male inmates would violate women's rights under Title VII and the equal protection clause.[97] Women cannot be excluded from large parts of the institution and from core duties of the correctional officer simply because of their sex. Certainly, institutions may establish reasonable efforts to diminish cross-sex supervision, but the legitimate demands of institutional security, efficiency, and worker rights all permit this practice.[98]

The courts have also considered the issues of what mail the inmates may receive and with whom and how they can have outside visitation.[99] Prison officials have wide discretion in limiting the mail and publications that inmates can send and receive.[100] The institution must demonstrate how restrictions are consistent with the needs of prison security and efficiency. Mail from those with a personal or professional relationship with the inmate, such as family, lawyers, and clergy, is generally allowed. However, rules concerning visitation vary considerably by institution. Contraband smuggled in by visitors is a constant threat to jails and prisons. Therefore, personal visits may be restricted by separating the visitor and inmate with a glass barrier and having them communicate by telephone. Contact visits, in which inmates and visitors are allowed to touch, have been deemed problematic by the courts and not a constitutional right. There is also no right to conjugal visitation.[101] Such visitation may help maintain the marital bond while the inmate is incarcerated, but it is up to the state to allow this practice, which is usually permitted for only a few inmates.[102]

PAUSE AND REVIEW

1. **What are the contributions of the Eighth Amendment to inmate rights?**

2. **What equal protections are inmates entitled to under the Fourteenth Amendment?**

This warning at the visitor's entrance to the New Hampshire State Prison in Concord alerts visitors to the rules against bringing contraband into the prison. What issues does contraband create for prisons and jails?

LEARNING OBJECTIVE **8**

Characterize how occupations within the prison differ from those outside the prison.

LEARNING OBJECTIVE **9**

Summarize the general functions of prison correctional officers.

Working in the Prison

Guards, medical technicians, doctors, treatment specialists, administrators, secretaries, and clergy all contribute to the prison dynamic. Most of these occupations are found in society, but unique demands are placed on those who serve in these positions in the prison. For instance, a secretary in most organizations is encouraged to promote good customer relations. In the prison, the "customer" is the inmate, and secretaries are cautioned to be wary, emotionally distant, and suspicious of every request, motive, and kindness offered by inmates. An occupational environment in which the potential for violence, escape, and duplicity is constant poses many challenges and is not for everyone. Those who work in the prison perform a job that, though important, is not always appreciated.

By far the most prevalent and problematic of these jobs is the correctional officer or guard. Correctional officers keep the institution secure, help to maintain the facility, manage its population of inmates, and assist in their rehabilitation. Generally, there are seven variations of correctional officer job assignments:[103]

1. Block officers. These officers are responsible for the security of the housing block, which can contain 300 to 400 inmates, and must see that daily work and activities are done in an orderly way. This includes ensuring that inmates are fed, attend medical and rehabilitative treatment programs, are released into the exercise yard at the appropriate time, and get their mail. This is all done in a noisy and hectic environment in which the officer may be surrounded by inmates with varying demands.

2. Work-detail supervisors. Every prison function that requires inmate labor must be supervised by a correctional officer, including commissary, laundry, library privileges, and recreational activities. Control of scarce resources may be accompanied by pressures from inmates as well as other correctional officers to stretch the limits of discretion to do favors. Although this gives officers some bargaining power with inmates, it is also a source of tension because the work-detail officers are accountable to the administration for getting the work of the prison done. These officers, who are evaluated on how well they can get felons to do their work, are in a vulnerable position.

3. Industrial shop and school officers. These officers perform security and order-maintenance functions by supervising inmates engaged in work or school activities provided by civilians.

4. Yard officers. The yard is the outdoor recreation area of the prison and is the closest thing to the street in the prison environment. The block is the inmate's home, and the school or work assignment keeps the inmate busy, but the yard is where the greatest potential for trouble exists. Yard officers must constantly be alert for signs of trouble.

5. Administrative building assignments. These officers have little inmate contact and perform various administrative functions. They control security gates; handle the storage of weapons; field telephone calls from the outside; and supervise visitations.

6. Wall posts. Some officers watch from a tower what is going on inside the prison yard and on the outside perimeter. This duty is devoid of the anxiety of dealing with inmates at close quarters, but it can be boring. Nevertheless, the position is essential to protect innocent people, especially fellow guards.

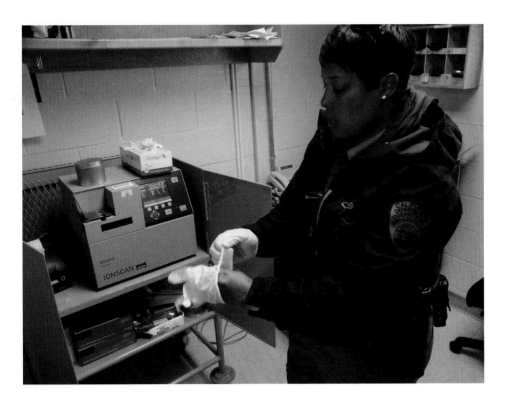

A correctional officer prepares to demonstrate an ion spectrometer that tests for illegal narcotics at Vacaville State Prison in California. What are some types of correctional officer job assignments?

7. Relief officers. These officers fill in for other officers who take time off. The job can be stressful because, without a regular post, the officers have not developed working relationships with inmates. Like substitute teachers, these officers are constantly tested by inmates pushing the boundaries of acceptable behavior. Written job descriptions exist for every post in the prison, but the relief officer must quickly learn any of these jobs while simultaneously performing the job for the first time.

Although the exact posting of the correctional officer dictates the type of duties he or she performs, some general functions are performed in every correctional institution. Over the years, bureaucratization has increased the number of specialist guards, but these general functions are still pertinent to the overall nature of the correctional officers' work:

> Human services. Officers perform many services for inmates, either as a formal part of their duties or because of informal relationships they develop. For example, some inmates may be mentally ill and require extra attention. The three aspects of human-services work are providing goods and services, acting as an advocate, and assisting in inmates' institutional adjustment.

> Order maintenance. Correctional officers maintain the social order in prison by earning the inmates' trust and cooperation. By enforcing rules in a consistent manner, showing inmates respect, and allowing them a certain level of dignity, the correctional officer can help establish an atmosphere in which inmates feel not only secure but also that their world is predictable and controllable. By maintaining order in subtle ways, as well as with the threat of punishments, the officer can reduce tension in the cell block.

> Security. Security is a passive function in which officers ensure that inmates are not acting out and are kept inside the institution.

> Supervision. Correctional officers supervise inmates who do prison maintenance work. Officers are responsible for seeing that the work is done efficiently and safely.

Correctional officers face many stresses primarily because they are actively engaged in controlling and managing a population held against its will.[104] Stresses include crowding, physical exhaustion, shift work, inmate violence, unsatisfactory relationships with co-workers and/or supervisors, vague institutional goals and policies, and poor organizational support.[105] It is estimated that 37 percent of correctional officers experience job stress, which is higher than the estimated 19–30 percent of the general working population who experience job stress. Correctional officers who are under stress may lose motivation and become less committed to their jobs. This could lead to actions that compromise the security of the institution and the safety of their co-workers, such as helping an inmate engage in criminal activity either inside or outside the institution.[106]

Stress factors are aggravated for correctional officers who work in overcrowded facilities.[107] In one survey, correctional officers told researchers that overcrowding leads to problems with safety, inmate/inmate violence, inmate/correctional officer violence, and job performance.[108] In particular, these officers noted that inmate/inmate violence increased in the more crowded areas of the institution and that the number of correctional officers had not increased along with the inmate population. The result has been that many institutions now have fewer officers supervising more inmates who have become increasingly violent as conditions become more crowded.[109]

Some studies have shown that different types of correctional employees have different levels of job stress. Correctional officers in custodial positions (meaning they directly supervise inmates) report more stress than both their supervisors and non-custodial staff.[110] Carceral facilities are strict bureaucratic hierarchies, and the order of command affects the relationships between the administration, the correctional officers, and the inmates. In many cases, the correctional officers are, as one officer put it, "the meat in the sandwich."[111] That is, the correctional officers are at a vulnerable point between the facility administrators, who are responsible for the facility but typically do not have day-to-day contact with the inmates, and the inmates themselves, who have their own needs and desires. The correctional officers must find a way to manage both their employers' expectations and the demands of the often intimidating populations they physically control.[112]

PAUSE AND REVIEW

1. **How do occupations within the prison differ from those outside the prison?**
2. **What are some general functions of prison correctional officers?**
3. **In what ways might the stresses of being a correctional officer affect how one performs the general functions of the position?**

LEARNING OBJECTIVE 10

Argue in support of and against private prisons.

Private Prisons

Interest in privatizing prisons began around the mid-1970s, and the first modern private prisons opened in the early 1980s.[113] Several factors that had their roots in the social revolutions of the 1960s contributed to this trend. By the mid-1970s, the United States was reeling from the loss of the Vietnam War, economic recession, gas and oil shortages, major paradigm shifts in civil society, and a skyrocketing crime rate. The government had become unpopular with Americans and probably not without good reason. It had participated in an unpopular war; President Richard Nixon had left office in disgrace, only to be pardoned by his successor President Gerald Ford; and the country seemed to be at the mercy of foreign powers such as the Organization of Petroleum Exporting Countries (OPEC) and Iran's Ayatollah Khomeini.[114] The government, many Americans believed, could no longer do anything right, including run prisons.

As states grappled with growing inmate populations (see Figure 11.3), the idea that private firms could handle inmates more inexpensively and more efficiently grew popular. It was thought that capitalism could solve a variety of problems because an open market would presumably force the providers of any good or service to produce the best value.

Currently, two companies—CoreCivic (formerly Corrections Corporation of America) and the GEO Group—are the major providers of private correctional services in the United States:

> › Founded in 1983, CoreCivic is currently the largest provider of private prison services in the United States. Working off the idea that the government "can't do anything very well," CoreCivic expanded quickly.[115] As of early 2017, the company operates 89 facilities in the United States, housing nearly 70,000 inmates.[116] Its revenues as of early 2016 were $1.85 billion.[117]

> › The GEO Group is an international company that currently operates 64 facilities in the United States, as well as facilities in the United Kingdom, Australia, and South Africa.[118] The GEO Group's revenue in 2016 was $2.18 billion.[119]

Although private correctional facilities have become big business, they have met with mixed success. State and local facilities still take in most inmates.[120] The arguments both for and against private prisons are numerous. The following are some of the arguments used in favor of private prisons:[121]

> › Money. Hypothetically, private enterprise can run prisons more cheaply than the government because government agencies have an incentive to grow in order to inflate their budgets. Corporations can operate many prisons across

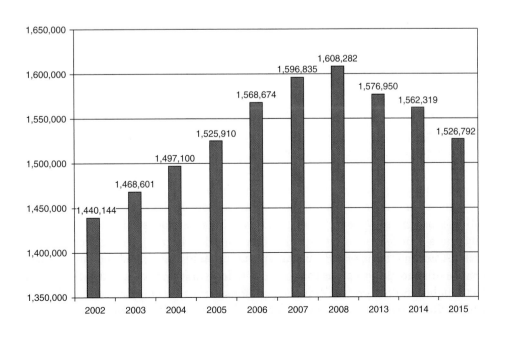

FIGURE 11.3 Number of Inmates Incarcerated under State and Federal Jurisdiction, 2002–2015 In which year did the number of inmates increase the most from the prior year? Decrease the most?

Sources: E. Ann Carson, Prisoners in 2014 *(Washington, D.C.: U.S. Department of Justice, Office of Justice Programs, Bureau of Justice Statistics, 2015), 4. Available at http://www.bjs.gov/index.cfm?ty=pbdetail&iid=5387. E. Ann Carson and Elizabeth Anderson,* Prisoners in 2015, *Table 1 (Washington, D.C.: U.S. Department of Justice, Office of Justice Programs, Bureau of Justice Statistics, 2016), 3. Available at https://www.bjs.gov/index.cfm?ty=pbdetail&iid=5869.*

several jurisdictions, which local and state agencies cannot do, allowing for economy of scale. The profit motive of private prisons demands less waste and more suppliers, which allows private facilities to spend money wisely and avoid shortages. Competition with other private-prison firms encourages higher quality and lower costs.

> Better employee control. Employees of private enterprises are more easily hired and fired than government employees, who have civil service protections, so private prisons can adjust staff sizes more quickly. Administration and staff have more incentive to do a good job and treat inmates fairly because their jobs are at stake. Furthermore, staff members are less likely to strike because they are more likely to be fired if they do so. In addition, private contractors may save money by paying employees less and providing fewer benefits, as well as promoting more effective personnel management and lower absenteeism and employee turnover.

> Accountability. Stockholders and corporate boards add another layer of review to decision-making but are immune to political pressures.

> Flexibility. Private prisons can be built more quickly and cheaply and designed for more efficient operation. Inmates can also be transferred across jurisdictions, allowing optimum residence levels to be maintained at all facilities.

The arguments against private prisons are as follows:

> Money. The first duty of a for-profit operation is to make a profit. Private prisons might cut corners to save money without concern for inmate rights or welfare. If the prison company goes bankrupt or is not making enough profit, it can leave a jurisdiction without facilities. Private prisons are actually more expensive than government prisons because their profit margins are added to the costs of running the prison.[122]

> Labor. Private prisons threaten the jobs, benefits, professionalism, and tenure of public employees, who have less incentive to do a good job because they are less secure and paid less. This increases the risk of strikes and high employee turnover in public facilities.[123]

> Control. Morally speaking, private enterprise should not have the degree of control over human beings that incarceration requires. Private prisons might make government prisons more difficult to manage by housing only the best behaved offenders and refusing to incarcerate the difficult ones. Prison corporations might lobby to build more prisons, thus increasing society's dependence on incarceration and weakening the use of alternatives such as parole.

> Accountability. Private corporations are less accountable to the public than those governed by legislatures of elected officials. The layer of managerial involvement created by the existence of stockholders and corporate boards introduces new opportunities for corruption.[124]

The final judgment on private prisons remains to be seen. The news is rife with their failures: escapes, employee and inmate maltreatment, closings, and falling stock prices. Whether they cost less to operate is questionable.[125] Additionally, there is little evidence that private prisons do a better job of reducing recidivism. According to one study, private prison inmates in Oklahoma had a greater chance of returning to prison than those held in state prisons.[126] Another factor that might limit the growth of private prisons is the new emphasis on faith-based

Critics condemn the GEO Group for its purported efforts to criminalize immigrants and people of color in order to profit from their imprisonment. What are some of the alleged advantages of private prisons?

initiatives that seek to fund religious-oriented prison programs. The federal government has developed a policy that provides public money for these types of programs in public institutions, and, as the overall prison population levels off, demand for private prisons may decrease.[127]

PAUSE AND REVIEW

1. **What are some arguments supporting private prisons?**
2. **What are some arguments against private prisons?**

Jails

A **jail** is a secure facility that typically holds arrestees, criminal suspects, and inmates serving sentences less than a year. Jails, a fundamental component of the corrections system, are a crucial institution that is connected to the law enforcement, courts, and correctional systems and serve as a major focal point in the administration of justice. Jails are controlled by either the local sheriff or an administrator under the auspices of the county or city.[128] Control of the jail can often be a political issue because it is such an important part of the community, the local criminal justice system, and the local power structure. Where the jail is placed organizationally can have a major effect on how it is funded, who is detained there, and the quality of justice.[129]

As of 2015, 728,200 people were held in jails.[130] Males accounted for 85 percent of inmates. Of all jail inmates, 47 percent were white, 35 percent were black, and 15 percent were Hispanic. Fewer than 5,000 juveniles were held in jails.[131] Alaska, Connecticut, Delaware, Hawaii, Rhode Island, and Vermont combine prisons and jails. Thus, the prison population in these states includes jail inmates, who are typically awaiting trial. In other states, prisons may hold a small number of

LEARNING OBJECTIVE 11

Explain the two major functions of jails.

jail—A secure facility that typically holds arrestees, criminal suspects, and inmates serving sentences less than a year.

unsentenced prisoners. At the same time, some states with crowded prisons place some sentenced prisoners in their jails.[132]

The jail serves two major functions (see CJ Reference 11.3 for a complete list). First, it holds suspects who have been arrested and are awaiting disposition of their cases. In 2014, about 6 in 10 jail inmates were defendants awaiting court action on a current charge, and about 4 in 10 were sentenced offenders or convicted offenders awaiting sentencing.[133] Judges and prosecutors decide whether suspects can be safely released before court hearings, so many people spend short periods behind bars ranging from a few hours to a few weeks. Other offenders spend months behind bars awaiting trial or release. The factors that determine how much time is spent in jail before trial include the gravity of the offense, the offender's reputation and ties to the community, and money.

The jail's second major function is the confinement of misdemeanor offenders who have been sentenced to less than one year of incarceration. In some jurisdictions, these sentenced offenders may serve their time on weekends and live at home during the week while maintaining their employment and family ties. Sentenced offenders often act as trustees and clean the courthouse, mow the grass, shovel sidewalks, or help feed and service the inmates awaiting disposition of their cases. A local jail can also be connected to a larger local corrections system that includes work-release programs, road crews, stockades, and local probation departments. There is a wide variety of local corrections structures around the country, each with its own concerns, funding issues, and punishment philosophies. For example, former Sheriff Joe Arpaio of Maricopa County, Arizona, was known for his "Tent City," an outdoor jail he set up in 1993 that housed about 2,000 inmates under canvas tarps in the desert in triple-digit temperatures.[134] After Arpaio lost his bid for re-election in 2016, new Sheriff Paul Penzone announced that Tent City would be closed due to its cost inefficiency and ineffectiveness as a crime deterrent.[135]

One of the major issues associated with jails concerns searches. There are no regulations governing the manner in which jails conduct searches as long as they do not unnecessarily humiliate or degrade the inmate. For example, a reasonable search may violate the Fourth Amendment if performed in an unreasonable manner.[136] Recall that not everyone in jail has been convicted of a criminal offense. Some inmates are merely suspects, whereas others are arrestees for minor

CJ REFERENCE 11.3
What Jails Do

- Receive individuals pending arraignment and hold them awaiting trial, conviction, or sentencing
- Re-admit probation, parole, and bail bond violators and absconders
- Temporarily detain juveniles pending transfer to juvenile authorities
- Hold mentally ill persons pending their movement to appropriate mental health facilities
- Hold individuals for the military, for protective custody, for contempt, and for the courts as witnesses
- Release convicted inmates to the community upon completion of sentence
- Transfer inmates to federal, state, or other authorities
- House inmates for federal, state, or other authorities because of crowding of their facilities
- Sometimes operate community-based programs as alternatives to incarceration[137]

The infamous "Tent City" at Maricopa County Jail in Arizona, seen here in February 2015, was considered one of the worst facilities in the United States for its alleged mistreatment of inmates. What are the two major functions of jails?

infractions such as having too many parking tickets. The following is a summary of search policies common to many jails.

> Cell searches. Jail staff can search the cells at any time without the presence of inmates. In *Block v. Rutherford* (1984), the Supreme Court stated that no cause was required for cell searches.

> Strip searches. Some jails call for the strip search of every inmate booked into the jail, as supported by the Supreme Court case *Bell v. Wolfish* (1979). Inmates may be strip-searched without cause after contact visits or trips outside the jail. Questions remain as to whether inmates in a jail's or prison's general population (as opposed to mere arrestees) may be strip-searched without cause.

> Body-cavity searches. Jails rarely conduct body-cavity searches, and most will not without at least reasonable suspicion. Many jurisdictions adhere to the stricter standard of probable cause and often require a judge's search warrant. Only medically trained personnel are allowed to conduct body-cavity searches.

> Searches of visitors and staff. Visitors and staff have more privacy protections than inmates do but less than they would have outside the jail. At minimum, visitors may expect any bags or parcels to be searched.

Another major issue involving jails is getting out of them. Arrestees and suspects who are in jail awaiting court action are supposed to be able to get out if they can post bail. However, many cannot afford their bail and may remain in jail for months or years awaiting trial. Sixty percent of jail inmates are awaiting disposition of their cases, not serving time for a conviction, and many of those inmates are accused of property, drug, or other nonviolent offenses. Keeping such suspects in jail is expensive, adding to the $22.2 billion local governments spend annually on jails.[138] Suspects and defendants kept in jail often lose their jobs, are unable to support their families, and are kept from doing anything that may help their cases. Researchers say defendants and suspects who can get out of jail, hold down a job, remain with their families, and are not abusing drugs or alcohol are more likely to show up in court.

Some see the jail as a place where society's "rabble" can be placed to improve the appearance of city streets.[139] Homeless people, drug users, drunks, and the mentally ill are all susceptible to being swept into jail for real or imagined infractions of the law.[140] The public demands that the police keep the streets safe for everyone, and those who appear to pose a security threat are often incarcerated in jail. This is not to say that jails are being used inappropriately, but rather that law enforcement is under tremendous pressure to maintain order, and jails are where those without community ties or resources often end up. Law enforcement's job would be much easier and jails less crowded if more community resources existed to help those in desperate financial or social trouble.[141]

PAUSE AND REVIEW

1. What are the two major functions of jails?
2. Why are searches a concern for jails?
3. Why is it so difficult for inmates to get out of jail, and what are the implications of incarceration?

FOCUS ON ETHICS   Keeping the Condemned Alive

Horacio Alberto Reyes-Camarena needs a kidney. His dialysis treatment reportedly costs $121,000 a year, and his doctor believes he is a good candidate for a transplant. Reyes-Camarena is also on death row in the state of Oregon. He has been there since 1996, when he was convicted of repeatedly stabbing two women, one of whom died from her wounds.

Acute medical care for inmates is a controversial subject, with many opponents citing cost as a major factor. Oregon has suffered massive budget cuts affecting such essential services as health care for the poor and education. However, even in a difficult economy, states are required by the Constitution to provide the medical care that inmates need, including organ transplants, regardless of the cost.

Opponents of such procedures question saving the life of a man who is going to die with an organ that could save someone else's life. They also point to poor, law-abiding citizens who do not qualify for placement on organ transplant lists because they cannot afford the anti-rejection drugs, as well as a state already ravaged by a desperate economy. Supporters of lifesaving

procedures for inmates point to the U.S. Supreme Court's decision in *Estelle v. Gamble* (1976) which states that denying necessary medical care to prisoners violates the Eighth Amendment.[142]

WHAT DO YOU DO?

1. Allow Reyes-Camarena to receive a new kidney. His dialysis treatments are expensive, and a new kidney would save the state money.
2. Allow Reyes-Camarena to receive a new kidney. He is a human being, and if he is eligible for the organ, he should receive it.
3. Deny Reyes-Camarena a new kidney. He is a criminal on death row. He is already on dialysis, which is a life-saving treatment, and does not deserve a new organ.

For more insight into how someone might respond to such an ethical dilemma, visit the companion website at www.oup.com/us/fuller to watch a video that connects this scenario to a real-world situation.

Summary

LEARNING OBJECTIVE 1 Define the concept of a total institution as it relates to prisons.	The prison is a total institution in which everything is tightly controlled and highly structured, including who inmates' cellmates are, what they eat, and when they can bathe. This system is designed to help the prison run efficiently, maintain order, and punish offenders by depriving them of goods and services, relationships, and discretion, thus limiting inmates' ability to influence the conditions of their confinement.
LEARNING OBJECTIVE 2 Describe the five pains of imprisonment.	Deprivation of liberty: Inmates are confined to an institution and then further confined within it. Deprivation of goods and services: Inmates do not have access to the food, entertainment, and services that free people enjoy. Deprivation of heterosexual relationships: The inability to engage in heterosexual activities sometimes leads to sexual deviation within the prison. Deprivation of autonomy: Inmates cannot make decisions about some of the most basic tasks. Deprivation of security: Inmates victimize each other by testing for physical or emotional weaknesses.
LEARNING OBJECTIVE 3 Frame how gangs affect the informal inmate social structure and prison security efforts.	Prison gangs based on racial identification promote violence, thus complicating administrative efforts to maintain security. Segregating inmates by race can increase safety; however, this prevents inmates from learning how to get along and does not promote diversity. It may also prompt accusations of discrimination; yet, when inmates have access to each other and violence ensues, prisons can also be accused of failing to protect the weak.
LEARNING OBJECTIVE 4 Identify how prison violence and overcrowding are dealt with.	Supermax prisons confine inmates to their cells with no work, recreation, or contact with anyone but a cellmate. This modern version of the separate-and-silent system keeps dangerous offenders incapacitated, ensuring their safety and that of prison staff, but it is costly to operate. Less expensive prisons with less inmate control are often overcrowded, which can encourage collective challenges from inmates that result in riots, shattering social control. To keep facilities within capacity, some jurisdictions are altering sentencing policies and lowering bond amounts to promote early release and decrease prison populations.
LEARNING OBJECTIVE 5 Outline how Elizabeth Fry improved prison conditions for women.	Fry advocated that female staff only should guard women. English prisons adopted her reforms, including separate facilities for women, female staffing, prisoner education, and less hard labor. Fry's efforts and visit to the United States inspired the creation in 1825 of a separate wing for female juveniles at the New York House of Refuge.
LEARNING OBJECTIVE 6 Discuss some of the health issues associated with women's prisons.	Female inmates are vulnerable to cervical cancer because the prison environment renders the screening process difficult. The lack of access to sanitary supplies makes menstrual care problematic. Sexual abuse and misconduct is common, and sometimes inmates become pregnant while incarcerated. Abortion care is not provided within the facilities. Pregnancy care is especially problematic because institutional medical regulations are not available to the public and facilities often do not adhere to standards because they are not enforced.

LEARNING OBJECTIVE 7 Recognize the contributions of the Eighth and Fourteenth Amendments to inmate rights.	The Eighth Amendment prohibits cruel and unusual punishments; however, it is not always clear as to what constitutes cruel or unusual. In thousands of cases, prison administrators have been faulted for policies related to food issues, heating, and discipline. *Wolff v. McDonnell* (1974) established that the Fourteenth Amendment grants some level of due process to inmates. The equal protection clause establishes that inmates cannot be treated differently based on their race or because they are male or female. Discrimination that is prohibited in society is not permitted in correctional institutions.
LEARNING OBJECTIVE 8 Characterize how occupations within the prison differ from those outside the prison.	In prison, guards, medical technicians, doctors, treatment specialists, administrators, secretaries, and clergy must be wary, emotionally distant, and suspicious of every request, motive, and kindness offered by inmates. In the prison environment, the potential for violence, escape, and duplicity is constant, whereas outside the prison, the likelihood is less so.
LEARNING OBJECTIVE 9 Summarize the general functions of prison correctional officers.	Human services: Officers perform a variety of services for inmates, either as a formal part of their duties or because of informal relationships they develop with certain inmates. Order maintenance: Officers maintain the social order in prison by earning the inmates' trust and cooperation. Security: The focus of security is to keep the inmates inside the institution. Supervision: The physical maintenance of the prison is accomplished by officers' supervision of inmate labor.
LEARNING OBJECTIVE 10 Argue in support of and against private prisons.	In support of: Private enterprise can run prisons more cheaply than the government. Private enterprise employees are more easily hired and fired than government workers, so private prisons can adjust staff sizes more quickly when needed. Stockholders and corporate boards add another layer of review to decision-making and are immune to some of the political pressures inherent in governments. Against: Private prisons put profit ahead of inmate welfare and threaten the jobs, benefits, professionalism, and tenure of public employees. Private enterprise morally should not have the degree of control over human beings that incarceration requires.
LEARNING OBJECTIVE 11 Explain the two major functions of jails.	1. Jails hold suspects who have been arrested and are awaiting disposition of their cases. 2. Jails hold misdemeanor offenders who have been sentenced to less than one year of incarceration.

Critical Reflections

1. If you were incarcerated, what would be your biggest challenges in adjusting to prison life?

2. Why is it necessary for the courts to get involved in issues concerning the legal rights of the incarcerated?

3. How does the experience of women in prison differ from that of men?

Key Terms

Endnotes

1 Mike Freeman, "Pro Football: Phillips Let Go after Troubling Signs," *New York Times.* November 21, 1997, http://www.nytimes.com/1997/11/21/sports/pro-football-phillips-let-go-after-troubling-signs.html. *New York Times,* "Pro Football: Notebook: 49ers Suspend Phillips and Plan to Waive Him," November 16, 1999, http://www.nytimes.com/1999/11/16/sports/pro-football-notebook-49ers-suspend-phillips-and-plan-to-waive-him.html.

2 Joe Rogers, "Former NFL RB Lawrence Phillips Hinted at Killing Before Cellmate's Death," *Sporting News,* September 12, 2015, http://www.sportingnews.com/nfl-news/4655085-lawrence-phillips-cellmate-murder-charged-letters.

3 Josh Peter, "Lawrence Phillips Found Dead in Prison at Age 40," *USA Today,* January 13, 2016, http://www.usatoday.com/story/sports/nfl/2016/01/13/lawrence-phillips-death-prison/78742058/. *Sports Illustrated,* "Lawrence Phillips Committed Suicide, Found with 'Do Not Resuscitate' Note," June 16, 2016, https://www.si.com/nfl/2016/06/16/lawrence-phillips-death-suicide.

4 Josh Peters, "Lawrence Phillips Seeks to Pay Murder Defense with NFL Concussion Settlement," *USA Today Sports.* September 26, 2015, http://www.freep.com/story/sports/nfl/2015/09/26/lawrence-phillips-seeks-pay-murder-defense-nfl-concussion-settlement/72881424.

5 James J. Stephan, Census of State and Federal Correctional Facilities, 2005 (Washington, D.C.: U.S. Department of Justice, Office of Justice Programs, 2008), 1. Available at http://www.bjs.gov/index.cfm?ty=dcdetail&iid=255.

6 Michigan.gov, Prisons, http://www.michigan.gov/corrections/ 0,4551,7-119-68854_1381_1385---,00.html. Utah Department of Corrections, http://corrections.utah.gov.

7 E. Ann Carson and Elizabeth Anderson, *Prisoners in 2015,* Table 1 (Washington, D.C.: U.S. Department of Justice, Office of Justice Programs, Bureau of Justice Statistics, 2016), 3. Available at https://www.bjs.gov/index.cfm?ty=pbdetail&iid=5869.

8 Georgia Department of Corrections, http://www.dcor.state.ga.us/Divisions/Facilities/FacilitiesOperations. Accessed February 2017.

9 California Department of Corrections and Rehabilitation, Reception and Classification Process, http://www.cdcr.ca.gov/Ombuds/Entering_a_Prison_FAQs.html. Accessed February 2017.

10 Federal Bureau of Prisons, Federal Inmates, https://www.bop.gov/inmates. Accessed March 2017.

11 Federal Bureau of Prisons, https://www.bop.gov/about/facilities/federal_prisons.jsp. Accessed February 2017.

12 Ibid.

13 Federal Bureau of Prisons, Sentence Computations, https://www.bop.gov/inmates/custody_and_care/sentence_computations.jsp. Accessed March 2017. Anne Berton, *Practical Tips If Your Client Faces Incarceration in a Federal Prison* (San Francisco, Calif.: Sentencing Advocacy Workshop, 2010), https://www.fd.org/pdf_lib/SAWII2010/SAWII2010_Practical_Tips.pdf.

14 Federal Bureau of Prisons, Voluntary Surrenders, https://www.bop.gov/inmates/custody_and_care/voluntary_surrenders.jsp. Accessed March 2017.

15 Patricia L. Hardyman, James Austin, and Johnette Peyton, *Prisoner Intake Systems: Assessing Needs and Classifying Prisoners* (Washington, D.C.: U.S. Department of Justice National Institute of Corrections, 2004), vii. Available at http://nicic.gov/library/019033.

16 Erving Goffman, *Asylums: Essays on the Social Situation of Mental Patients and Other Inmates* (Garden City, N.Y.: Anchor Books, 1961).

17 Tonisha R. Jones and Travis C. Pratt, "The Prevalence of Sexual Violence in Prison: The State of the Knowledge Base and Implications for Evidence-Based Correctional Policy Making," *International Journal of Offender Therapy and Comparative Criminology* 52 (June 2008): 280–295.

18 Victor H. Brombert, *The Romantic Prison: The French Traditions* (Princeton, N.J.: Princeton University Press, 1978).

19 Gresham M. Sykes, *The Society of Captives: A Study of a Maximum Security Prison* (Princeton, N.J.: Princeton University Press, 1974), 64.

20 Ibid., 65.

21 Stephen Katz, "What It's Like to Actually Eat the Food in Oakland County Jail," *Detroit Metro Times,* July 8, 2015, http://www.metrotimes.com/detroit/what-its-like-to-actually-eat-the-food-in-oakland-county-jail/Content?oid=2354552.

22 Sykes, *The Society of Captives,* 72.

23 Cindy Struckman-Johnson and David Struckman-Johnson, "A Comparison of Sexual Coercion Experiences Reported by Men and Women in Prison," *Journal of Interpersonal Violence* 21 (December 2006): 1591–1615.

24 National Institute of Justice, About the Prison Rape Elimination Act of 2003, November 6, 2007, http://www.nij.gov/topics/corrections/institutional/prison-rape/pages/prea.aspx.

25 Michael Windzio, "Is There a Deterrent Effect of Pains of Imprisonment?" *Punishment and Society* 8 (July 2006): 341–364.

26 Thomas Carnahan and Sam McFarland, "Revisiting the Stanford Prison Experiment: Could Participant Self-Selection Have Led to the Cruelty?" *Personality and Social Psychology Bulletin* 33, no. 5 (May 2007): 603–614.

27 David Skarbek, *The Social Order of the Underworld* (New York: Oxford University Press, 2014). Christian Parenti, *Lockdown America: Police and Prisons in the Age of Crisis* (New York: Verso, 2000).

28 Philip G. Zimbardo, Stanford Prison Experiment, http://www.prisonexp .org.

29 Ibid.

30 Ibid.

31 Ibid.

32 Ibid.

33 Ibid.

34 Ibid.

35 Ibid.

36 Tori Richards, "Murder Trial Yields Sharply Conflicting Portrayals of White Prison Gang," *New York Times*, July 14, 2006, 16.

37 Marie Griffin, "Prison Gang Policy and Recidivism: Short-Term Management Benefits, Long-Term Consequences," *Criminology and Public Policy* 6 (May 2007): 223–230.

38 Parenti, *Lockdown America: Police and Prisons in the Age of Crisis*, 172.

39 Jeffrey Ian Ross, "Supermax Prisons," *Society* 44 (March 2007): 60–64.

40 Craig Haney, "Infamous Punishment: The Psychological Consequences of Isolation," in *Correctional Contexts: Contemporary and Classical Readings*, 2d ed., eds. Edward J. Latessa, Alexander Holsinger, Jonathan R. Sorensen, and James W. Marquart (Los Angeles: Roxbury, 2001), 172.

41 Associated Press, "California Prisons to End Solitary Confinement of Gang Members after Pelican Bay Prisoners Sue," *San Jose Mercury News*, September 1, 2015, http://www.mercurynews.com/california/ci_28738123/solitary-confinement-california-pelican-bay-inmates-lawyers-have.

42 Gabriel Reyes, "The Crime of Punishment at Pelican Bay State Prison," *San Francisco Chronicle*, November 27, 2012, http://www.sfgate.com/opinion/openforum/article/The-crime-of-punishment-at-Pelican-Bay-State-3597332.php.

43 James Austin and John Irwin, *It's About Time: America's Imprisonment Binge*, 3d ed. (Belmont, Calif.: Wadsworth, 2001). See especially Chapter 6, "Super Max," 117–137.

44 Haney, "The Psychological Impact of Incarceration: Implications for Post-Prison Adjustment."

45 Ralph S. Turner and Lewis M. Killian, *Collective Behavior*, 3d ed. (Englewood Cliffs, N.J.: Prentice Hall, 1987).

46 Gustave Le Bon, *The Crowd* (New York: Viking Press, 1960). First published in 1895; see also Ladd Wheeler, "Toward a Theory of Behavioral Contagion," *Psychological Review* 73 (March 1966): 179–192.

47 Vernon B. Fox, *Violence behind Bars: An Explosive Report on Prison Riots in the United States* (New York: Vantage Press, 1956).

48 Sanya Mansoor, "Deaths of Three Guards, Two Inmate Trustees," *Christian Science Monitor*, August 13, 2015, http://www.csmonitor.com/USA/Justice/2015/0813/Death-of-infamous-inmate-triggers-California-prison-riot-Who-was-Hugo-Pinell-video.

49 Paige St. John, "Death of Inmate During California Prison Melee Is Second in a Week," *Los Angeles Times*, January 25, 2016, http://www.latimes.com/local/political/la-me-inmate-killed-third-prison-riot-20150819-story.html.

50 Peter Holley, "Mysterious Prison Killing Leaves California Inmate Sawed in Half with Organs Missing," *Washington Post*, July 11, 2015, https://www.washingtonpost.com/news/morning-mix/wp/2015/07/11/mysterious-prison-killing-leaves-california-inmate-sawed-in-half-with-organs-missing.

51 Randy Martin and Sherwood Zimmerman, "A Typology of the Causes of Prison Riots and an Analytical Extension to the 1986 West Virginia Riot," *Justice Quarterly* 7 (1990): 711–737; See also John Pallas and Robert Barber, "From Riots to Revolution," in *The Politics of Punishment*, ed. Erik Olin Wright (New York: Harper & Row, 1973), 237–261.

52 Karen F. Lahm, "Inmate-On-Inmate Assault: A Multilevel Examination of Prison Violence," *Criminal Justice and Behavior* 35, no. 1 (2008): 120–137.

53 Sari Horwitz, "Justice Department Set to Free 6,000 Prisoners, Largest One-time Release," *Washington Post*, October 6, 2015, https://www.washingtonpost.com/world/national-security/justice-department-about-to-free-6000-prisoners-largest-one-time-release/2015/10/06/961f4c9a-6ba2-11e5-aa5b-f78a98956699_story.html.

54 Joseph L. Martin, Bronwen Lichtenstein, Robert B. Jenkot, and David R. Forde, "'They Can Take Us over Any Time They Want': Correctional Officers' Responses to Prison Crowding," *Prison Journal* 92, no. 1 (2012): 88–105.

55 Horwitz, "Justice Department Set to Free 6,000 Prisoners, Largest One-time Release."

56 Sharon Bernstein, "California Eases Prison Crowding After Years of Trying," Reuters, January 30, 2015, http://www.reuters.com/article/2015/01/30/us-usa-california-prisons-idUSKBN0L301N20150130.

57 Melody Gutierrez, "California Prisons Have Released 2,700 Inmates under Prop. 47," SFGate, March 6, 2015, http://www.sfgate.com/crime/article/California-prisons-have-released-2-700-inmates-6117826.php.

58 Todd D. Minton and Zhen Zeng, *Jail Inmates at Midyear 2014* (Washington, D.C.: U.S. Department of Justice, Office of Justice Programs, Bureau of Justice Statistics, 2015), 1. Available online at http://www.bjs.gov/index.cfm?ty=pbdetail&iid=5299.

59 Holly Fournier, "Some Sentences Being Cut to Ease Macomb Jail Crowding," *Detroit News*, June 17, 2015, http://www.detroit-news.com/story/news/local/macomb-county/2015/06/17/macomb-jail/28864571/.

60 Carson and Anderson, *Prisoners in 2015*, Table 1, p. 3.

61 Ibid., Table 8, p. 13.

62 Ibid., Table 9, p. 14.

63 Harry Elmer Barnes, *The Evolution of Penology in Pennsylvania: A Study in American Social History* (Indianapolis, Ind.: Bobbs-Merrill Company, 1927), 72.

64 Russell L. Craig, "Women in Corrections: Elizabeth Gurney Fry," *Journal of Correctional Education* 57, no. 2 (June 2006): 141–144.

65 Ibid.

66 Mary Winifred, "Vocational and Technical Training Programs for Women in Prison," *Corrections Today* 58, no. 5 (August 1996): 168.

67 Utah College Named in Prisoners' Vocational Education Suit," *Community College Week* 13, no. 26 (August 6, 2001): 10.

68 ABCNews, "Inside a Maximum Security Women's Prison," November 2004, http://abcnews.go.com/Primetime/story?id=227295&page=1. Accessed January 2016.

69 Holly M. Harner, "Relationships Between Incarcerated Women: Moving Beyond Stereotypes," *Journal of Psychosocial Nursing & Mental Health Services* 42, no. 1 (January 2004): 38–46.

70 Catherine G. Magee, Jen R. Hult, Ruby Turalba, and Shelby McMillan, "Preventive Care for Women in Prison: A Qualitative Community Health Assessment of the Papanicolaou Test and Follow-Up Treatment at a California State Women's Prison," *American Journal of Public Health* 95, no. 10 (October 2005): 1712–1717.

71 Chandra Bozelko, "Prisons that Withhold Menstrual Pads Humiliate Women and Violate Basic Rights," *Guardian*, June 12, 2015, http://www.theguardian.com/commentisfree/2015/jun/12/prisons-menstrual-pads-humiliate-women-violate-rights.

72 Rachel Roth, "Obstructing Justice: Prisons as Barriers to Medical Care for Pregnant Women," *UCLA Women's Law Journal* 18, no. 1 (Fall 2010): 79–105.

73 Elizabeth Chuck, "'Frequent and Severe' Sexual Violence Alleged at Women's Prison in Alabama," NBCNews, May 2012, http://usnews.nbcnews.com/_news/2012/05/23/11830574-frequent-and-severe-sexual-violence-alleged-at-womens-prison-in-alabama.

74 Jael Silliman and Anannya Bhattacharjee, ed., *Policing the National Body: Sex, Race, and Criminalization* (Cambridge, Mass.: South End Press 2002), 1–81. Beth Richie, "The Social Impact of Mass Incarceration on Women," in *Invisible Punishment: The Collateral Consequences of Mass Imprisonment*, ed. Marc Mauer and Meda Chesney-Lind (New York: New Press 2002), 136–149.

75 Laura M. Maruschak, *Medical Problems of Jail Inmates* (Washington, D.C.: U.S. Department of Justice, Office of Justice Programs, Bureau of Justice Statistics, 2006), 1. Available at http://www.bjs.gov/index.cfm?ty=pbdetail&iid=786.

76 Roth, "Obstructing Justice."

77 Priscilla A. Ocen, "Punishing Pregnancy: Race, Incarceration, and the Shackling of Pregnant Prisoners," *California Law Review* 100, no. 5 (October 2012): 1239–1311.

78 Roth, "Obstructing Justice." Terry A. Kupers, "The Role of Misogyny and Homophobia in Prison Sexual Abuse," *UCLA Women's Law Journal* 18, no. 1 (Fall 2010): 107–130.

79 David Kaiser and Lovisa Stannow, "Prison Rape: Obama's Program to Stop It," *New York Review of Books*, October 11, 2012, 49–52. Available at http://www.nybooks.com/articles/2012/10/11/prison-rape-obamas-program-stop-it.

80 James B. Jacobs, *Stateville: The Penitentiary in Mass Society* (Chicago: University of Chicago Press, 1977), 105.

81 Bernard D. Reams Jr. and William H. Manz, *A Legislative History of the Prison Litigation Reform Act of 1996*, vol. 1 (New York: William S. Hein & Co., 1997), iii. Available online at https://www.law.umich.edu/facultyhome/margoschlanger/Pages/PrisonLitigationReformActLegislativeHistory.aspx.

82 ACLU, Know Your Rights: The Prison Litigation Reform Act (PLRA), https://www.aclu.org/know-your-rights/prison-or-jail-prison-litigation-reform-act-plra. Accessed January 2016. Kyle T. Sullivan, "To Free or Not to Free: Rethinking Release Orders under the Prison Litigation Reform Act after *Brown v. Plata*," *Boston College Journal of Law & Social Justice* 33, no. 2 (Spring 2013): 419–451.

83 Tasha Hill, "Inmates' Need for Federally Funded Lawyers: How the Prison Litigation Reform Act, Casey, and Iqbal Combine with Implicit Bias to Eviscerate Inmate Civil Rights," *UCLA Law Review* 62, no. 1 (January 2015): 176–235.

84 Bernard D. Reams Jr. and William H. Manz, *A Legislative History of the Prison Litigation Reform Act of 1996*, vol. 1 (New York: William S. Hein & Co., 1997), iii. Available online

at https://www.law.umich.edu/facultyhome/margoschlanger/Pages/PrisonLitigationReformActLegislativeHistory.aspx.

85 ACLU, Know Your Rights: The Prison Litigation Reform Act (PLRA), https://www.aclu.org/sites/default/files/images/asset_upload_file79_25805.pdf. Accessed January 2016.

86 ACLU, Know Your Rights: The Prison Litigation Reform Act (PLRA), https://www.aclu.org/sites/default/files/images/asset_upload_file79_25805.pdf. Accessed January 2016.

87 *Columbia Human Rights Law Review*, Chapter 14: The Prison Litigation Reform Act, *A Jailhouse Lawyer's Manual*, 9th ed., 2011, p. 302, http://www3.law.columbia.edu/hrlr/JLM/.

88 These reasons are best articulated by Philip L. Reichel, *Corrections: Philosophies, Practices, and Procedures*, 2d ed. (Boston: Allyn & Bacon, 2001), 517.

89 Jacobs, *Stateville*, 107.

90 James Bennett, "Who Wants to Be a Warden?" *New England Journal of Prison Law* 1 (1974): 69–79.

91 Reichel, *Corrections*, 522.

92 *Lee v. Washington*, 390 U.S. 333, 88 S.Ct. 994 (1968); *Holt v. Sarver*, 309 F. Supp. 362 (ED Ark. 1970).

93 *Cruz v. Beto*, 405 U.S. 319, 92 S.Ct. 1079 (1972).

94 *Cooper v. Pate*, 378 U.S. 546, 84 S.Ct. 1733 (1964).

95 *Hudson v. Palmer*, 468 U.S. 517, 104 S.Ct. 3194 (1984).

96 *Bell v. Wolfish*, 441 U.S. 520, 99 S.Ct. 1861 (1979).

97 *Grummett v. Rushen*, 587 F.Supp. 913 (1984).

98 *Johnson v. Phelan*, 69 F.3d 144 (1995).

99 *Kentucky Department of Corrections v. Thompson*, 490 U.S. 454, 109 S.Ct. 1904 (1989).

100 *Thornburgh v. Abbot*, 490 U.S. 401, 109 S.Ct. 1874 (1989).

101 *Tarlton v. Clark*, 441 F.2d 384 (1971).

102 Rachel Wyatt, "Male Rape in U.S. Prisons: Are Conjugal Visits the Answer?" *Case Western Reserve Journal of International Law* 37 (March 2006): 579–614.

103 Lucien X. Lombardo, "Guards Imprisoned: Correctional Officers at Work" in *Correctional Contexts: Contemporary and Classical Readings*, eds. Edward J.

Latessa et al. (Los Angeles: Roxbury, 2001), 153–167.

104 Caitlin Finney, Erene Stergiopoulos, Jennifer Hensel, Sarah Bonato, and Carolyn S Dewa, "Organizational Stressors Associated with Job Stress and Burnout in Correctional Officers: A Systematic Review," *BMC Public Health* 13, no. 1 (March 2013): 1–13.

105 Finney et al., " Organizational Stressors Associated with Job Stress and Burnout in Correctional Officers." Martin et al., "'They Can Take Us over Any Time They Want'."

106 Finney et al., ""Organizational Stressors Associated with Job Stress and Burnout in Correctional Officers." E. G. Lambert, N. L. Hogan, and I. Altheimer, "An Exploratory Examination of the Consequences of Burnout in Terms of Life Satisfaction, Turnover Intent, and Absenteeism among Private Correctional Staff," *Prison Journal* 90, no. 1 (2010): 94–114.

107 Martin et al., "'They Can Take Us over Any Time They Want'."

108 Ibid.

109 Ibid.

110 C. Dowden and C. Tellier, "Predicting Work-related Stress in Correctional Officers: A Meta-analysis," *Journal of Criminal Justice* 32 (2004): 31–47. L. H. Gerstein, C. G. Topp, and G. Correll, "The Role of the Environment and Person When Predicting Burnout among Correctional Personnel," *Criminal Justice and Behavior* 14, no. 3 (1987): 352–369. J. R. Carlson and G. Thomas, "Burnout among Prison Case Workers and Corrections Officers," *Journal of Offender Rehabilitation* 43, no. 3 (2008):19–34. E. A. Paoline, E. Lambert, and N. L. Hogan, "A Calm and Happy Keeper of the Keys: The Impact of ACA Views, Relations with Co-workers, and Policy Views on the Job Stress and Job Satisfaction of Correctional Staff," *Prison Journal* 86, no. 2 (2006):182–205.

111 Finney et al., " Organizational Stressors Associated with Job Stress and Burnout in Correctional Officers." Joseph L. Martin, Bronwen Lichtenstein, Robert B. Jenkot, and David R. Forde, "'They Can Take Us over Any Time They Want': Correctional Officers' Responses to Prison Crowding," *Prison Journal* 92, no. 1 (March 2012): 88–105.

112 Martin et al., "'They Can Take Us over Any Time They Want'."

113 David Shichor, *Punishment for Profit: Private Prisons/Public Concerns* (Thousand Oaks, Calif.: SAGE, 1995), 13–14.

114 The current members of OPEC are Algeria, Indonesia, Iran, Iraq, Kuwait, Libya, Nigeria, Qatar, Saudi Arabia, the United Arab Emirates, and Venezuela. As for the Ayatollah Khomeini, in November 1979, Iranian militants supporting Khomeini took 70 Americans captive at the U.S. embassy in Tehran. The ordeal lasted 444 days.

115 David Shichor and Michael J. Gilbert, *Privatization in Criminal Justice: Past, Present, and Future* (Cincinnati, Ohio: Anderson, 2001), 209, as quoted in E. Bates, "Prisons for Profit," in *The Dilemmas of Corrections: Contemporary Readings*, 4th ed., eds. Kenneth C. Haas and Geoffrey P. Alpert (Prospect Heights, Ill.: Waveland Press, 1998).

116 CoreCivic, Locations, http://www.cca.com/locations. CoreCivic, Who We Are, http://www.cca.com/who-we-are. Accessed March 2017.

117 MarketWatch, CoreCivic, http://www.marketwatch.com/investing/stock/cxw/financials. Accessed March 2017.

118 The Geo Group, Locations, http://www.geogroup.com/locations. Accessed March 2017.

119 Geo Group, The GEO Group Reports Fourth Quarter and Full-Year 2016 Results, February 2017, http://investors.geogroup.com/file/Index?KeyFile=38172520.

120 Carson, *Prisoners in 2015*, 16.

121 Charles H. Logan, *Private Prisons: Cons and Pros* (New York: Oxford University Press, 1990), 41–48.

122 Alex Friedmann, "Apples-to-Fish: Public and Private Prison Cost Comparisons," *Fordham Urban Law Journal* 42, no. 2 (December 2014): 503–568.

123 Doris Schartmueller, "People Matter More Than Numbers: Organized Efforts Against Prison Privatization in Florida," *Contemporary Justice Review* 17, no. 2 (June 2014): 233–249.

124 Rebecca Cooper, Caroline Heldman, Alissa R. Ackerman, and Victoria A. Farrar-Meyers, "Hidden Corporate Profits in the U.S. Prison System: The Unorthodox Policy-making of the American Legislative Exchange Council," *Contemporary Justice Review* 19, no. 3 (September 2016): 380.

125 Sasha Volokh, "Are Private Prisons Better or Worse Than Public Prisons?" *Washington Post*, February 25,

2014, https://www.washingtonpost.com/news/volokh-conspiracy/wp/2014/02/25/are-private-prisons-better-or-worse-than-public-prisons.

126 Andrew L. Spivak and Susan F. Sharp, "Inmate Recidivism as a Measure of Private Prison Performance," *Crime and Delinquency* 54 (July 2008): 482–508.

127 Richard F. Culp, "The Rise and Stall of Prison Privatization: An Integration of Policy Analysis Perspectives," *Criminal Justice Policy Review* 16 (December 2005): 412–442. U.S. Department of Justice, Center for Faith Based & Neighborhood Partnerships (FBNP), https://ojp.gov/fbnp/index.htm. Accessed February 2017.

128 Brandon K. Applegate and Alicia H. Sitren, "The Jail and the Community: Comparing Jails in Rural and Urban Contexts," *Prison Journal* 88 (June 2008): 252–269.

129 Thomas G. Blomberg, "Beyond Metaphors: Penal Reform as Net-Widening," in *Punishment and Social Control*, eds. Thomas G. Blomberg and Stanley Cohen (New York: Aldine de Gruyter, 1995): 45–61.

130 Danielle Kaeble and Lauren Glaze, *Correctional Populations in the United States, 2015*, Table 1 (Washington, D.C.: U.S. Department of Justice, Office of Justice Programs, Bureau of Justice Statistics, 2016), 2. Available at https://www.bjs.gov/index.cfm?ty=pbdetail&iid=5870.

131 Todd D. Minton and Zhen Zeng, *Jail Inmates at Midyear 2014* (U.S. Department of Justice, Office of Justice Programs, Bureau of Justice Statistics, 2015), 3. Available at http://www.bjs.gov/index.cfm?ty=pbdetail&iid=5299.

132 Carson, *Prisoners in 2015*, 3.

133 Minton and Zeng, *Jail Inmates at Midyear 2014*, 4.

134 Joe Hagan, "The Long, Lawless Ride of Sheriff Joe," *Rolling Stone* no. 1163 (August 16, 2012): 62–69. Maricopa County Sheriff's Office, Jail Information, https://www.mcso.org/Home/Jailsa#fifth.

135 Fernanda Santos, "Outdoor Jail, a Vestige of Joe Arpaio's Tenure, Is Closing," *New York Times*, April 4, 2017, https://www.nytimes.com/2017/04/04/us/arpaio-tent-city-maricopa-sheriff-penzone.html.

136 "The Fourth Amendment in Jail: Prisoner and Arrestee Rights While in

Custody," *Supreme Court Debates* 14, no. 8 (November 2011): 7–15.

137 Todd D. Minton, Jail Inmates at Midyear 2011 - Statistical Tables (Washington, D.C.: U.S. Department of Justice, Office of Justice Programs, Bureau of Justice Statistics, 2012), 12–13. Available at www.bjs.gov/content/pub/pdf/jim11st.pdf.

138 Tracey Kyckelhahn, *Local Government Corrections Expenditures, FY 2005–2011* (U.S. Department of Justice,

Office of Justice Programs, Bureau of Justice Statistics, 2013), 3.

139 Stan C. Proband, "Jail Populations Up—Racial Disproportions Worse," *Overcrowded Times* 4, no. 4 (1993): 4.

140 John Irwin, *The Jail: Managing the Underclass in American Society* (Berkeley: University of California Press, 1985).

141 Michael Welch, "Social Junk, Social Dynamite and the Rabble: Persons with AIDS in Jail," *American Journal*

of Criminal Justice 14, no. 1 (1989): 135–147.

142 Bryan Robinson, "Death-Row Inmate Seeks Organ Transplant," ABCNews.com. May 28, 2003, http://abcnews.go.com/US/story?id=90611&page=1. Oregon Live, Oregon Death Row, http://www.oregonlive.com/pacific-northwest-news/index.ssf/page/oregon_death_row.html. Accessed February 2017.

Community Corrections

Cornealious "Mike" Anderson leaves the Mississippi County Courthouse in Charleston, Missouri, with his grandmother (left) and wife and daughter (right) on May 5, 2014. Do you agree with the judge's ruling to release Anderson from prison?

In 2000, Mike Anderson was convicted of armed robbery after he and an accomplice used a BB gun to rob the manager of a Burger King who was making a night deposit at a bank. Anderson was sentenced to 13 years in prison. In July 2013 when the Missouri Department of Corrections was preparing to release Anderson, they could not find him.

Anderson never served a day of his sentence. After his conviction, his family hired a new attorney to handle an appeal, and Anderson bonded out of prison. The appeal failed, but because of a clerical error, a warrant was never issued to pick up Anderson. Anderson, meanwhile, went on to live an exemplary life. He married a woman who did not know about his criminal past and started a contracting business. By all accounts, Anderson was a good father and a devoted church member. He never committed another crime. Additionally, he never tried to hide, living only two blocks from his original address. He did not change his name. He got married at the courthouse, and he registered his business with the Secretary of State under his real name. Regardless, after discovering its error, a team of U.S. marshals in tactical gear raided Anderson's home in Webster Groves, Missouri, just after dawn and took him into custody.[1]

In court, Anderson's attorney argued, "My client has been his own parole officer for the past 14 years. He's been able to accomplish on his own what the criminal justice system often cannot accomplish." Judge Terry Lynn Brown agreed, telling Anderson, "You're a good man, and you're a changed man, and that makes a huge difference in my decision today. . . . You're not the man you were 14 years ago. I believe that continuing to [incarcerate you] serves no purpose."[2] Anderson was released after receiving credit for time served.

THINK ABOUT IT > In your opinion, what are the benefits of the Missouri Department of Corrections inadvertently allowing Mike Anderson to remain in the community for 13 years?

LEARNING
OBJECTIVE | **1**

Outline the assumptions about the nature of crime that lie at the heart of community corrections.

**community
corrections**—A form of corrections in which criminal offenders are managed in the community instead of in correctional facilities.

Community Corrections in Context

How does society send a message to offenders that they will be dealt with seriously and at the same time make the criminal justice response cost effective? Many jurisdictions have implemented **community corrections**. By partially restricting freedoms, requiring participation in treatment programs, and imposing fines, community corrections attempts not only to deter but also to rehabilitate. As of 2015, about 6,741,400 people were under the supervision of U.S. adult correctional systems. Of those, about 7 in 10 were either on probation or parole.[3]

Although not as visible as prisons, community corrections account for a major portion of the correctional efforts of the criminal justice process.[4] This chapter will cover four related community corrections strategies: diversion programs, probation, intermediate sanctions, and parole. The historical and philosophical underpinnings of attempts to reform and/or incapacitate offenders outside the prison will also be discussed.

Why do we treat and punish offenders within the community rather than just send them all to prison? The answer is both simple and complex. Simply put, we cannot afford to incarcerate everyone who violates the law.[5] It is not possible to build enough prisons to house everyone who breaks the law.[6] One of the functions of the criminal justice system is to remove offenders who pose a continued threat and place them in the relatively few prison cells.

A more complex answer to the question of why every offender is not locked up is that, for the most part, prisons work only in a limited manner. As we have discussed, the criminal justice system has multiple goals: incapacitation, retribution, and to a lesser extent, rehabilitation.

> Incapacitation. Prisons are good at achieving the goal of incapacitation. For the limited time offenders are behind bars, they cannot break any more laws outside the prison. Offenders might break the law within prison by victimizing other inmates or correctional workers, but this depends on how effective the prison is in keeping internal order. In addition, prison gang members may order fellow members to commit offenses on the outside, but the chance of this occurring is likely less than if the offender were free.

> Retribution. The goal of **retribution** is to punish the offender for transgressions of the criminal law. Prisons are somewhat successful in accomplishing this goal, but for financial reasons related to prison overcrowding, the public is generally unsatisfied with the amount of punishment they believe the offender is getting when they hear stories about early parole and "country club prisons," a designation often given to federal prisons that incarcerate white-collar offenders. Although the prisons are still uncomfortable circumstances, the media have dubbed them "Club Fed," owing to the availability of amenities such as college classes and recreational activities like volleyball and billiards, giving federal prison a somewhat distorted view.

> Rehabilitation. The goal of rehabilitation might not be met because of the meager conditions of confinement within most institutions, which seem to release inmates who are more antisocial than when they first arrived.[7] In this sense, prisons might not enhance public safety because they tend to embitter, harden, and alienate inmates.[8] Consequently, efforts are made to limit the deleterious effect of prisons by finding alternatives to incarceration for all but the most dangerous offenders. Consider the opening case of Mike Anderson, who became a productive member of society without going to prison. What might have become of Anderson had he served those 13 years in prison?

retribution—
Punishment that is considered to be deserved.

At the heart of the community corrections movement are some assumptions about the nature of crime and the benefits of using community resources to address the problems of crime. These assumptions include the following:

> Prison is an artificial society. Conformity in prison is not always a good indicator of the inmate's ability to adjust to the free world.

> The prison's total control does little to prepare inmates to take responsibility for their actions.

> The community has resources that are unavailable in the prison, such as drug treatment or work release, which enhance the likelihood of rehabilitation.

> The community can provide support networks to the offender that do not exist in prison. With the help of spouses, parents, children, and clergy who have bonds with the offender, the offender has a greater chance of leading a law-abiding life.

> The offender can contribute to the financial upkeep of his or her family and, if gainfully employed, pay taxes. Additionally, some community corrections programs require offenders to pay the cost of their supervision.

As part of an intensive drug and alcohol rehabilitation program, former prisoners grow and sell produce outside of Larimer County Community Corrections in Fort Collins, Colorado. What other types of community corrections programs do offenders participate in?

> The state spends less money on offenders in community corrections programs than it does incarcerating them. Prison cells are expensive, and the state can address many more offenders by handling them outside the prison setting.

> The state can accurately identify which offenders are dangerous and need secure incarceration and which ones are safe to release into the community with supervision.

> The number of trained probation and parole officers is sufficient to adequately supervise the offenders who are selected for community corrections programs.

Is it safe to make these assumptions about the efficacy of community corrections? For the most part, the answer is yes. Millions of offenders have successfully served sentences in community corrections programs during which, in addition to not breaking any more laws, they have completed treatment programs, supported their families, paid taxes, re-entered society, and contributed to the community (see Figure 12.1 for the number of adults who have successfully completed probation).[9] Many notable failures have occurred, however, in which offenders have killed, raped, or robbed, causing criminal justice officials to look incompetent and careless.[10] Such instances create tension around the use of community corrections. Despite calls for such radical initiatives as abolishing parole, those who understand the corrections situation in the United States appreciate that early-release mechanisms are necessary.[11] Therefore, community corrections will always be with us. Only the degree to which they are used is controversial. Which and how many inmates or offenders should be released into the community and what level of supervision they are subjected to are the key concerns.

PAUSE AND REVIEW

1. **What are some assumptions about the nature of crime that lie at the heart of the community corrections movement?**

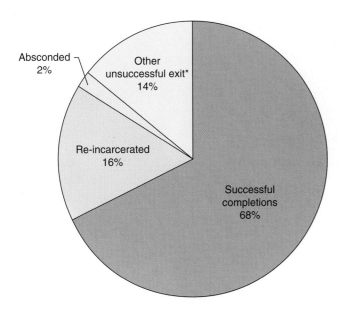

Absconded 2%

Other unsuccessful exit* 14%

Re-incarcerated 16%

Successful completions 68%

FIGURE 12.1 Adults Leaving Probation, 2015 Based on what you've read, do you think the number of probationers who successfully complete their sentences should be higher or lower?

*This category includes discharged probationers who failed to meet all conditions of supervision, including some probationers who had only financial conditions remaining, and some who had their probation sentence revoked but were not incarcerated because their probation sentence was immediately reinstated.

Source: Danielle Kaeble and Thomas P. Bonczar, Probation and Parole in the United States, 2015 (U.S. Department of Justice Office of Justice Programs Bureau of Justice Statistics, 2017), 4. Available at https://www.bjs.gov/index.cfm?ty=pbdetail&iid=5784.

Diversion

Offenders can be diverted to alternative programs at several points in the criminal justice system. These programs are based on **labeling theory**, which suggests that limiting the offender's penetration into the criminal justice system makes the offender less likely to adopt a criminal self-concept and continue to break the law. Diversion programs are especially popular when dealing with the first-time offender who has committed a relatively minor offense.[12] Typically, the offender's charges are held in abeyance (temporarily suspended) while he or she completes some type of treatment program or community service or simply continues to stay out of trouble for a specified period of time.[13] Once the conditions of the diversion program are completed, the offender is released from supervision without a conviction on his or her record.

Sometimes this brief encounter with the criminal justice system is enough to get the attention of young offenders, who are then successful in avoiding further contact with the law. For many young people who have college aspirations or hope for a career in law, medicine, or teaching, a clean record is crucial. Many prosecutors and judges do not want to spoil the record of young people who commit minor offenses. They see diversion programs as a method for sorting out those who respond immediately and those who will continue to be problems for the criminal justice system.[14]

Although diversion programs limit the number of people who enter the criminal justice system, they are not without critics. Given the present state of prison overcrowding and the heavy caseloads that probation officers carry, were it not for diversion programs, the state would dismiss the cases of many first-time offenders who commit minor offenses.[15] Because prosecutors must prioritize what cases to pursue, diversion programs provide an attractive alternative to dropping the charges. However, the overall effect of diversion programs is to widen the net of social control, a phenomenon known as **net-widening**. By that, we mean that the state controls more and more people who, with one more minor slip-up, could find themselves entangled deeply within the criminal justice system. Some programs have so many conditions and restrictions that clients are almost sure to violate at

LEARNING OBJECTIVE 2

Describe the connection between diversion programs and labeling theory.

labeling theory—A perspective that considers recidivism to be a consequence, in part, of the negative labels applied to offenders.

net-widening—A phenomenon through which criminal justice programs pull more clients into the system than would otherwise be involved without the program.

Seattle Police Officer Tom Christenson talks to Gailen Lopton (seated right). After having previously caught Lopton using heroin, instead of incarcerating him, the police offered Lopton the opportunity to participate in a drug rehabilitation program that tries to keep low-level drug offenders out of jail. How do such diversion programs help to curb the number of people entering the criminal justice system?

least some of them. This has been called "stacking the deck." Instead of diverting offenders from the system, some programs, with their multitude of conditions and requirements, actually suck the offender into a deeper quagmire of legal problems.[16] For example, it is one thing to be caught with a misdemeanor quantity of marijuana, but when an offender fails to attend a drug-counseling program or return the diversion officer's phone calls, the resulting revocation of diversion can mean incarceration.[17]

probation (from Chapter 1)—The suspension of all or part of a sentence subject to certain conditions and supervision in the community.

PAUSE AND REVIEW

1. **What is the connection between diversion programs and labeling theory?**

2. **What are the advantages and disadvantages of diversion programs?**

LEARNING OBJECTIVE **3**

Discuss how various actors in the criminal justice system view probation.

LEARNING OBJECTIVE **4**

Characterize the three universal functions that define the probation officer's occupation.

Probation

Probation is a chance for offenders to stay out of prison or jail if they promise to be good. At any given time, there are more probationers than prison inmates or parolees, with state probationers far outnumbering federal probationers (see Figures 12.2 and 12.3). Probationers are not completely free, however. They must agree to certain terms set by a judge, such as performing public-service work, abstaining from alcohol, getting therapy, and reporting regularly to a probation officer.[18] Those who violate these agreements are usually incarcerated for the term for which they were initially eligible. Probation is a widely used sentencing alternative because it accomplishes several positive outcomes. Depending on how one views the criminal justice system, one or more of these outcomes might be more attractive than others. Here, we will consider the practice of probation from the relative viewpoints of the key actors in the criminal justice system.

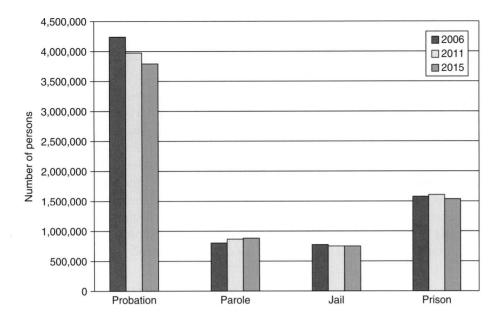

FIGURE 12.2 Persons under Correctional Supervision, Selected Years, 2006–2015 Why are more people on probation than under any other form of correctional supervision?

Source: Danielle Kaeble and Lauren Glaze, Correctional Populations in the United States, 2015, *Table 1 (Washington, D.C.: U.S. Department of Justice, Office of Justice Programs, Bureau of Justice Statistics, 2016), 2. Available at https://www.bjs.gov/index.cfm?ty=pbdetail&iid=5870.*

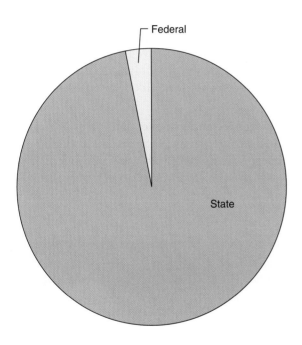

FIGURE 12.3 Comparison of Adults on State and Federal Probation, 2015 What are some possible reasons as to why there are so many more state probationers than federal?

Source: Danielle Kaeble and Lauren Glaze, Correctional Populations in the United States, 2015, *Appendix Table 4 (Washington, D.C.: U.S. Department of Justice, Office of Justice Programs, Bureau of Justice Statistics, 2016), 17. Available at https://www.bjs.gov/index.cfm?ty=pbdetail&iid=5870.*

> How the offender views probation. Probation can seem like a good deal for the offender. When faced with prison, many offenders embrace the prospect of probation like a lifeline. Probation allows the offender to remain at home, at work, and safe from the pains of imprisonment. Compared to life in prison, the restrictions of probation seem like a minor irritant. However, the conditions of probation do affect the offender's freedom and, after a while, can seem frivolous and nitpicky. Probationers do not enjoy the same legal rights as other citizens. Reporting to the probation officer on a weekly or monthly basis; abstaining from alcohol and drugs; and seeking permission to move to a different residence, change jobs, or travel outside the county can cause resentment and alienation.[19] These conditions must be taken seriously because their violation can bring swift and certain

punishment from the state. Because the time served on probation does not count toward a new prison sentence, revocation, even after many successful years of probation, may result in receiving the entire prison sentence for which one was initially eligible.

› How the prosecutor views probation. The prosecutor's foremost concern is to win the case. Having decided to file a charge against an offender, the prosecutor wants to dispose of the case positively and efficiently. As we discussed in Chapter 8, although often under pressure from the victim to seek prison time, the prosecutor has considerable discretion in fashioning **plea bargains** with defense attorneys.[20] Probation is a sanction that the prosecutor can point to as a victory, even though it requires little time or resources. As a plea-bargaining tool, probation allows the prosecutor to avoid costly trials for a large percentage of cases. Additionally, prosecutors may embrace probation when the facts of the case are weak and it would likely result in a dismissal if it went to trial.

› How the defense attorney views probation. The defense attorney also views probation as a victory. By keeping the offender out of prison, the defense attorney can claim to have preserved the offender's liberty with some reasonable compromises (i.e., the conditions of probation). The defense attorney is not overly concerned with the conditions because, for the most part, they will not hurt the offender and may serve as positive influences. Being required to get more education or counseling are not violations of fundamental human rights, and the defense attorney is not likely to object to such requirements.[21]

› How the judge views probation. Judges are under tremendous pressure from the public to punish offenders despite the fact that prisons are full. Probation allows the judge to impose a sentence that is less expensive than prison and, to some degree at least, satisfies victims and other citizens that

plea bargain (from Chapter 8)—A compromise reached by the defendant, the defendant's attorney, and the prosecutor in which the defendant agrees to plead guilty or no contest in return for a reduction of the charges' severity, dismissal of some charges, further information about the offense or about others involved in it, or the prosecutor's agreement to recommend a desired sentence.

In May 2017, model Dani Mathers (center right), shown here with her attorneys, faced invasion of privacy charges for photographing an elderly woman in a gym locker room and body-shaming her on Snapchat. Mathers pleaded no contest and was sentenced to probation and community service. In what ways does the defense attorney view probation as a victory?

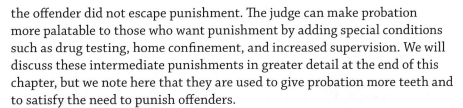

the offender did not escape punishment. The judge can make probation more palatable to those who want punishment by adding special conditions such as drug testing, home confinement, and increased supervision. We will discuss these intermediate punishments in greater detail at the end of this chapter, but we note here that they are used to give probation more teeth and to satisfy the need to punish offenders.

> How reformers view probation. Probation offers the offender a variety of treatment and community-service activities. Community resources such as schools, mental health centers, hospitals, and opportunities for gainful employment cannot be duplicated in prison. If used judiciously, these resources can provide the ingredients for successful rehabilitation and reintegration of the offender. Perhaps the major benefit of probation as seen by reformers is the avoidance of the deleterious effects of prison. By avoiding hardened, long-term inmates, the offender may still be able to learn productive work habits and positive social skills.

> How politicians view probation. On one hand, many politicians adopt a tough-on-crime stance and advocate sending vast numbers of offenders to prison for long sentences. On the other hand, these same politicians do not provide the funds needed to build enough prisons, hire enough probation officers, or establish effective community-corrections treatment services. To them, probation is a cheaper way to punish than prison. However, politicians can be expected to condemn parole when some parolee commits a heinous offense while under supervision.

Probation means many things to many people. The emphasis of probation in any given jurisdiction may vacillate between its twin goals of supervision and treatment. Because it is such a fundamental feature of the criminal justice system, however, it will always be used in one form or another.

Probation Officers at Work

The probation officer's job requires a variety of skills, a strong sense of self-worth, and a tolerance for other people not doing what is expected of them. Most probation work is done at the local level, although there are probation officers at the federal level. The probation officer spends time in the courtroom, in the office, and in the field visiting clients where they work and live. Each probation department has standards for monitoring offenders, and each probation officer works out how to accomplish the job's multiple demands. Many probation officers love this work because its discretion and flexibility allow them to use their particular administrative, interpersonal, and investigative strengths to help offenders and protect society. The probation officer's duties are many, but three universal functions define the occupation: investigation, supervision, and service.

INVESTIGATION

The probation officer spends a lot of time gathering information for decision-makers throughout the criminal justice system. The offender's case file contains data gleaned from police reports; prosecutors' files; and interviews with offenders, victims, witnesses, neighbors, teachers, and peers. The most time-consuming and significant report the probation officer writes is the **pre-sentence investigation (PSI)**.[22]

The United States has a bifurcated court process. The first goal of the proceedings is to determine if the defendant is guilty. This is sometimes done by means of a criminal trial, which is used sparingly; most cases are settled through plea bargaining.[23] With plea bargaining, the judge does not have the opportunity to

pre-sentence investigation (PSI)— The report prepared by a probation officer to assist a judge in sentencing; also called a pre-sentence report.

San Bernardino County probation officers search the room of a parolee during a probation compliance sweep. What are the three universal functions of a probation officer?

become familiar with the case or the defendant, so in the second part of the case proceedings, the sentencing, the judge has little information on which to base a sentence. Typically, the judge postpones the sentencing judgment while the probation department conducts a pre-sentence investigation.[24] During the PSI, the probation officer collects information about two important aspects of the case: the legal history of the incident and the offender's social history.

The legal history offers the judge two primary items to help make an informed sentencing decision. The first item is a complete report on the offense. The probation officer summarizes the police report, provides the offender's version of the incident, and includes additional perspectives from the victim or other interested parties. The goal is to give the judge a good idea of the offense's effects on the victim and the community.[25] This is especially useful when the case has been plea-bargained because the final charge might not reflect the seriousness of the offense or the dangerousness of the offender. For example, in a case of spousal abuse, a husband may be able to plead a savage beating down to a simple assault charge. This reduced charge limits the sentence, but the judge is well served in knowing exactly what happened and how violent the husband can be. With this knowledge, the judge may impose special conditions of probation, such as attending anger-management classes. Additionally, this part of the PSI alerts the judge to the dispositions of any co-defendants and to any further charges that might be hanging over the offender. The second item of the legal history is the offender's record. Is this the first time the defendant has violated the law or the fifteenth? If probation was attempted before, did the defendant successfully complete the probationary term without violating its conditions? Is there a pattern of increasing severity in the defendant's offenses? Did the peeping tom become a flasher who now is convicted of rape? Have other interventions such as alcohol and drug treatment been successful? The answers to these types of questions help the judge determine the risk of putting an offender back on the street.

The offender's social history also helps the judge craft an appropriate sentence. The probation officer gathers information on the offender's education, family, work situation and employment history, physical and mental health, and military history. If any of these factors are related to the case, the probation officer may describe in great detail how the offender may have special issues that require consideration. For example, if the offender has been convicted of child abuse, it would be important for the judge to be aware of his employment as a fourth-grade teacher or volunteer work for the Boy Scouts. In gathering this information, the probation officer includes names, addresses, phone numbers, and other information on family members, places of employment, peers, victims, and witnesses. This information is important not only for the case at hand, but to develop a record of attachments that can be used by future probation officers to monitor the offender. Sometimes the phone number of a former girlfriend or boyfriend becomes the one link to a probationer who has disappeared.

The probation officer questions the client on all of these issues and then spends a great deal of time attempting to verify the truthfulness of the answers. Some clients forget important details of their past, some try to put a positive spin on their actions, and some simply lie. A forthcoming and honest offender may find a judge to be more receptive than one who demonstrates that he or she cannot be trusted. The PSI is the probation officer's opportunity to provide the judge not only with facts but also with information on the offender's attitude. Because this document can determine whether the defendant goes to prison or is placed on probation, the probation officer must be fair to both the defendant and society.[26]

SUPERVISION

Once an offender is placed on probation, the probation officer advises him or her about what is expected. Each probation system has standard conditions. Typically, these include instructions on how often to report; restrictions on changing jobs, residences, or schools without prior approval; and proscriptions on alcohol consumption, drug use, and consorting with known felons. The probationer must cooperate with the probation officer and follow all lawful instructions. These standard conditions give the probation officer wide latitude in controlling the probationer's lifestyle. However, because of high caseloads, most officers cannot systematically ensure that all the conditions are being followed.

The judge may also apply special conditions to a particular case. For instance, in the case of a child abuser, the judge may prohibit him from loitering around schools or playgrounds.[27] Other special conditions may include community service. For example, an accountant convicted of a DUI may be required to provide free tax advice to senior citizens, or a college student involved in a hit-and-run accident may be required to speak at high schools and confess to her lack of judgment and the remorse she has for the harm she did to the victim. The probation officer must ensure that these activities are accomplished.

The supervision function of the probation officer's job accomplishes two goals. First, supervision is a form of punishment in which the probationer's life is disrupted by the many conditions of probation. This disruption obviously pales in comparison to the disruption of going to prison, but reporting to the probation officer and asking permission for simple things such as leaving the state to go on vacation can become tiresome after a couple of months or years. Second, the supervision function is a form of surveillance designed to protect society by alerting the probation officer that the probationer is drifting back into unlawful behavior.[28]

Because prisons are crowded, courts must place on probation some offenders who pose a risk to society. In such instances, surveillance is an especially important function.[29] To determine an offender's level of risk, probation departments

Judge David A. Tapp of the Pulaski County Courthouse in Somerset, Kentucky, assesses the willingness of offenders to participate in the Supervision Motivation Accountable Responsibility and Treatment (SMART) probation program, which provides medication to drug offenders. What are the two goals of the supervision function of probation?

measure the type of offense and the offender's legal and social history to inform the level of supervision and the frequency of probation officer contacts. The determination of probation risk is an internal management issue for probation departments and not a legal issue in which offenders are protected by the court. The courts have intervened only sporadically to limit the discretion of probation officers and judges. The risk assessment instrument does have some built-in bias. For instance, younger offenders are automatically assigned more risk than older offenders. Similarly, juvenile and adult first-time offenses are usually treated more leniently by the courts, but in probation risk assessments, they count against the offender as stringently as any other offense.[30]

The probationer's risk level dictates how much he or she will be watched. Typically, probation officers allocate more attention to new offenders until they can determine that they are adjusting to their status. If the probationer follows instructions and reports when required, attends school and/or holds down a steady job, and fulfills the standards and special conditions of probation, then the supervision is relaxed.

In an ideal world, there would be enough probation officers to ensure that every probationer is living a law-abiding life and following the conditions of probation. However, due to a lack of funding, many probationers get away with numerous minor violations, and some of them continue to maintain a criminal lifestyle. Doing so is precarious, however, because probation officers have surveillance powers that police officers lack. If the probation officer suspects that a probationer is breaking the law, then a search of the residence, car, or person can be conducted without the benefit of probable cause. It is understood that the probation officer may conduct almost unlimited surveillance on probationers. Because probation is a conditional release, probationers must agree to limited legal rights.

When a probationer is caught committing a new offense or violating the conditions of probation, the probation officer may decide to handle the violation informally by warning the probationer or the case may go back to the judge. In *Mempa v. Rhay* (1967), the U.S. Supreme Court determined that felony defendants must be allowed to have an attorney during hearings when probation may be revoked or a deferred sentence imposed. However, this is where things get dicey for the probationer. Although the court must afford the probationer all the required legal rights for the new offense, this new offense will also be considered a probation violation. The legal requirements necessary to revoke the probation and sentence the probationer on the old charge are far less rigorous than those needed to convict and sentence the probationer on the new charge.

Any plea bargaining the probationer does on the new charge can affect his or her probation status. For example, suppose Joe is on probation for five years for assault and has successfully completed four years of probation when he is arrested for selling drugs to an undercover narcotics officer. Because he cooperated with the police by ratting out his drug-dealing friends, he strikes a deal with the prosecutor on the drug charge for probation. However, Joe's prior charge of assault, which occurred in another jurisdiction, involves a different judge who determines that his arrest for selling drugs violates his conditions of probation. Consequently, Joe's probation is revoked, and the judge sentences him to five years in prison based on the assault charge. When Joe gets to prison, he is alarmed to find that his new cellmate is one of his friends who was incarcerated as a result of his testimony. Oops.

Most violations of the technical conditions of probation do not result in revocation. Many judges are reluctant to send people to jail because they failed to report to their probation officers or moved to a new apartment without permission. Judges do not want to be bothered with minor issues, and so they depend on the probation officer to use discretion and chastise the offender. On some occasions, the probation term may be extended for an offender who cannot follow instructions, or new, more restrictive conditions may be applied until it is clear that compliance is forthcoming.[31]

The probation officer must document his or her supervision of offenders because there is always the possibility that one will commit a serious offense and not only make the officer look incompetent but expose the officer to professional liability. If the probation officer did not follow protocol and failed to require the probationer to abide by the conditions of probation, then the offender's victims may be able to sue.[32] For instance, say a probation officer unknowingly permitted a child molester to move to a residence next to an elementary school, did not visit the probationer for months, and during this time, the probationer lured children into his yard and sexually abused them. It would be reasonable for a prosecutor to argue that the probation officer should have known the probationer lived next to the school. If examination of case records demonstrates that procedures were not followed and required home contacts not made, such inaction would subject the officer to legal implications.

A good example of the possible consequences of lax probation practices is illustrated by the case of Jaycee Dugard. Phillip Garrido kidnapped Dugard in 1991 when she was 11 years old and kept her in his backyard for 18 years, eventually fathering two children by her. Garrido was on federal probation for a kidnapping and rape in the 1970s, yet probation officers never discovered Dugard or her two daughters. Although a federal judge found no evidence that probation officers would have found Dugard or her children by searching Garrido's premises, the report called the probation office's handling of Garrido "clearly substandard." According to the judge's report, probation officers rarely visited Garrido at home, "never" talked with his neighbors and local police, and "largely ignored . . . frequent positive drug tests." Garrido's probation officer never confirmed that Garrido had registered as a sex offender in California and ignored fears expressed by his female co-workers.[33] In 2010, Dugard's family received a $20 million settlement from the state of California.[34]

One management technique to ensure that dangerous offenders are provided with an adequate level of supervision is to give their cases to probation officers with reduced caseloads, who can then be required to make more contacts. These reduced-caseload strategies are called intensive-supervision probation (ISP). Because this practice is similar to the parole function, we will discuss it in greater detail later in this chapter.

SERVICE

One reason why individuals decide to work in corrections is to help people. Although investigation and supervision occupy most of probation officers' time, they are still expected to provide some level of service to offenders who need help. Sometimes new probation officers are disillusioned when they discover the impediments to providing the help they believe is needed. These impediments include the following:

> High caseloads. Because probation officers must supervise so many cases, they have little time to establish a personal rapport with each client.

> Many offenders do not want the help and extra attention of the probation officer. Some officers are surprised that the very clients they are trying to help are liars, cheats, and con artists. Some officers become cynical after being betrayed a few times and replace their naiveté with an equally ineffective bitterness.

> Sparse resources. Mental health institutes, drug treatment centers, and all sorts of aid programs have been jettisoned because of budget cuts at every level of government. This can be frustrating to both the probation officer and the probationer. Sometimes a "treatable moment" appears when the probationer is motivated to seek help; however, being placed on a waiting list can mean a lost opportunity.

It is unfortunate that the service aspect of the probation officer's job is so limited. Some may argue that rehabilitation is a secondary activity, but evidence suggests that appropriate placement in a decent treatment program can have a positive effect. Although the investigation and supervision aspects of probation will always be the primary focus, the service component may well be the most important for the long-term behavior change of the offender and ultimately the protection of society.

Private Probation

private probation—A form of probation supervision that is contracted to for-profit private agencies by the state.

With probation caseloads rapidly expanding, many states have found it difficult to provide enough probation officers to adequately supervise everyone who is on probation. As a result, many states use contract, or private, probation services for misdemeanor cases.[35] **Private probation** involves contractual agreements between the state government and companies owned by private individuals whereby misdemeanor probationers are assigned by the judge to be supervised by agencies that are not part of a formal state government. Presumably, these offenders require little in the way of supervision as compared to people convicted of felonies, and relieving state probation officers of this responsibility seems to be an attractive way to focus resources on more serious offenders. These private agencies may charge probationers a cost-of-supervision fee that helps offset their personnel costs and overhead, while also allowing the private agency to make a profit. Although figures are not available as to how much profit is realized, it is potentially substantial.

There is considerable debate about the ethical issues of this type of for-profit probation (see A Closer Look 12.1), but it is not unlike the example of private prisons. When traditional government activities are privatized, it is assumed that the service will be less expensive and more effective. To this end, states have developed guidelines and requirements that dictate how private probation agencies supervise misdemeanor cases.[36] These requirements specify such activities as how often the probationers are contacted, the collection of fines and cost-of-supervision fees, and the provision for treatment alternatives, which also may be contracted to private agencies. Private probation has many advantages and disadvantages.

A CLOSER LOOK 12.1
Pay or Stay in the Modern Debtor's Prison

In 2008, Harriet Cleveland of Montgomery, Alabama, received several traffic tickets. Cleveland, 49, could not pay the fines, so she received two years of probation to be supervised by the private probation company Judicial Correction Services (JCS). She was to pay JCS $200 monthly: $160 for her fines and $40 for the cost of supervision. Although Cleveland lost her full-time job when a local factory closed, she continued to pay, but she sometimes fell short, so the money often only went toward the company's fee. In 2012, she paid $2,000, almost her entire income-tax rebate, but by summer, her fines and fees had grown from hundreds of dollars to over $4,000. As Cleveland fell further behind, JCS began calling her family to tell them that she would go to jail if she did not pay. Eventually, Cleveland was arrested and, under a policy called Pay or Stay, was sentenced to spend a month in jail unless she paid $1,700.[37]

Only six states and the District of Columbia do not charge for the costs of probation.[38] Many of the 44 states that do charge these fees have turned that process over to private probation companies. These for-profit companies not only collect the court's fines, but also their own fees. Many impoverished probationers fall behind on their payments because the companies often collect their own fees first before applying payments to the probationers' court fines. Critics of private probation companies say such practices create an endless cycle of inflating debt for impoverished people, many of whom initially owed relatively low fines.

In 1983, the U.S. Supreme Court ruled in *Bearden v. Georgia* that courts cannot revoke probation for the

inability to pay a fine. However, states are struggling with the part of the ruling that addresses the probationer's ability to pay. According to the ruling, if a probationer has the ability to pay, but "willfully" refuses, "the State is justified in using imprisonment as a sanction to enforce collection."[39] Although many jurisdictions interview probationers to determine their ability to pay, many probationers are still caught up in cycles of endless debt and jail terms.

While Cleveland was in jail, a team from the Southern Poverty Law Center (SPLC) convinced her to sue the court because her arrest seemed to violate both state law and the Fourteenth Amendment's equal-protection clause. Eventually, the SPLC not only secured Cleveland's release, but also discovered that she had already paid off one of the tickets. It was also revealed that JCS had sometimes deposited Cleveland's payments into its own accounts, applying little or nothing toward her court fines. One $200 payment went entirely to JCS instead of only $40 for their supervision fee.[40]

In 2015, the SPLC sued JCS alleging racketeering and extortion. By September, 54 jurisdictions had canceled their contracts with JCS.[41] In October 2015, JCS announced that it would cease operations in Alabama.[42]

THINK ABOUT IT

1. Should the privatization of government services in which one's freedom may be restricted be legal? Explain your answer.

ADVANTAGES

> Cost. The cost of supervising individuals on private probation is borne by the probationer. In a sense, this is a "user fee" similar to toll roads or impact fees charged to real-estate developers. The idea is for those who use the service to assume the cost of the service.

> Effectiveness. By shifting the burden for misdemeanor offenders to private agencies, state agencies can more effectively supervise and treat more serious felony offenders. Furthermore, misdemeanor offenders experience a greater degree of contact with probation officers, especially considering that the private agency has an incentive to collect cost-of-supervision fees. Most misdemeanor offenders do not require substantial counseling or rigorous supervision, so the high caseloads of these private agencies are not considered problematic.

> Public perception. Under traditional probation, misdemeanor offenders often fall through the cracks. There simply are not enough resources available to provide the type of supervision that the public and crime victims demand. With private probation agencies, it is clear to all that those convicted of misdemeanors literally pay a price.

DISADVANTAGES

> Staff qualifications. Most traditional probation officers are required to have a four-year university degree. Many private agencies have no educational requirement, and people with a high school diploma are put in charge of a large number of offenders. Most traditional probation officers get intensive in-service training when they join the agency. Private probation agencies offer little or no training. Although many private probation officers are dedicated and effective in their jobs, the lack of standards and guidelines makes this type of arrangement problematic.[43]

> Profit motive. The primary missions of traditional probation are to protect the public and provide treatment for their clients. In private probation agencies, the first order of business is that the organizations make money. This profit motive can conflict with the basic reasons why misdemeanor probation was established in the first place.

> Ethical concerns. Some people have raised concerns about the ethical position of punishment for profit. The government has a monopoly on the legitimate use of correctional coercion, and outsourcing it to private agencies is deemed questionable. A relevant analogy is the employment of mercenaries to fight the country's wars. Public safety is a basic government responsibility, and many believe that it should remain in the hands of the government and be accountable to the public.[44]

> Social-class bias. Charging misdemeanor probationers cost-of-supervision fees has a differential effect, depending on individual financial capabilities. Those who have enough money to meet their basic needs might be inconvenienced by the added expense, but those who are unemployed or living paycheck to paycheck may find the cost of freedom more than they can afford. Some agencies charge up to $50 per month for the cost of supervision, which can mean the difference between successfully completing the probation or being brought back before the judge on a technical violation.[45]

The use of private probation in the United States will continue to be a controversial issue. As state governments seek to provide services more efficiently without raising taxes, the outsourcing of misdemeanor probation is a tempting strategy.

Rachael Hamm, an inmate at the Rutherford County Adult Detention Center in Murfreesboro, Tennessee, is ensnared in a cycle of debt due to the fees she is charged for private probation. In 2016, Rutherford County was sued for its use of a private probation company, which profits from the collection of monthly probation and drug-testing fees. Why is the use of private probation a controversial issue?

PAUSE AND REVIEW

1. How do various actors in the criminal justice system view probation?
2. What is a pre-sentence investigation, and what sort of information does it contain?
3. What are the two goals of the supervision function of the probation officer?
4. List some of the advantages and disadvantages of private probation.

Parole

The origin of the word **parole** is French. *Parole d'honneur*, which means "word of honor," was used when prisoners of war were released on their promise not to fight anymore.[46] Many people use the terms *probation* and *parole* interchangeably, but significant differences make these practices distinct and worthy of separate consideration. Both deal with offenders in the community, but they differ in a number of distinctive ways.

> Probation instead, parole after. The primary difference between parole and probation is the point at which it occurs in the criminal justice process. Probation, on one hand, is a sentencing option that allows offenders to be placed under community-corrections supervision *instead* of being placed in prison. Parole, on the other hand, is a form of early release that happens *after* the offender has served part of the prison sentence.

> Governing authority. Although the bureaucratic placement of the probation and parole functions varies considerably across the United States, probation is usually associated with the judiciary, with the judge being the primary decision-maker. Parole is extended by the executive branch and is under the

LEARNING OBJECTIVE 5

Differentiate between probation and parole.

LEARNING OBJECTIVE 6

Summarize the major adjustments that stand as obstacles to successful re-entry into society.

parole (from Chapter 9)—The conditional release of a prison inmate who has served part of a sentence and who remains under the court's control.

auspices of the governor. Of course, there are many variations on this theme. In some jurisdictions, the agency that supervises parolees is part of the executive branch, but the parole board is an independent decision-making panel that is presumably free of political influence.

> Parolees and probationers are different types of clients in terms of risk factors, community ties, and social needs. Generally, parolees have committed more serious offenses, have readjustment issues after being incarcerated, and might not have the same support from family and friends because of weakened social bonds caused by long periods of incarceration. This may certainly be the case for many offenders; however, whether the client is on probation or parole depends on the last offense he or she was convicted of. Many individuals, especially the most problematic ones, have been on multiple probations and paroles. Therefore, it is misleading to judge the level of risk as higher for those on parole than for those on probation. In some ways, parolees may be more cooperative because they have already had a taste of prison life and are willing to abide by the conditions of their release in order to maintain their liberty.

> Probation and parole officers have different mandates and responsibilities. Depending on the jurisdiction, there are different expectations of probation and parole officers. In some states, parole officers carry firearms and arrest parole violators, whereas the probation officer would call the police to do any dangerous work.

Those on parole face many of the same challenges as those on probation. Being under state supervision means that restrictions are placed on the offender. Conditions of parole are not significantly different from conditions of probation, including the requirement to maintain contact with the parole officer and get permission to change residences or employment, and travel outside the jurisdiction.

A parole agent talks with a paroled sex offender during an unannounced visit to his home. What differentiates a probationer from a parolee?

When to Parole

The complicated decision of when to grant parole is based on three competing principles. First, there is the political issue of how much time the offender should spend in prison to satisfy the public demand for retribution and punishment. By paroling inmates too early, the parole board risks losing the confidence of politicians and society, who start to question whether prison is a sufficient deterrent and punishment. In fact, some states have abolished parole and others have greatly modified the discretion of parole boards by assigning fixed sentences to several types of offenses.

A second and competing principle when deciding whether to grant parole is the rehabilitation issue.[47] Can a parole board accurately determine when someone is emotionally ready to be released from prison? We have already discussed indeterminate sentencing, in which the offender is sentenced to serve an unspecified time: the prison officials and parole board are responsible for deciding when, based on the medical model, the inmate is "cured." However, ascertaining when it is safe to release an inmate is difficult, and because of prison overcrowding, few resources are allocated for treatment programs.[48] The third principle driving the parole decision is the limited number of prison beds. States cannot afford to keep everyone incarcerated for as long as they have been sentenced. To let new offenders in the prison, others must be released. With these conflicting principles in mind, the parole board attempts to make rational, fair, and informed decisions on when to grant parole. These decisions are based on several factors:

1. Time served. The parole board does not have unlimited discretion in the release decision. The length of the imposed sentence controls, in part, when the inmate may first be eligible to be considered for parole. Another influential factor is the time the inmate served in jail awaiting trial (in some cases this could be a year or more).

2. Prison adjustment. In many states, inmates are granted **good time** (time deducted) for behaving in prison, which can reduce an inmate's sentence by up to one-third. Some inmates can significantly reduce their sentence by earning **meritorious time** for completing treatment programs or educational degrees while in prison. By taking advantage of opportunities for self-betterment, inmates can demonstrate that they can compete for jobs or have acquired the social skills necessary to function in society.

3. Pre-parole plan. A parole officer develops a plan with the inmate and his or her family members (or those who will be involved with the inmate) for the inmate's release. This plan specifies where the inmate will live, how the inmate will survive financially, and what supervision level and treatment programs will be required. One reason for parole denial is an insufficient parole plan. If the parole board does not see a reasonable support network for the inmate, it will instruct all involved to develop a comprehensive plan before the next parole hearing. The longer an offender stays in prison, losing contact and trust with family and friends on the outside, the more difficult it is to develop these plans.[49]

4. Offender interview. The parole board (or hearing officers acting in its name) interviews the offender before the parole decision to get a feel for the offender's attitude, demeanor, preparedness, and sincerity. In these hearings, the parole board inquires about the offender's remorse, prison experiences, parole plan, and sensitivity to criticism. The parole board asks pointed and

good time—The time deducted from an inmate's prison sentence for good behavior.

meritorious time—Time deducted from an inmate's sentence for doing something special or extra, such as getting a GED.

Here, inmates attend a college class at the Monroe Correctional Complex in Monroe, Washington. Sometimes inmates can reduce their sentences by completing educational degrees while incarcerated. What other factors are considered when a decision is made to grant parole?

personal questions to ascertain how the inmate reacts to authority figures. Some inmates are defiant, but most attempt to determine what the hearing officers want to hear and then provide it.

5. Victim-impact statements. The parole staff contacts the victim(s) of the inmate's offense and asks them to comment on how they suffered as a result of the inmate's actions and how the inmate's release will affect them. Some victims who have been especially traumatized may write impassioned statements that sink any chance of parole. On some occasions, victims—or in homicide cases, their relatives—show up at every parole hearing to ensure that the parole board is aware of their opposition to the offender's release.[50]

As you can see, the decision to grant parole involves many factors and is often difficult to predict. One is never sure how the hearing officer or the parole board will respond to evidence, but some established policies and a given board's track record suggest what the "going rate" is for most parole authorities. Because so many cases are heard each year, patterns develop according to the length of time served and the appropriateness of the parole plan, so that even though an inmate has a parole hearing, parole likely will not be granted until a few more years have passed.

Re-entry and "Making It"

Most prison systems attempt to prepare inmates for re-entry into society. Generally, more inmates successfully complete parole than return to prison (see Figure 12.4). Some programs can last up to a year and include mechanisms of gradual reintegration such as furloughs (leaves of absence) and work release. Other programs last only weeks and include mock job interviews and/or studies to prepare for getting a driver's license. Regardless of how a prison prepares inmates, at least three major adjustments stand as obstacles to successful re-entry. One of these obstacles involves changes in the inmate, and the others involve changes in the world to which he or she is returning.

1. Prisonization.[51] Prison life is lived according to rigid rules established by both the administration and the inmate social system. The inmate quickly learns the boundaries of appropriate behavior and lives a life of predictability, routine, and boredom. The inmate is not required, or permitted, to make decisions, exercise judgment, be creative, or experiment in relationships or daily life. Some inmates find comfort in this atmosphere in which

all important, and even most unimportant, decisions are made for them. When these inmates are released, they are overwhelmed by the magnitude of decisions they must make. For example, in prison, deciding what to eat involves sticking out a tray and assessing what is served, whereas in the free world, the menu options can be daunting. The prison may have a soup of the day (sometimes it is the soup of every day), but a grocery store has dozens of different brands, flavors, and sizes. Moreover, consider the vast array of foods in the store, and the former inmate can experience decision overload. Other concerns have greater consequences. The interpersonal skills needed to survive in prison are not always conducive to getting along with co-workers in society. The necessity of demonstrating a willingness to use violence that can keep one alive in prison is obviously problematic in the workplace, where supervisors and co-workers give and accept criticism without worrying about their physical safety.

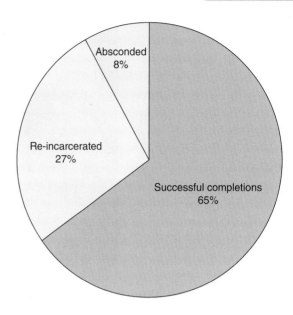

FIGURE 12.4 Adults Completing Parole, 2015 Based on what you've read, do you think the number of parolees who successfully complete their sentences should be higher or lower?

Source: Danielle Kaeble and Thomas P. Bonczar, Probation and Parole in the United States, 2015, Table 5 (U.S. Department of Justice, Office of Justice Programs, Bureau of Justice Statistics, 2017), 6. Available at https://www.bjs.gov/index.cfm?ty=pbdetail&iid=5784.

2. Weakened social ties. The world that the inmate left behind is not the same as the one he or she returns to. People have moved on with their lives, and the inmate must re-establish social bonds that have been weakened, twisted, or broken by incarceration.[52] Spouses, children, parents, friends, and bosses might act differently and be wary of how the offender has been affected by prison. At its most extreme, these changes in social bonds include divorce or estrangement from spouses and rejection by children. The inmate often comes home to find that someone else has usurped his or her former status as authority figure, breadwinner, and confidant. While in prison, a mother might remember her children in a highly romanticized way, but on release, she may return home to find them hostile, bitter, and attached to a new caretaker. The assumed social location of the inmate that was frozen in time by incarceration thaws out on release and melts into disillusionment, anomie, and alienation.

3. Stigmatization.[53] Sociologist Erving Goffman defines one type of stigma as a "blemish of individual character" and includes imprisonment as one of the stigmas that individuals must carry with them for a lifetime and constantly fight to overcome. This stigma is both legal and social. The legal stigma, depending on the jurisdiction, involves losing the right to vote, to parent, to hold public employment, to serve on a jury, to hold public office, or to possess a firearm, and it could mean being required to register as a felon. Perhaps the former inmate who concedes that there is a continuous price to pay for crime understands these restrictions. However, the social stigma can be even more frustrating. The stigma of "ex-con" can be as debilitating as that of "convict." For the former inmate who has served a sentence and has paid for his or her offenses, the continuing discrimination and prejudice seem unjust. A fresh start is nearly impossible and carries a **master status** that overwhelms all of his or her positive attributes and accomplishments.[54] Once parents hear that the new boyfriend is a convicted rapist, there may be no convincing them that he has mended his ways, learned his lesson, paid his debt to society, or is in any way a suitable future son-in-law.

master status—A personal status that overwhelms all others.

Depending on the former inmate's criminal offense, prison experience, and support system outside the prison, he or she will face various challenges upon

At San Quentin State Prison in California, inmates learn to code as part of The Last Mile Program, which prepares them for reintegration into society by teaching inmates skills that will help them find a job upon release. What are some obstacles to successful re-entry that inmates face?

reentering society. The stigma associated with being a convicted felon and limited opportunities for employment can hamper a former inmate's efforts to reintegrate into family and society. Leaving prison may relieve former inmates of several problems, but it can also introduce new ones.

PAUSE AND REVIEW

1. **What is the difference between probation and parole?**
2. **What three competing principles is the decision to grant parole based on?**
3. **What three major adjustments stand as obstacles to successful re-entry?**

LEARNING OBJECTIVE 7

Outline how intensive-supervision probation (ISP) is different from regular probation.

intermediate sanctions—Sentencing alternatives that are stricter than regular probation but less severe than prison.

Intermediate Sanctions

Several other community corrections tactics require examination if we are to truly appreciate how community corrections have developed over the years. Because of prison overcrowding and the heavy caseloads of probation and parole officers, intermediate sanctions have been implemented to make probation and parole more effective, more stringent, and more palatable to the public, who demand that offenders be held accountable for their actions.[55] **Intermediate sanctions** are sentencing alternatives available to the judge who finds regular probation too lenient and prison too severe.[56] With the pressures for parole boards to release inmates early to make room for new offenders, some of these intermediate sanctions are also employed at the parole stage of the criminal justice process.

Intermediate sanctions give the criminal justice system a broader range of mechanisms of social control and enhance the public's perception that crime does not pay. Although some of these newer intermediate sanctions are problematic, critics' concerns are being addressed, and the courts are beginning to recognize that the issue must be resolved. The following is a discussion of some of the more notable intermediate sanctions.

Intensive-Supervision Probation

Intensive-supervision probation (ISP) is simply what probation used to be before the advent of unreasonably high caseloads for probation officers.[57] ISP is actually a form of triage in which offenders deemed the most problematic are allocated extra supervision. Probation officers assigned to these troublesome offenders are given small caseloads and are expected to have more frequent contact with clients.[58] It is believed that if probation officers can concentrate on those who need help or really pose a threat to society, then they can recognize emerging problems and intervene quickly. Because it is more structured, ISP differs in several ways from regular probation:

> ISP clients have about four times as much contact with probation officers. More contacts occur at the probationer's home or place of work. Some regular probationers only have to report as little as one or two times a month, and home visits may occur as infrequently as once every six months.

> ISP clients are more likely to be required to participate in electronic home monitoring and random drug and/or alcohol testing.

> Unannounced job-site or home visits are more frequent.

> ISP clients are more likely to be brought before the court for technical violations.

> ISP clients are more likely to be required to maintain full-time employment or vocational training as well as have community-service requirements.

> Curfews are stricter. Some ISP clients must request permission to leave their homes or place of work at any time.

> ISP officers' caseloads are lower, typically 20 or fewer clients, although some might be as high as 40. Regular probation caseloads usually range from 30 to more than 100 probationers per officer.

The focus of the ISP program is up to the individual agency. Some are treatment-oriented, whereas others are more concerned with surveillance. Several tools are available to the intensive-supervision probation officer to aid in detecting wrongdoing.

Drug Testing

Rather than relying on behavioral cues or lifestyle changes to detect drug use, the officer can require that clients, on either a routine or random basis, submit a urine sample for analysis.[59] Because one of the conditions of freedom is to refrain from illegal drug use, and because probation and parole are conditional-release practices, the client has a choice of cooperating or going to jail or prison. Most offenders cooperate and retain their liberty, live with their families, hold down a job, and escape the pains of imprisonment.

Submitting a urine sample, though humiliating and insulting, seems a small price to pay for staying out of prison. This is not to say, however, that offenders do not attempt to frustrate the system by masking their drug use. Probationers use several techniques to deceive authorities. These techniques include submitting someone else's urine, eating or drinking various items that mask the presence of drugs, and missing or delaying tests until drugs have been diluted in the body. Probation and parole authorities counter these deceptions by increasing the sophistication of the drug tests (for example, using hair strands instead of urine), surprising the clients with random tests, and closely monitoring the administration of the tests.

intensive-supervision probation (ISP)—A form of supervision that requires frequent meetings between the client and probation officer.

House Arrest and Electronic Monitoring

House arrest is an old concept that has appeal today because it allows offenders to maintain family ties, remain employed, pay taxes, and take advantage of community resources such as school and counseling services. It also saves the state the cost of incarceration.[60] Typically, offenders are required to stay home except when they are attending approved activities such as employment, school, treatment programs, or religious services. They are especially restricted during the evening hours, when most offenses take place and when they can expect unannounced calls or visits from their probation officer. Although some citizens are concerned about some home-confined offenders being a danger to the community, for the most part these probationers are selected because they are low-risk individuals and have relatively stable residences in which to be confined.

Electronic monitoring is often used to supplement house arrest but is also used with other programs.[61] Like drug testing, electronic monitoring uses technology to address human concerns.[62] In this case, a device attached to the offender's ankle alerts authorities when it is moved too far from its transmitter. If the offender can slip off the electronic bracelet and leave it next to the transmitter, then he or she is free to roam at will, safe in the knowledge that the probation officer believes he or she is still home. Another limitation of electronic monitoring is that it can only tell the probation officer where the offender is, not what the offender is doing. Offenses such as child abuse, domestic violence, or drug sales could be happening, and the probation officer would not know.

A relatively recent electronic monitoring innovation is the Secure Continuous Remote Alcohol Monitoring (SCRAM) device. The SCRAM device measures the amount of alcohol in a person's body through the skin. When alcohol is consumed, ethanol is excreted through perspiration. The device measures alcohol levels by testing the wearer's perspiration and transmitting the data to the monitoring system. This device monitors defendants and convicted offenders for alcohol consumption and sends alerts to community corrections officers when alcohol has been consumed. SCRAM devices are used as a sanction or condition of pretrial

A Secure Continuous Remote Alcohol Monitor (SCRAM) company executive attaches a SCRAM anklet at the Municipal Court in North Las Vegas, Nevada. How do such devices allow probation officers to monitor offenders?

release for those who have been charged with or sentenced for driving under the influence or, sometimes, domestic violence offenses. SCRAM devices help relieve jail crowding and allow clients to remain in the community, drive a car, and remain employed during the course of their sentence or pretrial release period.[63]

In many ways, technological devices may lull us into thinking that offenders are adjusting to their limited freedoms when they are still engaging in serious offenses. Therefore, these tools should be considered merely as supplements to face-to-face supervision rather than as replacements for the traditional probation or parole officer. As technology becomes more sophisticated, so will the methods used to supervise criminal offenders. It is already possible to implant a small transmitter under an offender's skin and use a satellite to track his or her movements.[64] This way, probation officers can tell whether the offender is at home, at work, or at a bar.

Fines

The use of fines has been a consistent feature of the U.S. criminal justice system. For some types of offenses, especially some economic offenses such as tax evasion or insider trading, fines are an appropriate sanction.[65] For other types of offenses, the public does not think offenders should be able to "buy" their way out of trouble. Fines are often used in conjunction with other types of sanctions, such as short periods of incarceration.[66]

Fines have several advantages as a criminal sanction. Fines used as an alternative to incarceration not only are less expensive to administer but bring extra money to the criminal justice system's budgets. In fact, many probation systems require their clients to pay cost-of-supervision fines as a condition of probation, thus offsetting a major portion of the expense.[67] Another advantage of fines is the message they send to the public that offenders sometimes do literally pay for their crimes. A large fine levied on a tax cheat or an unscrupulous businessperson gives the public a sense of justice.

The downside of using fines as a criminal sanction involves fairness. For impoverished people who can barely afford to support themselves or their families, adding fines to their sentences places hardship on them that wealthy offenders do not experience. For this reason, in addition to having fixed fines for certain offenses, some countries have instituted a "day fine" system in which the offender is fined in proportion to how much money he or she makes. The fine is based on how much the offender is paid for one day of work and then multiplied by the degree of punishment the court wants to administer. Consequently, someone who makes $100,000 a year would pay 10 times the fine of someone who makes $10,000 a year. Although this fine system may be more equitable than a fixed-fine system, wealth still has its advantages. Someone who makes $10,000 a year has little discretionary money because every dime is used for rent, food, health care, and other necessities. However, for offenders making $100,000 a year, even though their houses may cost more and their children may go to more expensive schools, a certain economy of scale works in their favor and allows them to pay a percentage of their income without suffering as much as impoverished offenders.

Shock Probation

An intermediate sanction that employs fear as a main feature is **shock probation**. In these programs, the probation officer and the judge play a confidence game on the offender. The offender receives a bogus sentence of jail or prison time, and

shock probation—The practice of sentencing offenders to prison, allowing them to serve a short time, and then granting them probation without their prior knowledge.

then, after he or she has been incarcerated for 30 to 90 days, the judge converts the sentence to probation.[68] Because offenders think they are going to be imprisoned for a long time, the sudden release is presumed to encourage them to "turn over a new leaf" and start a new life of law-abiding behavior. There is a certain commonsense appeal to shock probation, but on closer examination, it has some flaws that make it a better public relations tool than corrections program. Incarcerating offenders for 30 to 90 days ruptures any stability they have. They lose their jobs, drop out of school, and sever ties with significant social networks. However, on release after their short stay, they are expected to instantly pick up the pieces of their shattered lives. Shock probation programs may also make the courts look hypocritical and duplicitous and further alienate and label the offender. When used sparingly with carefully selected offenders, this sanction has some corrections value, but for most offenders, probation or a short, planned incarceration is a better option.

Intermediate sanctions include several ways to make sentencing options between probation and prison more effective, severe, and politically popular. These sanctions are driven by a high crime rate with few traditional alternatives, a desire on the part of well-intentioned people to provide more effective community corrections services, and simple economics. If used intelligently, intermediate sanctions provide useful alternatives to incarceration at a low cost and without endangering the community.

However, intermediate sanctions, like diversion programs, are susceptible to compromise by the problem of net-widening.[69] Unless their use is monitored closely, intermediate sanctions can be diverted from their intended targets—those who require intense supervision—and used on petty offenders who would normally be released. On the one hand, judges want to teach lessons to vandals, small-time thieves, or marijuana users and place them in programs that capture their attention and alter their lifestyles. On the other hand, because these programs are evaluated constantly and must demonstrate successful **recidivism** rates, judges tend to select those who are the most likely to complete the sanction successfully. The result is that a greater proportion of citizens are brought under social control by the state, and scarce resources are frittered away on petty offenders instead of being directed at those who pose a genuine threat to society.

recidivism—Continuing to break the criminal law and returning to the criminal justice system after being processed for past offenses.

PAUSE AND REVIEW

1. How does intensive-supervision probation differ from regular probation?
2. What are some of the various forms of intermediate sanctions?

FOCUS ON ETHICS   Going Out on a Limb

As a probation officer, you are pretty tough with your clients. However, every once in a while, someone comes along whom you are willing to take a chance on. You have been burned a couple of times before by probationers who promised one thing and did the opposite,

but this time you think you have a client who warrants your trust and help.

James is a college freshman and gifted athlete with NFL prospects. He is on scholarship but was implicated in a brawl at a concert where several people were brutally beaten and hospitalized. Although the degree of James's involvement is unclear, his lawyer arranged a plea bargain for probation with the stipulation that the coach would allow James to remain on scholarship and play that season. Everyone, including you when you did the pre-sentence investigation, believed James was a worthwhile probation risk because of his bright future.

However, as James's probation officer, you suspect that he is developing an entitled attitude and believes that because he is a football star, he need not abide by the conditions of his probation or listen to you when you try to advise him. James is missing classes, not returning your phone calls, has had beer in his dormitory refrigerator even though he is not of drinking age, and violates the court-ordered curfew of midnight on weekends.

You have tried to correct the problem by contacting his coach and advising him of your concerns, but you are finding that the longer the football season goes on, the less anyone—James, his coaches, the judge, or your supervisor—cares about your complaints. Most of the issues are minor technical violations, but you have recently noticed a hostile attitude in James both on the field and off. Today, his girlfriend shows up at your office with a black eye and details about James's violent outbursts, gunplay, and steroids. This weekend is the big game against the cross-state rival, and everyone knows that James must do well for the team to win. However, you are afraid he might not make it to the weekend without hurting somebody unless you take action.

WHAT DO YOU DO?

1. Go to James's dorm room and have a face-to-face, heart-to-heart talk with him.
2. Go to the coach and threaten to get the judge to revoke James's probation before the game if he does not shape up.
3. Express your concerns to the judge and essentially place the issue in his lap, thereby covering yourself.
4. Say nothing until after the game and hope that once the pressure of football is off, James will behave in a more appropriate way.

For more insight into how someone might respond to such an ethical dilemma, visit the companion website at www.oup.com/us/fuller to watch a video that connects this scenario to a real-world situation.

Summary

LEARNING OBJECTIVE	**1**	Prison is an artificial society. Conformity in prison is not always a good indicator of inmates' ability to adjust to the free world.
Outline the assumptions about the nature of crime that lie at the heart of community corrections.		The total control of the prison does little to prepare inmates to take responsibility for their actions. The community has resources that are unavailable in the prison, which enhance the likelihood of rehabilitation. The community can provide support networks to offenders that do not exist in prison. Offenders can contribute to the financial upkeep of their families and, if gainfully employed, pay taxes. The state spends less money on offenders in community corrections programs than it does incarcerating them. The state can accurately identify dangerous offenders who need secure incarceration and which offenders are safe to release into the community with supervision. The number of trained probation and parole officers is sufficient to adequately supervise offenders selected for community corrections programs.
LEARNING OBJECTIVE	**2**	Offenders can be diverted to alternative (diversion) programs based on labeling theory, which suggests that the more limited the offender's penetration into the criminal justice system, the less likely the offender will be to adopt a criminal self-concept and continue to break the law.
Describe the connection between diversion programs and labeling theory.		

LEARNING OBJECTIVE 3 Discuss how various actors in the criminal justice system view probation.	Many offenders embrace probation because it allows them to remain at home, at work, and safe from the pains of imprisonment. The prosecutor, who has the discretion to fashion plea bargains, sees probation as a victory because it requires little time or resources and allows for efficient disposal of cases. The defense attorney views probation as a victory because the offender is kept out of prison and the offender's liberty is preserved with some reasonable compromises (the conditions of probation). Probation allows the judge to impose a sentence that is less expensive than prison and, to some degree, satisfies victims and the public in that the offender did not escape punishment. For criminal justice reformers, probation offers offenders a variety of treatment and community service activities. To politicians, probation is a cheaper way to punish than prison.
LEARNING OBJECTIVE 4 Characterize the three universal functions that define the probation officer's occupation.	1. Investigation: the probation officer gathers information for decision makers throughout the criminal justice system. The most time-consuming and significant report that the probation officer writes is the pre-sentence investigation, which assists a judge in sentencing. 2. Supervision: each probation system has standard conditions that must be met. The probationer must cooperate with the probation officer and follow all lawful instructions. 3. Service: probation officers provide services to offenders who need help, such as finding a job, counseling, or substance abuse treatment.
LEARNING OBJECTIVE 5 Differentiate between probation and parole.	Probation is a sentencing option that allows offenders to be placed under community corrections supervision *instead* of going to prison. Parole is a form of early release that happens *after* the offender has served part of the prison sentence. (Probation instead, parole after.)
LEARNING OBJECTIVE 6 Summarize the major adjustments that stand as obstacles to successful reentry into society.	1. Prisonization: life in prison is lived according to rigid rules established by both the administration and the inmate social system. Inmates are not allowed to make decisions, but on release, the magnitude of decisions to be made can be overwhelming. 2. Weakened social ties: the world that the inmate left behind is not the same as the one he or she returns to. Relationships have likely changed, and the inmate must reestablish these bonds. 3. Stigmatization: Imprisonment is a legal and social stigma that individuals must constantly fight to overcome. Legally, this may involve losing the right to vote, parent, hold public employment, serve on a jury, hold public office, or possess a firearm, and might mean registering as a felon. Socially, former inmates often face discrimination and prejudice.
LEARNING OBJECTIVE 7 Outline how intensive-supervision probation (ISP) is different from regular probation.	ISP clients have about four times as much contact with probation officers, more unannounced job-site or home visits, and stricter curfews. ISP clients are more likely to be required to participate in electronic home monitoring and random drug and/or alcohol testing, and to maintain full-time employment or vocational training, as well as have community service requirements. ISP clients are also more likely to be brought before the court for technical violations. ISP officers' caseloads are lighter than those of regular probation officers.

Critical Reflections

1. Which community resources should correctional agencies partner with in order to best supervise and help released offenders?

2. Why is it important to include the community in community corrections?

Key Terms

community corrections **p. 368**
good time **p. 385**
intensive-supervision probation (ISP) **p. 389**
intermediate sanctions **p. 388**
labeling theory **p. 371**
master status **p. 387**

meritorious time **p. 385**
net-widening **p. 371**
parole **p. 383**
plea bargain **p. 374**
pre-sentence investigation (PSI) **p. 375**
private probation **p. 380**

probation **p. 372**
recidivism **p. 392**
retribution **p. 369**
shock probation **p. 391**

Endnotes

1 Jessica Lussenhop, "An Oversight Allowed a Convicted Man to Walk Free for Thirteen Years. Now the Justice System Wants to Restart the Clock." *Riverfront Times*, September 1, 2013, http://www.riverfronttimes.com/stlouis/an-oversight-allowed-a-convicted-man-to-walk-free-for-thirteen-years-now-the-justice-system-wants-to-restart-the-clock/Content?oid=2506702.

2 Jessica Lussenhop, "Cornealious Michael Anderson III, Freed from Prison, Reunites with Family," *Riverfront Times*, May 6, 2014, http://www.riverfronttimes.com/newsblog/2014/05/06/cornealious-michael-anderson-iii-freed-from-prison-reunites-with-family.

3 Danielle Kaeble and Lauren Glaze, *Correctional Populations in the United States, 2015* (Washington, D.C.: U.S. Department of Justice Office of Justice Programs Bureau of Justice Statistics, 2016), 2. Available at https://www.bjs.gov/index.cfm?ty=pbdetail&iid=5870.

4 Belinda Rodgers McCarthy, Bernard J. McCarthy Jr., and Matthew C. Leone, *Community-Based Corrections*, 4th ed. (Belmont, Calif.: Wadsworth, 2001).

5 Jane Browning, "Coming to Terms with Prison Growth," *Corrections Today* 69 (October 2007): 18–19.

6 We are not suggesting that everyone is a criminal, but rather that almost all of us have committed offenses for which we could have been brought into the criminal justice system and punished with a period of incarceration. Our drug use, DUIs, and income tax creativity have largely gone undiscovered,

and hence we maintain our freedom and conventional lifestyles.

7 John Irwin, *Prisons in Turmoil* (Boston: Little, Brown, 1980).

8 Sasha Adamsky, "When They Got Out," *Atlantic Online*, June 1999, http://www.theatlantic.com/magazine/archive/1999/06/when-they-get-out/308517.

9 Francis T. Cullen and Karen E. Gilbert, *Reaffirming Rehabilitation* (Cincinnati, Ohio: Anderson, 1982).

10 Eric W. Hickey, *Serial Murderers and Their Victims,* 3d ed. (Belmont, Calif.: Wadsworth, 2002). See Hickey's profile of Henry Lee Lucas on p. 194.

11 Todd R. Clear and Harry R. Dammer, *The Offender in the Community* (Belmont, Calif.: Wadsworth, 2003), 226.

12 Thomas G. Blomberg, "Diversion and Social Control," *Journal of Criminal Law and Criminology* 68 (1977): 274–282.

13 Jeffrey Draine, Amy Blank Wilson, and Wendy Pogorzelski, "Limitations and Potential in Current Research on Services for People with Mental Illness in the Criminal Justice System," *Journal of Offender Rehabilitation* 45 (July 2007): 159–177.

14 Kristie A. Blevins, Francis T. Cullen, and Jody L. Sundt, "The Correctional Orientation of 'Child Savers': Support for Rehabilitation and Custody among Juvenile Correctional Workers," *Journal of Offender Rehabilitation* 45 (July 2007): 47–83.

15 James Austin and Barry Krisberg, "Wider, Stronger, and Different Nets: The Dialectics of Criminal Justice Reform," *Journal of Research in Crime and Delinquency* 18 (1981): 165–196.

16 Thomas G. Blomberg and Karol Lucken, "Stacking the Deck by Piling Up Sanctions: Is Intermediate Punishment Destined to Fail?" *Howard Journal of Criminal Justice* 33, no. 1 (1994): 62–80.

17 Kathy G. Padgett, William D. Bales, and Thomas G. Blomberg, "Under Surveillance: An Empirical Test of the Effectiveness and Consequences of Electronic Monitoring," *Criminology and Public Policy* 5 (February 2006): 61–91.

18 Heather Barklage, Dane Miller, and Gene Bonham, "Probation Conditions versus Probation Officer Directives: Where the Twain Shall Meet," *Federal Probation* 70, no. 3 (December 2006): 37–41.

19 Ricky N. Bluthenthal et al., "Perspectives on Therapeutic Treatment from Adolescent Probationers," *Journal of Psychoactive Drugs* 38 (December 2006): 461–471.

20 Douglas Thomson, "How Plea Bargaining Shapes Intensive Probation Supervision," *Crime and Delinquency* 36 (1990): 146.

21 Dane C. Miller, Richard D. Sluder, and J. Dennis Laster, "Can Probation Be Revoked When Probationers Do Not Willfully Violate the Terms or Conditions of Probation?" *Federal Probation* 63, no. 1 (June 1999): 23.

22 John Rosecrance, "Maintaining the Myth of Individualized Justice: Probation, Pre-sentence Reports," *Justice Quarterly* 5 (1988): 235–236.

23 David Sudnow, "Normal Crimes: Sociological Features of the Penal Code in a Public Defender Office," *Social Problems* 12 (1965): 255–276.

24 Marilyn West, "A Few Words about Interviewing in Pre-sentence Investigations," in *Correctional Assessment, Casework, and Counseling*, 3d ed., ed. Anthony Walsh (Lanham, Md.: American Correctional Association).

25 Anthony Walsh, ed., *Correctional Assessment, Casework, and Counseling*, 3d ed. (Lanham, Md.: American Correction Association), 106.

26 Anthony Walsh, "The Role of the Probation Officer in the Sentencing Process: Independent Professional or Judicial Hack?" *Criminal Justice and Behavior* 12 (1985): 289–303.

27 Fay Honey Knapp, "Northwest Treatment Associates: A Comprehensive Community-Based-Evaluation-and-Treatment Program for Adult Sex Offenders," in *Correctional Counseling and Treatment*, 4th ed., ed. Peter C. Kratcoski (Prospect Heights, Ill.: Waveland Press, 2000), 617–633. For instance, Knapp reported, "One of the most creative things we do with flashers who exhibit in their cars is to have them put their names on the front, back, and sides of the car" (624).

28 Fay S. Taxman, "Dealing with Technical Violations," *Corrections Today* 57 (1995): 46–53.

29 Nancy Rodriguez and Vincent J. Webb, "Probation Violations, Revocations, and Imprisonment," *Criminal Justice Policy Review* 18 (March 2007): 3–30.

30 Jeffrey J. Shook and Rosemary C. Sarri, "Structured Decision Making in Juvenile Justice: Judges' and Probation Officers' Perceptions and Use," *Children and Youth Services Review* 29 (October 2007): 1335–1351.

31 Shook and Sarri, "Structured Decision Making in Juvenile Justice."

32 R. V. Del Carmen and J. A. Pilant, "The Scope of Judicial Immunity for Probation and Parole Officers," *Perspectives* (American Probation and Parole Association) (Summer 1994): 14–21.

33 CNN, Federal Report Blasts Probation Officers' Handling of Garrido Case, July 9, 2011, http://www.cnn.com/2011/CRIME/07/09/california.garrido.probation/.

34 Maria L. La Ganga and Shane Goldmacher, "Jaycee Lee Dugard's Family Will Receive $20 Million from California," *Los Angeles Times*, July 2, 2010, http://articles.latimes.com/2010/jul/02/local/la-me-0702-dugard-settlement-20100702.

35 Christine S. Schloss and Leanne F. Alarid, "Standards in the Privatization of Probation Services," *Criminal Justice Review* 32 (2007): 233–245.

36 Ibid.

37 Sarah Stillman, "Get Out of Jail, Inc.," *New Yorker*, June 23, 2014, http://www.newyorker.com/magazine/2014/06/23/get-out-of-jail-inc.

38 National Public Radio, State-by-State Court Fees, May 19, 2014, http://www.npr.org/2014/05/19/312455680/state-by-state-court-fees.

39 Bearden v. Georgia 461 U.S. 660 (1983), Justia, https://supreme.justia.com/cases/federal/us/461/660/.

40 Stillman, "Get Out of Jail, Inc."

41 Southern Poverty Law Center, Cities across Alabama cancel contracts with company sued by SPLC, August 12, 2015, https://www.splcenter.org/news/2015/08/12/cities-across-alabama-cancel-contracts-company-sued-splc.

42 Kent Faulk, "Private Probation Company Once Called 'Judicially Sanctioned Extortion Racket' Leaving Alabama," October 19, 2015, AL.com, http://www.al.com/news/birmingham/index.ssf/2015/10/judicial_correction_services_i.html.

43 Ibid.

44 Celia Perry, Justine Sharrock, and Michael Mechanic, "Probation for Profit," *Mother Jones* (July 2008): 57–58.

45 Ibid.

46 Clear and Dammer, *Offender in the Community*, 182–183.

47 Melinda D. Schlager and Kelly Robbins, "Does Parole Work?—Revisited: Reframing the Discussion of the Impact of Postprison Supervision on Offender Outcome," *Prison Journal* 88 (June 2008): 234–251.

48 Irwin, *Prisons in Turmoil*.

49 Catherine Cuellar, "Investing in Second Chances: An Innovative Program Helps Prison Inmates Make a Fresh Start—and a Business Plan," *Sojourners Magazine* 37 (July 2008): 20–24.

50 Robert C. Davis and Carrie Mulford, "Victim Rights and New Remedies: Finally Getting Victims Their Due," *Journal of Contemporary Criminal Justice* 24 (May 2008): 198–208.

51 Donald Clemmer, "The Prison Community," in *Correctional Contexts: Contemporary and Classical Readings*, 2d ed., ed. Edward J. Latessa et al. (Los Angeles: Roxbury, 2001), 83–87.

52 Clear and Dammer, *Offender in the Community*, 213–214.

53 Erving Goffman, *Stigma: Notes on the Management of Spoiled Identity* (Englewood Cliffs, N.J.: Prentice Hall, 1963), 4.

54 D. Stanley Eitzen and Maxine Baca Zinn, *Social Problems*, 6th ed. (Boston: Allyn & Bacon, 1992), 305.

55 Schlager and Robbins, "Does Parole Work?"

56 Norval Morris and Michael Tonry, *Between Prison and Probation: Intermediate Punishments in a Rational Sentencing System* (New York: Oxford University Press, 1990).

57 Joan Petersilia, "Conditions That Permit Intensive Supervision Programs to Survive," *Crime and Delinquency* 36 (1990): 126–145.

58 Joshua Cochran, Daniel Mears, and William Bales, "Assessing the Effectiveness of Correctional Sanctions," *Journal of Quantitative Criminology* 30, no. 2 (June 2014): 317–347.

59 Beau Kilmer, "Does Parolee Drug Testing Influence Employment and Education Outcomes? Evidence from a Randomized Experiment with Noncompliance," *Journal of Quantitative Criminology* 24 (March 2008): 93–123.

60 P. J. Hofer and B. S. Meierhoefer, *Home Confinement: An Evolving Sanction in the Federal Criminal Justice System* (Washington, D.C.: Federal Judicial Center, 1987).

61 Padgett, Bales, and Blomberg, "Under Surveillance."

62 A. K. Schmidt, "Electronic Monitors: Realistically, What Can Be Expected?" *Federal Probation* 55, no. 2 (1991): 47–53.

63 Secure Continuous Remote Alcohol Monitoring (SCRAM) Technology Evaluability Assessment, https://www.ncjrs.gov/pdffiles1/nij/secure-continuous-remote-alcohol.pdf.

64 What Are Those Microchips That People Put in Their Dogs? Howstuffworks.com, http://animals.howstuffworks.com/pets/question690.htm.

65 Diana Marszalek, "Jail and Fines Proposed for Theft of Recyclables," *New York Times*, May 25, 2008, 2.

66 Sally Hillsman, Barry Mahoney, George Cole, and Bernard Auchter, *Fines as Criminal Sanctions* (Washington, D.C.: National Institute of Justice, 1987).

67 Dale Parent, *Recovering Correctional Costs Through Offender Fees* (Washington, D.C.: National Institute of Justice, 1990).

68 Clear and Dammer, *Offenders in the Community*, 255–256.

69 Dale K. Sechrest, "Prison 'Boot Camps' Do Not Measure Up," *Federal Probation* 53, no. 3 (1989): 15–20.

PART V

Contemporary
Issues

397

Chapter 13

Juvenile Justice

Ethan Couch enters the courtroom for his hearing at the Tim Curry Criminal Justice Center in Fort Worth, Texas, in April 2016. Should Couch have initially been tried in the adult system?

I n 2013, 16-year-old Ethan Couch was speeding along the highway in his family's truck when he swerved off the road and slammed into several people helping a stranded motorist. Four people were killed, and one was paralyzed. Couch, who had had run-ins with the law before, admitted to drinking alcohol.[1] At the time of his crash, his blood alcohol level was three times the legal limit and also contained valium, THC, and muscle relaxants.[2]

The case made national headlines, in part because Couch's defense team argued that Couch was stricken with "affluenza," a term they used to describe how children from privileged families sometimes develop a sense of entitlement, behave irresponsibly, and abuse drugs and alcohol. Couch's attorney was able to convince the judge that rather than incarcerating Couch until he turned 18, he should serve 10 years of probation. Because Couch's family is wealthy, he was also required to attend a California treatment facility at the cost of $450,000 a year.

In 2015, Couch, now 18, was revealed to have violated his probation after an online video showed him drinking alcohol at a party. Fearing a return to court, Couch fled to Mexico with his mother. They were located after Couch used a cell phone to order pizza. Mexican authorities arrested the pair and extradited them to the United States.[3] When Couch turned 19, he was transferred to the adult court system and sentenced to 720 days in jail.[4]

THINK ABOUT IT > How is the underlying philosophy of the juvenile justice system responsible for Ethan Couch's sentence to probation rather than incarceration?

LEARNING OBJECTIVE **1**

Describe the benefits and critiques of the modern juvenile justice system.

LEARNING OBJECTIVE **2**

Characterize the types of youths whom the juvenile justice system is responsible for.

LEARNING OBJECTIVE **3**

Outline the stages of the juvenile justice system.

juvenile delinquent—
A person, usually under the age of 18, who is determined to have committed a criminal offense or status offense in states in which a minor is declared to lack responsibility and cannot be sentenced as an adult.

The Juvenile Justice System

One of the most stable features of crime is that youths commit much of it. Even though many young people break the law, they desist once they get older and become more legitimately involved in society. However, youths who break the law are handled differently than adult offenders. Juvenile justice not only is a matter of degree but also involves a completely different justice system with its own philosophy, courts, and correctional system.[5]

Many Americans are dissatisfied with the criminal justice system, and much of this frustration centers on the perceived liberal tendencies of the juvenile justice system, as is evident in the case of Ethan Couch. As a juvenile, he killed four people and permanently injured another in a drunk-driving accident, yet received only probation, which he promptly violated. Many people think Couch should have been tried as an adult. However, the Couch case is an outlier. Although the juvenile justice system is based on a progressive philosophy, **juvenile delinquents**—individuals under the age of 18 who commit a criminal offense in states where minors are declared to lack responsibility and cannot be sentenced as adults—are often handled punitively.[6] Over time, the juvenile justice system has changed its focus from one of rehabilitation to one that also emphasizes deterrence and punishment. This should not be surprising given the public's concern for high crime rates, drug abuse, and gang violence. However, these competing philosophical perspectives complicate the juvenile justice system's mission and confuse the public as to what the juvenile justice system is supposed to do. In many ways, juveniles receive the worst of both the criminal justice and the juvenile justice systems.[7] They may not be getting the treatment and rehabilitation recommended by the juvenile court, while at the same time they are stripped of their legal rights because the juvenile justice system focuses more on social control than rehabilitation. This chapter will illustrate both the promise and the problems of the juvenile justice system, while considering how it contrasts with the criminal justice system.

In 1899, the first juvenile court was established in Cook County, Illinois, with the mandate to process the cases of children between the ages of 8 and 17. The social forces that led to the development of the juvenile court were entwined with the rapid social changes that occurred in the United States at the turn of the 20th century. The juvenile court relieved young people of their legal rights (many of which have since been restored) and operated according to what reformers believed was the best interests of the child. This was achieved by extending the philosophy of **parens patriae**, Latin for "father of the country," meaning that the state assumes the ultimate responsibility for the welfare of children. This philosophy led to the development of contemporary differences between the modern criminal court and the juvenile court:

> Focus on rehabilitation. The juvenile court operates on the idea that problematic children can be redeemed. Rehabilitation, not punishment, is the primary concern. Juveniles are not subject to capital punishment, and instead of sentences, cases receive dispositions. (In 2005, the U.S. Supreme Court decided in *Roper v. Simmons* that offenders who were younger than 18 at the time of their offenses cannot be executed.) At the beginning of the reform movement, many believed that keeping juveniles out of jails and reform schools would prevent them from being further tempted to break the law. Experts believed that they knew how to change the behavior of delinquent youths. It was assumed that delinquent behavior was a result of individual deficiencies and that youths could be cured of their propensity for such behavior.

> Informal hearing. The juvenile case is conducted as a **hearing** instead of a trial. The adversarial process is absent, and the court workers and judge determine how to best serve the youth's needs by correcting or counteracting social deficiencies such as inadequate schooling, poverty, faulty parenting, and substance abuse.

> Individualized justice. Each juvenile case is treated according to its own merits. There is little effort to produce uniform dispositions because each child has a different set of problems and a different social support network. The goal is to craft the disposition to the child instead of the offense.

> Private hearings. Juvenile hearings are closed to the public and the press, and after a period of time juvenile court records are expunged. Deviant behavior committed as a juvenile is not to be counted against the person when he or she becomes an adult.

In the 20th century, widespread dissatisfaction with the juvenile courts led to several reforms. Foremost among these reforms was the move to restore some

Juvenile Court Committee

Chicago

INCORPORATED MARCH 26, 1904

MRS. JOSEPH T. BOWEN, President, 136 Astor Street.
Miss Julia C. Lathrop, Vice-President
    Hull House, 335 South Halsted Street
Leroy D. Thomas, Vice President
    204 Dearborn Street
Mrs. Charles Henrotin, Vice President
    251 Goethe Street
        Mrs. George Bass, Chairman Court Committee
            150 Lincoln Park Boulevard
        Miss Julia C. Lathrop, Chairman Conference Committee
            Hull House, 335 South Halsted Street
        Mrs. Sadie T. Wald, Chairman Detention Home Committee
            3958 Michigan Avenue.

Mrs. Frederick K. Tracy, Recording Secretary
    545 Jackson Boulevard
Mr. James H. Eckels, Treasurer
    President Commercial National Bank
Mrs. Theodore B. Wells, Assistant Treasurer
    215 South Winchester Avenue

In order to continue the work of the Juvenile Court in a satisfactory manner, it is necessary to raise the sum of $15,000 annually.

The Committee in charge of this work is incorporated. We employ fifteen probation officers, without whose services the Juvenile Court would be useless.

We have assumed the management and certain expenses of the Detention Home, 625 West Adams Street.

We are asking every church in Chicago to give us $10 per annum, and it is earnestly requested that every pastor will put this matter before his congregation and urge upon them the necessity of supporting this most important institution. There is no better mission work than this saving of children; it is keeping them from becoming criminals; it is making them honest citizens. We look to you to do your share in guiding the children of this city towards clean and and reputable lives. If you are able, support a probation officer at $720 a year. If you are unable to do this, give us something—at least $10.

Make cheques payable to James H. Eckels, Treasurer, and send to Mrs. F. K. Tracy, Secretary, 545 Jackson Boulevard.

LOUISE DE KOVEN BOWEN,
President Juvenile Court Committee.

Women reformers who established the first juvenile court in Cook County, Illinois, also organized the Juvenile Court Committee to fund the court's operations. What led to the development of the juvenile court?

parens patriae—Latin for "father of the country," the philosophy that the government is the ultimate guardian of all children or disabled adults.

hearing—A session that takes place without a jury before a judge or magistrate in which evidence and/or arguments are presented to determine some factual or legal issue.

due-process rights—
Guarantees by the Fifth, Sixth, and Fourteenth Amendments that establish legal procedures that recognize the protection of an individual's life, liberty, and property.

due-process rights to juveniles, guaranteed by the Fifth, Sixth, and Fourteenth Amendments that protect an individual's life, liberty, and property. This was due to concerns related to police officers misleading juveniles about the consequences of admitting to offenses; perfunctory court hearings that failed to adequately consider the youth's best interests; reform schools that were little better than prisons; and the public's overall impression that the juvenile justice system fostered more crime than it prevented.

In several cases, such as *Kent v. United States* (1966); *In re Gault* (1967); *In re Winship* (1970); *McKeiver v. Pennsylvania* (1971); and *Breed v. Jones* (1975) (see Table 13.1), the courts provided that youths have the right to receive notice of charges, an attorney to represent their interests, the ability to confront and cross-examine witnesses, and protection against self-incrimination. Critics of these decisions say these changes contradict the juvenile court's original intentions, turning the juvenile court into a less formal version of the criminal court.

The Pros and Cons of the Modern Juvenile Justice System

The organizational structure of the juvenile justice system is parallel to the criminal justice system. This can be confusing because the two systems, though distinctly different in many of their goals, philosophies, and practices, also have

---

TABLE 13.1   U.S. Supreme Court Cases that Expanded and Abridged the Rights and Protections of Juvenile Defendants

	CASE	YEAR	RULING
Cases that Expanded Juvenile Rights and Protections	Kent v. United States	1966	A youth's due process rights are denied when his or her case is waived to criminal court without a formal hearing.
	In re Gault	1967	Youths have the right to an attorney, as well as the right to confront accusers and protection from self-incrimination.
	In re Winship	1970	If incarceration or loss of freedom is possible, a case against a juvenile must be proved beyond a reasonable doubt.
	Breed v. Jones	1975	Adjudicating a youth in juvenile court, then trying the youth as an adult in a criminal court violates the double jeopardy clause of the Fifth Amendment.
	Thompson v. Oklahoma	1988	Execution of a person under the age of 16 is unconstitutional.
	Roper v. Simmons	2005	The Eighth and Fourteenth Amendments forbid imposition of the death penalty on offenders who were under the age of 18 when they committed their offenses.
	Graham v. Florida	2010	Sentencing a juvenile to life in prison for a non-homicidal offense violates the Eighth Amendment's prohibition on cruel and unusual punishment.
	J.D.B. v. North Carolina	2010	A child's age is a relevant factor in determining whether the child is in custody for purposes of *Miranda v. Arizona*.
	Miller v. Alabama	2012	Mandatory life-without-parole sentencing for juvenile homicide offenders violates the Eighth Amendment's prohibition on cruel and unusual punishment.

	CASE	YEAR	RULING
Cases that Abridged Juvenile Rights and Protections	*McKeiver v. Pennsylvania*	1971	The Constitution does not require a trial by jury in the adjudicative phase of a state juvenile court delinquency proceeding.
	Goss v. Lopez	1975	Students do not have the right to a formal hearing before receiving a school suspension of fewer than 10 days.
	Swisher v. Brady	1978	Allowing prosecutors to appeal to juvenile court judges the "not guilty" recommendations made by court designees who hear juvenile cases (often called "masters" or "referees") does not incur double jeopardy.
	Fare v. Michael C.	1979	A youth's request to speak to his or her probation officer does not equate the right to remain silent and consult with an attorney.
	Schall v. Martin	1984	As long as procedures protect a youth's rights, detention of a juvenile is constitutional if it protects the juvenile and society from offenses he or she might commit before trial.
	New Jersey v. T.L.O.	1985	Searches of students by school officials are not subject to the warrant requirement of the Fourth Amendment and need only be justified by reasonable cause.
	Stanford v. Kentucky	1988	The execution of youths over the age of 16 does not violate the Eighth Amendment's prohibition on cruel and unusual punishment.

points of convergence in which they share personnel, interact on certain cases, and are jointly blamed by the public for the crime rate. In many cases, it is a tough call as to whether the juvenile justice system promotes or hinders the application of justice and the youth's best interests. What is the right balance between protecting children and holding them accountable for their actions? To answer this question, we must consider the presumed advantages and disadvantages of having a separate juvenile justice system. The benefits of the juvenile justice system are as follows:

> The philosophy of the juvenile justice system is different from that of the criminal justice system. Whereas the criminal justice system seeks to deter crime and punish offenders to promote public safety, the juvenile justice system is supposed to act in the best interests of the youth.

> The juvenile justice system seeks to reduce the stigma of deviant behavior. By shielding the names of juveniles from the press, keeping hearings private, and allowing juvenile records to be purged, the juvenile justice system seeks to prevent youths from being labeled "bad kids."

> Having a separate juvenile justice system keeps juveniles apart from adult offenders who might abuse, exploit, or teach them negative behaviors and attitudes.

> By addressing the social, emotional, and educational needs of young offenders, the juvenile justice system seeks to help them gain the necessary skills to become productive members of society.

> The juvenile justice system protects young offenders from receiving the harsh punishments meted out by the criminal justice system.

A teenager learns bicycle mechanics skills in a job training class at Farmington Bay Youth Center in Utah. In what ways is addressing the educational needs of juvenile delinquents a beneficial aspect of the juvenile justice system?

Those who are dissatisfied with the juvenile justice system critique it for the following reasons:

› Youths who commit serious offenses are treated too leniently. A 17-year-old who commits murder or rape does as much harm to society as a 20-year-old who commits the same offense and deserves to be punished as severely. Many people believe that youths can appreciate the consequences of their unlawful behavior and should be held accountable.

› There are great inconsistencies between the punishments meted out in the juvenile justice system and those meted out in the criminal justice system. For citizens to have confidence in law enforcement and the courts, punishments must be more uniform.

› Juvenile delinquents are not afforded all the due-process rights that are available in the criminal justice system. Although the juvenile court is supposed to be working in the youth's best interests, some believe that certain cases are dealt with more harshly because the youth does not have the full protection of the legal rights granted to adults.

Finally, juvenile justice cases exhibit many of the features of criminal cases; however, a different vocabulary is used to signify what happens at each stage. As we consider the processing of juvenile cases, we must be aware of these alternative terms (see Table 13.2). Because each state has its own structure and method of processing juvenile cases, the description of the system here will be general and simplified and will highlight common decision points and practices.

Who Enters the Juvenile Justice System?

The modern juvenile justice system is responsible for dealing with many issues affecting children's lives. Managing delinquent behavior is the most visible of these duties, but it is only part of the system's mission. The juvenile justice system is responsible for dealing with the following types of youths:

TABLE 13.2	Differences between the Adult and Juvenile Justice Systems	
ISSUE	**ADULT SYSTEM**	**JUVENILE SYSTEM**
Status in Question	The defendant's guilt in breaking a law.	The child's delinquency in breaking a law or committing a status offense.
Searches	Protections exist against unreasonable searches of one's person, home, and possessions.	Protections against unreasonable searches are limited.
Self-Incrimination	Both children and adults are protected.	
Goal of Proceedings	The defendant is assumed innocent until proven guilty.	The best interests of the child, whether guilty or innocent, are paramount.
Nature of Proceedings	Adversarial	Remedial
Arrests	A warrant is required.	Children are not arrested but taken into custody via petition or complaint.
Representation	Both children and adults have the right to an attorney.	
Trials	Open to the public.	Closed hearings. The right to a jury trial does not exist (there are no trials).
Result upon Conviction or Finding of Delinquency	Convicted adults are punished with possible rehabilitation and/or treatment.	Children are protected and rehabilitated.
Treatment	No right to treatment.	Right to treatment.
Release	Via bail or release-on-recognizance (ROR).	Parental or guardian custody.
Public Records	The results of the trial and judgment remain on public record.	Records are sealed and may be destroyed once the child reaches a certain age.
Incarceration	Prison or jail.	Children are held or incarcerated in non-adult facilities.

> Incorrigible youths. Some parents cannot control their children, particularly as they become teenagers and are lured by temptations outside the home. When children disobey their parents, refuse to go to school, leave home for days at a time, or physically abuse their parents and siblings, the court might remove them from their homes and find alternative living arrangements. Sometimes, parents give up on their children and ask the court to take them.

> Dependent youths. When children are abandoned or orphaned, the state becomes responsible for their welfare. Usually, the first option is to place the child with a relative, but if no suitable relative is available, the court will seek a foster home and oversee adoption requests.

> Neglected youths. Some parents are unconcerned, careless, or incapable of providing physical, emotional, and economic care for their children. The

juvenile justice system must ensure that neglected children have adequate food, shelter, clothes, and schooling. Sometimes this means working with the parent(s) to monitor the family's living conditions, and sometimes it means removing the child from the home and placing him or her in a more suitable environment.

status offense—An act that is considered a legal offense only when committed by a juvenile and that can be adjudicated only in a juvenile court.

› Status offenders. Many behaviors are considered legitimate for adults but deviant for children. These are known as **status offenses**. For instance, because of mandatory education laws, children are required to attend school until the age of 16, 17, or 18 depending on the state, whereas there is no such requirement of adults.[8] Underage drinking laws are another example of a status offense. Those under the age of 21 are subject to arrest for consuming alcohol, whereas adults are free to drink as much alcohol as they want as long as they do not violate other laws, such as being drunk in public or driving an automobile while intoxicated. Running away from home, violating curfew, and breaking other age-determined laws make juveniles subject to a range of restrictions that do not affect adults.

› Delinquent youths. Children must obey all the laws that apply to adults, with limited exceptions (for instance, a 15-year-old and a 14-year-old who have sex are treated differently than a 25-year-old who has sex with a 14-year-old). Upon breaking the law, children are brought into the juvenile justice system, just as adults are brought into the criminal justice system. However, what happens to youths, once taken into custody, can be quite different. In serious situations, the youth's case might be transferred to adult court (this will be discussed in greater detail later in this chapter).

Although we use multiple methods of assessing crime such as self-report studies, victimization studies, and official statistics, because much crime goes unreported, and a substantial amount of it can never be attributed to any individual or group, the actual amount of crime can never be definitively measured. When dealing with juvenile delinquency, this inability to accurately comprehend the

A Tucson Police officer takes a juvenile into custody. What types of youths enter the juvenile justice system?

reality of the crime problem is even more acute. In addition to the many reasons that people do not report crime, there are additional reasons why much juvenile delinquency never finds its way into official statistics or reports. These reasons include the following:

> Adults are unaware of the offense. Violence between youths is often unknown to adults who have the ability or desire to report it. Young people might get in a fight after school, and even though the combatants return home bloodied and bruised, they may not tell their parents or guardians about the cause. Youths do not define these conflicts as crime, and they may have good reasons not to make their parents or guardians aware of the problem. If the youth was the one who picked the fight in the first place, he or she may expect little or no sympathy. Consequently, many such activities go unreported.

> Some delinquency and status offending is consensual. Alcohol use, drug use, and sexual activity are all behaviors that would be included in the juvenile delinquency and status-offending picture if they were reported. However, because juveniles often enter into these activities freely, there is little incentive, and great disincentive, to make parents, teachers, or police aware of these transgressions.

> Status offenses are difficult to identify. It is difficult to define exactly when some behaviors become status offenses. For instance, if a 14-year-old runs away from home and is gone for two weeks but reconciles with his or her parents, should this count as running away? At what point does disobeying one's parents become incorrigibility? Additionally, schools have a great deal of discretion, and many have policies in place that allow them to work with students to keep them attending school before declaring them truant. For this reason, one school district's policy might result in more truancy being recorded than another school district's, although the behavior patterns are similar.

> Adults choose not to report. Adults do not report many minor transgressions by youths because they do not want young people to be subject to the juvenile justice system. In order to avoid the label or stigma of juvenile delinquent, teachers and law enforcement often give stern warnings for minor misbehavior in the hope that they were simply youthful transgressions and not indicative of a pattern of delinquency. According to **labeling theory**, it is often deemed wise to overlook and minimize the deviant behavior of young people so that they are not officially labeled as delinquent and, furthermore, do not think of themselves that way. The idea is to prevent a negative label from becoming a self-fulfilling prophecy.

labeling theory (from Chapter 12)—A perspective that considers recidivism to be a consequence, in part, of the negative labels applied to offenders.

These reasons explaining why much juvenile delinquency and status offending is not reported should not blind us to the fact that a great deal of it is reported and that it is a substantial problem. Efforts to measure juvenile delinquency have become more sophisticated, and because these measures show some stability in levels and trends, we can make approximations about the seriousness of juvenile delinquency. According to the Uniform Crime Reports, 41,335 people under age 18 were arrested for violent offenses in 2016. Most of these arrests were for aggravated assault, followed by robbery. Relatively few arrests were for murders/non-negligent manslaughters. However, most juveniles were arrested for property offenses, with 147,350 arrests. By far, the most common property offense was larceny-theft (see Figure 13.1).[9]

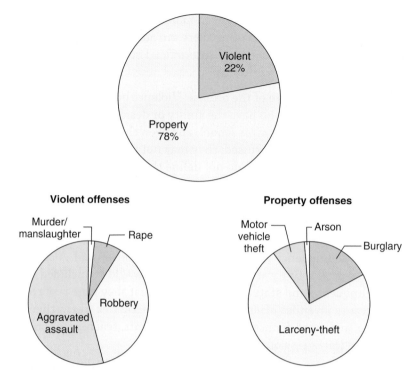

FIGURE 13.1   Arrests by Age Which violent offenses were juveniles arrested for most often? Which property offenses?

Source: Federal Bureau of Investigation, Uniform Crime Reports: Crime in the United States, 2016, Arrests by Age, Table 20, https://ucr.fbi.gov/crime-in-the-u.s/2016/crime-in-the-u.s.-2016/topic-pages/tables/table-20.

We must remember that these figures represent only known offenses and not the actual level of juvenile delinquency. Still, they are useful figures because they give some indication as to the volume of cases the juvenile justice system must handle. Regardless of how much delinquency juveniles are involved in, the juvenile court and juvenile corrections systems only have to deal with those who are identified by the police and taken into custody.

Entering the System

referral—Similar to a "charge" in the adult system in which an authority, usually the police, parents, or the school, determines that a youth needs intervention from the juvenile court.

Cases enter the juvenile justice system by a process called **referral**, in which an authority determines that a youth needs intervention from the juvenile court. There are two types of referrals. The first type of referral can come from schools, parents, or child welfare agencies that believe the child is at risk from others, as in cases of child abuse or delinquency. A parent may turn the child over to the juvenile court because he or she cannot provide an adequate home or because the child is incorrigible. A child welfare agency may turn the child over to the court if both parents are incarcerated and no relative is available to care for the youth.

The second type of referral comes from law enforcement. This type of referral is the functional equivalent of an arrest. Depending on the youth's age and the seriousness of the delinquency, the youth's treatment can closely resemble the arrest of an adult, although the process is often different. Based on the philosophy of doing what is best for youths, many large police departments have specialized juvenile units that are familiar with the community resources available to treat youths. As many as one-third of juvenile cases handled by law enforcement are diverted from the juvenile justice system, and the youths are either released or funneled into alternative programs.[11] Of the two types of referrals, the law enforcement referral is the most common by a large margin. Typically, law enforcement referrals account for 59 percent of the cases entered into the juvenile justice system (see Figure 13.2).[12]

PRE-HEARING DETENTION

When the police take a youth into custody, they may detain the youth for several hours at the police station in order to obtain information about the youth, such as name, age, and address. During this time, the police may decide to either release or take the youth to a shelter or detention facility until a decision about the case has been made. The rules concerning keeping youths in detention differ from state to state, but the following is typical.

Depending on the jurisdiction, the youth's age determines where he or she is held. For example, for youths under age 12, the jurisdiction may require a judge's decision as to whether the youth may be placed in detention. Youths older than age 12 may be held in detention for up to 36 hours without a court hearing. Law enforcement agencies are discouraged from holding juveniles in adult jails while the case is processed. Federal regulations require that youths be held no longer than six hours in adult jails and that they be kept out of sight and sound of adult inmates. After six hours, youths must be transferred to a juvenile agency that can provide secure detention. Some jurisdictions do not allow particularly young juveniles, such as those under age 15, to be held in adult jails at all.

The rules that determine the pre-hearing treatment of youths differ from state to state. Typical requirements for pre-hearing detention are:

> the youth is accused of an offense against a person;

> an alleged victim requires protection from the youth;

> the youth is believed unlikely to show up for the hearing or will commit another offense upon release;

> the youth is on probation, parole, or release from another charge; or the youth has run away from a court-ordered placement.

For youths in detention, there is usually a time limit, for example, 36 hours from the time of arrest, in which probable cause must be found that the youth committed an offense.

INTAKE

The intake function is a major decision point in the juvenile justice system. An intake officer, who is responsible to the juvenile probation department and/or the juvenile court judge, reviews the case to determine whether evidence is sufficient to prove the allegation against the youth. This review is often in the form of a preliminary hearing in which the youth and his or her parent(s) or guardian(s) are questioned about the youth's understanding of the offending behavior and the willingness and ability of the parent(s) or guardian(s) to correct that behavior. The youth might be released at this point if the evidence is weak; however, the burden of proof is low.[13] Consequently, a finding by the intake officer that sufficient reason exists to pass the case forward is enough to keep the case in court.

The intake officer, in conjunction with the probation department, may establish an informal way of handling the case that, if successfully completed, could allow the youth to escape formal processing and the resultant paper trail of legal transgressions.[14] A **consent decree** may be written at this point, in which the youth agrees to some conditions for a specified period of time. These conditions might include restitution to a victim, drug or alcohol counseling, attendance at school, or maintaining a curfew. Once the youth successfully completes the conditions, the case is dismissed. Because the probation department often monitors these conditions, this

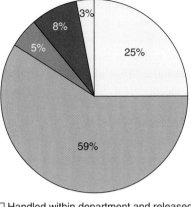

□ Handled within department and released

■ Referred to juvenile court jurisdiction

■ Referred to other police agency

■ Referred to criminal or adult court

□ Referred to welfare agency

FIGURE 13.2 Police Disposition of Juveniles Taken into Custody What happens to most juveniles taken into custody?

Source: Federal Bureau of Investigation, Uniform Crime Reports: Crime in the United States, 2015, Table 68: Police Disposition Juvenile Offenders Taken into Custody, 2015, https://ucr.fbi.gov/crime-in-the-u.s/2015/crime-in-the-u.s.-2015/tables/table-68.

consent decree—When the parties to a lawsuit accept a judge's order that is based on an agreement made by them instead of continuing the case through a trial or hearing.

informal probation— A period during which a juvenile is required to stay out of trouble or make restitution before a case is dropped.

diversion—The effort to deinstitutionalize delinquent and neglected children.

procedure is often called **informal probation**. This type of processing allows the case to be diverted from the system without formal charges being filed. If the youth fails to comply with the conditions, the case goes back into the system.[15]

DIVERSION

Diversion, a reform that took root in the 1960s and 1970s, is the effort to de-institutionalize delinquent and neglected children. Today, rather than incarcerate youths in prison-like reform or training schools, some jurisdictions utilize community correctional practices such as foster homes, halfway houses, and extended probation-like supervision.[16] By referring youths to programs that address their educational, counseling, and drug treatment needs, diversion seeks to avoid contact between casual offenders and more seriously troubled young people. Jurisdictions use various terms to refer to diversion, including informal processing, adjustment, supervision, proceeding, probation adjustment, deferred prosecution, civil citation, or consent decree.[17] Depending on the jurisdiction, diversion programs may be operated by one or all of the following agencies: law enforcement, the county juvenile probation office, the prosecutor's office, the court, a community-based service agency, public mental health agencies, and private organizations.[18]

Probation is a common method used to divert status offenders or first-time juvenile delinquents from the juvenile court. Some communities use probation to informally monitor at-risk youth and prevent more serious problem behavior.[19] Diversion may also occur at the detention stage, or at any of the following pre-adjudication points:

> Arrest or apprehension: when law enforcement has contact with a youth;

> Intake: when a youth is delivered to an office such as a police department or pretrial detention center that is authorized to book the case;

> Petitioning: when the court begins the process leading to adjudication;

> Pretrial probation contact: when a court or probation officer interviews a youth and family during the course of formal processing.[20]

A probation officer at Camp Kenyon Scudder in California meets with a new arrival during her intake at the detention center. At what stage of the juvenile justice system process does intake occur?

Jurisdictions that use diversion programs typically aspire to five major goals:

1. reduce recidivism
2. avoid labeling
3. reduce unnecessary social control
4. provide services
5. reduce system costs[21]

The goal of reducing recidivism is a typical measure of a program's effectiveness. The goal of avoiding labeling, based on labeling theory, is to prevent young offenders from thinking of themselves as criminals by immersing them in conventional schools, activities, and close contact with their families.[22] The goal of reducing unnecessary social control seeks to keep youths out of the juvenile justice system, although diversion sometimes has the opposite effect (see the following discussion on net-widening). Diversion programs try to provide services, such as drug treatment or job training, which may not be available in an incarceration environment. By achieving the four prior goals, it is hoped that the fifth, a reduction of costs, will be achieved.

A criticism of diversion is that it is sometimes self-defeating in terms of keeping youths out of the juvenile justice system. Some diversion programs actually pull more youths into the juvenile justice system than would otherwise be involved, a phenomenon called **net-widening** (also discussed in Chapters 7 and 12). For example, a correctly functioning diversion program would extract 300 of 1,000 youths processed into the system and divert them to foster homes, rehabilitation programs, and other therapeutic alternatives, such as ranches and camps (discussed later in the chapter). However, a program engaged in net-widening would draw in 300 youths in addition to the 1,000 who are already being processed. Under normal circumstances, these 300 youths might not enter the juvenile justice system at all: their cases would be dropped, and they would be released into the custody of their parents or guardians.[23] In some cases, the youths would only receive a lecture from the police.

net-widening (from Chapter 12)—A phenomenon through which criminal justice programs pull more clients into the system than would otherwise be involved without the program.

Shakespeare in the Courts is a program in Massachusetts that works with young offenders who have been given the opportunity to learn and perform works of Shakespeare as an alternative to doing community service or being placed in juvenile detention. What are the benefits of diversion programs?

Some research indicates that net-widening is pervasive. Many programs, instead of serving the intended nonviolent, first-time delinquents who are at risk of more serious delinquency, instead target low-risk youths who would probably be better off not participating in the program at all.

DETERMINING JURISDICTION

Once an intake officer decides that a case should be processed through the juvenile justice system and not diverted, it is decided whether the case will remain in the juvenile court or be transferred to criminal court. The states have various mechanisms for making this decision (see the Juvenile Waiver section later in this chapter). The prosecutor may file the case in criminal court, or the intake officer may file a petition waiver to transfer the case.[24] The decision is based on two factors: the seriousness of the delinquency and the history and demeanor of the juvenile. Only serious offenses, such as homicide, are bound over (transferred) to criminal court.[25] Most cases involving youths stay under the juvenile court's jurisdiction. If the youth has been before the court many times and has disregarded the authority of the judge and probation staff, waiver to criminal court may be deemed an appropriate way to handle the case. If the youth is not amenable to treatment and continues to break the law while under juvenile court supervision, the prosecutor may decide to kick the case up to criminal court where the protection of society is considered as important as the youth's welfare.[26]

For those who commit minor offenses, a different type of jurisdictional alternative is available in many juvenile justice systems. Teen courts are used to handle nonviolent juvenile offenders in the context of having their peers consider their case. In a teen court, the judge, jury, prosecutor, and defense attorney are all other teens who consider the case and pass judgment. It is thought that in the teen court context peer pressure can be used to resolve the case.[27]

ADJUDICATORY HEARING

adjudicatory hearing—The process in which a juvenile court determines whether the allegations in a petition are supported by evidence.

Within a specified period (this varies by state), an **adjudicatory hearing** is held to determine whether the youth committed the delinquent acts charged against him or her. This hearing is the equivalent of a criminal trial but with some important differences. First, the juvenile hearing is a quasi-civil proceeding (not criminal) and therefore may be confidential. Only official and interested parties are allowed in the court. The facts of the case and, most important, the names of juvenile delinquents and victims may be kept from the media. Second, the adjudicatory hearing is conducted by a judge who also acts as a jury. Third, the youth, if guilty, will be adjudicated delinquent, shifting the focus of the case from the delinquent act to the youth's rehabilitation.

adversarial process (from Chapter 7)—A term describing the manner in which U.S. criminal trial courts operate; a system that requires two sides, a prosecution and a defense.

Although not an **adversarial process,** the adjudicatory hearing has many of the aspects of a trial. Because of the legal reforms of the 1960s and 1970s, juvenile delinquents enjoy many of the rights afforded adults in the criminal court, including the right to have an attorney, the right to confront and cross-examine hostile witnesses, the right to present witnesses in defense, and protection against self-incrimination. Furthermore, the standard of proof in an adjudicatory hearing is set at the highest standard: beyond a reasonable doubt. Although youths have the right to an attorney, the youth or his or her parents can waive this right. This makes for a somewhat confusing situation. Attorneys are supposed to exercise independent professional judgment on behalf of their clients, but sometimes the juvenile's best interests conflict with the wishes of the parents, who pay the attorney's fee. At the end of the day, the juvenile's welfare must be balanced with his or her legal rights when the case is processed.

Additionally, the juvenile system has its own terminology, further setting it apart from the adult system. In the adjudicatory hearing (trial), the **petitioner** (prosecutor) will attempt to prove the youth delinquent and in need of **commitment** (incarceration), whereas the **respondent** (defense attorney) challenges the facts of the case.

An interesting controversy surrounding adjudicatory hearings is that in some jurisdictions, juveniles who have been in detention prior to their hearing are brought into court in shackles.[28] Usually, these shackles consist of wrist and ankle restraints chained at the waist. Many states and jurisdictions have stopped using shackles except in cases in which the youth presents a security risk.[29] One reason for discontinuing the practice is related to labeling theory, which asserts that if a youth is treated like a criminal, then he or she may begin to identify as such and retreat more deeply into a criminal lifestyle.

DISPOSITION

The disposition of the juvenile case is comparable to the handing down of the sentence in criminal court. The disposition can take two paths: residential placement (confinement) in a secure facility or referral to probation or a similar nonresidential program.

As a rule, placement in a residential facility is reserved for those adjudicated for the most serious offenses. **Residential placement** sometimes means being placed in a community halfway house or a foster home. However, residential placement often means the juvenile is sent to a training or reform school that is little different from a prison. Although the youth is confined with other youths, residential placement can, in many ways, be compared to "hard time" in an adult institution.

In some cases, youths can be sentenced to adult facilities in which relatively young adults are confined. Some youths are so advanced in antisocial lifestyles that officials believe that keeping them in juvenile institutions would not provide the proper security and the youths might negatively influence other young offenders.

petitioner—A person who files a lawsuit; also called a plaintiff.

commitment—An order by a judge upon conviction or before a trial that sends a person to jail or prison. Also, a judge's order that sends a mentally unstable person to a mental institution.

respondent—The party who must reply to a petitioner's complaint. Equivalent to a defendant in a lawsuit.

residential placement—Any sentence of a juvenile delinquent to a residential facility where the juvenile is closely monitored.

Boys sit in assigned seats while waiting to go to the gym at the Lucas County Juvenile Detention Center in Toledo, Ohio. What are some of the defining characteristics of residential placement?

Some dispositions for juveniles result in sentences in adult prisons. This typically occurs when the juvenile is tried as an adult and thus receives an "adult" sentence. The youths in such cases are usually accused of heinous offenses, which often involve homicide. Until recently, adults who had committed their offenses as youths could be executed, and many states mandated life-without-parole sentencing for juveniles convicted of certain offenses. This is no longer the case, although juveniles may still be tried as adults and serve prison sentences.

A disposition of juvenile probation can be linked to a set of conditions that requires the youth to participate in treatment programs, additional schooling, or public service activities.[30] Again, the philosophy of the juvenile justice system is geared toward rehabilitation, but by forcing the youth to engage in multiple activities, the distinction between rehabilitation and punishment may be indistinct to the youth.[31]

AFTERCARE

To ease the transition of the youth from residential treatment back into the community, the court may order some type of aftercare. This can be thought of as similar to the parole function in the criminal court. Aftercare may consist of programs designed to address the youth's problems, including drug or alcohol treatment, counseling, regular school attendance, or employment. The key to aftercare programs is the court's ability to ensure the offender's accountability. If the youth fails to complete the aftercare requirements, another period of confinement may be in store.[32]

Figure 13.3 shows that juveniles can be diverted from the system at many points. However, this does not mean that they are not under some type of control. Cases are held in abeyance (suspended) until youths successfully complete diversion programs or other court requirements. Sometimes this is as easy as not getting into trouble for one year. If the court's orders are completed, the case is dismissed, but if the youth violates the law or ignores the directives of the diversion program, he or she will again face a judge who may order more draconian forms of control.

Seated here is 20-year-old Michelle Carter in Bristol Juvenile Court in Taunton, Massachusetts. In June 2017, Carter was found guilty of involuntary manslaughter for encouraging her friend, Conrad Roy III, to commit suicide via text messaging in 2014 when she was 17. Should Carter have been tried as an adult?

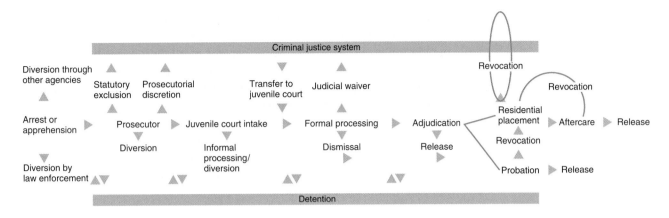

FIGURE 13.3   Juvenile Justice System Case Flow At what point does diversion occur? At what point does revocation occur?

Source: Office of Juvenile Justice and Delinquency Prevention, Statistical Briefing Book Case Flow Diagram (Washington, D.C.: U.S. Department of Justice), http://www.ojjdp.gov/ojstatbb/structure_process/case.html. Accessed March 2017.

PAUSE AND REVIEW

1. What are the benefits and critiques of the modern juvenile justice system?

2. What types of youths are the juvenile justice system responsible for?

3. Why are authorities unable to accurately assess the reality of juvenile delinquency?

4. What are the stages of the juvenile justice system?

5. What are the major goals of diversion programs, and how does net widening affect such goals?

Issues in Juvenile Justice

Despite the good intentions and concerns of those working in the juvenile justice system, some issues have not been resolved in ways that make youths more controllable or society any safer. In some ways, the juvenile justice system and our society in general have not addressed delinquency comprehensively and effectively. All the institutions that deal with children are partially responsible for this failure. The juvenile justice system is the institution of last resort; therefore, it looks more ineffective than the school, family, or community. If those other institutions were fulfilling their missions more completely, however, there might be fewer delinquent children. Any real reform of the juvenile justice system must be linked to the way these other institutions interact with law enforcement, the juvenile court, and treatment programs. To a large extent, the solution to effective reform is better funding, but other issues may be more politically feasible than raising taxes and allocating more funds to schools, recreational programs, treatment alternatives, or increasing the number of police officers. To reform the juvenile justice system, the following issues should receive greater scrutiny and consideration.

Chronic Offenders

Given the broad reach of statutes criminalizing the behavior of youths, we can expect many to come in contact with the juvenile justice system as they test the boundaries of appropriate behavior, seek to establish their identities, and have a bit of fun. The "kids-will-be-kids" behavior is not what concerns us most because boys and girls typically outgrow much of this deviant behavior.

LEARNING OBJECTIVE 4

Discuss why belonging to a youth gang is a predictor of chronic delinquency.

LEARNING OBJECTIVE 5

Classify the types of public facilities in which youths may be incarcerated.

LEARNING OBJECTIVE 6

Defend and criticize the process of waiver to criminal court.

A small percentage of youth, however, are long-term, chronic, and consistent law violators.[33] According to one landmark study, less than 7 percent of the juvenile population was responsible for 52 percent of all delinquent offenses. Out of a total sample of 10,000 boys, 627 accounted for 71 percent of the homicides, 73 percent of the rapes, 82 percent of the robberies, and 69 percent of the aggravated assaults.[34] Other findings suggest that going to juvenile court does little to deter youths from further delinquency.[35] Because research has shown that such youths share several factors such as behavior problems, poor grades, drug or alcohol use, family problems (such as criminal parents), abuse or neglect, and patterns of stealing or running away, the solution to chronic delinquency is necessarily complex, broad-based, and expensive.

Gangs

One predictor of chronic delinquency is belonging to a youth gang. The influence of gang ideas is prevalent in popular music, television dramas, and movies, and youths often adopt the style of gangs in clothing, tattoos, and use of gang signs. Graffiti in cities and towns of all sizes throughout the country suggest some level of gang influence.[36]

Regardless of the perceived growth and diffusion of youth gangs, they remain a particular problem in the largest cities, where there are contested neighborhoods, a critical mass of disenfranchised youth, and a long history and tradition of gang activity. For example, in 2016, large metropolitan areas, including Boston and Washington, D.C., dealt with renewed violence from members of Mara Salvatrucha (or MS-13), a Central American gang with roots in Los Angeles, California.[37] Police say the gang has been trying to re-establish itself in the Boston area by recruiting youths in schools, on sports fields, and on playgrounds. To acquire money, MS-13 members typically extort businesses, distribute drugs, and commit robberies.[38] Although large, traditional gangs remain a problem, in some areas small, local gangs cause the most trouble. For instance, in Augusta, Georgia, police officials say that the local gangs are more likely to be violent than the gangs affiliated with traditional, nationwide gangs like the Bloods or Crips because those gangs have more structure and control over their member gangs.[39]

A police officer encourages graduates of the G. R. E. A. T. (Gang Resistance Education and Training) program at the Gilpin Montessori School in Denver, Colorado. Why is belonging to a gang a predictor of chronic delinquency?

Because there are so many types of youth gangs, it is difficult to construct a general definition other than that they engage in criminal or delinquent activity.[40] Youth gangs are often focused around drug distribution, turf protection, robbery, extortion, or any number of other illegal activities. Many youth gangs are connected to larger, national gangs or gang alliances such as the Folk Nation and the People Nation, which also have adult members. At their most extreme, youth gangs are highly organized, have members who remain active well into their adult years, are connected with prison gangs, and have hundreds of members.

Race and ethnicity are another dimension of many gangs.[41] California has Hispanic gangs, black gangs, Asian gangs, and white gangs. This list is misleading, however, because the number and types of gangs can be subdivided in any number of ways. For instance, Asian gangs can be subdivided into Filipino, Chinese, Indochinese (Vietnamese, Cambodian, Laotian, Thai, and Hmong), Korean, Japanese, and Pacific Islander (Samoan, Fijian, Guamanian, and Hawaiian) gangs. There is a constantly shifting loyalty among gangs; sometimes certain ethnic groups will oppose each other one month and then merge to confront another group the following month. The police have established gang units and have recruited officers from many of the nationalities that contribute to the U.S. gang problem.[42]

Race and ethnicity have been shown to be significant factors in how the juvenile justice system deals with problematic youth. Research has shown that white youths consistently receive more lenient treatment from the juvenile justice system.[43] This bias is also evident when dealing with female delinquents.[44]

Although we typically think of the gang problem as being a male issue, research shows that females are also active in gangs. Previously, female gang activity was thought to be supportive of male gangs, but today, full-fledged female gangs provide many of the functions for their members that make gangs so attractive to males. From a feminist point of view, the social liberation of women and girls has enabled them to become more actively engaged in gang and criminal pursuits.[45] However, we should not make too much of this liberation hypothesis. The opportunity that young women have to form their own gangs does not reflect a greater freedom of choice.

Often, girls and young women are forced to enter gang life to protect themselves in a community that has lost (or never had) social viability. Female gang activity is not a step forward for females but rather an unintended consequence of so many young men going to training schools and prisons and leaving a void in the drug markets and power relationships on the street. As young women move to fill this void by engaging in gang activity, they are in danger not only of being further victimized by males, but also of victimizing each other and exposing themselves to the juvenile justice system.

Although youth gangs have engaged in crime for a long time, the effect of the drug culture since the 1970s has radically changed the nature of many gangs and greatly increased the amount of lethal behavior associated with gang activity. To some extent, lucrative drug sales have replaced the expressive gang activities of fighting, graffiti, and turf protection. Given the amount of money involved in the drug trade, neighborhood gangs are driven to act more like organized crime groups.[46]

Large, well-established gangs that require adults to run their major vice operations rely on youths to fuel their memberships. A 24-year-old man who had just quit the West Tennessee Vice Lords after 11 years describes his recruitment like this: "They took me in as their seed. That's what they called you. At the age of 13, I was called a young seed."[47] Most people who join gangs do so between the ages of 11 and 15, with 15 being the most commonly reported age of gang members. It is also important to understand that most youths leave the gang after a year and that longer tenures in a gang are not as common as may be believed. This is one reason that gangs recruit youths so actively: most will eventually drift away from the gang, leaving relatively few adults to take care of business.[48] However, even if youths do drop out of the gang, the effects of gang membership may be permanent. Compared to youths who never joined a gang, adults who joined a gang during adolescence had poorer outcomes during their adult lives, including higher rates of crime, incarceration, drug abuse, and poor health, as well as lower rates of high school graduation.[49]

According to a La Crosse, Wisconsin, police officer who works with youths on gang prevention, peer perception is an important part of educating young people about gangs. In an interview, the officer stated that youths think that up to half of the students in their classes are gang members, but that nationally only about 7 percent of youths are gang members. When youths learn that gang members are actually a minority and that not "all their friends are doing it," it affects their decisions about joining a gang.[50]

Another view of what makes gangs attractive to some youths comes from Father Gregory Boyle, a Jesuit priest in Los Angeles who runs Homeboy Industries, the largest gang intervention, rehabilitation, and re-entry program in the United States. According to Boyle, "Three types of youths become gang members. One is the kid stuck in despair so bleak that his future doesn't compel him; the second is in so much pain—so damaged that he can't transform his pain so he transmits it; and the third is a mentally ill kid. I've never met a hopeful kid who joined a gang."[51] Boyle advocates providing a sense of hope for young gang members, as well as providing mental health care.

Types and Conditions of Youth Confinement

The types of institutions available for juvenile delinquents vary widely across the United States. However, even when a state has many sentencing options, crowding often means there is no room in the most appropriate type of confinement. As of 2013, more than 35,000 juveniles were committed to some form of incarceration. Juveniles who are convicted in criminal court typically remain in juvenile facilities until they reach their state's age of adulthood, usually between 18 and 21, and then are moved to adult facilities.[52] Generally, three main types of facilities are available in many states.

> Adult prisons. Some young offenders convicted of serious offenses may be kept in adult prisons because of security risks and the harm they may do to other youths. Juveniles are kept separate from adult inmates, but are often placed in the most restrictive confinement possible. For many of these dangerous delinquents, this means protective custody in what amounts to solitary confinement.

> Ranches and camps. Ranches and forestry camps enable juvenile delinquents to work outside on public lands. The intent is to provide positive work experiences so that youths can find gainful employment when released. Additionally, by being away from the temptations of urban life and the confines of a training school, the more normal summer camp-like experience of these types of detention is thought to be less stigmatizing and harmful to the youth's self-concept.[53] Most ranches and camps are privately operated.[54]

> Traditional training schools. These often crowded and understaffed programs are where more serious delinquents are incarcerated for longer periods of time. Some training schools physically resemble adult prisons; others have the appearance of a college campus.[55]

The Youth Treatment Center in Toledo, Ohio, is a community-based alternative to prison for non-violent juvenile delinquents. What are the three main types of youth confinement institutions in the United States?

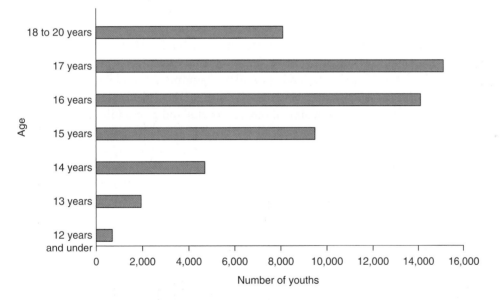

FIGURE 13.4 Juveniles in Residential Placement, by Age Which is the most common age for a youth to be in residential placement?

Source: M. Sickmund, T. J. Sladky, W. Kang, and C. Puzzanchera, "Easy Access to the Census of Juveniles in Residential Placement," 2015, http://www.ojjdp.gov/ojstatbb/ezacjrp/.

In addition to these types of public institutions are many public and private residential placement facilities, with juveniles in their mid- to late teens making up most of these placements (see Figure 13.4). There are more than twice as many small, privately operated juvenile facilities in the United States than public facilities, and more than half of these are group homes. Private facilities hold fewer than half as many delinquents as public facilities but more status offenders.[56] These programs offer the court, parents, and youths an alternative to traditional confinement. Although private programs can be expensive, some offer exceptional counseling. However, some private programs are controversial; at those located outside the United States, youths' legal rights can be extremely limited.

Much like adult prisons and jails, security is an issue at many youth facilities. The level of security varies with the type of facility, but generally, the most secure facilities hold the most troublesome delinquents. Private facilities, which typically house less serious delinquents, are less likely to lock youths in their sleeping rooms than public facilities. Locked doors and gates are often used for juveniles being held for offenses such as homicide, sexual and aggravated assault, robbery, arson, and technical violations. The use of fences, walls, and equipment such as surveillance cameras is common in juvenile facilities.[57] Detention centers and training schools are most likely to use razor wire to secure their grounds. One aspect of security is the facility's ability to protect some youths from themselves. Most youths go to facilities that screen for mental health problems, suicide risk, and substance abuse.[58] One recent government census found that of eight deaths of youths held in juvenile facilities, five were suicides.[59]

Critics of large residential facilities argue that they are ineffective and inhumane. According to the Annie E. Casey Foundation, up to 80 percent of juveniles released from state-operated youth corrections facilities are rearrested within two or three years for a new offense. The facilities are also expensive: in many states, the average annual cost per bed is more than $200,000.[60] In an effort to improve the conditions of and prevent unnecessary juvenile confinement, the Juvenile Justice and Delinquency Prevention Act of 2002 does not allow status offenders to be placed in secure facilities for long terms.

An alternative to prison-style incarceration is called the Missouri Model.[61] In 1983, the state of Missouri closed its two training schools in favor of group homes, camps, and small treatment facilities. Security is maintained through direct staff supervision rather than fences and surveillance equipment, and youth specialists run the facilities rather than correctional guards. The typical facility consists of cottage-style dormitories housing about 10 youths and two adult staff.[62] Proponents of the Missouri Model say that it results in lower recidivism rates. For example, only 8.5 percent of committed youths in Missouri ended up in adult prisons within three years of release as opposed to 26 percent in Maryland, 20.8 percent in Indiana, and 23.4 percent in Arizona.[63] Despite the success of the Missouri Model,

A 19-year-old transgender woman, who was a resident of a halfway house for juvenile delinquents, says she received death threats from fellow residents. Advocates state that juvenile detention centers in the United States are not equipped to securely house and counsel transgender youths, which increases the likelihood for bullying, assault, depression, and suicide. Why does security remain an issue at many youth facilities?

research indicates that youths are best served through home-based interventions rather than out-of-home commitments.[64]

Juvenile Waiver: Treating Children as Adults

One of the outgrowths of the get-tough-on-crime approach has been to treat serious juvenile delinquents as adult offenders. Rather than handling these cases in juvenile courts, these cases are waived to the criminal court where the protection of society is paramount. It is argued that the most serious juvenile delinquents require a minimum criminal sentence that is not available in juvenile court. All states have provisions for trying juveniles as adults. Some states lower the age for juvenile jurisdiction to 15 or 16 rather than 17 or 18. Other methods by which juveniles may be sent to criminal court are **judicial waiver**, **statutory exclusion**, and **direct filing** (see CJ Reference 13.1).[65]

Critics of the waiver process point out that sending a juvenile to adult court does not always protect the public because the youth may serve only a fraction of the sentence. Additionally, the criminal court might not have the treatment alternatives for young offenders that are available in juvenile court.[66] There is also evidence of racial bias in terms of who is waived to criminal court, with young, black males being disproportionately selected.[67]

The public approves of trying youths as adults in part so that they will receive a criminal disposition. Many people believe that a juvenile who commits a

judicial waiver—A form of waiving a juvenile to criminal court in which a judge sends the juvenile to adult court.

statutory exclusion—Provisions that exclude, without hearing or waiver, juveniles who meet certain age, offense, or past-record criteria from the jurisdiction of the juvenile court.

direct filing—A form of waiving a juvenile to criminal court in which a prosecutor has the discretion to file charges in either juvenile or criminal court.

CJ REFERENCE 13.1
Waiver to Criminal Court

JUDICIAL WAIVER

A judge sends the juvenile to adult court. The three types of judicial waiver are discretionary, mandatory, and presumptive.

- Discretionary waiver. Transfer of the juvenile to adult court is at the judge's discretion.
- Mandatory waiver. Automatic transfer to criminal court on the basis of the youth's age and the gravity of the offense.
- Presumptive waiver. The burden of proof shifts from the state to the juvenile, who must contest being transferred to adult court.

    Some states have "once an adult, always an adult" provisions, which means that once the youth is treated by the court as an adult, that youth will always be considered as an adult in any future proceedings.

DIRECT FILING (CONCURRENT JURISDICTION OR PROSECUTORIAL DISCRETION)

A prosecutor has the discretion to file charges in either juvenile or criminal court.

STATUTORY EXCLUSION

Also called legislative waiver, statutory exclusion comes from a state's legislature and does not require a juvenile court hearing. It automatically excludes some juveniles from juvenile court and sends them directly to adult court. Criteria include age, type of offense, and prior record. Statutory exclusion is used most for particularly heinous offenses, such as murder and aggravated rape. Some states without concurrent jurisdictions may also use statutory exclusion for minor violations such as traffic, fish or game, and local ordinance.

REVERSE WAIVER

Some states have laws that allow juveniles whose cases are filed in criminal court (usually through direct filing) to petition to have them transferred to juvenile court. Not all states allow it in all types of cases. Also, the burden of proof for the reversal may shift to the youth.

particularly heinous offense should not receive a lenient juvenile disposition such as probation or a sentence to a juvenile institution (although such dispositions are often anything but lenient), but a sentence that fits the crime. These sentences, which are sometimes mandatory depending on the state, include decades-long prison terms and, until recently, life imprisonment (*Miller v. Alabama* and *Graham v. Florida*) and the death penalty (*Roper v. Simmons*; see Table 13.1 for a summary of these cases). The line of reasoning that the Supreme Court took in *Miller*, *Graham*, and *Roper* was that the Eighth Amendment protection against excessive punishment includes the principle that a punishment should be proportional to both the offender and the offense. In the case of juveniles, their immature ability to reason, their susceptibility to peer pressure, and their inability to choose their parents, living conditions, and school environments are all integral to their status as youths. (See A Closer Look 13.1 for a case in which a youth sentenced as an adult was released from prison 16 years into his 45-year sentence.)

With the incarceration rate in the United States being one of the highest in the world, researchers have also looked at whether trying juveniles as adults, and

A CLOSER LOOK 13.1
Thaddeus Jimenez

When Thaddeus Jimenez was 13 years old, he was charged as an adult in the 1993 murder of Eric Morro, 19, during an argument on Chicago's Northwest Side. As a child, Jimenez was introduced to the Simon City Royals gang by relatives and by the age of 10 was building an extensive juvenile record. Because Morro's shooting was gang-related, it did not take police long to settle on Jimenez as a suspect. Jimenez was convicted in 1994 and sentenced to 45 years in prison.[68]

Jimenez spent his juvenile years of incarceration in a state youth facility and was transferred to prison upon turning 17. Jimenez's behavior landed him in segregation for years at a time. For years, he wrote letters begging attorneys and advocacy groups to consider his case. Finally, in 2005, attorneys and students from the Northwestern University Bluhm Legal Clinic Center on Wrongful Convictions looked into his conviction. Investigators discovered a recording of another suspect, Juan Carlos Torres, confessing to shooting Morro. Two witnesses recanted earlier statements that Jimenez had committed the murder, and in 2007, the Cook County state's attorney's office reopened its investigation.[69]

Jimenez's conviction was overturned in 2009, and he was released from prison after 16 years of incarceration and awarded $199,000 in state compensation.[70] In 2012, a jury awarded Jimenez another $25 million from the city of Chicago.[71]

Almost as soon as he received the settlement, Jimenez began recruiting members for his gang and racking up arrests. He was convicted in 2012 of felony narcotics possession and sentenced to a year in prison. In 2014, he and other gang members were convicted of misdemeanor reckless conduct for surrounding vehicular traffic while wearing masks. He paid large cash bonuses to new gang recruits and to members who tattooed their faces with the Simon City Royals insignia.[72]

In August 2015, while cruising the Irving Park neighborhood in a Mercedes, Jimenez pulled up alongside a 33-year-old former gang member, Earl Casteel, and shot him in the legs, allegedly because he would not rejoin the gang.[73] After his arrest, Jimenez pleaded guilty to a federal weapons violation and in March 2017 was sentenced to nine years in prison, with state charges in the shooting pending.[74]

In a letter to gang members penned from jail, Jimenez vowed to keep the Simon City Royals going. Jimenez wrote about life behind bars: "This is where I was created. This is my home."[75]

THINK ABOUT IT

1. Is 13 years old too young for a juvenile to be charged as an adult no matter how serious the crime?
2. Is 45 years in prison too long a sentence for a juvenile?
3. Would Thaddeus Jimenez have been more likely to have not engaged in further serious crime if he had been retained in the juvenile court?

punishing them as such, deters them from crime and prevents recidivism. According to research, not only does juvenile transfer not deter aspiring delinquents, it actually increases recidivism rates for violent offenders.[76]

PAUSE AND REVIEW

1. Why is belonging to a youth gang a predictor of chronic delinquency?
2. In what types of public facilities may youths be incarcerated?
3. What are some reasons supporting and criticizing the process of waiver to criminal court?

FOCUS ON ETHICS   Widening the Net of Social Control

The juvenile court is responsible for safeguarding the welfare of children, including protecting them from abusive or neglectful parents. You are a juvenile court judge who has been struggling with a particularly difficult case involving a 14-year-old boy who continually smokes marijuana, shoplifts, and recently has been running with a local gang and threatening other children with violence.

The experienced caseworker who has been working hard to help this young man tells you that the source of much of the problem is his parents and his family's dynamics. The boy ignores his mother's instructions and argues with his father. You order the family to see a psychologist who specializes in family matters, but the father refuses to cooperate and contends that the problem is not himself but the "rotten" boy and has discontinued therapy. After several attempts to resolve the situation, you order the boy to be placed in foster care because you believe the father is an unfit parent and a negative influence.

This boy has a 12-year-old brother whose behavior is exemplary. He is an honor student, star athlete, and all-around good kid. You order the 12-year-old out of the home also because the father is recalcitrant and refuses to cooperate with the courts. You think that if he is a poor father for one child, he is probably a poor father for the other and that your duty is to place both boys in foster care for their own well-being.

The 14-year-old seems to be responding well to his new home, but the 12-year-old has become a problem.

He runs away from home, is in danger of being dropped from the honors program because of slipping grades, and refuses to discuss his new problems with the psychologist. You are so angry with the father because of his attitude that you do not want to allow the 12-year-old to return to the home, but you are worried that your actions have resulted in a good kid going bad.

WHAT DO YOU DO?

1. Let the 12-year-old go home and keep pressuring the father to participate in family therapy.
2. Keep both children in foster care until the father starts to cooperate.
3. Return both boys to the home and let the situation run its course. You tried to help, but now it is the father's problem. If his sons end up in prison, it is not your fault.
4. Order the 12-year-old to live with you so that you can show the father that you care about children and are willing to go to great lengths to ensure that they are protected.

For more insight into how someone might respond to such an ethical dilemma, visit the companion website at www.oup.com/us/fuller to watch a video that connects this scenario to a real-world situation.

Summary

LEARNING OBJECTIVE 1 Describe the benefits and critiques of the modern juvenile justice system.	Benefits of the juvenile justice system: • it is supposed to act in the best interests of youths; • it seeks to reduce the stigma of deviant behavior; • young offenders are kept apart from adult offenders; • it seeks to help juvenile delinquents gain the necessary skills to become productive members of society; • it protects youths from receiving the harsh punishments meted out by the criminal justice system. Critiques of the juvenile justice system: • youths who commit serious offenses are treated too leniently; • many people believe that juveniles should be held accountable for their unlawful behavior; • the punishments meted out in the juvenile justice system are inconsistent with those meted out in the criminal justice system; • juvenile delinquents are not afforded all the due-process rights available in the criminal justice system.
LEARNING OBJECTIVE 2 Characterize the types of youths whom the juvenile justice system is responsible for.	Incorrigible youths: Some parents cannot control their children, particularly teenagers, who are lured by temptations outside the home. Dependent youths: When children are abandoned or orphaned, the state becomes responsible for their welfare. Neglected youths: Some parents are unconcerned, careless, or incapable of providing for their children. Status offenders: Many behaviors are considered legitimate for adults but deviant for children (i.e., skipping school, drinking alcohol underage). Delinquent youths: Children must obey all the laws that apply to adults, with limited exceptions.
LEARNING OBJECTIVE 3 Outline the stages of the juvenile justice system.	Referral: Cases enter the juvenile justice system by a referral. Referrals can come from schools, parents, or child welfare agencies that believe the child is at risk from others; referrals can also come from law enforcement agencies. Pre-hearing detention: When the police take a youth into custody, they may detain the youth for several hours in order to obtain information about the youth. Intake: An intake officer reviews the case to determine whether evidence is sufficient to prove the allegation. Diversion: To deinstitutionalize delinquent and neglected children, some jurisdictions utilize community correctional practices such as foster homes, halfway houses, and extended probation-like supervision. Determining jurisdiction: Once an intake officer decides that the case should be processed through the juvenile justice system, it is decided whether the case will remain in the juvenile court or be transferred to criminal court. Adjudicatory hearing: A hearing to determine whether the youth committed the delinquent acts as charged. Disposition: The disposition (like a sentence) can take two paths: residential placement (confinement) in a secure facility or referral to probation or a similar nonresidential program. Aftercare: Programs designed to address the youth's problems, including drug or alcohol treatment, counseling, attending school on a regular basis, or employment.

LEARNING OBJECTIVE 4 Discuss why belonging to a youth gang is a predictor of chronic delinquency.	Youth gangs engage in criminal or delinquent activity and are often involved in drug distribution, turf protecting, robbery, extortion, or any number of other illegal activities. Large, well-established gangs that require adults to run their major vice operations rely on youths to fuel their memberships.
LEARNING OBJECTIVE 5 Classify the types of public facilities in which youths may be incarcerated.	Adult prisons: Some young offenders convicted of serious offenses may be kept here. Ranches and camps: These enable delinquents to work outside on public lands. Traditional training schools: These schools are where more serious delinquents are incarcerated for longer periods of time.
LEARNING OBJECTIVE 6 Defend and criticize the process of waiver to criminal court.	Proponents of the waiver process argue that the most serious juvenile delinquents require a minimum criminal sentence that is not available in juvenile court. Critics of the waiver process assert that sending a juvenile to adult court does not always ensure protection of the public because the youth may serve only a fraction of the sentence imposed by the court. There is also evidence that the waiver process is racially biased.

Critical Reflections

1. Do children really need the same legal protections of the criminal justice system that adults have?

2. Does the juvenile justice system's philosophy of treatment and rehabilitation adequately protect the long-term interests of children?

3. Should age or seriousness of offense determine whether a youth is transferred to the criminal justice system?

Key Terms

adjudicatory hearing **p. 412**
adversarial process **p. 412**
commitment **p. 413**
consent decree **p. 409**
direct filing **p. 421**
diversion **p. 410**
due-process rights **p. 402**

hearing **p. 401**
informal probation **p. 410**
judicial waiver **p. 421**
juvenile delinquent **p. 400**
labeling theory **p. 407**
net-widening **p. 411**
parens patriae **p. 401**

petitioner **p. 413**
referral **p. 408**
residential placement **p. 413**
respondent **p. 413**
status offense **p. 406**
statutory exclusion **p. 421**

Endnotes

1 Tristan Hallman, "Attorney Defends Probation for Teen in Burleson DWI Crash that Killed 4," *Dallas Morning News*, February 11, 2016, http://www.dallasnews.com/news/crime/headlines/20131212-attorney-defends-probation-for-teen-whose-dwi-crash-killed-4-in-burleson.ece.

2 CBS News, Texas Deadly Drunk Driving Probation Sentence Leaves

Families Stunned, December 11, 2013, http://www.cbsnews.com/news/texas-deadly-drunk-driving-probation-sentence-leaves-families-stunned. Hallman, "Attorney Defends Probation for Teen in Burleson DWI Crash That Killed 4."

3 CBS News, "Affluenza" teen Ethan Couch moved to adult jail, February 5, 2016, http://www.cbsnews.com/

news/affluenza-teen-ethan-couch-moved-to-adult-jail/. Naheed Rajwani, "At Most, Affluenza Teen Ethan Couch Faces 120 Days in Jail and Another Chance, Authorities Say," *Dallas Morning News*, December 29, 2015, http://crimeblog.dallasnews.com/2015/12/authorities-to-release-details-on-ethan-couchs-capture-at-10-a-m-news-conference-in-tarrant-county.html/.

4 Naheed Rajwani, "Judge Gives Affluenza Teen Ethan Couch Almost Two Years in Jail," *Dallas News*, April 13, 2016, http://www.dallasnews.com/news/crime/2016/04/13/ethan-couch-to-appear-in-court-wednesday-faces-stricter-probation-terms-as-an-adult.

5 Mary Clement, *The Juvenile Justice System: Law and Process* (Boston: Butterworth-Heinemann, 1977).

6 Donna M. Bishop, "Injustice and Irrationality in Contemporary Youth Policy," *Criminology and Public Policy* 3, no. 4 (November 2004): 633–644.

7 Jodi L. Viljoen, Patricia A. Zapf, and Ronald Roesch, "Adjudicative Competence and Comprehension of Miranda Rights in Adolescent Defendants: A Comparison of Legal Standards," *Behavioral Sciences and the Law* 25, no. 1 (January 2007): 1–19.

8 National Education Association, Raising Compulsory School Age Requirements: A Dropout Fix?, http://www.nea.org/home/50897.htm. Accessed February 2017.

9 Federal Bureau of Investigation, *Uniform Crime Reports: Crime in the United States, 2016*, Arrests by Age, Table 20, https://ucr.fbi.gov/crime-in-the-u.s/2016/crime-in-the-u.s.-2016/topic-pages/tables/table-20.

10 Federal Bureau of Investigation, Crime in the United States, Offenses Cleared, https://ucr.fbi.gov/crime-in-the-u.s/2010/crime-in-the-u.s.-2010/clearances. Accessed June 2017.

11 Alexes Harris, "Diverting and Abdicating Judicial Discretion: Cultural, Political, and Procedural Dynamics in California Juvenile Justice," *Law and Society Review* 41, no. 2 (June 2007): 387–428.

12 Federal Bureau of Investigation, *Uniform Crime Reports: Crime in the United States, 2015*, Table 68: Police Disposition Juvenile Offenders Taken into Custody, 2015, https://ucr.fbi.gov/crime-in-the-u.s/2015/crime-in-the-u.s.-2015/tables/table-68.

13 Douglas C. Dodge, *Due Process Advocacy* (Washington, D.C.: Office of Juvenile Justice and Delinquency Prevention, 1997).

14 Eyitayo Onifade, William Davidson, Sarah Livsey, Garrett Turke, Chris Horton, Jill Malinowski, Dan Atkinson, and Dominique Wimberly, "Risk Assessment: Identifying Patterns of Risk in Young Offenders with the Youth Level of Service/Case Management Inventory," *Journal of Criminal Justice* 36, no. 2 (May 2008): 165–173.

15 James Austin and Barry Krisberg, "Wider, Stronger, and Different Nets: The Dialectics of Criminal Justice Reform," *Journal of Research in Crime and Delinquency* 18, no. 1 (1981): 165–196.

16 Clement, *Juvenile Justice System*.

17 The Models for Change Juvenile Diversion Workgroup, Juvenile Diversion Guidebook, March 2011, http://www.modelsforchange.net/publications/301.

18 Ibid.

19 Office of Juvenile Justice and Delinquency Prevention, Juveniles on Probation, http://www.ojjdp.gov/ojstatbb/probation/overview.html. Accessed February 2017.

20 The Models for Change Juvenile Diversion Workgroup, Juvenile Diversion Guidebook.

21 Ibid.

22 Thomas G. Blomberg, "Diversion and Accelerated Social Control," *Journal of Criminal Law and Criminology* 68, no. 2 (1977): 274–282.

23 Office of Juvenile Justice and Delinquency Prevention, Detention Diversion Advocacy: An Evaluation, Net Widening, September 1999, https://www.ncjrs.gov/html/ojjdp/9909-3/div.html#2.

24 James Howell, "Juvenile Transfers to the Criminal Justice System: State of the Art," *Law and Policy* 18, no. 1 (1996): 17–60.

25 Benjamin Steiner and Emily Wright, "Assessing the Relative Effects of State Direct File Waiver Laws on Violent Juvenile Crime: Deterrence or Irrelevance?" *Journal of Criminal Law and Criminology* 96, no. 4 (Summer 2006): 1451–1477.

26 James L. Loving and Nicholas S. Patapis, "Evaluating Juvenile Amenability to Treatment: Integrating Statutes and Case Law into Clinical Practice," *Journal of Forensic Psychology Practice* 7, no. 1 (January 2007): 67–78.

27 Kenneth S. Smith and Ashley G. Blackburn, "Is Teen Court the Best Fit? Assessing the Predictive Validity of the Teen Court Peer Influence Scale," *Journal of Criminal Justice* 39, no. 2 (March 2011): 198–204.

28 Brian D. Gallagher and John C. Lore III, "Shackling Children in Juvenile Court: The Growing Debate, Recent Trends and the Way to Protect Everyone's Interest," *UC Davis Journal of Juvenile Law and Policy* 12, no. 2 (Summer 2008): 453–480. Available at http://jjlp.law.ucdavis.edu/archives.

29 Jordan Steffen, "Colorado Public Defenders Want Children Out of Restraints in Court," *Denver Post*, September 1, 2015, http://www.denverpost.com/news/ci_26445494/colorado-public-defenders-want-children-out-restraints-court.

30 Grant Grissom, "Dispositional Authority and the Future of the Juvenile Justice System," *Juvenile and Family Court Journal* 42, no. 1 (1991): 25–34.

31 Erika Gebo, "Do Family Courts Administer Individualized Justice in Delinquency Cases?" *Criminal Justice Policy Review* 16, no. 2 (June 2005): 190–210.

32 John Whitehead and Steven Lab, "Meta-Analysis of Juvenile Correctional Treatment," *Journal of Research in Crime and Delinquency* 26, no. 4 (1989): 276–295.

33 Kimberly Kempf-Leonard, Paul E. Tracy, and James C. Howell, "Serious, Violent, and Chronic Juvenile Delinquents: The Relationship of Delinquency Career Types to Adult Criminality," *Justice Quarterly* 18, no. 3 (2001): 449–478.

34 Paul Tracy, Marvin Wolfgang, and Robert Figlio, *Delinquency in Two Birth Cohorts. Executive Summary* (Washington, D.C.: U.S. Department of Justice, 1985).

35 David E. Barrett, Antonis Katsiyannis, and Zhang Dalun, "Predictors of Offense Severity, Adjudication, Incarceration, and Repeat Referrals for Juvenile Offenders," *Remedial and Special Education* 31, no. 4 (July 2010): 261–275.

36 Wayne S. Wooden, "Tagger Crews and Members of the Posse," in *The Modern Gang Reader*, eds. Malcolm W. Klein, Cheryl L. Maxson, and Jody Miller (Los Angeles: Roxbury, 1995), 65–68.

37 Stephen Moss, "The Gangs of El Salvador: Inside the Prison the Guards Are Too Afraid to Enter," *Guardian*, September 4, 2015, http://www.theguardian.com/artanddesign/2015/sep/04/adam-hinton-el-salvador-ms-13-gangs-prison-portraits.

38 O'Ryan Johnson, "Lawmen Address MS-13 Scourge," *Boston Herald*, February 12, 2016, http://www.bostonherald.com/news/local_coverage/2016/02/lawmen_address_ms_13_scourge.

39 Bianca Cain Johnson, "Gang Activity Increasing in Augusta Area," *Augusta Chronicle*, March 11, 2017, http://chronicle.augusta.com/news/2017-03-11/gang-activity-increasing-augusta-area.

40 Malcolm W. Klein and Cheryl L. Maxson, *Gang Structures, Crime Patterns, and Police Responses: A Summary Report* (1996), National Criminal Justice Reference Service. Available at https://www.ncjrs.gov/App/Publications/abstract.aspx?ID=188510.

41 Matthew T. Heriot and Barbara "Sunshine" Parker, "Native American Youth Gangs: Linking Culture, History and Theory for Improved Understanding, Prevention and Intervention," *Journal of Ethnicity in Criminal Justice* 5, no. 4 (December 2007): 83–97.

42 Randall G. Shelden, Sharon K. Tracy, and William B. Brown, *Youth Gangs in American Society*, 3d ed. (Belmont, Calif: Wadsworth, 2004), 116.

43 Tina L. Freiburger and Alison A. Burke, "Adjudication Decisions of Black, White, Hispanic, and Native American Youth in Juvenile Court," *Journal of Ethnicity in Criminal Justice* 8, no. 4 (October 2010): 231–247.

44 Stephen M. Gavazzi, Courtney M. Yarcheck, and Lim Ji-Young, "Ethnicity, Gender, and Global Risk Indicators in the Lives of Status Offenders Coming to the Attention of the Juvenile Court," *International Journal Of Offender Therapy and Comparative Criminology* 49, no. 6 (December 2005): 696–710.

45 Jody Miller, *One of the Guys: Girls, Gangs, and Gender* (New York: Oxford University Press, 2001).

46 Jerome H. Skolnick, "Gangs and Crime Old as Time; But Drugs Change Gang Culture," in *The Modern Gang Reader,* ed. Malcolm W. Klein, Cheryl L. Maxson, and Jody Miller (Los Angeles: Roxbury, 1995), 222–227.

47 Justin Hanson, "Gangs Are Making Their Way to the Suburbs," WMCTV.com, November 13, 2012, http://www.wmcactionnews5.com/story/20086551/gangs-are-making-their-way-to-the-suburbs.

48 G. David Curry, Scott H. Decker, and David C. Pyrooz, *Confronting Gangs: Crime and Community*, 3d ed. (New York: Oxford University Press, 2014), 20, 72.

49 Amanda B. Gilman, Karl G. Hill, and J. David Hawkins, "Long-Term Consequences of Adolescent Gang Membership for Adult Functioning," *American Journal of Public Health* 104, no. 5 (2014): 938–945.

50 Kristen Barbaresi, "Police Educate Students about Gang Activity," WXOW.com, http://www.wxow.com/story/20199145/2012/11/27/police-educate-students-about-gang-activity.

51 Barbara Anderson, "Fresno's Gang Intervention Effort Requires Hope, Help," *Fresno Bee* (California), November 17, 2012.

52 M. Sickmund, T.J. Sladky, W. Kang, and C. Puzzanchera, Easy Access to the Census of Juveniles in Residential Placement, 2015, http://www.ojjdp.gov/ojstatbb/ezacjrp.

53 Thomas Castellano and Irina Soderstrom, "Therapeutic Wilderness Programs and Juvenile Recidivism: A Program Evaluation," *Journal of Offender Rehabilitation* 17, no. 1 (1992): 19–46.

54 Howard N. Snyder and Melissa Sickmund, *Juvenile Offenders and Victims: 2006 National Report* (Washington, D.C.: U.S. Department of Justice, Office of Justice Programs, Office of Juvenile Justice and Delinquency Prevention, 2006), 218.

55 Patricia Puritz and Mary Ann Scali, *Beyond the Walls: Improvising Conditions of Confinement for Youth in Custody* (Washington, D.C.: Office of Juvenile Justice and Delinquency Prevention, 1998).

56 Snyder and Sickmund, *Juvenile Offenders and Victims*, 196, 198, 218.

57 Ibid.

58 Ibid., 225.

59 Sarah Hockenberry, Andrew Wachter, and Anthony Sladky, *Juvenile Residential Facility Census, 2014: Selected Findings* (Washington, D.C.: U.S. Department of Justice Office of Justice Programs Office of Juvenile Justice and Delinquency Prevention, 2016), 17. Online at https://www.ojjdp.gov/ojstatbb/publications/StatBBAbstract.asp?BibID=272283.

60 Richard A. Mendel, *The Missouri Model: Reinventing the Practice of Rehabilitating Youthful Offenders* (Baltimore, Md.: The Annie E. Casey Foundation, 2010). Available at http://www.aecf.org/resources/the-missouri-model.

61 The Missouri Approach, http://missouriapproach.org. Accessed February 2017.

62 Solomon Moore, "Missouri System Treats Juvenile Offenders with Lighter Hand," *New York Times*, March 26, 2009, http://www.nytimes.com/2009/03/27/us/27juvenile.html?_r=0.

63 Mendel, *The Missouri Model*, 6.

64 Ibid., 3.

65 Howard N. Snyder and Melissa Sickmund, *Juvenile Offenders and Victims: 2006 National Report* (Washington, D.C.: U.S. Department of Justice, Office of Justice Programs, Office of Juvenile Justice and Delinquency Prevention, 2006).

66 Lisa M. Flesch, "Juvenile Crime and Why Waiver Is Not the Answer," *Family Court Review* 42, no. 3 (July 2004): 583–596.

67 J. Fagan, E. Slaughter, and E. Hartstone, "Blind Justice: The Impact of Race on the Juvenile Justice Process," *Crime and Delinquency* 53, no. 3 (1997): 224–258.

68 Jason Meisner, "Chicago Man Freed from Prison, Given $25 Million. He Spent His Second Chance Rebuilding His Old Gang," *Chicago Tribune*, March 9, 2017, http://www.chicagotribune.com/news/ct-gang-leader-multimillion-dollar-settlement-met-20170308-story.html.

69 Ibid.

70 National Registry of Exonerations, Thaddeus Jimenez, March 2017, https://www.law.umich.edu/special/exoneration/Pages/casedetail.aspx?caseid=3438.

71 Frank Main, "Feds Say Video Shows Multimillionaire Gang Leader Shooting Man," *Chicago Sun-Times*, June 22, 2016, http://chicago.suntimes.com/news/feds-say-video-shows-millionaire-gang-leader-shooting-man.

72 Meisner, "Chicago Man Freed from Prison, Given $25 Million."

73 Main, "Feds Say Video Shows Multimillionaire Gang Leader Shooting Man."

74 National Registry of Exonerations, Thaddeus Jimenez.

75 Meisner, "Chicago Man Freed from Prison, Given $25 Million."

76 Richard E. Redding, *Juvenile Transfer Laws: An Effective Deterrent to Delinquency?* (U.S. Department of Justice Office of Justice Programs Office of Juvenile Justice and Delinquency Prevention, 2010), http://www.ojjdp.gov/publications/PubAbstract.asp?pubi=242419.

Chapter 14

Criminal Justice in the Future: Issues and Concerns

A police officer uses her computer while on a call. What issues and concerns does the increased use of surveillance technology pose for the future of policing?

magine that you are sitting in a car in your neighborhood when somewhere nearby a firearm goes off. Using microphone-based gunshot sensors, the police pick up this suspicious noise, and a computer program analyzes the sound and pinpoints its location to within a few yards of where you are sitting. The police officers who are dispatched to the scene confront you and request your identification. When you refuse, they utilize voice-recognition software to match your voice with a digital recording of your voice that was stored in their database when you received a traffic ticket two years ago.

Investigating further, the police access your Facebook page and determine that you are a gang member because there are pictures of you and your nephews making gang signs with your hands and wearing professional sports jerseys that some gangs have adopted as their preferred mode of dress. Based on this information, which the police believe is reasonable cause for a search, they require you to submit to breathalyzer tests for alcohol and marijuana.

THINK ABOUT IT > In what ways does new technology challenge our ideas about privacy and the role of government?

LEARNING
OBJECTIVE   **1**

Compare the incarceration rate in the United States with that of other countries.

LEARNING
OBJECTIVE   **2**

Analyze the social cost of a high incarceration rate in terms of unintended consequences.

The High Incarceration Rate

The criminal justice system continuously attempts to maintain order in an environment of shifting laws, unstable social forces, fluctuating cultural politics, and changing social values.[1] As we have learned in the preceding chapters, there are many goals, demands upon, and resources allocated to the various components of the criminal justice system. These influences are not universal or evenly distributed throughout the system. For example, as noted in the chapters on the court system, there is a disparity between the public support of resources allocated for the prosecution of cases and for the defense of indigent people.[2] Similarly, the resources necessary to deal with the country's soaring incarceration rate has forced state and local governments to rely on private prisons, eliminate rehabilitation programs, and in some places, release inmates well before the completion of their sentences because of prison overcrowding.[3]

In the United States, one of the consequences of the war on drugs and the war on crime is that a significant percentage of American citizens are behind bars. Instead of relying on community-based correctional programs for providing a broad range of social services and educational programs that may help prevent individuals from breaking the law, the criminal justice system has put all its eggs in the incarceration basket.

According to a National Academy of Sciences (NAS) study, *The Growth of Incarceration in the United States*, the United States has the largest penal population in the world with over 2.2 million incarcerated adults (see Figure 14.1). This study points out that the population of the United States accounts for about 5 percent of the world population, but it incarcerates about 25 percent of the world's prison inmates. With nearly one of every 100 adults in prison or jail, the U.S. incarceration rate is 5 to 10 times higher than that of the rates of western Europe.[4] For a look at the increase in the number of inmates in the United States, see Figure 14.2.

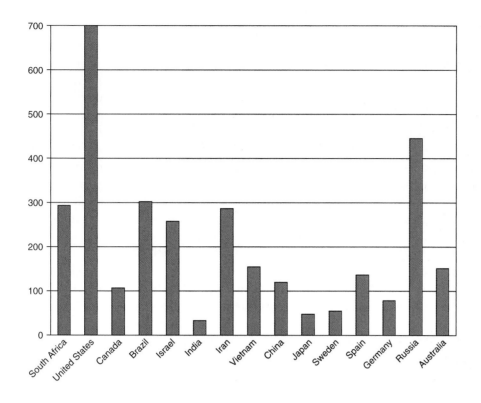

FIGURE 14.1 Incarceration Rates, Selected Countries What are some possible reasons as to why the United States incarcerates so many more of its citizens than other countries?

Source: Roy Walmsley, World Prison Population List, *11th ed. (World Prison Brief, Institute for Criminal Policy Research, 2015). Available at http://www. prisonstudies.org.*

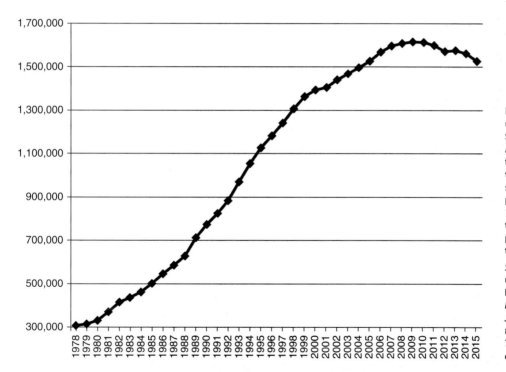

FIGURE 14.2 Inmates under the Jurisdiction of State or Federal Correctional Authorities, 1978–2015 This figure shows the increase in the number of people sent to state prisons, jails, and federal prisons in the United States since 1978. What are some reasons for the steep rise in the number of people incarcerated over the past three decades?

Source: E. Ann Carson, Prisoners under the Jurisdiction of State or Federal Correctional Authorities, December 31, 1978–2015, *Bureau of Justice Statistics. Generated using the Corrections Statistical Analysis Tool at https://www.bjs.gov/index. cfm?ty=nps, July 2015.*

Some observers and scholars argue that the United States' harsh incarceration policy has been effective in reducing crime. It is true that over the past 15 years, crime has decreased in many parts of the country, and many communities are safer than they once were.[5] However, it is difficult to attribute this phenomenon solely to increased incarceration. Several other factors, including economic forces, better target-hardening techniques (such as security cameras and more effective locks), and the stabilization of illegal drug markets, can also be linked to the reduction of crime.[6] In fact, the NAS study cautions against drawing any cause-and-effect relationships between the high incarceration rate and crime reduction, stating that high incarceration may have caused some decrease in crime, but that most research suggests that little, if any, of the decrease in crime was directly related to high incarceration policies.[7]

A significant problem of high incarceration is the unintended consequences it produces. It is difficult, if not impossible, to deprive so many people of their liberty without creating a ripple effect throughout society. These unintended consequences affect inmates' families; create more effective criminal offenders; disproportionately affect minorities and the impoverished; and damage inmates' physical and mental health, their chances at future employment and fair wages, and their communities. Let's look at these unintended consequences in detail.

Unintended Consequences of High Incarceration

A major unintended consequence of high incarceration rates is that prison does not make many offenders better citizens, but rather accelerates their criminal careers.[8] So much money is spent on the infrastructure of prisons in terms of institutional security, correctional officers, and weapons that fewer resources are allotted to actually changing the inmate's behavior. Because of mandatory-minimum sentence policies, state and federal prisons are packed with offenders serving sentences for relatively minor offenses. Overcrowded prisons mean that fewer resources are available for the rehabilitation and re-entry of inmates into society.[9] It is not surprising that the **recidivism rate** is so high when little is done to adequately prepare inmates for employment and social responsibility.

recidivism rate—The rate of ex-offenders who commit new offenses and are returned to prison.

According to the NAS report, prison inmates typically come from the most impoverished and disadvantaged constituencies. They are mainly minority men under age 40 who are poorly educated, addicted to drugs and/or alcohol, mentally and/or physically ill, and lack work training or experience. More than half the U.S. prison population is black or Hispanic. Blacks are incarcerated at about six times the rate of non-Hispanic whites, and Hispanics are incarcerated at nearly three times the rate of non-Hispanic whites (see Figure 14.3). Although the criminal responsibility of many inmates is real, it is entrenched in the life experiences brought by impoverishment, illness, addiction, and disadvantage.[10]

Inmates at the Northern Nevada Correctional Center in Carson City do gardening in the prison yard. This program is part of an initiative that seeks to prepare inmates for successful reintegration into society when they first enter prison, rather than toward the end of their sentences, the goal of which is to ultimately reduce recidivism. How do high incarceration rates negatively affect recidivism rates?

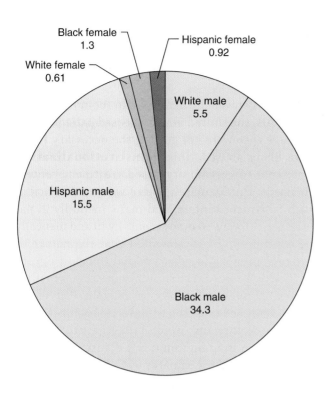

FIGURE 14.3   Rate of Incarceration by Race In 2015, there were 34.3 black male inmates per 1,000 regular population over the age of 18 as opposed to 5.5 white male inmates per 1,000 and 15.5 male Hispanic inmates per 1,000. How do the male inmate populations compare with the female inmate populations?

Source: United States Census Bureau, American Fact Finder, Annual Estimates of the Resident Population by Sex, Age, Race, and Hispanic Origin for the United States and States: April 1, 2010 to July 1, 2015, 2015 Population Estimates; Annual Estimates of the Resident Population by Sex, Age, Race Alone or in Combination, and Hispanic Origin for the United States and States: April 1, 2010 to July 1, 2015, 2015 Population Estimates, https://factfinder.census.gov/faces/nav/jsf/pages/searchresults.xhtml. E. Ann Carson and Joseph Mulako-Wangota, Estimated Number of Sentenced Prisoners under State and Federal Jurisdiction, by Age, Sex, Race, and Hispanic Origin, December 31, 2015, Bureau of Justice Statistics. Available at https://www.bjs.gov/index.cfm?ty=nps.

The intended and unintended consequences of mass incarceration have been so socially harmful that this policy is coming under scrutiny by both the criminal justice system and society.[11] A review of these consequences reveals that the old tough on crime policies have blossomed into new issues and concerns that call into question the over-reliance on jails and prisons to deal with what are essentially problems of impoverishment, mental illness, and drug addiction. There are also other unintended consequences of mass incarceration.

CHILDREN AND FAMILIES

Criminal justice policies that rely on incarceration have limited the ability of an offender's family to effectively raise children. Incarcerated offenders are unable to provide economic support for their families or to supervise and guide their children. Additionally, the children of incarcerated parents tend to have few or inadequate role models and instead often learn how to interact with other people from their peers and the habits they observe in their respective neighborhoods.[12]

Although many children visit their parents in prison, it is common for parents not to want their children to see them behind bars. Children may experience feelings of abandonment, grief, depression, shame, and, in some cases, even guilt over having an incarcerated parent. All too often, a parent's incarceration can lead to a child's eventual delinquency.[13] It is difficult to maintain a healthy relationship with children if incarceration is long term and if the spouse or partner has moved onto another partner. It is difficult for inmates to maintain healthy relationships with their partners as several factors work against their ability to stay in contact, share feelings, and develop trust.[14] In addition to the emotional strain on the relationship caused by incarceration, there is also an economic effect. Being connected to someone who is in prison can cost a great deal of money in collect telephone calls, travel costs, and sending money and packages to the inmate. Legal fees can also put a financial strain on the family. Typically, families of inmates also require more public assistance, including food stamps and Temporary Assistance for

Needy Families, and studies have found that families of inmates are more likely to experience homelessness.

PHYSICAL AND MENTAL HEALTH

deinstitutionaliza-tion—The policy of removing mentally ill people from public mental-health institutions and closing part or all of those institutions.

Because jail and prison facilities are so crowded, there is little room in budgets for medical professionals. In the 1970s, the United States released patients from secure mental health facilities where they were not getting the necessary treatment and, in many cases, were being abused. This **deinstitutionalization** was supposed to shift these patients to community-based treatment centers that could better address their needs. Unfortunately, there were not sufficient resources to build and staff such treatment centers, and many mentally ill patients found themselves on the street.[15] Today, so many mentally ill and mentally disabled people have been and continue to be incarcerated that the nature of the prison population has shifted from being largely criminal to being significantly mentally ill and mentally disabled, issues the criminal justice system is ill-prepared to address.[16] Additionally, many inmates have serious physical health problems. Prisons and jails are not equipped to deal with infectious and chronic diseases and do not provide adequate dietary and exercise programs to keep inmates healthy. Another growing concern is aging inmates. Because of shifts in sentencing policy in the 1980s and 1990s, many inmates were sentenced to extremely long prison sentences. As these inmates are becoming elderly, it is obvious that the prison and jail systems are not adequately prepared to deal with a geriatric population.[17]

EMPLOYMENT AND EARNINGS

Prisons and jails are not a good place to learn skills that are useful in legitimate society. One problem that many people face when incarcerated is that they did not have the sufficient skills and education to compete successfully in the first place. Traditionally, inmates have less than 12 years of schooling, score low on cognitive tests, and have low functional literacy. In addition, many have little work experience and are not employable. Prison does not help their chances for

Two elderly inmates sit in the dining hall at Federal Medical Center in Devens, Massachusetts, a prison for male inmates who require long-term medical care. How did changes in sentencing policies in the 1980s and 1990s affect the current aging prison population?

employment upon release.[18] Many inmates leave prison having adopted disruptive and debilitating qualities that help them to survive in prison but fail in society. These qualities include a taciturn demeanor, a suspicious approach to relationships, and resistance to authority. Over time, any useful skills they might have had erode. Prison also has a deleterious effect on job prospects because of restrictions in the employment market that prevent many felons from working in specific sectors. Although it is not unreasonable for daycares to restrict employment for those convicted of child abuse and for banks to decline to employ those who have been convicted of **embezzlement** or robbery, many people convicted of relatively minor offenses have trouble finding any employment at all. For example, a study in Florida found that 40 percent of jobs were unavailable to felons.[19] Negligent hiring laws expose employers to liability when they hire people with a criminal record, so not only do many employers worry about how ex-con employees might interact with customers, they also worry about their legal liability if those employees continue to be deviant in the workplace. One study found that, when presented with the résumés of applicants with criminal records and applicants without criminal records, employers were 30 to 60 percent less likely to call applicants with criminal records.[20] In times of economic recession, this problem becomes even more acute.

embezzlement—The theft or taking of money or property by a person who is charged by an employer or other authority to be responsible for those assets.

COMMUNITIES

The effect of high incarceration rates is not as direct for communities as it is for individuals, but it has a compounding effect because incarcerated people often come from the same types of communities.[21] This means that incarceration rates are not evenly distributed across the U.S. population, but rather are concentrated in specific neighborhoods characterized by high rates of poverty, violence, and failing social institutions.[22] Furthermore, the reciprocal relationship between disadvantaged neighborhoods and the detrimental effects of life in prison is reinforced when inmates are disproportionately released back into the same communities where they broke the law. The repetition of arrest/incarceration/return becomes a vicious cycle of crime and violence.[23] Simply taking law-breakers out of the community and punishing them does not solve the overall crime problem when the same individuals are repeatedly released into the same communities with little or no rehabilitation, job prospects, or life skills.

SOCIETY OVERALL

The high incarceration rate has a broad effect on society because thousands of people are denied full citizenship rights. Prisoners, parolees, probationers, convicted sex offenders, and others with criminal records are routinely denied rights and responsibilities, as well as access to many public benefits. Former inmates can be considered "partial citizens" or "internal exiles" thus increasing their social marginalization. People who have experienced incarceration are not only subject to greater unemployment and poverty, but are also denied full political participation.[24] Elevated incarceration rates also sap money from social programs designed to address the causes of crime. Resources are depleted for education, health care, economic development, and other key interventions and services that not only aid disadvantaged groups, but also improve the health and well-being of the entire population.[25]

If high incarceration is so detrimental, why did the United States expand incarceration? As we discussed in Chapter 10, from the 1960s to the 1990s, legislators and criminal justice administrators advocated that a punitive incarceration policy was the best way to address rising crime and rapid social change. New

three strikes (from Chapter 10)—In reference to criminal justice, a term that describes state laws that require an offender's third felony to be punishable by a severe sentence, including life imprisonment.

prison-industrial complex—The increased reliance on incarceration, surveillance, and law enforcement in the United States and its relationship to the establishment of for-profit incarceration and probation/parole services, and businesses that supply goods and services to prisons and jails.

policies that required incarceration for minor offenses and intensified punishment for drug offenses significantly increased the length of time people were sentenced to prison.[26] The political mandate to get tough on crime, along with mandatory minimum sentences and **three-strikes** policies, have resulted in unprecedented rates of incarceration and the creation of what has come to be known as the **prison-industrial complex**. This term refers to the increased reliance on incarceration, surveillance, and law enforcement in the United States and its relationship to the establishment of for-profit incarceration and probation/parole services, as well as businesses that supply goods and services to prisons and jails.

Appreciating the prison-industrial complex requires a short history lesson. In the 1950s, President Dwight D. Eisenhower warned the American public about the military-industrial complex, a runaway system in which corporations sold weapons systems to the U.S. government that it did not really need. Billions of dollars were diverted from the economy and wasted on obsolete, inefficient, and unneeded weapons, thus accelerating the diversion of economic resources toward defense at the expense of social programs.[27] Similarly, the prison-industrial complex has diverted resources from social programs and used them to build more prisons and put more people under the control of the criminal justice system.[28]

The future of criminal justice in the United States likely includes addressing the causes and consequences of the high incarceration rate. The next section of this chapter will discuss some of the causes of the high incarceration rate, such as the war on drugs, as well as other policies that exert a counterproductive influence on how individuals perceive justice in the United States.

In September 2015, Pope Francis visited the Curran-Fromhold Correctional Facility in Philadelphia, Pennsylvania, where he encouraged society to aid in the rehabilitation of the incarcerated. What are some of the effects of high incarceration rates on society?

The War on Drugs

"War" is a convenient and slippery term to use when referring to the work of the criminal justice system. The idea of war is easy to understand and easy to promote as a crime-fighting policy: criminals are the enemy, and we should use any and all resources to defeat the enemy. Because the enemy robs, rapes, steals, and sells illegal drugs, we are justified by the principle of self-defense to use warlike strategies, tactics, and weapons to fight crime.

But is fighting crime the same as fighting a war? Are Americans willing to endure the consequences of treating the crime problem as a war problem? The answers to these questions are elusive because so much emotion is involved in thinking about crime that sober reflection about how to prevent crime becomes difficult. Although many citizens applaud the idea of fighting a war against criminals, the war concept becomes problematic when we realize that the "enemy" consists of regular citizens, just like us. According to one researcher, there is also another problem with the war metaphor: "Among the characteristics implied in the notion of coping with a problem by declaring war on it are extra effort, expediency, ruthlessness, sacrifice, and subordination of the individual."[29]

The war on drugs in the United States is, by many measures, a failed policy. Although drug abuse has caused suffering in individuals, it can be argued that the war on drugs has had an even more deleterious effect on society. The diversion of resources from crime toward the war on drugs has overburdened the criminal justice system with minor drug offenders at the expense of dealing with other types of crime, such as white-collar crime, that have undermined the economic vitality of society. We must take a fresh look at the war on drugs and determine what types of policies can best enhance the health of citizens, ensure that the criminal justice system treats all individuals in an equitable manner, and preserves constitutional freedoms, individual rights, and the public's sense of justice. This analysis must address some difficult questions about exactly what negative effects drugs have on society.[30] In this analysis, the actual effects of drugs on human beings are separated from the effects of the war on drugs. Although a good deal of crime is related to drug abuse, it is difficult to gauge exactly how much social harm such crime actually presents. After all, research suggests that alcohol abuse does a great deal more damage to individuals and society than do illegal drugs.[31]

Drugs are related to crime in three ways, and these three types of crime could be eliminated by legalizing drugs. These are offenses committed by people who are on drugs; offenses committed by people who need money to buy drugs, and offenses committed among drug dealers. By regulating rather than criminalizing drugs, it is assumed that much of the crime and violence associated with the illegal drug trade could be eliminated.[32] However, as attractive as drug legalization may appear, it is unlikely that there will be any sweeping changes in the near future. Some drugs, such as cocaine, heroin, and methamphetamine, are highly

LEARNING OBJECTIVE | **3**

Describe why the term *war* is an inappropriate metaphor for drug policy.

LEARNING OBJECTIVE | **4**

Characterize the three types of crime related to drugs.

LEARNING OBJECTIVE | **5**

Discuss the perceived benefits of legalizing some drugs.

Both recreational and medical marijuana are legal in several states. How have the decriminalization and legalization of marijuana affected the criminal justice system in such jurisdictions?

decriminalization— Emendation of laws or statutes to lessen or remove penalties for specific acts subject to criminal prosecution, arrest, and imprisonment.

legalization— The total removal of legal prohibitions on specific acts that were previously proscribed and punishable by law.

addictive and can cause great physical harm, as well as deeply affect the behavior of those who use these drugs. Thus, they are unlikely to be legalized.[33]

The **decriminalization** (lessening or removing penalties for criminal prosecution, arrest, and imprisonment) and **legalization** (the removal of legal prohibitions previously proscribed and punishable by law) of marijuana present an entirely different story, however. In recent years, many states have made significant changes to their marijuana laws. Twenty states have legalized or decriminalized marijuana in one form or another and have established mechanisms and regulations for its control and distribution.[34] Other states are currently considering similar legislation.[35] There are several perceived advantages to the legalization of marijuana according to its proponents.

> Tax revenue. States that have legalized marijuana are finding that they are realizing millions of dollars in tax revenue from its legal sale.[36] The underground economy of illegal marijuana use has almost disappeared in states like Colorado where users can buy it legally.[37]

> Reduction in law enforcement costs. Jurisdictions that have legalized marijuana are finding that their law enforcement efforts can now be directed at serious crime. In many ways, marijuana enforcement was "low-hanging fruit" that diverted law enforcement resources toward behaviors that did not harm society as much as traditional crime. Police officers are now able to concentrate on homicide, rape, robbery, and burglary, as well as other offenses that directly threaten the safety of the community.[38]

> Avoidance of stigma. The war on drugs has had several consequences for illegal marijuana users, including incarceration, fines, and being labeled as felons.[39] Corporations and government agencies have developed policies specifying that those convicted of drug use (including marijuana) can be fired from their jobs, denied scholarships and fellowships, and prevented from pursuing many occupations. Perhaps the most visible of these policies

is the manner in which professional athletes are drug-tested and suspended or banned from participating in their sport.[40] Although it was once thought that marijuana use could be curtailed by making it illegal and levying occupational sanctions, the actual result was that it marginalized otherwise law-abiding citizens.[41]

The decriminalization and legalization of marijuana will present the justice system with many challenges in the near future, requiring a shift in how we consider the behavior once it has become normalized. No doubt, more states will make recreational marijuana readily available to adults in the future. Other states will likely continue to prohibit marijuana use. Future research comparing jurisdictions with legal marijuana use with those that prohibit it should provide evidence as to whether marijuana use is a significant social problem or if it is the war on drugs that causes so many social problems.

PAUSE AND REVIEW

1. Is "war" an accurate metaphor to describe the United States' efforts to control illegal drugs?

2. In what ways is the United States' war on drugs a failed policy?

3. What effect would legalization of some drugs have on the criminal justice system?

Predictive Policing

The task of the criminal justice system is to enforce the law with fairness and concern for the dignity of citizens. However, several factors, including the prevalence of firearms, the widening disparity between socioeconomic classes, and deeply rooted systemic problems in the way that race, sex, and gender continue to divide groups of people, will continue to create tensions between those who make and enforce the law and those upon whom the law is implemented. This tension between protecting the public and safeguarding the constitutional and civil rights of individuals is a major challenge of policing.

Despite these challenges, much can be done to improve and reform the criminal justice system so that it operates in a manner that is both more fair and smarter. Many recent incidents that have publicized the tension between citizens and the criminal justice system have been the result of mistakes, poor judgment, bad information, and flawed policies. Such incidents could have been prevented had criminal justice practitioners been better informed and better trained with the skills and information to help them serve the community without having to result to physical force. One goal that the criminal justice system will undoubtedly pursue in the future is preventing crime rather than simply reacting to it.

One of the more promising strategies is **predictive policing**, sometimes called "smart policing," which uses technology to gather information and analyze data to help police better target their resources toward potential crime. Rather than relying on the experience and intuition of individual police officers, data analytics allow law enforcement to roughly predict where crime will happen and what type of citizens will engage in it, thus allowing them to work toward its

LEARNING OBJECTIVE 6

Outline how future police departments will engage in predictive ("smart") policing.

LEARNING OBJECTIVE 7

Discuss how the new professionalism in policing will change the nature of police behavior.

predictive policing— The use of information technology to analyze vast amounts of data to allow law enforcement to better target their resources toward potential crime.

prevention. Computers can process a range of data (some of it seemingly unrelated to crime) to anticipate where crime is likely to occur. For example:

> › In Richmond, Virginia, the problem of random gunfire on New Year's Eve was addressed when police officers looked at data gathered over several years and anticipated the time, location, and nature of future incidents. On one New Year's Eve, the department placed officers at locations where gunfire was most likely to occur and were able to achieve a 246 percent increase in weapons seized, a 47 percent decrease in the amount of random gunfire, and a savings of $15,000 in personnel costs.[42]

> › In Arlington, Texas, the police department correlated the data on residential burglaries. For each unit of physical decay (a measure of neighborhood quality), the police identified and predicted an additional six burglaries. Working with other city agencies, the police department now works more effectively in addressing "fragile neighborhoods" as a means of indirectly targeting residential burglaries.[43]

The Smart Policing Initiative (SPI) focuses on the role of science in the study of police effectiveness. In the past, much of the knowledge about police work was based on the experience of individual officers and administrators who were unable to recognize broad patterns in apparently unrelated data sources. Officers would use hunches, biases, and intuition to decide how to deploy police resources, which citizens to confront, and which offenses to concentrate upon.

SPI has provided more than $12.4 million to 33 local law enforcement agencies, which have conducted 36 projects.[44] In Philadelphia, it was found that offender-based programs could significantly reduce violent crime. A Los Angeles study showed that the creative use of crime analytics coupled with targeted problem-solving approaches could reduce violent crime in historically extremely violent districts. In Boston, problem-solving teams were able to prevent violence in stubborn chronic hot spots. In Glendale, California, service calls to high-traffic convenience stores were reduced.[45]

Sergeant Charles Coleman of the LAPD Foothill Division utilizes predictive policing zone maps when on patrol in the Pacoima neighborhood of Los Angeles. How does predictive policing help police departments be more efficient?

Use of Technology in Predictive Policing

SPI incorporates crime science, evaluation methods, and police–scholar partnerships to improve the types of data that police agencies use to respond to and prevent crime. Perhaps the most obvious and visible components of SPI is the technology that has been integrated into the work environment of the police. Technology has greatly enhanced the effectiveness of police officers in the following ways:

> › Wireless video-streaming. Wireless video-streaming allows departments to increase officer accountability, ensure officer safety, and monitor police behavior during traffic stops and other encounters with citizens. In addition, wireless video-streaming is used on cameras attached to the robots deployed in investigations, helicopter surveillance, and barricade or hostage situations.[46]

> › License plate readers. This technology allows police officers to quickly and efficiently evaluate the status of automobiles. License-plate readers attached to a police car can determine if the vehicles it is passing are reported stolen, have parking violations, or have been reported in some other activity of interest to the police such as an Amber Alert. This technology allows for the quick transmission of information from the patrol car to databases stored at police headquarters.

> › Global positioning systems (GPS). GPS allows police officers to track the movements of criminal suspects. By obtaining a warrant and placing a GPS device on a suspect's car, a police officer is able to keep track of and/or follow suspects without being detected. (In 2012, the U.S. Supreme Court ruled in *United States v. Jones* that placement of a GPS tracking device by law enforcement constitutes a search and thus requires a warrant.) Additionally, police departments use GPS to track police vehicles so that dispatchers can be more effective in determining which units are in the best position to respond to calls for service. The GPS systems can alert police agencies as to the officer's exact location, whether they are in an accident, or whether they have been assaulted or are otherwise endangered or incapacitated.

> › Social media. Like many businesses and other government agencies, a social media page can be a police department's "front door" in its relationship with the public. Social media can be used to disseminate information and engage in community-policing activities designed to increase the accessibility and transparency of the police department. Many departments use social media to receive crime tips and other information from the public. Additionally, many departments monitor social media by reviewing the activity of suspected gang members who sometimes brag about the offenses they have committed or post otherwise incriminating information that the police can use to investigate a crime.

The use of technology in predictive policing is not without controversy. Technology can help police departments acquire as much information as possible and evaluate that information quickly and efficiently. However, Fourth Amendment issues related to the individual right to privacy has raised many concerns. For instance, in a situation in which predictive policing estimates that a certain neighborhood at a certain time is vulnerable to residential burglary, should police officers have more latitude in stopping suspects who look suspicious? Do the analytics of predictive policing constitute reasonable cause absent other characteristics of potential crime? In short, is it desirable for people to be stopped and frisked based on predictive factors rather than their actual behavior? By relying on databases

Palo Alto police officers visit with two young entrepreneurs. In 2015, the Palo Alto Police Department started a social media outreach campaign to encourage interaction with the community, especially children. For what other purposes do the police use social media?

that collect and analyze historical crime information, predictive policing may simply keep pointing officers toward impoverished and minority communities where the enhanced police presence simply uncovers more offenses and repeats the cycle.[47]

Some critics assert that predictive policing is not really new but rather a more sophisticated way of doing what police officers have always done. They have looked at historical data for patterns of crime and then allocated their resources accordingly. Predictive policing may be viewed as simply a more technologically dependent, expensive, and intrusive form of problem-oriented policing.

In looking toward the future, it will be necessary to ensure that police departments evolve not only in their use of technology, but also in ensuring that the police culture maintains its central goals of protecting citizens, apprehending offenders, and respecting the rights and dignity of everyone. Christopher Stone of the Kennedy School of Government at Harvard University and Jeremy Travis, President of the John Jay College of Criminal Justice, City University of New York, have called for police departments to emphasize four elements of what they call the "new professionalism":[48]

> Accountability. The police must account for their actions not only to the departmental chain of command, but also to city councils, citizen review boards, state legislators, inspectors general, as well as government auditors and the courts. Police departments must become more transparent in their actions, and individual officers must be expected to be able to defend their behavior. One initiative to increase the accountability of officers currently underway is to have them wear body cameras to record their interactions with citizens.

> Legitimacy. The police must be considered honest brokers in their interactions with citizens. In many communities, the police are viewed as an occupying force or simply another gang. Citizens have lost their trust and confidence in

the police, which greatly compromises their effectiveness, especially among young people and minorities. The quest to retain legitimacy has been weakened by police militarization and recent incidents of excessive use of force.

> Innovation. Future police departments should be willing to accept and adopt the innovations of other departments that have been properly evaluated. A commitment to innovation means an active investment in personnel and resources in adapting new policies and practices that have proven effective elsewhere.

> National coherence. True professionalism allows police departments to engage in a national conversation that extends good police practices, as well as knowledge and understanding that are transferable across police jurisdictions. The new police professionalism allows officers, supervisors, and executives to share a set of skills and follow a common set of protocols that have been accepted by the profession because they have proven to be effective or legally required. Conventional wisdom has always held that police officers could only be effective in their home cities where they had come up through the ranks and could appreciate the uniqueness of their communities. A commitment to national coherence suggests that good policing does not depend on the training in a particular department, but rather incorporates a universal set of practices and policies that can be effective in jurisdictions across the country.

Policing in the future will certainly incorporate much more technology, as suggested by predictive policing. However, technology is not the only concern important in developing more efficient, effective, and equitable policing practices. Maintaining the trust of citizens will require that police departments be considered legitimate by enforcing the law in a fair and impartial manner. This legitimacy can be obtained only by having measures of accountability that make the work of police officers transparent to supervisors, politicians, and the general public. This will be an immense task that some departments will undoubtedly perform better than others.

PAUSE AND REVIEW

1. **What is predictive policing?**
2. **What types of technology does predictive policing utilize?**
3. **What are the four elements of the new professionalism in policing?**

Technology and Surveillance

LEARNING OBJECTIVE **8**

Recognize how surveillance technology has conflicted with privacy issues.

One of the most challenging issues in the criminal justice system is the use of surveillance technology to expose the activities of criminals and terrorists. The Bill of Rights, particularly the Fourth Amendment, protects citizens against intrusions into their privacy by the government. This has always been a contentious issue and one that has engendered a great deal of legal opinion from the courts, which specify just how far the government can go in terms of invading the privacy of citizens while pursuing criminal convictions.[49] The **USA PATRIOT Act** of 2001 (Uniting and Strengthening America by Providing Appropriate Tools Required to Intercept and Obstruct Terrorism) drastically changed the rules of the relationship between security and privacy. Through legislation drafted in response to the terrorist attacks of September 11, 2001, Congress gave broad and sweeping authority to the government to do whatever was necessary to prevent further terrorist attacks.

USA PATRIOT Act—A law signed by President George W. Bush on October 26, 2001, in response to the terror attacks of September 11, 2001.

Much of the PATRIOT Act is purely administrative. It allots funds for government agencies to pursue terrorists, permits federal law enforcement to hire more officers and staff, and reinforces federal law against discrimination. However, other parts of the PATRIOT Act reduce judicial oversight of telephone and Internet surveillance. For instance:

> Under the PATRIOT Act, federal law enforcement agencies aren't required to determine if a suspect uses or is likely to use a phone before planting a "bug." Under Sections 214 and 216, the federal government is also authorized to sweep the records of Internet Service Providers (ISPs) and network administrators in both private and public sectors, and may monitor and intercept email and cell phone usage without first being required either to have a court order or to report such activities to judicial oversight. The federal government only has to believe that the information is "relevant," and does not need to show there is a "probable cause," as required under the Fourth Amendment. More important, the federal government can receive such warrants without the courts being allowed to determine if the allegations are truthful. Because the United States is essentially a "wired nation," with almost as many families having access to computers as they do to televisions, the problem of databases and possible privacy intrusions becomes even more severe.[50]

USA FREEDOM Act—A law signed by President Barack Obama in 2015 that reauthorized parts of the USA PATRIOT Act but limited the bulk collection of U.S. residents' phone records and Internet data.

The PATRIOT Act was forged during an emergency when it was deemed that the government needed these resources on a temporary basis to deal with potential future terrorist attacks. For years, it was politically unpopular to challenge the PATRIOT Act, and it was routinely touted as the "war on terror" continued both abroad and at home. However, the tension between the PATRIOT Act and the civil rights guarantees of the Constitution has become more contentious. In 2015, Congress passed a modification to the PATRIOT Act called the **USA FREEDOM Act** (Uniting and Strengthening America by Fulfilling Rights and Ending Eavesdropping, Dragnet-collection and Online Monitoring) that limits the government's ability to collect information that cannot be directly connected to terrorism (see A Closer Look 14.1). Specifically, The FREEDOM Act placed new limits on the National Security Agency's (NSA) practice of collecting every cell-phone call and

The NSA's mass surveillance practices stirred up a great deal of opposition from the American public. Why was the agency's collection of the phone records of U.S. citizens so controversial?

e-mail of all citizens in order to give it the ability to "connect the dots" when it found possible evidence of terrorist activities. Whereas the NSA did not read or hear communications individually, those concerned with privacy believed that the collection of all this data represented a broad overreach of constitutional protections.[51] Although the FREEDOM Act specifies that the government can no longer collect and keep this data, it does allow the government to look at the data that is held by Internet service providers and cell-phone companies.[52]

There will always be tension between those who value the constitutional rights to privacy and those who are willing to sacrifice some privacy for greater security. It is not a matter of one being more important than the other. The challenge is to find a healthy balance between privacy and security.

A CLOSER LOOK 14.1
The USA FREEDOM Act

In June 2015, Congress passed the USA FREEDOM Act in response to numerous complaints about the USA PATRIOT Act impinging upon the civil rights of Americans.[53] However, the FREEDOM Act was only partially successful in rolling back the powers granted to the government to gather intelligence in pursuit of the war on terror.

What the FREEDOM Act did:

- The act ended, at least partially, the National Security Agency's bulk collection of nearly every American's phone records.
- The act requires the government to limit its demand for phone data to those related to specific names, phone numbers, or addresses of suspected terrorists.
- The act requires the government to improve its Foreign Intelligence Surveillance Act (FISA) court process by requiring the appointment of lawyers during closed-door sessions to argue for privacy concerns.

What the FREEDOM Act did not do:

- The act did not end the government's practice of collecting enormous amounts of personal data on the communications of foreigners overseas even when they are communicating with Americans.
- The act said nothing about the National Security Agency hacking into overseas Internet trunk lines to indiscriminately gather data on millions of U.S. Internet users.
- The act does not stop the NSA from inserting vulnerabilities into computer networks and encryption systems so that the agency can more easily conduct surveillance.
- The act does not restrict police from obtaining location data about citizens from cellphones and Internet service providers.
- The act does not stop the government from obtaining, without probable cause or a warrant, the contents of any e-mail saved for more than 180 days.[54]

In a technological environment in which much of individuals' private information, from medical records to credit card purchases, is online, the FREEDOM Act legitimizes the U.S. government's ability to collect information that officials believe will help anti-terrorist agencies identify terrorists and prevent violence within and toward the United States. Critics of the USA PATRIOT Act contend that the FREEDOM Act takes a large step toward limiting the ability of government intelligence agencies to collect data on U.S. citizens without proper oversight.

THINK ABOUT IT
1. How does the FREEDOM Act affect how the government responds to terrorism?

PAUSE AND REVIEW

1. **Why did Congress give so much power to the National Security Agency to collect information about people in the United States?**

2. **Which practices authorized by the PATRIOT Act most concern its critics?**

3. **In what ways has the FREEDOM Act addressed some of the problems associated with the PATRIOT Act?**

The Future of Criminal Justice and You

What is the future of criminal justice in the United States? Many of the people taking this class who may pursue a career in the criminal justice system will doubtless answer this question differently. One of the most interesting benefits of being a criminal justice major is participating in a vigorously changing discipline. As social problems wax and wane, politicians demand new programs, the economy fluctuates, and new strategies to reduce crime are implemented, the criminal justice system tries to respond. Students of criminal justice can look forward to a career that will encourage innovation, reward success, recognize hard work, and foster creativity.

It is not too early to start preparing for a career in the criminal justice system. In addition to gleaning everything you can from your classes, it would be a good idea to pay attention to your personal characteristics and hobbies, as well as your interactions with criminal justice agencies. A long list of traffic violations can sabotage a career in law enforcement before it even begins. Arrests and convictions for drug offenses, domestic violence, and/or a host of misdemeanor convictions can disqualify you from being considered for criminal justice jobs.

In addition to keeping your criminal record clean, try to develop skills and abilities that criminal justice agencies can readily use.[55] This means staying in good physical shape, demonstrating that you can learn new skills quickly, and maintaining a demeanor that suggests you are resourceful, industrious, dependable, and honest. Those who desire to have extra advantages in seeking employment in the criminal justice system should develop special skills. Many agencies, particularly federal agencies, are always looking for individuals who can speak Spanish, Arabic, Chinese, and Russian. Other skills that criminal justice agencies may deem desirable include accounting, information technology, and general computer skills. In short, once you receive your degree, your education has only just begun and should be a lifelong endeavor.

In this text, we have only touched upon many of the challenges that the criminal justice system faces. The intent of this chapter is to give students an appreciation for the desirability of an education that will prepare them not only to react to some of the chronic problems that face the criminal justice system, but also to identify systemic issues that must be addressed. By appreciating the obstacles and limitations of working in the system, students will be better prepared to respond to, and even prevent, some of the harms and problems that criminal justice practitioners face.

At the New Hampshire Correctional Facility for Women, inmates learn how to translate books into braille, which are sent to schools for the blind. Constructive criminal justice reform and decreasing recidivism rates depend greatly on the access offenders have to opportunities for education and training while incarcerated. How can such opportunities positively affect outcomes for criminal justice reform in the United States?

 Changing the Law in the Future

Each year, Congress and state legislatures make new laws and remove old ones. Reaching consensus on new laws is a political activity. Congress and state legislatures supposedly reflect the will of the people and thus follow changes in the mood of society. Seldom are laws made that do not achieve a consensus from the majority of citizens, or at least the majority of citizens who take an active interest in legislative matters. There is, of course, a great deal of negotiation, conflict, and ill will between competing parties as the criminal law is constructed. It is probably beneficial to society that the political process makes passing new laws and revising old laws difficult.

Sometimes we as individuals believe that we can see what is necessary for society. If each of us were given the discretion and authority to make new laws, then we might do things differently than our legislative bodies did in the past. Imagine that for one day you were given the power to revise the criminal code.

- Which single existing law would you eliminate?
  - Is there a particular law that you believe is unnecessary, unfair, biased, impractical, subjective, or unworkable?
  - What would be the practical implications of abolishing this law?
  - Would it be expensive?
  - Would it be accepted by the public?
  - How would it affect crime?
  - Why would abolishing this law be beneficial to the quality of your life or the quality of others' lives?
- What new law would you institute?
  - Are there practices and activities that are currently legal that you believe harm society?
  - How would you construct your law so that it addresses its target problem without causing a host of new problems?

- Does your new law have regional or national implications?
- Do you expect your new law to be popular or unpopular?
- Why has this new law not already been passed?

You should keep some important issues in mind as you abolish an old law and develop a new one. Does your new law have constitutional implications? How will your new law affect criminal justice agencies? For instance, if you advocate the legalization of all drugs, will we still need the U.S. Drug Enforcement Agency (DEA)?

WHAT DO YOU DO?

1. What are the chances that your changes in the law will become a reality? Do you believe that you are in step with most citizens in the United States in terms of your attitudes toward crime and justice?
2. What might be some of the unintended consequences of your proposed changes in the criminal law? Will your changes make the country safer or less safe?
3. Recognizing that you do not have the power to single-handedly make these changes, what activities could you engage in to bring about the types of reforms that you are advocating? What type of evidence would you need to convince Congress or a state legislature that your ideas benefit society?

For more insight into how someone might respond to such an ethical dilemma, visit the companion website at www.oup.com/us/fuller to watch a video that connects this scenario to a real-world situation.

Summary

LEARNING OBJECTIVE **1** Compare the incarceration rate in the United States with that of other countries.	The United States relies on incarceration to a much greater degree than any other country. The U.S. prison population accounts for 25 percent of the world's prison inmates. The U.S. incarceration rate is five times higher than the rates of western European countries.

LEARNING OBJECTIVE 2 Analyze the social cost of a high incarceration rate in terms of unintended consequences.	The high incarceration rate in the United States has a disproportionate effect on minorities and the impoverished. One of the most pressing social causes of the high incarceration rate is the way prisons and jails are used to deal with mental illness and other health problems. A serious problem for the corrections system is aging prison populations. Incarceration seriously inhibits an individual's ability to obtain employment. Incarceration disrupts the bond between spouses, as well as parents and children. The high incarceration rate also affects communities; when incarcerated individuals are released into their neighborhoods, they bring with them a prison mentality that damages the social fabric of the community. Society is affected by the high incarceration rate because individuals are denied their full citizenship rights. Money is diverted from schools, recreational programs, and social programs to build and staff prisons and jails.
LEARNING OBJECTIVE 3 Describe why the term *war* is an inappropriate metaphor for drug policy.	The term *war* implies that society should be ruthless, expedient, prepared to make a sacrifice, and subordinate the individual to the overall goal of winning the war. Traditional wars have an external opponent, but the war on drugs concentrates on U.S. citizens and thus is an inappropriate and inaccurate metaphor.
LEARNING OBJECTIVE 4 Characterize the three types of crime related to drugs.	The three types of crime related to drugs are offenses committed by (1) people who are on drugs; (2) people who need money to buy drugs; and (3) drug dealers.
LEARNING OBJECTIVE 5 Discuss the perceived benefits of legalizing some drugs.	States that have legalized medical marijuana have been able to collect taxes related to marijuana sales. The legalization of some drugs means that fewer police officers are required to police the illegal drug trade, and law enforcement resources can be directed at curbing serious crime. Legalization also helps drug-users avoid the stigmatization of being arrested and sanctioned for drug use.
LEARNING OBJECTIVE 6 Outline how future police departments will engage in predictive ("smart") policing.	Predictive policing focuses on the use of new technologies and information systems to provide police departments with better tools to address and prevent crime. Predictive policing uses data analytics to better utilize available resources in targeting neighborhoods and offenders who historically have shown a propensity to break the law.
LEARNING OBJECTIVE 7 Discuss how the new professionalism in policing will change the nature of police behavior.	The new professionalism will incorporate commitments to accountability, legitimacy, innovation, and national coherence. These commitments will allow future police departments to ensure that the behavior of officers is more transparent and understandable, they have the support of citizens, they utilize the latest tools and techniques that have been proven effective elsewhere, and they operate in a manner that is consistent with the best practices of exemplary police departments across the country.
LEARNING OBJECTIVE 8 Recognize how surveillance technology has conflicted with privacy issues.	Many people are concerned that the war on terror has resulted in curtailing the privacy rights of citizens. The PATRIOT Act gave broad and sweeping powers to law enforcement to conduct surveillance on individuals' telephone and Internet communications. Although the FREEDOM Act curtails some of the most egregious activities allowed by the PATRIOT Act, critics still claim that the federal government has violated the constitutional protections inherent in the Bill of Rights.

Critical Reflections

1. What additional issues do you consider problematic for the future of the criminal justice system? Explain how new laws, improved training, and/or advances in technology may address these issues.

2. Develop some alternatives for the high incarceration rate in the United States. How can we better decide which offenders are truly dangerous and which ones can be provided with

alternative sentencing? How can incarceration be employed in a manner that does not affect minorities so disproportionately?

3. What type of organizational structure might be employed to minimize excessive use of force? Is there some way to change the police subculture to make it less militaristic and more effective in dealing with crime?

Key Terms

decriminalization **p. 438**
deinstitutionalization **p. 434**
embezzlement **p. 435**
legalization **p. 438**

predictive policing **p. 439**
prison-industrial complex **p. 436**
recidivism rate **p. 432**
three strikes **p. 436**

USA FREEDOM Act **p. 444**
USA PATRIOT Act **p. 443**

Endnotes

1 Amitai Etzioni, "Politics and Culture in an Age of Austerity," *International Journal of Politics, Culture and Society* 27, no. 4 (December 2014): 389–407.

2 Chris Dandurand, "Walking Out on the Check: How Missouri Abandoned Its Public Defenders and Left the Poor to Foot the Bill," *Missouri Law Review* 76, no. 1 (Winter 2011): 185–211.

3 Hadar Aviram, "Are Private Prisons to Blame for Mass Incarceration and Its Evils? Prison Conditions, Neoliberalism, and Public Choice," *Fordham Urban Law Journal* 42, no. 2 (December 2014): 411–449.

4 Jeremy Travis and Bruce Western, *The Growth of Incarceration in the United States: Exploring Causes and Consequences*, (Washington, D.C.: National Academies Press, 2014).

5 John R. Hipp, "Assessing Crime as a Problem: The Relationship Between Residents' Perception of Crime and Official Crime Rates Over 25 Years," *Crime and Delinquency* 59, no. 4 (June 2013): 616–648.

6 James M. Byrne, "After the Fall: Assessing the Impact of the Great Prison Experiment on Future Crime Control Policy," *Federal Probation* 77, no. 3 (December 2013): 9–22.

7 Travis and Western, *The Growth of Incarceration in the United States*.

8 Sophie R. Dickson, Devon L.L. Polaschek, and Allanah R. Casey, "Can the Quality of High-risk Violent Prisoners' Release Plans Predict Recidivism Following Intensive Rehabilitation? A Comparison with

Risk Assessment Instruments," *Psychology, Crime and Law* 19, no. 4 (May 2013): 371–389.

9 Cassandre Monique Davilmar, "We Tried to Make Them Offer Rehab, but They Said, 'No, No, No!'" Incentivizing Private Prison Reform Through the Private Prisoner Rehabilitation Credit," *New York University Law Review* 89, no. 1 (April 2014): 267–292.

10 Travis and Western, *The Growth of Incarceration in the United States*.

11 Michael Tonry, "Remodeling American Sentencing: A Ten-Step Blueprint for Moving Past Mass Incarceration," *Criminology & Public Policy* 13, no. 4 (November 2014): 503–533.

12 Randal D. Day, Alan C. Acock, Stephen J. Bahr, and Joyce A. Arditti, "Incarcerated Fathers Returning Home to Children and Families: Introduction to the Special Issue and a Primer on Doing Research with Men in Prison," *Fathering: A Journal of Theory, Research, and Practice About Men as Fathers* 3, no. 3 (Fall 2005): 183–200.

13 Kristin Turney, "The Intergenerational Consequences of Mass Incarceration: Implications for Children's Co-Residence and Contact with Grandparents," *Social Forces* 93, no. 1 (September 2014): 299–327.

14 Beth M. Huebner, "The Effect of Incarceration on Marriage and Work over the Life Course," *JQ: Justice Quarterly* 22, no. 3 (September 2005): 281–303.

15 Robert Weisberg and Joan Petersilia, "The Dangers of Pyrrhic victories

Against Mass Incarceration," *Daedalus* 139, no. 3 (Summer 2010): 124–133.

16 Kristine Artello, "Shifting 'Tough on Crime' to Keeping Kids Out of Jail: Exploring Organizational Adaptability and Sustainability at a Mental Health Agency Serving Adjudicated Children Living With Severe Mental Illness," *Criminal Justice Policy Review* 25, no. 3 (May 2014): 378–396.

17 Heather Habes, "Paying for the Graying: How California Can More Effectively Manage Its Growing Elderly Inmate Population," *Southern California Interdisciplinary Law Journal* 20, no. 2 (January 2011): 395–423.

18 Haeil Jung, "The Long-Term Impact of Incarceration During the Teens and 20s on the Wages and Employment of Men," *Journal of Offender Rehabilitation* 54, no. 5 (July 2015): 317–337.

19 H.J. Holzer, S. Raphael, and M. Stoll, "Will Employers Hire Former Offenders? Employer Preferences, Background Checks and Their Determinants," in *Imprisoning America: The Racial Effects of Mass Incarceration*, eds. M. Pattillo, D. Weiman, and B. Western (New York: Russell Sage Foundation, 2004), 205–246.

20 D. Pager, B. Western, and N. Sugie, "Sequencing Disadvantage: Barriers to Employment Facing Young Black and White Men with Criminal Records," *Annals of the American Academy of Social and Political Science* 623, no. 1 (2009): 195–213.

21 Mark L. Hatzenbuehler, Katherine Keyes, Ava Hamilton, Monica Uddin,

and Sandro Galea, "The Collateral Damage of Mass Incarceration: Risk of Psychiatric Morbidity Among Nonincarcerated Residents of High-Incarceration Neighborhoods," *American Journal of Public Health* 105, no. 1 (2015): 138–143.

22   E. Brown, "Expanding Carceral Geographies: Challenging Mass Incarceration and Creating a 'Community Orientation' Towards Juvenile Delinquency," *Geographica Helvetica* 69, no. 5 (December 15, 2014): 377–388.

23   Kayla Martensen, "The Price that US Minority Communities Pay: Mass Incarceration and the Ideologies That Fuel Them," *Contemporary Justice Review* 15, no. 2 (June 2012): 211–222.

24   Kamesha Spates and Carlton Mathis, "Preserving Dignity: Rethinking Voting Rights for U.S. Prisoners, Lessons from South Africa," *Journal of Pan African Studies* 7, no. 6 (October 21, 2014): 84–105.

25   Derecka Purnell, "Examining Disparate Impact Discrimination on Ex-offenders of Color Across Voting, Government Policy and Aid Receipt, Employment, and Housing," *Harvard Journal of African American Public Policy* (January 2013): 1–15.

26   John R. Sutton, "Symbol and Substance: Effects of California's Three Strikes Law on Felony Sentencing," *Law & Society Review* 47, no. 1 (March 2013): 37–72.

27   Charles J. Dunlap Jr., "The Military-Industrial Complex," *Daedalus* 140, no. 3 (Summer 2011): 135–147.

28   Rose M. Brewer and Nancy A. Heitzeg, "The Racialization of Crime and Punishment: Criminal Justice, Color-Blind Racism, and the Political Economy of the Prison Industrial Complex," *American Behavioral Scientist* 51, no. 5 (January 2008): 625–644.

29   Eugene H. Czajkoski, "Drugs and the Warlike Administration of Justice," *Journal of Drug Issues* 20, no. 1 (1990): 125–129.

30   David B. Kopel and Trevor Burrus, "Reducing the Drug War's Damage to Government Budgets," *Harvard Journal of Law & Public Policy* 35, no. 3 (Summer 2012): 543–568.

31   David J. Nutt, Leslie A. King, and Lawrence D. Phillips, "Drug Harms in the UK: A Multicriteria Decision Analysis," *Lancet* 376, no. 9752 (November 6, 2010): 1558–1565. Dirk W. Lachenmeier and Jürgen Rehm, "Comparative Risk Assessment of Alcohol, Tobacco, Cannabis and Other Illicit Drugs Using the Margin of Exposure Approach," *Scientific Reports* 5 (2015): 8126. Online at http://www.ncbi.nlm.

nih.gov/pmc/articles/PMC4311234. Peter N.S. Hoakena and Sherry H. Stewart, "Drugs of Abuse and the Elicitation of Human Aggressive Behavior," *Addictive Behaviors* 28 (2003): 1533–1554. Robert Gable, "The Toxicity of Recreational Drugs," *American Scientist* 94, no. 3 (2006): 206. Online at http://www.americanscientist.org/issues/pub/the-toxicity-of-recreational-drugs/4.

32   Tibor R. Machan, "Drug Prohibition Is Both Wrong and Unworkable," *Think: Philosophy For Everyone* 11, no. 30 (Spring 2012): 85.

33   Jonathan P. Caulkins, Beau Kilmer, Peter H Reuter, and Greg Midgette, "Cocaine's Fall and Marijuana's Rise: Questions and Insights Based on New Estimates of Consumption and Expenditures in US Drug Markets," *Addiction* 110, no. 5 (May 2015): 728–736.

34   NORML, State Info, http://norml.org/states. Accessed March 2017.

35   Jacob Sullum, "Which States Will Legalize Pot Next?" *Reason* 47, no. 3 (July 2015): 52–58.

36   Christopher Ingraham, "Colorado's Legal Weed Market: $700 Million in Sales Last Year, $1 Billion by 2016," *Washington Post*, February 12, 2015, http://www.washingtonpost.com/blogs/wonkblog/wp/2015/02/12/coloradas-legal-weed-market-700-million-in-sales-last-year-1-billion-by-2016.

37   Elizabeth Hernandez, "Colorado's Record January Marijuana Sales Yield $2.4M for Schools," *The Cannabist*. March 11, 2015, http://www.thecannabist.co/2015/03/11/colorado-pot-tax-results-january-2015/31462.

38   Robert G. Morris, Michael TenEyck, J. C. Barnes, and Tomislav V. Kovandzic, "The Effect of Medical Marijuana Laws on Crime: Evidence from State Panel Data, 1990–2006," *Plos One* 9, no. 3 (March 26, 2014): 1–7. Online at http://journals.plos.org/plosone/article?id=10.1371/journal.pone.0092816. Jérôme Adda, Brendon McConnell, and Imran Rasul, "Crime and the Depenalization of Cannabis Possession: Evidence from a Policing Experiment," *Journal of Political Economy* 122, no. 5 (October 2014): 1130–1202.

39   Joseph J. Palamar, Mathew V. Kiang, and Perry N. Halkitis, "Predictors of Stigmatization Towards Use of Various Illicit Drugs Among Emerging Adults," *Journal Of Psychoactive Drugs* 44, no. 3 (July 2012): 243–251.

40   Erik Brady, "NFL Eases Its Pot Rules, Leaving No One Satisfied," *USA Today*, October 23, 2014, http://www.usatoday.com/story/sports/nfl/2014/10/23/national-football-league-marijuana-testing-policy/17784021.

41   Nigel Duara, "It's Legal to Smoke Pot in Colorado, but You Can Still Get Fired for It," *Los Angeles Times*, June 15, 2015, http://www.latimes.com/nation/la-na-ff-colorado-high-court-employee-marijuana-20150615-story.html.

42   Beth Pearsall, "Predictive Policing: The Future of Law Enforcement," *NIJ Journal*, no. 266 (June 2010): 16–19. Online at http://www.nij.gov/journals/266/pages/predictive.aspx.

43   Ibid.

44   Smart Policing: Data, Analysis, Solutions. 2010. Available at http://www.smartpolicinginitiative.com.

45   James R. Coldren, Jr., Alissa Huntoon, and Michael Medaris, "Introducing Smart Policing: Foundations, Principles, and Practice," *Police Quarterly* 16, no. 3 (2013): 275–286.

46   Police Executive Research Forum, "How Are Innovations in Technology Transforming Policing?" 2012, http://www.policeforum.org/about.

47   Chris Baraniuk, "Caught Before the Act," *New Scientist* 225, no. 3012, (March 14, 2015): 18–19.

48   Christopher Stone and Jeremy Travis, "Toward a New Professionalism in Policing," Harvard Kennedy School, March 2011, http://www.hks.harvard.edu/criminaljustice/executive_sessions/policing.htm.

49   Randy Barnett, "Why The NSA Data Seizures Are Unconstitutional," *Harvard Journal of Law & Public Policy* 38, no. 1 (Winter 2015): 3–20.

50   Walter M. Brasch, *America's Unpatriotic Acts: The Federal Government's Violation of Constitutional and Civil Rights* (New York: Peter Lang, 10).

51   Charlie Savage, Jonathan Weisman, and Peter Baker, "N.S.A. Collection of Bulk Call Data Is Ruled Illegal," *New York Times*, May 8, 2015, A1–A8.

52   United States House of Representatives Judiciary Committee, H.R. 2048, the USA Freedom Act, http://judiciary.house.gov/index.cfm/usa-freedom-act. Accessed March 2017.

53   Walter Brasch, *America's Unpatriotic Acts: The Federal Government's Violations of Constitutional and Civil Rights* (New York: Peter Lang, 2005).

54   David Cole, "The New America: Little Privacy, Big Terror," *New York Review of Books* LXII, no. 13 (August 13, 2015): 18–22.

55   Jeffery T. Walker, Ronald G. Burns, Jeffrey Bumgarner, and Michele P. Bratina, "Federal Law Enforcement Careers: Laying the Groundwork," *Journal of Criminal Justice Education* 19, no. 1 (2008): 110–135.

Appendix: **Theories of Crime**

One of the challenges that criminologists face is to develop ideas about crime into systematic theories that clearly spell out perspectives and concepts in ways that can be tested and measured. As criminal justice grows as an academic discipline, criminological theories become more sophisticated and specific. This appendix will help us understand the variety and complexity of criminological theories. By looking at the explanations of crime that have guided the actions of people and the criminal justice system, we can better understand why and how crime remains a significant social problem and continues to demand serious study in the 21st century. By understanding the history of how our ideas about the causes of crime have evolved, we can learn to appreciate the fascinating complexity of the law, the criminal justice system, and other methods of social control.

The Classical School of Criminology

The **classical school of criminology** argues that people freely choose to break the law. The principle of "free will" allows us to consider various courses of action and then select the one we believe is most desirable. If we structure the criminal justice system in such a way that penalties for breaking the law are sufficiently severe, swift, and certain, then people will rationally choose not to break the law.[1]

The classical school of criminology is embodied primarily in the works of Cesare Beccaria (1738–1794) and Jeremy Bentham (1748–1832). Both men were more concerned with reforming the criminal justice system than with understanding why people broke the law or finding the causes of crime.[2]

Cesare Beccaria's ideas about reforming the ways in which society dealt with crime are detailed in his seminal work *On Crimes and Punishments*, published in 1764.[3] In this work, Beccaria presented nine principles concerning crime and the way society responds to lawbreakers. These and other ideas formulated by Beccaria have found their way into many of the principles that guide our criminal justice system today. Beccaria suggested that punishment should

only be stringent enough to deter crime. He also advocated the abolition of physical punishment and the death penalty. The presumption of innocence, the right to confront accusers, the right to a speedy trial, and the right not to be required to testify against oneself are all traceable to Beccaria.

According to Jeremy Bentham's theory of **utilitarianism**, people are guided by their desire for pleasure and aversion to pain.[4] To understand the actions of people, we need only understand how they comprehend pleasure and pain. Bentham believed people perform a mental exercise he called the **hedonistic calculus** when considering how to behave. A person attempts to weigh the pleasures that would accrue from breaking the law and the pain that would result if caught. In weighing pleasure and pain, the following are considered:

1. Intensity
2. Duration
3. Certainty or uncertainty
4. Propinquity or remoteness[5]

It is in this consideration of the balance between pleasure and pain that Bentham believed society could affect antisocial behavior.[6] Crime can be prevented by structuring the criminal justice system and the law in such a way that potential offenders can calculate that the pains of crime outweigh the pleasures. Modern sentencing patterns have a high degree of proportionality due to Bentham's ideas. For example, murder can get an offender the death penalty, but stealing a car will not. In Bentham's time, over 200 offenses demanded the death penalty. His work focused on reforming the system by introducing some logic into how, and how much, punishment was meted out.[7]

Bentham's hedonistic calculus is also apparent in the attempt to increase the certainty of punishment. More police officers, better crime-fighting technology, more efficient court systems, and other reforms are aimed at influencing the calculations that potential offenders make. The purpose of increasing the duration of prison sentences (such as life imprisonment) is to discourage severe crime.

The Neoclassical School of Criminology

Neoclassical criminology is a modern interpretation of classical criminology that acknowledges the possibility that human choices are affected by causes external to the will but holds that human beings are ultimately responsible for their choices. Neoclassical criminology emphasizes deterrence and retribution. Theoretically, those who are contemplating breaking the law can be deterred if they determine that the costs of committing the offense are higher than the rewards.

The idea behind deterrence is that the more serious a crime, the harsher the punishment. Theories based on deterrence introduce a degree of proportionality into the equation of matching punishments to the amount of harm caused by the offense. That is why people convicted of offenses such as murder may receive capital punishment, whereas those who commit simple assault are more likely to receive probation or a short jail term.

Severity of punishment is not the only aspect of deterrence; the swiftness and certainty of the punishment are also important considerations. Swiftness of punishment in the modern criminal justice system has a limited deterrence effect because the process can take so long. It is not unusual to see individuals executed many years after committing their offenses. The certainty of punishment also has limited utility as a deterrent because the resources to detect all crime are simply not available. Potential offenders, especially those who have been successful in the past, are able to plan their escapades in ways that can greatly limit their detection.

Not all law-breakers are equally adept at assessing the risks and potential rewards of breaking the law. For instance, those who rob a convenience store with a firearm expose themselves to long periods of incarceration for little potential reward. The $300 gained from robbing the store is a poor exchange for a 20-year (or longer) prison sentence if convicted of armed robbery. Several factors may go into this unwise decision, including an elevated opinion of one's confidence and ability, the influence of drugs or alcohol, or a proclivity for thrill-seeking. Many offenders who perform the risk/reward calculus fail to do the math correctly.

Neoclassical theories of criminology provide valuable insights into the factors that potential lawbreakers consider when deciding whether to violate the law and have the potential for policy implications. Rather than attempting to determine why offenders break the law, neoclassical theories allow policymakers to change the situational nature of the criminal act in ways that make crime riskier. Consequently, offenders choose to find other locations and more attractive targets rather than expose themselves to increased chances of apprehension and conviction.[8]

Rational Choice Theory

In criminology, **rational choice theory** is the idea that people consciously weigh the risks against the benefits of their actions, and choose the action they think has the most benefit. Developed by Derek Cornish and Ronald Clarke, rational choice theory seeks to capture the reasoning behind the decision to break the law.[9] Several factors beyond the expected benefits go into this decision. Offenders must also calculate the costs of committing crime, which include not only the potential sanction but also more mundane factors such as the equipment needed, the potential use of violence, and even the distance that the offender must travel to the crime scene.[10]

By understanding how potential lawbreakers think as they decide the costs and benefits of committing a crime, criminal justice policymakers can attempt to deter unlawful behavior by increasing costs. For instance, the severity of an offense is just one cost that can be manipulated by law enforcement. The cost can also be increased by shaming the perpetrator by publishing his or her name in the media, making a target less attractive by maintaining only a limited amount of cash (for example, at a convenience store), or increasing the likelihood of victim resistance (for example, arming a store clerk).[11]

Situational Crime Prevention

Situational crime prevention involves making crime less attractive to potential criminals by reducing the physical opportunities to break the law.[12] For example, "target hardening," or securing property by using padlocks, surrounding it with fences, security cameras, and increased lighting may help deter crime. The intent is to convince potential lawbreakers that the costs of physically committing the crime are unreasonably high given the expected potential benefits. When the target is sufficiently protected, potential offenders will presumably move on to more vulnerable targets. Situational crime prevention has been successful in reducing crime in public places, as evinced by the concentrated effort in MacArthur Park in Los Angeles, California. Increased police patrol, enforcement of misdemeanor laws, increased use of security cameras, and the posting of nearly 60 signs in both English and Spanish detailing the rules of appropriate behavior, as well as notices that the police would enforce these rules, are credited with influencing potential offenders to decide that committing a crime in the park is a bad idea.[13]

Routine Activities Theory

Routine activities theory states that crime is most likely to occur when three elements converge: motivated offenders, attractive targets, and the absence of capable guardians (such as police officers). According to the architects of the theory, Lawrence Cohen and Marcus Felson, the first element, motivated offenders, is the least important. The theory assumes that there will always be offenders motivated to break the law, so it is necessary to emphasize the other two elements: attractive targets and capable guardians. By making targets less attractive, that is, more secure, motivated offenders will be less likely to attack. Additionally, potential offenders will be deterred by providing adequate guardianship, such as regular police or security officer patrols.[14]

The Positivist School of Criminology

The classical school of criminology assumes motivation and treats all offenders equally. However, not all offenders are equal. People break the law for different reasons and are not affected by punishment in the same way. The idea that free will determines when and how people break the law fails to account for the complex nature of crime and the vast differences among people. There is no way to determine how one exercises free will in deciding to break the law.[15] The **positivist school of criminology**, theories that use scientific techniques to study crime and criminal offenders, is a natural outgrowth of the scientific method. By applying scientific disciplines, criminologists shifted the focus of criminology away from the law and the criminal justice system and toward the offender.[16] By looking to science to help understand patterns of crime, the question became, what factors influence people to break the law?[17]

Biological Theories of Crime

Scientists have long attempted to find a relationship between the body and behavior.[18] Here are some ideas that seek to cast light on the relationship between crime and factors such as heredity, hormones, blood chemistry, and environmental problems including alcohol and drug use.

BIOSOCIAL CRIMINOLOGY

Biosocial criminology utilizes genetic, neuropsychological, environmental, and evolutionary factors to explain crime and antisocial behavior across the life course.[19] The links between genes, hormones, the brain, and behavior are complicated, and scientists are still working out the connections. However, it is important to understand that there is no "crime gene"; that is, there is no single gene, or trait, that makes a person more likely to break the law. Scientists stress that environment deeply affects behavior.

Biosocial criminology is controversial, and the subject must be approached with caution. Some scholars criticize biosocial criminology by pointing out that researchers are trying to use physical traits (genes) to explain a socially defined phenomenon (crime). Another criticism recalls the debate about the focus on street crime versus white-collar and corporate crime. Studies tend to focus on violence, aggression, and impulsivity, all behaviors that are associated with street crime, rather than the more subtle behaviors that may be associated with white-collar and corporate crime. We should be aware that many ethical issues must be considered. At best, we hope to understand the interaction physical factors might have with social and psychological influences and pressures related to criminal behavior.[20]

Genes. The study of the possible effects of genes on antisocial behavior is part of biosocial criminology. A gene is a unit composed of DNA (deoxyribonucleic acid), which contains instructions for coding a protein for a particular function. Genes are the building blocks of our bodies, including our brains. The idea is that genes are partly responsible for behavior because they determine how our brains are constructed. For example, a gene that has been linked to violence regulates the production of an enzyme that controls the amount of the hormone serotonin. People with a version of the gene that produces less of the enzyme tend to be more impulsive and aggressive. Impulsivity and aggression are linked to violence, which in some cases may lead to antisocial behavior.[21] In another example, a study of twins and siblings tried to measure whether having delinquent friends and living in an impoverished neighborhood would cause a gene associated with violent behavior to express itself. The study found that without exposure to the risk factors, the violence-associated genes were not expressed. However, the more social risk factors a child encountered, the more likely genetics would play a role in any violent behavior.[22]

Hormones. The body secretes hormones for several reasons, but one by-product of this activity appears to be alterations in mood and behavior. For instance, a relationship exists between the release of testosterone in males and aggression.[23] A relatively new theory called evolutionary neuroandrogenic theory states that androgens (male sex hormones), primarily testosterone, promote competitive behaviors that may involve harming or victimizing another person. According to the theory, when testosterone levels rise, so does competitive, and often criminal, behavior. The evolutionary purposes of such behavior is to enhance the male ability to acquire resources and thus to attract females, who have evolved to prefer mates who are good at providing resources. According to a study by the theory's proponents, self-reported violent criminality was positively correlated with masculine traits such as high physical strength, high strength of sex drive, deep voice, ample body hair, and penis size.[24] At least one other study supports the idea that prenatal exposure of the brain to high levels of androgens increases the probability of criminal offending later in life; however, much more research is required to establish any firm conclusions.[25]

Brain Structure and Brain Chemistry. Brain chemistry is another area in which researchers are looking for the causes of antisocial behavior. Hormones such as norepinephrine, dopamine, and serotonin are of particular interest to criminologists because they regulate behaviors such as impulsivity, feelings of pleasure, and response to danger.[26] Techniques such as computed tomography (CT), magnetic resonance imaging (MRI), position emission tomography (PET), and single photon emission computed tomography (SPECT) allow researchers to observe how the brain is influenced by injury. This research is still in its early stages, and although there is no consensus about exactly how the brain influences behavior, some evidence suggests that it might eventually prove to be fruitful.

Psychological Theories of Crime

Although it is inadvisable, and maybe impossible, to separate the influences of the body and brain on behavior, criminologists distinguish between biological and psychological theories. Contemporary criminal psychology focuses on how antisocial individuals acquire, display, maintain, and (sometimes) modify their behavior and considers the influence of society, personality, and individual mental processes on behavior.[27] Modern criminal psychology utilizes cognitive and developmental approaches. Cognition refers to the act of thinking, which includes attitudes, beliefs, and values that individuals hold about themselves, other people, and their surroundings. Developmental approaches address individual human development from childhood to adulthood.[28]

BEHAVIORISM

Psychologist B. F. Skinner (1904–1990) theorized that behavior is determined by rewards and punishments. His theory, **behaviorism**, is based on the psychological principle of **operant conditioning**. That is, behavior is more likely to occur when it is rewarded and less likely to occur when it is punished or not rewarded. Operant conditioning is more complicated than it first appears. For example, slot machines are set up to pay on an intermittent schedule. They dispense just enough coins just often enough to keep gamblers pulling the lever. Slot machine designers calculate payoff intervals to encourage more gambling. If the schedule of reinforcement is too long—that is, if the machine does not pay off often enough—then gamblers will stop inserting coins. Like slot-machine designers, behaviorists study how people deal with rewards and punishments to see how good behavior can be encouraged and bad behavior eliminated.[29] In the criminal justice system, behaviorism is used extensively in therapeutic communities in which residents are placed on token economies that reward appropriate behavior.[30]

Some issues of behaviorism concern criminologists. First, rewards and punishments in the real world are not given according to predictable or dependable schedules. Hard work does not guarantee rewards. Often, the real world favors the strong, the lucky, the well connected, and those who cheat. Behaviorism works best in the artificial environments of the laboratory, the classroom, and the therapeutic community. Offenders can get frustrated quickly when they experience the inequities of the real world. Behaviorism is undependable as a guide for criminological policy because rewards come in many forms. What the middle-class, middle-age criminologist might think is a deterrent to inappropriate behavior might be seen by the impoverished, immigrant, or young gang member as a reward. For instance, incarceration evokes fear in most of us, but for some gang members it is seen as a necessary step in the development of a gang identity.[31]

OBSERVATIONAL LEARNING

Psychologist Albert Bandura focused on **observational learning** as a form of social learning, specifically "reciprocal determinism," which refers to how cognition (thought), behavior, and environment reinforce each other. That is, what we think affects how we behave and how we perceive our surroundings, including other people. In return, our surroundings reflect our behavior to some extent, which affects how we think. This has implications for the study of antisocial behavior, especially considering that much of Bandura's work concerns how aggressive and violent behavior is learned.[32]

Bandura's famous "Bobo doll experiments" used an inflated plastic toy called a "Bobo doll" that sits on the floor and pops back up when it is struck. Children of kindergarten age were shown a film of a woman punching the doll repeatedly as it popped up. When the children were led into the room with the doll, they immediately started punching and kicking the doll in imitation of what they had seen the woman do. This modeling behavior is not particularly surprising because the Bobo doll is designed to be used this way. However, Bandura conducted further experiments in which he showed the children a film of a woman punching and kicking a live clown. When the children were given the opportunity to punch and kick the clown themselves, they did so. The woman modeled behavior to the observers (the children), who then imitated the behavior.[33]

It is easy to see how this line of reasoning can be extended to antisocial behavior. When individuals routinely see others being abused or physically assaulted, they might imitate or model the behavior. Of course, there are many obstacles to overcome before this process takes place. Most adults have a certain level of self-regulation that prevents them from imitating everything they see. Also, the psychological processes involved in modeling behavior are complex and have certain limitations. Specifically, behaviorism considers external behavior and fails to consider individual cognitive processes.

COGNITIVE PSYCHOLOGICAL THEORY

According to psychologist Lawrence Kohlberg's **moral development theory**, human moral development proceeds through clearly defined stages of moral reasoning. Children learn the higher stages of morality from older children, teenagers, and adults. The level of an individual's moral reasoning is related to the decision to break the law.[34] The earlier stages are representative of egocentric behavior. In other words, the world revolves around the individual, who then acts in his or her best interest all the time. Criminal offenders are stuck at the lower stages of moral development because those who wish to simply avoid punishment are more likely to engage in antisocial behavior than those

who feel an obligation to the abstract principles of justice, equality, and respect for life. Cognitive theory suggests that the teaching of problem-solving skills could be useful in helping offenders to understand their motivations and actions, which in turn can prevent them from breaking the law again.

According to Kohlberg, moral development progresses in three main stages, with six sub-stages (see Table A.1).[35] Kohlberg believed that most law-abiding adults never proceed beyond the conventional level.[36] Kohlberg also theorized that the quality of our moral development is related to how we adapt to "cognitive disequilibrium," which is the thinking that occurs when we realize that what we learn does not match what we know and that we must consciously, or unconsciously, change the way we think about things. Cognitive disequilibrium can result from confronting moral challenges and conflicts and from talking to peers.[37] Progression through the stages is also marked with the development of empathy, or the ability to put oneself in the place of others. Studies have found that juvenile delinquents also show strong signs of being developmentally delayed in their capacity for moral judgment.[38]

PSYCHOPATHY

In common usage, the term *psychopath* refers to criminal offenders who commit the most heinous crimes, apparently without remorse. However, psychopathy actually refers to a specific condition that might or might not be paired with heinous criminal offending. According to psychologist Robert Hare, the three categories of psychopath are primary, secondary, and dyssocial.

> Primary psychopathy is manifested in pathological lying; a lack of remorse, empathy, or guilt; poor behavioral controls; irresponsibility; low empathy; and a grandiose sense of self-worth. These characteristics make for people who maneuver through society doing what they want, when they want, with little or no forethought, regardless of the consequences. Primary psychopaths are often in trouble with the law because of this behavior, but many manage never to break the law.

> Secondary psychopathy is characterized by engagement in antisocial and violent behavior because of severe emotional issues.

> Dyssocial psychopathy is characterized by learned aggressive, violent, and antisocial behaviors, not due to illness or inner conflict. A violent gang member is an example of a dyssocial psychopath.[39]

TABLE A.1   Kohlberg's Stages of Moral Development

LEVEL I: PRECONVENTIONAL

Children learn to avoid punishment by following simple rules. At this stage, children follow the rules because if they do not, they will be punished.

Stage 1: Obedience and Punishment Orientation	The punishment defines the rules.
Stage 2: Individualism and Exchange	Children learn that it is in their self-interest to avoid punishment, so the rules must be followed. Adult and older adolescent criminal offenders are "stuck" at this level of reasoning.

LEVEL II: CONVENTIONAL

At this point, which usually occurs during adolescence, people adopt and support their society's values.

Stage 3: Good Interpersonal Relationships	Young teenagers believe that being "good" and maintaining personal relationships are important. "Good" and "bad" are usually clearly defined at this point.
Stage 4: Maintaining the Social Order	Older teenagers and adults believe that the social order is of the utmost importance and that laws must be obeyed for the sake of the social order. Kohlberg found that most adolescents and adults function at this level.

LEVEL III: POSTCONVENTIONAL

Adults who reach this stage compare rules and laws to universal moral laws and ethics. At this point, adults question exactly what is required for society to be "good." Justice demands that everyone be treated equally and impartially.

Stage 5: Social Contract and Individual Rights	Some adults begin to think about the rights and values that a society should uphold. People in this stage believe a good society is a social contract into which people freely enter to work toward the benefit of all.
Stage 6: Universal Principles	A theoretical stage that is defined by a commitment to justice.

Source: William C. Crain, Theories of Development: Concepts and Applications (Englewood Cliffs, N.J.: Prentice-Hall, 1985).

Neither secondary psychopaths nor dyssocial psychopaths are considered true psychopaths because their conditions are caused by external factors, such as mental illness or their surroundings. There is some concern about the psychopathy diagnosis because it is difficult to recognize before serious crime has occurred. When researchers interview offenders who have committed heinous offenses, it is usually after they have been convicted. The critical issue in identifying psychopathy is to identify psychopaths who might commit serious offenses and prevent their behavior.[40]

Another condition often confused with psychopathy is antisocial personality disorder (APD). According to the American Psychiatric Association, APD "is a pervasive pattern of disregard for, and violation of, the rights of others that begins in childhood or early adolescence and continues into adulthood."[41] APD has much in common with psychopathy, but its definition is marked by behavior, while the definition of psychopathy includes cognitive and emotional characteristics. APD is also marked by aggression, violence, and irritability, while psychopaths might not display any of these symptoms. Those with APD, which occurs more frequently in males than in females, are almost certain to break the law repeatedly, while psychopaths may only break the law occasionally.[42]

Sociological Theories of Crime

The biological and psychological theories of crime focus on the mind and body to determine why people break the law. In short, these theories argue that something is wrong with the offender, either physically or mentally. Consequently, the policy implications of these types of theories revolve around incapacitating or treating the offender. However, another type of criminological theory finds problems not with the individual but with the social situation or environment. Several sociological theories consider social structure and social processes as explanations for crime.

THE CHICAGO SCHOOL

University of Chicago scholars developed several theories of crime as well as a method for examining crime. **Chicago-school** criminologists rejected the idea that crime is individual in nature, as the biological and psychological theories suggested, and turned to examining external factors. Two researchers connected to the Chicago school, Clifford Shaw and Henry McKay, studied the social disorganization of the neighborhoods of delinquent youths and concluded that something about bad neighborhoods caused crime.[43] According to their **social disorganization theory**, the neighborhood's structural and cultural conditions affect criminal behavior. What was it about some communities that contribute to crime? Poverty is not the only issue. Unstable neighborhoods cause a breakdown in the traditional bonds of social control.[44] The policy implications of social disorganization theory suggest that efforts to improve the physical blight of the community and the social interaction and integration of all citizens can reduce crime.

DIFFERENTIAL ASSOCIATION THEORY

Sociologist Edwin Sutherland (1883–1950) developed **differential association theory**, one of the most popular theories of delinquency. Sutherland's theory claims that antisocial behavior is learned and that young people learn antisocial behavior in intimate playgroups (friends and family).[45] What Sutherland's theory does not explain is how this learning takes place. One could question whether learning is really happening in these groups or whether it is simply a case of "birds of a feather flock together." If we accept that one's chances of being a delinquent are greater when one's friends are also delinquent, this still does not prove that delinquency is learned in intimate groups. Differential association theory is not an explanation for why individuals break the law, but how groups adopt attitudes favorable to breaking the law. Sutherland's work has stimulated other theorists to pursue the idea that antisocial behavior is learned.[46]

STRAIN THEORY

Sociologist Robert Merton made many contributions to the field of criminology, including the **strain theory** of delinquency. Merton was influenced by French sociologist Émile Durkheim's theory of **anomie** or "normlessness." In times of rapid social change, Durkheim contended that old norms break down and people lack controls on their behavior. Before new norms can be established, people experience a sense of normlessness and are more likely to engage in antisocial behavior. Merton looked at norms and recognized that society holds the same norms for everybody. The problem arises when there is unequal access to these norms. Those who share the goals promoted by society but find their means to attain these goals systematically blocked experience anomie. This anomie can be translated into antisocial behavior when the person attempts to adapt the barriers to the goal.[47]

For example, American society has a cultural goal of acquiring wealth. The goal of achieving financial independence is pushed by our families, schools, and the media. It is such a pervasive goal that we tend to take it for granted and assume that it is appropriate for everyone. As we attempt to reach this goal, some of us encounter obstacles. Sexism, racism, class bias, and age restrictions can frustrate our desires to become wealthy. For many people, simply working hard and saving money does not guarantee success. Does one disregard the goal when the means are lacking? According to Merton, the answer is no. One finds other ways of addressing the goal and adapts to the lack of means (see Table A.2).

Criminologist Robert Agnew expanded strain theory to encompass situations and conditions that may compel people to break the law. Merton viewed economic success as the predominant strain in lawbreaking. Agnew added three other major sources of strain.

› The disconnection between fair consequences and actual consequences. When it appears that rewards are not fair but, say, a result of inside information, favoritism, family connections, or class bias, people often feel that society is not fair.

› The loss of something valuable. Agnew states that much of the literature about aggression suggests that the removal of something valuable causes strain. This includes the loss of a loved one, divorce, job loss, or poor school performance.

› The presence of negative stimuli. Negative stimuli can take a physical form, such as unpleasant odors, distressing scenes, pollution, overpopulation, noise, heat, or cold. Sometimes negative stimuli consist of physical or sexual abuse, criminal victimization, physical punishment, bad relationships with parents or peers, physical pain, or verbal abuse.[48]

TABLE A.2   Robert Merton's Strain Theory

TYPE	EXPLANATION	EXAMPLE	GOALS	MEANS
Conformist	Most people fit this adaptation, accepting the goal of having money and adopting the culturally approved way to achieve it: hard work and deferred gratification.	Most university students are conformists. They work hard, defer gratification, and prepare for legitimate occupations.	Accepted +	Accepted +
Innovator	One accepts the goal of having money but rejects the culturally approved means to obtain it, finding alternative methods instead. Innovations can include crime or legal ways to make money, but adaptations do not fall within societal norms.	Drug dealers; bounty hunters.	Accepted +	Rejected or blocked −
Ritualist	The goal is rejected, but the means are accepted. Ritualists are not usually deviant, but they no longer have the goal of achieving wealth and success. Ritualists tend to go through the motions.	Professors who deliver the same lecture term after term and seem not to care if the lecture is current or if the students learn.	Rejected −	Accepted +
Retreatist	Both the goals and the means are rejected (or blocked), and nothing is substituted. Many retreatists end up as clients of the criminal justice system.	Drug addicts, alcoholics, hermits, and outcasts.	Rejected −	Rejected or blocked −
Rebel	Rebellious people reject culturally approved means and goals and substitute new ones.	Some domestic terrorist groups; hippies of the 1960s who dropped out of conventional society.	Rejected and substituted −	Rejected and substituted −

Agnew's general strain theory has several advantages over Merton's theory. In addition to considering more types of strain, he also considers the mechanisms that people use to cope with strain. For instance, because males are more often exposed to strains conducive to crime, they are more likely to cope with strain through crime.[49] This theory also suggests ways of reducing crime. According to Agnew, strategies for reducing exposure to strain include:

> Eliminating strains conducive to crime

> Altering strains to make them less conducive to crime, such as reducing their magnitude or perceived injustice

> Removing individuals from strains conducive to crime

> Equipping individuals with the traits and skills to avoid strains conducive to crime

> Altering perceptions and goals of individuals to reduce subjective strains

Strategies for reducing the likelihood that individuals will respond to strain with crime include improving conventional coping skills and resources; increasing social support; increasing social control; and reducing association with delinquent peers and beliefs favorable to crime.[50]

SOCIAL CONTROL THEORY

Travis Hirschi's **social control theory** does not ask why some people break the criminal law. Instead, it considers why most people do not. Rather than seeking to explain the relatively infrequent event of crime, social control theory explores the pervasive conforming behavior that makes meaningful communities possible. Hirschi speculated that the mechanism that accomplishes this is a social bond that links us to conventional society.[51] Only when this social bond is weakened is crime likely to occur. Hirschi contended that this social bond has four elements:

1. Attachment. When people are concerned with the feelings of others, they are less likely to do things that are wrong. A child who values his parents' approval and affection will behave in ways that maintain a good relationship. Hirschi believed that attachments to parents, schools, and peers help form the social bond that keeps people from engaging in criminal behavior.

2. Commitment. People are committed to a society when they are successful in it. People who have money, property, and good reputations are committed to the social system that allowed them the opportunities for that success. A frequent mistake in the study of criminal behavior is the assumption that most criminals are committed to conventional society when, in fact, they have not been able to realize their needs in that society. In a sense, then, most criminals have little or nothing to lose.

3. Involvement. People involved in conventional activities have less time and energy for crime. Involvement is the idea behind a vast array of programs designed to keep young people occupied. Although ballet lessons, Little League baseball, athletic programs, after-school day care, and parks and recreation areas for children have a number of positive features, a primary benefit is that they keep children busy.

4. Beliefs. Children who believe in the conventional value system of society are less likely to break the law. According to Hirschi, children who commit delinquent acts have weakened beliefs in the conventional moral code. Unlike other theories that speculate about deviant subcultures that supply contrasting codes of conduct, Hirschi's theory considers only the dominant culture and envisions that everyone is bonded to it to some degree. The strength of that bond is what determines whether one will become delinquent.

Critical Sociological Theories of Crime

The term **critical theory** encompasses a range of perspectives that critique the current manner in which justice is dispensed and that consider social justice to be a legitimate end. The following theories examine how power is distributed in society and how the criminal justice system often is simply a reflection of power and sometimes a tool of power.[52]

MARXISM

Karl Marx (1818–1883) was a social theorist whose critique of capitalism and its effect on social justice is important to the understanding of crime. Marx, who studied the 19th-century European capitalist system, asserted that the owners of the means of production (factories and such) paid their workers poorly and used the government to pass laws that prevented reform. Those with economic power controlled the system and used that power to make sure things did not change. According to Marx, the workers put up with this inequitable arrangement because they suffered from **false consciousness**. The owner class controlled the sources of opinion, newspapers, churches, and schools; therefore, they could make the workers believe they were lucky to have a job and that they should be grateful. Marx's solution to this state of affairs was for the workers to rise up and grab the means of production for themselves, through violence if necessary.[53]

Although Marx actually said little about crime and the criminal justice system, criminologists who study his tradition point out that those in power control the making and the enforcement of the law.[54] One need only look at how political campaigns are financed to see how big money influences lawmaking. When we consider the disparities between how the criminal justice system deals with street crime and corporate crime, we can appreciate why critical criminologists continue to consider the role of social class and power in society.[55]

GENDER AND JUSTICE

Feminism examines how women are treated differently from men in a society dominated by male power structures. As a starting point in addressing the social condition of women, feminists employ the concept of **gender**, which argues that society has different expectations of females and males. In addition to the obvious physical differences between men and women, gender asserts that there are also different rules, opportunities, and consequences that are automatically distributed according to sex.

Sexism is a way in which the contributions of males and females are valued according to different standards. Because men have historically dominated our social system, much of what we think we know about female offenders and female criminal justice system practitioners has been based on the study of males. Feminist criminologists (both female and male) have begun to correct this gap in our knowledge about crime.[56]

Crime can be appreciated from feminist perspectives in three ways:

1. Liberal feminism and criminology. Liberal feminists assert two ideas. First, women's opportunities are blocked by a social system controlled by men who reserve most of the power for themselves. Power should be distributed according to accomplishment rather than gender. Second, girls are socialized differently from boys. Women are systematically taught to be passive, nurturing, and dependent, whereas men are taught to be assertive, competitive, and aggressive. By changing the way women are socialized and removing barriers to power, women will be able to fully realize their talents and not be limited by a patriarchal, sexist system. As these goals are accomplished, however, women also have opportunities to engage in deviant behavior. As females become more equal, they will also find more opportunities for illegitimate activities and be treated more like males by the criminal justice system.

2. Radical feminist criminology. The radical feminist contends that sexism is not so much a product of class relations as it is of the patriarchal structure that places all women at a severe disadvantage, regardless of their social class or race. Radical feminists point to how women are victims of rape, acquaintance rape, pornography, and spousal abuse as evidence that the criminal justice system does not seriously address women's concerns. Traditional criminology has focused primarily on male street crime and has neglected the types of personal violent crimes that affect women. This is true even in the case of rape, in which stranger rape is considered easier to prosecute and more serious than that of acquaintance rape. Radical feminists call for a fundamental overhaul of patriarchal systems rather than the less ambitious legal changes advocated by liberal feminists.

3. Socialist feminist criminology. Socialist feminists use the combined effects of social class and gender to explain women's disadvantaged status in society and the criminal justice system. Women's opportunities for crime are influenced by the greater controls they experience in society. They are more closely supervised by their parents, husbands, boyfriends, and authorities for what is believed to be "their own good." This greater surveillance both limits their opportunities and increases the chances that their deviant behavior will be detected. Additionally, women are underrepresented in official positions of power and responsibility. If the disadvantages of race are added to the disadvantages of social class and gender, the combined effects produce even greater marginalization.[57]

Feminist theories of criminology also have relevance for men. By considering how power is concentrated in the privileged male sex role, we can begin to understand how race, sexual orientation, and gender determine how the criminal justice system treats practitioners, offenders, and victims. Feminist theories also have policy implications. Changing the way rape victims are treated by police officers and prosecutors is one example of how a feminist perspective can introduce some social justice into legal proceedings.[58]

CRITICAL RACE THEORY

Critical race theory begins with the observation that people of color are overrepresented at every decision point of the criminal justice system and suggests that race is a crucial variable for scholars to examine when attempting to explain the dynamics of the U.S. justice system and, to varying degrees, the justice systems of other countries. Critical race theory asserts that the concept that "we are a nation of laws and not of men" masks the function of the criminal justice system to legitimize white supremacy and oppress people of color.[59] As a theoretical perspective, critical race theory focuses on inequality, discrimination, prejudice, and differential law enforcement and explains issues such as racial profiling, interracial crime, and racial hoaxes. To understand the experiences of people of color and their treatment by the criminal justice system, some research should be based on personalized accounts of harm. Traditional criminal justice research methods do not uncover the types of injustices that are the focus of critical race theory.

Integrated Theories of Crime

Recognizing that traditional biological, psychological, and sociological theories are of limited utility, integrationists have attempted to link theories.[60] There is some question as to whether integrating theories is even desirable. Many theories have assumptions that contrast with the assumptions of other theories that make integration not only difficult but impossible. For instance, some theories are developed at a micro (individual) level, so combining them with theories developed at a macro (group or societal) level can violate the assumptions of both types of theories. Nevertheless, the integration of theories has produced several perspectives that are worth investigating.

INTEGRATED THEORY OF DELINQUENT BEHAVIOR

Scholars Delbert Elliott, Suzanne Ageton, and Rachel Canter combine strain theory, social control theory, and social learning theory to explain delinquency within the lower and middle classes. They assert that all youths experience issues with strain, social control, and association with delinquent peer groups regardless of class; however, the types of issues differ slightly depending on social class, class expectations, or aspirations.

For example, most youths want to achieve certain socially approved goals, seek control over their environment and others' perceptions of them, and have the opportunity at some point during adolescence to associate with delinquent or near-delinquent peers. An impoverished youth might aspire to go to a community college, get a blue-collar job, and leave the impoverished, socially disorganized neighborhood while being pressured to join a local gang. A wealthy youth might aspire to major in pre-med at an Ivy League university and eventually buy a home with a pool, but in the meantime be tempted to construct a fake driver's license in order to buy beer and get drunk with friends before attending a keg party.

The aspirations and expectations of each class are a matter of degree. Additionally, youths in each class may have equal amounts of difficulty in achieving their goals. In the prior examples, both the impoverished and wealthy youth may have poor grades, which would keep both from achieving their educational goals. Both youths could get into equally deep trouble by associating with their delinquent peers. This highlights the strain and social control aspects of the theory. According to the theory, youths who

experience more strain and weak feelings of social control are more likely to seek out delinquent peers. In fact, Elliott, et al. found that the best predictor of future delinquency, other than prior delinquency, was association with delinquent peers.[61]

INTERACTIONAL THEORY OF DELINQUENCY

Terence Thornberry's **interactional theory of delinquency** looks at low social control and exposure to delinquent peers over the entire course of adolescent development. Thornberry considers how parental attachment diminishes as youths grow older and how commitment to conventional values, such as employment and education, protect the youth from delinquent behavior. Furthermore, Thornberry demonstrates how the effects of delinquent peers and self-control change as adolescents are exposed to changes in sets of peers. Such changes as getting married and starting a family bond the youth to conventional society and thus result in a lower involvement in delinquency. According to Thornberry, association with delinquent peers increases the chances for individual delinquency, but individual delinquency also increases the chances for association with delinquent peers. In a sort of feedback loop, the group and individual aspects of delinquency feed one another until the youth is fully involved in delinquency, usually with a set of delinquent friends.[62]

CONTROL BALANCE THEORY

According to Charles Tittle, all relationships exhibit a power differential. Whether it is between parent and child, parole officer and parolee, or professor and student, this difference in power is an interesting and understudied variable and manifests itself in any type of relationship involving any number of people. A balance between the amount of control one has and the amount that one is controlled determines how or whether one will break the law. A person with too little social control or a powerful person who has too much is each at risk for breaking the law—in the first case to increase control or in the second to further extend control.

Tittle contends that those who have the subordinate power position attempt to balance their power through a variety of strategies, one of which is antisocial behavior. For example, if a teen is doing poorly in school, he or she might employ a number of strategies to regain a sense of dignity. The adolescent might drop out of school as a way of escaping the feeling of failure, claim that he or she is not interested in trying to succeed as a way of minimizing the feeling of failure, or might simply attempt to burn the school down or attack other students. Each strategy is aimed at reducing the humiliation of failure and restoring the sense of control the adolescent has over his or her life.[63]

Life-Course and Developmental Theories

Life-course theories are dynamic in that they use longitudinal data to observe how subjects grow and mature over long periods of time. In this way, life-course theories provide a broader context to their explanations of crime and demonstrate how continuity and change are important. Two life-course theories illustrate not only how the research is different from traditional criminological research but also how the results generated are more robust and theoretically rich.

PATHWAY THEORY

British criminologist Terrie Moffitt's life-course theory of crime focuses on two types of juvenile delinquent: "life-course persistent" and "adolescence-limited" offenders. By examining these two groups in greater detail, it is possible to appreciate Moffitt's pathway theory.[64]

1. Life-course-persistent offenders engage in antisocial behavior for long periods of time. Moffitt considers biological, psychological, and sociological variables in an attempt to explain why some individuals are continually in trouble throughout their lives. There is a cumulative effect of problems that start in early childhood and escalate into serious crime as the subject grows older.

2. Adolescence-limited offenders can be contrasted with the life-course-persistent offender by the absence of problems in childhood and the unlikely continuation of crime into adulthood. Although the offenses of adolescence-limited offenders might be serious, there is little continuity to the patterns of crime they engage in, and there are long periods where they do not break the law at all. Rather than being a way of life, crime for the adolescent-limited offender is episodic and instrumental. This type of offender usually breaks the law infrequently and does so to achieve a specific goal. Adolescence-limited offenders account for most delinquents, and most of them age out of crime and develop into normal productive citizens.

According to Moffitt, adolescence-limited offenders respond to shifting contingencies as they age. With the inevitable progression of chronological age, more legitimate and tangible adult roles become available to adolescents. Adolescence-limited delinquents gradually lose motivation for delinquency as they mature. Moreover, when aging delinquents attain some of the privileges they coveted as teens, the consequences of illegal behavior shift from rewarding to punishing, in their perception. Adolescence-limited delinquents have something to lose by persisting in their antisocial behavior beyond the teen years.[65]

PERSISTENT-OFFENDING AND DESISTANCE-FROM-CRIME THEORY

In the basement of the Harvard Law Library, criminologists John Laub and Robert Sampson found a dataset collected between 1949 and 1963 from 500 delinquent boys by influential criminologists Sheldon and Eleanor Glueck. Laub and Sampson followed up on this data and detailed how those delinquents either persisted in their antisocial orientation or desisted from crime over their life course. Upon tracing some of the subjects' lives until age 70, Laub and Sampson found that some of the subjects continued in a trajectory of crime while others became more involved in society and adopted conventional behaviors. Upon tracking some of the subjects down in late adulthood and old age, Sampson and Laub concluded that almost all of the delinquent boys eventually stopped breaking the law.[66] They found that desisting from crime is typically the result of youths experiencing a turning point in life in which they become connected to conventional society. This change can be summarized as follows:

1. The offenders experienced a structural turning point. This might be in the form of marriage, getting a new job, or joining the military. As the delinquents aged, they had increased opportunities to engage in conventional behavior and become bonded to a law-abiding lifestyle.

2. Conventional lifestyles resulted in greater social control over their lives. When one gets married, it is more difficult to go out "drinking with the boys" or engage in other activities that may present opportunities for crime.

A spouse has expectations that must be dealt with, which inevitably curtails any antisocial behavior that took place during bachelorhood. Similarly, when one enters the military, the rules and regulations that must be followed limit the exposure to crime-producing situations. Many of the study's delinquents became bonded to conventional lifestyles in this way.

3. The ex-delinquents' new lifestyles afforded them fewer opportunities to hang out with deviant peers, but more opportunities to engage in pro-social activities, such as going on family outings, going to church, and becoming involved in the community.

4. The new lifestyle required commitment. As one becomes successful in conventional behavior,

it is no longer acceptable to participate in activities that put the new lifestyle at risk. Additionally, the new lifestyle provides benefits that replace the social and emotional needs that were addressed by the antisocial lifestyle. For example, for many of the ex-delinquents, holding down a well-paying job meant that they were less willing to do anything that jeopardized that job.

Although the change to conventional activities simply happened to some of the offenders, some of the subjects made conscious choices to change their lifestyle. This idea of agency is particularly important because it suggests that an antisocial lifestyle begun in childhood does not always continue through the life course.

TABLE A.3 Criminological Theories

	NAME/CLASS OF THEORY	THEORY	PRACTICE	THEORISTS
Classical School	**Nine Principles**	Free will and punishment should be based on humane principles.	Promote deterrence through social contract, public education, and legal clarity and equity. Punish proportionally. Eliminate systemic corruption.	Beccaria
	Utilitarianism	People are guided by desire for pleasure and aversion to pain.		Bentham
Neoclassical School	**Rational Choice Theory**	People consciously weigh the risks against the benefits of their actions, and choose the action that they think has the most benefit.	Raise the costs of criminal behavior; shame the perpetrator by publishing his or her name in the media; make targets less attractive by maintaining a limited amount of the desired item (such as cash); increase the likelihood of victim resistance.	Cornish and Clarke
	Situational Crime Prevention	Make crime less attractive to potential criminals by reducing the physical opportunities to break the law.	Target hardening.	Clarke
	Routine Activities Theory	Crime is more likely when offenders are motivated, targets are attractive, and capable guardians are absent.	There will always be motivated offenders. Thus, make targets less attractive and provide adequate guardians.	Cohen and Felson

Positivist School Biological Theories	**Biochemistry**	Hormones, brain structure, and/or brain chemistry may cause criminal behavior.	Provide medication, make diet changes.	
	Biosocial Criminology	Genetics may affect criminal behavior.		
Psychological Theories	**Behaviorism (operant conditioning)**	Behavior is determined by rewards and punishments.	Reward reform, punish continued offensive behavior.	Skinner
	Observational Learning	Cognition, behavior, and environment mutually reinforce each other. Observers, especially children, imitate behavior they see.	Model good behavior.	Bandura
	Moral Development Theory	Human moral development proceeds through stages of moral reasoning. Criminal offenders are stuck at the lower levels of development.	Promote attentive parenting, effective schools, and public programs for children, such as Headstart.	Kohlberg
	Psychopathy	Psychopathy is a specific psychological condition that might or might not co-occur with heinous criminal offending.	For serious offenders, life-long incarceration or commission to a mental institution is common.	Hare
	Antisocial Personality Disorder	APD has much in common with psychopathy except that its definition is marked by behavior, as well as aggression, violence, and irritability.	As those with APD continually break the law, incarceration is common, as are counseling and medication.	
Sociological Theories	**Chicago School**	Social disorganization causes criminal behavior in individuals.	Institute social reform, ensure equal access to societal incentives and norms, improve environments.	Shaw, McKay
	Differential Association Theory	Crime is learned.		Sutherland
	Strain Theory	There is unequal access to societal norms.		Merton
	Social Control Theory	This theory questions why people do not break the law.		Hirschi
	Labeling Theory	Deviants conform to the "deviant" label.		Lemert
Critical Sociological Theories	**Marxism**	Those in power make laws to favor themselves.	Institute social reform, provide minority groups access to more power and decision-making, recognize oppression, allocate group-specific research.	Marx
	Feminism (gender)	Crime study and the criminal justice system are male-dominated and male-oriented.		
	Critical Race Theory	The criminal justice system targets and oppresses people of color.		

Integrated Theories	**Integrated Theory of Delinquent Behavior**	Strain theory, social control, and social learning theories are combined to explain delinquency within the lower and middle classes.	Institute social reform, ensure equal access to societal incentives and norms.	Elliot, Ageton, and Canter
	Interactional Theory of Delinquency	Low social control and exposure to delinquent peers over the course of adolescent development contribute to delinquency and antisocial behavior.		Thornberry
	Control Balance Theory	People seek to correct and balance power differentials in their relationships.		Tittle
Life Course Theories	**Pathway Theory**	Life-course-persistent offenders engage in antisocial behavior for long periods of time, possibly all their lives. Adolescence-limited offenders break the law in adolescence but desist upon adulthood.	Institute social reform, ensure equal access to societal incentives and norms.	Moffitt
	Persistent-Offending and Desistance-from-Crime Theory	As delinquents age, some continue to break the law well into adulthood, while others experience turning points in which they bond to conventional society.		Laub and Sampson

Critical Reflections

1. What is the classical school of criminology?

2. What are the similarities and differences between Beccaria's and Bentham's approaches to crime?

3. What is neoclassical criminology, and what two aspects of crime prevention does it emphasize?

4. Why is the idea of deterrence so important in classical criminology?

5. What is the positivist school of criminology?

6. How are biological and psychological theories of criminology different?

7. How are critical sociological theories of crime different from other sociological theories?

8. How are theories that focus on the offender different from theories that focus on the offense?

9. If most crime is committed by adolescents and young adults, why do some criminologists consider crime across the life course?

10. Can any single criminological theory explain the wide variety of crimes committed in the United States?

Key Terms

anomie—A condition in which a people or society undergoes a breakdown of social norms and values.

behaviorism—The assessment of human psychology via the examination of objectively observable and quantifiable actions, as opposed to subjective mental states.

biosocial criminology—A perspective that utilizes genetic, neuropsychological, environmental, and evolutionary factors to explain crime and antisocial behavior across the life course.

Chicago school— Criminological theories that rely, in part, on individuals' demographics and geographic location to explain criminal behavior.

classical school of criminology—A set of criminological theories that uses the idea of free will to explain criminal behavior.

critical theory—A perspective that critiques the current manner in which justice is dispensed and considers social justice to be a legitimate end.

differential association theory—A theory developed by Edwin Sutherland that states that crime is learned.

false consciousness— The idea that the attitudes held by the lower class do not accurately reflect the reality of that class's existence.

gender (from Chapter 6)— The socially constructed roles, behaviors, actions, and characteristics that a society considers appropriate for males and females.

hedonistic calculus— An individual's mental calculation of the personal value of an activity by how much pleasure or pain it will incur.

interactional theory of delinquency—The theory that low social control and exposure to delinquent peers over the course of adolescent development contributes to delinquency and antisocial behavior.

moral development theory—Kohlberg's theory that human moral development proceeds through clearly defined stages of moral reasoning.

neoclassical criminology—A modern interpretation of classical criminology that acknowledges the possibility that human choices are affected by causes external to the will but holds that human beings are ultimately responsible for their choices.

observational learning—The process of learning by watching the behavior of others.

operant conditioning—The alteration of behavior by rewarding or punishing a subject for a specified action until the subject associates the action with pleasure or pain.

positivist school of criminology—A set of criminological theories that uses scientific techniques to study crime and criminal offenders.

rational choice theory—The idea that people consciously weigh the risks against the benefits of their actions and choose the action that they think has the most benefit.

routine activities theory—A perspective that states that crime is most likely to occur when these three elements converge: motivated offenders, attractive targets, and the absence of capable guardians.

situational crime prevention—An idea that involves making crime less attractive to potential criminals by reducing the physical opportunities to break the law.

social control theory—A theory that seeks not to explain why people break the law, but instead explores what keeps most people from breaking the law.

social disorganization theory—The theory that the structural and cultural conditions of a neighborhood affect criminal behavior.

strain theory—The theory that the causes of crime can be connected to the pressure on culturally or materially disadvantaged groups or individuals to achieve the goals held by society, even if the means to those goals require the breaking of laws.

utilitarianism—A theory associated with Jeremy Bentham that states that people will choose not to break the law when the pain of punishment outweighs the benefits of the offense.

Endnotes

1 Erline Eide, *Economics of Crime: Deterrence and the Rational Offender* (North Holland, Netherlands: Elsevier, 1994).

2 Philip Jenkins, "Varieties of Enlightenment Criminology," *British Journal of Criminology* 24 (1984): 112–130. José Brunner "Modern Times: Law, Temporality and Happiness in Hobbes, Locke and Bentham," *Theoretical Inquiries in Law* 8, no. 1 (January 1, 2007): 21.

3 Cesare Beccaria, *On Crimes and Punishments,* trans. Henry Paolucci (Indianapolis, Ind.: Bobbs-Merrill, 1764/1963).

4 Jeremy Bentham, "An Introduction to the Principles of Morals and Legislation," in *Classics of Criminology,* 2d ed., ed. Joseph E. Jacoby (Prospect Heights, Ill.: Waveland Press, 1994), 80.

5 Cesare Beccaria, *On Crimes and Punishment* (Indianapolis, Ind.: Bobbs-Merrill, 1963).

6 Frank P. Williams III and Marilyn D. McShane, Criminological Theory, 4th ed. (Upper Saddle River, N.J.: Prentice Hall, 2004), 15–32.

7 Imogene L. Moyer, *Criminological Theories: Traditional and Nontraditional Voices and Themes* (Thousand Oaks, Calif.: Sage, 2001).

8 Ronald L. Simons, Callie H. Burt, Ashley B. Barr, Man-Kit Lei, and Eric Stewart, "Incorporating Routine Activities, Activity Spaces, and Situational Definitions into the Social Schematic Theory of Crime," *Criminology* 52, no. 4 (2014): 655–687.

9 Ronald V. Clarke and Derek B. Cornish, "Rational Choice," in *Explaining Criminals and Crime,* Raymond Paternoster and Rona Bachman (Los Angeles:

Roxbury Publishing, 2000), 23–42. Derek B. Cornish and R. V. G. Clarke, *The Reasoning Criminal: Rational Choice Perspectives on Offending* (New York: Springer-Verlag, 1986), 1.

10 Christophe Vandeviver, Stijn Van Daele, and Tom Vander Beken. "What Makes Long Crime Trips Worth Undertaking? Balancing Costs and Benefits in Burglars' Journey to Crime," *British Journal of Criminology* 55, no. 2 (March 2015): 399–420.

11 Marie Rosenkrantz Lindegaard, Wim Bernasco, and Scott Jacques, "Consequences of Expected and Observed Victim Resistance for Offender Violence during Robbery Events," *Journal of Research in Crime and Delinquency* 52, no. 1 (February 2015): 32–61. See also M. Lyn Exum, Joseph B. Kuhns, Brad Koch, and Chuck Johnson, "An Examination of Situational Crime Prevention Strategies Across Convenience Stores and Fast-Food Restaurants," *Criminal Justice Policy Review* 21, no. 3 (2010): 269–295.

12 Ronald V. Clarke, *Situational Crime Prevention: Successful Case Studies* (Albany, N.Y.: Harrow and Heston, 1997).

13 William H. Sousa and George L. Kelling, "Police and the Reclamation of Public Places: A Study of MacArthur Park in Los Angeles," *International Journal of Police Science and Management* 12, no. 1 (Spring 2010): 41–54.

14 Lawrence E Cohen and Marcus Felson, "Social Change in Crime Rate Trends in Activities Approach," *American Sociological Review* 44 (1979): 588–607.

15 Derek B. Cornish and Ronald V. Clarke, *The Reasoning Criminal: Rational Choice Perspectives on Offending* (New York: Springer, 1986).

16 Charles Darwin, *The Origin of the Species* (Cambridge, Mass.: Harvard University Press, 1859/1964).

17 Deborah W. Denno, "Human Biology and Criminal Responsibility: Free Will or Free Ride," *University of Pennsylvania Law Review* 137 (1988): 615–671.

18 Hans-Ludwig Kroeber "The Historical Debate on Brain and Legal Responsibility—Revisited," *Behavioral Sciences & the Law* 25, no. 2 (March 1, 2007): 251.

19 Kevin M. Beaver and Anthony Walsh, "Biosocial Criminology," in *The Ashgate Research Companion to Biosocial Theories of Crime*, eds. Kevin M. Beaver and Anthony Walsh (Burlington, Vt.: Ashgate Publishing Company, 2011), 3–5.

20 Ty A. Ridenour, "Genetic Epidemiology of Antisocial Behavior," in *Theories of Crime: A Reader*, eds. Claire M. Renzetti, Daniel J. Curran, and Patrick J. Carr (Boston: Allyn and Bacon, 2003), 4–24.

21 Karen Sugden, Louise Arseneault, HonaLee Harrington, Terrie E. Moffitt, Benjamin Williams, and Avshalom Caspi, "Serotonin Transporter Gene Moderates the Development of Emotional Problems among Children Following Bullying Victimization," *Journal of the American Academy of Child & Adolescent Psychiatry* 49, no. 8 (August 2010): 830–840.

22 Kevin M. Beaver, "Environmental Moderators of Genetic Influences on Adolescent Delinquent Involvement and Victimization," *Journal of Adolescent Research* 26, no. 1 (January 2011): 84–114.

23 Alan Booth and D. Wayne Osgood, "The Influence of Testosterone on Deviance in Adulthood: Assessing and Explaining the Relationship," *Criminology* 31, no. 1 (February 1, 1993): 93.

24 Lee Ellis, Shyamal Das, and Hasan Buker, "Androgen-promoted Physiological Traits and Criminality: A Test of the Evolutionary Neuroandrogenic Theory," *Personality and Individual Differences* 44, no. 3 (February 2008): 699–709.

25 Anthony W. Hoskin and Lee Ellis, "Fetal Testosterone and Criminality: Test of Evolutionary Neuroandrogenic Theory," *Criminology* 53, no. 1 (February 2015): 54–73.

26 Debra Niehoff, "The Biology of Violence," in *Theories of Crime: A Reader*, eds. Claire M. Renzetti, Daniel J. Curran, and Patrick J. Carr (Boston: Allyn and Bacon, 2003), 26–31.

27 Curt R. Bartol and Anne M. Bartol, *Criminal Behavior*, 8th ed. (Upper Saddle River, N.J.: Pearson Prentice Hall, 2008), 6–8.

28 Ibid.

29 G. Terence Wilson, "Behavior Therapy," in *Current Psychotherapies*, 4th ed., eds. Raymond J. Corsini and Danny Wedding (Itasca, Ill.: F. E. Peacock, 1989), 241–282.

30 Michael J. Lillyquist, *Understanding and Changing Criminal Behavior* (Englewood Cliffs, N.J.: Prentice Hall, 1980).

31 G. David Curry and Scott H. Decker, *Confronting Gangs: Crime and Community* (Los Angeles: Roxbury, 1988).

32 Curt R. Bartol and Anne M. Bartol, *Criminal Behavior: A Psychosocial Approach*, 8th ed. (Upper Saddle River, N.J.: Pearson Prentice Hall, 2008), 121–123.

33 C. George Boeree, Albert Bandura, http://webspace.ship.edu/cgboer/bandura.html. Accessed September 2015.

34 Carol Veneziano and Louis Veneziano, "The Relationship Between Deterrence and Moral Reasoning," *Criminal Justice Review* 17, no. 2 (1992): 209–216.

35 William Crain, *Theories of Development*, 5th ed. (Upper Saddle River, N.J.: Prentice-Hall, 2005), 154–158.

36 Eric K. Klein "Dennis the Menace or Billy the Kid: An Analysis of the Role of Transfer to Criminal Court in Juvenile Justice," *The American Criminal Law Review* 35, no. 2 (January 1, 1998):371–410.

37 Ibid.

38 Geert Jan Stams, Daniel Brugman, Maja Deković, Lenny van Rosmalen, Peter H. van der Laan, and John C. Gibbs, "The Moral Judgment of Juvenile Delinquents: A Meta-Analysis," *Journal of Abnormal Child Psychology* 34, no. 5 (October 1, 2006):697–713.

39 Robert D. Hare, *Psychopathy: Theory and Research* (New York: Wiley, 1970). Bartol and Bartol, *Criminal Behavior*, 188.

40 John Randolph Fuller, *Juvenile Delinquency: Mainstream and Crosscurrents* (Upper Saddle River, N.J.: Pearson Prentice Hall, 2009), 188.

41 American Psychiatric Association, *Diagnostic and Statistical Manual of Mental Disorders*, 5th ed. (Washington, D.C.: American Psychiatric Association, 2013), 659.

42 Bartol and Bartol, *Criminal Behavior*, 235.

43 Clifford R. Shaw and Henry D. McKay, *Juvenile Delinquency and Urban Areas* (Chicago: University of Chicago Press, 1942).

44 Douglas S. Massey and Nancy A. Denton, *American Apartheid: Segregation and the Making of the Underclass* (Cambridge, Mass.: Harvard University Press, 1993).

45 Edwin H. Sutherland, Donald R. Cressey, and David F. Luckenbill, *Principles of Criminology* (Dix Hills, N.J.: General Hall, 1992).

46 Ross Matsueda, "The Current State of Differential Association Theory," *Crime and Delinquency* 34 (1988): 277–306.

47 Robert K. Merton, "Social Structure and Anomie," *American Sociological Review* 3 (1938): 672–682.

48 Robert Agnew, *Pressured into Crime: An Overview of General Strain Theory* (Los Angeles: Roxbury Publishing, 2006).

49 Lisa Broidy and Robert Agnew, "Gender and Crime: A General Strain Theory Perspective," *Journal of Research in Crime and Delinquency* 34 (1997):275–306.

50 Robert Agnew, "Pressured into Crime: General Strain Theory," in

Criminological Theory: Past to Present, eds. Francis T. Cullen and Robert Agnew (New York: Oxford University Press, 2006), 201–209.

51 Travis Hirschi, *Causes of Delinquency* (Berkeley: University of California Press, 1969).

52 Bruce A. Arrigo, ed., *Social Justice/Criminal Justice: The Maturation of Critical Theory in Law, Crime, and Deviance* (Belmont, Calif.: West/Wadsworth, 1999).

53 Karl Marx, *Capital* (New York: International, 1867/1974).

54 [55] Michael J. Lynch and Paul Stretesky, "Marxism and Social Justice: Thinking about Social Justice Eclipsing Criminal Justice," in *Social Justice/Criminal Justice: The Maturation of Critical Theory in Law, Crime, and Deviance,* ed. Bruce A. Arrigo (Belmont, Calif.: West/Wadsworth, 1999), 14–29.

55 [56] Francis T. Cullen, William J. Maakestad, and Gray Cavender, *Corporate Crime under Attack: The Ford Pinto Case and Beyond* (Cincinnati: Andersen, 1987).

56 Sally Simpson, "Feminist Theory, Crime, and Justice," *Criminology* 27 (1989): 605–631.

57 Curran and Renzetti, *Theories of Crime*, 209–228.

58 Gregg Barak, Jeanne M. Flavin, and Paul S. Leighton, *Class, Race, Gender, and Crime: Social Realities of Justice in America* (Los Angeles: Roxbury, 2000).

59 The phrase "We are a nation of laws and not of men" originates from John Adams.

60 Francis T. Cullen, Jon Paul Wright, and Mitchell B. Chamlin, "Social Support and Social Reform: A Progressive Crime Control Agenda," *Crime and Delinquency* 45 (1999): 188–207.

61 Delbert S. Elliott, David Huizinga, and Suzanne S. Ageton, *Explaining Delinquency and Drug Use* (Beverly Hills: Sage, 1985). Delbert S, Elliott, David Huizinga, and Scott Menard, *Multiple Problem Youth: Delinquency, Substance Use, and Mental Health Problems* (New York: Springer-Verlag, 1989).

62 Terence P. Thornberry, "Toward an Interactional Theory of Delinquency," *Criminology* 25, no. 4 (November 1987): 863–892.

63 Ibid.

64 Terrie Moffitt, "Adolescent-Limited and Life-Course Persistent Antisocial Behavior: A Developmental Taxonomy," *Psychological Review* 100 (1993): 674–701.

65 Ibid., 519.

66 John H. Laub and Robert J. Sampson, *Shared Beginnings, Divergent Lives: Delinquent Boys to Age 70* (Cambridge, Mass.: Harvard University Press, 2003).

Glossary

A

actual-seizure stop An incident in which police officers physically restrain a person and restrict his or her freedom.

actus reus The physical action of a criminal offense; "guilty deed."

adjudication Administration of a legal process of judging and pronouncing a judgment.

adjudicatory hearing The process in which a juvenile court determines whether the allegations in a petition are supported by evidence.

adversarial process A term describing the manner in which U.S. criminal trial courts operate; a system that requires two sides, a prosecution and a defense.

affirmative defense A defense in which the defendant must provide evidence that excuses the legal consequences of an act that the defendant has been proven to have committed.

alibi A defense that involves the defendant(s) claiming not to have been at the scene of a criminal offense when it was committed.

amicus curiae A brief in which someone who is not a part of a case gives advice or testimony.

anomie A condition in which a people or society undergoes a breakdown of social norms and values.

appeal A written petition to a higher court to review a lower court's decision for the purpose of convincing the higher court that the lower court's decision was incorrect.

arraignment Court appearance in which the defendant is formally charged with a crime and asked to respond by pleading guilty, not guilty, or *nolo contendere*.

arrest Law enforcement's action of detaining and holding a criminal suspect or suspects.

arson Any willful or malicious burning or attempt to burn a dwelling, public building, motor vehicle, aircraft, or personal property of another.

Assize of Clarendon A 12th-century English law that established judicial procedure and the grand jury system.

attendant circumstances Additional conditions that define a given criminal offense.

authority The right and the power to commit an act or to order others to commit an act.

B

bail agent An employee of a private, for-profit company that provides money for suspects to be released from jail. Also called a bondsman.

bailiff Court officer responsible for executing writs and processes, making arrests, and keeping order in the court.

behaviorism The assessment of human psychology via the examination of objectively observable and quantifiable actions, as opposed to subjective mental states.

bench trial A trial in which a defendant waives the right to a jury trial and instead agrees to a trial in which the judge hears and decides the case.

beyond a reasonable doubt The highest level of proof required to win a case; necessary in criminal cases to procure a guilty verdict.

bill of indictment A declaration of the charges against an accused person that is presented to a grand jury to determine whether enough evidence exists for an indictment.

Bill of Rights The first 10 amendments to the U.S. Constitution, which guarantee fundamental rights and privileges to citizens.

biosocial criminology A perspective that utilizes genetic, neuropsychological, environmental, and evolutionary factors to explain crime and antisocial behavior across the life course.

blood feud A disagreement whose settlement is based on personal vengeance and physical violence.

bobbies A slang term for the police force in England created in 1829 by Sir Robert Peel's Metropolitan Police Act that was derived from the short form of Robert, Bob.

Bow Street Runners A police organization created circa 1748 by magistrates and brothers Henry Fielding and Sir John Fielding whose members went on patrol rather than remaining at a designated post.

broken-windows perspective The idea that untended property or deviant behavior will attract crime.

burglary Breaking into and entering a structure or vehicle with intent to commit a felony or a theft.

C

capital punishment The sentence of death for a criminal offense.

case law The published decisions of courts that create new interpretations of the law and can be cited as precedent.

cash bond A requirement that the entire amount of the bail cost be paid in cash.

charge Formal statement of the criminal offense the defendant is accused of.

Chicago school Criminological theories that rely, in part, on individuals' demographics and geographic location to explain criminal behavior.

child advocate An officer appointed by the court to protect the interests of the child and to act as a liaison among the child, the child's family, the court, and any other agency involved with the child.

circuit court A court that holds sessions at intervals within different areas of a judicial district.

civil law The law that governs private rights as opposed to the law that governs criminal issues.

classical school of criminology A set of criminological theories that uses the idea of free will to explain criminal behavior.

clerk of the court The primary administrative officer of each court who manages nonjudicial functions.

Code of Hammurabi An ancient code instituted by Hammurabi, a ruler of Babylonia, dealing with criminal and civil matters.

collective behavior A sociological term that describes how an individual's actions are transmitted into group actions that can exceed what any of the individuals in the group intended.

commitment An order by a judge upon conviction or before a trial that sends a person to jail or prison. Also, a judge's order that sends a mentally unstable person to a mental institution.

common law Law based on customs and general principles which may be used as precedent or for matters not addressed by statute.

community corrections A form of corrections in which criminal offenders are managed in the community instead of in correctional facilities.

community policing A policing strategy that attempts to harness the resources and residents of a given community in stopping crime and maintaining order.

concurrence The coexistence of *actus reus* and *mens rea*.

congregate-and-silent system A style of penal control pioneered by the Auburn System, in which inmates were allowed to eat and work together during the day but were forbidden to speak to each other and were locked alone in their cells at night.

consent decree An agreement whereby the parties to a lawsuit accept a judge's order instead of continuing the case through a trial or hearing.

constable The head of law enforcement for large districts in early England. In the modern United States, a constable serves areas such as rural townships and is usually elected.

convict lease system A system initiated in the late 19th and early 20th centuries in which companies and individuals could purchase the labor of prison inmates from state and county governments.

corporate crime Offenses committed by a corporation's officers who pursue illegal activity in the corporation's name.

corpus delicti "Body of the crime"; the criminal offense.

court administrator An officer responsible for the mechanical necessities of the court, such as scheduling courtrooms, managing case flow, administering personnel, procuring furniture, and preparing budgets.

Court of the Star Chamber An old English court comprising the king's councilors that was separate from common-law courts.

court reporter A court officer who records and transcribes an official verbatim record of the legal proceedings of the court.

courtroom work group The judges, prosecutors, defense attorneys, clerks, and bailiffs who work together to move cases through the court system and whose interaction determines the outcome of criminal cases.

crime The violation of the laws of a society by a person or a group of people who are subject to the laws of that society.

crime control model A model proposed by legal scholar Herbert L. Packer to describe the public's expectation of an efficient criminal justice system.

crime rate The number of crime index offenses divided by the population of an area, usually given as a rate of crimes per 100,000 people.

Criminal Division A division that is part of the U.S. Department of Justice and that develops, enforces, and supervises the application of all federal criminal laws except those assigned to other divisions.

criminal justice A social institution that has the mission of controlling crime by detecting, detaining, adjudicating, and punishing and/or rehabilitating people who break the law.

criminal law The law specifying the prosecution by the government of a person or persons for an act that has been classified as a criminal offense.

critical theory A perspective that critiques the current manner in which justice is dispensed and considers social justice to be a legitimate end.

D

dark figure of crime A term describing crime that is unreported and never quantified.

decriminalization Emendation of laws or statutes to lessen or remove penalties for specific acts subject to criminal prosecution, arrest, and imprisonment.

deinstitutionalization The policy of removing mentally ill people from public mental health institutions and closing part or all of those institutions.

Department of Homeland Security (DHS) A department of the U.S. government responsible for preventing terrorism and enhancing national security; securing and managing U.S. borders; enforcing and administering U.S. immigration laws; safeguarding and securing U.S. interests on the Internet; and assisting in the federal response to terrorist attacks and natural disasters within the United States.

Department of Justice The federal executive agency that handles all criminal prosecutions and civil suits in which the United States has an interest.

Department of the Treasury The federal executive agency that is responsible for promoting economic prosperity and ensuring the financial security of the United States.

determinate sentence A prison term that is determined by law and states a specific period of time to be served.

differential association theory A theory developed by Edwin Sutherland that states that crime is learned.

direct filing A form of waiving a juvenile to criminal court in which a prosecutor has the discretion to file charges in either juvenile or criminal court.

directed verdict of acquittal An order from a trial judge to the jury stating that the jury must acquit the accused because the prosecution has not proved its case.

discretion The power of a criminal justice official to make decisions on issues within legal guidelines.

disposition The final determination of a case or other matter by a court or other judicial entity.

diversion The effort to deinstitutionalize delinquent and neglected children.

docket A schedule of cases in a court.

double jeopardy Prosecution of a defendant in the same jurisdiction for an offense for which the defendant has already been prosecuted and convicted or acquitted.

double marginality The multiple outsider status of women and minority police officers as a result of being treated differently by their fellow officers.

due process model A model proposed by legal scholar Herbert L. Packer to describe the public's expectation of a just and fair criminal justice system.

due process rights Guarantees by the Fifth, Sixth, and Fourteenth Amendments which establish legal procedures that recognize the protection of an individual's life, liberty, and property.

E

embezzlement The theft or taking of money or property by a person who is charged by an employer or other authority to be responsible for those assets.

entrapment The use of extreme means by law enforcement to pressure someone to break the law.

F

false consciousness The idea that the attitudes held by the lower class do not accurately reflect the reality of that class's existence.

Federal Bureau of Investigation (FBI) The main federal law enforcement agency in the United States, which operates under the Department of Justice and deals with domestic crime that crosses state lines, as well as some types of significant crime within the states, such as terrorism.

Federal Bureau of Prisons A federal agency established within the Department of Justice to manage and regulate all federal penal and correctional institutions.

felony An offense punishable by a sentence of more than a year in state or federal prison and sometimes by death.

frankpledge system An early form of English government that divided communities into groups of 10 men who were responsible for the group's conduct and ensured that a member charged with breaking the law appeared in court.

G

gender The socially constructed roles, behaviors, actions, and characteristics that a society considers appropriate for males and females.

general deterrence A method of control in which the punishment of a single offender sets an example for the rest of society.

general jurisdiction court A court that may hear all types of cases except for those prohibited by law.

geographic jurisdiction The authority of a court to hear a case based on the location of the offense.

going rate A term describing how similar cases have been settled by a given set of judges, prosecutors, and attorneys.

good time The time deducted from an inmate's prison sentence for good behavior.

grabbable area The area under the control of an individual during an arrest in an automobile.

H

habeas corpus An order to have a prisoner/detainee brought before the court to determine if it is legal to hold the prisoner/detainee.

hands-off doctrine The judicial attitude toward prisons before the 1960s in which courts did not become involved in prison affairs or inmate rights.

hearing A session that takes place without a jury before a judge or magistrate in which evidence and/or arguments are presented to determine some factual or legal issue.

hedonistic calculus An individual's mental calculation of the personal value of an activity on the basis of how much pleasure or pain it will incur.

hierarchical jurisdiction The authority of a court to hear a case based on where the case is located in the system.

hierarchy rule A principle stating that when more than one criminal offense is committed in a given incident, only the offense that is highest on the hierarchy list is reported to the FBI's Uniform Crime Reports.

hue and cry In early England, the alarm that citizens were required to raise upon the witness or discovery of a criminal offense.

hung jury A jury in a criminal case that is deadlocked or that cannot produce a unanimous verdict.

I

impeach To discredit a witness.

inchoate offense An offense composed of acts necessary to commit another offense.

indeterminate sentence A prison term that is determined by a parole board and does not state a specific period of time to be served or date of release.

indictment A written statement of the facts of the offense that is charged against the accused.

infancy In legal terminology, the state of a child who has not yet reached a specific age; almost all states end infancy at age 18.

informal probation A period during which a juvenile is required to stay out of trouble or make restitution before a case is dropped.

information A formal, written accusation against a defendant submitted to the court by a prosecutor.

infraction In most jurisdictions, a minor civil offense that is not serious enough to warrant curtailing an offender's freedom.

inquest In archaic usage, the first type of jury that determined the ownership of land; currently, a type of investigation.

insanity defense A defense that attempts to give physical or psychological reasons that a defendant cannot comprehend his or her criminal actions, their harm(s), or their punishment.

intensive-supervision probation (ISP) A form of supervision that requires frequent meetings between the client and the probation officer.

interactional theory of delinquency The theory that low social control and exposure to delinquent peers over the course of adolescent development contributes to delinquency and antisocial behavior.

intermediate sanctions Sentencing alternatives that are stricter than regular probation but less severe than prison.

J

jail A secure facility that typically holds arrestees, criminal suspects, and inmates serving sentences of less than a year.

judicial waiver A form of waiving a juvenile to criminal court in which a judge sends the juvenile to adult court.

jurisdiction The authority of the court to hear certain cases.

just deserts A philosophy that states that an offender who commits a heinous crime deserves death.

justice The administering of a punishment or reward in accordance with morals that a given society considers to be correct.

juvenile delinquent A person, usually under the age of 18, who is determined to have committed a criminal offense or status offense in states in which a minor is declared to lack responsibility and cannot be sentenced as an adult.

L

labeling theory A perspective that considers recidivism to be a consequence, in part, of the negative labels applied to offenders.

larceny A form of theft in which an offender takes possessions that do not belong to him or her with the intent of keeping them.

legalistic style A mode of policing that emphasizes enforcement of the letter of the law.

legalization The total removal of legal prohibitions on specific acts that were previously proscribed and punishable by law.

limited-jurisdiction court A court that has jurisdiction only over certain types of cases or subject matter.

lower courts Sometimes called inferior courts, in reference to their hierarchy. These courts receive their authority and resources from local county or municipal governments.

M

Magna Carta "Great Charter"; a guarantee of liberties signed by King John of England in 1215 that influenced many modern legal and constitutional principles.

mandatory minimum sentence A sentence determined by law that establishes the minimum length of prison time that may be served for an offense.

marks-of-commendation system An incarceration philosophy developed by Alexander Maconochie in which inmates earned the right to be released, as well as privileges, goods, and services.

mass murder The murder of three or more people in a single incident.

master status A personal status that overwhelms all others.

mens rea "Guilty mind"; intent or knowledge to break the law.

meritorious time Time deducted from an inmate's sentence for doing something special or extra, such as getting a GED.

Metropolitan Police Act The first successful bill to create a permanent, public police force, created in 1829 by Sir Robert Peel.

misdemeanor A minor criminal offense punishable by a fine and/or jail time for up to one year.

Missouri Bar Plan A form of judicial selection in which a nominating commission presents a list of candidates to the governor, who decides on a candidate. After a year in office, voters decide on whether to retain the judge. Judges must run for such reelection each term. Also called merit selection.

moral development theory Kohlberg's theory that human moral development proceeds through clearly defined stages of moral reasoning.

N

National Crime Victimization Survey (NCVS) A survey that is the primary source of information on criminal victimization in the United States and attempts to measure the extent of crime by interviewing crime victims.

National Incident-Based Reporting System (NIBRS) A crime-reporting system in which each separate offense in a crime is described, including data describing the offender(s), victim(s), and property.

self-report study Research in which individuals are asked about criminal offenses they have committed, even those they have never been arrested for or charged with.

Neighborhood Watch A community policing program that encourages residents to cooperate in providing security for the neighborhood.

neoclassical criminology A modern interpretation of classical criminology that acknowledges the possibility that human choices are affected by causes external to the will but holds that human beings are ultimately responsible for their choices.

net-widening A phenomenon through which criminal justice programs pull more clients into the system than would otherwise be involved without the program.

no-bill The decision of a grand jury not to indict an accused person because of insufficient evidence. Also called "no true bill."

nolo contendere A plea in which a defendant does not accept or deny responsibility for the charges but agrees to accept punishment. From Latin meaning, "I will not contest."

normal crimes Routine cases that are considered in the context of how the court handled similar offenses.

O

observational learning The process of learning by watching the behavior of others.

operant conditioning The alteration of behavior by rewarding or punishing a subject for a specified action until the subject associates the action with pleasure or pain.

P

pains of imprisonment Deprivations that define the punitive nature of imprisonment.

parens patriae Latin for "father of the country," the philosophy that the government is the ultimate guardian of all children or disabled adults.

parole The conditional release of a prison inmate who has served part of a sentence and who remains under the court's control.

penal code A code of laws that deals with crimes and the punishments for them.

Pendleton Civil Service Reform Act of 1883 Law establishing that federal government positions would be awarded on the basis of merit rather than political affiliation.

peremptory challenges The right of both the prosecution and the defense attorney to have a juror dismissed before trial without stating a reason.

petitioner A person who files a lawsuit; also called a plaintiff.

plea bargain A compromise reached by the defendant, the defendant's attorney, and the prosecutor in which the defendant agrees to plead guilty or no contest in return for a reduction of the charges' severity, dismissal of some charges, further information about the offense or about others involved in it, or the prosecutor's agreement to recommend a desired sentence.

policeman's working personality The mindset of police who must deal with danger, authority, isolation, and suspicion while appearing to be efficient.

positivist school of criminology A set of criminological theories that uses scientific techniques to study crime and criminal offenders.

posse comitatus "The power or force of the county. The entire population of a county above the age of 15, which a sheriff may summon to his assistance in certain cases as to aid him in keeping the peace, in pursuing and arresting felons, etc."[i]

precedent A prior legal decision used as a basis for deciding a later, similar case.

predictive policing The use of information technology to analyze vast amounts of data allowing law enforcement to better target their resources toward potential crime.

preponderance of the evidence A term referring to the burden of proof in a civil trial, which requires that more than 50 percent of the evidence be in the plaintiff's favor.

pre-sentence investigation (PSI) The report prepared by a probation officer to assist a judge in sentencing; also called a pre-sentence report.

presumptive sentence A sentence that may be adjusted by the judge depending on aggravating or mitigating factors.

pre-trial motion A request made by the prosecutor or defense attorney that the court make a decision on a specific issue before the trial begins.

prison-industrial complex The increased reliance on incarceration, surveillance, and law enforcement in the United States and its relationship to the establishment of for-profit incarceration and probation/parole services, and businesses that supply goods and services to prisons and jails.

Prison Litigation Reform Act Legislation that restricts litigation by prison inmates based on the conditions of their confinement.

private probation A form of probation supervision that is contracted to for-profit private agencies by the state.

probable cause A reason based on known facts to think that a law has been broken or that a property is connected to a criminal offense.

probation The suspension of all or part of a sentence subject to certain conditions and supervision in the community.

problem-oriented policing A style of policing that attempts to address the underlying social problems that contribute to crime by integrating research and scientific problem-solving strategies to analyze instances of crime, with the goal of developing more effective response strategies.

procedural law Law that specifies how the criminal justice system is allowed to deal with those who break the law or are accused of breaking the law.

property bond The use of a piece of property instead of cash as collateral for bail.

pseudofamilies Groups established by women in prison to imitate familial roles in society.

R

racial profiling Suspicion of illegal activity based on a person's race, ethnicity, or national origin rather than on actual illegal activity or evidence of illegal activity.

racketeering A federal crime that involves patterns of illegal activity carried out by organized groups that run illegal businesses or break the law in other organized ways.

rape Sexual activity, usually sexual intercourse, that is forced on another person without his or her consent, usually under threat of harm. Also, sexual activity conducted with a person who is incapable of valid consent.

rational choice theory The idea that people consciously weigh the risks against the benefits of their actions and choose the action that they think has the most benefit.

reasonable stop standard A Supreme Court measure that considers constitutionality on whether a reasonable person would feel free to terminate an encounter with law enforcement personnel.

reasonable suspicion A suspicion based on facts or circumstances that justifies stopping and sometimes searching an individual thought to be involved in illegal activity.

recidivism The tendency to break the criminal law and return to the criminal justice system after being processed for past offenses.

recidivism rate The rate of ex-offenders who commit new offenses and are returned to prison.

redirect examination The questioning of a witness about issues uncovered during cross-examination.

referral Similar to a "charge" in the adult system in which an authority, usually the police, parents, or the school, determines that a youth needs intervention from the juvenile court.

release on recognizance (ROR) A written promise signed by a defendant who pays no money to be released from jail and promises to appear in court when required.

residential placement Any sentence of a juvenile delinquent to a residential facility, where the juvenile is closely monitored.

respondent The party who must reply to a petitioner's complaint; equivalent to a defendant in a lawsuit.

retribution Punishment that is considered to be deserved.

retribution model A style of control in which offenders are punished as severely as possible for a crime and in which rehabilitation is not attempted.

robbery The taking or attempting to take anything of value from the care, custody, or control of a person or persons by force or threat of force or violence and/or by putting the victim in fear.

routine activities theory A perspective that states that crime is most likely to occur when these three elements converge: motivated offenders, attractive targets, and the absence of capable guardians.

rule of four A rule that states that at least four of the nine Supreme Court justices must vote to hear a case.

rule of law In the context of criminal justice, the principle that government cannot punish any individual without strict adherence to clear, fair, and defined rules, laws, and procedures.

S

search An investigation of an area and/or person by a police officer to look for evidence of criminal activity.

seizure The collecting by police officers of potential evidence in a criminal case.

sentencing guidelines A set of rules concerning the sentencing for a specified set of offenses that seek to create uniform sentencing policy by directing the judge to consider certain facts about the offense and the defendant when determining the sentence.

separate-and-silent system A method of penal control pioneered by Philadelphia's Eastern State Penitentiary in which inmates were kept from seeing or talking to one another. This method is comparable to solitary confinement in modern prisons.

serial murder The murder of a series of victims during three or more separate events over an extended period of time.

service style A mode of policing that is concerned primarily with serving the community and citizens.

sexual assault Sexual contact that is committed without the other party's consent or with a party who is not capable of giving consent.

shock probation The practice of sentencing offenders to prison, allowing them to serve a short time, and then granting them probation without their prior knowledge.

show-of-authority stop An incident in which police show a sign of authority (such as flashing a badge), and the suspect submits.

situational crime prevention An idea that involves making crime less attractive to potential criminals by reducing the physical opportunities to break the law.

social control The rules, habits, and customs a society uses to enforce conformity to its norms.

social control theory A theory that seeks not to explain why people break the law, but instead explores what keeps most people from breaking the law.

social disorganization theory The theory that the structural and cultural conditions of a neighborhood affect criminal behavior.

sociological imagination The idea that we must look beyond the obvious to evaluate how our social location influences how we perceive society.

specific deterrence A method of control in which an offender is prevented from committing more crimes by either imprisonment or death.

stare decisis The doctrine under which courts adhere to legal precedent.

state courts General courts and special courts funded and run by each state.

status offense An act that is considered a legal offense only when committed by a juvenile and that can be adjudicated only in a juvenile court.

statute A law enacted by a legislature.

statutory exclusion Provisions that exclude, without hearing or waiver, juveniles who meet certain age, offense, or past-record criteria from the jurisdiction of the juvenile court.

statutory law The type of law that is enacted by legislatures, as opposed to common law.

statutory rape Sexual activity conducted with a person who is younger than a specified age or incapable of valid consent because of mental illness, mental handicap, intoxication, unconsciousness, or deception.

stop A temporary detention that legally is a seizure of an individual and must be based on reasonable suspicion.

stop-and-frisk A term that describes two distinct behaviors on the part of law enforcement officers in dealing with suspects. To conduct a lawful frisk, the stop itself must meet the legal conditions of a seizure. A frisk constitutes a search.

strain theory The theory that the causes of crime can be connected to the pressure on culturally or materially disadvantaged groups or individuals to achieve the goals held by society, even if the means to those goals require the breaking of laws.

street crime Small-scale, personal offenses such as single-victim homicide, rape, robbery, assault, burglary, and vandalism.

strict liability Responsibility for a criminal offense without intention to break the law.

subject-matter jurisdiction The authority of a court to hear a case based on the nature of the case.

substantive law Law that describes which behaviors have been defined as criminal offenses.

supermax prison An extremely secure type of prison that strictly limits inmate contact with other inmates, correctional staff, and the outside world.

surety bond The use of a bail agent who promises to pay the defendant's bail if he or she fails to appear for further court proceedings.

T

terrorism The use or threat of violence against a state or other political entity in order to coerce.

Thames River Police A private police force created by the West India Trading Company in 1798 that represented the first professional, salaried police force in London.

three strikes In reference to criminal justice, a term that describes state laws that require an offender's third felony to be punishable by a severe sentence, including life imprisonment.

tort law An area of the law that deals with civil acts that cause harm and injury, including libel, slander, assault, trespass, and negligence.

total institution A closed environment in which every aspect, including the movement and behavior of the people within, is controlled and structured.

trial by ordeal An ancient custom in which the accused was required to perform a test that appealed to divine authority to prove guilt or innocence.

true bill The decision of a grand jury that sufficient evidence exists to indict an accused person.

U

Uniform Crime Reports (UCR) An annual publication by the Federal Bureau of Investigation that uses data from all participating law enforcement agencies in the United States to summarize the incidence and rate of reported crime.

U.S. Attorneys The principal litigators of the United States who conduct most of the trial work in which the United States is a party. They prosecute criminal cases brought by the federal government; prosecute and defend civil cases in which the United States is a party; and collect certain types of debts owed to the federal government.

U.S. courts of appeals Intermediate courts that dispose of many appeals before they reach the Supreme Court.

U.S. district courts Courts of general jurisdiction that try felony cases involving federal laws and civil cases involving amounts of money over $75,000.

U.S. Solicitor General The person who determines which cases the federal government will send to the U.S. Supreme Court for review and the positions the government will take before the Court.

U.S. Supreme Court The "court of last resort." The highest court in the United States, established by Article III of the Constitution, hears only appeals, with some exceptions.

USA FREEDOM Act A law signed by President Barack Obama in 2015 that reauthorized parts of the USA PATRIOT Act but limited the bulk collection of U.S. residents' phone records and Internet data.

USA PATRIOT Act A law signed by President George W. Bush on October 26, 2001, in response to the terror attacks of September 11, 2001.

use of force "The amount of effort required by police to compel compliance from an unwilling subject," according to the International Association of Chiefs of Police.

utilitarianism A theory associated with Jeremy Bentham that states that people will choose not to break the law when the pain of punishment outweighs the benefits of the offense.

V

venire The list or pool from which jurors are chosen.

victim "[A] person that has suffered direct physical, emotional, or pecuniary harm as a result of the commission of a crime."[ii]

victim-impact statement An account given by the victim, the victim's family, or others affected by the offense that expresses the effects of the offense, including economic losses, the extent of physical or psychological injuries, and major life changes.

victim precipitation A situation in which a crime victim plays an active role in initiating a crime or escalating it.

victimless crime Behaviors that are deemed undesirable because they offend community standards rather than directly harm people or property.

visibility A term that refers to the fact that police work is most easily observed by the public and that police are accountable to the public, police supervisors, and legislatures.

voir dire French for "to see, to speak"; a phrase that refers to the questioning of jurors by a judge and/or attorneys to determine whether individual jurors are appropriate for a particular jury panel.

W

war on drugs Governmental policy aimed at reducing the sale and use of illegal drugs.

watch-and-ward system An early English system overseen by the constable in which a watchman guarded a city's or town's gates at night.

watchman style A mode of policing that emphasizes the maintenance of order and informal intervention on the part of the police officer rather than strict enforcement of the law.

white-collar crime A nonviolent criminal offense committed during the course of business for financial gain.

Wickersham Commission report The 14-volume report published in 1931 and 1932, which was the first comprehensive national study of U.S. crime and law enforcement.

writ of certiorari An order from a superior court calling up for review the record of a case from a lower court.

Z

zero-tolerance policing A form of policing that punishes every infraction of the law, however minor, with an arrest, fine, or other penalty so that offenders will refrain from committing more serious offenses.

Endnotes

i *Black's Law Dictionary*, http://thelawdictionary.org/posse-comitatus/. Accessed August 2015.

ii 42 U.S.C. § 10607(e)(2)(A). See www .law.cornell.edu/uscode/text/42/10607. Accessed December 2012.

Credits

Index

A reference that includes *d* indicates that the term is defined on the page. A *t* indicates that the information may be found in a table, and *f* indicates that the information is located within a feature box.

Index